D1314387

THE MOTHER'S ALMANAC II

MARGUERITE KELLY

Illustrations by Katy Kelly

DOUBLEDAY

NEW YORK   LONDON   TORONTO   SYDNEY   AUCKLAND

With everlasting thanks to my two editors, Karen Van Westering and Tom Kelly, whose patience is only exceeded by their skill; to Molly Friedrich, an agent of ability and honor; and to my children, Kate, Mike, Meg and Nell, whose love and friendship I treasure almost as much as I treasure them.

HQ
769
K3672
1989

ROBERT MANNING
STROZIER LIBRARY

AUG 29 1989

Tallahassee, Florida

Published by Doubleday, a division of
Bantam Doubleday Dell Publishing Group, Inc.
666 Fifth Avenue, New York, New York 10103

Doubleday and the portrayal of an anchor with a dolphin are trademarks of Doubleday, a division of Bantam Doubleday Dell Publishing Group, Inc.

Library of Congress Cataloging-in-Publication Data

Kelly, Marguerite.
    The mother's almanac II / by Marguerite Kelly : illustrations by Katy Kelly.
        p.   cm.
    Bibliography: p.
    Includes index.
    ISBN 0-385-26283-3
    ISBN 0-385-13155-0 (Pbk)
    1. Child rearing—United States—Handbooks, manuals, etc.
2. Mothers—United States—Handbooks, manuals, etc. I. Kelly, Katy. II. Title
HQ769.K3672   1989
649'.124—dc19   88-25650
                                CIP

Copyright © 1989 by Marguerite Kelly

DESIGN: Stanley S. Drate/Folio Graphics Company, Inc.

All Rights Reserved
Printed in the United States of America
May 1989
First Edition

For my two mothers—my own and Aunt Kay

CONTENTS

PREFACE

While *The Mother's Almanac* dealt with children from birth to six, *The Mother's Almanac II* takes them from Six to Twelve—the Middle Years. Like its predecessor, it is written from a mother's perspective (although a father can follow it too) and with a great deal of love.

Individuality is still encouraged, in the child and in the family, and excellence is still pursued, whether in the quality of discipline or the making of a quiche. The scope of the book is also comprehensive, as it was before, for a child is part of a family and must be seen in that context. But there is a difference. *The Mother's Almanac II* deals with more serious challenges, for these children make more serious demands on their parents. Problems begin to show up now—in the child, in the parents and in the marriage—and they must be treated in greater depth.

The book itself is divided into three sections. The first and biggest one concerns the child—how he grows and how he thinks; how his independence—and therefore his conscience—develops, and how parents can discover, and often solve, the physical and psychological problems that may make behavior worse.

The second section is about the family, whatever its size or shape. The stability of your marriage—the greatest gift you can give your child—is considered here and so is the role you may have as a working parent, a single parent or a stepparent. And then there are the traditions—the ones you continue and the ones you start—from the way you worship together to the way you work and play. These are the building blocks that memories are made of, giving a child the stuffing to handle the stresses of life, like moving and divorce and death. These events are discussed too, in case you have to walk your child through them—and you may. Life has a way of chilling our halcyon days. By learning how to deal well with one stress, however, your child will be able to deal better with all stress.

The world, and especially the school, is introduced in the third section; you find out what to expect and what to do if your expectations don't come true. The value of friendships is also reviewed here, as well as good times, parties and sports, for children learn at least as much from fun and games as they do from school.

All of this took an embarrassingly long time to research and a great deal of help from friends and strangers—many of them between Six and Twelve. Their patience with interviews and observations was significant and deeply appreciated (see Acknowledgments).

Choices were made in writing this book: what to include, what to emphasize, and exactly how to put the information on paper in the clearest way, even if it meant putting substance ahead of semantics. The book, therefore, usually refers to your child as "he" rather than "he or she," and the child is discussed in the singular, although you may have two children or more. It is too complicated and distracting to switch from one sex to the other, or from one child to several, especially when we know that each child is born to be one of a kind.

You won't, of course, have the time or energy to do all the things this book mentions (nor did I) nor will the suggestions stop you from making mistakes (it certainly didn't stop me). It is enough to try to do the best you can and forgive yourself for the rest, even as you forgive your own child when he errs. Just take from this book what you will, enjoy what you can and revel in your good fortune. A child is truly a blessing.

MARGUERITE LELONG KELLY
Washington, D. C.

THE CHILD

The Middle Years of childhood arrive just as your own are getting uncomfortably close. They are the still years, the forgotten years, yet this stretch between Six and Twelve is critical, for it will decide how the teens will go.

Children are easy to love now, but not to know. They shine for their teachers more than their parents. They try hard to conform, and yet their differences continue to grow, in size and shape and ability. They act self-sufficient but they need you more than ever. They treasure their friends, and let you know it, and adore their own families, but seldom show it. They talk endlessly but say little that grabs your interest. They are our young pioneers, stepping gingerly out into the world, where everything they have ever known or assumed is going to be challenged, beginning with Santa Claus.

School, of course, is the most affecting experience your child encounters in these seven years. There is so much to learn, so much to do. The challenges he meets will help him define his ideas and values, bit by bit, and so will his environment. Your community may be silk stocking or blue collar, urban or suburban, but it is his to conquer. It needn't be homogeneous and, with luck, it won't be. A variety of cultures, of churches, of neighborhoods, of incomes and interests, will give him a fine introduction to bigger worlds to come and help him feel comfortable in them. A child's understanding of the world is as important as his triumph over it. It takes hundreds of small culture shocks to turn this child into an open-minded, empathic, self-reliant person, as bright and as curious as nature meant him to be.

Above all, his talents and tastes will help him choose his own directions. The assorted enthusiasms at Six, Seven, Eight and Nine often turn into a single-minded devotion at Ten, Eleven and Twelve. This is all to the good. With at least 23,000 potential careers, your child needs to con-

sider as many as possible in an unhurried, casual way and to concentrate on those interests when he's young, dropping them when he's taken one as far as he wants to go. This gives him the sense of purpose that every child needs.

Eight-year-olds—who like to classify small objects, meet people and handle money—will be pleased to know they could run a first-class hardware store like the one on the avenue. And Nines, who have lost much of their interest in money, will be delighted to know they have the makings of a museum curator. They still classify every movable object and they still like to meet people, but now they like to meet most of them in history books.

Boys and girls will explore a variety of interests and consider many goals, however improbable, if parents let them spin their dreams without threats about grades or college, or fuss because these careers won't suit their sex or their social class or won't pay enough, in money or prestige.

Some parents want to give their children the world in a tidy, prewrapped package but this can't be done. Just as we don't own their tomorrows, neither do they have our yesterdays. It will be years before they can apply our past to their present and even then they will only choose what they think suits them best. All children are born with blinders. It takes experience—and daring parents—to let them see the world. The more glimpses they get in the Middle Years, the less they'll need to rebel in adolescence.

MOTHER

There is a time for nesting and a time for marching forth, and after six years with a preschooler you hear the band play louder every day. This is natural. After pouring so much love and creativity into the rearing of your child, you may not have much left to nurture you.

Now you are privy to one of maternity's best-kept secrets: motherhood plumbs deep wells of love, but it makes you draw up buckets of humility too. It's as if the confidence your child takes into first grade has been wrung right out of you, whether you've gone to work or stayed at home.

Everything may seem wrong. If you have an outside job, you may be exhausted and guilty too, sure that you're giving less than you should. If you've stayed home full-time, you may have a different response. It may have been better for the child (and for you), but six years of tears, tantrums, medical emergencies—and no paycheck to prove your worth—have probably cut your self-esteem in half. At parties you mumble that you're "just a housewife" or announce defiantly that you work at home, thank you. The laundry, which was once just a chore, has become an affront, and meals have turned into a small familiar cycling of foods your child will eat without a fuss. Every duty has been learned to the point of boredom. This is a normal reaction, a critical call for change and growth.

The time has come to broaden your focus from motherhood to womanhood. You begin this change when your first child starts first grade and complete it when the last one goes to school. The transition is as natural, as wrenching—and as beneficial—as the nudges it takes to make a little bird fly: the mother will feel as freed as her fledgling.

You'll find, like every woman before you, that compromises are at the heart of

this transition. Car pools, Scouts and ballet lessons are necessary, but they shouldn't be your main concern, nor should you feel as if you're shirking your duty if they aren't. Mothers aren't meant to be martyrs.

It's time, instead, to replenish your reservoir of self-confidence by seeking fresh directions: a different career, new skills, college courses, unread books, a diet that works, weekends away with your husband and clothes that have your own special flair. If you deny yourself this natural expansion, you will have less and less left to give your child, and at a time when he needs you more than ever.

When you spent hours swinging him in the park and taking turns at the cooperative, your thoughts could amble along a hundred paths that had nothing to do with children. Now he is a more private person, and it takes thoughtful attention to figure out what's going on in that dear young mind and how to make the hurts go away. There are no thermometers for the soul; no Red Cross manual for fractured feelings.

You probably ache a little too. Now your child is in the classroom five hours a day, five days a week, and the importance of the family may suddenly seem slight. This isn't true, as your child knows better than anyone. Whether he has one parent or two, working at an office or at home, he needs the kind of support that only his family can give. The people who work at the school, the church, the recreation center, the day-care agency and the camp will enhance his life and, if they're good enough, they'll reinforce your values and your love, but they can never replace his family. It is always there, around the clock, around the calendar: the only institution that can fulfill a child's deepest needs. Its strength and its continuity weave an emotional security blanket for him.

This psychological dependence can make you feel chained to the loom, and suddenly you discover the next well-kept secret of motherhood: it's the longest tem-

porary job in the world. While you never stop paying for the privilege of being a parent, no other investment brings such a high return. It may sound soupy, but the richest joy is the joy of giving, and a child is our gift to the ages.

Medical breakthroughs protect these gifts as never before. Now, for the first time in the history of the world, we can confidently expect our children to grow up. This leaves us free to concentrate on the quality of their lives, rather than the life itself. It also invites us to give them a wealth of material things. Time and attention, however, are what every child needs, and why parenthood is still such a formidable job.

You are learning to handle your child's problems with more finesse but they're not as simple as they used to be. Moreover, each problem seems to last a little longer than the one that went before, and so does each stage of your child's development. On top of that, you're going through some stages of your own. And that's the next surprise.

As you help your schoolchild find that competence brings joy, you instinctively begin to reach out, to confide in friends and family, and to try to do what's right, whether anyone agrees with you or not. This is the final polishing of your own moral code. Now you help the teachers and the PTA, the church and the Scouts, the lonely and the less fortunate, because you find out that it takes a lot of giving in order to get.

There's more of this ahead. In your own middle years, you'll instinctively need to help a broader society, to make a difference, to leave the world a slightly better place than you found it. Without this giv-

ing, you'll be haunted by a sense of irrelevance—that midlife crisis when you're likely to say, "You mean this is it? This is all?" It's the giving, stage by stage, that will take you into the sunset years and the pot of harmony you'll find at the end of your rainbow. When we recognize that we are all of us—mother, father, child—"in a stage," we begin to understand and accept—and enjoy—one another even more.

This isn't always easy now. While many parents find the child between Six and Twelve is more satisfying than ever, you may long for the originality and joie de vivre he showed as a preschooler. Now it's the teachers and coaches and recreation leaders who may know more about his abilities and fears and dreams than you do, for they see him in his prime time, while at home he is probably in about the same state as your marriage: reasonably quiet, rather easygoing—and slightly boring.

You have to work a little harder on both relationships. Not to discourage you, but it's a matter of relying on humor most of the time and some plain old courage for the rest.

Now you and your husband must stand side by side, with enough space between you to feel like valuable and valued individuals and enough time together to remember why you love each other. This keeps the dry rot out of marriage, but even then it's not easy unless you concentrate for a few minutes each day on the goodness within you. This concentration will give you—and your marriage—the strength and the patience to enjoy your child as he goes from Six to Twelve.

Your rapport with your child needs a new enrichment too, for it is as essential as the one you created years ago when you rocked him to sleep. Just as the confusions of a lifetime often begin in the first few years, the problems of adolescence are often shaped in the Middle Years.

The choice is yours, but you'll hardly know you're making it. When your child tells you the same moldy riddles you used to tell when you were Nine, it becomes mighty easy to say, "Run out and play, dear." Dear usually will do just that and often with alacrity, but if you seem impatient or disinterested too often he will stop speaking so freely, obeying the frown on your face rather than your polite if half-hearted "And then what happened?" One day you'll be suddenly and happily aware of his emerging wit, his style and his ideas only to have him pull away from you. This is the young teenager who turns to those who had time for him when he needed it, even though they may be poor choices, or simply turns to the only person he feels able to trust—himself. This is the start of a painful, lonely adolescence. The respect you give—or don't give—is always returned, sooner or later. You'll do better to put up with most of his prattle now, and treat him more and more as a friend, so you can keep a strong connection between you when he's a teenager.

By treating yourself to a fresh look at your child occasionally, you can appreciate your miracle all over again. This is the time to watch him in a crowd of children, as if he belonged to somebody else. As an impartial observer, you have to admit: he clearly outshines all the others.

Although your child is the architect of his own soul, you still embellish it, and in much the same way as you did before. Despite the stimulation of school, he requires continued enrichment at home and abroad, for he still absorbs everything he sees and hears. Each new experience will help him break old molds and grow up to be an imaginative, sensitive adult.

He still needs nutritious food, a good night's sleep, limits on television and a small unexpected present sometimes, as well as your attention, your respect for his time and his privacy, your praise for jobs well done, and the chance to make many decisions for himself. It takes a lot of practice to become a responsible grown-up.

It will be your repeated assurances, your listening, your open affection for your child as he is that will let him feel welcome to say the things on his mind,

without having them fester too long. You will, of course, put up with less backchat, laziness and general orneriness as he gets older, but most of your support will be positive, as it always has been. A child is made to be loved, whatever his disposition on a particular day. When he knows that this lifeline will never be cut, he accepts any reasonable discipline.

Follow your instinct to be kind, fair and steady. If this guidance grows slack, you can depend upon your child to let you know, with behavior that is outrageous and prolonged. This is the age-old way in which a child asks for clear boundaries and you must supply them—wide enough to let him have options but firm enough to keep him out of trouble.

You cannot be all-loving, all-attentive all the time, but no matter. Your child will settle for less. Nor will you always relieve your child of all woes and confusion. The best parents in the world (whoever *they* may be) have sad, bad days and odd little aches and pains that make them act badly—and so do their children. Every child develops some physical or emotional difficulty, and you won't always recognize it—and get help for it—right away. Don't let these delays add more guilt to your gunnysack.

We all make a thousand mistakes but they can be undone. Sometimes it's quite easy, sometimes it takes much effort, but always we find that love makes the undoing that much easier. It is surprising, in fact, how much parents do that is right, for there are so many forks on every road. When the map is finally charted, you will be amazed at how smooth the path looks in retrospect.

Motherhood, it turns out, has just enough turns to keep you interested and enough peaks to hide most of the valleys.

CHILD

The Middle Years are supposed to be latent, but they are about as latent as winter. Now boys and girls draw in the nutrition they need to bloom in the spring of adolescence. Even so, your child may act as if he's becalmed in conformity. A schoolchild is governed by a seemingly mindless need to be just like his friends, but that's only on the surface. Underneath his careful, watchful ways, his mind fairly seethes with the wonder of the world, and he stuffs knowledge into his head as hungrily as he stuffs food in his mouth. He knows instinctively that he must learn as much as he can to be competent, for competence is what this age is all about.

Although your child's behavior doesn't switch dramatically from month to month as it did in the preschool years, it is still peppered with sudden changes, which will surprise and exasperate you. It is hard to believe that anyone can be so smart yet tell such lies; be so cocky by day and have such fears at night; be so clumsy now when he was so surefooted a year ago. His behavior, uncertain though it is, is a sign of the backing and forthing all children go through between Six and Twelve, for the body, the mind, the psyche and the conscience grow in stages and each is based on the one that's gone before.

These stages are predictable—and always in sequence. While man is the most adaptable of animals, we still follow immutable laws. The mind and the spirit can no more skip a step than the body can grow its last inch before it has filled in all the others between. These stages, each more complex than the last, bring confusion when they come.

Sudden physical growth—the need to fit his new size into old spaces—often makes a child feel awkward, and he finds it just as difficult to enter new mental, psychological and moral stages. Each time he approaches the next one he is assailed by new doubts and will often act much younger than he is and more self-centered.

There is a push forward and then a drawing back—a minuet of gains and occasionally of losses. New goals must be conquered each time, and everything that has been mastered once must be tested again.

Old triumphs are often repeated—although there is no guarantee—but the real problems usually come when the body, mind, psyche and conscience are developing at different rates of speed. Instead of a smooth, equal growth, you have a spurt here and a spurt there, with as much as a three- to four-year time lag between them. The developments may blend fairly well, but they never truly synchronize and sometimes they can clash like cymbals. This gives us the Twelve who looks like Fourteen—and acts like Ten. The clashes will also be worse if there is tension, at home or at school, or if someone else in the household is making changes too or tries to hold him back. Resistance is both futile and unfair: a child is born to grow.

His progress seems slow to you now and even slower to him, after the fast-paced growth of early childhood. Suddenly everything seems to slacken, particularly at Seven, Eight and Nine, as the stages and accomplishments become much less apparent. Once a child can read a book, the number of pages is less notable, and once he can climb a tree with safety, the height he reaches hardly matters.

The requirements at this age are serious but subtle. The child will want you—or somebody—to be there when he comes home from school, even if he never says so; he will expect you to hear the nuances of his silences as loudly as his words and will need you to encourage him to be as brave and outgoing as he wants to be, instead of as fearful and shy as he often feels.

Now the grand image he has had of himself begins to fade (as it will fade again when he changes from the hotshot high school senior to become just one more college freshman or when he goes off to conquer the world with his new degree and finds himself at the bottom of the ladder again). The emotional hurts and stumbles of boys and girls at Six or Seven are at least as painful as the goose eggs and the nicks of a Two. There was a time when they took their pratfalls in public but now the bruises are inside and the only ones they know about are their own. This simply makes them feel more inept.

By the middle of second grade your child, who started school as a reasonably well-tended, self-reliant person, will surely be more timid and lonely—a person who spends most of his time trying to be just like his best friend, never suspecting that his friend wants to be just like him. It's as if he's used up a lifetime of curiosity in the first six years. Now he avoids the unusual even if it's dropped in his path.

There are other significant changes which seem more positive. Your child may be less demonstrative but more sensitive to the needs of others; he may seem less imaginative but more attuned to logic. He also is less scattershot than he used to be, concentrating on one thing at a time, particularly on himself. It may seem as if he spends his whole seventh year worrying about his appeal, his abilities—even his health—and he does it with an intensity that can be alarming. He may even borrow worries from his parents. Although your child will no longer mimic your mannerisms or copy your expressions, he will reflect your tensions and resentments, and display them much more openly than you do, which may both surprise and concern you.

An Eight sees your limitations and foibles with a new clarity, and is both shocked and elated. He knows, for sure, that you don't have eyes in the back of your head, and it gives him a delicious sense of victory. Now he can sit at the kitchen table and pick his nose while you stir the soup on the stove—and you'll never know. It's foolishness like this that will give him the courage to be his own person, and in time to find his own place in the sun.

He will soon be running around in a gang of boys, and she with a circle of girls. This instinctive division of the sexes is fine. This is not a good time to be playing doctor. While the sex drive is suppressed, the energy is still there. It's just channeled in ways that may seem odd to you, but they help a child think and move better.

Now boys and girls fortify themselves with one academic skill after another—even arithmetic and penmanship for a while—but extracurricular activities usually challenge them more. These children collect stickers and baseball cards, seashells and comic books—sorting and classifying them again and again, with the same precision they will use later to sort and classify ideas. They are laying the basis of logic and abstract thought and therefore of morality. Children can't have a true conscience until they able to think well in abstractions.

Sports and other activities are pursued at least as zestily as any collection, especially at Ten, Eleven and Twelve. Boys and girls play soccer, career on a skateboard, watch television, read books, tend their animals and build model planes in every spare moment and quite a few that are not. You will find your child weaving his latest interest into every story he tells—including the long, convoluted account of what happened (or didn't happen) on the class trip to the planetarium. The scenarios may bore you but treasure this child just the same. You're looking at a mosaic, a beautiful work of art made up of many parts—rich and shiny, utilitarian and tough—all constantly shifting but generally fitting together a little better every year.

While he follows the pattern of all children, your child remains unique. That is the most miraculous fact of all and this you should know, as well as you know the color of his eyes. There never has been—never will be—another person like him, because he has a special collection of genes that will never be duplicated. It gave him a temperament all his own, conditioned still more in the womb by the rise and fall of your hormones, and the motion and commotion your body transmitted. He was born to be basically outgoing or shy, tense or relaxed, but everything that has happened to him since then has changed him in some slight way. The Four who was warned to keep out of the street—for the very sensible reason that he might get smashed—grows up to be a slightly different (and healthier) person than he would be if he could have wandered wherever he wanted.

Your child has also been shaped by the size of your family and his rank in it; the number of years between your children; the ages of you and your husband; the joy of your marriage; the amount of time you each work and the money you earn; the kind of attention you give; the relatives he visits and the rituals he experiences; the illnesses he gets and the foods he eats; the abilities he acquires; the neighborhood he lives in and the school he attends; the friends he has. All of this—and much more—make a child develop just a little differently but none of them change his basic characteristics.

Just as you can predict the height a Two will be when he's grown, so can you predict the kind of adult he will be. The personality he had at Two is much the same as the personality he has at Eight and the one he will have at Twenty. The thoughtful child is the reflective adult; the rough-and-tumble scalawag is the rowdy young man; the flirty little girl is, yes, the flirty big girl. People are all of a unit. A child often needs some help getting back on the track when he strays, but the personality is still the same; only the strengths and weaknesses shift.

The more you accept your child's eccentricities, the easier it is for him to accept yours—and that's a blessing, since there never has been another person quite like you either. Empathy flowers when everyone understands that the world has as many drummers as it has people. When your child truly understands that both of you are one of a kind, and that you know his needs, his goals and his joys are very

much his own, he will understand that your style of parenthood can't be quite the same as the kind he sees next door. He will even see that each child in his own family has special needs, and each must be treated in some special way. Where one gets dancing lessons, another is sent to soccer camp, and where you give your daughter a puppy when she is going through a bad stretch, you take your son and his friends camping at the beach when he needs to show off a bit. It is really a matter of keeping in tune with your child.

His basic needs are few, although each one lasts a lifetime. He needs to be independent, he needs to be capable, he needs to be accepted, he needs to be loved and he needs to be needed. The child whose needs are met will be a success. This doesn't necessarily mean he will make good grades now or a great deal of money later, although the child who expects to shine generally will. Rather, a successful person is one who has self-esteem and a love for living; who can afford to be kind to others; who can think—and act—for himself, and who can dare to risk failure.

Studies show that the child with a high self-esteem has the most creativity, the best chance for success of all kinds and even the greatest popularity, for other children see a child the way a child sees himself. It works both ways. A child reflects the image he thinks others have of him, no matter how bright, how able or how handsome he is. Your little girl knows she is smart, not because she can figure out the right answers quickly, but because she feels that others find her lovable and worth-

while. Your ten-year-old son may spend secret hours flexing his muscles in front of a mirror, but it is the attitude of his family—and to some extent his friends—that tell him he has a body beautiful, and not his picture in that looking glass. A child will feel like a champion if he can count on support at home, but he can't learn enough or achieve enough to feel good about himself if he gets day-in, day-out criticism instead, even if it's only implied.

Someday he will marry the kind of person he thinks is right for him and take the sort of job he feels he can handle. Both choices will reflect not only his own inclinations but also how he thinks others see him. If his self-portrait is wrong, these decisions may be wrong too, which is one reason why the divorce rate is so high.

What you hope your child will perceive is a true picture of himself and that picture should be forming now. Reality comes most easily when a child knows his strengths—and his weaknesses. For this he needs the chance to try many things so he can discover his three or four natural talents. People don't have equal abilities, but everyone should have the chance to recognize his own. A child who is awful in math, mediocre in volleyball and extraordinarily good in sculpture has the right to know where he stands all along the line.

Talents must be developed and encouraged, with enough hard work and training to turn them into skills, for competence is his passkey to confidence and maturity.

Every child should do whatever he can for himself but never will a feeling of competence be as important to him as it is in these Middle Years. When he was younger your child would have been proud of the cookies he had baked, although some burned, or the coatrack he had built, although a nail fell out, but now he judges himself

by the results, not the effort. That's why he practices a skill over and over (to your distraction) until he has mastered it. This is the same tenacity he showed as a toddler when he climbed the stairs again and again. And again.

Not only is your child trying to provide himself with enough inner strength to last a lifetime but he also is balancing his ego against the awesome and often abusive power of school. Even the best school will disillusion a child a little bit—and it should to some extent because school is a reflection of the real world. He learns that no matter how hard he tries there is almost always someone bigger or smarter or tougher than he is. There is a teacher ready to correct him, a classmate to tease. This is a reality every child must learn to handle.

Your positive, realistic expectations will show him that you have faith in his abilities; that you expect him to do a job not perfectly but fairly well; to share with the family chores; to work for sweet charity; to learn something extra—just for the pleasure of learning; to respect the values of the family and to give as much to a friendship as he hopes to get. All of these expectations give a child his parameters.

It is a fine line for you to walk, for it takes experience to know just how much a child can do, and parents are likely to expect more, rather than less, particularly of a firstborn. They may also expect more if they are disappointed in their own achievements. Other parents may see their children not so much as their surrogates but as their clones, although they can, of course, be neither. We have no right to assign our own goals to our children. A child is not a toy, or a pet, or a trophy, and most particularly not a replica of his mother or father.

You can let your child be his own person by letting him accept the consequences, positive or negative, his behavior brings. This is how he will discover that luck—and the ambitions of others—are the least of life. We are what we make of ourselves.

SIX

A Six can seem like a human yo-yo. He can be lovable, adorable, shy, dramatic, dawdling, tattling, serious, angelic, anxious, rowdy, giggling, wiggling and still great fun, all in the course of a day. You appreciate the fun and hardly notice the variations. Once you have lived with a Two and a Four, a Six seems pretty tame, and besides—he's away from home a lot.

His moods swing in a wide arc, with good reason. Here he stands, on the threshold of tomorrow, his whole world changing around him and within him, and he has to find out where he fits. He is trying on a dozen different styles of behavior, the way you try on hats in a store. Sixes are fusing two different environments—home and school—and at the same time their minds and bodies are taking giant steps forward. No wonder they get a bit tense.

As they get closer to Seven, their minds will start tracking in new ways. They have learned to read and are almost ready to understand simple math concepts. Their bodies are changing just as fast. Now the knock-knees disappear, the swaybacks begin to straighten and, while their appetites get ferocious, their bellies continue to flatten. Their faces are making major changes too. The jaw is growing to accommodate the new molars and the rootless milk teeth are falling out in the same order in which they came in, for nothing is as systematic as nature. The new permanent teeth won't fit the face very well, however, and you find yourself saying that beauty, after all, is only skin deep.

This beauty principle applies to clothes too. No matter what a Six wears, it quickly looks worn. Even the best shoes turn into scruffy, wretched little sock-eaters and pants become ragtags with holes at the knees.

Now fingers lose some of their dexterity—sixes drop their forks at least once at every meal—but they control their arms and legs better and better. With practice, they can swim fairly well, hike a couple of miles, scramble up a tree and weave a bike down the sidewalk so skillfully it hardly ever wobbles.

A six wants to climb higher, jump farther and spin faster than he ever has before and with scant regard for the consequences. This is not because he is particularly brave but because he is a great optimist. Naturally this produces many pratfalls and maybe an occasional broken bone but far fewer tears than you might expect, for your Six is a cocky child.

Now you are dealing with a king—and a queen—of the mountain: boisterous, swaggering and with such a regal sense of self-appreciation that everyone else is expected to share it, including other Sixes. It is this bravado that gives your child his boastful ways, as well as the let-down feeling he gets when he doesn't think people are paying him proper obeisance. This is the boy or girl who will tease with ease but dissolve when teased in return, for the ego of a Six is as fragile as a butterfly's wing.

This is one reason why dolls and imaginary playmates are so comforting now—they never talk back. It also is part of the pleasure Sixes take in magic in general, and their faith in tooth fairies, Santa and other elves reaches a pinnacle now. Despite their growing sophistication, these children still will them to be true.

Most of their friends are not imaginary however: Sixes are too gregarious for that. You may notice that your child plays best

with one, three or five other children, and this is because Sixes don't really play in groups but two by two. A Six plays well with others for only about a half hour (at least without a referee) but in this brief time he'll still tattle a tale or two. Even the Friend of the Month isn't safe. Everything is exaggerated—especially the telling. It isn't that this dear child is lying, he simply sees everything from his own point of view.

Now he discovers that the world is bigger than he ever imagined; he is just one person among many. This new perspective can be painful, particularly to the more pampered child. Instinctively a Six knows that the best defense is a good offense and at home your Six becomes an aggressive soul, especially with Mom. The more Sixes can cut the ties, the easier it is for them to walk out into the world, and that is what a Six has to do. This new sense of independence is reflected not just in the way they play but in the way they stand and the way they talk. Now they delight in using bad words (usually scatological) to give many orders and to have a lot to say about everything. Moreover, they talk in two languages—verbal and body English. They squirm, they squeak, they wriggle and smirk. If your child feels comfortable with your friends he will behave like a paid entertainer and perform and perform . . . and perform, but if he feels ill at ease he burrows in the chair and becomes a fanny-scooching, nose-picking embarrassment.

While Sixes usually talk a good show, even alone with their parents, they are beset by the old and the new—one moment spilling over with self-confidence, the next as tentative as newborn kittens.

Their health is not quite as good as it was, with more nose and throat infections and more allergies, as new ones develop and old ones return. Fatigue is more common too, but since Sixes think it's babyish to take a nap, they may want to watch more TV—a face-saving way to rest.

Although they daydream much less, fears resurface again and they worry about wind, rain or lightning, tiny bugs or fanciful animals and places that get so dark, like basements, wells and attics. There are deeper fears too, born of all that they are expected to do and the fear that it can't be done. From now on you have to listen harder, leaving long silences for your child to fill, and repeating any complaints, almost in his own words, so that he can elaborate on them without getting sidetracked by your reactions.

As always your child becomes disturbed by things that may surprise you. He may weep because someone he barely knows hasn't invited him to a birthday party or be angry because someone older and wiser (like you) has something he does not. A Six can be as possessive as a banker at foreclosure (or a mid-Two). Tantrums, however, are easily diverted now, and just when you think you can't bear a minute more your Six becomes an angel—full of understanding and generosity. At this age a child is usually eager to do for others, as long as he gets the credit.

Their anxieties are much smaller than they were at mid-Five and many confusions have been resolved. By mid-Six such a sense of equilibrium prevails that they almost brim over with enthusiasm. This is the happiness that lets them start a hundred projects, although they will finish very few.

Most of this joy is built on school, for these children think about little else. They dream about it at night and at breakfast your child will call you Miss Brown, looking aghast as he remembers how often he has called his teacher "Mom." As much as Sixes like school, they still dillydally in the morning and then will rush out of the house without books or lunch unless reminded. If you went along, you would see your child running and skipping all the way, bouncing into the building and then sidling into the classroom, only breathing easy when the teacher welcomes him by name.

Like the other boys and girls, he plays outdoors at full tilt at each recess and in the classroom he works with a much better attention span than he had a year ago, even though—like everyone else—he will squirm in his seat and drop his pencil with a rat-a-tat-tat that should drive a teacher wild.

Sixes come home exhausted, with their stomachs empty and their heads full. They talk nonstop and then, eager to do their homework, they must be urged to play outside while there is still some sunshine. But be assured: when they do finish their schoolwork, they insist that their little brother or sister play a game called school—and the Six, of course, will be the teacher. This is the way Sixes not only relive the good times but they also right whatever went wrong, just as they worked out their problems when they used to play house in kindergarten.

At night they do their chores fairly quickly (if there is someone to keep them company in the kitchen), and if reminded, they bathe, forgo television and lay out their clothes all without too much fuss, and all because school is tomorrow. School continues to be the main factor in their lives for at least twelve years, but it may never be so appreciated again.

SEVEN

Seven is the year you've been waiting for: the Age of Reason arrives. Now, you hope, your child will begin to empathize, to compromise, to get on with the business of growing up. Actually the Seven, that lamb, is doing all these things, but often with such a dismal air that it is hard to praise his achievements. Although nobody can be as silly or as sweet or as cuddly as Sevens, their manner often seems overlaid with a patina of sadness.

Some of this is not sadness at all but a dreamy kind of musing that helps them arrange their emotional and mental puzzle in a new way. This is a pivotal year. They no longer think the moon and the sun follow them about and they begin to real- ize that they are not the center of the universe, although it will take years—or maybe a lifetime—for them to discover that each person has a universe all his own.

As Sevens become less egocentric, they see experiences, ideas and relationships in a new light and feel closer to those around them. Now they can admit that their teach- ers have quirks, yet they love them still and they tolerate the peculiarities of their friends for longer stretches.

How they respond to their brothers and sisters is determined as much by their positions in the family as by their person- alities. They tease the younger children and treat the older ones almost reveren- tially, especially if they are the same sex. Parents also are regarded with a new awareness. You and your husband are no longer seen as a functioning unit but as two separate people, capable of having completely different feelings.

By looking at others as individuals, your child begins to realize that they see him as an individual too. It is an awesome idea. The dawn of such an amazing percep- tion would make anyone self-conscious, but since a Seven usually goes overboard in whatever he does, his self-consciousness is magnified. The more your child agonizes over what others think of him, the more he may turn into a first-class worry wart. Now he frets over innumerable possibili- ties: of being left out, of being spanked, of getting an F, of being seen crying in pub- lic—or of being seen naked, even in pri- vate.

Most of all, however, Sevens worry about being accepted, and are hurt by the most casual remark, which may remind you of the old-fashioned picture of the sad little child who is saying that no one loves him so he may as well go out to the garden and eat worms. Surely this child was Seven. There's a reason for this. Children get their first taste of puberty now, as weak hormones start pumping into their bodies. This can make self-doubts reach such a point this year that one dreadful day your child may pack his bag and run away from home, only to sit pathetically on the curb because he can't cross such a big street without permission.

The rejection a child feels now is hard for him to explain to himself, since it has never happened before, and it is just as hard for you to explain really, since it isn't happening now. Exasperation rather than praise is apt to be your instinctive recourse, but it's praise and respect that he needs. Respect does not, of course, guarantee paradise, but if Sevens think their parents respect them they do feel more confident. This makes them fairly easy to live with, and they may even help around the house without being asked—although usually not alone and not for long—and they will try to remember to wash their hands before dinner, to use their forks and napkins and to eat new foods, especially if there is a dessert.

No matter how much respect you give, your child will stood brood and complain and sulk now and then. Sevens are truly shy, dear people, who try to be good and expect to be perfect. Their own expectations, rather than yours, are the ones that cause the most trouble, salting everything they do with a little disappointment. If your child decides that you still see him as the child he was a year ago, he will feel like a failure, for his behavior will reflect the opinion he thinks you have of him. A Seven, consciously or unconsciously, aims to please.

The fact, as you both must learn, is that it takes years and years to grow up. The child feels stuck in such a rut, it's enough to make anyone sad. As much as a Seven enjoys repetition, learning seems mighty slow. The first grade had been a world of wonders, where everything was new, but good old safe second grade, like

the fourth and the sixth, is a reinforcement of the years that went before. All lessons need to be repeated to make them stick, but it is a policy with built-in tedium.

Again and again you will have to remind your child how much he has learned in one year, for once Sevens can do something well they can't remember when they couldn't. To know the seasons and the months seems natural now, but what they don't know will trouble them. It doesn't matter that they can tell their lefts from their rights, when they still can't set a place across the table without getting the silverware reversed.

Telling time is one new trick that brings visible pride. A Seven can read the hour and the minute as soon as he can tell "before" and "after," and even though he may have a digital watch he may now pine for the old-fashioned kind—a prize that will last approximately five days or until he takes his next bath, whichever comes first. Whether or not it keeps working is irrelevant. This watch is like a merit badge, for all the world to see, but don't expect your child to check it much, for Sevens have a poor concept of time even though they can read it.

Sevens have many other and more notable accomplishments. Their growth is smooth and steady now, with well-coordinated arms and legs, and their permanent teeth are coming in so fast, the second grade looks like a roomful of bunny rabbits. Despite this similarity, the children come in all sizes and shapes now, for they are obviously growing at different rates of speed. Even their eyes are changing, and glasses may be necessary.

They are healthy little rascals with few colds, although they are so intense they may have some nervous, jerky mannerisms and they won't always be as lively as they were a year ago. Your child may have sudden attacks of fatigue, hanging around like an old shoe for hours, then suddenly bounding out of his chair to badger his little brother or throw himself into some game as if possessed. Bed is a Seven's heaven, a haven, a place to calm down, to cuddle with a teddy, and to sleep eleven long, hard hours at night, seldom interrupted by nightmares or potty trips.

School brings out the best in boys and girls now. They compute well, recognize words quickly, read to themselves at home every day and treasure the comics—especially the ones about nature. It is comforting to these children, whose inner world has been turned topsy-turvy, to know that there are answers and rules that govern spelling and subtraction. Rote alone is not enough, however; it must be underscored by concepts. They need to be able to make sense of information, and if the concepts are missing they substitute intuition—a process that can give them some pretty wacky ideas.

Activities are more focused too, and their collection mania begins in earnest now. They save and sort all kinds of trivia, as they will for the next five years. Children finish most of their projects now because their attention span is longer, their determination greater and their concentration deeper.

Their concentration is sometimes so deep that they may go about muttering to themselves or acting as if they have a hearing problem, for they screen out many noises now—particularly the ones they don't want to hear. At the same time their voices may actually get louder and higher, as if they were trying to pierce their own consciousnesses.

Perhaps the most thrilling side of Seven is the way their minds change as they grasp new ideas, one after another. While a younger child is interested in what happens, a Seven wants to know what caused it to happen. This introspection, coupled with new abilities, will open—and sometimes quickly close—new doors. They may beg for music lessons, only to find the daily practice more than the heart can han-

dle and that the lessons teach more humility than music. When Sevens feel comfortable about an activity, however, they'll do it willingly, over and over, almost endlessly.

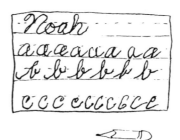

You will see your child put his body and his mind through repetitious paces the way he did when he was Two, practicing a skill over and over again until it is mastered. But being a Seven, he does it much longer and harder, whether it is giggling, jumping rope, practicing penmanship or holding his breath under water. This attitude extends to all facets of his life. If Sevens have done something that is fun, they beg to do it again, but they seldom do it as well as they remember, which just gives these champion complainers something new to grouse about.

At times television can be a savior, for a Seven will watch, zombie-like, while his head subconsciously gets itself together again. It seems a passive pastime, but he will insist that he is busy and, in a way, he is. Because a Seven has so much to absorb, he often needs privacy—the chance to think a thought through—and an hour of television is one way to get it. The programs he watches (and the fairy tales he reads and the movies he sees) need to be monitored carefully for violence, however, since fears are often swallowed whole and remain undigested. Even the most sheltered Seven finds something to fear. Strangers and goblins lurk like shadows and are just as scary, which is why he may become uneasy when you go out after dark. He also may be afraid of heights, depths and (whisper as you say it) cemeteries.

This timidity is reflected in his play. A

Seven is a great climber of gym sets and high trees, a lover of wild, physical games with his friends and a willing roughhouser with his dad, but there is, fortunately, an element of caution you haven't seen before. Now you have a child who thinks before he leaps, so that, while the clothes get torn more than ever, the body usually stays intact.

Since a child would rather do some things very well than do everything sort of well, you will find that both boys and girls are attracted to the games that are identified with their sex. This has at least as much to do with the way they are built as the way they are taught. Boys pursue baseball and especially football, since they have begun to throw a little better than girls, and girls, who outclass boys in the broad jump, gravitate to games like hopscotch. All of this separates the sexes, but it also reinforces their abilities and their self-confidence.

Some sports, like soccer, charm them both, now and for years to come. Even though boys and girls play on the same team, however, they still segregate themselves in their minds, for each sex wants less and less to do with the other. This is because the Seven, who retreats in many areas, retreats in sex too.

The experiments of a year ago are now embarrassing memories and a Seven only dares to think about sex in terms of new babies (expect a request for one) and how they are cared for, in and out of the womb, and particularly how *you* cared for *him*.

This is also the peak of the passion a little girl is apt to have for her daddy and a son for his mom—and sometimes the source of frightening dreams about the other parent.

Nevertheless, a child feels attached to both parents now. He likes the intimacy of being read the same stories again and again, and enjoys long conversations with you about serious subjects—like outer space and inner truths—as well as silly chatter. This child considers jokes to be the ultimate smart talk and is able to divide them into two categories. Jokes in the first category, which are told only to friends, either make fun of adults or they contain vulgarity and/or bathroom language—the favorite form of cussing at Seven. Jokes in the second category, which he will tell you and everyone else repeatedly, will teach you things you never thought you wanted to know, like why elephants fall out of trees (because rhinoceroses push them, of course).

The conscience of a Seven is as uncertain as his wit. It would be lovely if we could have full faith in the judgment of a Seven, but we can't. His conscience won't really be his guide for another five to nine years. Until then your child can resist if one or maybe two friends are naughty, but not if all of them misbehave, and not if his best friend does—a behavior pattern that will intensify in the next two years.

An occasional ill-chosen buddy is no cause for alarm, but you do have to monitor his friendships by making it more convenient for him to see some playmates than others. Even without that, the close friendships of the Seven ebb and flow and change as he seeks one mirror image after the next, according to his changing self-esteem and who else is living on the block.

Watch a group of five or six children playing happily together and one will suddenly shout that Janet won't give up the swing! Actually these children, although still more takers than givers, are much less selfish than they used to be, but they play so enthusiastically they get carried away by the game.

This child will bluff and brag too—particularly a boy, which often makes him the target of older boys. All of this underscores his sense of self-righteousness. Now he runs home with the weeps even though he started the fight, and once again you will see that a Seven is a rotten loser. Adult supervision, like the beady eye of the boss, does wonders for decorum.

At this age, clubs and gangs form over and over again, adding a couple of children here and dropping a few there. Who gets left out is as much the point as who is invited to join, and rejection always triggers a Seven's capacity for self-pity. Children are not cruel but they are incredibly direct, instinctively correcting one another by acceptance or rejection. Their reactions to these frank opinions can affect their behavior more than you do. Now you discover: The family is not enough.

Although Sevens are less likely to blame others when things go wrong, they still aren't ready to assume responsibility themselves; instead, they see luck everywhere. Each one thinks he has all the bad and everyone else has all the good. That's why so many Sevens are sure they were swapped in the cradle—a universal fantasy that, if true, would have us up to our knees in princesses and princes, with not a peasant around. After all, if a child is going to invent a new family, it might as well have class. These inventions are part of your child's love affair with adventure, mystery and all sorts of magic. The tooth fairy is another one and well regarded (at the rate he loses teeth, why not?) but a Seven is too sophisticated to believe in Santa Claus. Even God may come in for big doubts.

Although Sevens do fantasize, they lie much less, since they now can blame bad luck. The closest they come to lying may be through omission. A Seven is likely to bring home only his best papers, tossing them casually on the table (and aching inside if he isn't sufficiently praised). For all their honesty with words, however, Sevens may steal with few qualms for they don't think it's wrong until they're made

to understand that stealing hurts someone else.

These light-fingered ways tell you how hard it still is for a Seven to put himself in someone else's shoes. Empathy is no overnight virtue. When your child takes something from home to school without permission, you may think of it as little more than show and tell, but alas, he probably will feel just as free to bring home someone's brand-new ballpoint pen. The experts probably are right when they see this as a child's need to bridge two worlds, home and school, but a mother knows that her Seven only takes what he first covets.

Inexplicably to an adult, colored pencils seem to be the second-grader's favorite art supply, followed by felt-tipped pens and crayons, all in as many colors as possible. Even a plain old yellow No. 2 lead pencil has a certain charm, as long as it has an eraser. Your child may clutch his pencil so tightly in class that he drops it again and again as the tension makes his fingers numb. By the end of the year so much pressure has been exerted so often that the bump on his middle finger may last for years.

Seven is the age of paper, as well as pencils. There is the paper airplane, the paper doll, the paper anything, so long as it involves paste and that special delight, a pair of scissors. Where you once kept them out of sight because of their sharp points, you now may want to hide them to avoid all those snippets on the floor. Whatever comes from these efforts is likely to seem more prosaic than artistic, like so much else that he does. Take heart.

Nothing is as creative as the development of a child—even in these still years.

EIGHT

Eights are voracious. Not only do they eat everything in sight, but they are hungry for anything new. They need new trees to climb, new streets to cross, new treasures to hoard, new jokes to laugh at.

As silly as Eights can be, they will be even sillier when they're around someone younger, for they adore to perform. All the world is a stage at this age and they are front and center, and if they aren't on-stage, they are rowdy members of the audience. Anything vulgar tickles these boys and girls. Just the mention of an ''elevator-ful of buggers'' will bring the house down (says one whose house has often come down).

Now that your child has had a year to pull his world together, he is at peace with himself, free to flit here and there, probing nothing very deeply, but intent on touching every base. You watch him gauge each new situation, each new piece of information, trying to see where it fits into his life. It is this sorting of ideas that makes religion intriguing to him again, for it is a puzzle with so many pieces.

While Seven was his pivotal year, Eight will be yours. Once he has his new self firmly in place, you can expect him to have a big impact on the whole household. Suddenly this wonderful, exuberant, bouncy, brassy child is omnipresent. Every time you turn around, your Eight is right there, listening in, hanging around, getting inside your soul. This child exhausted you as an infant and nearly overwhelmed you at Two, but now you make the real discovery: he was just warming up.

From now on you and your husband will seldom have any time alone unless you go out of the house or set aside some of the dinner hour for yourselves. The ubiquity of your Eight may make you decide—if you haven't already—that you cannot afford any more babies. It isn't the money but the time and the space and the way this child invades the privacy of your mind. Even a year ago, you could nod and say, ''Ummm,'' while you wrote the grocery list in your head, but not anymore. Now he has opinions about everything and you are going to know what they are. Suddenly this child is a Person, who not only stays up almost as late as you do but takes up nearly as much space. One night he was in his nitey-nites, snuggling in your lap for story time, and the next, it seems, there is this someone in jeans who sprawls across the best armchair, eating popcorn, reading the newspaper (your newspaper) and listening, always listening, to everything that's said.

No matter how low you murmur or how cryptically you tell your husband that things aren't going well down the street, you can bet that Ears hears. Are the Smiths getting a divorce? he wants to know. Did Mr. Jones lose his job? Is Mrs. Johnson really sick? Is she going to DIE?

Even if well squished, you know your child is cataloguing the information to share with his best friend. Such bits of gossip are the trading stamps of the Middle Years. This isn't because your child is nosy or unkind or malicious but because he is old enough now to empathize, so he insinuates himself into every adult situation—in books, on television, in real life—by imagining how he would behave in that situation. It's one more way he figures out what kind of a person he is.

Your phone conversations are monitored too. Just when you think you can dream with your best friend about the degree you hope to get or the camper you want to buy, your Eight suddenly springs up like a mushroom with who?/what?/when?/where?/how?

His new fascination with money makes these discussions particularly intriguing, but he may panic if he hears you talk about "being broke" or "going to the poorhouse." These are the worries he locks inside, however, unless you notice his uneasiness.

As he takes more and more space in your house, he also takes more space in your mind, for the older a child gets, the more attention he needs. You have to decide how much responsibility a third-grader can handle and how much supervision he needs. He wants you to hear the undercurrents of his conversations, to pick up the signals of concern before they turn into Maydays. Now you must listen closely to what he says, rather than "um-ming" along. It is the interest of his parents that support an Eight's ego and tells him he is worthwhile. Never has the need for you to listen—truly listen—been so serious, and the need will grow and grow. Suddenly you are dealing with a full-fledged person, requiring more rights, more freedoms and more respect than ever before. Discipline is still needed but it must be much less direct.

The needs of an Eight are so unrelenting, you may feel a constant resentment, although it may not be spoken or even acknowledged. This puts an extra stress on your marriage, but you can prepare for it if you know you're in for the long run and are willing to deal with it honestly. This is no time to kid yourself: the family package isn't perfect—it never was (and never will be). You wouldn't know it, however, by the way your child acts. If imitation is the most sincere form of flattery, it is also the first sign of change. From Eight until Ten, children want to be just like their parents—your daughter like you; your son like his dad. An Eight who lives with only one parent because of divorce or death should have a regular replacement—if not the parent, then a friend, a neighbor or an experienced sitter of the same sex. Eights need the time and instruction and camaraderie that come from working alongside people they admire as they prune a shrub, clamp a plug onto an electric cord or rake and burn the leaves.

Such quality attention is good for any child, in any kind of family situation and at any age, but Eights require it. This is the time for heroes and parents are the heroes of choice. Even though they often take their mothers and fathers off the pedestal, they quickly put them back.

While both boys and girls give their parents a lot of affection, attention and praise, they demand just as much in return—particularly from their mothers. Whatever you say, whatever you do—even what clothes you wear—matters a great deal. Although your child tries to be stoic, he still may cry over your rebukes. This is a good time to reassess both your expectations and your demands. While they are not identical to those of another mother, they should be realistic, for you and your child are each unique.

Children like to prove that they're dependable, but they shouldn't have more responsibility than they can handle. They can't perform at top level all the time, and they can't perform very often or for very long. Eights, after all, are still pretty young. If they feel their parents' expectations are beyond them—whether they are or not—they may be afraid to try or they will try and fail and then feel guilty, and in either case they will resent it.

Because Mother means so much to an Eight, your child may also get very mad with you and call you some wretched name or, if he doesn't have the nerve to argue with you directly, he may get into a fight with his brother or sister. Once he's asserted his independence, however, he will get over his anger quickly—and may leave you quite cross.

Eights treat their friends the same way. Although sensitive to their criticism, they often ask for it and they bicker quite a bit when they play together, especially if they are unsupervised. Quarrels are inevitable, and in fact they can be good, for they help children practice the art of giving and getting. There may even be tears before the sunshine—which follows the most dramatic squabbles fairly quickly—for neither boys nor girls are as sophisticated as they pretend and will also cry sometimes when they're tired or a book makes them sad.

Although Eights play in groups more and more, they choose one special friend to hear their dreams of glory—for anything seems possible now—as well as their gripes about bratty little brothers and sisters who get into their things. This best friend may change from time to time, but not the need to have one—a need that will last at least until Eleven. Together this pair will re-enact real-life situations with their robots or their dolls—paper, Barbie or G. I. Joe—and will play almost endless games of Parcheesi, dominoes, checkers and even rudimentary games of chess. Since the most sedate game with Eights may get wild, it is a wise mother who stays near when they play in the house.

Any talk about a best friend means, of course, another boy, if you have a son, or a girl, if you have a daughter. Eights, Nines and Tens absolutely align themselves by sex and there is no need to do anything about it.

Because sex is sublimated, the only discussions about it will be the ones you initiate. At this age children need to understand that, while sex is a natural, positive process for most people, this is unfortunately not true for all and child abuse is often sexual. Although you began giving the first gentle warnings at Two, they become very important now,

since an Eight goes far afield. It is also the time to emphasize, once more, that sex is part of love. Those children who are told through the years that sex is more than a mating game will make responsible decisions about sex when they are older. You won't need to dwell on this now, for even small discussions on sex make our Eights uncomfortable, although a girl can't help wondering what it's like to have a *thing* (and a boy wonders, heaven help us, what it's like *not* to have one!). A little girl may even try to kiss her elbow now and then so she can turn into a boy but always quits in skittish alarm. What if she gets stuck that way?

This division of the sexes is one reason why clubhouses are built now. The basic purpose is still the same as it was when you were young: for little girls to let boys know where the clubhouse is, and then to keep them out—and for little boys to treat little girls the same way, except much more vociferously. Girls are willing to have clubs anywhere, anytime, but if boys can't have the fun of building a tree house or a lean-to of pine boughs, they would rather spend this time playing on their beloved teams or playing elaborate games of war, whether you know about them or not. It's all part of being in a gang—a preference which gets stronger and stronger for both boys and girls in the next two years. You see this in all the activities that Eights like best—Cub Scouts, Little League, Brownies, soccer, baseball, pajama parties, follow-the-leader, hide-and-seek—anything that gathers a herd.

Of all the gang activities, none has greater appeal to our crazy Eights than playacting. They spend a lot of time jockeying to write on the blackboard or clap the erasers in the classroom, just to be in front of everyone and to feel the sweet agony of performing. To be in a real play is simply terrific. It gives a child the chance not only to escape dull reality but to be applauded for it. Both boys and girls—but especially girls—enjoy producing their own shows, making them up as they go along, although the players and the plays sometimes end in tears, often in giggles and always in confusion. You are expected to watch and cheer and you will be astonished by your daughter's getup, as glamorous and as tarty as can be. Now you see how she will look as an adult—minus, one trusts, a great deal of rouge.

As the chrysalis of young childhood begins to shatter, you have a glimpse of the face of tomorrow, although it's too early to tell how the body will shape itself. Today's growth is usually slow and tells you little. Those who do grow fast now may become quite skinny; those who don't may gain too much weight. Eights go at everything full tilt, even the way they eat. Their bodies don't have time to register that they're already full before they take another helping.

Although some Eights may be too thin or too fat, and there may be a return of hay fever or asthma, they are generally healthy and graceful. Their bodies are co-ordinated enough for gymnastics, tumbling, biking, skating and swimming and their muscles are finally developed enough to dance *en pointe* in ballet without damaging the hamstrings.

Precise skills are easier now too, although handwriting takes great effort. Eights also can cut their meat at dinner, but so poorly it is kinder to cut some of it for them before their plates are passed or they will be embarrassed by the time it takes to do it and the mess it makes. Such sensitivity may surprise you, but much as Eights like to fool around, they do try to behave at the table. In fact, they hardly ever say, "Yuk," to your face—especially if they will have to eat alone if they do—and they even eat the required spoonful of the food they don't like, no matter what it smells like. This is a real concession now, for aromas entice or repel much more now than they will later.

There are other signs of civility for the next year or so. Eights take messages on the telephone quite nicely and are very polite when visiting, particularly if their parents aren't along. Some of these good manners come from a newfound empathy. Since they now spend so much less time thinking about themselves, they have much more time to think about others.

Parents reinforce this quality of mercy by supporting their new interests in other countries and other people and by condemning any signs of bigotry. Eights acquire a range of values from their friends, including some prejudices. The building of a conscience isn't easy, so it's important to encourage the right kind of playmates.

Generally, Eights are pretty good eggs because they want to be, particularly if they have been given some firm rules to lean on when their stuffings turn to dust. While it is true that they exaggerate, they are more and more opposed to lying, and although they have an alibi for every accident, they at least admit their wrongs. Temptation is less now too, but they still may think the dish of change in the kitchen is a common till and tap it from time to time, the way their parents do.

Self-discipline is a sign of self-confidence. Eights can dare to say no, even to themselves, for their new abilities give them courage. Few new fears bloom now, many subside and the rest are hidden away, for Eights have many public faces and bravery is one of their most important. You will see it in the way they skate like fury down the most dangerous slope in the neighborhood (it's always called Suicide Hill), even though they half expect to be in smithereens when they hit the bottom.

Since Eights live life so hard, they fall asleep, zonk, for ten deep almost dreamless hours at night, although they will like some reading in bed first to relax and perhaps some thumbsucking again too. Good old habits die hard—especially when you get so tired.

Other less charming habits are becoming ingrained now, which you can monitor but not prevent. At this age most Eights carry themselves in the same unkempt way. Shoes have knotted, broken laces, clothes have frequent new rips and the nails and the hair draw dirt like magnets and should be kept trimmed. When it comes down to it, shortliness is next to cleanliness. The less there is, the less there is to get dirty.

Cavities are more common now and teeth become a gray shadow of their pearly selves. Although your child may have a small allowance, some friends will have big ones and together they buy and share an extraordinary amount of sweet, high-calorie treats—a custom that will last for years. The results can be resisted only by your nagging to brush and floss. With ten to twelve permanent teeth in place, you can't wait any longer to get stern about this.

School, of course, is still the focus of Eights, and they hate to miss it, but these children are so casual about getting there that it is easy for them to be late. There are two reasons for this. They seldom have their gear together in the morning, and even if they do they take a long time to get to school, since they track new routes with the cleverness of Marco Polo. These children like maps in any form, but the best are the ones they draw with their feet. You help your child most when you see that he collects his things at night and gets up a little earlier so he has more time to get to school.

Once there, the Eights may seem to appreciate third grade more for the equality, fraternity and liberty than for the learning, but it is a closer race than you might think. They are entranced by pyramids, Vikings, knights, Greek myths and Mexican maidens who are tossed in the lake, even if they don't know what maidens are.

Full class activities have a strong appeal and spelling bees take on an icy thrill, but much of the best work is done in small groups. Here reading, math, science—whatever the subject—is broken down into any number of classifications, for a good third-grade teacher takes advantage of her students' fascination with structure.

Although Eights still guess new words phonetically, and old ones may be misread or their order confused, the meaning is clear. In math, they can add and subtract well, multiply and divide rather well and realize what simple fractions are about. Now they not only begin to understand the concept of space and size but they can differentiate between numbers, and become enchanted with money. Like baseball cards, money can be separated so many ways. It also can be the basis of a coin collection and the source of a thousand dreams, for Eights are the most acquisitive of children. They like to buy, to swap, to own, to enter into any exchange at all. Window-shopping is a delight, whether in a mall or a mail-order catalog, but the catalog helps them sort their dreams better, for they can go back to the pictures again and again to help rank their wishes. The more children can organize their thoughts, the more easily they will solve problems the rest of their lives. This is one way the intelligence is stretched.

These mental shopping sprees will inspire your child to earn money, and for the next year or so he will begin selling somewhat unsavory lemonade at the sight of an ad for a ten-speed bike—a savings project that will lose its appeal as soon as he makes enough money to buy a few comic books. The lure of these comics reaches its zenith in the next year. Although it may not be apparent at the time—for so much of a mother's wisdom

comes after the fact—comics are a reasonable, if unproductive, way to wind down after the rigors of school or the wild action of the playground. Of course, you would rather your child spread out on the bed with a good book, but don't fret. If you have to choose between the habit of reading and the books themselves, the habit is surely more important. Bad writing will make a child appreciate good writing, although it may take a while. Comic books and joke books tease a child to read more, and so do the bookshelves in the bedroom, a personalized bookplate, a handsome volume on art or animals and especially the stories you read aloud in the family.

Television, like comic books, is another big escape for an Eight and it isn't a bad one for you either. It is true that most shows have little educational value but they pay other dividends if they are limited to an hour or so a day, if they aren't offensive and if they give the family an oasis of calm before dinner. There is another advantage to television now. By watching some of the same shows as their friends, your conforming Eight can conform still more.

Your child had days last year when he wanted to be like someone else—anyone at all—but now he wants to conform more than ever. He accepts himself best if he can act and think like his buddies and wear the same kind of tennis shoes. It seems that the more Eights look like individuals, the more they want to be like their friends—and the more their friends want to be like them. This is no cause for alarm. Underneath it all, your child is just as original as before, seeing the world in a way that it has never been seen before. That's the miracle of people—conformity is only skin deep.

NINE

The Nine is a paradox, full of highs and lows—outgoing one day and introspective the next. It's as if all his past emotional stages were taking turns in his head. You will see him change from chipper and con-

tented to tense and forgetful—from humming a tune off key to picking his nose or his cuticles or whatever is handy—but basically he is still an easy person to have around and easily disciplined too. He will fail to meet the standards now and then but a little time alone will help him contemplate his sorry deeds and accept a share of the blame, although he is sure to tell you that someone else really started it all.

This brooding about justice, about rights, about fairness, can be tiresome but it is healthy, for it tells you his sense of ethics is becoming better defined every day. Nines, bless their hearts, are trustworthy people, with honesty their hallmark. At this age one child may find reinforcement for his ideas of right and wrong at Sunday school, while another feels a need to depend on himself. In either case both boys and girls are less and less interested in lectures at home, and search instead for new ways to put themselves to the test and to keep most adults, including their parents, at a distance. To be allowed on their own, alone in the house, for an hour or two—especially if it isn't a regular routine—lets them know the joy of being trusted and responsible for themselves.

This is one way they practice being adult. Now Nines study you and your friends—and the soaps and the sitcoms—like textbooks, gathering the ideas and values that help them decide what kind of people they want to be. They aim to please when they feel close, but thumb their noses at the world, or at least at their mothers, when they're feeling more aloof. Your husband will get better treatment, however, for children usually bond more tightly with their fathers now.

For all that they try to act like grown-ups, they still want to be most like their friends, wearing the same kind of jeans and sneakers, having the same haircut and the same toys as the other children in their class. This conformity shows a lack of self-confidence that will become more apparent in the next few years. This is not to say that Nines are a stuffy lot. They still roar at riddles and revel in bathroom language. Just an old-fashioned toast like "Bottoms up!" will make these children collapse.

Physically, they're pretty healthy—although allergies may still be a bother—and growth is slow and even. You can expect your child to add about an inch to his height again this year. Eating becomes moderate and nutritious as they savor good plain foods, even if they're covered with gravy. As for sleep, they still need ten hours a night, but it may be clouded with bad dreams. For Nines, the anxiety of the day hangs over their heads, and although there are few fears now, there are many worries—most of them about themselves. These worries are behind their sudden bouts of babyishness, until sometimes they need as much sympathy as they did at Seven and you wonder: will your child ever grow up? Actually, that's just what he's doing. Nines may get discouraged quickly but, unlike Sevens, they keep on trying, for these children are little pluggers. Problems are there to be solved.

They are planners too—figurers—and lists are integral to their lives. Lists help children compete against themselves, not only setting a goal but trying to meet it in the time allowed. This is why interruptions are resented so much. You practically need an appointment—or at the least a family calendar—for they have little time for surprises.

Although they quickly denigrate themselves when some scheme goes wrong, they go back to their drawing boards for another try. It is this self-motivation that is perhaps the essence of the age—the force that will carry them forward for the rest of their lives. You must learn to nourish it in your child as you never have before, reminding him only to do those important things that he's apt to forget, like brushing his teeth—since you pay the dentist—or washing his hands before dinner, since you have to look at those hands while you eat. In other areas, you show your faith in him when you expect him to answer his own alarm

clock in the morning, to make his bed and to grab his books from the hall table. Children can only care about meeting these particular demands if they've first been allowed to be reasonably self-sufficient. This is where their competence and confidence come from.

Nothing makes a child feel so competent as camping. Nines love it. This is not just that the nights are dark and magical and the food so smoky and good, but that it satisfies the primitive need to know that they can take care of themselves, anytime, anywhere. Biking and hiking trips bring the same rewards as long as the children have a serious destination, a large amount of food and a thrilling conviction that peril may be just around the bend.

To be capable, Nines not only seek new horizons but work hard to perfect old skills. Their successes are obvious and so are their failures. In school, reading problems are almost impossible to ignore, thank heavens, although a math disability is harder to spot since somehow parents, and even teachers, treat it as an acceptable, if unfortunate, fault, particularly in a girl, which, of course, is silly. Your child may need tutoring to get on track and feel successful.

When a child does something well, he likes to do it abidingly, whether he (generally he) is building with an elaborate construction set or she (almost always she) is playing with a doll whose wardrobe is bigger than yours. Nines are still fanatics about comic books and television and will read the same books endlessly and often. All of these pastimes can be addictive. If they interfere too much with school or chores or exercise for your child, you will have to set some limits, but it won't be easy and you never will be altogether successful.

Sports are pursued with this same dedication and the best-loved ones are those that take the most dexterity—baseball, football, kite-flying, swimming, karate or skating, whether on ice or sidewalks. They also usually involve one or more friends, for friends are more and more important to a child's happiness. The plain old friends of Eight are called "best friends" now, and if they can't go out to play together they visit by telephone. Either way, they spend hours telling each other small yarns and begin to do it rather well, although their stories do go on and on. No matter. Friendships are built now on words much more than deeds and quantity seems to count.

Nines constantly think in terms of others—not as a matter of generosity, but as if they were plural. A picnic is only fun if they can invite a guest or, better still, if they can go picnicking with the families of their friends. You either have an extra child or none. This need to be with friends is part of the familiar compulsions to conform, to organize, to be in a group. That's why school is still a beloved place. Nothing else in their lives is so organized. Even the most open classroom has a tight if invisible structure that gives order to the rowdiest fourth grade.

Nines, like Eights and Tens, cling to rules—rigid rules—which they and their pals usually make up. It is their form of power, their way to control the situations that challenge them on every side. Clubs become gangs now and the children—especially girls—block the sidewalk as they walk arm in arm, a veritable parade of friendship. They might as well carry "no trespassing" signs written in blood. This ardor does not imply permanency. Over the months, a teacher sees her classroom of Nines form into three or four loose groups, disperse and form again, adding a few members here, dropping others there, almost spontaneously, as interests change and arguments erupt.

There will be fights now—no doubt about it—but they are more likely to be with their wits than their fists, unless, of course, someone is teased about liking *a member of the opposite sex.* Such affection is unthinkable. Nines are aware of sex, of course, but the only way you will know it will be by all the swearing they do, for the

expletives are often sexual now. If you're lucky, they'll also be out of earshot.

When their friends are away, sick or angry with them, Nines always have their collections, for they have two kinds of intense friendships—animate and inanimate. A collection is as much fun as a companion for an hour or two a day, any day. If the collection is as small as a stack of baseball cards, they carry it in a pocket or even in a file box, flipping through and rearranging it wherever the opportunity presents itself, including at Sunday school. You never know where they will be seized with the need to classify the players by their batting averages rather than their teams (or their hometowns or their years in the majors).

The Nines' need to collect a whole variety of things is so overwhelming, you may fear that your child's room will begin to look as if the Collier brothers lived there. It might, unless there are shelves to display them and baskets or boxes to contain them. This collection mania takes many forms. A super Nine named Julie, who inherited her father's New England frugality and her mother's eye for beauty, crammed her room with lead soldiers and china dolls; gold jewelry and tortoiseshell combs; laces and little quilts, almost all from neighborhood yard sales. It was a better collection of little antique wonders than the town museums.

In our family, the children collected indiscriminately—the "it just might come in handy" theory—but they specialized too: horse chestnuts from the park, rocks of no distinction at all, and wretched stuffed animals bought at the sort of yard sales young Julie would ignore. We hoped that this too would pass, and so it did. May you be comforted.

In the meantime, you can expect your Nine to display each collection as proudly as diamonds—and guard it as highly. Nines hang on tight to almost everything they have, for they know, somehow, that the minute they let go, a big chunk of childhood goes too.

TEN

Ten is the dawning. Now you see the promise of what's to come in the next three years. The metamorphosis will bring much of the old excitement back to parenthood. This is not to say, of course, that all children begin to bloom at the stroke of Ten. Growing up seldom happens right when it should, but you can count on the order of the growing. If all is going well, your child will develop according to the pattern, give or take a year or even two.

Tens who are on target often act before they think, and their exaggerated emotions run the gamut in the space of thirty minutes. Tears come quickly (especially to girls), followed by giggles, and grudges are a thing of the past. These children, once so serious and solemn, become positively flighty now, skipping from one thing to the next until you think superficiality is here to stay. And it is, at least for the time being. Just as the body grows in one direction at a time, so does the psyche. Now it seems that their emotions are a mile wide and an inch deep. After those years of introspection, the change is welcome as the past blends with the present and produces a stable, balanced person who is energetic, easygoing, honest and—in spite of their what-the-hell ways—fairly dependable. Like Fives, they are good eggs to have around—good in sports, good in school, good in getting along.

While Tens are happy with just about anybody, most of the time, they do have some trouble with their juniors—from Six to Nine—and also with young teenagers. A Ten's sudden, surprising bursts of anger are likely to be directed at children in these ages. If you have a Ten with brothers and sisters in one or both groups, you can expect an extra dose of sibling rivalry. As parenthood teaches us so well, everything good has at least a small price.

Even with this tension, Tens are interesting, interested people who fit in well with their families. They like to spend time reading and playing with the preschooler and enjoy lunch with a jolly old aunt and they make their parents feel like real winners. All the hero-worshipping at this age—and there is a great deal—is consolidated in their affection for good old mom and dad. Their loyalty to both helps weld the family into a strong unit, the center of their lives. This, in turn, encourages parents to treat them more as adults, which is just what they need, for it produces an upward spiral of good behavior.

Tens are great social assets for short and long family jaunts, for charades, for sharing hobbies. Family chores are performed reasonably well too, as long as you're willing to work alongside, for without company the Ten will barely get a job done, and never with embellishments. Even when working with their parents, their attention spans are short and they need many small breaks. Talking is their favorite respite, and a break for them means a chat, which gives you a chance to know your child that much better.

Whether talking, listening or reading, Tens surround themselves with words. You also will find them more entertaining than they've been in years. Whether they are going on about their loves—horses or dogs or sports (but not the opposite sex!)—or about the state of the world, their conversations are sharper than they used to be, their arguments more logical. It is their love of words and their love of mom that irritates the older children. They know that any secret, any overheard confidence, is likely to be funneled to Mother. It isn't that they want to be tattletales, it's just so hard to resist.

Certainly the rest of their ethical sense is getting more solid every day, and at an accelerated rate. By now they probably have a moral code that despises dishonesty, injustice, drugs, cigarettes, and all the wrongs of the world and they are mighty self-righteous about it. Traditional prayers may be dropped now in favor of talking directly to God.

This doesn't mean that Tens are spiritual sorts but rather that goodness is one of their many, many new interests. It leads them to feel it their duty to make the world a better place, and they are sure that they can. It's a matter of figuring out how. Every encounter teaches them something. They look to people, books, television, adventures—good and bad—to help them understand the problems that adults have, so they can learn how to solve them.

Now all knowledge, no matter the source, whets their curiosity and the result is a fresher, more spontaneous person. You will watch them dip into one enthusiasm after another until suddenly an interest becomes a passion that may last for years. The Scouts, a horse, gymnastics, the drill team, Little League, all have the power to enrapture, and no enthusiast was ever more willing than a Ten.

The outdoors is a great lure in itself, perhaps because Tens are so full of sunshine they want to wrap themselves in more. While there are rushes of energy for the daredevilish things they like to do—for these children are well coordinated—it is the free and easy neighborhood play that brings the most consistent pleasure. This appetite is likely to be both intense and short-lived, for the club of a Ten is almost always so noble in concept that it is impossible to maintain. Besides, the casual curbside gatherings suit their style better. Here a boy hangs out with a gang of boys, including his two or three good buddies, while a girl has her own circle of girls, and within it one best friend. These alliances may last for years since a Ten chooses a friend with great care and gives complete loyalty. These friends are so special, your child would like to bring them home for dinner every night. Tens are as proud of their friends as they are of their parents and, like matchmakers, they bask when showing off their favorite people to each other.

Collections—old ones and new ones—continue to be important for both boys and girls but they have become a little more sophisticated as Tens refine their interests.

Although there are many exceptions, much of their play still follows along traditional lines. Girls still may play with the teenage doll and her elaborate clothes collections, but they begin to put aside other dolls in favor of the sort that sit on a shelf—stuffed animals or tiny glass figures—while boys develop an overblown interest in sports. You will see your son—and sometimes your daughter—support a specific football team fanatically. This child assembles anything that has the team's insignia on it and records all information about the players in his head, with the computer-like memory you once hoped he would have for history.

Boys, generally rougher and more active now, concentrate on the sport of the season while girls tend to write and produce dreadful plays or put on fashion shows—the favorite entertainment at a slumber party. For both sexes, the pastimes that call for teamwork, for rules and, on good days, for a chance to be the leader are the best activities, especially if they make dreams of glory dance in their heads. Therein lies the real joy.

Even though the interests of boys and girls are often different, there is a growing camaraderie between them. You'll find them playing Scrabble, Parcheesi, Monopoly, Clue, table tennis and wild card games like pig and spit—all of which allow new friendships to thrive under a disguise of name-calling and outraged reactions.

In public, the behavior is less friendly but excitingly aware. A band of girls—some barely budding beneath their T-shirts and as conscious of their bodies as Hollywood starlets—will talk together and smirk as they march past a knot of ten-year-old boys. In response, the boys will ignore, catcall or make ill-phrased, possibly ribald jokes while the most debonair of the lot will stuff his hands in his pockets and whistle as he rides his bike in circles—a stunt he's been practicing in the alley for weeks. It's all a lovely part of growing up.

Tens watch each other's bodies with fascination. No one is more aware of the progress of her breast development than a ten-year-old girl except, perhaps, a ten-year-old boy. Although he'd be mortified to be seen naked by any female, he spends a lot of time thinking about naked females, and catches any looks he can, by way of keyholes, windows or centerfolds. He may even swipe a racy magazine from the drugstore, stealing it not because of the cost but because he can't imagine nonchalantly sauntering to the counter to buy it—especially if the druggist knows his folks.

While Tens are embarrassed by sex, they are still deeply interested in it and, like any true scholars, they look everywhere for information. Although pictures are preferred, particularly by boys, both boys and girls can quote whole paragraphs from the brochure in your box of tampons, although they won't admit it.

Now your child needs to talk about sexual development, about desires and about the sex act itself in straightforward detail, or to be given some books that do it for you. Even though you have had these talks before, your child is sure to have some facts wrong. It is both wise and natural to bring up this complicated subject again, for all important, complex information must be reviewed many times and sex is both important and complex.

No matter that they never ask; they need to know, they want to know and they have the right to know.

Tens are intensely curious to find out how babies are born, although in this enlightened age you will seldom find a child as naive as my childhood friend, who blushed with shame at Ten to realize that her grandmother had obviously Done It nine times (she had nine children, hadn't she?). Part of the admitted interest in sex comes from the changes in the child's body. A son is more solid-looking, a daughter's waist more accented and feminine. She may gain weight rapidly now, on both her body and her face—a sign that puberty is near; the nipples may swell and there is some downy pubic hair. She may even have begun to menstruate. As many as one out of ten start this early.

Both boys and girls have good health now with allergies much less troublesome than they were last year, and they even see better with both eyes at once, rather than monocularly, but not with the precision that will come in another year. Nevertheless, Tens don't like glasses even if they're needed and they may even refuse to wear them. This is a decision you can do little about, short of keeping them on a leash. When they care more about what they see than how they think others see them, they will wear their glasses.

Teeth cause some problems too. There are fourteen to sixteen permanent teeth now, which finally seem to fit the face fairly well, but unless you push lots of natural toothbrushes—like raw celery, carrots and apples—or fuss a lot, your child may wear the badge of the fifth grader: gray teeth. As conscious as Tens are of growing up, they still keep their bodies in the same old way, except more so.

This is obvious in their disdain for cleanliness, which is getting worse. Baths are taken under duress and the tub is left a wreck (if it isn't, it's because they forgot to get in). It may be several years before your child thinks success and acceptance depend on a shampoo every morning, so

parents do best when they convince both girls and boys that short hair is in style. Although they are getting better about losing things, they are sloppy souls with sloppy rooms and sloppy clothes. A Ten, particularly a boy, seldom even ties his sneakers (but then, neither does a Twenty).

The one concern all Tens have is food. Before breakfast is done, they are thinking about lunch, and at lunch they look forward to dinner. Now they like more and more food and tuck a lot of it away. Fast foods were created for this child. Food, in fact, is so important that it even makes the manners of Tens improve. By now they have eaten around enough to find out that other parents also think forks were made before fingers. If they don't want to be stared at (and no Ten does), and they want to be invited for another meal (and a Ten always does), they have to act the way grown-ups expect. At home, of course, the Ten will need the reminder of an uplifted eyebrow or a tickle on the elbow to maintain a few niceties of the dinner table, but you'll never try for all.

This child needs reminders to complete every duty, even getting to bed on time. Otherwise, the Ten will miss some of the nine and a half to ten and a half hours of sleep both boys and girls—but especially boys—require, although all Tens—and especially boys—tend to bounce out of bed easily and early in the morning.

Except for bedtime, Tens do manage to juggle their time reasonably well, are seldom late for appointments and never for school, which they still love. You can expect your child to be happy there as long as the lessons are interesting and the teacher is fair, for discipline only works in elementary school if the child can see its justice.

Part of the joy of school is in the new talents that begin to emerge—the results of so much new knowledge, so much encouragement and such a freeing of their own ten-year-old spirits. No matter that the handwriting has turned to hieroglyphics; it's the love of learning that counts. They probably read more now and they've begun to use fractions, but they're most intrigued by the ideas that others have and how they fit in with their own. Tens do, however, find it hard to connect all the facts that pour in on them. Any help you can give on ways to study, to review, to outline, is appreciated now, as long as you don't demand that they get only A's and B's.

Even though the Tens, those lambs, like school, they only want to do as well as their friends, not better, because they care about others more than they care about marks. All in all, friendships are better than a fistful of A's.

ELEVEN

An Eleven is an inspiration—for a perpetual motion machine. This child twists and wiggles from the time he wakes up until the time he falls asleep. He eats as casually as a goat and as constantly as a cow. He talks fast and often too loudly, argues with everyone and often insults them.

He is also a laughing, sociable, silly soul who can charm you right down to your socks. You just never know what to expect. These mood swings reflect the fermentation inside. While an Eleven is as effervescent as champagne, this is generally not a vintage year.

Children seem to go through the anguish of uncertainty during each odd year. Elevens are especially like Fives when they get close to Six—at one moment trying to get there too soon; at another, afraid to move on. This isn't just a storm before a calm but a whole new phase, a breaking free, so they can think and act in new ways.

One day these Elevens may look back at the venture with fondness, but they don't always enjoy it at the time. Now they are painfully conscious of themselves, their awkwardness and their confusing need for privacy one day, conviviality the next. These children try to pace themselves and put their priorities in order, and this won't be easy until they're Twelves.

Now the chemical and nervous changes in their bodies trigger tension, affect behavior and unsettle friendships. Both boys and girls cry unexpectedly, to their great embarrassment. Emotions plummet over a minor quarrel with a brother or because another sixth grader didn't wave back. Even the language of an Eleven is highly charged. Such words as "hate" and "desperately" pepper one child's vocabulary, while another may "love" and "is dying for" even the least of his wishes. Since an Eleven acts so excessively, parents tend to behave the same way, setting up contests of emotion that can continue for years. Let your child be. His sensitivity right now is much greater than yours.

Elevens aren't happy with their own confusions and they don't need to have them pointed out. It's as if they're jerked about on their own marionette strings as they try to deal with a new crop of fears. They can't depend on themselves as much as they did a year ago and may even feel cross when they wake up in the morning.

Your display of faith in him will bolster your child's self-confidence and keep him from being sullen and resentful much of the time. You express this faith by granting new liberties—a way of saying that you

trust his judgment. Telling an Eleven what to do—and when—can leave both of you with a fine sense of outrage and you may be tempted to tighten rather than loosen the reins, but a little loosening is what he really needs. But not too much. No matter how much extra freedom they get, Elevens will demand more than they can handle. They are spreading their wings but that doesn't mean they're ready for flight.

As in any watershed year, Elevens must figure out who they are, and they do this by finding out first who they are not. In the process they treat their psyches the way they used to treat their blocks—knocking down the images they have of themselves so they can build new ones. Elevens do the same things in their relationships with people, confronting everything and everybody. It's one more way to define themselves better.

They are now so self-centered that they will not notice that they are being a little rough on the rest of the world. Their harsh judgment of others is part of their growth, a way to shape their own moral code. They are critical of those around them—including their parents—because they are now looking at themselves with a sterner eye.

You may find your Eleven counting every drink you and your husband take or asking you earnest questions to make sure you didn't cheat on your income tax. He feels almost as responsible for you as you are responsible for him. If you can't do what's right, how can he? Since every parent slips up somewhere, the Eleven's only totally trustworthy deities are rock stars, ballplayers and other adults who are too far away to scrutinize.

This is just as well: a parent is not a perfect person, and it's time your child stopped looking to you for miracles. He may find the clay extends right up to your knees, but he loves you both just the same, although at the moment he may prefer to be with one of you more than the other. The favored one should spend extra time alone with him, whether at some special event or simply running errands together in the car. With the radio off, you create a quiet island, with nothing expected of either parent or child. When you have plenty of time for both of you to talk and listen, your child can share a great deal with you. Most of it will be inconsequential, but it's the sharing that counts.

Despite their testiness with each other, Elevens throw themselves into their relationships and their friends seldom leave their thoughts or, when it's possible, their sight, which can make a solitary vacation to Grandma's quite lonely. A girl of Eleven compensates by spending hours finding just the right trinket or postcard for her best friend as well as for everyone in the family, including the dog. A boy is not as dutiful about buying gifts but his passion for friendship is just as strong.

This is a great age for overnighting; for writing letters to friends who move away; for playing endless pickup games of baseball, soccer and touch football; for marathons for fun and walk-a-thons and carnivals for sweet charity.

When Elevens are together, any time that isn't spent sharing serious dreams or arguing about ballplayers, clothes, politics or music is spent hooting in laughter. Old slapstick movies are a delight and a pie in the face is a triumph of wit. Your child is now as experimental in his handling of humor as in everything else, and cracks many puns and sex jokes now. He instinctively knows it's better to try and fail than never to try at all.

Birthday parties change significantly. A girl of Eleven has a slumber party, and if a cake is served it is incidental to the rest of

the evening. A boy prefers to flash some cash and invite a few buddies for pizza and shakes. Here only the best friend might give a present—but never in front of anyone else—and the cake is reserved for the family.

While he loves each member in his fashion, it is the family itself that is most dear. It gives him a great sense of belonging, no matter how badly he may be jibing with some of its members. His big brother may think he is a pest, which is true, and his little sister may find him a bully, which is also true, but when an Eleven is at home he wants to be with them and all the family and to be getting a lot of love and attention. Friends and family and people in general are more important to an Eleven than games, books, parties or treats. He gives as good as he gets, with both his love and his backchat. One way or another, this is one of the givingest years your child will have.

What Elevens really want to do is walk, talk, dress and act just like their friends, which means they want to act like teenagers at least half the time. From now on they follow every high school fad, getting particularly interested in clothes and music, but Elevens—and Twelves too, poor dears—are always too late. The trend setters seem to find some new style just before the younger set adopts the last one.

As radio and tapes become more important, books and television take second billing, unless the plots are full of action. In sports, a boy usually charges into ball games as if the next world cup depends on him, while most girls like noncontact activities, such as tennis and swimming.

The passions that were beginning to blossom a year ago become full-blown now, and not in such disarray. Their focus, once so scattershot, is aimed at just two or three interests: ballet, a dog, a single sport, a board game (as long as it lasts five to six hours or more) and perhaps some weekly event, like a Scout meeting. Merit badges are worth more to some Elevens than a mink to a matron. If a child were limited to just one delight, he would pick a bike and she would choose a horse. Anything that moves fast and feels sexy is heaven at Eleven.

Most of these interests cost money. If your child doesn't get as much allowance as he would like—and he shouldn't—he will take on a newspaper route or invent a hundred odd jobs in the neighborhood to pay for his habit. This is something you want to encourage. Specific goals inspire a child to open a bank account and learn a little about thrift. You may find yourself dealing with a person of substance—maybe even someone who can save enough to buy the bike all alone or pay his own stable fees.

Most Elevens have had their fill of collecting and classifying and the seashells and model planes gather dust. These children no longer spend much time in their rooms—and parents, having seen these rooms, know why. They may admit that their nests need attention—although they hate the implied criticism—but they will still try to avoid cleaning them and when pressed they'll do the work badly. Many a parent is sure a child's slovenly ways will change if she gives the room a paint job and a new bedspread—and many a parent will be disappointed. While it is a good idea to start junior high school with a newly done room, don't expect a reformation. An Eleven will dismantle his bike at the spin of a wheel (and put it back together fairly well), but he is basically anti-work. With dogged nagging—and supervision—he'll get his room cleaned once a week—probably because his mother gets so impatient she'll do half the work. Elevens may have lost interest in classifying seashells but they still know how to classify parents.

Good hygiene is also too much to expect now, although it is better than it was. At this age a boy bathes only slightly more willingly than a Ten, and a girl only slightly more willingly than a boy. Both only scrub what they can see, and then only if they remember to look. Furthermore an Eleven is so active that the dirt is almost imbedded and a long soak is not always long enough. You can expect to do some fussing here too, when the occasion is worth it.

Actually your Eleven wants to look nice—according to the style of the gang—but he seldom thinks about it until it is time to leave for the party. That's when he realizes that he hasn't brushed his teeth in three weeks. Since he figures it is too late to make them shine, he does the next best thing—he tries hard not to smile. This only embarrasses him later when he suddenly realizes that everyone must have thought he was unfriendly, which can cause grievous reflections when he gets home. The possibilities for agony at this age are not to be believed.

All of their emotions are exaggerated. While Elevens enjoy each other's company, things seldom go smoothly when they are together. Arguments abound with friends as with the family, for the Eleven, like the Six, goes on the offensive when he defends himself. Anger is sudden and fierce—the start of a new, more challenging kind of blowup that will take full form in the teenage years. Right now he will hold grudges but not for long—an Eleven is such a chatterbox, he doesn't have the patience for sustained feuds. He gets mad at his friends, makes up, gets mad and

makes up with the same pushing and shoving that went on when he was Two. He is learning that the art of friendship is like everything worth having: it takes practice to perfect it.

Occasionally a child will try to hurt one particular person—a sign that he needs help—but generally an Eleven is as democratic in his furies as in his flattery. Any target is a good target, although he usually has the discretion to pick on those who are younger or smaller or weaker.

Each year a new epithet of scorn seems to sweep classrooms across the country. One year the new child in school is a "retard," no matter how bright he is or how appalled you are, and another year one child after another is called a "gay," as if the sixth-grade classroom were one big closet. Although an Eleven usually feels pretty good about himself, he resorts to this name-calling when he feels low, and that's why he gets jealous of his buddies too. Their privileges, their records, their clothes, their friends, their allowances all seem more and better than his.

Other problems cause anger. Between Eleven and Twelve your child realizes that motives are important and that misbehavior is a lot worse if it's intentional than if it's accidental. This is why he gets furious with the child who cheats or steals or lies. It's hard for him to refrain from such behavior himself; it's inexcusable for someone else to give in. And occasionally he too will succumb and then your sweet child will lie to save his own skin, although he will rationalize it. It's the best he can do right now. Shoplifting may occur too, but usually only when he's in a group of three or four, so you will want to take special notice of the company he keeps. It's tough enough for a child to balance his parents' expectations against those of his friends; he can't afford for the gap to be too great.

As your child wrestles with vice and virtue, he may want to attend church or temple instead of Sunday school. This is partly because he is a bit more interested in religion and partly because he knows he needs every bit of help he can get. The more he can strengthen his character now, the more he will be cushioned against the rough edges of adolescence. That's why the parents of an Eleven do well to go to services regularly themselves.

You can also help your child cope by seeing that he gets the right amount of food and sleep. An Eleven is growing so much and playing so hard that he may need more sleep than he did a year ago, not less. He also may need extra time to make his bed and eat his breakfast. The first is necessary for your peace of mind; the second one is necessary for his. A child doesn't think or act well on an empty stomach. Although an Eleven is often too discombobulated to eat properly before school, he is willing to eat steadily for the rest of the day. This can create a weight problem, with self-esteem going down as the pounds go up. Now you have to emphasize good nutrition all over again and quietly strike junk food from the grocery list.

The body creates other dilemmas for an Eleven. There is more throwing up, more asthma, more colds, and your child may need glasses. Moreover he may get what our Tante Margot grandly called *chaleurs*, turning hot and cold by turn. These hot flashes—or cold ones—are one more sign that the body of an Eleven, like the mind, is being pulled in different directions.

Some of this is obvious. Suddenly you realize that the hair on your daughter's legs is darker and thicker and if she dares to let you see her naked you realize that she is starting to grow pubic hair too. Her hips are broader, and she weighs nearly half as much as she will as an adult. This is normal. A girl usually reaches 90% of her adult height before menstruation begins and most of the rest within the next year. Even though you have given her a book and junior tampons or a box of sanitary napkins, the classic mother-daughter talks you initiate will be basically one-way. As curious as she is about puberty, an Eleven feigns disinterest because she may be dismayed at the idea of growing up or haunted to think her first period might start without warning—and when she's wearing white. She will talk about it with her friends but, where adults are concerned, Elevens are a modest lot, both in private and in public.

She will try to hide her budding breasts by rounding her shoulders or by wearing three T-shirts. This is especially true if one breast is growing a little faster than the other, which often happens. A girl whose chest is well developed—or worse, still as flat as her little brother—is mortified either by her progress or by her lack of it. Nothing suits.

With such hormonal changes, girls become increasingly interested in the opposite sex, but Nature knew what she was doing when she made sixth-grade boys. Since boys are one or two years slower in their sexual development, they hardly take this young girl's fancy. Nevertheless, both sexes are as aware of each other as they are wary and there may be some grappling, particularly if some of the boys are older. This calls for more supervision now than you might think is necessary and perhaps more than your child will need in a few years, when, with luck, the conscience is as developed as the body.

Not all boys are grapplers at this age, but it isn't for lack of interest. Even though only one eleven-year-old boy in four has any downy pubic hair, he still may rub his chin for signs of fuzz that probably won't sprout for another five years. He does have frequent erections, however, and is becoming adept at the fine art of masturbation, although we know of one boy, in a more innocent age, who was amazed to find he needn't climb a streetlight pole to get the same effect.

A boy at Eleven is not only slower in his development than a girl, he may be shorter too, for he has only reached about 80% of his adult height and less than half of his projected weight. The bones of any boy seem heavier, though, and his chest a bit more brawny. His endurance is also much better than that of a girl of Eleven and the chores he prefers are those that call for strength, which he will do more willingly if you say they need "brute strength." This builds the muscles and the ego at the same time.

Because an Eleven is so curious and so competitive, you will find the body, the mind and the spirit need a great deal of fortification to do well, especially in school. The sixth grade, like the age itself, is pivotal; you don't want anything to hold him back. Although an Eleven begins to think in abstract terms, any weaknesses are likely to catch up with him now. The child who started school a little earlier, who was a bit slower to read or is shorter than anyone else in class may be in for a tough time this year. A gifted child may be too, for a very high I.Q. or a particular talent can be harder to recognize than a learning disability. All of these problems are compounded by the confusions of the age, causing many sixth graders to flounder and even turn against school.

The teacher is another critical element. She must be interesting and must, above all, be fair. The call for justice—a constant requirement in elementary school—is never more in demand than it is right now. The teacher also must take the child seriously, starting with the first day when she tells the class just what she expects them to learn, by month and by semester. Your child spends thirty hours a week at his job and he has the right to know how he will be spending his time, particularly at this age.

An Eleven seldom feels in charge and the less a person feels in charge, the more order he needs around him. This need is behind his challenges and confrontations, which can be a bother to live with, but it's productive. The more a child questions, the better he thinks.

TWELVE

If every emotion were a thread, a lot of your child's snarls would get untangled this year. There is a new harmony about Twelves, a promise of things to come. Although they have shown a unity in earlier years, they were still clearly children. Now you see the image of an adult, the way you once caught a glimpse of tomorrow when your Six was playing dress-up.

By now your child has had twelve years of living and has learned enough about the world, about people, about nuances, to see life through your prism quite a lot of the time.

Never before have so many skills coalesced so well. Most Twelves have traveled a bit—perhaps visiting relatives alone—and have learned to like the food of a dozen cultures, read some of the books you read, listened to the news and know that laws and social conditions touch everyone's life. Although they still repeat the political opinions of their parents, they now consider what others say and seek out new ideas.

These wider horizons give the Twelve enough self-confidence to talk with adults about abstract ideas and worldly matters and to use a developing wit. While most attempts to be funny are still tentative, the Twelve is overjoyed when the audience laughs from amusement rather than just good manners. A blessed sense of the ridiculous may seep through their humor too. Twelves can take some teasing from others and have enough esteem for a little self-mockery—especially if they have read *The Secret Life of Walter Mitty* and found that everyone has hidden dreams. Their new understanding of people—including themselves—encourages greater tolerance for others, although Twelves will brood about their own failings, both real and imagined. In trying to hide them from others, they become a bit more private about themselves.

They think in new ways too, not just looking at ideas individually but arranging them to fit into concepts—the process that helps them make sense of an adult's world. Now your child understands why many rules are made, and challenges them much less.

If this seems to present the Twelve as a paragon, however, relax. His behavior will continue to fluctuate and he will act younger on some days and older on others.

"Love" and "hate" remain part of this child's vocabulary—particularly when talking about school—and anger is a common reaction. Although both boys and girls usually know they're too old to hit people, they may do it anyway or at least rush to their rooms in fury. The degree of such reactions tells you how much your child needs to talk about it.

There are many more good days than bad ones, however, and they light up most days with their inner excitement. At first you may think that Twelves plunge into life with all the exuberance of a treeful of monkeys, but then you realize that your child now deliberates and usually comes to a personal decision whatever the rest of the gang might do.

Twelves will still ask, of course, for advice from friends, as well as from parents and from an older brother or sister. This in itself makes them less annoying to older siblings; anyone who seeks wisdom isn't entirely a pest. This adds up to a more balanced person and a much easier one to have around the house. The Twelve is less affectionate, to be sure, but also more willing to compromise, to reason, to try to act the way adults are supposed to act. Now they are sure they can handle every project they try (and therefore they will succeed in most) and your old dreams of "My child, the President" suddenly seem less silly.

Your child is more levelheaded in many ways, even when walking down the stairs. Since a Twelve doesn't need to hold on to the wall anymore, you can finally quit washing fingerprints. The body, like the rest of the Twelve, is stabilizing. It's true he may twitch and pull his hair or even suck his thumb, but this usually only happens when he's tired—and he will get tired.

Despite many enthusiasms, a Twelve can usually handle only one or two after-school activities a week and still needs plenty of time to unwind and at least nine hours of sleep a night. This much rest is essential now and affects the cadence of the day. Your child will drift away to school early to hang out lazily with his friends, then throw himself into schoolwork or some rowdy field trip, and after school come home and sprawl in a heap. A child who puts out a lot of energy will need time to do nothing, so the body stays on an even keel.

Appetites need a lot of refills too. Twelves may not be able to stomach an early breakfast, but they want—and need—a midmorning pickup, a good lunch, a hearty after-school snack, dinner and maybe a little something at bedtime, despite the few extra pounds of puberty weight that they may be carrying. Even a truly overweight child needs meals this often, although they should be low in calories.

You can expect Twelves to take good care of their bodies—comparatively speaking, of course. Now teeth are often brushed without reminder and baths are taken every day, whether they're needed or not. Many girls and some boys may even shampoo their hair every day, not to be clean but to be more like teenagers. As for ears, neck and fingernails—it's better not to look.

Conformity is still big and they want the same clothes everyone else is wearing, still hoping that the style, the fit and the flare could disguise the growing differences in their sizes and shapes. The sameness of their wardrobes is not as boring as it was at Seven, Eight and Nine, however, for some eccentricities do flower. A Twelve is proud of being an individual and this has to show.

These clothes mean so much that your child, boy or girl, will be willing to wash and iron them if need be—and by all means let this be needed, even though the job won't be perfect. It's part of folk wisdom: never look a child's gift in the mouth. When you expect your Twelve to do a fair share of the laundry you are encouraging a new sense of responsibility.

Although a daughter is often still eager to be a veterinarian—and he to be a baseball player—she now worries at least as much about people as about animals and he thinks about the homeless as well as home runs. It's this caring for others—and a certain amount of nagging—that inspires a Twelve to write thank-you notes and to eat with a fork more often than with fingers, but again, don't expect perfection. Twelves will still talk with a mouthful of peas and jab the air with their knives while they talk. Growing up doesn't happen overnight, but at least this year your child is growing up a little faster.

Twelves are more mature in other ways too. They will help with the housework and the yardwork when it needs to be done—with some nudging—and tackle something major without being asked. Now this kind child surprises you by giving the living room a first-rate cleaning, but never notices that the playroom looks eligible for a disaster loan—and neither should you. One big project a day is all children can handle at this age and, even then, their eyes may be too big for their abilities—and, especially, their patience.

Twelves will also clean their rooms with a certain grace, although they would rather decorate them. Expect both boys and girls to hang pennants and street signs on the wall, keep travel souvenirs on their bureaus and to do it all with more esprit than good taste.

One child likes to sew, another to build model planes or customize his roller skates, while still another invests all his spare time playing football—real or electronic or both—and they now earn money to pay for their projects in a more systematic way, although they don't get very far. Never mind. This helps them understand money better, and they may even bankroll the family, lending small sums to their profligate parents as long as they're paid back promptly. Twelves want others to care as much about their interests as they do, which is a lot.

The Twelve does all things with zest, for whatever is tackled is tackled for the love of it. Now he finds that the fun is in the game itself, and he's the only person worth competing against, which he does with a vengeance.

Twelves may cheat enthusiastically at games, for this is now allowed and the source of great hilarity. Cheating usually isn't done at school, however, unless it seems the only way to handle some serious pressures either in class or at home. To lie, in anything that matters, jeopardizes their own new sense of integrity and even bragging is considered excessive. This helps you breathe a little easier, for you know your Twelve believes that being good is always better than being bad, but be forewarned: if Twelves go without supervision for long stretches, it will get much harder for them to make the right choices.

It's difficult to know when to leave Twelves completely on their own, especially if their parents go out for an evening. They think they're too old for sitters (by at least a year) but they also think—although they won't admit it—that burglars are lurking behind the rosebush, ready to break in at the first opportunity. That's why you pay someone a little older, not to sit but to keep your child company when you go out for a late night, but it's your child who gets the instructions and calls in the evening report. Twelves know that all's well with the world, but they still need parents, God—and company—to help them feel secure.

They need friends too, in every situation. They write to pen pals they've never met—when their handwriting is good enough to do it with ease—and talk almost endlessly with their buddies, swapping news, guffawing over sex jokes and double entendres, and when parents aren't around, they use their favorite verb—the one that starts with *f*.

Your son is more likely to hang out with a small group on a street corner—clubs are childish now—but your daughter may do most of her visiting by phone, as if the receiver grows out of her ear. No matter how you fight the cartoon stereotypes of boys and girls, they continue just the same.

Although Twelves shouldn't have phones of their own, or even an extension (this is no way to learn about sharing), it's important that they be able to talk with some privacy. It's true that gossip will be a large part of these conversations for the next few years, but they also will be sharing their secrets, and that's important. Children—especially boys—often become guarded now, laying the basis for the isolation that plagues so many adults. The telephone can be preventive medicine, for it's much easier to confide when you don't have to look the other person in the eye.

The exchanges between boys and girls, which are almost always face to face, are more comfortable now, but still feisty. At school a girl can almost gauge her popularity with boys by the number of times they run away with her books and hide her jacket and she acts foot-stamping furious (and feels very smug) when they do.

Boy-girl parties begin to be quite popular now, with the best ones usually built around an occasion, like Christmas, a farewell or the end of school, and they incorporate an activity—swimming, skating or dancing. If the boys have their way (and the girls too, though they won't admit it), they will try to start an old-fashioned game of spin the bottle—a good reason for both bottles and parents to be handy. Nevertheless the best-planned parties bring both pain and pleasure to a Twelve. They are so deliciously awful. If the party is a big one, girls cluster together or march in small bands, striding from room to room with no purpose whatsoever. In contrast, boys show their savoir faire by eating constantly, spilling quite a bit and, as we recall, on one memorable night tossing finger sandwiches into the whirling blades of an electric fan—an ant lure that could be patented, if people wanted ants on the ceiling.

Dancing will be successful but only if you have thoughtfully put twenty-five-watt bulbs in the lamps to hide the poor footwork. To a twelve-year-old boy, sex is always lurking in the heart of darkness, which is why you don't let them dance completely in the dark.

As boys and girls reach Twelve, the differences between them become more apparent. By the end of the year a girl is about 95% as tall as she ever will be. Most girls finally welcome menstruation and are ready to grow up, which is fortunate since their bodies do the deciding for them. They are rounder, their waists are smaller, their breasts are bigger and, almost without exception, they are pleased about it and the boys are too.

While only some boys have started their rapid growth spurts, others stay embarrassingly short for another two to three years. Sexually, however, the penis and scrotum begin to get larger, the pubic hair darker and coarser, and the *Playboy* magazines under the mattress give his bed a lumpy effect. Masturbation is part of his lexicon now, though usually by another name. It even may be carried out in groups, as immortalized in the movie *Amercord*. This is not, of course, a sign of homosexuality, nor is homosexuality indicated if your son has one or two sexual experiments with another boy.

While a girl seldom experiments, she can feel just as guilty if she has a crush on another girl or on an older woman, if no one has told her this is quite normal. These encounters, like any other, help a Twelve decide who she is by realizing who she is not.

You also help your Twelve resist promiscuity or drugs by helping him understand how much you care about him, as a person, not as an extension and reflection of you. Once more, you do it by listening and by giving encouragement and acceptance. A child who feels loved at home doesn't need substitutes.

Twelves thirst for information—they would cram the whole world into their heads if they knew what to ask—and they rely on parents to provide a lot of it. Now the importance of television, books and certainly comic books dwindles as people become the source of most new ideas.

This need, and their growing ability to think in abstractions, is what makes school so interesting this year. Whether it is exciting or frustrating depends on the teacher. Your child doesn't need her good opinion, the way she did a year ago, but she does require her respect. She's getting it if the teacher talks to the students as you talk to young people—as intelligent, thoughtful human beings—and gives them more time for independent study and more freedom to move around than they had last year. This is the secret to a well-run classroom, which is possible, even in junior high.

The teacher also shows respect by the way she gives homework. Most seventh graders resent it on the weekend, unless it is something special like a book report or a research paper, but they should do their nightly assignments without much grousing. It's the busywork they hate and work that apparently isn't necessary enough to be graded for weeks. A Twelve thinks his time is too important to be wasted—and he's right.

Although you think you know your child's general talents, you'll be surprised at the breadth of his horizons now. It was Nell, our science-mad Twelve, who stopped writing a short story long enough to ask dreamily, "Is there anything in the world more fun than writing fiction?" This is the age you'll hug tight to your heart: the last true year of childhood.

Sixes and Sevens accept their bodies as casually as they accept the rest of their immediate world. An ache, bump or bruise will make them complain, of course, especially at Seven, when anything makes them complain, but children are usually Ten before they begin to scrutinize their bodies. Girls take an interest because their bodies change as puberty approaches, and boys get interested in their bodies because they're good in sports—or because they're not, and want to know how to improve them.

Unfortunately, most parents limit body talk to food, teeth and sex, which isn't too successful. Dental hygiene and nutrition make for dreary conversation, and sex, plucked out of context, can be downright embarrassing. It needn't be this way. Wise parents explain early and often how the body works, for the space inside a child's skin can be at least as fascinating as all the space outside.

Children between Six and Twelve are usually quite interested to learn that they come in one of three basic shapes—endomorph, mesomorph or ectomorph—and that each has its own special temperament. This isn't an exact science, of course, nor do most children fit precisely in one of these slots, but it is comforting to children—and moms—to know that a certain temperament goes with a certain body build. If nothing else, it makes expectations more realistic.

The true endomorph has small hands and feet, a short neck, a soft, round body and a digestive system so big he tends to eat more—and weigh more—which makes some people say he lives to eat, but that's not quite true. This open, easygoing child is so sociable it's hard to know what he likes more: people or food.

The mesomorph has big bones, a strong heart, heavy muscles, straight posture and a go-go-go behavior. These children like to eat too, the way they like to do almost everything. They live with gusto and noise and let you know it with their rowdy, assertive ways. They are the ones who like to run the show, and because mesomorphs are so popular, they usually do.

The long, thin ectomorphs have small appetites, lightly muscled arms and legs, rounded shoulders, and seem to sit on the middle of their spines—a posture that drives teachers wild. These children are sensitive in a dozen ways, physically and socially. They are easily bothered by noise (although they may have a keen appreciation of music); they jump at the touch; and they tend to be shy, introverted and uneasy at parties. You can see why they may need extra understanding, especially when surrounded by rowdy mesomorphs.

Children vary quite a bit in the Middle Years, but they follow the same general growing pattern. Just when baby cheeks lose some of their cheekiness, a Six starts losing his teeth—a little sooner for girls than for boys. As the permanent teeth come in, the child gets that dear little rabbity look that often lasts until adolescence, when the nose and the jaw finally catch up with the rest of the face.

Their bodies follow a growth pattern too. The average Six is about 40 pounds and 3½' tall and will grow another 12–18", doubling his weight in the next few years.

The real growth spurt begins after that—as early as Ten and as late as Sixteen. Usually a girl begins the spurt around Ten or Eleven, when the breasts bud, and will keep growing until about a year after her period begins. A boy, however, will grow about an inch a year between Six and Eleven—which doesn't explain why his pants get two inches shorter from one birthday to the next—and start his growth spurt around Twelve or Thirteen.

You can tell the big growth spurt is beginning when your child gets a little swaybacked and loose-jointed, a sign that the body is about to be a bit out of sync with itself and the muscles can't support the bones as well as before. The trunk, the arms and legs and the hands and feet will then grow at different rates (slow, fast and faster), causing awkwardness for a year or two. As sturdy as he seems, his bones remain fairly soft and spongy until he is in his twenties. In the meantime, he needs to wear well-fitting shoes; sleep on a mattress that is either firm or has a bed board under it; and use a light comforter instead of heavy blankets.

As your preteen's body prepares to make its final leap forward, you usually can expect the mind and the psyche to lag behind. This is the daughter who is interested in dolls and boys at the same time, and the son who stops playing war games long enough to eye the girl next door.

This new awareness of their bodies makes them sure they know how to care for themselves. Now your child decides how his hair should be cut and what clothes he should wear and may experiment to see how much trash his body can handle and whether it's going to be junk food, tobacco, alcohol, pills or pot. He'll be much more likely to decide wisely if he has a clear understanding of the body and its needs and limitations.

You will have to be alert and as sensitive as possible. The preteen who is aghast about her split ends or his scrawny chest (or her scrawny chest) must be taken seriously. To say, "It doesn't matter," or "You're too young to worry about that," will only make it worse. By adolescence, children need knowledge and empathy in equal measure.

DEVELOPMENT

Children normally reach certain physical and mental milestones around certain ages. Some matter most to parents, some to children, some to both.

Six—These children usually can ride a bike, skate, walk backward, spread butter with a knife, tie their shoes (but won't), and know their left from their right.

Seven—They can cut their meat with a knife and fork, but not very well, comb their hair (but won't), count by twos and fives, tell time, repeat five numbers forward and three backward, follow a line in a maze, and balance on their toes while bending forward at the waist.

Eight—They can write cursive, move with increasing grace, touch each finger to all other fingers, count backward from twenty; give you the right change (but sometimes won't), and stand on one foot.

Nine—Now they can skim a book, multiply and divide, join letters neatly (but often won't), judge weights in order of their heaviness, and stand on one foot with their eyes closed.

Ten—They can skip double dutch and build model planes, jump while clapping their hands three times, repeat a twenty-syllable sentence, understand numbers greater than 100, remember to get home on time (and usually will), and balance on tiptoes with their eyes closed.

Eleven and Twelve—The time of these achievements is harder to pinpoint exactly, but during these two years children learn to catch a ball with one hand, jump up and touch their heels with both hands, reproduce a geometric figure from memory, wash the car and do other chores (but probably won't, if they're Eleven), and stand on one foot with the sole of the other foot pressed against that leg, like a stork.

FOOD

One of the surest (and cheapest) ways to keep your child content is to see that he eats the right foods and resists most of the wrong ones. What he puts in his body in the morning can decide how he feels—and acts—in the afternoon and even the next day. It can also decide how you feel. A cranky child will make you cranky too.

Nor is that the only effect. Next year's cavities depend on this year's candy bars and raisins. Try to persuade your child to brush his teeth after a sticky snack or at least drink a glass of water to wash some of the stickiness away. A poor diet now can also affect the speed with which a broken bone will heal a year or two later. If his undernourished body has been leeching vitamins and minerals from his bones, there may not be enough left to mend a break quickly. Having to hop about in a cast for an extra week or two will be no fun for the hopper—or the hopper's mother. Between Six and Eight the snacks he fixes for himself will be reasonably good ones (with a little guidance) and he will be dutiful enough and hungry enough to eat the lunches you pack. By fourth grade, however, he begins to shed some of his better eating habits and by junior high he'll question your ideas on nutrition just like he questions everything else.

It is not easy to make sure your child is well nourished, particularly as he gets older. Your meals are nutritious but he's out almost half of his waking day and, even at home, he's too old to be spoon-fed.

His appetite may be his salvation. Your child goes from a moderate eater at Six to an eating machine at Twelve. By then he is so consistently hungry that he usually will eat the right things if you don't have much junk food at home, if his allowance is fairly low and if you tell him why he should eat the good food you serve. You don't tell a child to eat greens "because they're good for you," of course, but because they strengthen his pitching arm or make her hair even shinier. Even broccoli tastes better when it's approached from the child's point of view.

You give other lessons on nutrition, both direct and indirect. When you make fun of a television ad that promises a breakfastful of vitamins in a fortified doughnut, the child is more impressed by your comments than by the ad because you have much more influence than a stranger on a screen. And when your child says Jenny—the junk-food champ—is the biggest crab in class, you wonder

if it's because Jenny eats so many junky things—and that's all you say on the subject.

Your child also learns about nutrition when he helps you plan menus and make grocery lists and when you explain why the family needs certain foods. In talking about nutrition, as in talking about sex, you add more and more information as he gets older. Children take in knowledge easily, if it is clear and offered in terms of their own interests. As our Meg once told us in exasperation, "You know, even a child will do something if she knows the reason why!"

Your child needs to know that a healthy body needs about 30%—or less—of its intake in proteins; another 30% in fats—most of which are part of the foods he eats—and the rest in carbohydrates. He also needs to know which is which and why each is needed.

He should learn that proteins—meat, dairy products, nuts, beans, seafood and eggs—build and repair tissues, which is much more important than it sounds; that a simple carbohydrate, like sugar, gives only energy while complex ones—bread, cereals, fruits and vegetables—give bulk and nutrients too; and that fats give energy and keep away hunger better than anything else, since it takes longer to digest them. It's also smart to teach a child that each gram of fat has more than twice as many calories as a gram of carbohydrate or protein—a lesson to be learned before weight becomes an issue, since fat calories are supposed to be the hardest to lose.

Aside from the calories, some fats are all right for you and even necessary. The saturated fats are not, however. Butter is the obvious one, but most fats are hidden in meat, eggs, cheese and in manufactured foods, where they're listed as "vegetable oil," rather than coconut or palm oil—two major offenders. The polyunsaturated fats, like the cold-pressed oils, are fine, however, and should make up two thirds of the fats we add to our diet since they contain linoleic acids and vitamin E and also break down cholesterol. Doctors rank flaxseed oil first, followed by olive, walnut, peanut, safflower and corn oils, with most margarines ranked at the bottom, because they've been heated and chilled.

We not only eat more fats than we think, we often eat too much meat when other foods can be combined to make a protein that can be better for us. When you have your child make peas with mushrooms, spinach salad with walnuts, macaroni with cheese—or simply add milk to his cereal—he is getting a complete protein. This kind of information intrigues a child in the Middle Years when facts are so fascinating.

Nutritionists have also found that combinations of vitamins and minerals interact in positive ways. The vitamin C that comes in orange juice, tomatoes and kale helps your child absorb four times as much iron as he would take in otherwise, but only if he eats the foods that contain C and iron at the same meal.

The freshest food is the most nutritious. The more it has been refined, frozen, canned, reconstituted or processed in any way, the more vitamins and minerals have been lost. If some of the nutrients are returned chemically, the label will read "enriched," and if vitamins and minerals are added to foods that never had them before, it will say "fortified." Manufacturers are allowed to add seventeen of the forty vitamins and minerals that healthy people are known to need but essential trace minerals can't be added since no one knows how much is necessary. Moreover, our individual needs vary.

Vitamin pills and other supplements have value but should be used with cau-

tion. Fat-soluble vitamins—A, D, E and K—in both food and pills can accumulate and cause problems; too little iron is bad for anybody; and too much iron can be bad for some. A further caution: many vitamin pills contain the very colors and preservatives you may have been avoiding in foods, and most packaged vitamins are grown on yeast or bound with wheat or corn or sugar, which can bother some allergic children. Other multivitamins can cause problems if they exacerbate a marked imbalance of minerals in the body. If you think your child needs more vitamins than the daily dose his pediatrician suggests, find a well-trained nutritionist to recommend the right supplements.

Generally it's better for your child to realize that good, natural food is much cheaper and tastier than pills or foods sprayed indiscriminately with vitamins—and that water is the best fluid he can drink. You don't want him to become a food faddist, but you should encourage him to be a food purist. Although he may turn into a junk-food fanatic in his teens, he'll eat well when he grows up if he associates home cooking with fine ingredients. That's one more reason why the rice you cook should be brown, not white; the flour unbleached or preferably whole wheat; the cheese should be natural and uncolored; the cereals sugar-free and processed very little; the bread made from whole wheat flour and the pasta from pure durum wheat; and the fruits and vegetables as fresh as you can find, before the natural sugar has turned to starch. He should know, however, that perfect foods are as rare as perfect people. Everything is short of some vitamins and most have impurities.

This is particularly true of meat, which may contain any of 10,000 hormones, antibiotics and other chemicals that the animal was given as medicine or that was added to the fodder or the water. Most of these additions will be stored in the fat and the offal, including the liver, and the best way to avoid them is to cut away the fat before you cook the meat. You also may decide to serve liver less often, which should make your child a believer in good nutrition.

Washing helps clean fruits and vegetables, but unless they're organically grown they'll never be entirely free of pesticides or herbicides. Even your own tomatoes may have a high lead content if they're grown less than 100′ from heavy traffic.

It's pointless to worry about the additives that can't be avoided, but wise to be concerned about those that can. Altogether there are about 2800 enhancers, stabilizers, thickeners, extenders, antioxidants, artificial colors and flavors that can be added to our food to make it look better or last longer, or to disguise cheaper ingredients (or missing ones), or to let you think you're buying food that is fresher than it is or has more of some expensive ingredient. The additives permitted after 1958 have been tested, although usually only by the manufacturer, but most of those in use before that simply went on the government's "generally recognized as safe" (GRAS) list. Indeed, many are so ordinary, like sugar and salt, that we don't even think of them as additives, and yet these are the ones we abuse the most—and don't even know it. Most of the sugar we eat is added—in some form or another—before we ever buy the food, which is another good reason to cook for ourselves.

It doesn't take an expert, or even another mother, to tell you that the more salt and sugar your child eats, the more he wants, for if salt whets the appetite, sugar makes it sit up and beg. A baby just a few days old likes sweetened water better than plain, and the sweeter it is, the better he likes it. Put that sugar in a candy bar and a child may go wild.

Michael was only Eight when he would dash to the corner store for that forgotten loaf of bread for school lunches, only to come home with three telltale clues: less change than he should have had, a pair of ears that glowed bright red (for lying gets harder at Eight) and a telltale aura that caused his sisters to whisper, "Michael, you have *chocolate* on your breath!" And all this before 8 A.M. By Ten, Michael's penchant for chocolate was replaced by a passion for hamburgers. Just let him whiff a burger as he passed a fast food parlor and, like the thirsty young man in W. C. Fields's classic, *The Fatal Glass of Beer*, he had to rush in for his hamburger fix. At least it was better than beer.

While hamburgers and fries give children much more grease than they need, they also give them some basically nutritious food. Chemical shakes and fried pies, on the other hand, give no nutrition at all. Fortunately, homemade soups and gingerbread, baked beans and oat bran muffins can compete with junk food very well, because they smell so good that they satisfy the senses as well as the tum. They have other advantages too. The food a parent and child prepare when they work side by side enriches their relationship the way convenience food never can. Home is more than the family: it is all the special smells and tastes and customs that bind it together.

MEALTIMES

You can affect your child's diet most by the foods you serve at breakfast, lunch and dinner.

Breakfast

The first meal of the day is the most critical. To skip it puts the body under a heavy strain and to eat something sweet or floury on an empty stomach will lower blood sugar that is already low.

Despite the furor over cholesterol, an egg cushioned with whole wheat toast is a good breakfast for a growing child and so is French toast or a piece of fish with a patty of leftover potatoes. Cereal is fine too, if it is processed as little as possible, and still has a lot of bran (for bulk) and germ (for vitamins). If your child does eat a presweetened cereal, choose one with no more sugar in a serving than the teaspoonful you would let him add to plain cereal.

It may be old-fashioned, but the best cereal is probably a hot one—a lesson we learned when Nell, at Eight, had oatmeal for the first time. That was the day she said with wonder, "I wasn't hungry until lunchtime!" She hadn't mentioned that she was hungry every day by recess—until she wasn't—and neither had her big brother or sisters.

Maybe, as our foremothers said, a hot cereal sticks to the ribs better. Certainly there is more of it to stick. A child gets up to three times as much hot cereal as cold in his bowl, even though one serving looks as big as the other. Hot or cold, the cereal should be eaten with milk, to make it a whole protein.

Any meal should also have some vitamin C, to absorb the iron better. Frozen or canned juice is pretty good, despite its coloring, but fresh juice is much better and a piece of fruit is best of all, because it has roughage and enough bulk to fill a child quicker and last longer. This makes the caloric intake less—an important consideration if your child is overweight. As for powdered drinks or chemical "juice"— forget them. They're not good enough for your child.

A healthy breakfast will take extra effort on a busy morning, but it beats a tantrum later.

Lunch

You know your child eats a good lunch on weekends because you're around, but school is another matter. It isn't even easy to pack a good lunch for your Six as he badgers you for a cupcake ("like all the others get") in place of an apple, and chips instead of celery sticks stuffed with cheese. You can make conformity work for you if you ask the first-grade teacher to teach nutrition with a lunchbox show-and-tell

---

CHILI MILLET

YIELD: 2 cups

A Twelve will like to make this filling because the taste is terrific—and you'll like it because it's good for him, it's cheap and it keeps well in a covered dish in the refrigerator. In the top of a double boiler:

COMBINE	3½ c. water
	1 c. millet
BOIL	5 minutes
SIMMER	40 minutes

It's done when it's still a bit crunchy. Drain any water that's left.

ADD	¼ c. olive oil
	1½ t. chili powder

Tuck some into pita bread for a summer lunch. For extra flavor

ADD	lettuce OR sliced tomatoes OR sliced avocado OR small chunks of natural Cheddar cheese

Cover the rest of this stuffing and store in the refrigerator.

---

every day. Blue stars go to the children with the most nutritious lunches, gold stars to those who win the most each week, and favorite menus are copied and distributed to the students by the room mother (probably you).

The lunch of the Six won't do for the Nine. Now your child won't eat those nutritious lunches you pack, because a Nine is an entrepreneur. This is the age of trades and, unless you're careful, lunch may become more junk than food. It almost defies analysis, but the explanation may simply be that a few pampered children in every classroom have far more goodies than they need and they share their largess freely. A few others, in an eager attempt to win friends, may trade their candy bars for peanut butter sandwiches. There is also a certain amount of giving between good friends and since most children have too many sweets and treats in their lunches, they can afford to be generous.

In this way the banana gets swapped for some potato chips and carrot sticks for bubble gum, two granola cookies for a half of a doughnut, and the money your child got for helping the fellow next door is spent on peanut brittle in the vending machine. And then somebody in the class has a birthday and everyone gets a chocolate cupcake from the supermarket.

If your child is a good trader, you'll be lucky if he takes two bites of his tuna fish on whole wheat and he won't even open his thermos of minestrone. And to make the problem universal, the banana, the carrot sticks and even the cookies may scarcely be touched by the children who wind up with them. Since you can't change the folkways of the fourth grade, and you can't expect your child to be an oddball of the class, you have to make your requirements mesh with his reality. To do it you have to understand the mystique of the school lunch.

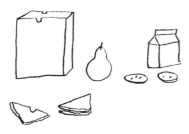

Whether it's a cafeteria special or a bag lunch, each child has the same object—to eat anything except his own food, unless of course he has something that is sweet or fried, or both. Bartering gives a child a reason to socialize, to classify—which he does when he rates one fireball against three gingersnaps—and to conform. You can't find three activities that bring more satisfaction between Eight and Ten.

PEANUT SPREAD

YIELD: 3 sandwiches

An Eight can make this nutritious filling for whole wheat bread, but use unsweetened peanut butter, for the banana makes it sweet enough.

MASH	1 large, ripe banana
ADD	½ c. peanut butter
	1 T. shredded coconut
	1 T. raisins OR dates
	¼ t. cinnamon

BROILER TREAT

Preheat oven to 350°

Peanut butter becomes much nuttier when it's broiled. A Six can smear it on a slice of bread rather thickly, but broil it yourself for it gets brown and bubbly in about a minute.

We know four lovely sisters who went all through grade school dreading lunch, because they couldn't conform. Their elegant mother—a gourmet cook who believed that fine food and a small waist could go together—packed the fanciest sandwiches for her girls. There was no bologna or peanut butter or egg salad, but such fine leftovers as sliced tongue and homemade pâté. And to keep her beauties slim the sandwiches were open-faced, for all the world to see. The girls not only couldn't trade, they could only show them to their very best friends.

And then there were the three children who couldn't trade because they always had slightly damp peanut butter and jelly sandwiches. Their mother hated to make school lunches so much that she took a whole day to make and freeze 275 pbj's each September and January—enough to last the whole semester.

You can avoid these extremes and still limit your child's ability to swap most of his lunch. Pack a sandwich on whole wheat, chosen from a list you've tacked on the bulletin board—it's easy to forget favorites if you have more than one child—and two to three cookies, fresh fruit or soup and white milk or juice. He'll also be less likely to swap his lunch if he's the one who makes a soup, banana bread or some of the sandwich spreads every week. The more a child has invested himself in the lunches, the less he will want to trade.

There should, of course, be some frivolity: self-righteousness has no place in the lunchbox. Give your child an extra treat—gooey, fried or sweet—every week or so. It will help his class standing.

The same is true for an allowance. Even though you know your child will only spend his money on candy and gum, he still needs a little bit (a very little bit) to squander each week, so he won't turn into the class moocher and so he can feel like part of the gang. While it's true that lunch should fill a third of a child's nutritional needs, he has other appetites to feed.

Afternoon Snack

A famous nutritionist once said that a child's best snack is an apple, a glass of milk and a piece of whole wheat bread spread with peanut butter. It's fortunately a favorite too, although a Six may want only half as much and a Twelve will fix a double helping.

It's one of his mother's favorites too, for the fruit raises the blood sugar quickly, the bread satisfies the hunger and the milk and peanut butter stretch a child's energy, so he won't be so cross by dinnertime.

Other good snacks, to be eaten with fruit or milk or 100% fruit juice:

- apple or pear slices covered with cheese
- 2 bran muffins or a few highly enriched homemade cookies

BANANA POPS

This snack calls for 3 bananas, 6 skewers and 5 friends.

Cut peeled bananas in half, crosswise, sticking a Popsicle stick in the end of each one as if it were a long, skinny lollipop.

FREEZE	30 minutes

In a blender

CHOP	5 oz. pecans or peanuts

In a long skinny glass jar

COMBINE	12-oz. pkg. chocolate chips
	1 oz. butter
	¼ c. hot water

Put the jar in a saucepan half filled with water, heating it to melt the chocolate.

Dip the frozen bananas into the sauce, then quickly roll them in the broken nuts.

Lay the Banana Pops on wax paper.

FREEZE	1 hour

GINGERBREAD

YIELD: 50 squares   Preheat oven to 350°

Gingerbread always smells good, but no other gingerbread smells (or tastes) as good as this one. A Nine can do everything but pour the boiling water; a younger child needs more help, but less than you might think. In a bowl

COMBINE	2 t. soda
	⅛ t. hot water

When the soda is dissolved

ADD	1 c. unsulfured molasses
	1 c. sugar
	1 c. butter, softened
	3 eggs
	1 t. ginger
	1 t. cinnamon
	1 t. ground cloves
	⅛ t. salt

Beat well with a mixer.

ADD	2 c. flour

Beat again.

ADD	2 c. boiling water

Beat this thin batter quickly and pour it into two greased, floured pans, 8″ square.

BAKE	45 minutes

It's done when the gingerbread shrinks from the sides of the pans or a wooden toothpick comes clean when your chef pokes into the center. Cool the pans on cake racks for 10 minutes before cutting into squares.

- half a bagel, some graham crackers, or fruit, vegetable or nut bread spread with cream cheese

- a small pita stuffed with hummus
- a slice of whole wheat bread covered with a layer of apple slices or drained Olive Salad (see Cooking), covered with a layer of natural Cheddar, and then broiled briefly.

Dinner

You can have light, nutritious meals at night by serving more chicken, fish and vegetarian meals and cutting back on meat, bread, pasta and sweets. A salad or a lightly cooked green vegetable, a yellow vegetable like carrots or squash and milk, juice—or water—go with it, followed by fresh fruit, with a real dessert maybe two or three times a week, depending on how well your child eats.

He'll eat dinner (or any meal) better if you ban snacks for an hour beforehand—except, perhaps, raw vegetables—so he'll be hungrier, and if he does some of the cooking. With direction, a Six can make the salad—from washing the greens to mixing the dressing—and by Eight should be so proficient he can graduate to vegetables: stir-frying the broccoli, cooking rice and learning a dozen ways to fix potatoes. Each dish a child masters will encourage him to eat a greater variety of foods.

SLEEP

Your baby's long hours of sleep helped knit up your "raveled sleave of care." It meant fair moods instead of foul ones—for both of you. Now that your child is older, he may say he doesn't need any more sleep than you do—and he will be wrong.

At Six a child needs at least ten to eleven hours of sleep and at least eight to nine hours by Twelve—and often much more. The stirrings of puberty, and puberty itself, can turn a child into a sleepaholic. You may grant a later night at Eleven and Twelve, but limit them to one a week unless it's for a party and never in response to a bedtime scene. If you yield to a scene, the scene will become a habit.

What is best for your child is also good for your marriage. You and your husband need some time together as a couple, and the end of the day is usually the only time to get it. You don't need a child, as dear as he is, to hang around while you read the paper or chat or cuddle or watch television. You have your evening rituals and he has his; they shouldn't be the same.

Your child benefits too. The third grader who learns to go to bed without a fuss will be the sixth grader who can decide for himself when he's tired, without coercion. Just knowing what he needs and why is often enough to make him go to bed. The body is logical—and so is a child.

BEDTIME

There are four times a day when children appreciate soft words most: before they leave for school, when they come home, at dinner, and at bedtime. Unfortunately, parents are likely to feel their least loving—and most frazzled—at breakfast, dinner and bedtime—and they're often not home after school.

Make the most of these opportunities. You'll pay for it if you don't, especially at night. A bedtime scene haunts everyone's dreams. Once more, harmony at home comes from the respect you give and the limits you set. The rituals of Two have changed with the years but not the need for rituals.

This means a Six is tucked into bed at a regular

time—bathed and pajamaed, with his school supplies and homework set aside, the room tidied a little, a story read and prayers heard. He then has fifteen minutes to read in bed before the timer rings to tell him it's time to turn out the light. Life never goes quite so smoothly as this, but that is the goal, and it's worth going after every blessed night.

An Eight should have perhaps thirty minutes to read—a blissful habit that will be at least as strong and as lasting as television, for we revisit the havens of childhood the rest of our lives.

If this bedding down is difficult, you may want to follow the lead of one clever mother, who turned a little spiral notebook into a "bedtime bankbook." Into it she entered ten minutes whenever her son went to bed on time, without any calling or fooling around (and ten minutes were docked when he didn't). It was time to be spent staying up on a weekend—time so treasured he was seldom docked during the week.

A Nine or a Ten usually needs no set bedtime but is simply expected to douse the lights between eight-thirty and nine-thirty or between nine and ten. The hour before should be fairly quiet and spent in his own room, listening to the radio while puttering around until sleepy—which is usually reached when the body temperature drops.

Despite the advance of years, your Nine may have trouble with this independence at first, staying awake until the last possible moment and then oversleeping in the morning or being cranky. If that happens, bring the hour forward by thirty minutes, "until you need a little less sleep." If bedtime doesn't become an issue now, curfews are less likely to be an issue six years from now.

By making his nightly retirement gradual, you not only help your child monitor his body but you let him wind down at his own pace and adjust to your schedule and the schedule at school. Even a born night owl will change his body clock after a few weeks, although he may grow up to choose a job that suits his innate timing, working nights and reveling in late morning sleeps. That's fine. Those will be his years to schedule; these are yours.

DREAMS

Dreams are luscious, luxurious, wacky stories of the night, some of the time. The happy dream frees a child's soul, which may make him chatter or laugh out loud. He levitates, he performs onstage, he pedals a bike at gale force. Your child must balance the anxieties of his day (and his week and his month), and he does his best balancing at night.

Dreams follow a wonderfully regular pattern, changing on schedule year by year. A Six usually has happy dreams, but he's beginning to have some bad ones too, for it's becoming clear to him that the world isn't as safe as it seemed when he was an unsophisticated Three. Scary dreams will be fewer when he's a Seven and an Eight but they'll be back when he's Nine. This child is a worrier, and why not? His responsibilities are growing. The sanguine Ten sleeps pretty peacefully but the Eleven will have occasional nightmares, more frequent and more violent than any he's had before, while a Twelve will be more at peace with himself both asleep and awake.

Dreams do, of course, have meanings and a child is usually entranced when he's

SLEEPWALKING

Fifteen percent of our children are sleepwalkers or sleeptalkers, and the experts don't know why. They do know, however, that it's not a sign of distress and that it usually goes away by Fifteen.

If your child is a night traveler, he'll be safer if you keep a gate in his doorway and a stop on his window, so he can only raise it a few inches.

told that they're mazes of symbols which can be deciphered, at least some of the time. Since dreams are seldom interesting to anyone but the dreamer, you may suggest he keep a Dream Book.

For this, a simple empty notebook, with a pencil attached, sits on his night table, so he can record his dream as soon as he wakes. If he waits even a few minutes it will slip out of his mind, but sometimes it returns if he gets into the same position he was in when he awoke. This is an interesting sort of diary; it helps his writing skills, and it's a great way to explain himself to himself, especially if the dream was a bad one. He'll be less likely to have it again if he can unravel the puzzle. There is one more benefit: by the time he's finished writing about it, he'll have forgotten how scared he was.

Nightmares

Nightmares last only a minute or two, but each one is accompanied by a flash of fear that will make a child shudder and perhaps even wake up and run to you. They begin early and pop up now and then probably for the rest of his life.

Your child may be bedeviled by ghosts, dogs that bite or bad men who frighten small children or bears. Meg was Four when her sleep was troubled by a ferocious bear who simply wouldn't stay away until finally one night Kate and Mike helped their dad chase it out of the house with a broom. Harry the Bear, they said, wouldn't bother her anymore. He had gone to live down the street with Uncle Tom, where he was very happy wearing electric socks night and day, except when he was taking a bath (to which he was very partial). And that was the end of the bear-mares, although Harry remained so memorable that Meg, at Seven, was still dropping in on Uncle Tom, hoping to find Harry at home.

Most nightmares can be banished by identifying their possible causes. The goriest fairy stories bother many children and violent shows on television bother them much more. Both should be forsworn. Books are safer: a child takes whatever television offers because the picture is imagined for him, but a child seldom draws more from a book than he is ready to handle.

Nightmares also may be caused by the food a child eats or by drinks, like chocolate or milk. Many doctors now think allergies or sensitivities cause enough discomfort at night for a child to dream a story that makes sense out of the tummyache or the tender ear. A drop in the blood sugar also may cause nightmares, which may be prevented by giving your child a spoonful of peanut butter at night, or smeared on apple or banana slices. Protein stabilizes the ups and downs of the mind as well as the body.

Night Terrors

Wild, wild nightmares that leave a child frightened and shaking are called night terrors, and they scare the parents almost as much as the child. He jumps up suddenly, perhaps clutching something or somebody, and may sweat or weep or see things that aren't there for as long as fifteen minutes. He then falls asleep suddenly and with serenity, and without any memory of it in the morning. More and more doctors think night terrors, like bedwetting, are caused by an allergy, but whatever the reason, relax. They usually go away as the child gets older.

EXERCISE

Boys and girls need to know that exercise makes all the muscles strong, including the heart. The family that exercises—swimming, tennis or building a playroom in the basement—will be healthier and probably happier, for exercise is fun and it wards off depression and a hundred other ills.

At the very least, children need some sports equipment—a bike or roller skates, a soccer ball, a jump rope—and the chance to use them often. A child will bike to the store, or run, if you need the celery in a hurry (and the chocolate chips to make some cookies), but give him a ride to soccer practice if that's the only way to get there. All of this teaches children that exercise is important and merits a fair share of their day.

THE ROBICS

Some exercises use a small amount of oxygen and some use a lot, and the second are much better than the first.

Anaerobics—a dash to the corner, for example—take less than two minutes and use little oxygen, and they don't do the body much good, but aerobics involve both the arms and the legs and are terrific if they last at least fifteen or twenty minutes. Jogging, biking, hiking, dancing or swimming (the crawl) can make a child breathe in up to seventeen times more air than he would if he were sitting still. By sending oxygen to all the muscles, including the heart, he will burn more food and, even though he'll eat more, he'll have the energy to exercise more.

Aerobics make the heart beat faster and get stronger, so it can beat slower when it's resting—the secret to greater endurance and a long, long life—and if the arms and

THE CRAB

Not all exercises involve running, jumping and deep breathing, of course. Our Aunt Kay insisted we each touch our toes daily, brush our hair until it crackled, walk up and down steps with books on our heads—so we'd learn to glide like ladies—and, when we were just sitting around, she would urge us to rotate one foot and then the other, round and round. ("You don't want to have fat ankles, do you, honey?")

And when there was nothing left to do, Aunt Kay had each child stand with her back to the wall, throw back her head, put her hands flat against the wall and walk them down, until they were doubled back and flat on the floor, and then we would walk, belly up, around the small house.

No wonder we had such a good time.

the upper torso work as hard as the legs, the heart and the lungs benefit much, much more. To be the most effective, your child should play hard at school for a half hour every day and play a half hour of aerobic sports three to four times a week, including a five-minute warm-up and another five minutes to slow down.

Your child will know if he's working hard enough by testing his pulse rate with a clock or a watch that has a second hand. The test itself will fascinate a Ten. Teach him to find his pulse by placing his index and middle fingers either on the underside of the wrist about an inch below the base of the palm or just under the jaw and to one side of the windpipe. He then slides his fingers up and down his wrist or his neck—either one will do—until he can feel the throb. When he finds it, he stands still and starts counting when the sweep hand hits twelve and stops when it reaches ten. He then multiplies these beats by six to find out how many times his heart beats in a minute: his pulse rate. In the Middle Years, it's usually between 70 and 100 when he's just hanging around.

He then takes it while he exercises. A preteen's body is working well if the rate goes up to 140–170 during a five- to ten-minute exercise and drops to normal within forty-five seconds after he quits.

Exercises that seem so hard at first, like jogging or jumping jacks, will soon be easy and then his pulse rate won't go up so high—a sign that the heart is stronger and needs to beat less, even though it's delivering more blood. This means he'll need to bike at a lower gear, jump higher on the rebounder or snap light weights on his ankles when he runs, but this will just give him the heart—and the energy—to exercise more.

Jogging

Jogging is great for a child; it can rest his emotions while exercising his body, and let him get in touch with nature whether he runs with his best friend, his parents, his dog or alone. It will also, of course, increase a child's strength and build endurance, particularly for young girls, since they tend to be more efficient runners than boys.

In jogging, as in any form of aerobics, the muscles expand and contract in a pumping action, turning them into auxiliary hearts that help to push the blood through the body. This changes the metabolism and keeps the body slim.

Jogging—or running, which is a little faster—lets a child drink in oxygen and enjoy its exhilaration—a splendid and safe addiction and a lot of fun. But not at first. It takes a few weeks until the new runner knows the ropes and follows these rules:

- Run on a fairly empty stomach.
- Warm up with a few toe touches or by bracing against a tree—so the muscles are stretched before they're tested.

- Run on bike paths or asphalt, rather than concrete.
- Run slowly at the start and the finish, so the heartbeat can build up and slow down.
- Keep the back straight, the forearms and the chin more or less parallel to the ground.
- Breathe deeply enough to expand the belly, a sign that the lungs are filled too.
- Run slowly enough to be able to talk while jogging.
- Lope or even walk if there is pain in the chest or breathlessness.
- Work out side stitches, if possible, by stopping to bend the body at the waist in every direction and by taking deep breaths.
- Drink lots of water after a run, particularly in summer, even if you aren't particularly thirsty.

Running shoes, which add a great deal of style, are good if you can afford them, but a child should do all right in a decent pair of sneakers since his height-to-weight ratio is less than yours, and so is the impact on his spine.

If you run with your child for about fifteen minutes, three to four times a week—slowing to a walk when one of you is tired, but always keeping up an effort—

he will soon be ready to push for longer distances. The Boston Marathon is pretty unlikely, but you may both be ready for a 10K race by the time he's in junior high.

RELAXATION

The right kind of relaxation is almost as important as the right kind of exercise, and meditation heads the list. Although it usually takes a week or two to learn the techniques, some children meditate naturally when they daydream, staring out into space, letting vague ideas flow through their heads.

The boys and girls who keep themselves tightly programmed, however, may need to have their meditation programmed too. Do it together until he learns the routine, then each go to your own separate, secluded and tranquil part of the house or the backyard where you'll have as few distractions as possible.

Your child should be comfortable when he meditates, sitting on a soft pillow on the floor, legs crossed in the lotus position like Gandhi—a position he'll achieve much easier than you will—and his hands in his lap. He breathes deeply as he repeats a special sound of his own invention, his mantra, over and over again softly—the same one each day, a sound no one else need know. This has an exotic appeal to a child, but counting actually works just as well. He inhales, drawing in the air slowly, deeply and evenly, then he holds it for a couple of slow beats and exhales: 1001; 1002; 1003; 1004; 1005. By repeating the same sound each day, again and again, for twenty minutes, the mind is emptied; the body uses less oxygen; the blood pressure goes down; the pulse rate and the breathing are slower, and the relaxed brain makes the special, slower, calming alpha waves.

You'll be following the same program in your corner and, when you're both done, the world will seem a more reasonable place and you'll both feel livelier and able to concentrate better. In time meditation will be so easy you may wish to drop the mantra, or at least keep quiet about it.

Because a child can feel just as pressured as an adult, he needs to grow up knowing he has the right to put some time aside just for himself. It's a lesson for parents to learn too.

HYGIENE

Each generation of young people seems to worry about its sex appeal a little earlier, especially girls. Now they're fretting over makeup at Eleven or Twelve, using deodorant before it's needed and mouthwash even though they still forget to brush their teeth. They have sound enough reasons. Looks do matter to both the looker and the one who is looked at and every preteen knows it—especially a girl. She must look attractive to be fully accepted by her friends and therefore, by herself.

Rather than dismiss these whims and wishes, let her learn how to take care of herself in a natural way, as her foremothers did. She can experiment with makeup by rubbing her cheeks with a cut beet and, when they're dry, by patting her face with rice powder, made by grinding dry rice in

RAG DOLL

If meditation takes too much time, tell your child to stand as limply as he can and shake out first one arm, then the other; then one leg, then the other; and finally his whole self, as if he were a floppy rag doll. It's a fine and silly relaxer.

FACE FIXER

Modern folk medicine finds that vitamin E—the pure, viscous kind without color or scent—often cures or at least improves bad skin and keeps any skin in good condition. If your child has an early case of acne, she should use it three times a day for at least three days, either on isolated zits or on her whole face. Use once a day on normal skin. It's dandy for mothers too.

the blender. It was considered very daring a century ago.

Give her a ribbon with People Polish (see Gifts) to make her feel elegant, a bunch of parsley to freshen her breath and some fine conditioners and rinses from the kitchen cupboard. This is the time for a child to learn that the best tricks are the oldest, the cheapest, usually the safest and certainly the daffiest.

TEETH

Your child's teeth probably need more care and protection than any part of his body, for the sake of the family, as well as his own. The price of dental work can cut a week at the beach into a weekend.

To keep his teeth in good condition, your child must brush and floss at least once a day—and keep a chart in the bathroom to check when he does; use fluoridated water or a fluoride mouth rinse and eat a balanced diet, including plenty of raw apples, celery and carrots, which scrub the teeth between meals. And if that's not enough, put up our dentist's favorite sign: DON'T FLOSS ALL YOUR TEETH; JUST THE ONES YOU WANT TO KEEP.

Your child will be more likely to follow this regimen if he knows that bacteria in his mouth form a thin, colorless plaque on his teeth—and especially in the grooves—in only twenty-four hours, unless he brushes it away. Every time he eats any-thing sweet, the bacteria in this plaque changes the sugar to acid for the next twenty minutes, which erodes the hard enamel that covers his teeth. Once a spot is eaten away—fortunately a slow process—a cavity is quick to follow. When a child knows how cavities start, he'll take much better care of his teeth.

Even with the best of care he'll need to see the dentist at least once a year and to get a custom-made mouth guard if he's on a football or soccer team. Because it's more comfortable than one from a sports store, he'll be more likely to wear it. If a tooth does get cracked, chipped or out of line, however, take him straight to the dentist. Most teeth can be patched and saved.

BATH

The ubiquitous dirty-neck syndrome—a badge of the Middle Years—is the result of bathing alone, for privacy is essential to most children by Seven.

The best you can do is insist on a nightly bath, allowing enough time to soak even the nails clean. Expect the neck to get washed when the head is shampooed. There are very few occasions when a neck should be scrubbed at the expense of a child's dignity.

HAIR

As the sixties taught us, hairstyles can tear a family apart—and they shouldn't. Parents have the veto, but most styles aren't worth the fuss.

Your daughter will be about Eight and your son around Eleven or Twelve before the haircut really matters, although both boys and girls usually feel strongly about bangs—one way or another—and should have the right to decide whether to wear them or not. Otherwise your wishes will probably prevail.

A short cut usually works best if your child's hair is curly or has a lot of body, while a longer style is better if the hair is straight or fine.

You'll know your child is in the hands of a good barber or hairdresser if he talks to you and your child separately, to make sure you agree on the cut, and then reconciles any differences before he makes the first snip. He'll also expect you to wander away from his chair for the fifteen minutes or so that it takes to give a good cut. If you hover, your child will turn his head to talk with you, and some cutting mistakes are sure to be made. The haircutter should be deft enough, and friendly enough, to chat with your child as he works, however, because he'll time his comments better.

Hair Care

Brushing and braiding may drive your daughter wild at Six—especially if she's a touchy little ectomorph—for the scalp is as sensitive as her neck and face at this age. Brush her hair in quick little strokes, starting from the bottom, and show her how to do the same.

By the seventh grade your daughter (but not your son) will fret about the sheen, the condition and the color of her hair. If it doesn't match the standard set by Miss Perfection at school (and it never does), she will blame her hair for any popularity problem she thinks she has. No wonder nobody likes her! Take her com-

plaints seriously, not because they're true, but because it shows that you take her seriously.

You can boost her self-image by helping her make natural conditioners and rinses, inventing new styles for her to wear and teaching her how to brush her hair 100 times a day—50 times over, 25 times under and 25 more on top. This may be boring enough to make her find something else to fuss about, and if not, that's all right. So much brushing is great for her hair.

Shampoo

A son with longish hair won't want help to wash his hair, and if its short he won't need it. Just tell him to scrub his scalp in the shower and hope he gets caught in the rain a lot.

A long-haired daughter can—and should—get help until she learns how to do the job herself. She won't mind if you treat her on a grown-up level—one woman to another—and give her some beauty parlor secrets. Tell her that baby shampoo isn't good for her hair, since it contains a drying ingredient to get rid of cradle cap, and that homemade rinses and conditioners are best. She won't even need the conditioner if she only washes her hair twice a week—which is all she needs to do—and uses the rinses sparingly.

She'll probably want to hang her head over the sink or tub to wash her hair (so she can stay dressed) and will need you to help her get her hair wet all over and to squeeze on the shampoo. Show her how much to use so she won't use too much when she washes her hair by herself. Give her scalp a few rubs "the way they do it at the beauty shop" and then busy yourself cleaning out a cabinet while she scrubs. Now show her how to squeeze out the extra suds, run her head under water, and then do it all once more, running it under much more water than she thinks necessary. She has to learn that it's clean and soap-free when she can pull a clump of hair between her thumb and index finger and have it squeak all the way from the scalp to the ends. After a few months your Eight will be able to wash her hair fairly well herself, although you'll want to supervise before any special occasion.

The child who is worried about "split ends" is always a girl and probably Twelve.

HOT OIL TREATMENT

This treatment works well, but double the recipe if it's for both of you, or if your child's hair is quite long. In a saucepan

HEAT   ½ c. mayonnaise

When it's cool enough to touch, have your child put a towel on her shoulders, pour the mayonnaise on her dry hair and rub it in well. Cover with a towel for 20 minutes, and then shampoo.

It's such a messy, drippy thing to do, she'll be sure it was worth it, although it will take a few shampoos to get rid of all this oil.

By Eleven or Twelve, your beauty-minded child begins to use enough shampoo to wash a Shetland pony, and then complains that her hair is dull. Now is the time to teach her that it takes a final rinse to cut the soap and give her hair its sheen.

Plain old salt-free seltzer probably takes out chlorine, salt water, suntan oil and soap residue better than anything else. An acidic rinse removes the shampoo buildup but may strip the hair and may remove many natural oils too, which is why sun can bleach the hair in summer.

Nevertheless, it's all right to use one of these rinses occasionally if only because they make a preteen feel glamorous.

FOR BLONDES

Fresh lemon juice can be squeezed directly on the hair, then rinsed, but add 3 parts of water to 1 part of any commercially bottled juice.

FOR REDHEADS AND BRUNETTES

Rinse No. 1

COMBINE   1 pt. warm water
               5 oz. cider vinegar

Pour all over wet, clean hair and towel dry.

Rinse No. 2
Substitute leftover coffee for the vinegar. It not only cuts the soapy film but gives the hair a glow, a slightly darker color—and a delicate coffee aroma.

SKIN

A child's skin—taken for granted by the casual Ten—is anxiously studied at Twelve as the fear of acne becomes real, particularly for a girl because she reaches puberty sooner. A little motherly advice will teach her how to care for her skin.

The fine art of face washing appeals to a preteen. Teach her to wash her face first

SKIN CONDITIONER

This once-a-day treatment makes a Twelve feel fancy and her skin look better, because it restores the right acid level to the skin and helps prevent acne.

MIX   1 oz. cider vinegar
            3 oz. warm water

Splash it on the face freely and let the skin air-dry.

FACIAL

Oatmeal has another reason for being.

MIX   **2 oz. oatmeal (any kind)**
                1 oz. water

Have your child pat this mixture all over her face and let it dry into a tight mask. She rubs it off with her fingers to remove dead skin and blackheads, then washes her face well.

with hot, soapy water—to open the pores; to splash them with cold—to close them again; and then to pat her skin dry with a towel. This is the same thing she'll do before and after a facial or a freshener.

SEXUALITY

Since grade school children can't think in abstractions, they don't think much about sex. They are very conscious, nevertheless, of being boys and girls and with good reason. Something sure feels good down there.

As much as they may ask about babies, a Six or Seven doesn't really believe sex has anything to do with making them, no matter how well you explain it. At this age they believe only in what they can see or remember. They accept the connection at Eight but most of them aren't particularly interested.

The energy they'll devote to thinking, dreaming and sometimes experimenting with sex in adolescence is now spent learning how to keep their world in reasonable control. In the preteens—Ten, Eleven and Twelve—the energy pours out, and they throw themselves into physical activity, baseball or ballet, with a passion you can hardly believe. Their growing understanding of sexual concepts is reflected in their behavior. While more discreet in their language, particularly around adults, they begin to define their masculinity and femininity in more sexual ways. Now boys talk and fantasize about sex with each other in

terms of conquest and girls turn into romantics. Here the pigtailed Twelve forlornly plucks a daisy, petal by petal, saying, "He loves me; he loves me not"—and she doesn't even have a special fellow in mind.

This alarms some parents. Despite years of helping your son to be caring and gentle and your daughter to be athletic and assertive, the prepuberty boy still thinks like a caveman and the girl dreams of building her nest. Accept the inevitable and feel blessed. Your earlier efforts will still give your child a broader understanding and the chance to be a more complete person.

Of course boys and girls should know (and can hardly avoid knowing) the mechanics and consequences of sex. We are almost back to Chaucerian days, when the book of sex was wide open, and even if you don't mention it at all, your child will find out about it. It's obviously much better for parents to do the teaching, openly and honestly, so children will feel comfortable about their bodies, accept their sexual feelings and regard sex as a healthy endowment, rather than a weapon or a commodity.

More than anything else, however, the facts of life give children a lifetime of protection so they know they have the right—and almost always the power—to protect themselves against sexual experiments and sexual abuse. To expect children to have the physical strength—and the strength of character—to say no is unrealistic unless they also know why. This gives them the courage to say, "I won't," to even the most persuasive friend, the most persistent adult. It isn't always easy for them, which is why some kind of supervision is necessary, even in the early teen years.

The lessons at Six should be unhurried, one gentle step at a time, and the lessons should be verbal, not visual. A Six is too old to see her parents walk around naked or to shower with them, especially a parent of the opposite sex, for this could arouse confused desires and fill the child with guilt. By Ten, he'll need the backup of a sex ed class and the chance to read a few well-chosen sex books written for that age. Most of the information should come from you and your husband, however, because it includes your values. To protect your child from wrong information, you have to teach what's right.

By talking about sex openly, throughout the Middle Years, you clear up most of the confusion generated by ill-informed friends, popular music, television, movies and magazines. At first these conversations may make you blush, but they'll be less embarrassing if you simply admit that they do. Your child will appreciate your honesty. The experience will also give you a new assurance. Once you can talk easily with your child about sex, you can talk about anything.

These talks are never easy, but you'll be more comfortable if you also talk about sex in casual, matter-of-fact asides when it's appropriate, and have Big Talks a few times a year. If you don't, you'll find yourself answering questions in the middle of a department store—and not very well.

You can initiate the more serious talks by using a story on television or an incident in the neighborhood as your springboard. Use clinical terms, like "penis" and "vagina," rather than the babyish names you may have used when the child was younger. Formal and grown-up words help both boys and girls understand that sex is for grown-ups, and they get a child used to this vocabulary, so he can talk about sex with a counselor or the family doctor without too much embarrassment.

The subject probably will be brought up every few months by one of you, and each time you'll give as much information as you think your child wants, repeating what you've already talked about and adding a little more. This is much better than giving the full story in the beginning, since this would only be confusing. There will still be some misconceptions, but if you ask your child what he knows, you can clarify errors as you go along. It's also important to explain how love and commitment give sex the significance and beauty that nature intended. This is the thread you'll want to weave through your talks.

When you explain sex to your child, do it as you would explain anything else— at the child's own level of understanding. This varies from year to year and child to child. The younger child wants to find out where the baby lived before his birth rather than how he got there. As clear as you try to be, some of the information will be garbled. If a Six still has trouble understanding cause and effect—and many do— he can't imagine a world before he was born or that a sperm and an egg could possibly turn into a baby.

Another Six may think on a slightly older plane but still believe that babies really come from a factory or a baby store, despite your best explanations. That's why you'll want to give your child a fine picture book of the baby in the womb and ask the pregnant neighbor to let your child hear her baby's heartbeat in her belly. At this age a child needs to know simply that it takes males and females to make babies, whether parakeets or people, and that most of them do it the same way.

The mind of a Seven usually can understand the mechanics of baby making and yet may refuse watermelon since she's sure the seeds have something to do with pregnancy. Why else would that neighbor be walking around with a watermelon in her stomach?

An Eight begins to be more sophisticated. Now the child can understand that a baby is made up of the genes from both parents—although that's hard to believe—as well as their love, which is not.

By Nine your child—boy or girl—should know about menstruation and why it's necessary, just as a Ten, boy or girl, should know about erections and how hormones turn into desires and how to handle them.

Even at Eleven or Twelve, your child may realize that it takes a sperm and an egg to make a baby and yet think that one or the other is really a very, very, very tiny baby, ready to grow. Your child probably will be on the verge of adolescence before the whole process becomes clear.

There still will be many missing bits and odd confusions. You help your child understand when you talk about sex indirectly, including gay rights, living arrangements and abortion in your matter-of-fact discussions of the news. When you assume your child already knows what you are talking about, you discover an amazing fact: he does. Any child who reads Ann Landers—and they all do—knows about sex, including some of the fancier fetishes.

It's still hard to talk about sex and values with a Twelve, and you may be hurt that he prefers to ask the counselor at school for guidance rather than you, but try to understand. Parents can seem judgmental to their children now, since the preteen, like the young teen, may do a bit of groping until his conscience catches up with his hormones.

Talk about sex as a biological wonder—a warm, happy, exciting interlude that depends on love and commitment to reach its ultimate pleasure. Only a parent can make that message so clear.

Parents must also teach their children the physical and psychological dangers of early sex, so they can hold their own in the young teens, even though friends will insist that virginity is obsolete. This standard line from your mid-teens is now used much earlier.

You also want your child to understand that sex is the most habit-forming drug in the world. Once tried, it continues to appeal, whether it's been a good experience or not. If children are well grounded in values, they will also know that sex is a treasure that requires the greatest protection. Your child needs to feel a responsibility not only for the feelings of another but for the life of another. By defining values now, children are able to stand by them better as they grow up, because they realize that sex is a matter of maturity and morality as much as pleasure.

That's why you want your child—boy or girl—to grow up knowing that people must forgo sex until both parties are old enough to pay its emotional and financial price—that is to say, until your child is not a child anymore.

PUBERTY

Around Seven the adrenal glands start releasing weak androgens in both boys and girls, causing a milder version of the same mood swings they'll have in adolescence. A sketchy explanation of puberty at this early age may help your child handle the hormones with greater equanimity and a certain amount of pride.

The real signs and feelings of puberty begin when their brains release a flow of hormones while they sleep. This will continue around the clock as girls produce estrogen and boys make testosterone—the essential ingredients that will make them grow tall, take shape and turn them into

several years. She should know that her two ovaries will start growing and producing the hormones to make her breasts develop; one breast may grow faster than the other for a while, before they become the same size, or her nipples may develop small bumpy bits of glandular tissue which will soon dissolve. Neither problem is reason for concern. She will also be growing taller and the shape of her breasts may displease her. The pain of adjustment will be forgotten when puberty is past and her body is once again in balance.

By Ten a girl should know the practical needs of menstruation and be prepared with a box of slim tampons, a box of sanitary napkins and some panty shields, so she can choose what she needs when her period starts. It's comforting to have her supplies ready, even though she may not menstruate for years. Just having them on her closet shelf and knowing she can take them with her on a trip will make her more comfortable, especially if many of her friends have started to menstruate. The longer she waits the more she will worry that it will happen in the middle of class and all the world will know or, even worse, that it will never happen at all.

Talk to her about this possibility before it becomes an issue. She should know that a doctor doesn't even start to worry about a late bloomer until she's Sixteen and then only if she's shown no other signs of development. She also should know that a girl needs to weigh about 90 pounds to menstruate and that she may start a couple of years late—and be irregular too—if she has been a serious competitive swimmer or runner for several years. The ratio of body fat to lean affects the hormones, and so do stress and weight loss. Your matter-of-fact attitude should be enough to calm her, but if it isn't, a visit with a sympathetic gynecologist—preferably a woman—can give her the reassurance she needs.

The same straightforward manner is necessary when her period does start, so she'll recognize that menstruation is just a simple, rather tiresome biological proce-

men and women. This happens to most girls around Twelve and to most boys around Fourteen. There's no reason to worry if the hormones don't follow this schedule, however. Some children start a year or two later, others begin as much as three years earlier—a good reason to give children a complete picture of puberty at Nine.

Girls

Menstruation has been starting earlier and earlier—perhaps because our diets are better—but the flow will be so irregular at first that your daughter will have time to get used to the idea. Her body will have already changed a great deal even before her first period. She will probably have grown a few quick inches; her hips will have started to spread; her breasts will have started to bud; and she will have grown some pubic hair. She also will have shown a tendency to be moody, antsy and rebellious; hormones are a new experience. These are the real growing pains, so be gentle. Your child doesn't like this behavior any better than you do.

She won't take her anxieties quite so seriously if you tell her in detail what to expect and that the whole process will take dure. Her first period has its own once-in-a-lifetime name: menarche, which sounds like monarchy, and it does make a girl feel special—though not necessarily in charge of all she surveys. The least fuss is best, although some mothers find that a small, special, today-you-are-a-woman gift is appreciated, to signify the gift of womanhood.

Certainly you won't want to pass on any of the nonsense of our foremothers' day. Menstruation is not "the curse"; you have not lost your little girl; and she can still exercise and swim when she has her period. You do, however, want to review the processes that take place inside her body so she'll know what's going on. Tell her that her ovaries will take turns sending an egg to the womb each month. This may start before menarche, or even a year afterward, and when it does, she can get pregnant. She also should know that menstruation is just the lining of the womb that thickens to cushion the egg and, if it's fertilized, to cushion the baby. If it isn't, the lining breaks down to become the menstrual flow, carrying the broken egg with it.

She'll be relieved to know that the vagina is open just enough to release the menstrual flow and to accept a slim tampon without tearing the hymen—a fear of many young girls. Tampons may alarm your daughter at first, even though she has watched you insert one, but she probably will want to use them once she gets used to the idea, for they will give her the most freedom, the tidiest and safest absorption, and if they're changed before the blood is exposed to the air, they are odor-free.

You do need to teach your daughter to be responsible about her period, by keeping a supply of tampons in the bathroom at home, a couple of emergency tampons in her purse and some special change to buy some more if needed. She'll also have to remember to wash her genitals a couple of times a day when she menstruates to avoid any odor.

There will be some problems, of course. When ovulation begins, there may be cramps caused by the conflict of hormones in her body. If they've already begun, suggest a little exercise to help the uterus contract and activate the flow; a couple of aspirin every few hours; an old-fashioned heating pad; and a cup of hot tea. Aside from a hug and a kiss, she shouldn't need anything else after a few hours. Babying a child too much won't help her grow up.

Premenstrual tension also can be a problem but don't mention it beforehand or it will make her anxious. If your child gets headachy and depressed and her behavior ranges from cross to unbearable the week or two before she's due, there are many ways to make it better or even get rid of premenstrual syndrome (PMS) entirely. It helps to ban caffeine, because it ups the body's need for B vitamins; to cut down on salt, which makes her retain water; and to exercise regularly, but especially the two weeks before her period is due. This boosts the body's output of endorphins, which kill pain. She might also go on the hypoglycemic diet—four to six small meals a day, few fruits and no junk food—since the blood sugar tends to vacillate with PMS. In addition, some doctors suggest over-the-counter nutrients, such as 100 units of vitamin B_6 a day to make the neurotransmitters work better, or 8 capsules of gamma linoleic acid, such as evening primrose oil, every day for several months, to help the production of prostaglandins. If all this fails, the doctor may have your child keep a basal temperature chart. If her temperature drops early in her cycle, natural (but not synthetic) progesterone may be prescribed.

The fear of staining also presents a problem. Your daughter may feel better if she has dark underpants to wear or enough underpants to wear two pair at once, but brush off the possibility of an accident by teaching her how to take care of it if it happens. A quick rinse of cold water usually gets any blood from her underpants and pajamas—and sheets—but if there is a stain, she can soak it in a mild bleach solution.

Practical answers make many problems go away, especially those that haven't happened yet.

Boys

Boys are at least as conscious of puberty as girls, although its arrival is less noticeable. A boy of Ten or Eleven will produce the hormone that makes the testicles grow and, when they get big enough, they will make sperm. Other changes become more apparent during the next two years. The testes continue to grow and the scrotum that holds them gets so big it wrinkles. This gives the sac the space to hang loose when it's hot, for the testes must be cooler than the body to produce sperm—the reason fertility experts tell husbands to wear loose boxer shorts.

Now a boy's pubic hair, which had come in soft and downy, begins to grow curly and coarse—the sign that puberty is about midway—and some soft hair may grow on his face while his voice gets deeper (most of the time).

A boy does most of his growing after this point, and until then he may be sure that he'll be short all his life. He is also likely to be worried about the size of his penis. Tell him that after puberty the average penis is 3–4″ long and about 1¼″ in diameter when it's flaccid, and about 6″ long when it's erect and that the joy of sex doesn't depend on its size.

He is almost sure to be concerned and embarrassed with the discovery that the penis has a life of its own. Although he's always been able to have erections, he no longer can trust it to behave when it should. It reacts not only to a passing girl but to a vagrant thought, whether he's watching TV or singing in the choir. The best you can do is include the problem in one of your talks on sex, by assuring him that erections take all boys by surprise and that other people don't notice—and then give him fitted shorts so they won't.

Your son also should know that he will ejaculate in his sleep, that there's nothing wrong with it and that the frequency of these wet dreams depends on how often he masturbates, for, one way or another, his body has to make space for the new sperm he's constantly making. And give this child a rubber doorstop. You may forget to knock.

HOMOSEXUALITY

This subject is seldom considered by parents or children in the Middle Years, but you'll need to know some facts in case your child gets worried about it—or you worry about your child.

One out of four boys is said to have a homosexual experience, although no more than an estimated one out of ten males is homosexual (a figure many think is too high) and four out of a hundred females. There have been homosexuals throughout history, and always, apparently, to about the same degree.

If you think your child might be one, look at the situation realistically. There is no known cause. The parents of homosexuals may be weak or strong; permissive or authoritarian; hovering or scarcely around. Homosexuality seems to be as inborn as heterosexuality: it can't be caught or taught or reversed. It also may show up very early, but since it often isn't apparent until late adolescence a young person has good reason to be celibate or at the least to be discreet about it until then.

You will want to protect him from sexual encounters (as you would any child) and give him what he deserves most: your love. He is your child, first and last.

The elasticity of a child's mind is as awesome as its originality. The more it's stretched, the more it can be stretched. Children want to learn everything they can and a few things they can't, but circumstances—and parents—block them a little here, there and everywhere.

By Six it's clear that children are smarter in some areas than others, depending on which parts of their brains have developed best—a pattern that will last all their lives. Although they still have patches of confusion, most of them have also absorbed the basic skills they need for school by now. To read, children must be able to pass something from one hand to the other without putting it down. It's a seemingly simple skill but they need it to track their eyes from left to right, instead of up and down, which is more natural. If their eyes don't track, they can't read across the page. They must also be able to remember simple shapes and relate them to sounds and to put them in the right sequence. Phonics are fairly easy if they are familiar with rhymes and alliterations and can hear the nuances. To write, they must move their fingers in the direction they need to go—a hard task even for children who seem well coordinated. It's especially hard for a child who's still a clumsy climber and has trouble on a balance beam. This child needs patient instruction to learn how to move in an orderly way and encouragement so he doesn't lose heart, and his ego with it.

No child should be rushed in any direction, however. If he is learning faster than he's being taught and is begging to learn more, by all means teach him what he wants to know, but don't force-feed him. He needs to set his own pace, particularly in school. Remember: children learned very well before there were any books at all.

There is a universal pattern of learning among children. In the early school years they recognize quantities—an underpinning for math—and later lengths and heights and volume are understood and in a certain order, with each concept taking about a year to absorb. Moreover, they acquire this knowledge with or without help from parents or teachers, whether they live in the most advanced culture or the most primitive one, and with no more than a two-year difference between them. Children also understand the concept of time better by first grade, and they won't demand an immediate response to their requests, unless they're used to getting their way.

Even the most organized, school-ready children will learn better if parents let them solve problems on their own, as soon as they can. Children who are allowed to find the shortest route to school or the store, the cheapest school supplies, the best cookie recipe will quickly learn to trust their own minds to find answers, which will make them still more inquisitive. This challenges children without overwhelming them. Even those who aren't encouraged to make their own decisions will still try, for that is their nature. Children instinctively make comparisons to figure out how they fit into the world around them. Now the picture becomes more complete, as they also begin to take other people into account. They are developing the ability to reason.

This doesn't mean a child in the Middle Years can reason well or is always a reasonable person. Most of his answers are incomplete and many are incorrect, because a child must go through many stages before he can think like an adult. Moreover, his answers can only be drawn from what he knows, and his conclusions shift like earth plates to accommodate new facts. Each new piece of information is tested against the old. In the process, some old ideas are thrown away and others are blended together. This creative friction can make a child tense, but it sharpens the mind and builds self-esteem. The search is more important than the answers. When children are encouraged to think for themselves and do for themselves, they are encouraged to succeed, which feeds their self-confidence. This produces more motivation, more success, more confidence.

Children learn more easily when parents and teachers are sensitive to their individual learning styles. While all children learn better by doing—for doing makes learning come to life—some learn best by seeing new information, some by hearing it, some by touching it, and some need to put their whole bodies into it. A good teacher tries to vary her approach, so all the children can learn.

Visual children, for whom picture books were once a glory, are quick to remember words by sight and may find that reading brings them more knowledge and pleasure than anything else. Other children are primarily aural. The words they hear are imprinted on their minds, long after the picture they see has drifted away. These are the children who learn best in discussions, in or out of the classroom. And there are the tactile children who learn through their touch—the ones for whom sandpaper letters were invented, or who like to form letters and numbers out of snakes of clay or even trace them on their arms with their fingertips. Finally there are the kinesthetic learners who like letters so big they can actually climb through them and who remember best when they can use their bodies to act out a history lesson. Whatever style your child prefers, he will experiment over and over with new knowledge, realizing instinctively that practice—from writing poetry

to riding a bike—is the secret of all learning.

By Seven children begin to delight in order—not in their rooms but in their collections, which are usually the same ones as their friends'. Even if you start a collection with your child, he'll want to do the sorting, for children need to classify many things in many ways. The physical organizing of possessions now will help them organize their ideas in their early teens, so they can begin to think in abstractions.

You help your child when you encourage mnemonic learning—the classifying of things by their similarities. Here you help him see that apples and pears fit in one group, citrus fruits in another and the big-pitted ones, like plums and peaches, in another. Only then do you point out the details that distinguish one apple from another, comparing the bumpy blossom end of a Delicious to the smoothness of a Rome. By going from the general to the specific, a child learns to think in a logical, sequential way. This is particularly important for girls. All children need practice in logic, but studies show that most boys are instinctively good at it while intuition is the great strength of girls. By teaching your daughter the causes and effects, you help her discover the logic behind her intuition, so she can understand and defend her beliefs better. And by teaching your son to trust his intuition more, you broaden his perceptions.

Now that society has finally recognized that boys and girls (and men and women) have the same rights, we can admit that they don't always think in quite the same way. It seems to be easier for boys to see the whole and for girls to see its parts—two accurate pictures, but each is improved when they are combined. It's up to parents to help their children strengthen their shortcomings and share their strengths, so they can be more thoughtful, more complete adults.

No matter how children think, their minds consider not just what happens, but why, and the scope of their inquiries is huge. Their speech won't quite reflect it—for speech is never as advanced as the mind—but in the Middle Years they begin to focus on the biggies—death and divorce; space and infinity; heaven and hell and God by many names or none. These mental investigations are stressful but they provide the friction that spurs the mind and makes it grow. Imagination—which seems to hide in a cloak of conformity between Seven and Ten—must be stirred repeatedly with mythology and fairy tales in the primary grades and science fiction in the fourth, fifth and sixth grades.

At this age children instinctively know they need knowledge to develop their dreams. Life is real and earnest now; it thrives on the facts that will prepare them for all the mind-boggling ologies ahead. By using the globe to point out the rivers in the oceans that flow just like the rivers on the land, you can explain that running water purifies itself by taking oxygen from the air, much as we clean our blood by taking air into our lungs. A child is fascinated by the universal rules in nature and the order of the universe.

The astonishments of the world—whether he meets them in ideas, on museum trips or in books—help him see and talk and write with precision. You can expand your child's vocabulary by answering his question with another familiar word that is a little more exact than the one he just used or by using new words that he can understand by their context. Words are the tools of thought and this is how they're honed.

A child's knowledge depends on a flexible memory. This is enhanced when you play cards and games of concentration; when you encourage your Seven to be the family archivist, keeping the vacation maps and the matchbooks and the scorecards of miniature golf, and when you evoke the past with stories of your own childhood and your parents' childhoods too. Examples from the past help children put their own experiences into context.

The photographs you hang in your child's room—not just of distant family members but of the good times you shared with them—will help recall that Thanksgiving at Grandma's house, when he wasn't as tall as the dining-room table. Seeing is not only believing, it's remembering, and pictures in the mind and on the wall help the past stay alive.

When your child was little you compared him with other babies and swore you'd quit the habit. Now, just when you thought you had, you walk into his classroom and are struck by the children: their freshness, their dearness—and their differences. As much as they want to look alike, act alike and sound alike, their complexions, their hair and their height all vary more and more. They are as different on the inside as they are on the outside. It's the difference between the minds that bothers some parents, especially with their firstborns, and they may find it hard to accept their children as they are. If you are one of those parents, please try very hard. Acceptance makes a family work. Never mind that your child isn't a genius; very few children are. Never mind that he isn't learning as fast as some other mothers say their children learn; he shouldn't have to compete with your dreams (or theirs). Instead, he needs a healthy balance of attention and benign neglect, good genes, a healthy diet and a happy home.

The magic of the mind is its vastness. Even if a child has had the best of care and teaching, his natural boundaries are so wide, so elastic that his limits will never be reached. It's necessary to help a child go as far as he can, but there is a mild sadness in the prospect. The more your child uses his mind, the further he goes from you. Whatever he thinks and learns become his thoughts, his knowledge. You may exchange ideas but you may not invade this privacy, even if you're invited: outer space is closer than the far edge of his mind. As you help him explore his world, he will understand it better and get nearer to the next galaxy, and the next and the next. The mind is his ticket to freedom.

MEMORY

The memory is a sly rascal, hiding when we need it, then blowing in unexpectedly on the wings of a fragrance, a tune, a dandelion puff. It is as mysterious as it is elusive. Some events encourage memories, others block them, and by the Middle Years a child remembers nothing that happened before he was Two and not much before he was Three or Four, but from now on he adds to his own selective history, making his memory as individual as himself.

There are at least two kinds of memory—the short-term and the long-term. Your child, like you, first filters any information he gets—as well as smells and sights, and a honking horn—in less than a second, and then chooses a few of these to break into bits and ship to his short-term memory. It considers them for less than a minute, throws almost all of them away— to protect him from an overload of silly or useless information—and files the rest in his long-term bank: the human mind is the only 100 billion K computer in the world.

It's the long-term memory that catalogs this information, and the more important it is, the better it's remembered because a great joy, or a great fear, triggers a big release of chemicals, etching the memory deeply into the mind. Even the smallest bit of information makes each cell release a chemical spurt to carry it to the next. If the stress is too great or your child uses his mind too long, the chemical buildup blocks more and more information from reaching the brain.

That's when his mind calls "Time out!" and he begins to dream, whether he's awake or asleep. He will, like you, automatically let his mind drift for five or ten minutes and then reel it back and put it to work to simplify, sort or solve his problems. The dreams of the day (like the dreams of the night) take about a third of his time and help him work through his worries. The more he thinks, the better he thinks, but the little respites are necessary to consolidate his memories into logical thoughts, which lets him remember better and learn better.

You can help your child if you teach him to rhyme what he wants to remember or to learn such doggerel as "Thirty days hath September" or to link facts together. The letter *S* fascinates the first grader when he finds out that it looks like a snake and sounds like a hiss.

A child's memory also will be sharper if he's encouraged to repeat new information to himself, either in pictures or in words—hearing it and seeing it as well as thinking it—but it's strongest of all if he passes it on to someone else. A younger brother or sister will appreciate the attention (and an older one may not).

CREATIVITY

Creativity gives wings to the mind, art to the world and joy to both parent and child. It's often hard, however, for creative boys and girls to feel comfortable with their gifts, and schoolchildren—particularly boys—may feel awkward when they try to express themselves.

You have to be the one to introduce the crochet needles, the camera and the clay tools and look for activities he might never consider. The child who can't keep still when the band plays may be too shy to sing, but a harmonica can draw out tunes he never knew were in his head. The one who can't help rubbing his hand along the dining-room table may delight in carving soapstone or soap, or even refinishing fine wood. Children who are encouraged to notice color may not like to paint pictures, but they may sew beautiful clothes or plant brilliant gardens. A child doesn't have to throw pots or play the guitar to be creative.

If your Nine helps you solve a carpentry problem or figure out how much you should pay on each bill this month, you can bet he's being creative. Science and math, in their way, can be just as expressive as music and art. It's a matter of finding out how your child likes to use his special talents best and giving him the chance and the tools he needs.

You encourage creativity when you ask your Six to smell some herbs, choose the one he thinks would taste best with lemon and chicken and then let him sprinkle the herb on the bird and drizzle the juice on top, for who is more creative than a good chef? The young cook also needs a friendly welcome in the kitchen; a cookbook, so he can learn the principles as well as the precision of cooking; and some fine, simple recipes to win so much honest praise he'll want to try again. When a child exercises his imagination in one area, he will dare to reach for others.

Before long he will talk about finding solutions—the greatest creativity of all. You'll hear how wars can be averted, crops planted, bridges built. Some ideas will be daffy, some will probably have been in use for centuries and a few will contain new bits of wisdom. Listen well and join in—the two compliments that do the most to keep creativity alive and children lively. They deserve to be heard. They are the statesmen, the magicians, the inventors—and the parents—of tomorrow. And as you know so well, nothing takes more creativity than that.

DAYDREAMS

Every child is born with a special brand of originality, and daydreams help him keep it. Fantasy lets a child dare to think the unthinkable, do the undoable. He imagines how he would react in a desperate situation (heroically, of course). He may never have the chance to rescue seven children and a dog from a burning building, but just to imagine how he would do it will give him new confidence.

If you give your child enough time to dream and enough privacy—and if he knows you won't criticize him—he'll share some of these fancies with you. This will help you keep them within a reasonable range, so reality is never too far away, and to get to the bottom of his feelings when he seems down.

Since fantasies also let a child shape his goals, you need to take them seriously.

Mike was Nine when he was struck, suddenly and overwhelmingly, with a Great Idea: a wooden submarine. And he would build it himself. His dad was openly delighted.

That night they scrutinized the plans, looking for flaws and ways to correct them, and the next day Mike drew a bigger and better sub. And so it went, night after night. And then one night he met his dad at the door and said, "I have to tell you something about the wooden submarine. It won't work."

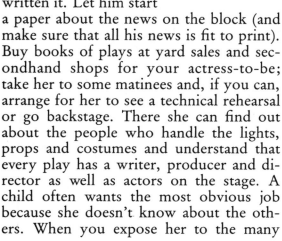

By giving children the chance to play out their dreams, you allow them to find out that the job is more fun than the glory at the end of the road, and that the more glamorous the goal, the harder the journey.

Your attention will also help your child clarify his dreams. Your son says he wants to be a journalist? Great. Ask the newspaper to give him a tour. Study a particular story. Ask how he would have written it. Let him start a paper about the news on the block (and make sure that all his news is fit to print). Buy books of plays at yard sales and secondhand shops for your actress-to-be; take her to some matinees and, if you can, arrange for her to see a technical rehearsal or go backstage. There she can find out about the people who handle the lights, props and costumes and understand that every play has a writer, producer and director as well as actors on the stage. A child often wants the most obvious job because she doesn't know about the others. When you expose her to the many

related jobs in any area, she can see how many choices she has within the same discipline.

Whatever the dreams, give your child the right to have them, and to change them too, but you needn't give the negative side of the picture. The child who plans to be a merchant mariner doesn't need to be told that the ships will be too dirty for her or the job too hard or that it's no place for girls. She wants to be treated seriously instead, with a trip to the docks and a tour of a ship, and the child who wants to be a forest ranger needs long tramps in the woods, to see how he and solitude get along. The sound ideas will hold up; the others will be springboards to something else.

All of this helps your child integrate his dreams with reality, so fantasies don't take over his life, and it does something more: it gives him the right to dream.

INTELLIGENCE

There's no use pretending. Children deserve an equal chance to do their best but they're not all created equal. Some are born bright as pennies; others find objects and actions more accessible than ideas and information. They also think at different rates of speed.

A child is born with an intelligence that falls within a certain range, but it can be kept twenty to forty points below par by poor prenatal care and, in the early years, by poor nutrition, little visual stimulation, limited loving and especially by poor communication. The same kind of blockers can stunt the mind in the Middle Years. It is hard for a schoolchild to grasp new knowledge when the basics are badly taught, the goals seem out of reach, the brain relies on junk food to think and home is a place where children are talked at, rather than with. All of this can lower his intelligence just as good nutrition, encouragement and enrichment at school—and particularly at home—can improve it.

No matter how good the school or how rich the home life, however, differences remain from child to child although all of them have brain power to spare. The mind is a reservoir no one has ever filled. Your child will keep on trying, as long as you encourage him to do his best and use his own special kind of intelligence. No one is equally good in all of them, nor do the experts agree on exactly what they are. Theories abound. One of the most persuasive divides the intelligence into seven separate categories, each located in specific parts of the brain. One of them, an intelligence for language, gives children the skill to use words and understand their nuances, while musical intelligence—which has been with us since the Stone Age—lets children compose a new song or repeat a tune heard only once, until, around Nine or so, they can master the technical skills. Some children may be strong in logic—and therefore in math and in many of the sciences—while other children have an intuitive sense of space: the architects, the graphic designers, the sculptors of tomorrow. Children can even think with their bodies too. The dancer, the actor, the boxer, the inventor, the outfielder who knows where to run the minute the bat meets the ball, all are kinesthetically smart. And finally, there are the children who know themselves and others so well that they know how to lead—the executives, the politicians, the union leaders.

Every discipline draws on one of these strengths in particular and often on several, mixing and matching to make the child's mind as unique as the body and the spirit.

INTELLIGENCE TESTS

An intelligence test can explore your child's mind, so you can help him build on his strengths, or perhaps understand why he's having trouble in class. A good test will indicate his capacity to learn new information, to put old knowledge together in new ways and to discover a learning disability, but it can't measure a child's

personality or motivation; his originality, creativity or talents; his stability or common sense; his conscience or his values or how well he can solve problems or learn from experience. Moreover, it doesn't measure some kinds of intelligence very well, and the younger the child, the harder it is to measure his mind at all.

The average I.Q. score is 100 and the higher a child scores over that figure, the better he probably will do in school, but this score can vary from week to week. For most this amounts to as much as ten points and one child in ten may change as much as thirty points. A child who is sick or tired may also score lower than a healthy, well-rested child. Practice with tests can also up the score six to seven points but it's the child who grows up with books and attention who is more likely to improve substantially than the child who has had little of either. Boys show greater growth over the years than girls because they take longer to mature.

If the score really reflects the full range of a child's intelligence, that's fine. And if it's a little too high, that's fine too. Tests show that teachers who think a child is smarter than he is will usually expect him to do better work—and he will. It is the child who tests below his ability, for one reason or another, who will suffer, for many teachers dismiss this child without even realizing it, particularly if he also has a learning disability or some other handicap. Moreover, the results will be posted in his school record, following him even through college.

There are two types of I.Q. tests—group and individual—and they can only be given with a parent's consent.

Group Tests

Group tests, which deal in language and logic, are usually given for a standard length of time, with the children writing or drawing their answers. Unfortunately, they can cause more problems than they solve. While these tests are much cheaper and more commonplace, they are also much less precise than the individual ones—so imprecise, in fact, that they are seldom accepted by the better independent schools.

Many factors can change the score. The child with a wide frame of reference has a definite edge, although a brighter child, whatever his background, is more likely to have a better memory and to compare what he remembers to the information he already has. Even so, it's pure luck if the Six who comes from a semiliterate household has ever heard that it's about 3000 miles from New York to Los Angeles—a question on one popular test.

Where and how your child is tested will matter too and so will his attitude. The child does better on a test if he *wants* to do well. The adrenalin of competition gets him going. Scores can be lowered too. A child won't be able to mark a lot of little blocks if he has an astigmatism or if he can't focus well after the first column because his eyes get tired. Another child may react poorly to the fluorescent lights in the room, particularly if they flicker. Fear is another problem. A child may be afraid to disappoint his parents—or himself. Risks are scary in the Middle Years, and an I.Q. test can be pretty risky, if adults have made a big fuss about it.

This makes the group I.Q. test about as accurate as the weatherman, which may be all right most of the time—especially for storm warnings—but it isn't perfect and, when blindly followed, it may cause poor decisions that will haunt your child for years. Unless he can have an individual test, it may be better to have none at all.

Individual Tests

These are given by a trained diagnostician to one child at a time, take several hours and are much more reliable because the score is based on a complicated formula figured against a national average. Generally your child's magic number will be a combination of the verbal I.Q.—which reflects his ability to answer questions and to reason in five or six subtests—and the performance I.Q., which shows how he analyzes and comprehends situations, without talking, in another five or six subtests.

The average score of each subtest is 10. The results are added to get the verbal and performance scores and then they are added together and compared to the norm, giving the diagnostician the child's mental age—in months—which is multiplied by 100. This is then divided by his chronological age—also in months—to get the final score.

If the child is roughly equal in all areas, the total will be valid, but there is often a difference of fifteen or sixteen points between the subtests. The child with this deviation can pay a heavy price if his parents only know that his total score is impressively high and then expect him to do well in every subject. This may be the child who is very adept with words and yet at sea in arithmetic—who is bored in English class, because it seems like needless repetition to him, and bewildered in math. The parent or teacher who only knows the child's I.Q. may feel he isn't "working up to his level." Watch out for this catch phrase. Water seeks a single level but intelligence does not. If a child is expected to do equally well in all subjects at school, even though he isn't equally smart in all of them, he will judge himself by his lowest grades rather than his highest.

There are other problems in accepting a child's total score, for there are differences between tests. The Wechsler Intelligence Scale for Children-Revised (WISC-R) is probably the most popular and respected individual test, quickly followed by the Stanford-Binet.

The WISC-R divides its verbal tests into math, reasoning, ability to make comparisons, vocabulary, general knowledge and common sense, and the performance tests judge a child on his ability to put one special puzzle together and to find out what's missing in another; to work with building blocks; and to see how well he can copy and understand pictures.

The Stanford-Binet, on the other hand, puts more stress on the ability to plan, to invent, to respond under stress, to solve problems, which gives a child of Ten or more an advantage if he's just gone through a verbal growth spurt. In fact, some parents choose this test if they're trying to get their preteen into private school, where verbal aptitude is often prized.

A parent should know the scores of the child's subtests and what they mean. If there is a twenty-point spread between the math and the verbal scores he needs some tutoring in the subject that is so much lower. The total score doesn't matter but it is important to know his percentile in the national level, if he goes to public school, and his independent rating if he goes to a private school, where the competition is much tougher. This will give you a realistic sense of how he should be doing in school.

An individual I.Q. test will give you a better understanding of your child's strengths and weaknesses but he shouldn't be placed in a more or less demanding class on the strength of it alone, since even the best test of intelligence is incomplete. You also need an objective classroom observation and a review of his annual achievement test, which will show how well he has learned that year—and how well the teacher has taught. When lower scores still can't be explained, the child should have a full physical before he's put in a remedial class.

Whatever the results, you're legally entitled to all the test information compiled by the school and you can ask for more tests if you're in doubt. You also can have any inaccurate conclusions removed from his school record. This is not only your right but your obligation. You can't expect all future teachers to overlook mistakes in his record, and some of them may act on it—to his cost.

THE GIFTED

While every child has three or four natural abilities, there are a few children—as many as five in a hundred—who are really born to shine. These gifted and talented children are, by definition, rare. One or two children out of a hundred are academically gifted with I.Q.s of 130 or more; two to three more may excel as natural athletes, leaders, inventors or artists; and some of them are strong in several of these areas. These boys and girls grow up rich, poor or middling, in the city or the country, in stability or chaos—occasional wildflowers in a field of clover.

Born athletes win early recognition, in school or out of it. The child who combines strength, fine timing and good coordination may become the ranking tennis star, the pro ball player or the Olympic contender—or he may simply be good enough to have a marvelous time on his high school or college team.

You'll know the child who will one day lead a nation—or a civic club. He's probably leading his neighborhood buddies now. More than anything else, he needs his parents to help him take the high road and not the easy one, so he'll never lead his flock astray.

The dexterous child is gifted too and will be much admired. He's the one who fixes the doorbell, the alarm clock or the two-wheeler and can do it with little or no instruction. Even though he may try too soon and fail at first, he will master these skills before other children even attempt them, because he has a problem-spotting, problem-solving sort of brain, as nimble as his fingers. He has a good chance to find and fill the right slot in life, but his chances are much better if he grows up knowing that tinkering can bring success—not just fame and fortune, but the inner joy that comes from doing a clever job and doing it well.

Artistically gifted children send out their own special signals. They are galvanized by the beauty of shadows on a moonlit wall or by motion, by dance, by rhythm, by design, by words or by color and will feel—and perhaps express their feelings—with intensity in one or several creative areas. When you find the born storyteller, the songbird, the doodler, the gourmet, the Six who must make her own skirt when you can barely mend—you may be looking at tomorrow's novelist or opera singer or illustrator or chef or designer. All it takes is some guidance and a little luck to help these children carry their gift from promise to practice.

Most of these managerial, athletic, inventive, creative, gifted and talented children are well rewarded by the popularity their friends bestow on them and by the honors they win. It's the intellectually gifted child who needs to be handled with the most sensitivity. Although there are early stories about the loneliness of gifted children, they are usually happy, well-rounded, interesting people who get along well with others. So will yours, if you are so blessed—providing you help him play his cards right. If you don't, this child can feel very alone and resentful for the "gifted" label can embarrass this child and should be used with discretion. Like any special package, he needs special handling.

Children who are bogged down in

classes that go too slow for them and who have no champion at home or at school will feel far out of the mainstream and bored. This is particularly true for the child with a gift that must be learned in sequential order, like math or science. It's no fun to wait for the class to catch up with him—and wait—and wait.

The gifts show up early. By Five, an academically gifted child usually knows he is different and by first grade this knowledge can begin to gnaw at his confidence. Even though he may wish to act like everyone else at this age, he won't be able to keep his special flair in check, and the sense of difference will grow each year. It's hard to find a playmate who will giggle and roller-skate for a while and then talk at length about dinosaurs or the DNA. Many of these children learn to slip easily between conformity and nonconformity, but others need extra support, and if they don't get it, they may become quite skilled at acting dumb. Many an underachiever—or a dropout—has been gifted. Other very bright children breeze through high school without ever feeling challenged, and then drop out of college. They may still be bored or they may not have learned to study and do complicated research.

Some who achieve so much—and so easily—in one area expect to be first-rate in all areas and without effort, and then may think of themselves as failures when they, of course, are not.

There are other pressures. Adults may expect this child's social behavior to keep pace with his mind, and it won't. The body, the mind and the spirit each grow at their own rate, and the gifted child—particularly if his intelligence is of the highest level—can be far out of kilter. This child will feel at war with himself and may be very hard to handle unless his lopsided development is fully accepted by his family and understood, one hopes, by his teacher.

It's as hard for the supercharged mind to hold back in the normal class as it is for the slow child to keep up with it. Unfortunately, teachers recognize the gifted child's abilities only about half the time. Genius or even high intelligence can be hard to spot in the child who doesn't seem to pay attention to what's taught and who invents most of the mischief in class. The teacher may see him as a troublemaker or as unmotivated or angry—and she'll be right on all three counts—and yet she still won't know why he acts the way he does. If your child is rowdy or withdrawn, he may simply be bored and working far below his ability. It will then be up to you to recognize the problem.

The gifted child who is healthy in body and mind should be full of energy. He sleeps less and runs more than others. The teacher may even decide he is hyperactive, which probably isn't true. Hyperactive children are not all gifted by any means, and all gifted children are not hyperactive by any means. It's just his active mind that makes his hands and feet and tongue so lively. A stick must be whittled, a sheet of paper demands a picture, an idea begs to become a short story and everything that needs to be invented is waiting for him to invent it. There's never enough time for all the things this child wants to do.

CHARACTERISTICS

There is a quickness about gifted children. They observe keenly, learn fast and remember well. They follow instructions, even complex ones, but only when they think they make sense—a reason to explain with care. They are also fascinated by new ideas but take very little for granted and want to know not just what is happening

but why. They process this information differently too, linking people and ideas and events together in such unorthodox ways that their conclusions may be quite original. Like all children, they fill in gaps with guesses, and take great leaps of intuition getting from here to there.

They see inconsistencies the way a Dutch housewife sees dust, and they modify their conclusions as they take in more information. This may make them look as if they daydream too much, but they must. It's their need to know that has them chasing the sunbeams of their minds. These children tie knowledge to imagination and consider a dozen solutions for every problem. It is by having so many possibilities that they hone their judgment and evaluate so well.

They are so empathic because they have absorbed knowledge in many ways, and more deeply than other children. Even if their parents hadn't asked them "what if?" questions at Four, they would play the game on their own. They see themselves when they see the tycoon, the park bum, the parent of triplets or the crane operator. They let their minds take them anywhere.

Their vocabularies are bigger, richer

and more precise than those of most children and they may revel in words, spinning them into poetry, telling rather good jokes (for their humor is above average too) and asking questions rat-a-tat-tat. They read more than most children—a skill they may have learned on their own before they ever started school—and they understand books quite beyond their years. They always prefer basic toys that allow them to invent their own games and to create new problems as soon as the old ones are solved.

Their ability to reason is good. They were often thinking in abstractions before first grade, which means their consciences will develop much sooner if they're encouraged, and they should be, for the academically gifted, like the born leaders, will accept poor values as well as good ones. They may be smart, but they can't invent the Ten Commandments.

It is the huge curiosity of the gifted child that is so striking. Even as a baby he found strangers too fascinating to be frightening. At Eight he focuses this curiosity on one or two interests at a time and does it with the passion the average preteen devotes to horseback riding or baseball. When he is Eleven he devours a favorite subject, like history or science, with the quick grasp of a high school senior or even a college student. Because he is so bright he sees his abilities in a realistic way and has a good idea where they will take him, although he probably will go further than he expects.

An abundance of books at home is a blessing for these children and their library cards can be passes to heaven. In addition, they still need to be encouraged to talk about books and to read and discuss newspapers, magazines, reports and research. This helps them focus and define their own ideas, and their ears and their voices 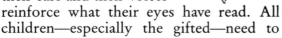 reinforce what their eyes have read. All children—especially the gifted—need to

muddle an idea out loud and to do it without being challenged at every turn. If ideas are judged before they're barely expressed, children eventually learn to keep these ideas to themselves. Even a gifted child needs practice to learn how to think in an orderly, responsive way.

Some academically gifted children excel in all subjects, peaking in some. Others, with good across-the-board intelligence, have their gifts sharply concentrated in one or a few areas. It is important for a child, and especially an academically gifted one, to know his strengths, for he may have real doubts about himself, particularly if his abilities are uneven or if he doesn't have physical or creative abilities that invite attention. He needs open approval to boost his confidence and, when he gets it, it's as if he has been given permission to be smart.

Special tests can help define the areas in which the child is specifically gifted. In the fifth grade, when he has learned enough math skills to make the results valid, he can take the Academic Promise Test (APT) or the Scholastic and College Abilities Test (SCAT). In the seventh grade, the scientifically minded child can take the STEP Science Test and children who have marked abilities in any area can take the Scholastic Aptitude Test (SAT), the same one that millions of high school juniors and seniors take to get into college. A seventh grader who scores in the top 3% against this competition is clearly very talented and a child in the top 1% deserves the chance to take accelerated courses.

The Torrance Test of Creative Thinking is a good, complicated, sophisticated measuring stick which can help parents choose the right enrichment. Special children of all kinds need special attention.

SPECIAL CLASSES

Every child should have the joy of learning what he likes best and at his own speed, whether it's slow, average or fast. Finding the right classes and the right school is the hardest part of the job, and many public elementary schools still don't have special programs, although the number is rising. Even private schools may not have accelerated courses or good enrichment programs.

Many states provide special, free classes and other learning opportunities for gifted children, including those with learning disabilities. If your school district is not in the forefront, or if you feel all alone as the parent of a gifted child, it's time to get involved with—or start—a parents' support group for gifted children, for the best public programs are the ones that parents have pushed so hard to get. This may seem like an elitist thing to do—and some dear friend will surely tell you it is—but you should seek special help just as you would if your child were extremely talented in music or art—of if he were retarded or crippled or deaf.

In an accelerated class, a child goes as fast as he likes. He is tested to discover what he knows, and then taught what he doesn't. It suits a gifted child fine; he hates to waste time. An enrichment class, either in school or out, is different. It gives a broader scope, greater depth, bigger subjects and is especially good for history, writing and reading.

Some school systems have fine magnet schools for these bright children—which is great for them but may make the other children feel rejected. Others have elaborate, all-day programs with a separate curriculum within the regular school but this can create social problems, for it isolates these children from all the others and makes them feel apart, and again, it can hurt the feelings of those who aren't chosen.

Other schools have one to three classes a day for the gifted, which is more manageable, or just a two-hour class once or twice a week for which the children are plucked out of their various grades. These pull-out classes may be all the help that's needed. Here a group of children, of different ages but with the same interests, meet with a special teacher and get the motivation to keep going on their own. It's not unlike a one-room schoolhouse where each child is part of the group but moves along at his own pace.

If classes for the gifted are taught by smart, enthusiastic teachers who ask thoughtful questions and give few answers, the children will be able to work out the answers themselves—the best instruction of all. The biggest problem is finding a teacher good enough and well enough trained, which is another reason many school systems rely on a special cadre of teachers who go from school to school, like judges who ride the circuit.

It's often hard for schools to recognize the mathematically gifted child in time to keep his interest alive, particularly if his teacher is a woman. Arithmetic is still considered so unnecessary for girls that those who become teachers often pass on the math lessons in a predictably spiritless way, even if they have a flair for it. If you find your mathematically apt child in this situation, you might get a high school teacher or a college student to tutor him. However, one-to-one classes can intensify the loneliness that often plagues the gifted. This is why an after-school group program is a better possibility, even if it's across town, for he can be with his own kind and, for once, think he's the one who's normal.

Classes in many subjects are taught in museums, art galleries, private schools or the education departments of colleges. If the course is too expensive, ask for a working scholarship for which you or your child give help in exchange for part or all of the tuition. Another alternative is college itself. Really. Some of the most prestigious universities in the country have programs to identify twelve-year-olds who can learn at a college level and have special classes for them. They offer evening, Saturday or summer classes in Latin, Greek, algebra, calculus, creative writing, great books and many other disciplines and give counseling, special recognition and awards as well.

Many states have day or residential camps in the summer for gifted children in the fourth grade and up, giving them several weeks to immerse themselves in such subjects as marine biology, anthropology or medieval history.

If you think your child would profit by an enrichment program in your school system—and not because his enrollment will reflect well on you—then you should apply. If he's admitted, fine. If he's turned down, you can find out how these choices were made and perhaps question the decision. Usually a committee in the school reviews the recommendations of the teacher and of the children in the class (studies show that children are right more often than the teachers) and to see if the child fits most of the ten to twelve criteria the county or state systems use to describe the gifted child best. These cover the child's personality and behavior and his patterns of thinking, reading and studying. The test scores are considered too, using whatever cutoff the system chooses. This either may be the top few percentile points in a national achievement test or the I.Q. score—generally around 130.

If it matters a great deal to you, and if your child has scored only one to five points below the I.Q. threshold, you can have him tested privately, at your expense. If the score jibes with the school tests, you can accept his class assignment better, but a higher score should be enough to get him admitted to the special program on a one-semester trial basis. There is, however, a big qualifier here. If you think this transfer might cause a full-scale scene at school, you should proceed only if the child is now suffering from a terrible teacher and a complete lack of enrichment. You should also consider the stigma of labels. To be "gifted" can make a child feel smart, but to be "almost gifted" will simply make him feel dumb. Your expectations are bound to be high—what mother doesn't expect her baby to grow up brilliant and beautiful too?—but it's important to be realistic, no matter what you or your husband have achieved. Your child is neither your extension nor your clone and, even if he is gifted, he may not want to express it now or in this way.

If he is already in special classes and begins to act more infantile, he may be telling you that the pressure, at this time, is just too much. Reassurance, rather than enrichment, is what he wants.

SPECIAL NEEDS

And reassurance is primarily your job. This is because he is a child, first of all, and he has the needs of a child. Every boy or girl is exceptional—whether retarded, normal or gifted. Each has certain needs and a few have many. Any child needs love—great, heaping amounts of unconditional love—no matter how smart he is or how he behaves that day.

The gifted child needs to see his pictures and awards hanging on the family bulletin board, as you would hang the achievements of any child. Some may be excellent, some may not be so fine, but there they hang in perspective.

And he needs his parents to read to him, even though he can, of course, read to himself; to explore places together and to have fun with him. As always, these good times won't happen unless you're doing something you both enjoy. To do something just because you think you should will bring nothing but tension. Above all, your gifted child needs you to listen to him. When you let him talk about the problem, ask about it, brood about it, wish about it, you're helping him learn how to be a critical thinker. Then, and only then, is he ready to hear what you say on the subject, so he can consider the alternatives you offer. This pattern of give and take, talk and listen, will make the teenage years go more smoothly for a gifted child, as it will for any child. Gifted children are children first and they need the same mix of care, encouragement and attention all children need but they often need it more often and more emphatically.

Gifted children need not only the encouragement to be creative but the time to be lazy, for a bout of creativity often requires a bout of laziness first. And if they can't read yet or write—which may happen when a gifted child has a learning disability—they need a parent to record or copy the poetry they spill forth, the yarns they tell, the ideas they have to solve the world's problems.

It's also important for gifted children to be competent in as many ways as possible, for they are so zesty they will need more skills than most children—typing; cooking; filing; tennis; swimming; ice skating; a foreign language. They need to know how to set up a tent and take it down; how to use the library and its computers; how to take care of their own clothes—washing, mending and ironing them—and how to get around town and how to hammer and saw and hang a plumb bob (and why).

When they get an interest—and gifted children always have at least one interest going—you can bet it will be serious, and they will depend on you to help them find out everything they can about it, with trips to museums and libraries, with magazine subscriptions and long conversations. By opening new avenues you let them know they exist, but don't expect your gifted child to follow them until he's bled the old ones dry.

By seventh grade a gifted child needs a mentor too—someone to turn to for guidance and for career information, for a gifted child always wants to know where he's going. This older friend is especially important if you're divorced; a single parent is spread thin enough. This is the person with whom he explores a career, and not in general terms. If he considers law, his mentor wonders whether he should go into admiralty law or international law, criminal law or tax law, and whether to teach law or write laws or be a judge. This lets a child roll ideas around his mind like so many marbles and examine each one as seriously as the last. So should you. When he knows you appreciate his dreams, even if they don't fit the image of your family or race or class or of his sex, your child has the joy of knowing that he is truly one of a kind. This is the best way to make a child—any child—feel special.

He should also know that he has been blessed and with that blessing comes a need to do a job better than others or learn a lesson more thoroughly and, if he doesn't fill this need, he will feel disappointed in himself.

Because he may think so fast he must be reminded to be patient with a slower child who has the gift, perhaps, to make people smile when he walks into a room or to be the stabilizing force on the playground when everyone else gets tense. Your child has to learn that gifts come in many packages.

Perhaps the hardest part of having a gifted child is your secret fear that one day he will think you're dumb and he won't listen to you anymore. Don't worry. Your child could get along fairly well without the books and special classes, but not without the love and respect and kindness and discipline that only a parent can give. And yes, there will be days when he's sure he knows more than you, about everything, and days when he won't listen, but that would happen whether he was gifted or not. Life, and children, are like that, but he'll love you just the same.

LEARNING DISABILITIES

Mrs. Malaprop probably had learning disabilities and so did the Reverend Mr. Spooner. Albert Einstein certainly did and so did Thomas Edison, General George Patton, Woodrow Wilson and Nelson Rockefeller. And so have millions of other children, yesterday and today.

These children may be brilliant or retarded or in that big sea in between, but they have a physical problem—probably a four- to eight-year lag in their neural development—which affects the way they think and act and move. Classically this is the child who turns his *b*'s into *d*'s and his *p*'s into *q*'s or he writes in mirror images or says he's going to shake a tower when it's a shower he wants to take. This is pure dyslexia, but few learning-disabled children have this symptom alone and many children don't have it at all. Experts can't agree on the number of disabilities—possibly a hundred or more—but they do agree that the children usually have more than one, and that they vary from child to child.

In fact, every child, learning disabled or not, undoubtedly has some small learning disability—perfect people are hard to find—but usually it is so minor, he compensates for it automatically or overcomes it or avoids it. There are some embarrassing moments if he plays poor baseball, but the consequences are grave if he can't read or write or add.

One child may not be able to add because he can't read from left to right; another can't spell because the sounds get scrambled; and a third can't read because his brain can't record symbols: the same old word is a new image every time and even faces may be forgotten. Or a child may remember letters or faces with precision but quickly forget the sounds. Mitt, mat and mutt are the same. He also may

have trouble repeating the cadence when you rap three times on the table—a sign that he can't follow sequences yet, which he must do before he can read. Another child can read flawlessly but can't comprehend the words.

These children have other problems too. One may be unable to use the past tense or subtract or step backward while another has such trouble integrating the two sides of his brain that he can't carry an idea or a movement from one side of his body to the other. To transfer a pencil from his right hand to his left without putting it down is as impossible as it is for him to put one group of pictures on the left side of the page and another on the right. It takes a well-trained, up-to-date teacher to realize this is something other than obstinacy.

His handwriting may be shockingly bad, not because he is lazy but because he can't direct his fingers well or he wants to hide his poor spelling or he can't figure out where the letters belong. You may see him squinching his name into a corner of the page or scrawling it so big it can't fit, all because he has a bad time handling space. Time may be an almost impossible concept too, and when you realize that time and space govern every aspect of learning, from history to geometry, you see how overwhelming this can be.

Whatever the disability, these children have a poor memory in some area and often know a set of facts one day and forget it the next. And yet they often are so verbal, so quick, it's hard for the most attentive mother to recognize that they have difficulties at all. A child with learning problems may get along pretty well in his early years—although he tends to be a bit babyish—but school turns into a nightmare until, as one little second grader said when he stumbled home in tears, "I saw a policeman today. I wanted to ask him to shoot me." Fortunately his sensitive mother took this for the cry of alarm that it was and had him thoroughly tested. That's when she learned that her gentle

little boy, a straight B student in one of the richest school systems in America, couldn't read at all. But because he was so bright, he could remember a story and fake it, and because he was so quiet, the teacher didn't notice how little he knew. It took six years at a special school for him to train his brain to think the way most people do, but after that he could—and did—go to a tough academic high school and on to college too.

It's estimated that one child in ten needs special tutoring to learn one or more of these intellectual skills, and one in twenty needs special classes. No one really knows why. Almost everything has been blamed, from problems in pregnancy, delivery or illness afterward, to heredity, diet, stress or an abnormality in the brain.

This child—usually a boy—has symptoms that get worse when he's hungry or when the weather is hot, hazy, humid or before storms and some say when there is a full moon. Health problems also may play a part. For some reason, allergies, respiratory infections and hypoglycemia are common in these children. Cerebral palsy, however minor, causes some learning disability too, because the same part of the brain is affected, and doctors are finding abnormal brain patterns in some children who are truly dyslexic.

No matter what the cause, however, any learning disabled child can be helped, with most problems corrected by mid-adolescence, although they may come back briefly under stress or fatigue all through his life. This is particularly true with spell-

ing, which requires information to be in the right order—the hardest job of all.

It takes skill, love, great effort, a specially trained tutor and lots of patience on everyone's part to let this child take longer to learn. The damage a learning disability can do to the child's ego is hard to believe. It starts to accumulate in the preschool years, when a child judges himself by how well he can handle his body. Because learning problems often have physical effects, this judgment may be pretty low. The same brain development that makes reading so difficult may also cause a child to talk as late as Three and use poor syntax and baby talk for years. Or this child may use either hand—but not too well—or be clumsy or even accident-prone, because he doesn't know how to use his body as a gauge. This child may trip over his own feet for another simple reason: the further the muscles are from the brain, the longer it takes to get them under control.

He also may have trouble making the hands and the eyes work well together, which is why his pictures never come out the way he meant and he never could stack his blocks right when he was little. The sweet joys of accomplishment are lost to him. Another learning disabled child may have fine coordination but behavior can be the tip-off. He may be sluggish or hyperactive or just everyday bouncy, but he is immature socially, as he is in everything else. Children with severe learning disabilities are at a constant disadvantage because their senses are under a steady barrage, to at least a small degree.

This child is crippled in a special way. The deaf child hears nothing, the blind child sees nothing, but in the worst cases the learning disabled child gets it all at full strength. There are no background sounds or distant images: everything is perceived with the same intensity. The fly that buzzes around the blackboard may be heard as clearly as the teacher's voice and the children yelling in the playground. In this peaceless land, a child either may withdraw and become very quiet or he may rush about frenetically, trying to obey every impulse, which is one of the reasons he gets tired so easily and has trouble getting along with others. Until a child can put everyday sights and sounds and smells into perspective he will feel pummeled by the world.

The bombardment has other effects. The child who can't take in two sounds at the same time is the one who can't walk and spin a yo-yo at the same time. He is set apart in both big and little ways. One learning disabled child may play with a toy for only minutes at a time, while the next will play with the same one long after he's called to dinner, almost as if he were hypnotized. This child keeps on doing the same thing so he can deal with all the mental clutter that comes from taking everything into his senses, full strength. He programs his life to bring some order to it. A new activity, a variety of choices or a slight change in plans may cause anxiety while a move to a new school, a new house—even a new room—can bring panic.

Since there are no nuances in his world, he doesn't understand innuendos and subtle jokes. He is so literal, he may blurt out obvious but embarrassing truths. He may be a rigid perfectionist or a poor loser. He may cheat, not because he is dishonest but because he just can't take another sign of failure. This is particularly true if he lives with a lot of criticism.

Sharing a toy or a friend may also be hard, for the learning disabled child is more self-centered than most, insisting on getting his own way and getting it immediately. He can't step back and look at the world but is a part of it all and all of it is a part of him. Most children emerge from the egocentric stage at Four or Five but for the learning disabled it lasts years longer. Since everything is an extension of himself, he can't put things in sequence or judge sizes or differentiate and these are all skills he needs to read and write and do math.

There is no way this child can do well in school without help, especially since he is away from his parents for the prime part of the day. Even though they may have shrieked, despaired, threatened, bribed and begged their way through the first six years, he always knew he was loved. First grade is something else. He may adore his teacher—most first graders do—but the kindest one will add new humiliations every day, just by the impossible work she assigns. Everything about the classroom will be a disappointment. The learning disabled child goes to school looking for a miracle—something magic to make sense out of things—and instead he feels like a fool, which only makes matters worse. No one wants to look dumb in front of a teacher he loves, and especially in front of a roomful of children.

The learning disabled child may be slow in many ways but he still has the same psychological needs as his classmates. Like them, he wants to be as popular as the most popular child and, above all, he wants to learn his lessons at least as fast as everyone else. Since he is sure other children hear and see and feel in the same jumbled way he does, he is devastated when he can't do the work that comes so easily to them. Even though he tries much harder than anyone else (until he quits trying at all), he can't think and act the way they do.

While it's true that he may shine in some areas—particularly creative ones—he is obviously outranked when he does basic work. This turns the sunniest classroom into a jail—and he's the only one in it. Like any inmate, he either tries to change the conditions or break out. In his first six years he learned some tricks of survival and now he invents some new ones. He becomes the model citizen, the class buffoon or the loner, the dreamer, the bully or the braggart, subconsciously hoping his behavior will attract enough attention to hide his ignorance.

He may insist he would do the work if it weren't so boring, or say, "I won't"—because he can't. Getting out of the room is another ruse. He may beg to run every errand for the class or say he's sick or, in desperation, act rowdy enough to be sent to the principal's office, once more avoiding the work and the ridicule when he can't do it. Punishment also helps assuage the guilt, for he is sure to feel at fault. It's almost as if he courts failure.

The teacher is quite likely to blame the child too, for many teachers and most doctors aren't trained to spot learning disabilities. This child is often so artistic, so articulate, so clever with his hands that it's hard for a teacher to believe something is wrong and so the teacher says he is willful, lazy, disturbed or dumb. How else to explain a child who can be lyrical about dinosaurs and the stars but can't count or recite the alphabet, the days of the week or the order of the seasons?

The more this child falls behind, the more isolated—or obstreperous—he's going to get. With each disappointment at school he will try harder and harder to win at home, controlling the situation by setting parent against parent and brother against sister. The center may hold, but it won't hold very well. This is particularly true if the child is also hyperactive, which is the case in nearly half of all learning disabled children. The most normal child adds stress to a household, but a learning disabled one can tear it apart when his handicap is mistaken for "spoiled bratism." Husband and wife are going to blame each other for his poor behavior, even as they blame themselves. It can be a cyclical horror. The more dissension you have at home, the more upset your child will be at home and at school.

The mildly disabled child is, not surprisingly, often the hardest to recognize since the signs are less obvious. He may have been slow to talk and now he is messy, disorganized and finishes his work first, because he doesn't follow instructions or double-check either. He reads slowly, spells poorly, concentrates badly and often has a shaky memory. Of course, every child will reverse letters occasionally

and have some trouble organizing his thoughts but you should suspect a disability if you think you see a pattern. If something seems wrong, or if you think school somehow makes your child unhappy—particularly if you've noticed symptoms long before first grade—you should ask that he be tested. You may have to insist, in fact, if neither the doctor nor the teacher agrees with you, but insist you should. It's a right now guaranteed by national law in all public schools, upon demand of the parent. The sooner the problem is identified, the quicker your child can get help, and this is essential, for learning is cumulative.

EVALUATION

The choice of the tester is crucial. She can be either a psychologist or a diagnostician, but she needs more than a degree. Look for someone who is warm and caring, who has tutored or counseled learning disabled children—rather than emotionally disturbed ones—and who has a good deal of experience. This usually makes a diagnostician so intuitive she almost smells the problem. It's up to you to review her credentials and if you have any doubts—or if you can't find a tester at all—write the Association for Children with Learning Disabilities (see Resources). They have a list of recommendations.

The diagnostician will get a full case history from you, including the details about your pregnancy, the delivery and the early years and any symptoms you have noticed, both physical and psychological. After that she will arrange for your child to take a four- to five-hour battery of tests, which is given individually in an uncluttered, peaceful setting.

The diagnostician will begin by explaining just what she will do and why and for how long, for she knows your child will be even more worried about himself than you are and he has a right to know what's going on. More than anything else, he needs to know that the tests aren't given to find out how smart he is (or how dumb), but how he learns best, so the teacher can tailor the lessons to suit him and he can build on his strengths.

The main test will be a well-rounded one, such as the WISC-R (see Intelligence Tests), although it won't grade creativity, for that is quite difficult to do. Reading, spelling, composition, arithmetic and perception are checked too and other tests—both formal and informal—are added as possible problems emerge. The child may also be asked to draw a picture of a person, not to judge his talent or his intelligence, but to see how the lines are connected—or not connected—a measure of what the child thinks of himself.

The tester also watches how the child holds the pencil—a learning disabled child almost always holds it in an uncomfortable grip. She'll also notice how he approaches each task. If he can't understand where he is in relation to up, down and around, he won't understand the teacher when she tells him to print his name in the upper right-hand corner.

It will be the pattern and the quality of the errors, as well as the scores of the subtests, that matter to the diagnostician. This will be the basis of several pages of information and an hour-long conference, which is shared to some extent with the child.

When you get the final results you and your husband will have to make some evaluations too. It's important that you think the diagnosis makes sense, for no one knows your child as well as the two of you, and no one cares so much. This doesn't mean it's easy to accept bad news. In fact, you will find yourself going through all the stages of grief—from denial to depression—before you reach a sense of rightness, even as you wonder where you go from here. That's why the parents need to talk regularly with other parents who face the same dilemmas.

The recommendations of the diagnostician may range from conservative to radical, depending on the disabilities and how hard they will be to correct. If they are mild, or if the problems are in only one area, the diagnostician will help your child's teacher figure out new ways for him to learn. The child who scrambles some sounds can learn visually and the one who can't decipher letters can learn with tapes and talking books loaned free by the Library of Congress to any child a doctor says is word-blind.

If the problem is more complicated, the teacher may send your child to the resource room each week for tutoring, where another teacher or a librarian will work with a small group of children who come from other classes and have similar learning blocks.

The next step—individual tutoring—is given to more impaired children one to five times a week for thirty to forty-five intense minutes, but not, it is hoped, at the expense of too many ball games and birthday parties. A learning disabled child feels odd enough at school; he shouldn't feel odd afterward too.

The tutor you choose for your child should be inventive, kind, firm in her discipline and endlessly patient in her teaching, for it will take a long time for him to learn—always longer than anyone seems to imagine. In the process she probably will report regularly to a clinic or a psychologist. This gives your child someone else to guard his interests, for a tutor may get too involved and it may take an outsider to notice when the teaching plans should be changed.

A good tutor, unlike a good teacher, focuses on only one to four children at a time, and breaks all learning into tiny steps, so it is more easily understood. She also gives the child short-range goals and describes each assignment for what it is: hard. That's because a good tutor is a realist. She knows that school may be easy for the average child but not for this one. Besides, a child gets a psychic reward for doing tough work, but if he can't do it yet, he at least keeps his dignity if he's been told it isn't easy.

PARENTS' ROLE

As tempting as it is to help the child yourself—especially when you know how much he needs it—few parents have the training and skill to tutor a learning disabled child and still fewer parents are detached enough to do it well. It's also rough on the child who is ashamed to tell his parents how little he knows. It's hard enough to disappoint himself; it's awful to disappoint them. Aside from himself, there is no one else he loves so much. Just as it is the tutor's job to teach your child, a parent has a special role too and no one else can fill it so well. You only have to be careful that you don't take too much time away from the rest of the family, which would be resented, and rightfully so. You also must keep a little time for yourself, or your own resentment will undercut all your efforts. This is why so many mothers of learning disabled children find that they can't work full time, especially in the early grade school years. There are just so many ways a mother can be pulled.

The most important help you can give your child will be your affection. It will be his solace on grim days, for he knows your love is so assured he can dare to talk about his fears. He also needs your compliments for trying so hard. The results may not be great, but they are at least as significant as the A's another child brings home. After all, the hill he climbs is a mountain to him and he still must carry a rock on his back to get to the top. Your warm humor helps too. If you don't jolly him along he will be somber indeed, which will affect everybody's disposition.

It will be your expectations that help him the most however. He needs to know you think he is smart, and that one day he will be able to do the work, and that you expect him to work at his own level and not the level of the child next door. With realistic goals he won't feel so much pressure, particularly if you back them up with graphs and charts, so he can look back and see how far he's come. They should not, however, be tied to a calendar, for you don't want to mark the delays. He knows them well enough.

SPECIAL SCHOOLS

In some cases, the best tutor and the most supportive parents are not enough. Some children need help on a full-time basis in a special classroom or a special school. You can expect him to be there one to eight years, depending on the problem.

With luck, this special school will be

like any good school. The child will find it friendly, exciting, respectful and overflowing with knowledge. But this school also will be well structured, so each child knows where he sits and how to get from here to there. A learning disabled child is confused enough without having to make a lot of choices. The classes follow a well-charted course, but they are highly imaginative and usually use different teachers for different subjects. The job is still exhausting, for every teacher is expected to teach toward each child's particular learning style and, as new tests show that the style is changing, the teaching methods must change too.

Although a learning disabled child processes information years later than other children, his interests are still the same as those of his friends. That's why the plots of his books must be as interesting, the problems as spellbinding and the ideas as sophisticated as they are for anyone else his age. The materials, however, must be quite simple and the projects have to be as graphic as possible, with sight, sound, touch, smell or even taste to reinforce a lesson.

One clever teacher brings a spicy spaghetti sauce to her history class so the children will always remember that Columbus was trying to find a short cut to India to get those spices, and not to find America at all. Another teacher has her class learn about pyramids and mummification, but only after she has the children divide an apple, covering one half with plastic wrap and leaving the other half exposed, so they can see that apples—and people—last a lot better when they're all wrapped up.

A learning disabled child may be taught to add and subtract by measuring wood and making a table in a workshop class, and he might get ready to read by learning how to dance, so he can follow sequences better. A child who has trouble planning and organizing his material is helped by making a videotape, for many things fall in place when he can relate an effect to a cause. He won't even use the word "because" until he understands this concept.

A computer is particularly helpful to the learning disabled child, because it makes him follow a logical, sequential pattern, which is eventually transferred to his reading and writing.

While these ideas help any child learn well, the learning disabled child requires them. It takes concrete examples to make him remember and believe, which he must do before he can think in abstract terms, and this is what it takes to develop a strong character. The older he gets the more complicated his decisions will become and there won't be any rulebook or parent or teacher to tell him what to do. That's why he has to learn how to think in abstract ways.

Although all learning disabled children can be helped, they don't advance at the same speed, and there will be some backsliding too. However, once the basic skills are there, the child fairly gallops forward, taking big leaps around Eleven and Fourteen when the body—and apparently the brain—grow so quickly.

The progress also depends on the child's motivation, his self-esteem and basically his willingness to take a risk, which is what education is all about. It can take a child more nerve to challenge his own mind than to take on the biggest bully in the block. One memorable child was so overwhelmed by all he had to learn that his mind seemed frozen. Nothing he was taught would register. Finally the teacher wrote two lists for him on a piece of paper. In one column were all the things he could do well and in the other were all the things he had to learn. And then she tore the list in half, giving him the one with the work he could do, and said she was responsible for the rest. That was all he needed. Once a child realizes that it is the teacher's job to figure out how to help him learn, he can concentrate on the learning itself.

HOME ENVIRONMENT

A learning disabled child does best in a household that, like his school, is structured and has few distractions. It's better to change the picture in his room every week than to have five on the wall at the same time. Conflicting noises are bad too. When the radio in the kitchen can be heard at the same time as the music in the living room it can shatter whatever equanimity he has.

If he has trouble with time, he needs you to help him get where he's going when he should and yet learn to depend on himself—and he can. Even the child who can't read the dial or a digital face well enough to wear a watch can pull out his own preset alarm at night and phone for the time by day, if not by reading the numbers, then by remembering the pattern it takes to dial or to punch the buttons on the phone or even by repeating the beeps that this phone number makes. The kitchen timer—much less complicated than a clock face—is another good device to help him remember to stick with the job. He sets it for the ten or twenty minutes he thinks it will take and if numbers confuse him you can color-code the 10 and the 20 with a felt pen and he decides if he can do it in blue or in red.

It will be the day-in, day-out problems you help your child solve at home that will matter so much, using the same ingenuity it takes to circumvent a Two. The more a child can accomplish, the greater his self-confidence will be, and this child needs a lot of it to make up for all the knocks he gets.

You build it at home by your reliance on him to do his share, even though it may be much easier to do the work yourself at first. He may need pictures and a check-off calendar to remind him, but when he keeps the dog groomed, the canary fed and the rose bed weeded, he is taking his place in the family sun. Responsibilities teach learning skills as well as self-esteem. When he sets the table he slowly overcomes his problem with lefts and rights and when he sorts the socks he is learning to classify, which he must do before he can read. As long as a job is broken down into the smallest steps, he has a much better chance of doing the work well, whether it's dressing himself or sending away for a free sample. A learning disabled child also needs to plan menus, to shop and make change, to fill forms, as well as to cook, so he can measure and decipher at least part of the recipe.

You and your husband are the only people who can teach the social graces so well and you do this by requiring—and using—better manners than you would of other children. He needs to see and hear everything more clearly than they do. The discipline will have to be much clearer too, and again, it must be broken into small segments, as if he were years younger, even though the tone of your voice holds as much respect as ever. It doesn't pay to talk down to any child.

The words you use are important. His vocabulary gets bigger and bigger when you choose concrete words—rather than abstract ones—to fit the way he thinks and add new words as soon as the old ones are well understood. Although conversation shouldn't turn into a lesson, you may have to use games of tag to show him what the prepositions mean. About, under, behind and beyond are nebulous concepts to this child.

A family story time every day is excellent too, for the words, the closeness and the story itself. Choose a classic on the child's own interest level, with the parents taking turns to read, but not the children. A round robin family session might be embarrassing if one child stumbles too much or has to be left out of the reading.

Your learning disabled child also needs a few hours of special time with you or your husband each week, involved in something he knows quite well. The insect zoo may not be your favorite place to visit, but when he knows a subject well he should be encouraged to know it better.

Any learning experience gives him a sense of accomplishment.

Television will help in different ways, especially the situation comedies and detective shows. These plots are so simple that he can pick out the main focus, the sequence and the cause and effect, as long as you watch the show with him and ask questions afterward. These are the same learning principles he needs to think straight.

Board games bring advances too. Strategy games, Monopoly and gin rummy emphasize cause and effect; Ping-Pong, miniature golf, tiddlywinks and pick up sticks—and a nail and a hammer—teach precision and coordination; and video games on a home computer not only teach coordination but they also make a child track his eyes so he can read better.

The learning disabled child discovers a great deal through the arts, both at home and at school, but the goals must be clear and the methods structured. When an artist, even a Six, paints a picture, he is finding a logical solution to a problem—in balance, color and composition, although he may need you to help him focus on the problem. Music—its beat, its reasonance, its mood—helps this child listen for pace differences and sequences, which he eventually can apply to his reading, math and spelling. Dance is good too, not just to learn how to follow patterns but to figure out where his body belongs and eventually where the letters belong on the page. The better a child can control his body, the better he can think.

One mother whose son still drooled a bit at Seven discovered this was an unusual sign of a learning disability—a sign that part of his brain was affected too. To help him she would hold the boy on her lap for a few minutes every day and sing silly songs while he tried to lick away the peanut butter she had dabbed on his nose, his chin and his cheeks. By strengthening his tongue muscles, he also was strengthening his mind, and because she made a game of it, he thought it was a lark.

Sports of course make muscles stronger and better coordinated too, which is why they are so important to a learning disabled child. He gets the most from bike riding, ice skating, swimming and skiing. Even though competition is usually hard for this child to handle, he likes tennis, if he can play well, and adores soccer, since it is easier to kick a ball than catch it. A swim team can be good too, for it lets him be part of a group and yet depend solely on himself. All of this helps his self-confidence at least as much as his mind.

Getting a child to afternoon practice and watching the Saturday games may seem more like the last haystack than the last straw, but since the value of these sports is so high, it should take precedence over many other activities. When a child can't read or write or spell, he has an extra need to be proud of something else.

Despite your many-pronged efforts, it may seem that he still isn't learning much reading, writing and arithmetic in the early years but progress will be very fast when the brain switches to "go." That's because all the information he's been fed at home and at school is in his head, like money in the bank.

Often a learning disability will improve—sometimes dramatically—if you can get rid of a chronic health problem, like hypoglycemia or allergies. Dyes, preservatives and foods, as well as pollens and odors, can affect a child's behavior and concentration and send his handwriting into confusion, and you can test much of this yourself (see Allergies and Aggravants and Hyperactivity).

By giving your child a variety of supports, as soon as possible, you give him the heart to try. And will so much time and energy spoil him? Not a chance. When loving is constructive, any child profits by it, but when he has a learning disability, he needs it to survive. His success as an adult will be built on the confidence and knowledge you help him gain now.

The spirit of a child is both fragile and fierce, resilient and reactive. It is of a type, yet one of a kind. More and more geneticists believe that the child's basic personality is set in the womb and in the genes, and it is fixed for life.

Bless your prepackaged child. He was born to have eyes a certain color and skin a certain shade: his ears were shaped and his fingertips whorled and his voice is one of a kind.

His personality is as individual as his body. One child is introverted, another is extroverted. One thinks logically, stacking facts one on the other before making a judgment, while another leaps to a conclusion intuitively, relying entirely on his perceptions. Moreover, there are degrees within each classification. The miracle is not that these differences exist but how much the world is enriched by such a variety.

Generally a healthy, well-accepted child is reasonably lovable and happy, most of the time, as long as his body chemistry is in balance. Since there are at least sixteen basic temperaments, however, it's sometimes hard to tell the difference between a personality and a personality problem, especially when one child is strikingly different from the rest of the family. Be patient. His drummer is just beating ragtime while the rest of you are in tune with the classics.

Although your child is still accountable for the choices he makes, genetics set the course, and you and your husband direct it with the environment you create. This defines his character, his joy, his industry and, to some extent, his intelligence in the Middle Years. While he is guided by many outside influences, children still respond to their parents more than to anyone else. Everything you do, or don't do, changes a child, at least a little bit. Just the simple admonition, "Don't run in the street. You'll get smashed," prunes the child a trifle differently than nature intended.

Some of this is necessary, but it's easy to overdo it.

Tensions arise when a child is expected to be the clone of his brother or sister—or his mother or father—instead of being himself, or when he must act docile when it's his nature to lead, be gregarious when he's born to be shy or aggressive when he is gentle. These tensions create the conflicts that could haunt him as an adult. If you make your child act in foreign ways, you undercut the one trait you want him to have more than any other: integrity. It is the core of the soul, to be preserved at all costs. The child who can be true to himself will grow up to be true to his values.

The best you can do is be attentive to his spirit and guide him to follow its natural bent. To do this you must be responsive to his feelings and his budding conscience and still encourage the behavior that suits him—and his family—best. You need rules to govern his behavior and corrections to change it sometimes, but don't change the essence of the child: the spirit.

By supporting his spirit you encourage him to be himself, quirks and all. Do it enough, and he'll hardly notice yours.

FEELINGS

The child who shows his feelings is always welcome—if the feelings are joy, enthusiasm and love—but that's not enough. He needs to show his unhappy emotions too and particularly to say how he feels. These are the ones that often get a child into trouble, however, especially if he walks out of a difficult conversation or yells or says, "Damn!"

A child must use good manners, even when he's mad, but it's no help to tell him that he shouldn't feel hurt or angry or scared. When you tell your son he *really* doesn't hate his new teacher or tell your daughter that you know, deep down, she's glad to be taking piano, you're denying the child's own firsthand perceptions. It even has physical repercussions. Once adrenalin is released, it has to be used, somehow or other.

The best way to get rid of a dark thought is to express it. If you don't give a child the right to be angry or sad, he'll learn to swallow all feelings, including joy.

You can't kiss away a schoolchild's feelings as you once could kiss away a booboo. Now he needs you to say, "You're right. It *is* awful that Susie didn't ask you to her party. I'm so sorry."

It's easier to understand a child's feelings if you and your husband are candid about your own, both with each other and with your child, and this is particularly true for boys, since society shushes them much more than girls. When a child can see that you empathize, he will be stronger for it. And when he sees that you have setbacks too, that you can be sorry, and that you handle them without too much bitterness or grief, he sees that he can work out his own disappointments.

If you don't talk about your emotions, however, he will feel responsible every time there's tension in the air. It's all right to be angry about the way your husband behaved at a party or that your dress must have shrunk or that the payment for braces will make you miss a convention. Those are the breaks. Your child would rather know, very briefly, that you're just cross with his daddy or mad because the diet didn't work, or because the braces cost so much, than think that you're mad at him. He will accept your right to say what you think, as long as you give him the same right. This gives him a sense of psychological safety. There is a pound of hate for every ton of love in each of us, and if a child knows it, he won't be frightened by his wicked thoughts. All feelings are legitimate, but a child won't believe they are, unless you tell him.

Even the bad feelings have some virtue. If a child doesn't have some anger, he'll never get outraged enough to stand up for what's right as an adult. If he has no anxiety, he also will have no ambition, and if he has no fear, he will have no caution—and little imagination either, for fear helps to nurture it.

The child who is never aggressive becomes the adult who can't assert himself, and the child with no shame or guilt will be the amoral adult who only obeys the law when it's convenient. It takes more than consequences to give a child a conscience.

Even jealousy has merit. A child grows up with a sense of his own worth according to his accomplishments and how they compare with the accomplishments of others. This measure is painful to take, but by analyzing—and wishing for—the talents of others, he can learn to analyze, appreciate—and enhance—his own.

All feelings—in proper measure—are reasonable.

ANGER

Anger is normal and healthy but children must learn to express it within limits if they are to be normal, healthy, happy adults. The let-it-all-hang-out approach only leads to more rage and some very hurt feelings.

Control isn't easy to learn, however, for anger is the emotion parents most often try to stifle. A child loves his parents so much, he tries to say what he thinks they want to hear and act the way he thinks they want him to act, but he may hurt himself when he hides his anger from himself and pretends it isn't there. He may get furious at the world and be full of accusations or he may rebel silently, skimping on his schoolwork or homework, or he may become sarcastic or a tattler or even get sick.

Other anger is more open and it's frequently aimed at a teacher, a sister or a parent—someone who will accept it anyway—rather than the person who made him mad. You need to figure out why your child is angry and how often and then help him deal with it constructively.

One or two brief displays of bad temper a day in an otherwise sunny child are signs that he has a temporary problem which will go away if it's faced. He needs to learn how to admit the source of his anger to himself and to you, because anger dissipates only when he talks it away, like a bad dream, but that won't happen unless he knows and acknowledges the reason for it, and talks about it without getting too mad. If the anger is habitual, you can still do much to help your child find the real cause, although therapy may still be needed.

In general, your child probably handles his anger the way you and your husband do, for, as in so many things, parents are the models a child tries to follow. The way you argue, negotiate and make up all teaches your child that people can love each other, get mad, resolve the issue and even be the better for it.

You have to express your anger with your child as carefully as you do with your husband. Admit your irritation with him when it happens, privately, in a clear, firm, quick way and then forget about it, so your child will know that anger's not so bad. If you don't talk about it, it will simmer in the back of your mind, popping out later when he does something else. This kind of moodiness frightens a child, who will know his latest behavior doesn't deserve such a big reaction.

You help a child avoid some anger by congratulating him for good work, since he may feel like a failure if he thinks his work isn't appreciated, and this will make him mad. You also help when you notice what he's doing and offer to help if the work is too complicated. He won't mind this interference, as long as he knows you won't take over his project.

A child also needs a little benign neglect so he can learn to handle frustration and irritations, a little gentle humor so he won't take himself so seriously—and a lot of exercise to work off his bad mood.

And when none of this works? Give a hug and a kiss if he gets truly out of hand, and walk him out of harm's way—and your way. No one ought to put up with attacks, either physical or verbal. You want your child to be assertive—to stand up for his rights—but not to be so aggressive that he would hurt anything or anyone.

When a child learns how to confront someone without being aggressive or self-righteous or accusatory or explosive, and without accumulating resentments, he is learning how to be civilized. The child who can do this is accepting responsibility for his own feelings and that is the stuff that maturity is made of. Even getting angry is an art: it takes years to do it well.

SHAME

Shame can be the price a child pays when someone he loves is always telling him what to do, particularly when that someone is a parent. He is ashamed that this very important person doesn't think he can take care of himself.

There is also the shame of being under-weight or overweight or of having braces (or not having them), a squeaky voice or a high-pitched laugh. A child may be ashamed of being the baby in the class or the tallest or smallest, or have parents who are foreign or whose clothes are out of date or because his sister, his brother or his house embarrasses him.

Some shame is inevitable and a little of it has value, for it helps a child grow up with a stronger character, but a child shouldn't grow up with too much. Sunshine and self-confidence are the best way to get rid of the rest. The more a person feels in charge of himself the more independent he is, and every decision he makes for himself, every task he masters, will make him prouder.

Shame is assuaged by confession, of the most private kind: the diary. It's excellent for a Nine or Ten. You may think a child so young could have no serious secrets, but this isn't so. His very lack of knowledge makes him awash with the fears, confusions and doubts you forgot you ever had. Give your child a book with a lock, for his peace of mind, although privacy should be such an ingrained idea in a family that no one in the house would glance at it even if the book were wide open.

Tell your child that everyone needs someone to tell their troubles to, and the best person is usually the child himself. He may, and probably will, repeat most of it again to his friends and his family, but by writing them down first, in this secret book, he can explode without hurting anyone's feelings. To go public too soon would only give him something else to feel ashamed about.

GUILT

Guilt, like shame, is a specter that haunts us all. No one is free of it, and to some extent that's fine. A smidgin of guilt is the governor of the conscience, but a smidgin is enough. Small amounts make a child obey traffic signs and write his thank-you notes—not because the rules say so, but because he knows it upsets you when he doesn't. Your child takes what you say even more seriously than you do, and his own imagination adds weight to your words.

Children who get too many complaints may seem to deny them, ignore them or volley with some of their own, but they also will absorb them and add their own strictures, until one day, when the expectations and complaints seem unfair, they may turn angry, vengeful—young rebels with a cause. It is the accumulation of guilt that makes children react like that.

You can help your child realize that it's safe to admit he did something wrong, that he's sorry, that you accept his apology and that the debt is paid. A crystal of guilt will remain, but it won't be enough to weigh him down. If the transgression is serious, he needs the chance to correct it or pay for it, with either time or money, but he doesn't need to be reminded of it next week or next year. He's learning to rely on his conscience, not yours.

ANXIETY

Some children seem to have been born with a frown. They are as destined to be anxious as their eyes are programmed to be blue or green. Anxieties grow if they sense anxieties at home—the frequent "watch outs" and "don't falls." It's a cyclical situation.

The more anxious a child feels, the more rigid his behavior and the more sure he is that everyone else is just the same. All of this leads to a need to control others. He wants to put all his ducks and his friends in order and the friends don't like it at all. This is the bossy child, the scourge of the playground. Another anxious child may be so fearful he waits through two red lights before he crosses the street, and then only makes it across before the light changes again. This dear child Chicken Littles his days away.

Any anxious child needs to see a lot of self-assurance in his parents—perhaps more than they feel—and to live in a predictable, orderly household, where surprises may be expected, even if he doesn't know what they will be. He needs few warnings of the dangers ahead—his own head is always full of them—but he needs to learn by his own mistakes instead. Strangers, streets and skates are hard enough to handle without extra advice, and "I told you so's."

Every skill this child can master will peel away another layer of anxiety but he never will be your carefree, madcap sort. Instead he will learn to let his anxiety work for him: to live by his lists; to be on time; to try only as much as he thinks he can do and always to do it well and in a pinch to do a little more, and do that just as well.

Anxiety may not make the world go round, but it can make the difference between a good job and a bad one. Properly handled, and in small amounts, it can be a blessing.

JEALOUSY

Jealousy and its twin, envy, are growing things that crowd the soul and wear life to a nubbin. In jealousy, the child may be afraid to lose something he has—like the love of a parent—while envy makes him long for something that someone else has.

There's a seed of both in all of us, and every time a child finds a new inequity to gripe about he looks for something more. In these Middle Years he often thinks that life is unfair, and that it's only unfair to him.

Although you won't tell your child that such feelings are silly—no feeling is silly to the one who's feeling it—you will want to point out that they are futile. There always will be someone bigger or brighter or more powerful. A child needs to understand this so he can accept his limitations. Even the President knows he and the Pope can't be King. A child may discard both jealousy and envy if he realizes that they are a waste of time.

It also helps if you update a cautionary tale to encourage your child to appreciate his good luck. Have him write down each of his griefs on slips of paper: "my nose is too big"; "I can't draw"; "I'm always picked last on the baseball team"; "my jacket is a hand-me-down." There will be many complaints. And then you tell him you're going to list the complaints that might be made by other children you both know—who should, of course, go nameless: "my parents are getting divorced"; "my grandmother is dying"; "my father lost his job"; "my mother drinks, a lot"; "I can't read." And when you're done, have him pull these slips from the basket to see what complaints he would rather have.

Even if he has a few clinkers of his own, most children would rather keep what they've got than live with the heartbreaks of someone else's life.

FEAR

Timidity and anger often have opposite results but their cause is the same: fear. When someone is frightened, he either attacks or withdraws. The insecurities that tear us apart can also tie us together—the basis of both treaties and wars. Fear is a universal thread. Every child is afraid of something and so is every adult—which is fortunate, for it is fear that keeps us from being foolhardy. It is the unreasonable fears in a child—or the heightened ones—that trouble a parent.

A schoolchild's fears ebb and flow, depending on his age. You can expect them to increase at Six, as he faces so many new challenges; intensify at Seven; and begin to disappear at Eight. Now he acts out his fears, daring himself to climb to the highest branch and dive from the highest board, and then to do it day after day until by Nine he will have sent most of his fears packing. But not for long. A Ten finds more to fret about, and an Eleven, now a full-fledged worry wart, finds still more. His concerns fade a bit at Twelve, but fears still haunt this child. Once again physical, mental and emotional changes make these reactions worse.

Fear comes from both a lack of knowledge and a lack of power. The child who doesn't know what's going to happen to him is going to be fearful, whether he's starting first grade, junior high or puberty. Moreover, teachers now wield such power that a child may feel eager to control each small part of his life and yet be unable to do it. His fears encourage a natural need to be orderly, structured and conforming, which makes him less creative.

Immediate fear causes physical changes too, as his body instinctively gets ready to fight—or to flee. He quits digesting his food well or even making spit, and instead uses the energy to pump adrenaline into his blood so his heart can beat harder and faster and the lungs can breathe deeper. This sends more oxygen to the heart, the muscles and the lungs and if he gets in a tussle and scrapes his knee, the blood will clot quicker too.

The hair gets bristly—some say to look ferocious—and the sweating begins, so the body will stay cool for the action. The pupils of a fearful child will open wider and his eyes may bulge or look shifty, moving quickly from side to side or they may look glazed, as if someone had pulled down the shades.

This is the sort of information a child should know, especially if he spends much time worrying about what he would do if the class bully started to pick on him. Just to know that his body would rise to defend him and that the alarming symptoms are perfectly natural will make your child feel much better.

There are of course many causes of fear

besides the bully. At Six there is the strange beggar, the blood test at the doctor's office and, of course, the dark. The Unknown will be shaped from whatever patch of information the child has at hand. A creak on the stair is the tread of a ghost (what else?); the early morning buzzzz of the neighbor's new power mower is the prelude to a swarm of killer bees. Dear child. All you can do (or should do) is help him admit the fear and then identify the cause. Dispel the dark with a night-light. Fix that creak by helping him drive a finishing nail into the exact source of the sound or ask the neighbor to let your child turn the mower on and off a few times.

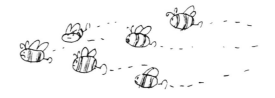

The whole world can frighten a child. Even God is scary, if He's a vengeful one, but most fears are more mundane. He is afraid to be late for school; afraid of the principal; afraid to be laughed at; afraid of "poison candy," which Sixes think is rampant on Halloween.

There is not only the fear about the first day of school but, for a while, the fear of school every day, as well as the fear of a recital, the first Scout meeting and the baseball game. There is fear about going to camp—will the old campers make room for him?—and coming home from camp—will the gang still have a place for him? A new neighborhood, new glasses, a new skill all scare a child, no matter how happily they are anticipated.

Many of his fears are spawned by violence on television or in fairy stories (no matter how they end) and especially by stories rehashed by other children, which get exaggerated at every telling. These fears often can be alleviated by anticipating the reaction and talking with your child before it sets in. Begin by getting the fear out in the open. It's perfectly reasonable for a child to be afraid of looking foolish, or feeling foolish, and your child needs to know he can admit his fears, no matter how wacky they are, and have his questions answered truthfully.

The kindest thing you can do, as a parent, is to admit your own fears, sensible or silly, in one of those lights-out, snuggle-up conversations that bond parent and child that much better. Now you tell him it's fear—and common sense—that makes you wear a seat belt in the car and put up smoke alarms at home, and it's fear that keeps you from walking under a ladder or opening an umbrella in the house, even though you're sure you won't really have bad luck. A child isn't so embarrassed about his irrational fears if he knows you have them too.

Most of all, a child is afraid when his parents have a big scene at home. This feeds the most pervasive fear in children: the fear of abandonment. It is this fear which parents should handle with the most sensitivity although it is one most children never mention. It is the deepest, longest-lasting fear of all and the most common one too, even among teenagers. You hear this fear when a child asks, "When are you coming back?" "Where are you going?" And you hear it in the games he plays too, never stepping on a crack, so he won't break his mother's back. Until boys and girls feel they can survive on their own, they are terrified that one of their parents might leave or get sick or die.

Fear of abandonment is especially prevalent today since divorce is so common. A big scene at home can leave a child quaking, and to make matters worse, he probably can't rely on relatives nearby. Today's extended families extend all over the map and a child may hardly know his aunts and uncles. The idea that a parent will disappear is particularly ominous if one parent is dead or if they are divorced. He particularly needs to know what would happen to him then, and he needs to be told enough to reassure him, without waiting for him to ask (since he probably won't).

Death is an inexplicable concept for years, but the fear of it is not. This fear shows up unexpectedly. If you ask your child a question in the car, he may not answer until you've driven past the cemetery, because he's holding his breath to keep safe. Gentle Nell, at Seven, was dismayed when we stopped for a wayside picnic in a village graveyard since she knew she couldn't hold her breath the whole time.

WISHES

Children in the Middle Years are usually so secretive, so private, that it can be hard to believe the depths of their souls. That's why it was such a surprise when our friend Tom, more trusting than most Nines, called his mother into his room for a serious talk in the dark.

"Mom," he asked, "would you rather have Truth and Glory or Freedom and Hope?"

Ponder that, if you will.

Other fears are more legitimate but if you warned your child of every possibility he would be more frightened and less confident—and so you shouldn't. You do have to tell him matter-of-factly of any real dangers, however, and how to prevent them—how to handle a fire or evacuate a house, deal with a friendly stranger or a strange family friend. Just knowing how to handle possibilities makes many fears go away. The more a child knows, the better he can put the pieces together, until there is less and less room for fear.

The sunshine of truth makes many fears vanish, and so does that night-light. Not only will it get rid of the child's spooky shadows but it will keep you from stepping on a roller skate in the middle of the night.

THE CONSCIENCE

For a while in the seventies it seemed as if the conscience had gone out of style. Somehow a child's own healthy self-esteem was supposed to make him behave. That was silly, of course. We were following a fashion instead of listening to our hearts and our heritage. Conscience is there, just as it's always been, although it needs encouragement to develop. Even then, we can't expect too much of it, too soon.

Your child may understand what you tell him to do but that doesn't mean he has a well-developed conscience. If he did, he wouldn't have been such a handful at Two. He doesn't even have a true conscience at Seven—the Age of Reason—for reason and conscience are not the same.

In fact, he will be at least Eleven or Twelve, or more probably Fourteen, Fifteen or Sixteen, before the conscience fully flowers. In between it will develop in predictable, sequential stages, just as the mind does but usually a couple of years after it. Boys and girls must be old enough to think well in abstractions, to put away their magical thinking and to consider the consequences of their actions before they know what they shouldn't do and why—and so they usually won't. After that the conscience may go on to reach a still higher level in their twenties. Here you have the adult who does what he thinks is right, even if he must act all alone.

The years between Six and Twelve set the basis for the years ahead. You can help your child move from one stage to the next a little sooner—by helping him try to figure what is fair and right—but he will still go rather slowly, and even slip back and forth. He will never skip a stage, however.

When your child enters first grade he carries his preschool rules and taboos with him, not because he understands and accepts them philosophically, but because he knows they keep him out of trouble. He's so egocentric, however, that he'll sometimes forget that the rules apply to him.

By Seven your child will invent the Golden Rule for himself. Doing Unto Others As He Would Have Them Do Unto Him will keep him in line now, for he values his friends and will want to do what's right by them. Out of this will come the support, the cooperation and the equality he needs to define his sense of right and wrong.

As this sense of fair play is honed, you may find it a bit of a burden. "It isn't fair!" is practically the password at Seven, Eight and Nine. And quite often this is true, for grown-ups often ignore the rights of children. Parents and teachers need to be particularly evenhanded in these sensitive years.

Your child will make another leap forward around Nine or Ten, once more because he wants his friends to like him. As a parent, conformity is your greatest ally, as long as his friends are good influences. This is of prime importance. You can't expect your child to hang around with the twisters and still stand straight.

By Eleven he may stick with the rules because they are the RULES, but the interpretation will depend on the sex of your child, for now boys and girls begin to see duties and decisions from somewhat different points of view. A girl worries about the needs of others while boys worry about rights—his own and others. This leads a boy into a lifelong king-of-the-mountain game—he's competing against the world—while a girl strives as part of a network of friends. She's competing as part of her world. By understanding these differences, you can help each sex develop some of the other's strengths, so your daughter will become more aware of the rights of others—and her own—and your son will be more sensitive to their needs.

Although you'll do all you can to help, the building of a conscience is a private, personal job and in some ways one of the hardest your child will ever have. He wants so much to live by the rules but he'll still make mistakes, just as he does in arithmetic. At times he will even seem to unlearn the rules you believed were imbedded in his skull, particularly as he moves from one stage of development to the next. Such transitions are unsettling, for a child always resists changes in his body, his mind and his spirit. You can only remind yourself that the conscience often grows most when it seems to be growing least.

You'll find his conscience stronger at Six if you've already drilled him with your own rules of good conduct. When a child identifies with parents, all will go fairly well, as long as you practice the rules that you preach. Dishonesty is very disturbing to children and so is blind conformity. That's why you don't say, "What will the neighbors think?" It's dandy for the teacher or the minister to teach values to your child—providing they are much like yours—but your own attitude and behavior teach them best. Parents have more influence over their children than anyone else. You'll watch your own child develop values very much like yours, but they'll never be exactly the same. That's all right. If we want our children to be strong individuals, their standards will have to be their own.

Your child will evolve his own personal code slowly as he compares the values— the "shoulds" and "shouldn'ts"—he hears at home, with those of his new friends and his teachers. As one wise soul said, "Values are chosen, not given." The choosing is sure to lead to some dissension of course, but your own clear and stable principles will help your child accept your corrections more easily.

He learns in other ways too. When you let him argue points of behavior with you, using his mind rather than just his emotions, he'll be learning to examine all ideas, including his own. A certain amount of friction strenghtens the conscience. The child who is conditioned to do exactly as he's told, without questioning or testing, will grow up looking for somebody else to tell him what to do. He may have a conscience, but it won't be his own.

Independence strengthens it too. The more everyday decisions a child makes for himself, the easier it will be for him to make moral choices. It helps if you talk together about the Big Issues, by discussing which course the country—or the family—should take, and if you listen to his ideas too. The more he considers cause and effect, the more he begins to recognize that the high road is the better path. Opportunities to make choices, to explore ideas, to imagine a walk in other shoes stretch a child's mind.

You help your child develop a strong character by the standards—and limits— you set and the encouragement and explanations and plain old patience you give. Praise for his good behavior, disapproval for the bad and an open, frequent show of love will help fortify the conscience—another reason (if one is needed) to have lots of love in your house.

A child will find his conscience more easily if you often remind him of the intrinsic goodness that is in him (and in everyone). Traditional religious faith, as well as family standards and traditions, bolsters these inner resources and makes the inevitable rough patches a little smoother.

Even sorting and classifying his collections now, as prosaic as this seems, will teach him the same mental skills he'll need to arrange the abstract ideas later. Practice in one area leads to mastery in another.

Although a child has been taught to think morally, he will still have to make an effort to resist temptation. Each time he succeeds, the next test is that much easier. There once was a time when we took an anxious Nell, at Ten, to shop at the big department store for Christmas, with the $5.00 she had so laboriously earned and saved. And then, like magic, she looked down and saw a $20 bill on the floor, all

by itself. With her heart in her mouth and the bill in her hand, she said she had to ask the guard if anyone had lost it. He told her he'd keep the money until closing time—a whole hour away—and if no one claimed it by then, the money was hers. And no one did. That was the night that honesty won a solid place in her heart.

You'll know your child has a conscience when he at least struggles before he gives in to a sorry impulse; when he admits a misdeed; when he feels bad when he's done one; when he needs to be forgiven; and when he tries not to do it again, even if no one is around to know.

There will come a time when he will always think of the consequences of his behavior on others as well as himself, so that the fewest people are hurt and the most are helped, most of the time. And by then he'll be a grown-up.

BEHAVIOR

Your child's behavior is a barometer, giving you fair and foul weather readings for his body and his mind. It will never change in the Middle Years as suddenly and dramatically as it did before, however, when his moods would swing wildly within the same day and his general behavior would change radically about twice a year.

By contrast, there may seem to be a sea of sameness between Six and Twelve. Now moods swing, not on a daily basis but over the months, and each stage lasts about a year, with the changes more gradual and the differences more subtle. Because the shifts are less dramatic and less frequent, each phase may seem endless and permanent—a satisfaction in the good years but a concern in the bad. Only one thing is certain: there is never a simple, steady advance. A child only grows when his good behavior breaks apart and then comes back together in a more adult way.

He is also more private. Now that he's older, and his vocabulary and understanding are broader, you might expect him to tell you how he feels about everything. He

won't. He can talk so well, but he tells you about movie plots and classroom scuffles to your exhaustion and keeps most of the serious thoughts to himself. The Five who told you about his dreams and fears and terrors will become the Nine who may only tell them to his best friend. This is the time for shutting out and shutting up. Consider this a positive retreat—one more step to independence—but if you retreat too, your child may stay in this cocoon through his preteens, even when he is ready to confide in you again. This would be a pity. If parent and child haven't learned how to talk to each other by the time he is a teenager, adolescence will be a tough passage.

Since his conversation is often superficial in the Middle Years, you need to pay closer attention to him than you ever have before, picking up signals he may not even know he's sending. This is especially true if there is a behavior problem and truer still if the problem has a physical base. People—especially young people—usually think their chronic aches and anxieties are normal and adjust their personalities, schedules and interests to explain them away.

Until the third grade a child seldom realizes that his coat isn't warm enough or his shoes hurt his feet. Instead he thinks of his clothes as part of himself and, though he feels grumpy, he puts the blame somewhere else. Playing outside, he says, is "no fun" or "Johnny is mean" or to go to the supermarket with you would be "dumb"—and with so many aisles to walk

through in pinchy shoes, he would be quite right.

On the other hand children may blame their toys or their clothes for some misfortune, as you'll discover when your son kicks his "stupid bike" when he falls or your daughter says the dress she wore to school is "babyish" when, to tell the truth, she felt babyish when she wasn't picked for the spelling team. It takes a long time for children to accept a reasonable share of responsibility for their own misfortunes, but they'll do it sooner if parents help them understand why they feel and act the way they do.

Now your child needs you to be his doctor, his teacher, his therapist and his friend, gentling him to say what hurts. First search for an external cause or a physical problem. If there is none, you know the pain is in his heart. He needs to talk about his feelings and, if possible, to work out his own solutions before you give any advice. The more answers he can discover on his own, the stronger he will be.

Boys and girls usually begin this middle era of growth as a pleasant, fairly self-assured people at Six, become rather clingy and given to self-pity at Seven and then so convivial in the next three years that they must have not only friends but a gang of friends. Although the characteristics of age often vary by a year or so—as always—the sequence is the same. The Eight is generally a roustabout, the Nine tends to be more sanctimonious and rather gossipy, the Ten is outgoing, enthusiastic and a tad

superficial, the Eleven is cute but cantankerous and the Twelve is cool and collected.

If you're like most parents you are so pleased with your child during the good times that you can endure the rest, but you may despair if you and the child both hit a bad year at the same time. Even if you're having a productive period yourself, you still may feel guilty when your child is in a slump. Modern-day parents have been told that everything they do—or don't do—affects their child (which is true), but no child is an island. His own moods also affect the way he acts and so does the great big world. Outside of his family, he is influenced most by his school and his friends, followed by books, movies and television.

His basic nature is pulled in many different ways and his behavior is the culmination of a hundred impulses, internal and external. Some are mighty hard for him to resist. These pulls on his conscience may disturb you, but they are valuable. Consequences—good and bad—will teach your child, for strengths are born of error as well as success.

No painting was ever painted, no poem ever written and certainly no child—that greatest work of all—ever grew without some creative conflict. A certain amount of abrasion is good for the soul. It's friction that helps the egocentric Six turn into a more empathic person in another year or two and that's just what you want. When he can put himself in someone else's place, he can decide to change his behavior when it's annoying. Friction also helps him change friends when they won't act the way he thinks they should. Even the smallest contrast forces a child to become more objective, defining the values he'll depend upon as a teenager.

A Six won't follow his buddy over a forbidden fence but in another few years he'll say he didn't hear you yelling, "Don't you dare!" and when he's Twelve you'll wish his escapades were still so simple. This is part of life.

No child under Thirteen (and not many Thirteens) will make the right choice every time, so you still need to monitor his friendships, supervise his activities and listen to him well throughout these Middle Years. It takes an adult to keep a child on target, and it still is easier to prevent bad behavior by setting limits, giving support and helping his personality mesh with the behavior that suits your family best.

This doesn't mean your child can be molded like putty. He fights against control because he instinctively knows that he must act from his own experience if he's going to be his own person. He still knows you're an essential part of his life, but you aren't treated with the same awe you once were. When he was young he watched you intensely, copying the way you moved and talked, and he still spends a lot of time concentrating on you, but there's a difference. Now he gauges what you tell him to do against what you do yourself. He reflects the person he thinks you are and the way he thinks you feel.

If you are aloof, he is withdrawn; if you are critical of him, he is critical of others—including you. Your shame is his shame, but your joy is his joy too, and so are your caring and your generosity.

With your support he'll move in the right direction. Seventeenth-century philosophers debated whether children were naturally evil or whether society had corrupted them. Mothers, however, have always known: a child is born to be good—and with any luck at all, he stays that way, most of the time.

It's the rest of the time that will shred your nerves.

When a child misbehaves, he either doesn't feel accepted by others—usually his parents—or he hasn't found the right way to express himself or he may feel that too much is expected of him—the sign of the helpless child. If he is consistently failing to meet your expectations, it's time to lower them.

A child also will regress under stress, either at home or at school. Poor behavior is the classic sign that something is amiss. It is a time for investigation but not for alarm. All children have rough passages, a little backsliding, and a lot of experiments. A child is sure to pull every kind of behavior, good, bad and weird, while he is growing up.

There are weeks and even months when your child may not think he's getting enough attention, so he will try to get it by being super-good, which is a cry for help that's seldom heard, or he acts quite wretched, without even realizing that he has made this decision. It's necessary for you to correct him, but some poor behavior is inevitable and even necessary. If a child can't have a scene in his own house, where can he have it? Where else does he dare to show anger? despair? frustration? Where can he cry? Where in the world is he safe?

Your child needs you to accept his negative emotions, so together you can exorcise them like any demons. This is one of your many important jobs as a parent and it's what acceptance is all about. With this bedrock, he will feel safe to follow your advice, for he knows you'll always stand by. This allows a child to forgive himself, and therefore to forgive others, which will minimize much of the rebellion in the teen years.

Independence should not, however, be confused with rebellion. The independent child stands up for himself because he thinks he's right. The rebellious one stands up for himself to prove that someone else is wrong.

If you want your child to be a capable adult, he must be a curious child; if you want him to be a loving mate, he must be a well-loved child, and if you want your child to be a person of substance, you must set high standards for yourself—and keep them. The standards you expect him to follow now, however, should be no higher than your own. Once you recognize that, you'll know he will be perfect as soon as, but no sooner than, you are. Fortunately, every day gives a fresh chance, for both mother and child.

THE GREAT MOTIVATORS

A child will behave, most of the time, as long as he's treated well. It takes a balance of incentives and limits to rear a child who knows he can think anything he'd like, as long as he behaves well; that he can say whatever he thinks, as long as his manners are good; and that he can gripe about something he has to do, as long as he does it anyway. Like everyone else, he responds to encouragement in a variety of forms, and they all amount to love.

Your child knows you love him when you act at least half as considerate of him as you are of your neighbor; when you ask him to do a job, instead of ordering him; when you listen closely to what he has to say, so he knows his ideas matter too.

Your reasonable expectations also help him grow and flourish. He is much more likely to have good manners and get good marks if they're expected, rather than demanded, because a fair expectation subtly tells him that he is capable. As long as your expectations aren't too high or too relentless—or raised too often—a child will try to meet them because you clearly think he can.

The need to be needed is in us all and

this encourages good behavior too. A child wants to learn new skills and use the ones he has, but only if they serve a purpose. The child who is given a "make-work" job knows it and feels insulted, but the one who is depended upon to do a real task feels complimented.

The straightforward compliment is a fine incentive too, although most parents find it hard to give. When you congratulate your child for a specific bit of good behavior—and especially when you notice that some poor behavior is getting better—he learns to act his best. Any child thrills to be told "Great job!" especially in front of one of your friends.

He also responds well to the attention you give to his work, for this is unspoken praise. Just going to the Wednesday afternoon assembly to see him in the chorus is praise in itself. It says that you value his time and effort as you value your own.

Your patience is another kind of encouragement. When you let a child do as much as he can for himself—even though you could do it faster and better—he will be getting more independence, and all the self-esteem that comes with it. The child who feels treasured will give his best. His efforts won't be constant of course, and they surely won't be perfect, but bit by bit they will get better with incentives, and a lot quicker than they would with punishments.

Since your child is sure to imitate you, your own good behavior is one of his best incentives. He will find it easier to live within his limits if you remember that your word must be golden if it's to be accepted—a good reason to reconsider before you make a promise or a threat. When he sees you and your husband work out a tough marital problem or deal with some tensions at the office, he decides he can overcome difficult problems too. And when you tolerate frustrations, laugh at your own foibles and realize that you're not the most important person in the world, your child takes his cue from you.

You also offer incentives by your attitude as well as your actions. It's literally true: if you don't discourage a child, you don't take his courage away.

This is the kind of caring that translates into love. You may think your child is too young to understand, but that's not true. Love is the native language of every child.

Respect

If you want your child to honor his father and mother, you have to honor your child. It takes mutual respect to make a family work, not because parents and children are equals, but because they have an equal right to be respected. It's the parents who must set the pace and who can change the atmosphere in the house.

The parent who is attentive and conscientious, but who still talks down to her child and treats his time and his privacy lightly is in for trouble. She may think she gets respect in return, but often the child is just anxious to please, always hoping that goodness will be rewarded. Another parent may give presents instead of respect, or drive more car pools than anyone else, but her child isn't fooled.

You show respect when you listen to your child as thoughtfully as you listen to your boss; when you take the time to teach him grown-up skills, like cooking, sewing, painting and plastering, and when you expect him to join in the family work as well as the family fun.

You also show respect when you give phone messages without being asked; knock on his door before you enter; ignore any notes that are left around his room— no matter how tantalizing they are; and surprise him with a small present, "for lending your room to Aunt Jane." This tells him that he has rights too, and you know it.

And you give respect when you give your child choices whenever you can; when you let him waste his time—because it is his time, not yours; and when you accept his choice in music and books as you hope he will accept yours one day.

Of all the signs of respect a mother can give, the greatest of all is when she lets go, and it is the hardest one too. The respectful parent tries to be less protective and less solicitous each day, keeping reminders to a minimum. A little neglect, you'll find, is good for the growing soul. If you clean up after your child, you're telling him that you don't think he can take care of himself, the same message you give when you tell him how to spend his allowance or how to do his homework, when he hasn't even asked for help. A child must feel independent before he wants to obey.

The child who is respected is the one who is free to grow.

Acceptance

All the world loves a winner, but a child needs to know his parents love him when he wins, when he loses and when he just chugs along. This tells him he is accepted as a person, no matter what he does. Nothing else makes a child feel so secure. If he only felt loved for what he could do, he would feel he had to do more and more, or if he thought his failure would lessen your love, he might not try at all.

A child who is often criticized will feel worthless and act that way too, being moody, mad, whiny, testy, nervous, bored or bad, usually concentrating on two or three of those characteristics. Criticism never made anyone work harder, except out of an "I'll show you" sort of anger, but it does make anyone resentful. You want your child to achieve, of course, but for his own joy, his own sense of accomplishment. If you said he should make A's because his daddy always did, you would be saying he had no right to be himself, and of course he would have to prove you wrong just to show you that he was an individual too.

Nor do you urge a child to achieve to "make you proud" or because he must use his "God-given talents" or because it will help him get into a better college one day or make a lot of money. None of these are valid reasons either to accept or reject someone you love.

A child has certain inalienable rights and one of them is the right to be accepted by his parents, with all the quirks and confusions that come with him. Never mind that your son's ears stick out a bit or your daughter's knees are knobby. They are his ears, her knees. You no more have the right to criticize them than you would have the right to criticize the looks of your neighbors.

You may ache for your child in the rough times, and thrill with him in the good ones, but you have to accept him, always. It's the only way he's going to accept himself.

Appreciation

Acceptance is essential; appreciation is the frosting on the cake. A child's need for it is particularly keen after he starts school. Now there are new challenges each day, and although some can be won the first time, most must be tried again and again and not always with success. On top of that are the tumbles on the playground; the teasing from the older students; some high-handed corrections from the teacher. It's hard to feel good about yourself when you have so many defeats, and have them so publicly.

A child needs a great deal of reinforcement to offset these setbacks and it all comes down to the right kind of praise. Some kinds are excellent; others can be more damaging than the defeats.

The child who is praised too often or too much may become so addicted to compliments that their absence seems unfair, or he may not trust his parents at all. Instead he needs to be appreciated for specific acts—for using his inborn talents, not for having them or even for being "good."

If a child is praised for being "good," in an all-enveloping way, he might feel that he had to be good to be loved, and that you will love him only as long as he is well behaved. He might become a goody two-

shoes, trying to live up to your expectations, or get depressed, because your standards seem so high, or even act quite dreadful, to show you how bad he really is. A child is distressed by false pretenses.

And if your child feels it is his looks that matter to you, he will be devastated by baby fat at Twelve; by acne or by any real or imagined blemish, no matter what his age. He may become the adult who constantly seeks perfection—and is always disappointed. And if you praise your child for being so good or smart or beautiful, he will know you can make negative judgments too, just as sharp and sweeping.

While an occasional, unexpected reward for good work is always welcome, the promise of prizes, money or treats puts a price tag on work that he does for himself or his family and might make him fear failure. He does, however, like to be judged—if the assessment is positive, if it's fair and if it's for his accomplishments. This is what makes a child feel cherished.

Instead of saying that her hair is so lovely, compliment your daughter for the way that she braids it, and rather than tell your son that he's a fine artist, notice how well he balances the yellow sun in the upper right corner of the picture with the yellow wheat field in the lower left. When he sees why you like the picture, he'll know for himself what a fine artist he is. When a child is praised for his real skills, even when they are still quite raw, he learns to identify his strengths and have the heart to perfect them. The more you reinforce these strengths, the more he lives up to them.

Most middle-class parents praise their

children for the good work they do in school, but children know that it's the survival skills that matter. It's the painting, sewing, cooking, building that make a child proud, and with good reason. When you get down to the basics, it's the basics that count. Competence gives a child self-esteem.

The praise that's overheard is also treasured. When your child hears you tell a friend how well he's doing, he knows it must be true. After all, you wouldn't lie to your friend. And because you notice how hard he is trying, he will want to try even harder.

Even if you aren't used to this style you can still adapt to it, and your child will thank you by behaving better.

The timing of your praise is important too. Good behavior is reinforced best if you give a compliment as soon as you notice it, but you can also leave little notes of congratulations on his bureau, which you can bet will be kept and read again months later—words of quiet cheer when a lift may be needed most.

While parents often feel overcome by the pleasure their child brings them, it is usually hard for them to admit it. Don't hesitate. If your child makes you feel happy, say so, just like that, or give a hug for no reason at all. Touching is an important way to talk to a child and is as necessary now as it was when he was little—and it always will be. There will be times ahead when words get so angry, so easily, that a mother who is used to giving hugs and kisses can let them speak for her instead.

A child also feels appreciated when you reflect with him about some misery at school or a problem with his best friend. It's important for a parent to appreciate a child's pain as much as his pleasure. Some appreciation is intangible.

A child knows he is appreciated when you look pleased when he comes home from school or to the dinner table, and when you sometimes check to see if he's warm enough at night, even though he's years past tucking in.

You teach him to appreciate himself when you have him say his prayers at night, or at least count his blessings for all the things that went right in his day and what he did to make them happen. This recognition gives him praise from the one person who means more to him than anyone else—himself.

Listening

Listening to anyone is an art; listening to a child is a necessity. It is a sign not just of courtesy but of caring. When your child was little you would let him talk while you skimmed the newspaper, gave a few "umms," or hugged and kissed him when he cried. You read stories to him, pointed out the funny clouds in the sky and gave him almost as many orders as he gave you. There weren't many real conversations, but your child needed your attention and was amusing enough to catch it. Now it's hard to be interested when your Eight runs through a dozen knock-knock jokes while you're trying to measure the ingredients for a cake. Although his subjects aren't too exciting, he needs to be heard more than ever, so you will stay close when he's older.

Indifference would make him feel rejected, which can be overwhelming to a child—a sign that he isn't worth much. And rejection is what it is when a child talks to a parent who clearly isn't listening, or who leaves the room when he's speaking or who doesn't answer or who grunts a response and flicks on the television or picks up the newspaper. These techniques tell a child that he isn't important enough or amusing enough to be heard. A good yardstick: would you treat an adult like this? a coworker? a boss?

To communicate well, you have to listen to your child at least as much as you talk. This doesn't mean you drop everything when he has something to say. If it's inconvenient, give him an outright, "Honey, I'm so weary (or worried, or whatever), I'm not hearing you well. Can we talk after I've had a good soak in the tub?" This sort of response tells your child he is a friend: you expect him to understand you, just as you try to understand him. And try you must.

Every member of the family has the right to be heard, especially the child in these self-absorbed years. The chance to sound off, to complain about real (or imagined) wrongs, to seek solace, is vital now. When you listen, do it well. Put down the rake; quit stirring the pot; turn off the television—and listen as if it is the most important thing you can do, because it is. This is the only way tones can be caught, and nuances and body language can be deciphered. The words that matter are often obscured by hundreds of others that cloud the subject. A child may hide his true feelings even from himself until it seems safe to pull them out from the depths of his mind. Just being able to put them into words can help, and you need neither approve nor disapprove. If you agree with your child that he was right to be furious with his friend Max today, you can bet that they'll make up tomorrow—and you'll be asked why you said such mean things about his best friend.

It was Nell who would come home from the fourth grade, slump down at the dinner table and, with a rolling of Rrrrrs, say, "Oh, Rrrrrats! Talk about a Rrrrrotten Day!" Every child will play a variation of this scene sometime, often frequently if he is in a continuing bad situation. Sometimes you can do something about it but often you just listen. When your child comes in, kicks off his boots and drops his lunchbox, you hug and say, "Not too good today, eh?" not "For Pete's sake, you're dropping your things everywhere!" He won't go to the crux of the problem right away but if you say, "Really!" often enough, and react with a nod, or a frown, he'll elaborate and tell you in detail the dreadful things that Max did.

When you repeat what he says, almost in his own words, to make sure you understand and to give him a chance to clarify,

he will peel another layer of the onion, admitting his fears and hurts to himself as well as to you. You don't stop the story and tell your child that everything is fine when it isn't. It's sympathy and empathy he wants and a little clucking, which gives him the framework to work through his own problems. He'll appreciate your patience. As our Meg would say at the end of a long litany, "Thanks for letting me whine."

When he's finished, it's your turn, but not to say, "You should have . . ." or "Maybe now you've learned . . ." You would never say that to a friend when she told you of her awful day at the office—and your child is your friend. He needs to hear you say, "Things must be pretty bad for Max to act that way. I guess he needs special understanding now," or perhaps, "I wonder if there was anything anyone could have done. . . ." The child who is allowed to play out his own emotions may, by the end, be able to consider the other side.

The same rules apply when you find yourself in an argument. Listen to yourself. If you are rational, gentle and understanding, your child will try hard to be the same but if you're repeating your own familiar catch phrases—no matter how clever they once were—your child will hear them as another way to shut him up.

And when he asks for a special privilege, let him make his whole presentation before you pass judgment. No matter how strange the request may seem initially, a child deserves the chance to be fully heard.

He should, of course, be encouraged to listen too. If you are willing to endure recitals of the ins and outs of the plots of Encyclopedia Brown and the detailed account of the ball game, because he's your friend, then he will be more willing to hear you talk about your day—because you're his friend.

You should also confide in him about your concerns, although not much about marital problems or money, since he'll think it's his responsibility to save you from divorce or the poorhouse and will be distressed because he doesn't know how. Your child will have ideas about the kind of car you should buy, however, or where to go for a picnic. You'll get some good and perhaps unexpected suggestions when you consult with someone who looks at life from the underside. As long as you either incorporate his plans into yours, or take the time to explain why you won't, your child will feel fairly treated.

The best conversation is, of course, two-way. You ask him to *guess* who's going to have a baby? Again? And should you and his dad vote for more school bonds? This is how he learns to talk with grown-ups and you learn what he thinks about babies—and maybe abortions—and what he thinks the school needs and if your money is getting wasted.

Talking—and listening—is all practice for the Great Big World that awaits. How else can he learn how to be a parent?

Expectations

Every day you telegraph a thousand unconscious signals to your child, and although you may find it hard to believe, he acts on them whenever he can—even when it's a bad idea.

If you make it clear that you think he'll catch a baseball with the ease of a major leaguer, he probably will. And if you tell him he is going to break that cup if he doesn't watch out, he'll break a lot of cups.

You have expectations because you know and love your child. From the beginning his health and his personality and his interests have conditioned you to expect a certain kind of behavior, and you in turn have let him know what these expectations are. You also have other expectations that

Promises, Promises—Sometimes we forget how literally a child listens to our promises. Even the silliest one is apt to be believed, especially if the child really wants it, for he takes himself so seriously in the early grades.

Nevertheless, silly promises have their place, for they sometimes help a child feel big and brave. Our friend Buddy was Eight before he knew for sure (although he always suspected) that we weren't going to let him clean our three-story chimney by tying a rope around his middle, covering him with honey and letting him slide down. By the time he knew the truth he was ready to realize that maybe it wasn't such a good idea.

But it was Nell who taught us that a silly promise can be taken too seriously if it isn't quite silly enough. She was Seven when we said, sure, we could get a horse to live in the stable of the big old house we had bought in the middle of Washington, D.C. It just couldn't cost more than $2.00. That didn't faze Nell. At the Amish auction in Maryland she asked her daddy to bid $2.00 on an old plow horse and, with some embarrassment, he did. The next bid was $75, but she stoically accepted that. She asked her big brother to help her look in the classified ads, and he did, but again there was no $2.00 horse. She accepted that too.

And then one magic day, standing with us on a corner in New York City, quiet little Nell went berserk and chased a bus down the street. When caught, she wept to explain what she had missed: a horse, ''a $2.00 horse!'' There was a sign right on the bus, she said, and she was right—a sign for off-track betting. It said: BUY A $2 HORSE.

And that's when we learned that, when it came to promises, a Seven can't always tell the difference between the silly and the serious.

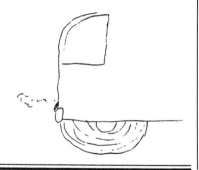

reflect your own anxieties and frustrations and dreams, for we can't stop thinking of our children as extensions of ourselves.

When expectations are too high or too low or simply irrelevant, a child rebels. To give him goals that are always beyond him will tell him that life is hopeless. This is the child who becomes rowdy or destructive when he decides it's time to quit the race.

If extremely high expectations are harmful, and they are, low ones can be much worse. A child seldom doubts the judgment of his parents; instead he doubts himself. If they don't believe in him, he certainly won't.

It's the realistically positive expectations that help a child so much, giving him the freedom to excel—or not to excel. No one is first-rate in every area or even always first-rate in one. Once more, a parent is meant to walk with the child down the middle of the road—expecting the best he can do but not demanding more. By having faith, you give him the courage to try anything and the right to fail. This is the little engine that could.

Harmony

Harmony helps a child behave and it's the parents who create it. You do this when you make sure the radio, the record player and the television stay on only if someone is listening or watching, and that the volume even then is kept at a reasonable level. Your preteen may say his music must be loud to be appreciated, but since loud, loud music can damage his hearing (and your disposition), insist that it stay reasonably low. A child who learns to consider the rights and needs of the rest of the family will grow up to consider the rights and needs of everyone around him.

You also help create harmony if you talk in a normal voice, even when you're mad, and if you don't answer anyone who yells at you in anger. If you don't scream at your children, they will be far less likely to scream at each other.

You don't even shout from room to room, since yelling is noise and noise creates tension. When your child calls you, just say where you are—"I'm down here in the basement"—and nothing else, so he will come to you. And if you're the one who needs to talk with him, call his name to find out where he is, and then go to him, unless you're terribly busy—and then ask him, politely, to come to you. Parents have some perks.

If you talk softly, you don't have to carry a big stick.

LIMITS

There can be too much obedience in the world, as the world discovered in Germany in the thirties, and too much disobedience, as we found in America in the sixties. We also learned that some wars must be joined and that all wars must be stopped. The family mirrors the bigger scene.

The permissive parent and the autocratic parent reap about the same amount of trouble—a lot. If a child is reared with few limits, it will be hard for him to set them for himself. This may leave you with one of those charmers who does what he wants and when, without taking other people into consideration. On the other hand, if a child is stifled too much he may become rebellious or angry or hostile, or he may lose his creativity and his sense of joy. This is the child who looks sad and withdraws from new ideas and people too. He chooses daydreams and fantasy instead, playing with imaginary friends in the primary grades or relying on television or escapist fiction. He may eat too much or get sick or depressed or act babyish, or as a preteen he may use drugs or run away.

Basically, you want to guide your child in your own style, with whatever limits, expectations, incentives—and corrections—help him stay on the track. He'll do best with as few rules as possible, for the more small decisions he can make, the easier it will be for him to make the big ones. Your limits must also make sense. If you set them capriciously, you'll show your child who's boss, but you won't do much else. He needs rules that are born of reason, because he is actually a reasonable person.

The greatest persuader is your own calm set of expectations. If you expect to be obeyed—not as a dictator but as a caring adult—you won't get too much flak. An effective parent is one who acts as if she is in charge, because she knows she is.

There is almost nothing a child won't do, or try to do—or at least promise to do—if he is consulted first; if his plans are considered; if he knows it's necessary, and if he isn't expected to put as much enthusiasm into daily chores in July as he does the week before Christmas. And that's fair. You certainly don't try as hard over a Monday night supper as you do for a company dinner. A child also can live with almost any rules as long as he feels safe to say what he thinks about them (within the bounds of good manners) and perhaps to change them with some ideas of his own.

If he can't, it's time to wonder if you're letting go soon enough and in the right way.

Your child also must know his limits. You certainly couldn't work efficiently or happily if your boss didn't tell you what you were expected—and not expected—to do.

You must also allow for differences between your limits and the ones set by your friends and neighbors. No two parents require exactly the same kind of behavior from a child, and teachers, grandmothers and housekeepers have styles of their own. This is part of the variety that spices a child's life but parents must trust their own judgment. Your limits must be yours, not those of the mother next door. This helps to give your family its individuality. If it doesn't bother you for your child to ride his bike in town, that's your business. And if Saturday cartoons do bother you, that's your business too. Your rules are meant for your own family. This doesn't mean that they are right for everyone else, or even anyone else. They may even be fairly strange but your neighbors will respect them, as long as you respect the limits they set.

If some new fad or activity seems wrong to you, even after you've talked about it with your child and your friends, then there is only one conclusion: it is wrong, for your household at least. Your child only fits into the family if he follows its rules.

When you do set a limit, you have to take full responsibility for it, even if it's the neighborhood standard. If you were to tell him that all the other mothers have the same rule, it would be no time at all before he would want to do something "because all the other kids can." Never mind what the other children do because some children need more freedom than others—

even in the same family—and some need more in one year than another. If you can adjust to suit the times and the child, you'll enjoy motherhood much more. This is the child you'll be loving all your life.

POSTING RULES

Every family has its day-to-day rules, and rules, like lists of chores, are heeded best when they are posted.

In our house it begins with a general statement and a code to live by: A family is a community, and each member owes it—and each other—respect.

*Be as cheerful as you can, even when you don't feel like it.

*Be loyal to one another.

*Give about five times as many smiles as you get, so you will get more—and so will everyone else.

* * *

If these rules seem familiar, you may recognize them in their old-fashioned, more succinct form: Do Unto Others As You Would Have Them Do Unto You.

Some rules also shift a little since no husband and wife can completely agree on what they should be. And that's all right. Just tell your child that you and his dad have agreed to disagree and the one who cares most about it will prevail. A child is never too young to learn that parents can still be united even if they don't think alike. That's the real consistency of discipline. This elasticity is simply another way to tell your child how special he is.

This doesn't mean that you betray your own standards—heavens no. You aren't supposed to renegotiate the rules every time they're applied, but you should break them when there is a real need and keep them quite firmly the rest of the time. There are times when you not only have the last word but the only word.

When you act with assurance your child will feel safe, for he knows that sometimes he is his own worst enemy. There's nothing like a mother to protect him from himself.

Even if your limits have been quite tentative so far, you can start setting firm rules, although he will rebel at first and it will take a bit longer to make them stick. These limits will be followed better if everyone helps to make them and if they are posted too. One mother announced a new set of standards by making this kitchen banner for her family: WE CAN NO LONGER AFFORD THE LUXURY OF DOING OUR OWN THING.

As much as your child may object, he will be secretly pleased to have limits. Without them he would drift in a limbo, which is scary. A child needs freedom, but only if he's earned it and only if he knows where the edges are. He cries out for boundaries, although his cries are often made in strange tongues. It's human nature for a child to push for more than he can have, but when he does it, he's really waiting for you to push back. As a parent, you have the duty to say no to anything that doesn't suit your way of life.

And if you relax a boundary and think better of it, don't hesitate to tell your child you made a mistake and why, and that unless he has some better alternative, you'll have to go back to the old way.

In all of these cases it's up to you to make the final decision on anything that could affect, damage or hurt the safety or the character of your child or the pleasure and harmony of the family. Unless your child regularly cooks the meals, cleans the house, waits for the repairman, tars the roof—and pays the mortgage—he hasn't earned the same rights that you have and he knows it. This won't prevent a certain amount of backchat, but that's all right too.

There was a time when Mrs. Einstein knew a lot more than Albert.

Giving Orders

Every household needs somebody in charge, somebody who tells a child what to do. The most effective orders are often unspoken, and this is why you post the weekday and weekend schedules—for mealtimes, bedtimes and piano practice—

and an assignment list for routine jobs. You still will have to give some verbal reminders but it's harder for a child to ignore his duties when they're written down, especially when they're checked off daily (see Work).

☺ ☺	Make Bed	Set Table	Clear Table	Walk Dog
Alex	✓	✓		✓
Jessica	✓		✓	✓
Catherine	✓	✓	✓	

Some orders, of course, must still be spoken out loud. "Stop," when a child is in danger, is quite properly shouted, but most orders are heard better if they're spoken in a pleasant tone of voice and phrased as requests, with a "please" and a "thank you" attached.

Requests should be clear and specific, so the child will know what is expected, how it should be done and how long it should take. The more his feelings are respected, the more willingly he'll work. Order giving is an art—if you want the orders to be obeyed.

The Nag Level

Nag levels evolve. With Kate, our first-born, we could reach the remarkable height of nine before blowing our stack. From then on, the level diminished. With Mike it was four; with Meg, three; and with Nell, the youngest, it hit two. Two, we then realized with a sense of triumph, was the right and proper level.

The first nag would be the warning and the second was the signal to move it, RIGHT THEN AND THERE. It worked but the third nag kept creeping in until we finally learned that it could be avoided if the child told us when the job was done, so he wouldn't be asked again. Neither the nagger nor the naggee enjoys nagging.

If you don't establish a traditional limit you will find yourself yelling hollow threats—"One more time and . . ." that invite the child to prolong the agony, if only to keep his self-respect.

Instead he needs to be told gently but firmly, "We'll need you to rake the yard today," and then give him a choice of starting at eleven o'clock, noon or one o'clock. He picks the time and that's the last time you mention it until the time arrives. Perhaps he'll begin on schedule but probably not. You give him five minutes of grace and then say, "Sorry, sweetie. You'll have to quit what you're doing now and start on the yard," lifting the book (or whatever) from his hand, kissing the top of his head and sending him on his way.

You watch him when he starts (since there's many a slip between the book and the rake) and compliment him when he's done, noting the time when you do. If he works much too slowly or too sloppily, give him a nudge—tell him to wrap it up, properly, in the next ten minutes or he'll lose a privilege, like the use of the telephone for a couple of days.

You, of course, have your own responsibilities when he might be tempted to nag you. When your child asks a question, avoid the temptation to say, "Ask me later" or "Maybe" or "We'll see." Your little kvetch will change his style if you stop what you're doing, consider his question carefully and give a thoughtful, complete answer. If he asks the same thing later, he is telling you he didn't quite understand what you said or he wants to make sure you still remember.

If he asks a third time, ignore the question, give a hug and tell him that all nag levels, yours and his, stop at two.

CORRECTIONS

Good discipline usually works—not just once but time and time again—and it works no matter how tired or angry you are.

Off-the-cuff discipline, however, only leads to emotional overreactions and ill-said words which will give your child a grievance. He may not know what's fair, but he sure knows what's unfair, because this child is out in the world now. His judgment is based not just on what you do or don't do but on the discipline exercised by the many other adults he meets now. These comparisons can be tough on you, since a child usually sees his own parents get much angrier than anyone else. Teachers, recreation leaders and other mothers lose their tempers but they are more contained simply because he's there. Even when they get mad at him they don't get as mad as you do because they aren't as involved with him as you are. The deeper the love, the stronger the emotion.

Signals

Parents and children argue with each other in a hundred ways. The trick is to understand when an argument stems from a mistake or a misunderstanding and when it is a battle of wills. A child will misjudge time occasionally and slough work rather often, and he needs you to be patient yet firm, but when the infractions are regular, take heed and look for a hidden cause. Routine misbehavior is another of a child's many ways to ask for help and, if you can catch his signals and make changes, you'll improve his behavior much more easily than you would by a head-on clash.

Even if you can't diagnose the problem precisely, your efforts will show your child that you feel responsible and want to make things better. If his conduct is worse on school days, better on weekends and good on vacation, something is almost surely the matter at school. If the behavior is bad, day in and day out, he may have a physical problem, or he may be reacting to problems in the family or to the degree and type of discipline he's getting.

If you think your style of discipline is at fault, keep a record of the number of times you say no, how often you nag and when you give an order too vague to be followed. A mother who acts like a fuss-and-feathers general gets about the same results. She may win the opening maneuvers, but she'll lose the war.

Rules and Consequences

Rules are given with notice and with reason, whenever possible. But not always. If you're annoyed by something your child is doing, and you don't quite know why, tell him to stop. It's more important to follow your instincts than to justify each thing you do.

While a child needs to have his views considered, parents still must give the orders. In discipline, however, less is more. The fewer orders you give, and the less you repeat them, the better your child will behave. You help him along through fair corrections, a few lectures and inconspicuous supervision, but consequences will teach him most.

The truth is, you can't eat for your child, you can't sleep for your child, you can't pee for your child—and after a while you can't even say no for your child. He has to learn for himself. When you expect him to take the consequences for his actions, you're saying that you think he can handle them. He may watch a special show on television when his schoolwork goes well—or miss it if he was late with a project (obviously he needs more time to study). Or if he is expected to save part of his allowance to buy Christmas gifts and spends it on candy instead, you may have to keep that amount from his allowance, since he must need help in handling his money.

When your child forgets his lunch money, he goes without lunch—unless you have rushed it to school or have had the office lend him money or unless his classmates have shared their food. His friends won't share forever and if you stop rushing to his rescue you'll find that the child who goes hungry today remembers his lunch tomorrow. And if he dallies in the morning and is scolded by the teacher for being late, you can bet he will be on time the next day (or the day after), as long as you don't send a note to say it was really your fault.

He can leave an unmade bed and a messy room when he goes to school, but he will have to clean it before dinner, since mess is offensive to others, even in his own room. Whatever the assignment, he should know that he either must do it well and on time, or he'll have to do it later—and more, even if he has to miss a ball game to do it. You have to teach him that bad luck follows bad work, but he'll only learn this lesson if you make sure that he does it. This is one of the most important tasks of discipline, and the one that's most forgotten.

When there is no built-in consequence, it's up to you to impose one. A child needn't always know what it will be in advance, but only that he must pay his own piper.

This isn't enough, however. There is still that wretched behavior that gives you a knot in the tum: the intentional disobedience; the unkindnesses to others; the repeated offense. A responsible parent must curb her child whenever he steps over the limits of good sense, good manners or good taste, even if he's passing through a stage or has a bad teacher. If he hurts someone, either by what he does or by what he says, or if he destroys property, or refuses to obey the rules of family or society, you must correct him fairly and quietly and he must apologize and make amends. And then, since a child shouldn't

be tried twice for the same crime, the act is forgiven and the mistake isn't mentioned anymore.

Negative Techniques

To figure out the right style of discipline, you first must figure out the wrong ones, so you can impose some necessary limits on yourself.

Some corrections are much worse than others. The parent who disciplines by turning cold and distant will devastate a child. If love is conditional, he won't feel safe enough to trust, and trust is the keystone of his whole emotional development. Without it, he'll find it hard to depend on anyone.

Spanking is another very poor correction. The occasional swats you gave to your preschooler's fanny—which relieved your temper but taught him so little—should be banned completely now. The body of the first grader, and certainly of a seventh grader, belongs to him and shouldn't be abused in any way. And no one knows this better than a child. It will make him furious or afraid or even ashamed (for spanking can be a sexual stimulant).

A spanking not only hurts your sense of dignity—and his—but it doesn't work very well and it doesn't teach a child self-discipline either. He surely isn't going to

spank himself when he's bad and he may even misbehave again, as if the spanking gave him credit on the ledger.

Effective discipline is a matter of words, not actions, but the wrong ones can make matters worse. It's all right to say, "That was a dumb thing to do," but it is disparaging to say, "You are so dumb!" You know it isn't true, and if it were you wouldn't say it, because you wouldn't expect so much of him. Unfortunately, your child won't know that. Even if he still thinks he's smart, he won't believe you know it and after a while he may even think it isn't worth proving.

The effect of harsh words and long tirades varies from child to child, but it is always much worse than most parents think and the message will be remembered much longer. If it happens too often, he may decide to live up to your bad opinion.

Other negative techniques have other negative results.

- Complaints that start with "You," either spoken or implied, invite shame and eventually rebellion in even the most stalwart child, until he starts hurling accusations of his own and you'll be the target. Poor discipline always comes back to haunt you.
- Absolutes beg for an argument and teach you the most humbling lesson of all: a parent *must never* say *"always"*—or *"never"* or *"must."* These are the words you'll eat.

- Demanded promises are also fraught with trouble. To make a child promise to "be good" or "never to tease your little brother again" is to ask him to break his word and you'll both feel let down when he does.
- Sarcasm is another poor correction—a verbal spanking that leaves a child defenseless. You may tell yourself you're just being witty, but he won't see it that way. Humor is essential in a happy life, but it should attract, not divide.
- Comparisons won't make a child act better either, if he's on the down side. His big brother, his dad and the child down the street may never have done such a thing, but it's irrelevant to say so and it hurts and shames a child. It is also redundant, since he already compares himself to others when he's low. It's a game he never lets himself win and your comments will only add to his freight.
- Threats and bribes bring trouble too. If you tell your child he can have something special for being good, you're offering a bribe; if you say he will forfeit something he wants if he's bad, you're making a threat, and in both cases he—or you—will keep upping the ante as he gets older.

Threats and bribes also make a child anxious. "I'm going to tell Daddy if you don't do what I say" simply teaches a child that his behavior is for sale and teaches him to be afraid of his daddy too. And a Six who is bribed to go to bed on Tuesday is sure to demand a bigger treat by Friday and yet he won't feel good about it. A child who is manipulated feels helpless, but he feels even worse when he's allowed to pull the strings. He knows he can't handle such responsibility.

All of these verbal corrections should be avoided, but if you slip occasionally, it's not the end of the world. Only constant criticism, repeated day after day, makes a child feel worthless, and, to a lesser degree, so does the criticism he hears you make about him to someone else.

Since there are so many wrong ways to correct a child, it may seem there are no right ways. Not at all. There's just no point in using corrections that don't work or that make a child feel guilty or ashamed or afraid or angry. Positive discipline is much easier on everyone.

Positive Techniques

A wise parent is involved with the child and not with the problem, which is easier if you remind yourself how much you love him. This will help you separate him from the wretched thing he did and put the situation into perspective, so he will know that you believe in his innate goodness, whatever he has done. A child judges himself so sternly, he needs to know that you don't think he's such a bad person after all.

He will feel better about himself if you make many of your corrections in silence: a raised eyebrow; a frown; a negative nod of the head; a touch to the elbow that sticks out at dinner; a patting up with the palm of the hand to remind your child to stand when an adult comes into the room; or a closing of the thumb and the index finger until they almost touch, to remind him to lower his voice. A noisy child will also get quieter if you speak softly and any child will listen harder if he has to concentrate on what you say.

Whispering, in fact, is one of the best tricks you can use to correct your child in public. This may not suit Miss Manners, but it's better to whisper than to chastise a child in front of the sister who teases so much, or before his friend (or yours) or a teenage neighbor. And when you can't talk with him privately, tell him you will discuss the matter with him later—and be sure that you do.

First ask your child if he did the rotten deed and then listen carefully to his answers before you say what you feel, for your child won't pay attention to you until he's had his say. He needs to talk long enough to explain why he feels the way he does, for even a disobedient child has the right to be heard. If he feels no one is listening, he'll soon stop talking and you'll lose the most important link you have.

If he denies the deed, however, leave it at that but ask him if he knows why you would be so annoyed and then tell him how you would have felt, being as serious about it as if he said he had done it. A child usually will admit the truth when he understands how much it matters and, if he does, you kiss him and simply thank him for having the courage to be honest. This is enough to teach him a lesson.

He needs to know that it's love—and often fear—that makes you angry when he's late for dinner, because you are concerned about him, and not about the meal getting cold. And it's rejection that makes you mad when he forgets to wash the dog. The dog certainly doesn't mind—and deep in your heart, you don't mind either—but you do feel unloved when your child doesn't seem to care for you enough to obey. If you explain your feelings in a loving, detached way, you and your child will at least be dealing from the same deck. Candor is the key to a good relationship.

You need to stick to the point throughout the conversation, without calling him any names or using your standard clichés.

You'll want to be at eye level when you talk, and either hold his hand so you can tell quickly if you're going too far or saying too much, or sit a few feet from him, so he won't feel so threatened. The parents who seem to abuse their power are the ones who are most likely to lose it.

When none of this works—and it often won't—a child can be respected and still be scolded, by telling him that his behavior is annoying, boring, terrible or inappropriate, but not that he is a bother, a bore or a holy terror. A child always must feel he is accepted, even when his behavior is not.

Not all scoldings will be rational, if your child has provoked you too much. It's better to rely on a short if not so sweet reaction—perhaps a simple shriek of "I'VE HAD IT!"—on those occasions. Anything else is redundant, and likely to be personal and unkind too, unless you're quite disciplined yourself.

Or you can say, "Let's stop and replay this. If we could do it over again, how would you have acted? What should I have answered?" And then play it again and if you think he's learned from it—and you've learned—a correction may not be necessary at all. Little children re-enact their bad times when they play with their dolls—working out their anger and their anxieties until the scene seems right or they feel vindicated. Now you and your child can use each other—real live people.

While most poor behavior is spotty, it is much more frequent in some children, and they do better if only one problem is corrected at a time. Decide which habit bothers you most—the dallying or the nose picking or the interrupting—and concentrate on that habit until it's cured. It may take only a week for each correction, but expect two or three, so you won't be disappointed.

If you must punish your child for acting poorly, do it sparingly, without mentioning the errors of the past, but be sure to reward the good behavior too—in both cases as soon as it's noticed. You're trying to change his behavior, not score a point. Even occasional improvement merits a compliment or a hug, and he deserves a small, unexpected present or a thank-you note when he's behaved well many times. Behavior modification is the name of this game, and it works.

As long as you don't suffocate your child with demands to do more and more, he will learn to work for his freedoms, taking responsibility for ones that he loses temporarily, just as he takes credit for the ones he earns.

You also should handle all poor discipline yourself, if it occurs on your watch, unless it's so serious you and your husband must handle it together. By the same token, tell your child when you correct his behavior because it bothers someone else, even if you admit that it's not bothering you. If you don't, he'll notice the discrepancy and disobey, and that will make you angry.

No matter how understanding and fair you try to be, there will of course be times when you make mistakes. As you may have noticed, parents aren't perfect. To admit that you have bad feelings gives your child the right to have them too—and to admit that he does. This is especially important for a boy, since he is so often urged to "act like a little man." As long as a child knows he can express his anger with words—if he uses good manners—he's less likely to resort to action. When a child sees that you aren't Supermom, he doesn't feel he has to be Superchild.

And sometimes you're provoked too easily. It's important to tell your child that you may seem more stern than usual because you're depressed or anxious, and tell him exactly why, if you can be that open about it. It makes him feel better when he knows that you're fallible—something he's suspected for years—rather than think he's the cause of your unhappiness.

And when you overreact—out of either fear or anger—be sure to apologize, even if you have to wake your child in the night. You both will sleep easier for it. Love and kisses and sweet notes undo almost any mistake. You're teaching your child that people who love each other can disagree; that solutions can be found; that all can be forgiven; that we pay for our mistakes; that there are no yesterdays—and that parents must decide how much freedom the child has earned, which is seldom as much as he thinks.

You're on course if you can ask yourself, "How would I feel if my boss talked to me like that?" or "What if my husband did this to me?" or "What if my friends could see this scene on TV?"

If you don't flinch too much, you're doing all right.

Tantrums

Tantrums begin and end at home. Some schoolchildren continue them long after

nursery days, flailing at anyone who crosses them, but whether they are chronic or only occasional, they can't be tolerated. Even if there is a physical reason—which you'll need to check—your child can't be allowed to hit other members of the family. It just isn't civilized.

Stand behind this wild child, wrap your arms around him to contain his swings and rock him as you stand there, as gently as you can. And when he calms down—and you calm down—listen hard to what he says. A child doesn't resort to violence unless he feels he can't be heard any other way.

Even if he hits you, you shouldn't hit back, whether he's a slight Six or a husky Twelve. Nothing is going to make a child feel more ashamed than to hit someone too proud to run away and too controlled to fight back. If you respond, by action, words or (the most painful response) laughter, he will feel justified and will throw another tantrum the next time he's angry. It's the prospect of more guilt or shame that will control him, not your threats or your countermeasures or your own physical reprisals.

What a tantruming child needs, more than anything else, is isolation and, if that's not possible, restraint, but always with dignity, whispers and, if at all possible, privacy. Like any shouter, he also needs you to talk in a low voice, with an "I can't hear you, sweetie, for all the noise in the room." Whispers often do more to defuse anger than anything else, for they make the child concentrate on what's being said and this breaks the mindless replay that tantrums follow.

Sulks, Whines and Other Wretched Moods

Moodiness is another weapon in a child's arsenal—a tantrum turned inward. The occasional moody silence—perhaps once or twice a week—deserves tea and sympathy but, when a child is sulky, surly or whiny he deserves no more attention than he would get for a tantrum: almost none at all. If you reward a wretched mood you will surrender your authority, rather than seek a solution. Instead you have to teach your child to reach out for help when he needs it, by encouraging him to say exactly what's wrong. Otherwise, you probably will console him for the wrong problem, which will get him mad—because he'll think you should read his mind—and you'll get angry because you can't understand what's going on. Pretty soon you'll spend less time with him and your child will decide that even angry attention is better than none at all and pull the same stunt again and again. By the time he's a teenager his moods will control the household.

You have to change the behavior before it becomes a pattern. You do it by first asking what's wrong—and being patient enough to listen to some trivia before he gets to the point. However, if he says loftily, "It's nothing," or "You wouldn't understand," you tell him he obviously needs some time alone and send him to his room or on a walk until he feels better. When he returns, ask if he wants to talk, but if he's still cross, he goes back to his room, just as he would for a tantrum.

And when he's himself again—and any other time he's good company— give the best of yourself by confiding, listening, laughing, enjoying. This is what encourages a child to do the same.

Sassiness

There are many things you don't need from a child and one of them is backchat. If your child gets sassy, it's the steely eye, the raised brow, the stern jaw and the low, low voice that asks, "WHAT-DID-YOU-SAY?"

A child bold enough to repeat what he said deserves a terse "Please go to your room." Every parent has the right to be respected, and the duty to insist on it.

Sarcasm

Sarcasm is the traditional weapon of a bully who isn't big enough or daring enough to fight. The victim may try to soothe his own wounded feelings with

"Sticks and stones can break my bones
  But words will never hurt me."

However, anyone who has ever known the whip of mockery remembers its sting a long time.

You can only console your child when he's been hurt by sarcasm, helping him understand his friend—and helping him find other friends who are kinder. If, on the other hand, your child is sarcastic, he is probably copying someone he sees regularly: his best friend, his teacher—or his parents. This will tell you that it may be time to change your way of talking. Sarcasm only leads to more of the same, and more hurt feelings too.

Tattling

The tattletale is a lonely child, if not at first, then surely later. No matter how right he is, other children will resent and beware of him.

However, it takes two to make a tattle work, and the second player is usually good old Mom. It's a routine that is almost always learned, or at least perfected, at home. If your child hasn't a ready listener

to run to, he will soon get out of the habit. Even a visiting tattler should discover that it doesn't pay to play his game at your house.

You break the pattern when you block each new "Do you know what Johnny did . . ." with "STOP! Is anyone hurt? Is there blood? Is anything broken?" If the answer is no, then you say you don't want to hear about it. And don't listen, and don't go near the scene of the alleged crime. If you do, the child will know the tattling has worked.

Occasionally blood may run or something may break, but basically the children are learning to solve their problems all by themselves. And that's just what you want.

Selfishness

There is some selfishness inside us all and no one is more obvious about it than a child. In his early years he was like a primitive caveman, protecting his food and his possessions against invaders, and then he learned to make others—most often his parents—give him what he wanted. By first grade your child is probably more subtle. Now he begins to negotiate and trade with his buddies, and because they are just as selfish as he is, the exchange is usually rather equal.

If a child wants far more time and toys than are good for him, however, alarms should sound in your head. This will be a lifelong pattern unless you discover the cause and stop it now.

A child may be so coddled that he thinks he deserves it all, so unsure of himself that he tries to prop up his ego with things, or he may think that things are more important in his house than people. No matter what the cause, selfishness should be discouraged. You and your husband must first make an objective and possibly painful analysis of your own lives to see if his self-concern is a reflection of your own. If it is, you'll have to make a determined effort to change.

In any case you'll want to make sure your child learns the joys of giving—of making presents, of helping the poor, of sharing himself. If he's been coddled you might give him less of your attention and demand more of his, letting him know how much he matters but that you matter too. You may give him fewer presents too, limiting the number and cost to what you can realistically afford at birthdays and holidays, and never giving as many as the richest children get (even if you happen to be rich) or as much as he asks. Babies are born to make demands, so they will be protected, but children don't have to be babied now.

Rebellion

Every person in a relationship has offensive weapons—ones that are used to annoy others most—and they're nearly always subconscious. In a marriage the weapon may be money or sex or late nights at the office. Let the wife (or husband) show that some type of behavior hurts and husbands (or wives) will unknowingly use it when their own feelings get hurt.

In school the child may do his homework messily, because he's mad at his su-

per-neat teacher who makes him recite even though she knows that he lisps. She in turn will call on him to recite because he turns in such messy work.

A parent and child have weapons too, with one sending off signals and the other responding like clockwork. Each chooses the other's weapons, by being more upset by some misdeeds than others. Now your child learns to be sassy or lazy or to use more dirty words than most children his age, and he does it to show you who's really in charge when you draw a line in the dust. And when he goes too far, you may retaliate with the weapons he gave you, so you yell—because he looks scared when you yell—or you forget to tell him where you are, even though that's made him cry before. It's hard to resist using these tricks, but you can break the pattern if you're honest about your upsets when they happen. This teaches a child to be the same.

When he rebels, it's almost never over the matter at hand but over a piece of power that might be lost. This is because rebellion is born of fear—the fear that someone is blocking his path, taking away his right to grow. And because we never stop growing, it is the cause of rebellion at every age and in every relationship.

The child is especially vulnerable. If he is given too many orders, he doesn't have the chance to think for himself, which makes him angry, and if he's given too few, he doesn't learn to work with others—the skill he needs most of all. Without a proper sense of his own power, he feels not only angry but isolated, for only other rebels will want to be his friends.

You'll find rebellion peaks around Eleven, as it did at Two and Four, times when a child feels he must defy others so he can define himself. This breaking up extends to the tip of the toes he taps on the floor, as his body jumps and twitches with all his energy and emotions bursting to get out.

You'll need to correct him for specific misbehavior but try not to make an issue of his new attitude. It may not be too charming, but it is necessary. You also have to remember that your child isn't a puppy in obedience class, nor is he someone to moan to your friends about. This would only embarrass him and put a distance between you, as it would if your husband told everyone that you were cross because your period was due.

Even if some of your child's emotions are triggered by hormones of his own, he still needs to feel he is in charge of his behavior. He knows it's a bit different, and it isn't lovely, but he still is doing what he should: growing up and out.

If these episodes are handled well, and if a child is allowed to grow in spite of his fidgets and fusses, the rebellions of the high school years should be no worse than those between Six and Twelve, although the issues will be more important.

Dillydallying

Dillydallying can drive a parent bonkers, which is probably why most children develop it to an art. It's another game that takes two to play and, if you wait for your dallying child, you're playing. You may not realize it, but when your child is late—he's demanding that you obey him. And when you permit it (even though you shriek, threaten or punish), you're permitting it.

The way to break his habit is to quit waiting, which is especially effective when it means he will miss something he enjoys. If he is late for dinner, start without him. And when he ambles in twenty minutes late, make no special comment about it—just hand over his plate. Finish eating (and rather quickly too) and pull a dessert from the freezer—a treat he won't have time to have. Food isn't used here as a reward but to help your child decide if dillydallying is worth an ice cream sundae.

When you plan to go to the movies, tell your child you'll give him only one advance call, and then one more when you're ready to leave. He either is ready or

he stays with the sitter you have arranged, promising her a cancellation fee if she isn't needed, or an extra fee for staying and sticking to some special rules: no treats, no television, no stories, no late bedtime—just a sitter who sits and reads or sews or talks on the phone and invites neither the company nor the conversation of the dallier.

Repeat as often as needed: an invitation to join the family, and a treat that's missed when he's late, and of course an occasional surprise treat when he's on time. This will work, but only if you don't shout or argue or fuss or beg or hurry him, and you never, ever negotiate. Instead, you keep your temper and smile. It isn't so hard. After all, you're making the rules.

Running Away

Some children try to handle their problems by running away, especially that dear drear, the Seven.

This is the age when his own good sense tells him that (1) nobody loves him; (2) he was swapped in the cradle; and (3) you'll be plenty sorry when he's gone.

Since the last is terribly true, this is no time to help him pack. Instead he needs you to forbid the going—so he can change his mind in dignity—and to hold him close, so he can know what's in your heart. You don't hold back extra loving when a child needs it most.

Your child also needs you to do some serious listening. Like any mother who has wanted to escape (and what mother

hasn't?), this child is full of anger and despair. When he can get rid of these feelings, home will seem like heaven and he will know he's still an angel to you.

Messy Room

Nowhere else does a child express his feelings so clearly as in the way he keeps his room. It is, after all, HIS ROOM, as he will tell you plonkingly, and, as he will say in his sassier moments, you don't even have the right to go into it. You do, of course. You not only have the right but the responsibility. It's the parent's job to check the storm windows, the state of the sheets, the general level of garbage. Your child may think it's his room, but no roach or mouse honors a threshold.

There also has never been a child who always remembered to shut his door every time he walked out of it. The chaos it exposes is sure to make you mad, which is normal. A child doesn't have the right to offend you—or your friends—with his mess, any more than you have the right to leave a messy living room that would embarrass him before his friends. Each person in the house is a member of a community, and each is required to help make life pleasant for the others.

Your child also doesn't have the right to cause a scene every morning or make his sister late for school because he can't find his homework or because all his clothes on the floor have turned out to be dirty.

This is not to say that a child is supposed to keep a perfect room. All children are fairly messy because they don't know how to organize either their possessions or their time. Even though your standards can be reasonably low, a child must try to keep his space presentable and succeed at least some of the time. Good habits, planted now, will become ingrained. He may rebel when he's a teenager, as a declaration of independence, but he'll return to tidiness when he's grown.

Right now he must be taught how to

housekeep and schedule his efforts. A child learns best if he is expected to pitch in with the general family housework and to help clean some neutral area, like the den. Here he works alongside you, learning how to tidy a room, one table at a time; to sweep—from one side of the room to the other; to vacuum without tripping over the cord at every turn (still a tough trick for this mom); to dust the things that are low and high as well as those that are at his eye level.

He will begin to translate some of this into his own roomkeeping, but not much, unless you help. Compliment him on his room whenever you can and don't kid him about his collections. You certainly wouldn't like it if he made fun of your things.

Have him begin by making the bed because it is so conspicuous it makes the whole room look cleaner. After that it's one thing at a time, so the job doesn't seem so formidable. First it's the bureau top; then the night table, then the desk, and finally, after all the surfaces are picked up, he sweeps the floor, including the part beneath the bed although a leaf rake often works better. Those things are then put away. As long as you let him decide where things go and what to do next, and you have him do most of the work with as much praise as you can muster, he'll learn how to keep his room better, some of the time. While you may vacuum and wipe the furniture and the fingerprints, you only do it when he leaves the room fairly clean. It's not a mother's job to tidy the room of a Six, and certainly not of a Twelve. Your once-a-month bit of help won't be enough for him to keep the room neat for the other twenty-nine days, but it will improve after he finishes college (several years after, in fact).

The child who is outrageously messy all of the time requires more specific attention. He is acting not only out of habit and ineptitude but out of a need to show you that he has some control over his own life. For this you have to examine why he feels so crowded and what restraints, corrections and orders you can abandon. The weather forecast can tell a child whether to wear a sweater as well as you can and if it's wrong—well, no doubt your own forecasts have been wrong once or twice.

In a month or so this super-messy child will keep his room cleaner, because the pressure is less and he's no longer so angry. Now you realize that he doesn't hear you when you say, "You're so sloppy I can't stand it." He does, however, when you say, "I'm proud to see the work I put into painting this room and making the bedspreads and curtains, but when it's messy my work seems worthless." The first puts him on the defensive, the second calls for his understanding.

His empathy won't be enough to make him neat, of course. You will also have to institute a new program but only if you're willing to spend a month or so as a policeman and think you can do it with a reasonably good temper. Theres's no point in giving your child an opportunity to drive you out of your mind.

Have him begin with a clean room, which you have helped him clean without rolling your eyes or making any negative comments. From then on he'll have to get ready for bed ten minutes earlier than usual, to get his gear ready for morning and to put dirty clothes in the hamper, shoes in the closet, trash in the basket and to put away the things that are on and under the bed and all over the floor, all without listening to the radio.

And then he calls you to have it checked—a key part of the plan. It takes no time at all for a child to learn to say, "I'm finished," if he knows you won't look at it.

And if it takes longer than ten to fifteen minutes to clean the room, he'll have to go to his room that much earlier the next night, and each night he goes up earlier and earlier if he must. If it takes him more than a half hour to clean his room at night, you or your husband should sit in the room with him, read a book and say nothing at all while he picks up his things. If a clean room doesn't mean that much to him, you'll have to show him it means that much to you. In the morning he should only have to hang up his pajamas and make his bed (a matter of dragging a quilt over the sheet should be fine).

If he improves too slowly, you may decide to collect anything left out of place at night and keep it until he's earned it back with a clean room, except, of course, school clothes, shoes and books and anything else that would make you return it the next morning—while he smirks. This routine is going to take a few weeks to instill, and then only if you check it each night. Do it all with a tolerant eye and a decent amount of humor. A messy room is not a great sin; it shouldn't be treated like one.

The child who remains determinedly messy may have to pay you to clean his room—a painful moment when he receives his allowance with one hand and forks most of it back with the other.

Slowly your child learns the key to good housekeeping, and a little sooner than it was learned by the father of our flock, who kept house for himself for a few days—the first time in thirty years.

"Do you know," he said with awe, "if you pick up as you go along, everything stays neat!"

Laziness

There is no such thing as a lazy child. He may be a quiet, thoughtful sort of person who thinks before he moves or he may be bored or he may be afraid or depressed or he may be growing so fast he needs extra rest. Maybe he's even slightly sick all the time. But lazy? Nonsense.

When a child drags around doing the least amount of work he can but has all the energy he needs for the things he wants to do, he's just telling you that he and his time are important—and that he resents it when you act as if they're not. No one likes to be ordered around, especially if he can't see the reason or if he has had no voice in making the plans. He may act lazy if he feels your expectations are beyond him, because he hasn't been taught how to do a job.

Mothers, like children, are new to their game. It takes experience before you know how much a child can handle, not just once, but time after time.

Sibling Rivalry

If you have more than one child, you have sibling rivalry. No family is immune. The third child resents the fourth; the second resents the third—and the first resents them all.

Actually, a little sibling rivalry does no harm. Although he won't be so bald about it, your child will use the same techniques,

on a team or in a crew or in a dormitory or an office, and they will work about as well—or as poorly—as they work now. Much depends on the allowances you make—and don't make—now.

The rivalry may take its sharpest form in disputes over turf. Each child deserves a nook to call his own and a few things that are particularly his, but you don't want to encourage possessiveness much further or the children will be in constant contention. A parent caters to this touchiness if she insists that each child has his own room and each is sacred; that they take turns using the playroom; that toys should be duplicated, rather than shared; that clothes shouldn't be handed down to a child who objects. Just because a child feels sensitive about something this Tuesday is no reason to take it seriously every day of every week.

Nor do you want to let your children trade malicious insults or hit each other. An explosion or two a day is normal, but they should end quickly and be fairly low key and quiet, because nobody has the right to upset the harmony of the house— or the parents. Your children may also say what's on their minds a couple of times a day but they'll have to learn to say it more quietly until eventually they become the best little hissers on the block.

If they get into a squabble you can't ignore, don't join the fray. It's one thing for them to be rivals for your attention but you'll be the target if you get in the middle. Instead walk away with one of the contestants, talk to him, defuse him by listening. And yes, chastise a little. And then talk with the other child privately and sympathize and empathize (and chastise). By then both children are so tired of this talking and understanding and chastising that they are usually quite glad to make up and drop the whole thing. If not, send them to sit in separate rooms—preferably with a chore to do—until they're less disagreeable to have around.

Basically, siblings rival not out of anger toward each other but out of competition.

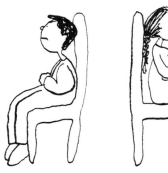

Each child wants more than an equal share of his parents. They also may think you or your husband favors one child more than the other (and the one who's talking never considers himself the favorite). You fan this flame if you tell one child you can't give her tap classes because you have to buy glasses for her sister. In truth, you can't afford the lessons because you also must pay for food, mortgage, utilities and, incidentally, glasses. In a family, money is dipped from the common well.

Attention, however, is not. Each child still needs ten to fifteen minutes a day from each parent just as you gave them as preschoolers. This is their sacred time, when they only talk about their interests, without being corrected or told what you want from them. Each child also deserves a special treat occasionally, going out for supper or fishing or to look at the stars with one or both parents, but no other children. If you treat children as separate individuals, you show them that each is like no one else in the world and each is loved as an individual.

If you're still accused of favoring one child more than the other—then maybe you are. Parents are human too. This is inevitable to some degree if the favored child is handicapped, but it happens in all families. You're likely to give extra attention to the child who is going through a more charming stage, or is in such a rough patch that he needs more handholding. Analyze the situation as objectively as you can and explain to the jealous child why the other one needs so much attention. You then compensate as much as possible by taking the child who feels neglected on routine errands that turn into interesting expeditions. If you can treat this child more like an equal, some of the envy will disappear, for he sees that he is special too.

Sometimes the younger child feels jealous, especially if the children are of the same sex. A Seven is the ultimate hero-worshiper and yet the older child may respond with disdain to this tagalong who's always in the way. It's up to you to explain to the other child how much attention means to the younger one and ask him to give fifteen minutes a day too, without making a production of it. He can challenge the younger one to a checker game, talk with him about school or, if he's busy with homework of his own, give him some easy arithmetic problems or ask him to look up some words for a paper he's writing, so the spelling will be right. These small attentions—and a few overheard compliments to his friends—may seem like a bother at first to the other child, but he'll find it's much less trouble than a child who teases, pokes and tattles to be noticed.

The fine art of friendship is learned at home.

Lying

All children lie and that's a fact. Parents have to distinguish between defensive lies, which are symptoms of other problems, and tales simply told out of exuberance.

When a child defends himself by lying repeatedly—and it's amazing how a child can stand you down—he may come to enjoy it, getting a fresh dose of adrenaline every time he gets away with it. It's addictive stuff, which is why you can't let a single lie go by. Habitual lying may even require family therapy. It's important to heal the family as well as cure the symptom.

Your child won't lie often, however, unless he's very bored, needs to feel like a hotshot, painfully wants attention—or is afraid of what will happen if he tells the truth. If any of these possibilities seem likely, it's important to find out which, so you can handle it the right way. You'll want to give him more loving if he feels low and more adventures if he tells tall tales to add pizzazz to his life.

Six-year-olds tend to tell whoppers, although they aren't as extravagant as they were at Four. Once again you congratulate your child for being a fine storyteller and ask him to write the story down. Instead of noticing the spelling, punctuation and handwriting, praise the tale and type it,

but without errors. It's a fine compliment to your child, whether you ask him to hang it on the bulletin board or enter it in a contest in a children's magazine. Either way, it helps him separate fact and fancy.

Perhaps nothing encourages a child to lie more than a baited question. To ask, "Who spilled the milk?" when the spiller is obviously either the child or the canary, invites a child to blame the canary, or at least say, "I dunno." Instead you ask, "How did this happen?" or simply say, "Come on, sport" (or "Dammit to hell" or whatever), "when you spill milk, you clean up milk."

And you both get down on your hands and knees with two sponges (for you would expect his help if you had spilled something) and clean up the mess together. You then have him do a bit more until the floor looks better than it did before. You don't fuss any more about it and you surely don't cry over spilled milk. Save your tears for the important calamities.

It's the lying out of fear that should trouble you most. Despite white lie alibis at every age and some slipups at Eleven, honesty is usually one of the hallmarks of the preteen. If it isn't, you want to take a long, serious look at your relationship. This is the child who would rather hide behind a lie than be yelled at or embarrassed in public or punished—or risk losing love and respect. He may lie to protect his friends too, for he loves them almost as much as himself. These lies are also born of fear—that his friends will be yelled at or embarrassed or punished or they might feel unloved if he told the truth.

Even if your child keeps lying in the face of logic and understanding you still don't call him a liar. Instead you tell him that you are unhappy because you can't make yourself believe he is telling the whole truth—and then a long pause to give him time to tell it. You may have to talk five to ten minutes, with more long pauses, but be careful neither to accuse nor disparage him. If you accuse and you're wrong on even one point, he will feel vindicated. This conversation may get emotional, but it won't escalate into a bad argument if you talk about your feelings and his, rather than his failings. A child fights back most when he's pinned into a corner.

If he still doesn't come clean, the subject is dropped. You don't discipline a child at all on incomplete evidence. Even if your intuition were right, it wouldn't be fair, because sooner or later he would be in trouble for something he didn't do and he wouldn't feel safe enough with you to tell the truth. The only time you charge a child with lying is when your judgment is supported by unimpeachable eyewitness reports, more objective than those given by a sister or brother—or a hysterical neighbor. Otherwise, give him the benefit of the doubt. If he is guilty he may confess when you sit by his bed at night in the dark and say you love him, no matter what (although you won't mention what What is), or he may need quite a few conversations, involving quite a number of lies on his part, to feel secure enough to tell the truth.

And when he does, he is thanked and congratulated for being brave enough to admit what he did. And if he must be disciplined, make sure he knows that it's for the deed and not for telling the truth. In fact, the truth should lessen the price he pays, and he should know that too.

He may lose one of his freedoms temporarily or have to make amends in some other way, or you may do nothing at all, if you think the talk has caused anguish enough. It's a matter of your own style and your own heart. You want your child to understand that liars who get away with it still carry a sack of shame, and truth weighs nothing at all.

Cheating

A child cheats for many reasons, and they vary with the age. It's so important to win a game at Six or Seven and sometimes at Eight that a child will cheat outrageously and lie in the face of discovery, for winning to him is a sign of competence. At the same time he may accuse others of cheating or disparage the practice: we are all inclined to see our own worst traits in others. It's like a mirror for the wicked witch.

A Nine and certainly a Ten should feel secure enough to lose a game. There may be some slipups the next year, however, for Eleven is not such a moral age. By Twelve any cheating you see is a sign of a problem, of a self-confidence too low or pressure too great, unless he's just being a dear big brother who is letting his little sister win.

A child may cheat at school if he is told he must get straight A's regularly if he "ever wants to get into a decent college" (or "have a decent job" or "earn a decent amount of money"). Pressure can also come from children in the class, who pass on the warnings they get at home. Still more pressure comes from teachers, particularly in private schools, who press for these goals or look the other way when children cheat, as if the good marks of their students mean they're successful too.

You can offset their effect, directly and indirectly, by curbing the cheating urge early. At Six and Seven you chuckle or raise your eyebrow in a card game and say that you remember when you used to make up special rules too, and how mad your brother would get—and then you stop playing competitive card and board games until your child can handle them better.

You have to handle cheating in school differently, asking your child if there is much cheating in class, the way you would ask if there is much homework. And if he says "Only Joey," you can say, "What a waste," and point out how tempting it can be to cheat, how happy you are that he doesn't, how bad it would make him feel inside, and how futile it is.

If he says that almost everyone cheats, he needs to be told, and told many times, that he goes to school to learn, not to pass tests. That's why you congratulate this child—and any child—on the effort he makes to prepare for a test and the imagination of his answers, not on the grade. Even a failed test probably has something that deserves a compliment, as well as sympathy. Your child also needs to know that a failure tells him what he needs to study, perhaps in a different way, and not that he is stupid.

A child judges himself harshly, and may feel the teacher judges him with such finality that he needs as much support from you as you can give. It also eases the pressure at home. The child who is criticized on all sides may feel he has to cheat to escape it.

The moral question of cheating is almost as great for the cheatee. To be asked if someone can look on your paper, or to know that someone is looking, can mortify a child. It's best to advise him how to handle this problem before it happens, if you can, especially if he is the class whiz. If he says he hates to have anyone use his answers because he would hate to have anyone copy his mistakes, it won't seem quite so snippy as a simple no. And if that doesn't work, he'll have to see the teacher in privacy and ask to move his desk, so he can pay attention better, without mention-

ing the cheating problem at all. Some teachers might make a scene about it.

Since cheating is a problem as early as the first grade, your child may as well get a philosophy about it as soon as he can—and it might as well be yours.

Fighting

A child must fight his own battles if he is to be his own man—or her own woman—but nothing makes a parent wince more.

It was Mike, a Seven, surrounded by sisters and still holding his own, who decided to take on the world, starting with the rough and tough ten and twelve-year-olds who played in the schoolyard next door.

Every day he would go forth and join them, only to come home weeping: the big boys had pushed him around. His sisters clucked; his mother intervened; the big boys squirmed, and the little kid got another chance. And then one day it became clear from the kitchen window: Mike was taunting the big boys. Once again he came home in tears, but this time he was sent back alone, to finish what he had started—a scene that was watched in tears too, for he certainly didn't win. He did, however, learn an important lesson: that a child who taunts must take the consequences.

Fighting is normal in childhood, but it's not to be encouraged. Much of it is curbed by the limits you set and by circumstances too. Many fights have been stopped before they started by something as fortuitous as the bell after lunch (it's amazing how many fights begin just a little too late), while others don't get started because the children are visiting somebody whose parents put a stop to it. Children instinctively learn to allow for a graceful retreat.

Other fights never happen because of the rules at school or camp but it's the limits you set that prevent most fights. You do it by teaching your child not to hit anyone smaller or weaker than he is, be-

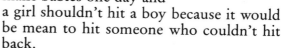

cause he would have an unfair advantage, or not to taunt anyone younger, since that child may not have the wisdom to argue with words. He also can't hit anyone who wears braces, which could cut the child's mouth, or a child with glasses, who couldn't see well enough to fight without them. And, of course, a boy shouldn't hit a girl because she may make babies one day and a girl shouldn't hit a boy because it would be mean to hit someone who couldn't hit back.

Fighting is off limits at home, of course. There will be some wrestling among children—especially between boys—and if it's rough enough they may have to be sent to different rooms until they're bored enough to be sociable, but actual fighting should never be permitted in the family. It's uncivilized.

Some experts will tell you to let a child hit a doll or a punching bag, and pretend it's her sister, but mothers know better. A child needs to take out his anger by doing something constructive, like washing the dog or planting some bulbs. To hit someone, even a substitute doll, would emphasize the child's most negative feelings. Never forget: a family is a microcosm of society. If a child can learn to negotiate at home, then maybe wars will end. Make sure your child finds the peaceful solution whenever he can, which is more likely if you regularly listen to his side in the family arguments, almost as hard as you listen to yourself. The child who feels he's never heard anyway is much more likely to let his fists do the talking for him.

Neighborhood Quarrels

Sooner or later every child causes a scene between his parents and a neighbor unless you live so far out of town that you don't have any neighbors. If it isn't tulips stolen for the teacher, it's a baseball through their window or dirty words shouted in their yard when he thought they were away. While you want to listen to the neighbor with care, and with an apology if she was offended, you still withhold judgment until you've talked with your child. Every story has at least two sides.

First tell your child that he has been accused—but not that you accuse him—and tell him if there were any eyewitnesses too—for you don't want to set him up. Only then do you ask him what happened and how. If he was with other children, assure him that his involvement is the only one that matters to you and, if he wants to accept sole responsibility, that's fine with you. If the charge is true and he's not too scared, a child usually will admit it, and then he has to apologize to the neighbor, by note or in person, either with you or alone. For the younger child, it's best to visit, so he won't be so embarrassed to see her next time, but he'll need your company.

A face-to-face encounter also helps a child realize how his friskiness can upset someone and lets him explain how it happened, with you slipping in some points of defense he may be too rattled to remember. You don't, however, say it really wasn't his fault or tell your neighbor the names of other children involved.

The matter should end on a reasonable note as long as no one makes direct accusations. If there is any damage, your family pays the cost as soon as possible (for families stick together). Your child—even a first grader—then pays you back, in money or services, although it may just be a token of the whole price. To him it will seem like all. And if your child caused some of the damage and some unnamed friends caused the rest, he still must pay it back by getting what he can from those friends. Since a true friend will come forward on his own, this is a tidy lesson to help your child choose his friends a little better.

For the child who swears he wasn't involved, stand by him, no matter what niggling doubts you have. That's what a family is for. A child's honor—and a family's honor—comes before your neighbor's regard. And if your child admits he was the culprit a month (or a year) later, you go to the neighbor as if it happened yesterday and make amends. And because at least one belated admission usually happens, sooner or later, it's best to make no ringing accusations of your own when you first defend your child.

Crow tastes terrible.

Cruelty

A second grader rushes to another child in the playground and says, "Nyah, nyah, nyah! Your mommy took one look at you and she got all crippled!" and the other child flies home without permission, running pell-mell against traffic, wailing to her arthritic mother to say it isn't so. And the teacher clucks and says, "Children are so cruel." Actually, they aren't.

Two years before, that little boy had walked into a room in time to see his father have a heart attack and die, and he thought he knew a terrible secret: he was too ugly for his father to stand. This wasn't a cruel child; this was a child who had a pain too big to keep inside. Every now and then he had to pass a piece of it along to someone else.

Other cruelty—verbal or physical—reflects the confusions at home, the way he is disciplined, the insecurities he feels, the frustrations he can't handle, or simply the manners he hasn't been taught. There also are times when words don't come out right, or they come out when they shouldn't.

Ordinarily a child won't try to hurt someone else, although it happens. This isn't because he is mean but because he is direct, he is honest, he is inept in the social graces, or he doesn't know how to handle his anger and it erupts in wild words, or a kick in the shins.

Whether the child is awkward or anxious, and whether he is your child or someone else's, he still gets treated the same way. You take him aside, as inconspicuously as possible, and help him understand why he has made someone quite sad, and that you expect him to apologize. And not only that, but you say it without hurting his feelings, for you can't ask for empathy unless you're being empathic yourself. You ask this child how he'd feel if someone said that to him and he'll say, "Fine," but slowly he learns what is acceptable and particularly what is not acceptable in your house.

Bigotry is another form of cruelty that hurts as much as any other, and it shouldn't be tolerated either. Perhaps the best way to make your child understand is to tell his own latest ethnic joke back to him—but make the people belong to his own nationality or religion or school or even his own street. It's amazing how unfunny a joke can get when it lives in your house.

And if your child is the victim of some particularly cruel comment, you hold him close and let him spew out his anger—quietly and in private, if possible—and then wonder out loud why the other child needed to hurt him so much and if something else could be bothering that child. By helping your child imagine how he would feel if his parents were separated or if his kitten had just died, he begins to put that comment into perspective. This may seem too advanced for a child, but it's not. Even a preschool child is sensitive to others and by Seven is quite understanding if you let him grouse before you explain. It will be years, however, before he can appreciate the sorrow of another person half as well as he appreciates his own.

It's as important for your child to understand the pain in others as it is to understand it in himself and to realize that it is the unlovable child who needs love the most—a concept he won't come by unless you say it first (and second and third).

The emphasis a family places—or doesn't place—on kind words and gentle

deeds will guide your child's behavior and help him choose friends wisely. This will help him keep that generosity of spirit he was born to have, so he will be blessed down all the days—and so will all who know him.

Stealing

Stealing is serious but not necessarily alarming, especially at certain ages. In the first grade a child is still so egocentric, he feels that what Johnny wants Johnny must have, and since his horizons have broadened he sees many things he wants, and is likely to take direct action now and then. The urge to steal is also strong among many preteens, when shoplifting often becomes a fad at school. This kind of stealing is serious, but it shouldn't be a cause for despair at these or any ages.

You can help curb the urge and prevent some, if not all, stealing by emphasizing the hard fact that your child would be taking someone else's property, causing

THE TALISMAN

When a child thinks his rotten character may take over in spite of his best intentions, he can always resort to magic.

Find a small, round stone, so unusual it can't be confused with any other and so smooth it begs to be rubbed in the hand. Wash it, oil it and give it to your child in great solemnity, telling him it's full of magic. He just has to keep it in his pocket and rub it in his hand whenever he feels the slightest temptation to steal or to do anything he shouldn't do. It will give him strength, you'll tell him—and indeed it will, for he will remember your words and your wrath when he gets the urge.

For the child with holey pockets or careless ways—or the girl who wears dresses instead of jeans—the talisman can be a handsome foreign coin, which you can buy at the main office of a city bank. Shine it very well, have a jeweler drill a hole near the rim and put it on a leather thong so it can be worn around the neck. The purpose is the same: to rub it when the will gets weak—and no one need ever know why.

Until a child can build his character from within, a little help from without is much appreciated.

that person to suffer a real and often painful loss.

When Sam was Six his mother found that he had swiped some change from her purse again, but this time she didn't say much. Instead she took him with her to the bank and cashed her paycheck without depositing any of it. Then she brought him home and spread the money out on the table. Sam was in awe. There seemed to be so much—twenties and tens and fives and ones; half dollars; quarters, dimes, nickels and even some pennies. Clearly they were rich.

He wanted to go out for hamburgers and fries right then and there but first, his mom said, they would divide it up and see how much would be left after the bills were paid. And so they did. They counted out the money for the phone bill and tucked it into an envelope marked TELEPHONE. And then the money to pay the gas bill and the electric bill and the rent and the insurance and the two department stores and the gasoline credit card and the sitter went into their own envelopes.

They also set aside the typical hefty amount for food—the ordinary day-in, day-out meals they had at home; a little for the cleaners and the shoemaker; some money to buy new jeans for his sisters and a present for Sam to take to a birthday party on Saturday. Finally there were the routine expenses, like bus money, lunch money and allowances for all so mother and children each had a little for treats and for church.

Some money was reserved for an emergency, since everyone has to expect the unexpected, and a few dollars for the savings account. They then counted what was left: $9.82 for the next two weeks. This went into an envelope of its own marked PLAY MONEY, to be used by the whole family.

Sam's mother also talked about the people to whom she paid her money and how hard it would be for the sitter if there wasn't enough to pay her (and how hard it would be on their mom if her boss gave

her less salary than usual). This, she explained, was why the money in those envelopes couldn't be spent any other way.

It was almost all Sam needed to go straight. From then on he knew that if he took money from an envelope with a bill from a creditor in it, he would be taking it from somebody, and if he took any Play Money, he would be taking it from everybody.

And then, to be safe, his mom put most of the money she owed others back in the bank, for Sam at Six could think of others, but naturally he thought of himself first. There was no point in putting temptation in his way. It takes a long time for a child to walk in someone else's shoes, but Sam had learned a certain amount because his mother knew a young child needs concrete examples to learn about abstract principles.

Sonny, at Six, had a different problem. He was a person of great charm and bravado and humor, and he usually had great confidence too. When first grade began, however, he found it quite different from day care, kindergarten and visits to Grandma: all the confidence he had stored began to flutter away like feathers in the wind. So he began to look for comfort and reinforcement and he found it in things. And like most other Sixes, his conscience was rather undeveloped and his eyes were bigger than his allowance.

First he slipped a tiny silver penknife from his baby-sitter's key chain. He was soon found out—since he displayed it rather openly—and he had the embarrassment of taking it back, with a written apology.

Still he moved on to greater crimes. He picked up the housekeeper's wages from the kitchen table and stuffed the bills in his coin purse. He was soon apprehended and wailed as he told her he was sorry. He also lost his right to go trick or treating, for the next day was Halloween. It was a just, if not a sweet, dessert.

And then he took four silver dollars from his best friend at school and said he found them on the sidewalk. He had to apologize to his friend while his mother, his friend's mother, the principal and the school social worker all stood around him in a grave circle. It was, everyone thought, an unforgettable scene. And to make it more unforgettable, his beloved, old-fashioned uncle warned that he'd get an old-fashioned pants-down spanking if he ever did it again.

Like many an embarrassed rake, Sonny publicly embraced religion. He asked that grace be said at every meal, and led it himself. Sanctimony could have been his middle name.

It was a week later that his mother opened his lunchbox to add a piece of fruit and found his auntie's tiny antique clock beneath his peanut butter and jelly sandwich. Despair hung over the household. And then a month passed and Sonny was Seven and he never stole again. He had been, it turned out, an enthusiastic, sensual Six, under new pressures, and he just couldn't resist very well.

Most children don't get such virulent urges, nor have such rich and eclectic tastes, but you'll have to deal quickly and firmly with any kind of stealing, at any time. If the evidence is clear, ask why your child did it, not if, for that only invites an evasion. And if the intensity continues in the second grade, consider some family therapy to get him back on the track. This is the same solution you'll need for any child who steals for years—even though he may not take much—or when you have a preteen who steals from friends rather than stores. In this case, it may reflect anger, or a need for revenge, or such low self-esteem that the child thinks he needs money to impress people.

For Sonny, however—and for most children in the primary grades—stealing was irresistible but temporary and much of it revolved around a need to integrate his life so that home and school had more unity. Although Sonny was disciplined at home—and certainly deserved it—the displeasure of his teacher and his friends

probably would have stopped him anyway and so would his developing sense of empathy.

Shoplifting

After a few years, when you've forgotten all about the wayward ways of your light-fingered first grader, you may find yourself living with a shoplifting fool, whether you have a boy or a girl. An Eleven is almost as egocentric now as he was at Six. These are the times when he thinks of the shopowner as a rich merchant (if he thinks of him at all), while he's one of the deserving poor.

In both cases, however, a child steals whatever seems irresistible. When he's young, he takes from anyone—friend or stranger—and from anywhere—private homes or the most public stores—but for most preteens the store is the only target and the items they take fit in nicely with the grown-up things they want now.

Some children shoplift if they feel cheated by Life and they think they can take whatever they want, but basically, shoplifting is a puberty rite. While it usually happens at Eleven, it may occur at Twelve (or later or not at all), with the time depending on the influence of his friends and the sophistication of the child. Cer-

tainly the preteens in south-side Chicago grow up quicker than the ones in south-side Virginia, and they may experiment with many things much sooner too, and not always wisely. The younger the child, the harder it is to juggle abstract ideas and behave according to the consequences.

Much of the shoplifting would never happen, however, if there were more supervision of preteens and better security in stores. This is not to excuse the shoplifter—for a preteen is old enough to know right from wrong—but to remind you to speak out against shoplifting before it happens—by talking about it openly, commending the children who can resist temptation and pitying those who need to steal to show how grown up they are.

You also will want to ask your child if there is much shoplifting in his crowd and to avoid the children who do it, especially when they go shopping together, because he wouldn't want the clerks to suspect him too. It's important for children to do much of their own shopping now, but they should do it within a reasonable time. To wander about a shopping mall for hours with their friends—long after everyone has spent their money—invites temptation as well as embarrassing comments from clerks who have learned to suspect any aimless young shopper.

Shoplifting should be considered a real possibility if your child has a surprising amount of shampoo, comic books, trinkets or maybe a package of cigarettes, for this is embarrassing to buy and yet many children experiment with smoking now. You may be told they were presents from his friend (for whom he was just holding the cigarettes), and if by chance they are, he should be expected to return them, since he can't accept more than he can afford to give.

If you think your child shoplifts and he doesn't admit it, you should tell him what you suspect and why. Tell him as gently as you can, allow for the possibility that you are wrong and say the suspicion itself is causing a break between you. If he

CORRECTIONS FOR PARENTS

A child doesn't deserve all the corrections. Take five minutes at the end of the day to review what went right, what went wrong and what you did to help it go in either direction. When you recognize your part, you'll be encouraged to repeat the good techniques and replace the bad ones.

still denies it in the face of your logic and instincts, let the subject lie.

If you know for a fact that your child shoplifts—either because he told you or because he got caught—you will have to take the sternest of measures: a tough lecture and the return of the goods to the store manager—with you at his side to make sure he does it. Your child may have to lose privileges too, unless he is clearly so dismayed that a punishment would be redundant.

Getting caught may be the best (as well as the worst) thing that can happen to a child, for it is so mortifying that the practice usually ends. Otherwise the problem may escalate, making him think of himself as a successful rebel—and act accordingly. Once you've whistled on Sunday, there's no turning back.

One boy we know succumbed to the shoplifting fad at his school and got caught on his third theft—slipping away with a candy bar and a dirty book. His father was finally located after he'd spent a teeth-chattering hour with a burly security guard at his side. The bill was paid, the child signed the mortifying pledge to keep out of the store for six months and he went home to an hour of somber disappointment from his parents. In this case, there was no need for further punishment because guilt and shame so obviously prevailed. Not only did he steadfastly refuse to steal but he began to make his shoplifting friends return what they took, and when they demurred, he slipped the items back on the shelf himself. Store-stuffing had replaced shoplifting.

Even the most remorseful shoplifter should get more than a stiff lecture if this is a second offense. You'll want to guide him into more supervised activities—and perhaps new friends—so he won't be tempted so much, and he should lose selected privileges until you have proof that he is more mature, but don't take away more than you can monitor.

If shoplifting is treated as a minor occurrence, or if your child's sudden accumulation of pocket knives, makeup or batteries is ignored as a swap with a friend, you will be ignoring your own responsibilities and at your child's expense. Shoplifting should never be treated lightly at this or any age.

Dirty Words

The vocabularies of boys and girls have changed a great deal in the past fifty years—especially the dirty words. Over a half century ago on a little island in Maine, a Six named Faith said the first four-letter word she'd learned. The father told her it was a word she shouldn't say aloud and, when she asked why, he said that if, for example, she said it to old Mrs. Jones down the road, Mrs. Jones would drop dead with the shock, and that would be the end of their weekly tea parties. And that is how little Faith learned to mind her *p*'s and *q*'s (and *f*'s).

Bad words—especially scatological words—are the secret treasures of elementary school. Jokes about the bathroom are considered uproarious in the early years, but by preadolesence it's the sex words that matter the most. Don't be too

alarmed. That doesn't mean, however, that your child should be allowed to use language you find offensive or which may embarrass others.

After the first correction or two, your child still will use these words at home, but in disguise. ("Do you know what that terrible Jamie said to my teacher today?" And before you can stop him he repeats it with glee and then sanctimoniously says, "I'm *only* repeating what Jamie said!")

Your child will test you from time to time, to see if you think he's as old as he thinks he is, and he may challenge you directly if, like many mothers, you use bad language too. If you do, remind your child that, since you have more responsibilities, you have more freedoms too, and then try to start cleaning up your own language. That's the trouble with admonishments. You have to listen to them.

Your child won't listen that well, however. He still will use playground words on the playground, and a few other places too, because conformity is so important, he doesn't want to be the odd one. He is learning that there is a time and a place for almost everything.

You can ignore much of this rough language, unless it's brought rather firmly to your attention, and you can ignore some at home too. You don't have to let your daughter know you heard what she said to her friend in the next room, nor do you have to make an issue over an occasional slip at the table. A raised eyebrow will do nicely.

As your child gets older, you can liberate a racy word, like "arse," into the family vocabulary. We allowed one Nine after another to use "shat" occasionally—as in, "Do you know what the dog just did?" It amused this frisky age a lot and, since the word was changed a bit, it didn't sound so bad from the mouths of babes.

Soft Porn

Girls usually don't read the girlie magazines, except as a passing curiosity, but

expect a boy to be enraptured as young as Eleven. Every centerfold is another sugar-plum to dance in his head. By Twelve you're apt to find a mountain stacked under your son's mattress where only some molehills had been before.

You will want to forbid the hard-core porn, of course, because it has no place in your home, but a few issues of some soft porn like *Playboy* are inevitable, some-where. They shouldn't hurt if you've given your child a sense of honor about sex. The pictures, stories and letters can hurt, how-ever, if he thinks the message tells him that women are meant to be used and that, therefore, they're inferior.

The magazines also might encourage future promiscuity by implying that sex is a mechanical act. It's up to you to teach your child that sex is a gift from one person to another, not a theft, and that it is love, commitment and responsibility that make it so magical. Because parents have so much influence, it will be your values, honestly stated, that offset the mes-sage in these magazines, and so will a little gentle humor about them.

If he does have a few magazines, let them stay in his closet so they don't offend others, rather than sit around in plain view. However, if you find a stack of, say, sixteen issues of *Playboy*, you have to won-der where they came from. Few preteens have the chutzpah to carry them to the counter and many stores don't sell them to children. You may be the parent of a bold boy with a light-fingered touch or one who has an allowance too big to spend wisely.

You can't censor your child's mind or, at this age, his reading matter, but you can cut some fat from his allowance and en-courage him to spend his time in other ways. Cold showers, for instance.

Sex Play

Adults did not invent sex. The joy is born with the child and the experiments proba-bly start in the womb, with a pleasant touch to the tush. By first grade, most children are too self-conscious to join in much sex play, and if they do, you should discourage it whether you have a son or a daughter. This is easier to do if you only let one child in the bathroom at the same time and ban any doctor games.

Rather than walk in on a pelvic exam, you'd be wise to tell your child that this has always been popular but it's not a good idea, that his body is his own and not a plaything. And because these rules are of-ten forgotten, the door should stay open when a boy and a girl are in a room alone. This is a good idea at any age, although not one to worry much about between the second and the fifth grades, when the sexes have so little to do with each other. They do, however, think about and taunt each other. A little girl would rather die (or so she says) than wear a dress to school and, if she does, you can bet some little boy will try to flip her skirt or make bawdy comments about what's underneath.

Children do quit investigating each other's bottoms in the Middle Years, but masturbation still occurs, although less of-ten than it will in the young teens. You don't encourage it, of course, but your child should know that it is nothing to be ashamed about, although it is a private pastime and so it should take place alone and in private. This is one good reason why you knock before you go into his bedroom.

You do have cause to worry, however, if your child is preoccupied with mastur-bation—a sign of too much isolation, too little supervision and too few interests. He needs even more attention, rewards, respect, hugs and "I love you's" than most children, to strengthen his self-esteem and his sense of trust and to remind him that he is always accepted by his parents, no matter what he does.

The child who feels loved will be able to love others and, by Ten, you can bet that he will. Some form of spin-the-bottle is as popular at birthday parties as it was in your grandmother's day. Crushes are epidemic, although they're usually denied, and they are healthy, for they prepare a child for commitments in the mid-teens. Until then, the crushes become increasingly intense but short term and conducted at a distance. With guidance, happy, busy, well-adjusted children will be juniors or seniors in high school before they have their first big romances.

Even reasonably contented children usually become a bit wayward at Eleven, however, especially if puberty starts early and if they have little or no supervision after school and no structured activities. They need both, but there'll probably be a certain amount of groping anyway. This isn't a sign that your child is immoral, however; he's just doing what comes naturally.

Other children—usually girls—send real danger signals. These are the ones who are so wild or lonely or anxious to please that they are setting themselves up to be promiscuous in adolescence, or even now, using sex like a game, to forget their troubles. And if one of them gets pregnant, she will say she doesn't know how it could have happened—and mean it—for she will still be thinking of herself as a child—and children can't, of course, have babies. She also may be using sex as a replacement for the love she is looking for at home, and be trying, unconsciously, to get pregnant. If she can't be somebody's baby, she'll be somebody to a baby of her own.

A third of all adolescents have sexual encounters in their early teens, another third in their middle teens. With luck, knowledge, a strong ego and a loving fam-ily, your child will be one of those who wait a little longer, if only so that sex will be as rich as she—and he—deserves.

MANNERS

Good manners is another name for kindness—the glue that holds things together when the going gets tough. You want your child to be polite to others, to be friendly, to be appreciative, to be gracious, because it is kind and he will feel good for it.

A child has a hard time acting mannerly on his own, not because it's against his nature, but because it's embarrassing to do anything in public if you don't know how to do it right. He would rather look like a fool by doing nothing than by doing something and doing it wrong. A child needs to know he's supposed to walk on the right side of the sidewalk so people don't bump into each other, and that a boy walks nearest the curb so the girl won't get her long skirts splashed with mud from the horses' hooves and the carriage wheels. No child minds that the purpose of the custom is a bit out of date.

Your child will learn the right way to behave if you give him thoughtful explanations, a certain amount of practice and the chance to copy you. Nothing else will be imitated as much as your own good (or bad) manners. He needs you to look happy

when he comes in the room; to ask if he's had a good day; to look at him when he talks; to speak in complete sentences; to knock before you go into his room; and to keep your eyes and your ears out of his business. He needs to be asked for his help far more than ordered, and never without a please, and for you to notice his work and thank him as soon as it's done. Above all, he needs to be corrected in private and with civility.

Manners always matter, but never so much as they do in a family.

Company Manners

The way to greet company is with pleasure. A visit is a compliment to be appreciated, even when the compliment is given a little too often. It's especially important that your child be well mannered with the elderly, for they appreciate it so much. In time he, too, will realize that the older he gets, the more age should be venerated.

Your example is your child's best instruction, but he'll behave better if he has occasional opportunities to run through the rules before company comes. Many children seem rude simply because they don't know how to act. Remind your child to stand when a visitor enters the room—a universal welcome—to shake hands and to give a smile, but he needn't offer his cheek for a kiss. A child usually permits special grown-ups to give a hug but a handshake is often preferred, and it makes a positive impression on the visitor since it's such an adult thing to do. Your child should also be taught to introduce himself if he's overlooked—a social grace that's reasonably easy at Ten and often possible at Eight. After that he offers to hang up a coat if it's needed, joins in the conversation briefly and then goes back to his own business.

When the company is for him, your child is expected to go to the door with a smile, to offer something to eat or drink (if you don't mind), to play with reasonable grace, and to walk his departing guest to the door and say the equivalent of

"Thank you for coming" though the phrasing can be left to him. It's sure to be sarcastic or silly but the sense of pleasure should be there.

There are also rules when he goes visiting, which he is expected to follow, once he's deciphered the code. You'll have to explain that when Billy's mother says, "Won't you stay for dinner, we're just about to sit down," she means "It's time to run along, sweetie."

Adults should also help visiting children understand the social scene. You make it easier for the hesitant young person by reaching out your hand and introducing yourself, or by saying, "Hi, Johnny. Great to see you!" And if he forgets to stand, he will remember when he realizes that your hand is out of reach unless he gets up. This isn't as awkward as it sounds, for the child will stand and be pleased at his own good manners, not even knowing what prompted him. You also do this with a child when you both reach the door at once—you may have to rush to get there at the same time—and you just stand there. If you don't open it, he will, and then you slip through first, fast as a flash, and thank him SO MUCH for opening the door for you, as you, in turn, hold it open for him.

Any time you can help a child use better manners, you're making it much easier for him when he's grown. Courtesy isn't just the open sesame to high society—it's the key to all society.

Table Manners

You may often despair over the table manners of your child in these Middle Years. How can he be so bright and still need 4,982 reminders and seven years to learn that his left hand lies in his lap while he eats and his right elbow stays close to his side? Manners take much longer to learn than multiplication tables and this is trying, since it is you who must do the teaching.

No longer can you give him an early dinner so you and your hungry husband

can eat late but in style. This is particularly true if you have more than one child. Now the dinner hour is a daily opportunity to bond the family, to gather together for good times, sharing news, and warmth. If the tone at your table is right, your child will come when called, most of the time, and may even go back to wash his hands without much grumbling. He will taste everything on his plate when reminded and try to keep his mouth shut when he chews. Eventually he will learn to sit straight in his chair, keep his elbows off the table, usually, and eat with his fork instead of his fingers. The lessons that are learned at dinner are remembered occasionally at breakfast and lunch and are often used when he's visiting, especially if you're not there, although you may find that hard to believe.

You surely can't expect a child to have perfect table manners at home, even for five minutes at a time, but the bobbles will be more bearable if you don't make each one a big issue. The fewer the lectures, the more pleasant the dinner and the more automatic good manners become. It will be even more pleasant if you expect to spend a leisurely half hour with the telephone off the hook, the television, record player and radio silent—unless you like some low background music—and there is plenty of give-and-take conversation, for conversation is also a skill to be learned. After a half hour, your child will be delighted to be excused and you and your husband can have your coffee in peace.

Basically, family dinner is a matter of aiming high and ignoring as much as you can. Although you do expect your child to

swallow his food before he talks, you don't want to correct him too much at the table for this or any faux pas. At the most you should niggle his elbow or murmur a low "Use your fork the right way, sweetie," although the simple hike of your eyebrow should tell him he's holding it like a shovel, again.

And when you can see improvement, congratulate your child for his good manners and surprise him, maybe with a Sunday brunch at a restaurant to show them off. He will try to be as elegant as the occasion.

Fanciness helps at home too, which is why your table should be lit by candlelight at least once or twice a week. A glass of wine for Mom and Dad can have the same effect. The more formality you have at the meal, the better the table manners are likely to be. That's why you have your child—boy or girl—pull out your chair at the table and push it in as you sit down, just as he'll do for any grown-up lady who visits.

If you start the meal with grace or a moment of silence, your child won't pick up his fork until you do (if you move reasonably fast), and then you can smile at his good manners. Once he knows it isn't polite to eat before his hostess does, the lesson will be remembered, at least when he is trying his best. Starting "while the food is still hot" may seem more logical to the child but it detracts from the general tone and it adds to the confusion if the first person served is asking for seconds before the others have hardly begun. If you must have the food hot, have your Ten warm the plates in the oven before dinner. The dinner table will also be less confusing if you teach your child to pass salt and pepper and condiments around the table rather than across it, and to sit properly at the table. All children like to stretch and squirm and lean and tilt so the Sit-Straight-in-Your-Chair rule is an important one to teach, if only to avoid a big regluing job in a few years. Rather than give a daily lecture, have your child pretend there is a thumbtack pushed through the back of his chair to nip him whenever he leans. And if he keeps forgetting, have him poke a tack through the sticky side of masking tape, and press the tape in place. A child would rather have a nip than a lecture.

The use of the napkin is an art in itself, starting with a napkin ring at the left of the plate, which reminds the child to spread his napkin on his lap as soon as he sits down. Cloth napkins—permanently pressed of course—are recommended too. They may seem unnecessarily formal but they're cheaper than paper ones and they don't float to the floor so easily. Teach your Six to touch the corner of his napkin to the corner of his mouth, which will make him giggle and carry on, but eventually he learns that if he has to wipe his whole mouth he's stuffing too much food into it at once. After dinner he folds and slides the napkin back into its ring to the left of his plate—the sign, you'll tell him, that he and the ring are permanent adornments: only company leaves napkins tossed and unfolded on the right, because they're not coming back. When a child knows the logic, he can remember the code. The napkins can be used for several days—boardinghouse style—if each person has his own special napkin ring, so he gets back his own napkin each night. When a child sees the dried splash of spaghetti sauce reappear night after night he is silently reminded to eat more neatly.

He needs to master the rules of silverware, you'll tell him, so he'll know what to do when he's invited to the White House. Even though you probably use just a knife, a fork and a spoon, some families are more formal and your child will feel safer if he knows that he uses his silverware in order, working from the outside to the inside, starting with soup and ending with dessert. When in doubt he can watch his hostess, since she will be the first one to start eating each course—another reason to wait.

A child also needs to know that salad forks have flat tines to cut through the lettuce, so knives don't have to be used; that pie and cake are eaten with a fork and other desserts with a spoon—or a fork and a spoon—and that soup requires special attention. A child not only learns that it shouldn't be slurped but that the spoon is filled only partly and then gently brushed across the far edge of the bowl to catch any drips before it's brought to the mouth, while dessert, being more solid, goes straight from bowl to mouth. Good table manners are simply techniques to make us eat comfortably and keep our shirtfronts clean.

Your child needs to learn to lay the knife and fork across the top of the plate when he wants seconds, and across the middle when he's done, so they will be less likely to fall when he clears the table. Leave it to the etiquette books to decide how the tines are placed—American or European style—when he's a grown-up.

And if he goes to a fancy dinner where there are waiters, he can expect to be served from the left and to have dishes cleared from the right—information that lets him know when to lean a little this way or that. Children who know what to expect aren't so self-conscious.

Learning good table manners takes time as well as effort and, if you don't embarrass a child with public corrections, both the meals and the manners will be more pleasant. Along the way you will of course still have chaos and comedy at your table, spilled milk, dropped silverware and a nine-year-old comedian who puts asparagus up his nose.

Raise your standards as you think your child can handle them, and acquire a certain stylish quality in the process. In time you may even be like the Smith College housemother who would watch her charges cut their fried chicken until they could cut no more, and then she would smile graciously and say, "Ladies, you may lift your bones."

Clean Plate—Children are corrected more often at the dinner table than anywhere else, which is one reason they fuss about their food. As important as it is, you can't correct too much, or food becomes a weapon and your child will limit his diet more and more.

Some exceptions should be made, of course, since a child feels foods as sharply as he tastes them and the texture of liver or the grittiness of grits may be more than he can bear. Simply scratch these foods off your list for a few years. The consistently finicky eater, however, is a pain. This is the one who swears he's not hungry, meal after meal, condescending only to eat some special foods you prepare for his dinner, and filling up with snacks before and afterward. He'll change if you stop making those special treats or buying those snacks, and tell him to eat raw carrots if he gets hungry. If he still picks at his dinner, no matter what you serve, and refuses to take at least a taste of everything you offer, simply take his plate away at the end of the meal, say you realize that people don't always need to eat a lot, give a kiss and serve dessert—even if it's not a regular custom—serve it to the rest of the family. When you ignore the scene that follows, he'll begin to change, for his appetite is getting larger every day. As long as he doesn't eat for an hour before dinner—except raw vegetables—or have a snack at bedtime, he'll eat dinner in spite of himself.

You and your independent-minded child can both keep your dignity if everyone serves himself from a side table, buffet style. He should be expected to eat a bit from each dish, but let him decide how much to put on his plate, for he'll have to follow the "waste not, want not" sign that hangs in Pennsylvania Dutch smorgasbords—YOU TAKE WHAT YOU WANT BUT YOU EAT WHAT YOU TAKE—before he can have a piece of bread or a second helping of a particular food or, of course, dessert. This is the only situation in which you expect your child to clean his plate, since you don't want to teach him to eat just for the sake of eating.

Most parents simply serve their children and expect them to sample everything, even though they say they're going to hate it. We wrestled for years with that problem until one day we found ourselves saying, "This may be the day that you like it!" Such a straightforward message worked, because it has a certain logic to it. Even a Six can remember when he once hated something he has come to adore.

In no case should your child be allowed to be rude, however. If he says a certain food is "yuk," explain that he has just used up the last of his yuks. And the next night, when he looks you eyeball to eyeball and says, yuk, he hates it, you take his plate away and you do not give him a kiss, a smile, a lecture—or anything else to eat, not even a crust of bread. The subject is closed, and if he complains he goes to his room. An empty tum for one night won't hurt him and unless you let it become a two-way scene—or let him eat later—it seldom will happen again.

You can instill either good habits or bad ones, but you'll like living with the good ones better.

Telephone Manners

By the time a child is Six he should be answering the phone with "Hello. This is the Joneses' residence. Henry speaking" (if you are the Jones family and he is Henry). This is a formal way to answer, but a child likes that and it tells the caller that he is being treated seriously.

If you attach a pen to each phone with a pad beside it, and are scrupulous about writing down messages for your child and always post them in the same place, he will do the same for you, usually.

By Seven or Eight the formality and the novelty will have become a simple "Hello," and at about Nine your child will get a virulent case of telephonitis, a disease that will last at least ten years. It has its social value but you don't want your child to monopolize the phone. Put a ten- to fifteen-minute limit on each call, with a break between calls and the proviso that he must answer if he's interrupted by the call-waiting service. This is a good way to solve some arguments before they happen. The service is much cheaper than a phone in his room, and it teaches him how to share. If you must have two numbers, they should both be for parents, with the child allowed to use only one of them—a subtle distinction that reminds him that parents are in charge.

The total number of calls should also be controlled: just a few in the evening, incoming or outgoing, and none at all during a meal. To keep the peace, answer the phone yourself, or use an answering machine.

CAR MANNERS

In a car good manners can spell the difference between life and death. No one can drive well if a passenger is jumping about, shouting or even making a lot of noise, and the older that person, the more these actions will distract you. You will be able to handle the routine decisions of driving, but you can't give your best in a sudden situation. Seat belts or other restraints must be used. They'll give you not only safety but serenity too, if you and your child buckle yourselves in place before you turn on the motor, and if your child's place is in the back seat. It puts his voice farther away from your eardrum.

When he's invited to sit in the front, you're asking him to share your privacy. This is the time for pleasant conversation, not lectures, arguments or loud music. If you do turn on the radio, pick the station yourself. You may not mind the music a Six chooses, but the choice of a Twelve, and the level at which he plays it, may drive you wild. It's best to set the rule now

so "driver's choice" becomes a standard family rule.

If your child acts up or acts out—which is more likely if you're fussing or if there is more than one child in the car—pull quietly over to the side of the road even if you have to leave the freeway to do it and even if it makes you late. Stay there without saying anything, for misbehavior deserves no further attention. It would be better to take a five-minute walk by yourself than to lose your temper. It doesn't take too many of these episodes for a child to learn that the smaller the confines the better his manners must be.

Thank-You Notes

Children naturally love gifts but not the writing of thank-you notes. It may seem easier just to write them yourself, but that's unwise. You want your child to become so accustomed to meeting this important obligation now that it will be automatic for the rest of his life. Your contribution: have stationery, stamps and addresses ready and a determination to see that they are sent.

They should be written soon, since the fresher the gift the more sincere the thank-you sounds. One or two days is best but make this rule for the Great Procrastinator: until the note is written, the gift check may not be spent, the gift book read or the gift game played.

It's of course hard for a child to express proper appreciation for a gift he doesn't like. No matter. If the present itself isn't appreciated, the donor's time and effort should be. He can thank Aunt Jane for going to so much trouble instead.

You can always tell him that if he doesn't like this year's gift he may like the one she sends next year (or the year after). And just to be safe, ask him to show you the note in case there's an embarrassing line. If a child can't be both kind and candid, it's better to be kind.

PERSONALITY PROBLEMS

Some boys and girls are born shy, some quiet, some aggressive, some outgoing—and then there are those who grow up without proper self-esteem, which makes them carry their natural inclinations too far. This child may try too hard to be good or become too dependent or a loner or a fighter or a bully or he may get too bossy or play the fool in class. Such children will be noticed but not admired and this will cause new damage to their self-esteem—a cyclical situation.

Every child has moments (or weeks) when he tries out an exaggerated posture, but if the posture seems to be becoming permanent you have a problem and so does he. When extreme behavior—good or bad—becomes chronic, it's a plea for more understanding, more respect. It's time for you and your husband to examine your own behavior and perhaps do some changing too. A child usually tries to handle a problem the way a parent does and this knowledge can be humbling, since the parent he copies is usually the one who objects the most. There's nothing like a pint-sized mirror to keep mothers and fathers in line.

You can help your child by encouraging him in what he does best—by driving the sports buff back and forth to baseball practice; giving the A-plus English student a secondhand typewriter; or counting on the great snack maker to fix dinner once a week. The child who gets such encouragement will get self-esteem too. This is because he is learning skills you think worthwhile.

THE BULLY

The bully is the misfit everyone resents. The loner, the clown and the goody two-shoes may be ignored or endured but this child draws fire.

A bully may use his body sometimes and sometimes his mouth—depending on the ability and the agility of both—but he combines them whenever he can. The more he prevails, the worse he becomes.

If your child has this problem, you should tell him that bullying won't be tolerated anymore. The next time he does it you say, "Stop that this instant!" and escort him to a place where he can't taunt or hit someone else. He should stay there until you both cool down. Then you invite him to return, but not to talk about his performance, no matter how much he wants to argue the matter or involve you in the fray.

A bully is so unsure of himself that he feels good only when he can control or frighten someone else—and, although it may not be apparent, he feels awful afterward. That's why you look for the origin of this behavior. He may be embarrassed because he is older or bigger than the other children in his class, or he is ashamed of some problem at home, like a crippled brother or a senile grandparent, or he may feel insignificant because he is the middle child. He even may be reflecting an abuse of power that goes on in your home, by either one parent or both, and in that case

family therapy is called for. Whatever the cause, your child needs to get a better picture of himself.

A chance to ride a pony regularly or build a tree house will strengthen a child's self-esteem and a preteen will profit from a good class in photography or a clinic in basketball. All children need to be proud of themselves but you have to teach this child some constructive ways. He will feel much more confident if he learns to use the power within himself, rather than his power over others.

Because a bully has few friends, he will respond very well to the one living thing that won't turn against him—a pet. Every child thrives on loving and caring for an animal, but the child who has social problems truly needs one. A puppy—even with the obedience classes and the newspapers to lay on the floor every night—will teach the bully to be gentle with others and so will a kitty or a bird.

A baby is another great way to help a child be gentle. One of your friends may be willing to pay your child a small stipend to play with her baby when she does some chores around the house (while you, in turn, do a big favor for your friend). When a child can recognize the vulnerability of others, he won't be so embarrassed about his own.

If your child is more likely to be the bully's victim, you must teach him the same lessons, although from a different point of view. Help him see how the bully uses other people to try to make himself feel better. You will want to help your child talk about the bullying incidents in detail, to discover the pattern. The person who is picked on regularly is probably setting it up, directly or incidentally. Your child may get attacked for wearing the cute little mittens with the snowmen on them— so he should have new mittens—or he may

tease the class bully about his red hair or big feet, which he must stop.

Over the long haul the frequent victim requires the same sort of bolstering the bully needs—the kind that comes from competence. Once a child feels proud of himself, he feels no need to bully or to be bullied, although it may take a full-fledged fistfight to give the victim this pride. Even if he loses the fight, he wins in the long run because a bully doesn't pick on people who fight back. Self-esteem is at least part of the cure for any behavior problem, especially this one.

THE BOSS

There are natural leaders—children with true executive ability whom other children naturally trip along behind. They are usually leaders in some but not all fields: in sports, in the classroom, in creativity. They are also content to follow in a game or a project when someone else can lead it better.

The boss, however, is not the natural leader. This is the child who tells everyone what to do and where to go, no matter how much they protest. The other children don't follow, but they sure do get mad. When a child feels so unsure of himself, so vulnerable, that he must be the boss, he almost surely has been given too many absolute orders at home, too many times.

To keep your child free of such frustrations, step back, relax and let him make a damn fool of himself now and then, just like the rest of us. He won't have to tell everyone what to do if he's allowed to tell himself.

THE LONER

Perhaps nothing makes a mother's heart break more than watching the loneliness of her child. Like most problems now, it bothers both boys and girls and to about the same degree—a lot. In fact, there are few conditions that bother children more.

Every child doubts his own popularity

quite often. The whims of a group change almost with the weather, usually focusing on the leaders—one week they're wonderful; the next, they're terrible. Other members gain or lose influence, depending on who's running the show.

The groups themselves change too, with members drifting in and out, making most loneliness short-term and inevitable and with some positive consequences, for it gives a child time to discover his strengths. There usually are one or two or three children however, who are in no groups at all, and they're bereft about it. Too much loneliness will make a child feel abandoned and afraid. He may be susceptible to headaches, stomachaches, muscle cramps, chest constriction and even an inexplicable lack of growth. In the Middle Years self-confidence depends so much on the opinion of others, especially on the parents. They can give too much attention or too little, only to find that too much may do more damage.

A lonely child is often protected by such a loving mother and father that he feels inadequate: they wouldn't do everything for him, he thinks, if they thought he could take care of himself. This is a merry-go-round. The more you do for your child, the less confident he feels, and then the less he tries, the more you have to do for him. Other children won't cater to him, however, and he not only becomes ostracized but thinks he should be, for he's sure he isn't as good as they are.

Nor can you make it better for this child by inviting other children over for little parties, or by giving your child a bike so fine and shiny that all the other children will be friendly so they can ride it. A child is no fool; these treats would only make him feel embarrassed and used by his make-believe friends. The best you can do is invite one child over for the movies (so your child won't have to talk much) and out for a snack afterward (so there will be the movie to talk about), or to ask a child and his parents for supper.

For the short term you can, literally, buy him a friend—a kitten or a puppy who will teach him to accept and give friendship. For the long term, help your lonely child by helping him change his self-image, by letting him fend for himself more and more, but without making an issue of it.

Instead of saying, "It's time you learned to make your bed," you say, "Let me show you how to make your bed," and from then on you expect him to make it without any further advice or help. You only notice that it's done by complimenting him for doing it well or for doing it quickly or for getting the spread on straight. You do not do this because some book has said you should let him take care of himself but because he can. By giving him a minimum of criticism and a maximum of compliments, he'll learn the same lesson.

He also needs competence in other areas, so he will be on a par with his classmates. Have him enroll in a Saturday class in graphics or photography or something else he fancies, or give him a regular chance to go cross-country skiing or swimming—something he can do in company with others, but essentially alone, so he doesn't feel so much social pressure yet. What he needs is the chance to learn how to do something he likes, and to do it frequently, so he can do it better than almost anyone else (or he thinks he can). As he gets this confidence, you'll find he gets some friends too.

THE DEPENDENT CHILD

Some children have a year or more when they depend on others for everything and a few seem to have a lifetime. This isn't because they're lazy or ornery, but because they don't dare to rely on themselves. They doubt if they can and so they protest, hoping to be reassured. When they're not, they let someone else tie the shoe or make the phone call and they collect one more piece of evidence that shows they're incapable.

The dependent child, like the lonely child, needs to be made to feel competent every single day, by having other people depend on him. Ask this child to do some small, simple, interesting job, but not one he's had trouble doing recently, for the idea of repeated failure will overwhelm him.

And when you give him the assignment, you ask him so matter-of-factly that you obviously think he can do it. In fact you're so confident you don't even tell him how. If he asks, you say, "Well, I'm not sure. How would you do it?" for he may just be asking for more reassurance. If he says he has no idea, talk it out with him, breaking the job into small steps. And then you go about your business—somewhere else. If he can't do the job, make no fuss about it, but try something else a little later—something you know he can do.

When your child does complete a job—any job—inspect it as soon as possible. Note some specific part of the work that was good—the speed, the care, the delicacy—but don't make a big production out of it or he'll think you're surprised he could do it at all. This child is so sensitive, he reads a book of lectures into every nuance. While his dependency probably is an outgrowth of his natural shyness, he will begin to take care of himself as soon as he learns that he can. The more you depend on him, the quicker that will be.

THE SHOW-OFF

Every class has its clown. Like the walk-on actor who catches invisible flies while the star gives her monologue, this child craves more attention than anyone else—and he'll do anything to get it. The other children laugh, the teacher laughs or scolds—and the child, deep inside, knows that he is paying a terribly high price to be

noticed. He wears his clownish behavior the way he might wear a funny hat—to distract from his vulnerable self. It's better to show off than be shown up.

If your child regularly shows off by acting silly—at home, at school and at play—he needs a physical checkup to see if he is hyperactive and a lot of ego building as well. If he only shows off at home, however, you and your husband need to take a good tough look at yourselves, to see if you give most of your attention when he is showing off, rather than when he's being quiet and unobtrusive. If the child shows off at school or at play (but not at home) he's still looking for an accepted place among children his own age and hasn't the grace, the experience or the confidence to get it in the conventional way. He needs more help to be as competent as he can.

If the problem is limited to school you need to observe for a half day to see if it's right for your spirited child, and if the teacher treats him well. Try as she might, a teacher can't help choosing pets and targets and every child in the class reacts to her choices.

He also may be trying to disguise some problem he has, like a learning disability, or a difficulty in hearing the teacher or seeing the blackboard. You might think this would be obvious, but a child always thinks he learns and hears and sees just like anyone else. Because he thinks the others somehow know how to try harder, he hides behind buffoonery instead.

Like all behavior problems, this one is cured by treating the cause, not by disciplining the result.

GOODY TWO-SHOES

Some children hide their troubles so well, you might not know they're there. These are the "goody two-shoes"—both girls and boys. They delight most parents and teachers but they drive other children wild.

They are first to jump up to find your purse or clear the table, the first to recite at school and to bring in their milk money. Usually they work against a foil of at least one laggard child, which makes the contrast clearer. Attention is a sign of love and this child gets it by being very, very good.

Unfortunately, this is an idea he has picked up at home. His parents criticize him more than he can take and raise the ante whenever he begins to reach their expectations. When a child thinks he is loved for his work alone, he works harder and harder to be reassured.

This pattern may continue for life, but quite often a child will eventually simply say, "What the hell." Today's goody two-shoes may be the teenager who gives up: love isn't worth it, he thinks, if it's that hard to get. The child who is too good to be believed—shouldn't be. Instead he needs you to notice him when he's not doing anything, to give him a smile and a kiss when he spills the milk, to compliment him on the B's and C's as well as the A's. He needs permission to fail.

And he needs you to tell him that nothing he does could ever make you stop loving him, nothing could push you away. To let a child grow up thinking that love is for sale would be a terrible mistake.

NEEDS

Boys and girls must fill both tangible and intangible needs to be competent, and therefore to fill their greatest need of all—independence.

Your child needs enough liberty to get around on his own if he can, and enough knowledge to do it safely. He requires privacy to house his possessions and his treasures and the right to decide what those treasures will be. He also needs sturdy, decent clothes, with one or two faddish items to feel part of the gang, and the responsibility to care for whatever he owns. An allowance is necessary too. Make it small enough to keep him out of trouble but big enough to spend a little, save a little and give a little, so he can learn how to handle money long before he leaves home.

The meeting of these needs builds your child's self-confidence, so he will dare to go forth on his own.

GETTING AROUND

Today a mother feels safe to let her Five go alone on a plane to see Grandma a thousand miles away but is afraid to let her Ten take the bus to a swimming lesson five miles away. The buses are infrequent, the schedules are unknown, the destination is hard to find—and besides, the car is in the driveway. Even if it isn't, there's always a car pool, which everyone knows is the easiest, cheapest way to get children from one place to the next. This isn't as easy as it seems and you can pay a hefty price. The mother who drives and uses car pools exclusively is building a pair of prisons—one for herself and one for her child—and his walls will be higher and last longer. Even though your child is allowed to walk or bike in his own neighborhood, he will feel helpless if he has to depend on an adult to take him everywhere else.

Food, shelter and sex may be the three primitive urges, but right after that comes independence, and to a child independence means the right to get around on his own. When a preteen is often allowed to be his own keeper, he'll keep himself safer as an adolescent. While you want a child under Ten to travel in carefully prescribed areas, an Eleven who can find his way around a huge shopping mall is able to move around town. By Twelve, he should be ready to go almost anywhere and be eager to do it as long as you haven't passed on your own fears. That's hard to avoid, particularly if you live in the suburbs, for the farther people live from the city, the more they seem to be afraid of it.

Public transportation is almost nonexistent in some areas, but perhaps your child can get around on commuter trains and buses, if they are an option in your area. You also may find that a motel or an apartment building will let your child ride their shuttle.

Take a few rides with him in the beginning—whatever the transportation—so he (and you) will feel more secure. If you're riding a bus, talk with the driver, so your child will feel that even a grouchy one is accessible. Teach the younger child to stay near the front, even when the driver says to move back, or to sit next to some nice chatty lady. He'll find it more entertaining than you would. Your child also must be taught to give his seat to adults, but especially to pregnant women, senior citizens and the handicapped. This will be easier for him to do if you have him offer his seat at least once while you ride together, just to show him how it's done without feeling too embarrassed. On these test rides, point out the landmarks, the way the bus meanders around to serve more riders and how long it takes to get from one place to another. All of this helps a child remember the route, so he won't panic when he's alone.

It makes the transition smoother if you have an older child take him on his first ride or you can drive him to his destination and then let him take the bus home, since it will be easier to recognize his own stop. It's the unfamiliar that is frightening—not just the routes but the possibilities. A child feels relieved to have an extra fare, in case he boards the wrong bus, and some change to call when he's reached his destination or if it's dark when he gets to his stop. You don't want him wandering about after hours. He'll also like the ride better if he goes with a friend, but in the Middle Years a child likes anything better with a buddy.

Of course there may be some rumbles with young riders he doesn't know, particularly if your child rides the bus when the other schools are dismissed, but even that's not so bad. There was a time when our Kate came home with a black eye and a

great deal of fury, but she learned something she never knew before: she could protect herself. This alone gives a child a sense of assurance—an aura—that keeps troublemakers away.

Moments of alarm are inevitable on public transportation. The only really bad possibility is the very infrequent encounter with the creepy old (or young) man we all remember from our childhoods. All girls and boys should be warned about him ahead of time. When a child knows that it's better to cause a commotion than to put up with any indignity, she (and he) will feel better. When she knows that the time-honored "I'll scream" is not only an honest defense but the best one, the child will also feel competent. The problem that has a solution isn't a problem anymore.

Some city children start their bus rides as young as Six. Charlotte, a beautiful blonde in our neighborhood, was put on a 45-minute bus ride every morning to get to her fancy private school, from which she would call to say she had arrived safely. Her daddy would take her to the stop and sit her next to the driver, a patient fellow who listened to her chatter as the rush-hour bus barreled through riot-torn slums, and along the way she picked up a knowledge of reality that money couldn't buy. The child who has a chance to be a part of the world, and yet still be protected, discovers that knowledge is security in itself.

This doesn't mean, of course, that you won't have some uneasy moments. When your child is a half hour late, you'll be angry one moment, frantic the next, only to find that it wasn't because of a wreck or an abduction but because he was fooling around and missed the bus, or because he slept past his stop. You can bet he was just as scared and mad as you were, although nonchalance will be his trademark and, with effort, it will be yours too.

After this litany you may feel that car-pooling and nothing but car-pooling is better than ever, but it is not. Public transportation frees both mother and child. It also sets a precedent: a child is important but the household does not revolve around his comings and goings, any more than it revolves around yours. The family is interdependent but it works best when each member is as independent as possible.

OUT-OF-TOWN TRAVEL

An Eight is old enough to take a train, plane or bus out of town—and love it—to see his auntie, if he promises not to run up and down the aisles, and to act more grown up than he ever has in his whole life. The stewardesses and conductors will look out for his safety, but they don't have time to baby-sit and they shouldn't be expected to do it. Your child will travel happily for two to three hours as long as he has magazines, books, quiet toys and a headset for some story tapes, a small amount of money for a few treats and a window seat. You might even dare to send two children on a shorter trip, for there's nothing the young like better than an adventure together.

PROTECTION

The innocence of children is one of the most precious things they have and yet they won't be safe unless parents take some of it away. This is one of the saddest jobs you have, and one of the most necessary, particularly if you have a daughter, for girls are usually more vulnerable than boys.

You want your child to be wary and to listen to her own instincts most of all. If someone seems peculiar, he probably is, and even if he isn't, it's better for her to be mistaken than sorry. Teach her not to make eye contact with a stranger or with anyone who makes her uncomfortable and not to look into a parked car when someone calls her. Tell her not to laugh at a joke she doesn't understand or that seems risqué or to play any game she's told to keep secret. She should know that the old line, "All right, but I have to ask my mom first," will often end the wrong game right there. All of this gives your child a set of rules to follow until she can figure out how to say no for herself (see Sexual Abuse).

You want to teach her to be suspicious of a stranger—teenager or adult—who wants to join a child's game or tries to talk to her at the movies or asks if she wants to earn some money. She also should refuse to ride with a stranger or someone she's never ridden with before, even if it's raining or the driver says you sent him or if he says he's a little lost and can't follow her directions unless she shows him the way. Tell her it doesn't hurt a child to get wet an adult to be lost. To be extra sure she'll obey, you can give her a code word known only to her and you and the few people who are allowed to pick her up without prior notice.

You also need to teach your child to refuse a treat—whether comic books or candy—if she has to go into someone's house to get it. By now she should know whose homes she can visit, but even then she should call as soon as she gets there so you will know where she is.

Many unpleasant situations can be avoided if your child goes to and from school the same way every day and always walks with a friend. She should also go with a friend to the movies, the park, the store, the swimming pool, or on a bus ride, and avoid alleys and empty buildings even with a buddy. In addition, you have to teach your child to stay in a public rest room for only as long as it takes to use the facilities—a rule that is especially important for a boy to follow.

The child who is home alone must learn to peek out the door to see who's

FROM DRUGS

Some child molesters deal in drugs, rather than sex. Your child should report anyone who asks him to sell something for him, or to keep it for a while, and he shouldn't eat or drink anything offered by a stranger or even someone he knows if the offer makes him uneasy.

there but not to open it, even if the person just wants to make a phone call. There are other doors on which to knock.

It's also wise to have your child off the neighborhood streets by 6 P.M. or by dark—whichever comes first—unless she is playing in a neighborhood game and has someone to walk her home. This is particularly true in the city. The occasional child who walks alone after most children are in their homes is most likely to attract the child molester or the exhibitionist, because he thinks no one is watching out for her.

You also protect your child by screening sitters with great care (see Child Care), by paying attention to your own antennae and by teaching her how to protect herself.

ON THE PHONE

A child must be protected on the telephone too. Make sure your child—particularly a daughter—only tells callers that you can't come to the phone—not that you're out for a while—and that she knows how to handle obscene phone callers. Tell her to hang up immediately if a caller refuses to give his name; if he uses bad or suggestive language; or if he says he is "taking a survey." (A reputable survey taker would want to talk with an adult, if only to get permission to interview a child.)

He probably will call back repeatedly, which your child should know, and if you're not home, teach her to hang up immediately at the sound of his voice (or his heavy breathing), and to do it without saying a word. This is a lot of self-control to expect of a young person, but she will obey you if she realizes that an obscene caller gets much of his pleasure from the reactions he gets. If he calls a third time she should take the telephone off the hook for a half hour.

This will not, of course, remove the sense of violation your child will feel and, if this problem persists, you or your husband should answer the calls when you're home for the next few weeks and if he calls again say, "Are you there, operator? This is the call I asked you to trace." It also is a good idea to tape the caller—and tell him so, for voices now can be printed as well as fingertips. All of this will make your child feel more in control of the situation.

Even if you've had a run of nasty phone calls, she can still answer the phone when she's home alone if you arrange a code. If you ring twice, hang up and dial immediately again, she'll know it's safe to answer the second time around. It's a code her friends can use too. And if none of that works, get an answering machine. It won't give the obscene callers their jollies.

IN TRAFFIC

When your child was little you made a big fuss about the red and green lights and the signals to walk, but now you may figure he knows what to do and go back to your own more careless ways. Please don't. This is a frisky age.

A child tests himself enough without getting a silent go-ahead sign from his parents. You still must warn a Six—and even a Seven—to look both ways when he crosses a street, and when he gets out of a bus or steps off the curb to buy a treat from a vendor. He also must be reminded not to enter the street behind a parked car or to jaywalk or to dart suddenly from the curb. Out-of-the-ordinary behavior surprises the daydreaming driver, or the one who is under the influence of alcohol or other drugs, and he may not react wisely. Even if your child crosses the street at a crosswalk and with the light, he still can't count on a car to stop. Just the difference in size makes it harder for a driver to see a child than an adult.

Your traffic rules will work, but only if you take the time to explain why they're necessary and continue to set a good example yourself.

PRIVACY

All boys and girls need a nook, if not a room, to call their own, or at least a shelf, a cabinet or a special drawer that is inviolate. A guarantee of privacy is an easy promise for the mother of a Six to make and much harder for the mother of a preteen to uphold. No matter how much you might worry about the company this older child keeps, he needs to know his mail is sacred, his pockets won't be emptied or his bureau investigated. The strength of a family is built on trust. A letter, once sealed, is to be read only by the person to whom it's addressed—and a diary belongs to its owner.

Not only does your child deserve a normal share of privacy, but he will revel in a special hideaway. Two of our favorites—Jennifer and Heather—each had bedrooms so beautiful they were truly their castles, but it was their tiny 3' x 6' hideaway that made their privacy so special. Their dad made it for them by cutting a small Alice-in-Wonderland door in the plaster wall, framing it and hanging a large cupboard door to get to the space beneath the eaves, only 5' high at its peak. He plastered and painted the little cranny, put down a rug of carpet squares and wired a lamp to light their way. The girls added their most precious books and many, many dolls. This was their snuggery, the place where they were safe.

Even the smallest pocket of privacy can be a marvel. It was nine-year-old Mike, surrounded by three sisters and feeling harassed, who recovered as soon as his dad made him a secret hideaway—a sliding piece of tongue-in-groove that seemed part of the basement paneling, so he could stow his treasures between the studs. Try as they might, his sisters never found it.

A child needs spiritual privacy too. He has the right to be alone, to have secret thoughts and silent dreams, to absorb what

happened at school before he's expected to talk about it. When you ask him how his day went, and he says only, "Okay," he's not ready. There also will be hours when he just hangs around, playing solitaire or staring out the window, preferably in a room by himself. Every child needs the chance to imagine the poems he will write to the butterflies next spring; the game he'll invent that will outsell Monopoly; the language he will translate from the cat's meows. There are also muscles to be flexed and high heels to be danced in and this requires a mirror but not an audience.

Even though your child wants privacy, he may not be happy in it, any more than you are always happy when you're alone. He just knows he needs time by himself to regroup, rethink, replay what's happened so he'll know what was right, what was wrong and what to do the next time.

Private time is growing time.

MONEY

The love of money may be the root of all evil but only to those who haven't learned to earn it, save it, give it and spend it in a balanced way. The whole concept of money fascinates a child, even at Six, and yet it is usually explained to him so broadly that it's beyond his comprehension or so narrowly that it's confusing. He needs to know how money affects him and his family before he can understand the bigger picture.

There's no need to tell him exactly what you earn, but he does need to know where it all goes, including the part that goes to taxes. Even though you may not like all of the ways that your tax money is used—and who does?—your child needs you to connect the payment with the style of his life. Point to the public swimming pool, the tulips that bloom in the park and the potholes that got fixed; tell him that the family paid for some of that. By stressing the positive side of government giving, your child grows up with a sense of his own responsibility to the community.

Your child understands the cost of running a household if you ask him to help you with the family budget sometimes, making a pie chart for him so he can see what portion of the family income is spent on the hidden expenses—not just the taxes, but the mortgage, the telephone, the heat and lights. He should know that the budget is a serious but not a frightening business, and that you and his dad are in control of the expenses. If he only hears you say things like, "What are we going to do?" or "We've never been so broke!" he'll be afraid. He won't know that you can make budget cuts together and that you still have options and resources, lines of hope and credit. A child won't even know you're just letting off steam if he doesn't have some grasp of the whole picture.

An Eight, that money-mad rascal, can help you with the bank statement, calling out the canceled checks so you can see how many are outstanding. This not only lets you figure your true cash balance, but it teaches him that a checking account is just a convenience and not an endless money source. By Twelve he can sort the bills into categories, adding the amounts on his calculator and even writing some of the checks for you to sign. You wouldn't do this every month—family bookkeeping is tense enough without giving an arithmetic lesson—but if you have your child work on the household budget with you every few times, you'll be surprised how much less he will fuss for expensive toys— and how much sooner he'll turn out the lights.

He'll also contribute to the common good much quicker if he understands that there is more money in the general till when he cleans the gutters or shovels the snow, so you don't have to hire someone. And he'll believe you because you'll sometimes say, "Davy saved us so much money last week, we can go out for pizza!" This teaches the child that a family is a team— and sometimes everyone wins the prize.

EARNING

A child who earns money is learning to rely on himself before asking help from somebody else. The ability seems to come naturally to children whose parents give them unspoken permission to try.

Peter, one of the most enterprising workers in our neighborhood, was only Four when he slipped off on a door-to-door mission to sell wire coat hangers— the kind that breed in closets—for two cents each. Already he had learned that work is like love: it's better to try and fail than never to try at all.

There are two basic rules. A child should be expected to work toward a specific goal—to help pay for a bike or a flute or a fancy pair of sneakers or jeans—and shouldn't get paid at home for doing work at home (see Work). One of a parent's persistent small temptations is to offer to pay a child for a family job to help him make his dreams come true. Fifty cents may not mean much to you and the child may be so wistful, but if you put a price on a family chore, you undermine the family's sense of sharing. Even big jobs should be done free unless his working to pay for that big expense or unless he has

to turn down a paid job so he can work for you. This doesn't happen very often, even at Eleven or Twelve. Although a child can be a good worker now, he will not be overwhelmed with outside offers.

There should also be a time limit on the number of jobs he is allowed and expected to do, inside or out of the family. A primary grader can manage a half hour of work a week, with occasional breaks, as long as the work is varied. By Twelve he can work for an hour several times a week. In both cases, however, the demand should be matched with the child, and he should know exactly what's expected of him and when the goal will probably be reached. The younger he is, the shorter the overall effort should be. He also needs supervision, although it should be less and less obtrusive as he gets older. He will have the chance to work for neighbors when he has worked enough at home to learn the skills that are needed and the attitude that is wanted. It's scutwork around the house that teaches him to do the dull as well as the exacting and compliments that make him work harder.

You should also keep an eye on your child when he works outside the family. It's surprising how much he doesn't know, especially about the ways of other households. You even have to teach this young worker how to get paid, for often adults who seem to be kind and honest may try to shortchange a child. He should know what rate he hopes to get and how low he will go, setting the amount before he starts, by asking, "Would you rather pay me by the hour or the job?" He also should know that the money may not be handed over easily, so he may have to ask for it, not only because he deserves it, but because these employers may hire other children who may not be nervy enough to stand up for themselves.

Some employers may offer outgrown clothes or toys or even a handful of pennies. ("You never know when one will be worth thousands of dollars!" they'll say.) In this case, your child should be taught to say, "Thank you but I'd rather be paid like we agreed because I've been counting on buying something special"— a line he says with a smile. And if the employer says he doesn't have it, he should be ready to smile again and say, "That's okay. My mom says she can cash your check."

It may seem backward to worry about the problems of getting paid before a child ever gets a job, but many children are afraid to try for work because they don't know how to handle the pitfalls other children have told them about. When you teach your child how to deal with employers, you also let him know that you're taking him seriously. And earning money is the best encouragement he can give to himself. Once a child has been paid, he'll want to get paid again. Work, he finds, is satisfying, but it's a lot better if he gets a little glory and money too.

Your child will still dream of both. He'll tell you his plans to become a rich and famous lawyer when he's grown (or a rich and famous doctor or a r. and f. movie star). Meanwhile, he'll have to do many piddling jobs along the way and he'll need the right to stumble and to fail. Even if a friend hires your child to do a job that's good and safe but still beyond him, it's best to keep your mouth shut. While you'll tell him you don't know if he's ready for that, don't make a fuss about it. Your child has the first right to your loyalty. Just give him a lot of encouragement and you may be happily surprised. But not always. If his employer is unhappy, send him back for another try, and if the work is still unsatisfactory, they both should cross it off as experience.

No matter how good a preteen's work, his enthusiasm may not last as long as yours. Hilary and Elizabeth were Eight and Nine when we asked them to wash our blond dog Daisy each week. The bath took an hour the first week and the results were a wonder. Except for her ears, Daisy was clean, damp and fluffy all over. The bath didn't take as long the second week, and both the tail and the ears stayed dirty. By the third week it took even less time and Daisy's tail, ears and face were untouched. The fourth (and last) week the girls were done in ten minutes and Daisy's tail, ears, face, legs and even her feet were dry, but somehow her back was clean, damp and fluffy, which was a wonder too.

Finally we learned: children between Six and Nine need work—and should work—but don't expect them to last very long, especially if they work together. As an old neighborhood plumber used to say, "One boy is one boy; two boys is half a boy; and three boys is no boy at all."

A preteen no longer is a clone of his best friend and often prefers to work by himself—if only to keep all the money. He still needs short, specific jobs and a grown-up nearby, and he also needs help to find work. Most children between Six and Twelve don't design interesting (or even dull) businesses for themselves. A younger child will need your help to decide what he can do and to write and duplicate a flyer listing them: pick up the trash that's blown around; help at a two-year-old's birthday party; run an errand; walk a dog—even snap the heads off dandelions so they won't go to seed. Even if the flyer doesn't win him a job, your child will think of himself as a worker, and so will the neighbors. This is the child who gets called first when there is a small job to be done.

The older child also needs encouragement. When this child wishes he could buy a bike, you offer some thoughtful suggestions, and perhaps promise to match what he makes, since he has to raise such an awesome sum. And that will only be the beginning. You still have to supervise, remind, encourage and set limits so his plans don't overwhelm him. A Ten, an Eleven and a Twelve are great ones for taking a preschooler for an hour-long walk in the afternoon, digging up plantains, delivering the weekly paper in the neighborhood or washing cars—a job done with lots of vigor and a fair degree of competence.

It's still the more original jobs you help him invent that will bring him the most pleasure—to make school-lunch cookies or grow fresh herbs and sell them door to door or go into the lamp rewiring business. Employers are much likelier to hire a child who helps them discover a need than the one who asks for work because he needs the money.

In politically conscious Washington, D.C., we passed on a funny campaign slogan to Mike, an Eleven, helped him find a printer and staked him to $20 to go into the bumper sticker business. The rest was up to him. It meant slipping into the House and Senate office buildings on Saturday mornings to hustle his wares among the partisan staffs and it netted him $80 and a somewhat broader knowledge of politics. While bird-dogging your child's business, you might as well steer him toward something that will amuse both of you.

It's your child's attitude toward work that will be more important to you than the work itself. You want to teach him that it's important to give his best, to be honest, to be proud of what he does—no matter what it is—and that his attitude is even

more important than making a lot of money. With that philosophy, he's sure to make a reasonable amount.

GIVING

Giving is one more thing a Six learns to do by doing. That's why he needs a special bank on his bureau—in addition to his piggy bank—to hold 10% of his allowance—his tithe—to give to church or the Salvation Army, to a soup kitchen or a settlement house. Sharing is part of growing up, even sharing with people he'll never see, but drive through the seedier parts of town sometimes, so he'll know who the poor really are. He can give to charity regularly or save it for an occasion, but either way a younger child needs a lock on the bank and the key checked with his mom. A bank full of nickels can be mighty tempting.

SAVING

To be responsible about money, children should work to save for what they want to buy, not work to pay for what they've bought. The first gives them control over their lives; the second makes them resent their commitments.

Seven is a splendid age for a child to switch from a piggy bank to a real bank, even if you have to add to the kitty so he has enough to make the opening deposit. You'll also have to see that he adds to it, which is a bother, but it's worth it. The child who makes a bank deposit on the first of every month will be a much more serious saver than the one who socks it away in a sock.

Some say that long-term saving is meaningless to a child, but it doesn't have to be a vague and abstract routine. Show him how to roll a hundred pennies into a wrapper, exchanging it for a crisp dollar bill at the bank before he deposits it. Later you'll listen to his dreams about money, how he can use it, travel on it, wear it or study with it, but be slow to take him to

the bank to withdraw it. He'll get more interested in saving now to withdraw later, as he understands time better, and cause and effect.

Others say a child shouldn't have a savings account because inflation will eat up most of his profits. These folks forget that the lump sum seems much more than its parts and a five-cent profit on a dollar makes a child feel awfully clever.

The opening of an account should be full of ceremony. Have your child dress up, even if he has to wear his good clothes to school or leave school a little early to change. The choice of banks should be made with care. Although banking services vary from one part of the country to another, you should still be able to find one that doesn't charge to maintain small savings accounts; that is open on Saturdays or after school—so he can do his own banking as he gets older, and, if possible, one that will take his picture and issue him a plastic identification card. The card is important. A preschool child mostly wants to matter to his parents, but a schoolchild wants to matter to the whole world. He loves to see his own name on a set of pencils or the family name in the phone book but identity cards are best and the only ones he can get are from the library and the bank. Both, if well used, will teach him a great deal, but since almost everyone has a library card, the banking card has a special cachet. It really seems to say that he's somebody.

If his bank is old-fashioned, he may get a passbook too, which is great. The smallest deposit brings a large amount of pride.

Meg was so pleased to open an account with a $5.00 windfall that she wanted to add to it immediately—and so she opened a lemonade stand in front of her bank, charged what the traffic would bear, and

made deposits all day long. The teller, a patient woman, stamped her passbook like this:

Deposit	
$5.00	$5.00
17c	$5.17
11c	$5.28
33c	$5.61
17c	$5.78
23c	$5.91

And so it went all day long, for two pages. What better proof that she was a productive member of the working class?

SPENDING

Your child's approach to saving and spending is shaped by your good or bad examples. You see it so plainly in children of the very rich or the very poor. The child of poverty seldom tries to save or budget his money, for in his home there is little space for choices, and the child of the very rich usually spends without reflection. If either you or your husband tend to be stingy or spendthrifty, you'll be wise to curb your impulse if you can. Money can be a chronic cause of trouble.

Basically, you want your child to realize that money, like time, can be spent only once. Let him deliberate, even when he buys something as inconsequential as bubble gum. When he weighs the pros and cons to buy small things, he'll weigh the big buys later on. Your Six or Seven will learn the ways of the marketplace if you have him run into the store alone to pick up the bread and milk, making sure he knows how much it is before he buys it and that he counts his change before leaving the register.

You can put the new money madness of an Eight to work and help him understand your planned economy by asking him to write down a full list of what the family needs at the grocery store—including what he'd like—and to take your dictation so that he is part of the decision making. When the list is complete, have him read it back so you can tell him which items to star as essentials. After you've bought these you can add as many extras as the budget allows. A child may not agree with you about which are the essentials, but he will accept your decisions if you take the time to explain them.

Have him check the sales and unit prices, to see which brand is cheapest, while reminding him that it isn't cheap if the jar is too big for the family, or too little, or a brand nobody likes. You will also teach him to resist the impulse items—the goodies—at the end of the aisles and near the registers; the springy, fast-paced music that makes shoppers want to buy more; and the higher-priced convenience food that isn't very convenient. When a parent pokes fun at advertisers' tricks, the child soon does the same.

ALLOWANCE

Every boy and girl deserves a small share of the family income by the first grade. It's a matter of honor. Even a dime tells a child that he's important. A child also needs an allowance so he can handle money often, which is how he learns to handle it well. If he depends on money as it's needed, he only learns to beg for it and to pit one parent against the other. This is the child who brags to his friend that he can get anything he wants if he brings his mom some tea when she's tired or smiles at his dad's jokes. You don't want to teach your child to manipulate you or anyone.

The money you hand out should be seen for what it is—a token of your affection. It isn't earned by doing chores or getting A's, nor is it docked for F's or misbehavior. If an allowance depends on performance, you are telling your child that he only belongs to the family when he does well.

The amount should be in keeping with your income, unless you make a lot of money. It's unfair to expect a young child to handle large amounts of money well, nor is it a good preparation for the future.

UNDERSTANDING MONEY

A Ten can learn much about money by playing the stock market, if only in a make-believe way. The lesson begins with a family discussion about businesses and how they sell shares to raise money to improve or expand. One member of the family plays broker, giving each player $500 worth of Monopoly money, in all denominations, to pay for some stocks listed on the financial page and to keep track of all purchases and sales.

The players check the financial page each day, comparing the ups and downs of their stocks and buying and selling to try to recoup their money or make more.

After a month or so—before the game loses its kick—the scores are tallied to see who did best in the marketplace.

If the whole family joins, your child will get not only a good understanding of the financial world but a sense of grown-upness too. Both are good, but the second is better.

No matter how much money you have, your child probably will start adult life with very little.

When he turns Eleven, you'll realize how important your policy of early restraint can be, for the children with the biggest allowances are often the first ones to buy drugs. Let your child's allowance be more than the lowest, if possible, but less—and often much less—than the most.

Regularity and dependability matter most. Your child should be able to expect the same amount, in cash, at the same time each week, and know that it will be raised by a regular anticipated amount each birthday, or at the start of each school year. If you follow an annual plan, there will be no dreary negotiations for a raise every month.

In addition to the allowance, your child needs an extra sum each week for lunch and milk money, transportation, field trips, school supplies and birthday gifts. This is a floating amount that varies each week. In the first few grades it's handed out, bit by bit, as needed, and by the fourth grade it's given at the same time as the allowance, but still separately. By the fifth grade a child should be able to combine these two amounts. This teaches him how to budget so the habit becomes ingrained by adolescence.

Some children find budgeting easier if the parents set up a tangible plan. If both you and your child enjoy details, he may prefer an account in the "family bank," for which he writes out an index card, or even a check, for a sum as he needs it, and you hand over the cash.

Other families find an envelope system works well, with the allowance in one envelope and the rest divided into separate envelopes marked "Lunch," "Transportation," etc. This is especially good at Eight, when a child enjoys categories as well as the feel of money. Whatever the system, the only way your child will learn to budget his money is by doing it himself.

When his budget needs a boost—during the holidays or at summer camp—you might give him a bonus or double the allowance (just as you give yourself extra for vacation and Christmastime) or you can create some big, extra job he can do for you for pay. This shouldn't undercut your money-managing principles, and it will keep your child from being overwhelmed by a painful lack of cash. It's important that money doesn't become a god or a weapon.

It's also important that your child doesn't hoard money—a sign of insecurity; that he isn't borrowing money without paying it back or isn't using his money to buy friendships. Although you'll watch for these signs of trouble, you don't want to monitor your child's spending. That's the joy of it for him. He doesn't have to account for it at all. It's just as well. If someone did a study on the way allowances are spent—and no doubt somebody will—it probably would show that most youngsters buy movie tickets once or twice a month and spend the rest on food, either sweet or salty. An allowance is one big yum.

Nothing is more natural and you might contribute now and then with a special treat. A double-dip ice cream cone or an egg roll after school might satisfy his tummy enough to let him go to an extra movie or buy a few baseball cards, or you can steer him to some yard sale treasures which whet a child's appetite for thrift like nothing else.

Even though most children spend their money on goodies, they spend at different rates of speed. Kate would spend only after due deliberation, Meg with deliberate speed and Mike with no deliberation at all. If he had money in his pocket he seldom made it past a fast food parlor. Hamburgers were heaven to him.

Nell was different. With her first allowance, she asked to be walked ten blocks away to an elegant wine and cheese shop where she borrowed fifteen cents from her next allowance and bought a small package of a delicately flavored French cheese. That day, and each day thereafter, she would cut a slice of bread into four squares, thinly smear the cheese on each one, and ask if anyone would like one, holding her breath until we dutifully said no. On the last day she used the last of her cheese, got her allowance, paid back her fifteen cents, and blew the rest on penny candy.

That's when we knew she was normal.

CLOTHES

A child expresses himself in many ways, including the clothes he wears. This can be awkward in the early school years. One understanding mother let her first grader wear a most becoming pair of shorts and cowboy boots to school every Friday until January. It shocked other mothers but it gave her daughter an almost overwhelming and gratifying sense of self-confidence.

Although a child seldom minds if the special outfit is dirty, torn, or fits poorly, he usually has an almost psychic sense of the styles and colors that look best on him, and, if he can carry out this individuality, he will feel more comfortable about himself. He may even take better care of these clothes, for they are part of his personal-

ity, but don't count on it. A child generally hangs all his clothes in the same place: on the floor.

If you're lucky your child will have a continuing stream of grandchild gifts and you probably will have hand-me-downs from friends as well. In both cases he should be able to choose which ones he wants to wear and which he does not, even if it means that you will have to wash the favorites twice as often. If your child wants to wear certain clothes badly enough, he'll learn to look after much of his own laundry by Ten, and that's a proper goal for both of you.

SHOPPING

You and your child should do his shopping together, at thrift shops and rummage sales as well as department stores. Before you go, however, you should agree on the clothes he needs and how much you're willing to spend, so he will understand your vetoes better. You should also agree that if either one of you dislikes something it stays at the store.

If you took him along just to make sure that the clothes fit, he would feel that his own, often intense, opinions were being ignored. The child who is allowed to make many of his own decisions will have more self-confidence because he knows that you're saying, "You're smart," every time you second his choice.

Choosing clothes is a skill and it takes practice. Your child learns when you show

him which clothes have growing space; what seams are tough; when a material is washable; which styles are lasting; and what's easiest to put on without help. This teaches him the difference between fad and fashion, quality and schlock.

Kate had her first lesson at Nine and showed a natural flair. In a spurt of dizziness, we took her to a branch of a classy and expensive New York store, relieved to see her go straight to the rack marked SALE. It took her just five minutes to flip through the dresses in her size, hardly looking at most of them before she chose a cotton jersey sailor dress that cost very little, fit very well and was the perfect choice for an interview at the new school. The saleslady was as baffled by her methods as we were and asked why she only looked at some of the dresses.

"Well," said Kate, "first I look at the tag to see if we can afford it and then I look at the material to see if I have to iron it and then I look at the dress to see if I like it."

These have been the criteria for our family ever since.

Shoes

Any parent who says she likes to take a child shoe shopping is either a kidder or a masochist. Shoes, like wheels, are symbols of freedom, and although clothes sometimes may not matter, shoes always do. Your child will run all about the store, look at dozens of shoes, insist the salesman could find some more or that you could try another store and then another. Time is no object to the shoe fool. Money isn't either, unless you insist on it.

Although there's no reason to let your young child have something that is both fashionable and inappropriate, it's fine to let him pick a particular pair if he is willing to pay the difference between the brand you can afford and the kind he wants. He pays, of course, with money already earned for jobs done outside the house, not the promise of work he will do later. If a child wants those special shoes bad enough to work for them, he's entitled to spend his own money, but most children find that fashion usually isn't worth the price.

No matter what shoes your child gets, sneakers will be worn most. A child likes to keep them clean as long as possible—which will be much longer if he sprays them repeatedly with liquid starch before the first wearing, but expect them to be worn with the strings untied. Bear with it. It is a custom that usually ends by the time he's old enough to vote. But not always.

MENDING

Children can learn simple mending techniques by Eight, which won't be put to use very often but will help them feel more in charge of their lives.

Preliminary mending doesn't even need a needle and thread. When your child remembers that his costume must be hemmed in fifteen minutes for a school pageant that afternoon, give him the stapler and a smile. He'll be satisfied and so will you. He can learn to sew a real hem when there's a little more time. With supervision, a Nine is adept enough to iron on denim patches, and by Ten he can use the iron to apply gossamer underside patches on some special shirt.

It's in the preteen years that your child learns how—and why—to use a little preventive mending if you put aside the pants that need a button tightened or the skirt with the falling hem. You'll still have to inspire most of this mending, however, by handing over some of it to your child while you watch television together. If this habit can be established now, it's more likely to last, but don't expect a boy to be clothes-conscious enough to do this willingly until the early teens. If then.

A preteen usually finds the sewing machine interesting enough to sew two seams together and, if the machine has a free arm, to sew a patch in place with a hundred zigs and zags. This teaching requires more effort of you than you would spend if you did the work yourself but a child can't be productive until someone teaches him how to produce.

You'll still have to repair most—but not all—of the boring rips and tears in his clothes, but only for a while. With praise, a child in the Middle Years is willing to learn the skills of life, and the more he learns, the more he'll do.

Buttons

A child of Nine is old enough to sew on his own buttons and by Ten it should be required. He should know that this trade has its tricks too, if the button is to stay in place and if he's to feel successful about his work.

Teach him to sew it through a half dozen times, and if the button has four holes, he should just use two holes, knot the thread and then start again for the second pair, so that the button will still hang on if the other thread breaks. Before tying the final knot, he should wrap it under the button a couple of times to shank it so the button stands up as it should.

And if the button is metal, he should know it probably will cut the thread soon, unless he first runs the threaded needle through an old candle to wax it and then paints the thread with clear nail polish when the button is sewed in place. It's a bit of fastidiousness that few boys or girls will bother about, unless they're about Twelve and the party is mighty special.

Hems

When a child learns a job she'll use for life—like hemming—she may as well learn to do it right. A Ten can do the job especially well. Have her open the seams, measure and fold up the hem so the seams meet and pin it at those points, so the hem will hang smoothly and evenly. She then measures the hem all around, inserting the pins vertically and taking tiny, tiny tucks in the hem if the skirt or pants leg is flared, to let the hem lie flat. As a final check, have her model it for you, to make sure the hem is straight.

She then doubles the thread, for strength, so each length is 12–15″ long for easy sewing, and unknotted, for neatness. Several little stitches on the edge of the hem, each on top of the other, will make it secure. She then starts to hem by taking a stitch and throwing the thread over the needle to lock it in place before going on to the next.

Remind her to keep the stitches small and even and as invisible on the top side as possible, and to smooth out the material as she goes so the thread stays fairly loose and pucker-free.

WASHING

A child of Nine or certainly Ten can wash and dry almost all of his own clothes, and many do it at Eight. He should keep the dirty ones in his own hamper and empty his own pockets, though you may want to supervise if he still uses crayons. At any rate, he'll learn to check once he's had too many of his baseball cards dissolve. It's been years since children's clothes faded or shrank but you'll have to take care of clothes that need bleaching or scrubbing or those that are dark and new and might bleed a little. It's just a matter of going through his laundry basket occasionally and doing the extra wash maybe once a month.

You will have to show your child how to set the dials, how much soap to use and about how many clothes your machine will hold but little else. The dryer is just a matter of dials and a lint filter. And will your child make a bit of a mess? Yes, but only for a while. And will it be worth it? Absolutely, after a while.

IRONING

This chore is a bother if your child has many cotton clothes but he still should know how to take care of them. A Ten can iron napkins or press a new hem under a damp cloth to get a sharper edge. A Twelve can handle a long-sleeved shirt—and should. If he can iron that, he can iron anything: it has all the problems. And if he irons it in a certain order, he'll solve them.

Have him sprinkle his cotton shirt lightly, wrap it in a tight ball and leave it for 15 minutes. With a hot iron—and your supervision—he irons the shirt in a certain order so it won't be wrinkled when it's done, although he may try it his way for a few times. Have him first press the inside of the yoke, the facings, and the undersides of the cuffs, the collar and the pocket, and then the collar and cuffs, the yoke and the tab, the sleeves, the two front panels, and finally the back.

It is amazing how a 100% cotton shirt loses its appeal when it has to be ironed by the fellow who wears it.

A mother may be the first to joke about the shortcomings of her child—just to show how objective she is—but secretly she knows her daughter or son is brilliant, beautiful, charming, winsome, witty and graceful. Never mind that this child bumps into displays at the supermarket, answers in words of one syllable, gets straight C's or has ears that fly away. If the signs of superiority are not obvious this week they surely will be next week or next year.

The child is not so sure. From his point of view he is stupid (not even one A on his report); ugly (he has the biggest feet in the class, and his ears flap like Dumbo's); tongue-tied (just let a grown-up visit and he freezes). And graceful? Then why did he knock down the stack of canned peas at the store when he was trying to hide from Mary Sue, the blabbermouth who gets straight A's?

Your child needs only to be teased a few times or to overhear some candid comment to have a minor flaw turn into a first-class cause for travail. Reality, of course, is somewhere in between, but the child believes his own perceptions, not yours.

One otherwise sensible and charming Twelve decided that her toes were strangely long, and when her sisters agreed and said that was why her feet were bigger than theirs, she decided that her feet were elephantine. Being a child who kept her problems to herself, she said little about it except to make fun of her "gunboats"—an invitation to be teased—and when she bought new sneakers she would soon insist she needed a bigger pair. By the time she was up to size 7½ she had become awkward and tripped a lot—not unusual at that age—and the tap class she begged for only made it worse. It wasn't until a shoe salesman insisted on measuring her feet that she found she still wore size 6. Instant beauty.

The moral: if your child thinks his feet (or his hands or his nose) are too big, they are sure to grow bigger—if only in his head. Your child needs you to help him cope with all such problems, real or imaginary, without any jokes or lectures which would dismiss his concerns as frivolous. They may be to you, but not to him.

Without such help your Twelve probably isn't going to feel charming, witty, winsome or graceful even if he is; for beauty, at this age, is in the eye of the holder. Unless boys and girls feel good about the way they look and how they move their bodies, they'll never get that stellar air.

While trimming noses (or toeses) is rarely called for, nature does sometimes need a positive nudge. There's nothing immoral about having a child's ears pinned back or getting that slight operation on the breastbone so the posture straightens up; the belly button tucked in or the nipples popped out. Most of these solutions are quick one-time operations and will do far more to improve a child's self-esteem than any compliment or present you can give. Some children are not fazed by such problems, but it's unwise to assume that your child is one of them.

Other children need help to hear better or see better—and they don't even know it—or they have a minor chronic problem, like stuttering or an overbite, or they're bothered by something unmentionable (so it isn't, at least not yet). Some problems affect the whole family. A child may be overweight, which calls for the rest of the family to be understanding, tactful and willing to give up any junk food at home.

Another child may have a mild to middling behavioral problem, which you may be able to resolve by changing his teacher or his school or by encouraging him to take up a new hobby or sport, where he can make new friends. If none of this makes a difference, your child should get a thorough workup to rule out the many physical problems that can cause emotional reactions, and then a psychological evaluation and possibly some psychotherapy.

Whether the problem is in the body, the mind or the spirit, your child needs the right diagnosis to get the right treatment, and to get what every child deserves every day: the chance to be joyous, to feel well and to learn easily.

HEARING

If a child is deaf, his parents are in essence deaf too, for if he can't speak, they can't listen. No other handicap is so isolating and, unless it is corrected by surgery, by hearing aids or by developing other ways to talk, it will inhibit him for life. When sounds can't be heard at 90 decibels, the loss is called profound. A serious hearing loss—when sounds that register at 26 decibels seem muffled to him—is usually noticed by first grade.

It's the child with a mild hearing loss who is the hardest to spot. Whether genetic or the result of an illness or accident, it can be undetected for years. A somewhat deaf child automatically learns to lip-read without realizing it, and if he is part of a loving, unified, articulate family the other members learn to talk to him a little louder and face to face, again without realizing it.

This mild impairment is usually overlooked in school too, but a child seldom gets the automatic, sympathetic adjustments he finds at home. Instead, the hard-of-hearing child is teased by others for being slow, or he is shut out of games on the playground because he may not respond to a teammate, which makes him sure he is either dumb or disliked. Unless this child is helped, there is no way he can feel like a successful person or even know he has a problem. It's hard to believe, but no matter how poorly a child hears, he is sure the rest of the world hears just the same as he does.

If the teacher doesn't recognize the problem, she may tell you that you have been too lenient and your child is disobedient, willful and stubborn and that he huddles in the back of the classroom, refusing to take part. She calls him and he's too busy to answer. She explains the math and he won't even try to understand it.

"Go to a psychologist," says the teacher. "Your child has a problem with authority." Perhaps he does—and he surely will have one if this keeps up—but take an inventory first. The child who seems withdrawn, who mumbles, who turns up the television louder than anyone else, who watches your face when you talk and answers questions you don't ask needs to be taken to an otologist or a licensed clinical audiologist. There is a critical need to diagnose the problem as soon as possible, but the cause may not be serious. Sometimes deafness can be caused by nothing more than a chronic sinus blockage—especially if it's much worse in the morning—for the eustachian tubes are more horizontal in children than in adults and they don't always drain well. It also may be caused by a plug of wax that has blocked the canal for years as well as by other, graver possibilities, such as an eardrum that has been ruptured by a high fever or a sharp object.

There can be a neural loss affecting frequency too, caused by either a genetic problem or some very loud noise, like firecrackers or his big brother's stereo. Music played all day, as loud as a rock band, is twenty to thirty decibels above the danger level set by the government for an eight-hour period and affects everyone within earshot. After each long, loud exposure, the hearing in the high (or low) frequency will spring back like a rubber band in a couple of hours, but each time it will be a little less springy until finally there is a neural loss. Here the soft *p*'s and *t*'s and *s*'s merge into a single slur, the church bells stop ringing and the birds don't sing anymore.

If your child has a hearing impairment that can't be fixed (in some cases malformed bones in the middle ear—so often inherited—can be rebuilt), he will need you to help him understand that everyone is handicapped in some way and each person must get the help he needs to do his best with what he has. And then you must help him do exactly that, first by learning all about hearing aids and how different people need different types. An audiologist will fit him with a hearing aid that suits his particular needs, but be prepared: it may take awhile to find the best aid, for all of them have some drawbacks. Your child also will learn exactly how the aid works and how to change the batteries so he can take care of it himself. Since it is an extension of his body, he should be responsible, although a Six will need you to check it often to make sure it still works well.

Getting your child to use his hearing aid won't be easy, particularly at first. A child doesn't want anything that sets him further apart from the class, especially at this age, and the sudden new intake of noise will be jangling. It will bother him less if he uses it for just an hour or two a day and if he wears it in the quietest room in the house, so he can listen to only one set of noises at a time: a bedtime story he has never heard before or some gentle music on the record player. Teach him to work with a tape recorder, letting him talk and sing and whistle into it, so he can hear it played back. This particularly should be done in privacy at first; like everyone else, he will be embarrassed when he first hears his own voice reproduced.

It's also important to go on walks together in a quiet park, and for him to describe the sound of a bird, if he can; the splash of the water fountain; the thudding of the stone he throws on the grass. When he can identify the background noises, they won't make him so anxious and he can screen out the unnecessary ones, just as you do, although this will be easier if his aid has special circuitry to help him do the job better. You also encourage your child to rely on the aid if you don't face him when you speak and if you stop talking so loud. Otherwise the volume he sets on the aid will be wrong when he is with others and he will be uneasy.

If your child still can't adjust to the aid after a couple of months, he will need to try other brands, some more audiotherapy and maybe some psychotherapy too. In time you can bet on it: your child will want to wear the aid all day, for the joy of hearing is its own reward.

An irreversible loss of the hearing nerves needs much more intensive help from parents and it needs their acceptance too. With counseling, a support group (see Resources) and the comfort of other parents of deaf children, a mother can even accept the haunting knowledge that a particular deafness might have been caused in early pregnancy by a virus, German measles, the Rh factor or venereal disease. The child with a very serious or profound hearing loss needs whatever aid he can get to improve the hearing he has, and special education as well. Although he may be mainstreamed in the regular classroom, many deaf graduates who have gone through both systems say they felt less isolated when they went to school with deaf classmates, for they all talked the same language there.

Sign language (six are used in the United States alone) is the universal bridge, but there is also finger spelling; oralism—a very difficult process in which a child reads lips and learns to speak with his own voice (although he can't hear it); and cued speech, in which lip reading is combined with a small international phonic vocabulary of signs—a technique that works especially well for the children who started before Four and have at least some hearing.

If you're the parent of a deaf child, you

spend hours helping him understand simple ideas, for the whole world is like a foreign country to him and you are the principal guide. The frustrations are many, but somehow the pleasure is greater. The more you invest in motherhood, the more you treasure the child.

EYESIGHT

A pair of eyeglasses can do wonderful things for a child—and so on occasion can the lack of a pair. One young mother named Chris remembers when it turned her into a saint—the only seven-year-old saint on record. This wasn't because she was so good (although the honor certainly made her act better) but because the trees had started talking to her and people walked around like shimmering visions, especially in the lamplight. She even saw a halo around her head when she looked in the mirror, just like the statues at church. It wasn't until Chris got glasses that the halo disappeared and she found people standing next to those trees. Sainthood had a short run.

A child's eyesight can change around Seven or Eight—a time of growth—just as it may change when he shoots up as a young teenager. Although the eye doesn't get much bigger, compared to the rest of the body, it still adds about nine millimeters to its length between birth and maturity. As this happens, the cornea changes its curvature and a child may lose the

farsightedness he was born with—the kind of vision his ancestors needed to hunt for food, and which he'll probably lose as he gets older.

The child who didn't have great distance vision at Four may now get nearsighted—or, as the doctor says, myopic—and faraway objects will become a blur. This is the child who tries to adapt in class by snuggling up to the blackboard, but don't wait for him to tell you about the problem if he's under Eight or even a little older. A young child is sure that everyone else sees just like he does and thinks the new and misty distance outside is normal, as we learned when Mike asked us in amazement, "You mean you're supposed to see the baseball coming?"

While many children need glasses to see in the distance, only a small number are farsighted—which means they can see things in the distance better than they can read a book, since reading takes only three units of focusing power and they have about twelve.

There are many signs that a checkup is needed. A child needs a test if he is clumsy or extrasensitive to sunlight; tilts or turns his head to see better; gets dizzy, queasy or headachy after doing close work; has trouble with this work or puts his face very near to a book or the papers on his desk; often squints, blinks, frowns or rubs his eyes; has a whitish reflection in the eye or has red or watery eyes or frequent styes or says his eyes are itchy, scratchy or that they burn. He also needs a test if he can't read the calendar across the room or tell whether that blob down the block is a dog or a cat, or when he has trouble with the 20/20 vision test at school—or if he suddenly decides he's a saint. A child also needs an eye checkup, as well as an ear test and a full neurological exam, if he withdraws so much, physically and emotionally, that he seems slow in school.

The kind of eye test your child needs depends on what kind he has had before. Ideally, he has seen a pediatric ophthalmologist, since it takes an M.D. to give the special eyedrops to dilate the eyes and discover amblyopia—lazy eye—a condition which affects one child in fifty. Here one eye does more work than the other, causing the lazy eye to lose some of its sight unless the strong one is covered with a black patch. This simple technique cures 90–95% of children at Four, but if treatment is delayed until Eight, success drops to 25%, and after that the eyesight quickly gets much worse and may even be totally lost in that eye.

A checkup also can pick up color blindness, although you can't do a thing about it, nor do you need to do anything. A genetic problem, it usually affects only boys, and seldom very much.

Since eyesight changes, your child should see the ophthalmologist or an optometrist every couple of years in grade school.

One child in twenty-five has some kind of muscle problem—crossed or wall eyes or some difficulty with the vertical alignment—and if it is bad enough he may need an eye patch, exercises, glasses or surgery—or all of these treatments—to correct it.

Any unequal vision requires glasses and so does an astigmatism, when the far or the near images are blurred, either in one eye or in both. There is also the possibility that there may be a millisecond of difference between the time it takes each eye to register a picture. Some say this can cause learning problems, a situation usually only recognized and diagnosed by a developmental optometrist and treated with eye exercises, but both the diagnosis and the treatment are controversial.

If a child does need glasses, he should be the one who chooses them—within your price range of course—for the choice is very personal. Even so, a child—particularly a boy—may refuse to wear them until his need is bigger than his vanity. (Peacocks are male, after all.) He can, however, use contacts (in fact, even babies can) although most children don't want them until their early teens. No single type of lens is best for everybody—hard, semisoft or soft—although soft lenses generally are better for active children, since they are bigger and pop out less often, but keep up with the latest information on this type of eye care, for it is rapidly changing.

CROOKED TEETH

When your child was Three you probably began the first of his annual checkups with the dentist. Now, at Seven, he may have to see an orthodontist if he has an overbite or if the teeth are crowded, crooked or widely spaced.

Although a bad bite usually runs in the family, it may be caused if a child sucks his thumb or pushes his tongue against his teeth or loses his baby teeth too soon (or not soon enough). Whatever the reason, the problem won't go away by itself and it has other effects. Crooked teeth will make any child—particularly a teenager—self-conscious and can cause extra cavities and gum problems in an adult. While teeth can be corrected at any age, there is a best time for everything and it's simpler to start now.

You need an orthodontist rather than the family dentist for this work. He has had at least two extra years of dental school to learn how to straighten teeth—a very precise job—and enough experience to know that every mouth is different, so every treatment plan must be different too. Look for an orthodontist who is university-trained and either board-certified or in practice with someone who is. He also should be so interested in his job that he takes part in study clubs or regular seminars and has done work you have seen and admired. And, with all that, he should be a person both you and your child like, for you're going to see a lot of him over the next eight years.

Even though your child won't go into a full set of braces until he's around Twelve—or until his mouth is about as big as it ever will be—the orthodontist often does some preliminary work in the Middle Years. He may need to pull some teeth to make room for the rest to grow well or, in radical cases, to foreshorten the jaw. He may have your child wear a little hardware to move the teeth slightly, and at the least he will want to check him periodically to see if the mouth is ready for braces. It's this supervision that will make the braces work faster and the job look better, and at a cost that is included in the overall price, no matter when it starts.

In the first visit the orthodontist will measure the size of your child's teeth, whether erupted or not; the size of the jaws; and his profile. He also will gauge his emotional maturity, to see if he is old enough to cooperate, for this is the key to success. From now on the doctor—not the parent—handles the habit of thumb-sucking or tongue-thrusting, either by jollying the child along or by having him wear a tongue guard for as short as two weeks or as long as a year.

There are many contraptions that can make significant changes in these Middle Years. One is a lip bumper, usually worn only between the lower lip and the teeth—so the second set grow in straighter and less crowded. Another is braces, worn only on the back teeth. Perhaps the most common is the retainer, worn either on the roof or the floor of the mouth to tighten the gaps. Although retainers have a certain status symbol at this age, the first day can be discouraging to your child. Have him read aloud in his room to learn how to talk without spitting or lisping, for if he masters this quickly he won't be tempted to pop the retainer out of his mouth when other children come around. It's not a habit to be encouraged, since it not only is disconcerting but any appliance a child wears is delicate. If left on a table top, it might be dropped; if it's stashed in a back pocket it can be sat upon; and if your child

tucks it into a paper napkin, some tidy soul—probably you—may throw it away.

Headgear is one device that is hard to lose, but it is fragile too. It is also quite effective. Worn at night for twelve to fourteen hours for three to six months, it can move the teeth permanently as much as two millimeters. Since every style of headgear looks like something from outer space, a child may get self-conscious if it has to be worn to school too. One thoughtful mother helped her daughter accept it by pasting different hair ribbons on a half dozen straps, so she could change them to match her clothes.

If your child still has a bad bite after the orthodontist has done his preliminary work—and he probably will—braces will be required. Metal, plastic or even porcelain brackets will be glued to each tooth with a light wire running through a slot on each of them. Every month this wire is checked, twisted, turned and usually tightened by new bends or it is replaced with a stronger wire occasionally. These are all processes that make the mouth hurt for a day or two, for which kisses and perhaps even aspirin are prescribed. The metal also may conduct cold straight to the teeth, so any cold drink is best when sipped through a straw.

Usually the braces are worn from nine months to three years and a child might be in and out of them before he's Thirteen. How long it takes depends on the problem and the progress. There is no gain at all if the child misses an appointment or has a bent or broken wire for weeks, which can happen easily. The wires are so frail that hard or sticky food or bubble gum is strictly forbidden.

Braces sometimes prevent cavities, since they are stuck to the teeth so tightly, but they may cause them too. Decay may set in if a bracket gets loose, or if your child doesn't floss every day and brush that small space between the braces and the gums—which is hard to do—and if he doesn't rinse his mouth right after eating sweets. The job still isn't quite done when the braces are finally removed. Your child will have to wear a retainer for six months until the teeth are set in place and occasionally even after that. In fact, he may be old enough to drive a car before the bite is right, and you surely will be broke enough to have paid for at least a secondhand one. The cost of braces, paid for on a monthly basis, should include evaluations, records, X rays, impressions, materials and appointments, starting at Seven, but not lost retainers or broken headgear.

STUTTERING

Stuttering is the claustrophobia of speech. Even though stutterers can speak fluently 95% of the time, that other 5% is agony. Nothing else causes so much panic and so many cold sweats, such rapid heartbeats and heartfelt embarrassment; and, unlike claustrophobia, it isn't limited to an elevator or a crowded train, but occurs any place where there may be another human being. The problem can be so acute that isolation may become a way of life for this child.

All preschoolers have some "disfluency," as it's called, repeating a word several times, perhaps because they have so much to say now that they can talk. This repetition or hesitation usually cures itself but a true stutterer has a much tougher time. This child stumbles over the same sound or the same "part words" again and again and in any of many patterns. Although half of these children—perhaps even two thirds—cure themselves, you don't know if your child will be one of them and this is critical. If he is still stuttering at Six he needs professional help. The longer therapy is postponed, the harder it is to cure, for patterns, once set, die hard. If nothing else, stuttering is sure to cause some psychological problems.

First have your child evaluated by a speech-language pathologist—someone who has a good deal of experience, is sensitive to children and trained to recognize and work with the interplay in a family as well as with the stuttering itself. Your child will have therapy with this person and perhaps the whole family will decide to work with a psychotherapist too, to make sure the problem is not psychological and to help your child undo the damage that stuttering can cause.

Some experts think such problems are almost always psychological, partly because a child who stutters is more apt to do it with those who mean the most to him, like his parents or his teacher, and to stutter if his parents are also strivers and the child may feel he must achieve for them. These experts use family therapy or hypnosis—with or without drugs—to help the child face his anxieties.

More and more experts, however, consider it a physical problem—an argument made more reasonable since stuttering, like learning disabilities and retardation, afflicts many more boys than girls—in this case by a factor of 4 to 1. To these therapists, stuttering may be caused by an allergy or a poor rhythmic control or faulty learning or, more likely, a neurological malfunction that makes the speech commands short-circuit in the brain. These therapists either change the child's diet or change his behavior, using a kind of earplug to drown out other sounds or a dubious device, the metronome, to help him pace his words; or they use biofeedback, which is perhaps the most successful program because it monitors the throat muscles which may block speech.

In any case you'll need to be as patient with your child as possible, looking him straight in the eye as he talks and listening to what he says, not how he says it. This tells a child that he is loved, without any ifs, ands or buts, which gives the stutterer the acceptance he needs so the therapy can work better and quicker.

HEIGHT

Growing pains hurt the psyche most of all. The girl who suddenly shoots up at Eleven—and is sure she'll never quit shooting—is as miserable as the boy who barely inches along, lagging behind his friends.

Generally you can figure that tall people reach their full height early and short ones take longer than usual to grow. Boys can keep growing until they're about twenty-one but grow very little when they're a year or two past puberty, although some may grow until they're nineteen.

The tallest girls in the class may suffer from this problem in the preteens. If your daughter is afraid of growing too tall, subscribe to a fashion magazine for her so she can identify with the willowy models; enroll her in a modern dance class so she will learn how to carry her body with grace, and join the Y for some mother-daughter workouts, where she can develop a healthy pride in her body.

The shortest boys in the class are as dismayed as the tallest girls. These are the ones who need to know what to expect for themselves so they can either lay their worries to rest or adjust to the inevitable. Although doctors have a more scientific gauge, you can predict your child's height as an adult by finding out how tall he was at Two and doubling the inches, unless he was very tall or very short, or unless he has a serious illness or accident before he

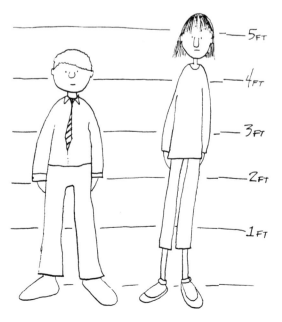

is grown. And if you don't like the results, or your child doesn't believe them, his ossification rate can be tested by a physiatrist to measure his bone age and therefore his future height.

The prediction may be disappointing but your child will feel more in control of the situation if he does what he can to reach his full growth. Old-fashioned doctors insist that plenty of nutritious food, exercise and sleep will add an inch or two to a child's height. In any case, he'll have years to adjust to his height and if you accept it with equanimity, rather than concern, he will feel better about it—the same acceptance a daughter needs when she feels too tall. If this isn't enough, a few visits with a thoughtful counselor can help children appreciate the height they're going to be. Compared to years of anxiety, this is a small price to pay.

POSTURE

There's probably never been a mother who didn't tell her young to sit up straight, stand up straight or keep his shoulders straight, but it isn't always easy or natural. While some children are born to sit up straight with shoulders squared, you'll find that round-shouldered children tend to sit on the middle of their backs, no matter how much their mums fuss.

Since good posture is a sign of harmony in the body, however, it's wise to have the doctor check your child for scoliosis—curvature of the spine—so he can start treatment with special exercises or even a back brace to prevent a serious problem later.

The doctor should also check your child's balance, especially if he has headaches, backaches and fatigue. These problems can come not only from poor posture but from a bad fall that has thrown a child's structure out of balance, causing the muscles to be weaker on one side than the other. This is the child who always tilts his head to one side or whose hands have one palm face backward more than the other when they're hanging at his side. Even without a doctor, you can tell if the body is symmetrical by hanging a plumb bob in a doorway and having him stand behind it, quite still, to see if the shoulders are level and don't roll forward; the waist has an equal curve on either side; the legs are straight, not knocked or bowed; the feet don't roll over on either side when standing. A well-balanced child even opens his mouth evenly, with the jaw dropping straight, without leaning either to the right or the left, and his gait is even when he walks or runs, and the arms swing at the same rate.

If you think your child's balance is a little askew, don't nag, because nagging doesn't make muscles stronger. Karate or dancing might, however. A good teacher who understands the structural alignment of the body will help your child straighten his body—and make it fun.

FEET

Bad feet, like bad tires, can throw the whole body out of alignment. After a while, nothing is on an even keel, including the child's disposition.

In one big Eastern city, nearly a third of the preschool and elementary children tested had some sort of foot problem. They included the ones a mother could see—blisters, hookworm or a virus, like a plantar wart—but many had symptoms that seemed unrelated to the feet. If your child has pains in his legs—the ankles, calves, knees or thighs—or his head, his neck, his shoulders, his back or his hips, his feet may be responsible, especially if the aches wake him up at night.

There are other signs that a child seldom will notice—or mention—so it's up to you to notice if he stumbles a lot; avoids running or walking much; gets overtired; walks strangely or has poor posture; has ankles that bulge a bit on the inside or feet that perspire more than normal.

The problem is almost sure to be minor and either the pediatrician or the podiatrist can treat it easily; quite often the shoe salesman can too. A child under Eight will almost never mention that his shoes have gotten too small.

WEIGHT

Mothers have many rights, but they don't have the right to let their children get fat. A little pudginess is all right, of course. Since children grow in only one direction at a time—up or out—an extra 10% over the ideal weight is nothing to worry about. In fact, to make these children lose weight could slow their growth. It could also put a child, particularly a girl, at particular risk, for unnecessary dieting can lead to an unfortunate preoccupation with her weight. It might even encourage her to act out psychological problems later if depression or stress first trips a case of anorexia nervosa or bulimia—the tragic weight loss syndromes that strike so many young women (and almost no young men).

When children are more than 20% overweight, however, they are at the beginning range of obesity. It's especially important to take care of a serious weight problem now, because the condition can color a child's whole life. If this happens he might not live as long or be as healthy as nature intended.

A weight problem is not caused by diet alone, however. Genetics play a big role. Even if children are adopted, they have four chances in ten of being fat if their

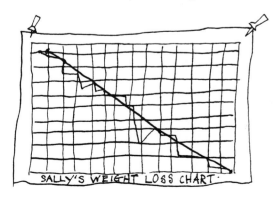

SALLY'S WEIGHT LOSS CHART.

biological mothers are fat, and eight chances in ten if both biological parents are heavy, for a low metabolism can be inherited. Nevertheless, it is possible to help overweight children change their diets—and therefore their set points—so they won't feel hungry before they really need to eat.

Other weight problems are triggered in the first two years of life and in adolescence, when the body makes bigger fat cells, and more of them, which makes obesity more likely as an adult. Babies don't mind being fat but schoolchildren do. Psychologically, the effects begin now, for they grow up thinking that fatness is inevitable. The problem peaks around the fifth grade and the effects are often lasting. A woman is particularly apt to judge herself by the way she looked and moved between Ten and Eighteen. No matter how slim—or fat—she becomes, the mental picture stays the same. Time softens the intensity, but the underlying pain or pleasure remains.

When children are fat, they are embarrassed every day of their lives. This is the girl who never feels truly good about herself and weeps in the dressing room with the three-way mirror. This is the boy who is never chosen first (or fifth) on the baseball team; who is pitied by the kind child in the class and mocked by many others.

While the tendency to be obese is often inherited, the eating patterns a child chooses are almost always set by the person who markets and cooks. Moreover, the child follows the gains and losses in the family, so that everyone is likely to get fatter, or thinner, at about the same time. And that's the key to the problem. A child seldom gets fat all alone. When you can admit that, you realize that it's a matter of breaking old habits—yours and his. The longer he has been overweight, the more help you both may need.

The pediatrician is usually the best adviser, to make sure your child is well, to rule out metabolic problems and to tell both of you exactly how much the child should lose. You'll need a second opinion, however, if the doctor says he will outgrow a serious weight problem—since this isn't too likely—or that an extra 20% hardly matters, even though his rubber tire is considerably more than an inch when it's pinched.

You also may want to enroll him in a medically directed weight control clinic for children at a teaching hospital. They're hard to find but worth it, since individual or group counseling is usually part of the package. You will learn a lot from it too. Sometimes it takes an outsider to teach you that you can't tempt a child to lose weight by buying his clothes a bit too small or promising him a trip to Disneyland "if you lose twenty-five pounds by Christmas." The only expectations worth having are the ones your child sets for himself. Your job is to help him make this goal realistic and a little easier to achieve.

Most doctors call for a child to lose no more than a half pound a week, so the weight stays lost. Your child won't lose that tire overnight at this pace, but he didn't gain it that fast either. He will need a lot of encouragement until the metabolism changes and the hungries go away—which takes about two weeks—and until the loss begins to show enough to win compliments outside of the family, which takes longer. He also will need extra encouragement when he reaches the plateaus—when the weight stays the same for two to three weeks—and near the end of the diet, when all the processes in the body slow down and fewer calories are burned.

Whether you monitor the diet or not, your child must decide what he eats, now and for the rest of his life. If you expect him to choose wisely, he has to know how and why. When he changes his habits he will lose weight, and if the new habits stick he won't gain it back, although he may fight the problem all his life if he has inherited it.

LOSING WEIGHT

Before starting, your child needs six helpers: a graph; a calorie chart; an exercise chart; two scales, and a small memo book. You make the chart for him on graph paper, a block for every half pound. On it he will draw a line from where he is to where he wants to be, and every week he draws another line to show his progress—hopefully on top of the first one, so he should use a different color.

He needs the calorie chart to count the calories he eats and the exercise chart to count the ones he burns. The scale in the bathroom is for his weekly weigh-in, always done at the same time of day, and a small counter-top one in the kitchen is used to weigh his food in grams and ounces. He can translate a gram of carbohydrate and a gram of protein into four calories each, and a gram of fat into nine—a sobering thought, but a dandy way to learn arithmetic.

The memo book is for writing down what he eats—the secret of most successful dieters and something that the list-keeping Nine might like to do, although he won't do it very well. No matter. You study it together once a week to help him see the pitfalls, but don't get mad when he succumbs to what our flock lovingly calls a "blubbo attack." It's bound to happen.

Your child should know that a calorie is a unit of energy and that he needs 1500–2400 of them a day to run, to study and to sleep, depending on his build and his exercise, but he won't be healthy unless most of his calories come from the four basic food groups. This leaves precious little room for sweets and fats. He also should know that it takes 3500 more calories to gain a pound—and 3500 less calories to lose it unless he's been eating a lot of fatty foods, like potato chips. Some new studies say that these calories are much harder to lose.

Your child has to learn how to think the way thin people do, although he probably will never think cantaloupe tastes better than cheesecake. Who could? To think thin, your child must

- eat only when he's hungry;
- measure his food before he eats, at least when he's at home;
- eat only when he's sitting at the table, whether at home or at school, and always at the same time;
- put down his fork after each bite;
- stop during the meal to talk;
- skip seconds of everything but his own birthday cake.

And between meals he has to do the hardest thing of all:

- wait at least ten minutes if he wants to eat something special—usually long enough for the yearning to pass.

Exercise is one helper a child gives himself, but he may not want to start an ambitious exercise regimen until he is in better shape. This usually takes about a month of very mild exercising—just an extra ten minutes every other day—which will accelerate his heartbeat enough to improve his conditioning 80%. The more he exercises, the more energetic he will feel, for every muscle works as an auxiliary heart, taking in more oxygen (see Exercise).

It even helps if you park on the far side of the mall, so your child has to walk to the store, and if you climb a flight or two of stairs when you take him to the dentist. A child might like to wear a pedometer—on his belt, to be accurate—to see how many miles he walks each day, although it will seldom be as many as he thinks.

When your child does start to work out (don't call it exercise), he needs privacy, with no other company in the garage or the basement but the timer, so he can skip rope or touch toes without feeling silly. Overweight children shouldn't be expected to jog or bike publicly until they are ready to be seen and possibly teased. This is particularly true for boys.

FAMILY SUPPORT

Your child also needs the privacy of silence from the whole family. The checker at the store needn't know about his diet, nor the neighbors, nor your company, nor even the children who sleep over, and they won't if everyone in the household is discreet. When a child hears his secret blathered about, a lot of heart goes out of the project.

It is the familial support that will help him the most and you're the one who sets the tone. You do it by calling the family together for a pep talk on loyalty, telling them that Jamie—or Janey—needs their help, by keeping temptation out of the way and by praising the child when any weight is lost. You also must insist that teasing is absolutely forbidden, just as it would be if he had acne or a limp. Fatness is no joke.

It is the practical side of the diet that may make the other children mad, since this diet means the end of the frozen waffles, the cupcakes, the cookies, the sodas and the potato chips in the house. Even after those pounds are lost, there shouldn't be much of this food around. If it can make one person in the family gain too much weight, then everyone is vulnerable—the best argument you can make to get cooperation. There is sure to be some grumbling anyway, if only for psychological reasons.

In the meantime, you should look into your soul to see if you or your husband treat your overweight child differently from the thin child in the family. Do you ask the thin one to run most of your errands? Does the fat child beg for an ice cream cone—and get it? Does one always get board games for Christmas and the other get the sports gear? Do you give big allowances, even though you know your heavy child spends every cent on the vending machines? A little evenhandedness is necessary, but if he has a savings account, he can bank any money sent by doting relatives and all but a minimum of his allowance.

Much of the weight problem your child has can be prevented by the measures you take. Serve meals low in protein and especially in fats, and with a high amount of complex carbohydrates—grains, vegetables and, to a much lesser extent, fruit. You should also stop getting whatever food the overweight child likes to eat in quantity, every day, like peanut butter. It not only is a temptation, but it may signify an allergy—the sort that makes him feel bad if he doesn't get a daily dose. If this is the problem, the diet will be even harder at first, but much easier after four or five days, when the food—and therefore the craving for it—is out of his system.

The way you store food matters too. Use opaque containers, if you can, both on the counter and in the refrigerator, so the sight of it doesn't get the taste buds going. You also should store any fattening foods like butter and mayonnaise in the back of the refrigerator, behind the celery and carrot sticks.

At dinner, use candlelight and flowers—things that help the eyes make up for the tastes that might be missed—and try new recipes. Not only does oriental cooking have fewer calories, but the Japanese in particular have a culture based on scarcity, so food comes in slivers and not in chunks.

Whatever you cook, cook less of it. To put one potato in the stew for each person and one for the pot is foolhardy: you know whose pot it's going to fill. From now on, food is boiled, broiled, baked or braised, but never sautéed, fried or breaded. Fish is preferred, then chicken, and both are cooked without their skin. Meat, when you do serve it, must be free of fat and you'll have to strike bread, rolls, sauces and gravies from the dinner menu, and serve fruit for dessert. Nondieters can eat other foods when they aren't at home and fruit can satisfy their sweet tooth when they are. The roughage of fruit also makes it more filling than juice, and less fattening; it takes a lot of oranges to fill a glass.

If the bread is dark and hearty and the food is unrefined there is much more roughage and more vitamins too. This means that you will skip many mixes and manufactured products, which is just as well. They seldom give much bulk and they usually are full of some form of sugar—the only food the body can't use. Besides, sugar, like salt, whets the appetite for something else to eat. Even substitute sweeteners and diet sodas are a bad idea. They have no food value; they mask the taste of pure food and they don't change eating habits, so your child will eat as many sweets as ever when the diet is done.

When you serve the foods that satisfy the appetite most, you help your child lose weight much quicker, and you help the eating habits of the whole family.

To help your child stay on his diet, he needs a good breakfast—eggs or instant oatmeal, instead of dry cereal; a midmorning snack, if possible, so he doesn't get ravenous by noon and overeat; a sensible lunch; a snack to sustain the blood sugar; and—hold on to your hat—a three-course dinner.

This meal isn't as complicated as it sounds. If you and your husband have a drink before dinner, serve raw vegetables at the same time as an hors d'oeuvre for everyone. This isn't an appetizer but an appetite-killer, so your child won't be as hungry twenty minutes later when he sits down to eat. Otherwise, start dinner with a thin soup or a salad, using an oil and vinegar dressing. By tossing it vigorously, like a good French chef, you'll coat the leaves so well you can use much, much less. The main course is served from the head of the table, which lets you regulate the size of the servings, and the dessert is one of a dozen combinations of fresh fruit.

When you serve the meal in segments, it will last a half hour and by then everyone will feel full. It is also a civilized length of time for a family to sit together and share the news, and it will be pleasant as long as you don't allow gripes, complaints, corrections and especially any talk about the foods people can or can't eat.

Since adult dieters find the remains of a meal hard to resist, you can't expect more of your child. That's why you have to help with the cleanup. When a patrolman walks the beat, the burglar stays home.

Altogether these changes may seem like a lot of trouble, and they are, but if a family has one basic function, it is to support each member in it. While you won't get a thank you, you can't give your overweight child a present that will be appreciated more. It will be like handing him a plateful of self-esteem.

SHOEBOX DIET

The easiest time for your child to stick to a diet is when he's full and the best time to start one is right after dinner—every night.

This diet begins with a new pair of shoes or, at the least, a shoebox. Together fill the empty box with all the food he may eat the next day—including his share of the food you will cook for dinner, or little notes that say "2 oz. frozen cauliflower" or "¼ c. spaghetti sauce," checking the calories with your child as you prepare the box. By measuring all the calories at one time he gets a graphic idea of how much he can eat in a day and still lose weight.

The bread slices, cereal and meat are stored in sandwich bags; the milk is measured into a jar and capped; the oil is spooned into an empty herb bottle; and things that can't spill—like peanut butter and tuna fish—are put in those little glass custard dishes. All goes into the shoebox, the box goes into the refrigerator, and every meal, every snack, comes out of it. This not only keeps impulse eating within bounds but it changes a child's bad eating habits too, for there are some built-in lessons in this diet.

Even though the food is planned into meals, your child is allowed to eat whatever he wants from it, whenever he wants, but when the box is empty—that's it. Lesson #1.

Since the fear of running out of food scares anyone who is fat, your child at first will be much more likely to have food left at the end of the day. This is either put back in the larder or counted into the next day's allotment. Since there is no hoarding, there can be no food binges. Lesson #2. It doesn't take long to learn that moderation is a reward in itself.

For a child on 1900 calories a day, the contents of a shoebox might look like this:

Breakfast:
(Poached Egg on Toast)

4 oz. tomato juice	22
1 egg	80
1 slice whole wheat bread	60
½ oz. butter	51

Snack:
(Celery Boats)

2 celery stalks	10
1 1½ oz. cream cheese	150

Lunch:
(Tuna Salad Sandwich)

2 oz. oil-packed tuna, drained	113
1 celery stalk, chopped	5
1 T. lemon juice	8
1 T. mayonnaise	100
2 slices rye bread	120
1 3″ apple	100
8 oz. skim milk	85

Snack:
(Unbuttered Popcorn)
(Peanut Butter on Banana Slices)

½ c. popcorn, unpopped	50
1 T. peanut butter, sugar-free	95
1 banana, sliced	119
8 oz. skim milk	85

Dinner:
(Baked Chicken with Vegetables; Broccoli; Salad)

1 skinned chicken breast	120
baked with ½ c. water, tarragon and	
1 medium potato	105
3 carrots	90
½ yellow onion	10
1 broccoli tree, steamed with	45
¼ lemon, squeezed	8
¼ head Boston lettuce, mixed with	5
½ tomato, sliced	13

½ T. olive oil	65
½ t. vinegar	
8 oz. skim milk	85
½ c. fresh strawberries	28

Bedtime:

½ orange	65

Because the calorie content may change from brand to brand, teach your child to become a label reader. He'll also learn how many chemicals are added and realize how junk food got its name.

ALLERGIES & AGGRAVANTS

Most of us know that penicillin or a bee sting can send some people into shock, but even pediatricians often forget that simple allergies can cause chronic problems, physical and emotional, and upset the whole family. People—children and adults—can be allergic or simply sensitive to anything that can be breathed, eaten or touched, particularly if it's new to our culture. Our diet and our environment have changed radically in the past two hundred years, but not our bodies. We just can't evolve that fast.

A common food or substance, such as milk or chalk dust, can cause a lot of trouble too, giving your schoolchild a sore throat or a cranky mood every time he comes in contact with it. Fifteen to 20% of all schoolchildren have allergies but only one out of three is being treated for them. That's why a mother should look to an allergy or an intolerance if the child has any chronic problem, of either the body or the behavior. Reactions may scarcely be noticed—particularly when they are overshadowed by a major symptom—or they may be so alarming you rush your child to the emergency room or to a psychiatrist.

There are many unsettled questions in the field, but most doctors agree that these sensitivities can be expressed in hundreds of ways including the classic allergic salute—a swipe of the forefinger under the nose; dark circles or puffiness around the eyes; a headache, including a migraine; a stuffy nose (or a runny one); a sneezing bout; weepy or itchy eyes, or itchy ears, nose, mouth, throat or skin; red ears or earaches; poor hearing; blurry vision; toothaches; postnasal drip; swollen glands; tonsillitis; laryngitis; bronchitis; stressful breathing; yawning; asthma; bloating stomach or puffy hands or feet; belching; upset stomach, colic or stomachache; vomiting; urinary infections; frequency of urination; bedwetting; colitis; constipation; flatulence; dizziness; aching joints; rashes; acne; hives; eczema—the list goes on. Allergies can affect behavior and lifelong fits of crankiness can become so routine that no one suspects the cause—even the child.

Consider allergies if your child has anxiety; nervousness; temper outbursts to the point of violence; drowsiness; fatigue; depression; confusion; erratic behavior; concentration difficulties; mood swings; clumsiness; hyperactivity and hypoactivity; and one of the best indicators of any reaction: handwriting that is suddenly unreadable or letters that are reversed.

Allergies can start (and stop) at any time. They are often inherited, but they surface when the person has tripped some body gauge by eating a great amount of peanut butter for weeks or by spending too much time around timothy grass or roses. The breast-fed baby who gets colic after his mother drinks a cup of coffee or eats an orange has probably had this sensitivity triggered in the womb and is likely to have allergies later in life.

A new allergy often surfaces, or an old one resumes, when the body—or the mind or the psyche—has been under major, prolonged stress. A nasty illness, a broken leg, an embarrassing learning disability, a move, a death in the family, a divorce—all of these can cause a sensitivity. A change of hormones also seems to coincide with the beginning, or the end, of allergies.

An allergy, or an intolerance, can come from kapok or chlorine to gasoline or paint, and indeed, from everything under the sun—and even the sun itself.

Mold—the most ubiquitous allergen of all—has dozens of varieties that float through the air. Their spores shower on us before it rains; blanket the city when the pollution count goes up (for pollution is mold); grow invisibly on bathroom tiles and on leaves that fall from the trees; and they can make up much of our house dust.

The child who showed symptoms as an infant is likely to react to foods now and to the mold in foods. It is found in any leftovers refrigerated for more than twenty-four hours, and in such things as yogurt, pickles, canned tomatoes, canned or frozen juices, cheese, mayonnaise, smoked meats, hamburger (unless you have just ground it yourself), mushrooms, dark, yeasty breads and coffeecakes, vinegar and the wine (especially the reds) a Twelve might be allowed to sip at Christmas dinner. Milk, however, is the food that bothers children (and adults) most, followed by many other fine, natural products—grains; eggs; the salicylates in orange juice and aspirin; pork and beef; peanuts; chocolate. Or some of the 2800 additives and preservatives permitted in our foods can be the culprits.

Once an allergy begins, the reactions will be worse under certain circumstances. The child who can eat an occasional tomato without distress may react to one if he is particularly tired or cold or under tension, or when the air is redolent with smog or fresh-cut grass or ragweed. It is a case of too much, all at once.

And now for the good news: almost all allergies are reversible. They can disappear of their own accord, just as they spring up. About 80% of all allergies will go away if you simply avoid them for several months and then introduce them quite slowly—provided, of course, there are no aggravants around, the child has been getting a lot of rest and he is relatively free of stress—good or bad.

Another 20% of all allergies are fixed, particularly those that cause an anaphalactic reaction—the syndrome that begins with hives and wheezing and in rare cases can escalate to shock or even death. Although there is a new vaccine to control this reaction to bee stings, avoidance is the only safe course for the child who is subject to shock from something else, like peanuts or seafood, and adrenaline may be necessary if he has eaten some by mistake.

Other fixed allergies can be treated by limiting the number of encounters, so the child can tolerate an occasional dose; by avoidance if he can't; by using medicine to control the symptoms or by taking regular shots to get rid of the cause—a solution that works for inhalants but not for foods. In this treatment, antigens are injected once or twice a week for six months to two years, in increasingly strong doses, to build resistance the way the diphtheria/whooping cough/tetanus series immunizes a baby.

The serum, however, is not sovereign and should be made up of only those antigens that can't be avoided, like mold, rather than all of a child's allergies, since that would make it too strong. When the course is complete, the child's body should make enough antibodies to overcome not only these allergies but others too, with only an occasional maintenance shot needed.

TESTING FOR ALLERGIES

Although there are many tests you can make yourself, you probably will be more assured to have a doctor test him too, and make up a serum tailored to his own sensitivities for an inhalant. Your main difficulty may be in finding a good allergist, or a pediatrician with more than cursory knowledge in this field. The search, however, is worth it. So many children bring so much havoc on themselves and their families, all because of an egg or an orange.

Look for a board-certified specialist—preferably one connected to a university—who knows the value of taking a long case history, asking not only about your child's early years but whether he was overly active or hiccuped a lot when you were pregnant, which can be signs of a prenatal allergy. During this process he will check for symptoms and when they occur; ask which foods the child eats every day (and which ones he hates or loves); where and how he plays; and if he has seasonal attacks, indicating a pollen. He also will investigate the child's heredity, to see if allergies run in the family. If one parent has allergies, the child has a 50% chance of having them; if both parents are affected, the odds go up to 75%. Some doctors also think a history of physical or mental problems in the family, like alcoholism, diabetes or obesity, are the precursors of allergies in children.

The diagnosis is much easier if you keep a diary of your child's symptoms and enter the information at least three times a day. Unsupported recollections don't work for the I.R.S. and they don't work for allergies either. The diary should include not only when and where he spends his time, but whatever he eats or inhales. The allergens are often the things he hates or the foods he eats day after day or the substances he is often around.

There are many ways to isolate allergies, from a change of pillows to a change of diet, and there are intradermal tests—the best skin test so far—or tests which identify allergens in a test tube. In each of these cases, however, the tests can usually recognize only inhalant allergies and about 10% of those caused by foods. Other food allergies must be checked by diet, since you can't see the reactions unless your child eats much more of a food than he can take in a capsule and since it can take two or three days for some reactions, like bedwetting, to show up. Such a diet can be tough to administer, however, unless your child sees the diet for what it is—a scientific experiment—and unless he's both the subject and the scientist. It's only fair for him to be in charge. After all, it's his body chemistry you want to examine, although the whole family may want to go on the diet with him—and may find a few allergies of their own.

Try the diet when all is calm, the pollen count is low and the child is well, or the results may be skewed and record the tests and the results in a diary several times a day so you—and he—can draw valid conclusions.

Test Diet

The day before the diet begins, give your child everything he eats normally and include the most common food allergens: milk, chocolate, eggs, wheat, sugar, pork, beef, corn and colorings, to make him more sensitive to them when he is tested. Then restrict his diet to these ten least allergenic, and healthful, items: chicken, lamb, veal, sweet potatoes, yellow squash, carrots, pears, bananas, rice and distilled water in glass bottles; and have him brush his teeth with baking soda, in case he is allergic to the colorings or the salicylates in toothpaste; and skip his vitamins, unless they are free of colors, additives, corn, wheat, sugar or yeast.

The child may have some obvious physical or behavioral problems for the first few days if an allergen is cut from his diet. He may even crave a certain food, for some people can be addicted to a food as well as a drug, only feeling bad as the fix wears off. He gets much better in about five days, however, when the withdrawal is over. Now his sensitivity is most acute and he's ready to be tested.

Add one of those suspicious foods to his diet each day, and always in its pure form—wheat germ that hasn't been opened and perhaps gotten moldy; a glass of milk; a soft-boiled egg; a pork chop that's been steamed or broiled, without spices. Whatever you test, note the results in the diary, including dark circles around the eyes, hyperactivity and poor handwriting. Altogether this diet takes about fourteen days, although after the tenth day a child may be able to tolerate a food a few times before having a reaction.

LIVING WITH ALLERGIES

Any child who has respiratory or digestive symptoms caused by allergies will need a first-class lesson on the sinuses and how they work. If your child is old enough to read, he's old enough to understand what you're talking about. He needs to know that if he gets cold—particularly his head or his feet—the mucus in his sinuses may solidify and block one or all of these eight tiny pinprick holes. When this happens, the air can't get through the passages and a vacuum is created, and often pain too. For a graphic illustration, a Ten can try the Bacon Test. Have him sauté some bacon in a skillet, drain it and, when the pan is cool, have him wash it in cold water. He'll see the grease congeal like the mucus in his head when he drinks cold orange juice first thing in the morning, but when he rinses the pan with hot water he'll see the grease melt, the way the mucus melts when he drinks something hot.

When a child discovers that there is a scientific reason to feel the way he does, he is glad to do something about it. And here's what he should do:

- Drink something hot the first thing in the morning, the last thing at night and before meals.
- Never drink anything cold on an empty stomach.
- Avoid nose sprays unless ordered by the doctor.
- Sleep with a foam wedge or a pillow

TIME	FOOD	STRESS	DRUG	ACTIVITY	PLACE	WEATHER	PHYSICAL SYMPTOMS	PSYCHOLOGICAL SYMPTOMS
THE NIGHT								

THE ALLERGY DIARY

between the mattress and the box spring, so the head of the bed is elevated 4″.

- Hock any phlegm that collects, but don't blow the nose, for this may block the holes again.
- Keep warm, wearing a hat outside in cold weather, and slippers inside.

Obviously, these rules could cause real parent-child warfare, if you started following him around with a cup of hot tea and telling him, again, that he *does* have to spit, but NEVER in public. You'll have to explain the principles behind these rules more than once, but do it as clearly and patiently as you can, talking to your child as an equal, and without nagging. As satisfying as nagging can be, it doesn't work.

Daily Diet

It can seem overwhelming to have an allergic child, especially when the allergy is to a food, but it's a problem to be solved, like anything else. Begin by reading everything you can about allergies, and read the labels on the processed foods you buy. You also have to skip almost all junk food and most convenience food, which saves money, and do some shopping at the health food store, which does not. Many of the dietary changes you make will benefit everyone in the family, since you only want to buy and serve those foods your child can eat. When one person has a food allergy, the whole family follows his diet too, at least at home, or it will be too hard for him to keep. Besides, it's the loyal thing to do.

He—and you—will also need a list of foods and plants by family (see Recommended Reading). You'll learn that the child who is allergic to chocolate can't have coffee ice cream, since coffee and chocolate belong to the same family, and that, if he is allergic to peas or peanuts, he can't have carob either, since they are all in the legume family. Relatives are sometimes like that—surrounding us from every side.

On top of that, you have to make sure your child still gets a balanced diet. To keep this regimen in perspective:

- Don't beg your child to eat.
- Don't become a food faddist.
- Don't serve something if you don't know what's in it.
- Don't berate him when he cheats (and he will), or he won't tell you the next time and you won't know why he's sick or cross. Besides, his body is punishing him enough.

Home Environment

There are a number of changes you can make at home if you think your child is allergic to something in the house. Take any plants out of his room—the soil usually contains mold—and remove the rug too. Exchange his feather pillow for a Dacron one, put cotton or acrylic blankets on his bed, rather than wool ones or a down comforter, and remove any pillows or animals stuffed with kapok. Keep the dog and the cat, but not in his room, and run a vaporizer every night, all night, to put some moisture back in the air. This keeps the mucous membranes from drying, but clean the vaporizer regularly, for mold can collect in it. If there is still a problem, cover the mattress, box springs and pillows with allergen-free casings.

You'll also have to dust and vacuum his bedroom weekly, wash the curtains often, wipe the bathroom tiles each week to remove mold and spray the walls with mold killer.

School Environment

Because allergies cause more chronic diseases—and absences—in children than anything else, the more advanced school districts not only ask parents to give the office any allergy information about the children but they try to eliminate the most common trouble spots in the school. It's a policy you might try to get your own school board to adopt.

These standards usually prohibit carpet underpadding made of animal hair, even washed or coated; synthetic fibers not treated by heat; kapok, cotton linters or down; sawdust; old upholstered furniture, which is often moldy; smelly paint, paint thinners and cleaning products; disinfectants; formaldehyde; chlorine; chemical sprays with camphor or tar and insect sprays containing pyrethrum. Moreover, any furred or feathered animals are kept in the halls, rather than the classroom.

The standards also require rugs to be shampooed regularly and vacuumed daily and the filters in the heating and cooling systems to be cleaned once a month.

These schools also notify the parents of allergic children before any painting or major renovation is started, assigning the children to another part of the building for one to three days until the job has been done and all the fumes are gone.

These children also are given other activities, instead of gym, for several days after an allergic attack, although each illness may have to be certified by a doctor.

BEDWETTING

Bedwetting may cause the schoolchild— and the schoolchild's mother—to shed more tears than almost any other minor problem. Nothing is more exasperating, troublesome or embarrassing. Toilet training is a basic 101 course in growing up and failure is hard to admit.

Because we live in an age of Freudian fallout, many parents—and many doctors—still think bedwetting is a psychological problem. If your child still wets the bed, this attitude is going to make you feel angry and guilty. You try so hard to be a good mother—and then your child pays you back like this? It seems so unfair that you explode sometimes, which only adds to the problem.

For there's one thing you can count on: a child of Six (or Five or Four or even Three) doesn't want to wet the bed. By now he—and the bedwetter is usually a boy—is mortified and feels the failure more keenly than you. To be such a baby; to be so different; to miss the overnights— and often the friendships; to wonder if he

will still wet the bed when he's an old man: these are awful burdens. If, on top of that, a child thinks his parents believe he wets the bed because he is trying to get attention, or is lazy or thoughtless, he will be devastated, for he knows how hard he tries to wake up. When he fails, he not only feels he lets his parents down, but he feels he can't manage his own body. This is sure to hurt a young ego, since independence is so vital in the Middle Years.

You can protect your child somewhat from the guilt and the embarrassment that enuresis brings by promising never to tease him about it or blame him or tell anyone without his permission. His dignity is suffering enough. You also need to reassure him that it isn't his fault, that he's terrific and that the problem has a cure, although it may take awhile to find it.

Anxieties or dreams or fears or bad habits may cause an occasional child to wet the bed—or to wet a bed occasionally— but the reasons are usually physical. Some doctors believe bedwetting is caused by a shortage of magnesium, since this mineral can affect the muscles—and the bladder is a muscle. If this is the case, he'll order the mineral or food that contains a lot of it, like spinach and parsley and apples.

There is the possibility that low blood sugar, caused by eating sweets or drinking sodas at night, will make a child sleep so soundly that he won't pay attention to the message that goes from the bladder to the spinal cord to the cortex—the one that says, "Get up and go!" For this child, a high-protein bedtime snack, like a handful of nuts, is suggested instead.

The most promising answer of all is a food allergy or sometimes an environmental one. Doctors have discovered that an allergic reaction can stop the valve of the bladder from shutting completely when it gets full and can cause a muscle in the wall of the bladder to swell. This reduces its capacity to two to three ounces, rather than the eight to twelve ounces it needs for your child to last through the night. Although the allergy may continue, the bladder's capacity almost always gets bigger one to two years before puberty starts, as the pelvic cavity expands to accommodate the growing size of the organs in that area.

Milk is the most common trigger, and so are other favorite foods, like wheat, chocolate, or fruit juice, and a feather pillow or the cat in his bedroom can make a child wet the bed too. This child also may urinate more often during the day—although no one notices it—and be more cross than most children, or more sluggish or hyperactive.

If an allergy is the cause, the bedwetter is usually cured in about five days after the allergen is removed from his diet or his room (see Allergies).

Other parents report great success by treating the symptom. They use a battery-operated buzzer device under the sheet which rings (loud!) at the first drop of moisture, and after a few weeks the child generally is conditioned to jump up before the deluge, although he may have to use the alarm for two to three years. Just the use of this device, however, can be embarrassing for a child unless he is included in the decision to try it. Have him help you order it from the mail-order catalog (its principal source); let him unwrap the package and learn how to work it by dripping a little water on it and turning off the buzzer himself. This lets him feel in charge of his alarm, if not completely in charge of himself.

Even if none of these cures work, be consoled. One percent of all children spontaneously stop wetting the bed every month anyway, and almost all children stop about two years before puberty begins, when the hips expand and give the bladder more space.

In the meantime, you'll have to put up with the inconvenience and the extra laundry with as much grace as you can, and you don't, of course, make your child wear a diaper at night. It would only embarrass him more. You do, however, want to follow the most simple laundry routine, so the wash won't cause a big problem—and a big fuss. Zip a plastic cover over the mattress, and use a rubberized flannel sheet under a large crib pad instead of a bottom sheet. You or your child can flip off the wet pad and replace it with a dry one in the middle of the night, which is much easier than changing the sheet. With luck the top sheet needn't be changed at all, and if your child wears a nightshirt or a long undershirt, he may not have to change that either. In any case, there should be fresh sheets, pads and nightclothes near the bed so the midnight change is a fairly minor production.

If you're visiting, pack a shower curtain, extra sheets and pads and prepare the bed yourself at night, washing the linens in the morning with as much discretion as you can. Any hostess will appreciate your thoughtfulness. You'll also want to use the plastic curtain in a motel. This is not only for the sake of subsequent guests but to teach your child that he is responsible for the condition of the bed, even though he didn't wet it on purpose.

Some learning experiences are more poignant than others.

HYPERACTIVITY

Even today some educators believe, like the Greeks, that children come in four flavors: phlegmatic, sanguine, choleric or melancholic. As a million families know, there is at least one more variety, the hyperactive child. This is nature's own disturber of the peace.

This is not the child who whoops around the house for the pure love of whooping or who throws an occasional tantrum because he's bored. The hyperactive child is the one who can seldom stay put. He not only listens to his own drummer, he is marching in double time and the music is discordant.

It may be called an attention-deficit disorder, minimum brain dysfunction, hyperkinesis or just plain old hyperactivity, but whatever it is, this child has whirled about since infancy—touching this, dropping that, springing out of control like a jack-in-the-box. He never stops wiggling or tapping his pencil. His hands, his mouth, his feet—some parts of his body—have to be moving, moving all the time. He sleeps maybe six hours a night and may wake up screaming. He talks loud and often. He gets mad easily and explodes in a tantrum with little provocation as if he were still Two. And then he is good and there is no apparent cause. Suddenly he slows down, cuddles in your lap and for once lets himself be kissed. These are the halcyon moments, made all the sweeter by contrast. He may even weep and tell you how embarrassed he is to be so wild, that he can't help himself. And you know it's true. Someone so dear wouldn't try to make you so sad.

If your child is hyperactive, you probably are almost as distraught as he is. Nothing could be more understandable. His condition is sure to leave you exhausted, both physically and emotionally. You feel as guilty for your own bad temper as you do for loving this child so much, for it almost seems as if the old Irish adage is true: the one who makes trouble the mother loves double. Investments are like that. The deeper they are and the harder they are to make, the higher the return. There's only one drawback. With a hyperactive child, it may take years to reap the dividends, but reap them you can. All it takes is good luck and a lot of endurance.

Much of your strength will come from your belief in his goodness, which won't be easy after living through his first six years. If he is your only child, or your first, you may have gone for a long time thinking his behavior was normal. There was always someone to tell you that a mother was supposed to chase her toddler constantly, get frantic, even cry herself to sleep sometimes.

Your sense of incompetence was reinforced by the experts, for there is nothing like a mother's insecurity to make an expert act superior. When you told the pediatrician that your Two was more terrible than any other Two he may have looked amazed. The hyperactive child is often angelic in the doctor's office—perhaps because there are few children to distract him or because he is in awe of the place. To this doctor your child was just "all boy" (and the hyperactive child is usually a male) or "a little tomboy," and you were told "Just relax, dear. Children will be children."

The nursery school teacher didn't agree. He was so frenetic in that enriched, stimulating atmosphere, she probably said he needed less attention—especially from you. He was too much of a "momma's boy," she said, and why didn't you get a job, dear? And when you did, the day care teacher noticed he was different too. In the beginning she may have delicately, almost smugly, given you tips on how to care for your active little child, but after a few months she grew noticeably cooler toward him—and to you—and in time even seemed angry. There she was, with her degree in child development and years of experience, and yet nothing seemed to work. After that she tried to make the best of it, sending out "What can I do?" messages that the other children in the class were sure to pick up. This alone would have made them treat him more warily, although they probably would have anyway. A hyperactive child is a burden, particularly to himself. He is neither a comfortable nor a popular playmate.

The problem continues in first grade.

The contrast between his behavior and the behavior of other children grows more marked as the children around him mature. You may become so embarrassed you even find yourself avoiding a good friend and her gentle little child and—much worse—your friend avoids you, without ever saying why.

Your own sister and brother, parents and in-laws, are more candid, and because the opinions of these people matter so much, they hurt much more too. One asks why you can't be more affectionate to your child, even as he squirms away from every kiss, and another is sure he would behave if you were more patient. If someone says, "If only you spanked him more," someone else says, "If only you didn't spank him so much!" And they want to know when you are ever going to teach him that "no" means "NO." It seems impossible to explain that there are only so many "no's" inside of one body on any given day, especially when it doesn't do any good anyway and besides—it seems so heartless to say no at his birthday party and so counterproductive to say no in church or in the line at the supermarket. He'll only act wilder. It's like waiting for a time bomb to explode.

Finally the dear young first grade teacher, two years out of ed school, tries every trick in her rather slim book and then suggests—what else?—family therapy. And at that point the teacher may be right. The strain a truly hyperactive child puts on a family is tremendous and often heartbreaking, and divorce can be a tempting repercussion. The strain on the child is even more unbearable, however, psychologically and even physically.

The hyperactive child is simply difficult, twenty-four hours a day. Asleep, he may wet the bed or have nightmares; awake, he runs like wildfire. In school he may even have more trouble than his short attention span should cause, which may mean learning disabilities too. Forty percent of the learning disabled are hyperactive, although not all hyperactive children are learning disabled, of course. Just as there are many degrees between "normal" and severe hyperactivity, there probably are much milder cases that go unrecognized.

COPING

Doctors agree that hyperactivity is not a disease or a virus but a syndrome—a broad collection of symptoms—and a child may have some or all of them. But that's about all the doctors agree upon. For every symptom someone has documented, there is at least one cause, and "cures" go in and out of fashion. According to computerized electroencephalograph readings, 15% of the hyperactive children have an abnormality in the brain, but a number of other causes have been cited, and many mirror those in learning-disabled children. There could have been an illness in pregnancy or perhaps the mother drank too much alcohol at a critical point. It may not have been too much for her body but too much for that particular fetus, who absorbed more than he could filter. Also the tolerance for a drug varies from one adult to the next, and it varies between unborn children too; nobody knows how much is too much.

Other research blames a traumatic delivery, with loss of oxygen for a few critical moments at birth, or an overactive thyroid or hypoglycemia or parasites. A shortage of food or sleep in a child can cause it too. Studies also attribute hyperactivity to a chemical or allergic reaction to something that's eaten or inhaled, and others cite a vitamin deficiency; too much lead or copper in the system; a high uric acid level in the urine or a low level of serotonin. Still other reports claim it's caused by the low-level radiation emitted when television sets or fluorescent lights are turned on or when the child is wearing—are you ready for it?—tight underwear.

Many doctors feel that hyperactivity is a stage, or that it's brought on by a parent's hysteria or by difficulties at home or at school, but that seems unlikely and an easy out for the doctor. A healthy child should be able to handle all kinds of unpleasant situations without falling apart for more than brief periods, and certainly he shouldn't be difficult from birth.

Individual therapy may be needed to keep up a child's self-confidence, and family therapy to help everyone live with the behavior, but neither will get rid of a problem that has a physical basis. If hyperactivity persists, psychological problems will follow and the child will need counseling before adolescence. Even if it's eventually conquered—and it often is—the young person who has gone for years without knowing how to control his body or his emotions is going to have a lot of patterns to unravel and so will everyone else in the family.

Some doctors tell parents one thing, some another and the best of them are these: be patient; give the child choices; enroll him in a structured school; and keep things as orderly and as consistent at home as you can. All of them help, but they don't help enough.

One possible addition is drugs to treat hyperactivity. Some doctors prescribe amphetamines which slow down, rather than speed up, the central nervous system in this child. While this often works, at least for a time, many parents complain that their children act like "zombies." They may also worry that amphetamines will restrain growth—which is possible—or cause other physical or mental problems or that it may encourage the child to experiment with other drugs later on.

Some doctors put the hyperactive child on the Feingold diet, named for a California allergist who found that almost half of his hyperactive patients had a chemical—not an allergic—reaction to preservatives, dyes or salicylates—salts found in aspirin, toothpaste, many fruits and a few vegetables and nuts. They became gentle souls when their diets were changed—a solution that also helps the child who is mildly or occasionally hyperactive. More and more

scientific evidence—and some doctors—back these findings, to a greater or lesser degree, but to the parent who has success with it, the results are 100%. The Feingold diet is not everyone's panacea—few things are—but it surely is about the cheapest, safest home remedy a mother can try, and as long as the child gets enough fruits and vegetables, it is nutritious too.

CHEESE CRACKERS

YIELD: 4 dozen   Preheat oven to 350°

As any dieter knows, the hardest time to give up special foods is when everyone else is enjoying them. Here's one a hyperactive Eight can both make and eat, but you may have to do the grating. In a bowl

MIX	1½ c. unbleached flour
	2 c. grated Cheddar cheese, uncolored
	½ t. salt
ADD	5 T. ice water
	3 T. butter
	3 T. peanut OR safflower oil
	⅛ t. white pepper

Have your child beat the ingredients with an electric mixer, then make ½" balls out of the dough. Space them 2" apart on greased cookie sheets and press each one with the flat tines of a fork, then press them in the opposite direction, to make a grid.

BAKE   15 minutes

The thinner they are, the quicker they cook. Remove when they're a light, golden brown and smell good. Let crisp on a cake rack and store in an airtight tin.

Other doctors recommend Feingold Plus diets, taking away other foods that frequently bother children, like milk and wheat and chocolate, and then having parents test the children with the same Test Diet that allergists use (see Allergies & Aggravants). They look carefully at the child's environment, for mold or paint or that static-free material you throw in the dryer, which can send some children into a tizzy. You will want to note these responses in the diary too, to see if you can find a pattern.

The allergy approach might do it, and if not that, then something else. One day you're going to figure out how to take the hyper out of the active and motherhood will bring the happiness you always knew it would. Even if you can't find out what's wrong, your child may either outgrow the condition or, if his self-esteem is strong, he'll put his temperament to good use later, becoming the adult who gets where he's going because he works so much harder and longer than anyone else.

HYPOACTIVITY

There are some sluggish children who need a great deal of sleep and these children are hypoactive rather than hyperactive. A low thyroid can cause this problem—which takes a TSH test to discover—or he may be reacting to something in the air or some food, like corn (see Allergies & Aggravants).

Because hypoactivity is so easy to have around—unless you want your child to do the yard—it is often ignored, and this is too bad. A hypoactive child deserves the same careful appraisal a hyperactive child would get, experimenting with his surroundings and his diet, so he also can get the most out of his young life.

THE UNMENTIONABLES

There are some small problems that are simply too embarrassing to talk about, but let's do it anyway.

PINWORMS

All children have their ups and downs in school, but the teacher only calls you in when your child is down. He looks tired, she says, and she adds that he's irritable in class and picks fights on the playground. He wiggles more than he listens. His marks are getting low.

And you on reflection agree, although not necessarily out loud, that his problems aren't limited to school. He's cranky half the time; nothing pleases. He may go to bed early, but he tosses all night and has nightmares, and often a stomachache too. Since the cramps may come when it's time to leave for school, and since there is no fever, the doctor may say your child is upset because he doesn't like his teacher. And if he doesn't like her, you think, the doctor may right.

It's time for the old pinworm check.

This parasite, which may strike a schoolchild as often as the common cold, lives a hand-to-mouth existence: a child goes to the bathroom, wipes his bottom, forgets to wash his hands and then shares a cupcake with his pal—your child. That's all it takes.

Pinworms can put a child off his feed, wreck his sleep and his disposition and sometimes make the intestines feel like they're tied up for parcel post, but even the doctor may not think of pinworms unless your child mentions the most embarrassing symptom—itching around the anus or, in a girl, perhaps the vagina too.

Although a Seven, that modest soul, may be mortified at the idea, he either has to examine his stool for the tiny, squirming white worms or save it for you—and possibly the doctor—to examine. To catch the movement, have him use a clean, empty cottage cheese carton.

To get rid of pinworms, your child will have to take a simple prescription medicine and you will have to wash his clothes and sheets in very hot water and dry them at a high heat, so the eggs will be killed.

Pinworms are only a bother but other parasites, like roundworms, hookworms and toxicara (which dogs and cats carry), can be more serious. Symptoms range from abdominal pain to weight loss, blood in the stool, diarrhea and even some kinds of pneumonia, and in rare cases they localize in other parts of the body. All of these worms can be picked up by someone who either lives near poor sanitation or has traveled to other countries, and all of them are transmitted by poor hygiene. That's why our foremothers made children wash their hands well before they ate, and it's why we still must do it today.

LICE

No other childhood problem may embarrass both mother and child so much as a crop of lice, but lice are remarkably commonplace and they're not a sign of poor hygiene. They also don't hurt; they're cured rather quickly and they don't carry any disease.

Lice live full lives on the human head—because it's the best source of the blood they need for nourishment—and they usually get from one head to another by using the backs of bus seats, upholstered chairs, beds and combs as transfer points.

The adult—a tiny, dark brown creature only two to three millimeters long—lays three to four little gray nits a day about a quarter inch from the scalp. Ten days later the nymphs break out of these eggs and begin to bite the scalp, which causes the head to itch—the first symptom.

You can see if your child has lice by shining a strong light on his hair. If they're there, have your doctor prescribe a special shampoo or buy an over-the-counter pediculocide. You'll shampoo your child's head once, to kill the lice, then repeat it in another eight to ten days to kill any nits that survived. You and your husband should also check your own hair, using the same treatment if you find nits too.

Since they can live in clothes, either send all the hats, scarves, coats and bedding to the dry cleaner to kill any traveling lice; or wash everything in 140° water; or put the clothes and bedding in a well-sealed plastic bag for thirty five days—five days beyond the bug's life cycle. You'll also have to soak the combs and brushes in a solution of the shampoo and vacuum the carpets, mattresses and upholstery very well.

While it's essential to rid the house and the child of lice, it's also important for the child to realize that it's just one of those dumb things that happen to people, and no fault of his. By using discretion with friends and humor with him, he'll barely remember the incident a few months later.

DRUGS

One of the great misfortunes of our age has been the willingness of adults to accept the use of stimulants and depressants—amphetamines, tranquilizers, alcohol, tobacco and pot—as a necessity or an inevitability. They are neither, of course, but we give these drugs our tacit seal of approval when we use them ourselves.

Even if your child is only Six, it's time to examine and perhaps adjust your own behavior, for you and your husband have great control over your child, by example as much as by insistence. In the process you may discover just how grown up you must be. The giddy carefree days of your youth are over now.

Your new caution should also apply to prescribed drugs and patent medicines. You don't want your child to think he can solve life's problems with casual chemistry. From now on toss away the prescriptions when an illness is over and keep only the basic medicines: a pain reliever; an antihistamine; a cough syrup; a digestive aid; and something for diarrhea. Even these should be used with discretion since you'll want to depend on good nutrition, natural foods, exercise and vitamins to stay healthy, treating most minor illnesses and viral infections with a vaporizer, lemon and honey, a lot of juice, cups of tea and extra vitamin C. In these subtle ways you tell your child that drugs don't have much magic, no matter what he's told on television.

Stronger pills should be set aside in a locked drawer—and, with luck, never used. You may need a tranquilizer or a sleeping pill at times of severe distress, but a wrenched back, a parent's funeral or a divorce hearing doesn't happen every day, or even every week. Pills can't turn a continuing crisis into a manageable problem. They may buy you time, but they only postpone what must be faced and if you feel you have to take more than a couple of these pills a month you're treating the symptoms rather than the problem. Both physical therapy and psychotherapy are more direct and they have fewer side effects.

If you rely on pills regularly you tell your child that you (and therefore he) aren't strong enough to reckon with reality. There will be many times in his life when he'll want to quit a school, a job, a marriage—not out of wisdom but out of fear. The memory of your grit will help him persevere.

You need to be cautious with other drugs too. You may say, "I can't wake up without a cup of coffee," or "I've got to have a cigarette," or "I really needed that drink," or even "I'm more creative if I'm stoned." You're only teaching your Six to say the same thing at Sixteen (or Thirteen or Eleven). Dependency is a contagious notion.

A child—even a first grader—also needs direct instruction. Information on drugs, like sex, should be part of a continuing process. As he gets older the approach becomes more indirect. You won't forbid the use of drugs; you'll assume your child won't try them—and you'll say so. This will become part of his image of himself by the time he's Ten. When you talk with a preteen you don't condemn pot; you express sorrow that some people—adults and children—think they can't get along without it. You'll tell him that many people don't handle alcohol well, especially young people, and that the wise don't drink with their friends until college, when their bodies and their brains have stopped growing and that they are much more likely to become addicted to any drug if they start using it before then. It's also essential that he know if aunts, uncles or grandparents have been alcoholics, since

the disease is usually inherited. All of this teaches your child to say no if you speak knowledgeably about drugs, rather than with emotion.

He may disagree with you but there will come a time when he'll use the information to get out of a sticky situation. Tell him that the use of any drug—alcohol, pot or the pill of the week—is never obligatory. You're really teaching your child that he has the right to say no all his life and the duty to say it until he's old enough to be on his own. A preteen is too young to believe he could die of cancer (or anything else) or that he might lose his memory or his motivation or his energy, but well-documented arguments will give him the ammunition to resist. He'll also be able to refuse drugs more easily if he knows that you simply won't tolerate them. Period.

Circumstances also help a child say no. Because boredom encourages drugs, it behooves you to keep things as interesting for your Eleven as you did for him at Four. You do this by doing things with your child, not for him. Let him know the family depends on him; that it functions better because he's in it; that you need him for the joy—and the hard work—he brings. When you rely on a child, he's less likely to let you down.

Supervision is another essential at Ten, Eleven and Twelve. You have to monitor the friendships of a preteen very closely. A child seldom smokes or uses drugs or even acts sassy without the encouragement and example of a best friend.

All children aren't offered drugs in the sixth and seventh grades, nor are they tempted to try them if they are, but if parents are prepared for the worst, they can usually prevent it. A small percentage do start smoking at Eleven and using pot or drinking at Twelve. These are mindless party capers to them, and usually infrequent, but because the preteens who experiment with drugs tend to have friends who do the same, the problem is likely to escalate in adolescence as friendships narrow into cliques.

If anyone in your child's crowd is using pot or drinking or even smoking, now is the time to mobilize other parents, but not just your own friends, who may pat you on the head and say, "Now, now." Perhaps they can't believe that your child (and especially their children) is involved, but strangers will be more objective. Call the parents of your child's friends for a meeting at your house, to see how they think things are going. Compare notes; tell them why you're worried; ask what they have seen. You will get responsive answers although you may get some denials, and perhaps some anger at first. As long as you're not accusatory, however, or blame their children for leading yours astray, these meetings should help all of you protect your children better. This can be the start of a support group that may continue for years—an idea that is catching on all over the country.

When parents have the same general rules, or at least know what rules other parents have, their children are less tempted to say, "But all the other kids . . ." You can also agree to call before a party to make sure the parents know they're giving it, and to help chaperone or drive. The more parents are involved now, the easier it will be to stay involved later, when the stakes are considerably higher.

Even if your child never tries a drug, he may be hurt by it. If two or three children in class are on drugs, the atmosphere gets chaotic in the classroom. It's your responsibility to protect your child and the rest of the class and to do it quietly and quickly. Although he wants you to do something about it, he doesn't want to know what it is. Tattletales are given short shrift at Eight and narcs are despised at Eleven. Arrange a confidential conversation with the teacher and tell him what's going on but don't name your source, out of loyalty to your child, even if you have to say that you heard it somewhere else.

You don't have to mention the culprits by name, nor should it be necessary. Children on alcohol or marijuana are fairly obvious when the teacher knows what to look for. Do, however, tell her what the children are doing and, if it occurs in a public place, where the smoking or drinking is going on and when. Tell her you know it makes teaching very hard and that you will be glad to help her do something about it, taking it to the principal or even the police. This gently tells the teacher that you intend to see the problem solved, which will encourage her to do something.

If you suspect that your child is directly involved, you must act more directly. Insist on new friends and new activities, turn down your child's sudden requests to sleep at a friend's house after a party and keep him busier with more chores and more family movies, ball games and interesting activities, particularly day trips out of town on a weekend to avoid Saturday night temptations.

Caution will be your guiding principle when your child is a teenager. Let precaution guide you now.

CIGARETTES

Both boys and girls are tempted to smoke somewhere between Ten and Twelve, and many succumb. The Great Smoke-in usually happens in the fifth grade, just as they become genuine smart alecks. There he is, on the verge of Eleven, and as ready to prove he's in charge of himself as he ever was at Four. Smoking seems such a grown-up way to outfox grown-ups.

Its danger is that it may not be a one-time caper. Most youngsters who smoke more than one cigarette go on smoking. Almost half of all Twelves and Thirteens smoke once a week, and a fifth of all high school students smoke every day. The number of boys and girls is about the same, but smoking is potentially more dangerous for girls since it can cause reactions in women on the pill.

Whether your child begins or not will depend on his opportunities, on his best friend and on you. If you or your husband smoke, he already is physically conditioned to try. For every twenty cigarettes smoked near your child, he smokes one, simply by inhaling the smoke around him. He is psychologically conditioned too. Even though he has begged you to quit—for children are terrified that cancer might take a parent away—a part of him still approves of the idea for a basic reason: he approves of you.

If one parent smokes, the child is twice as likely to smoke; if both parents smoke (or one parent and a brother or sister), the likelihood is four times and the bad influence does not end at home: if the best friend smokes, the chances are nine times greater. Your child will find it hard to say no when this friend says, "Why not?" They get still more encouragement from the models who advertise cigarettes and never have singed eyelashes, stains on their teeth or holes burned in their clothes, and nobody ever backs away from their bad breath. Instead your child sees people who can say anything and do anything with style, apparently because they smoke.

It takes an independent person to reject the pressure. Once again you need to make your child feel good about himself, every day of his life. A child with a strong self-image is much more likely to follow his own instincts. You can give added support. Treat your daughter to those much-wanted ballet lessons, where she will need her breath to dance well. Give your son time to shoot baskets every day and even though he is still sixteen inches too short, he'll see himself on a professional team one day.

You should also repeat the arguments against smoking regularly, beginning at least a couple of years before the problem looms. Your child needs to know that smoking is now a major factor in many diseases besides lung cancer; that smokers use more medicines, including antibiotics, than nonsmokers—for they don't resist disease as well—and that many of these medicines are less effective for them. They also should know that smoking makes the body use proteins poorly, so it absorbs less nitrogen and makes it require more vitamins just to stay even.

Most of all, a child needs to know that smoking is hard to quit, and for good reason. Nicotine reaches the brain within seconds and then goes to the organs in twenty to thirty minutes. This withdrawal of the drug from the brain creates anxiety, which makes the urine turn acidic and the body pass it more quickly. Because some of the nicotine goes with the waste, the smoker wants another cigarette to put the drug back in his system.

And will these horror stories stop a preteen from smoking? Not alone. Children may worry that parents will die, but they think they are immortal. Supervision will help. It's opportunity that may make the most stalwart child smoke. The more time children spend on their own, the more they are likely to try something different—like cigarettes. Keep an eye on your child and his friends, but keep it friendly. Even this is not foolproof. You can't supervise children in a tree house, on an overnight camping trip or during their rambles around town, and you shouldn't. All of this is part of growing up. If you want your child to be daring—and you do—you can't have it both ways.

If there is any sign that your child is smoking regularly, withhold some of his allowance. Obviously, he has money to burn. And when you intervene, as you must, do it with the same no-nonsense determination that you would use to protect him from any drugs, and make sure he knows you're doing it for the same reason—because you love him.

MARIJUANA

Of all bad habits that tempt a child, smoking marijuana is the most frightening. It is so easy to get; so fashionable to try; so inviting to continue. And so habit-forming.

The likelihood that your preteen will try marijuana is small but not nonexistent.

Four percent of our Twelve and Thirteen-year-olds are current users. They may be from close, churchgoing, middle-class families as well as from poor or broken homes. Fads—good and bad—spring up freely at this age, usually followed because a best friend (or an older brother or sister) shows the way. That's why you need to know about pot now and the pattern it usually takes.

The occasional puff is first tried after four or five offers, and then a joint is smoked at an occasional party. There are seldom any effects the first few times, which makes the drug seem innocuous, overrated and an easy way to be accepted by the gang. Even when its effect is felt, it seems safe. It takes very little for a young user to feel the euphoria that has made pot so beloved—a peace, a bliss, a sense of gentle joy. It's a revelation! Who couldn't do with a little of that?

It's hard for a preteen (or a young teenager) to believe a little pot could ever turn into a lot. In fact it continues to seem safe, no matter how deep the dependency. This may be its greatest deception, for its use is progressive. The child who started smoking pot as a preteen finds it especially hard to stop when he enters adolescence. His need to conform will be at its peak then: to quit would make him different.

Purists make a fine distinction between a habit and an addiction but parents who have been there know it doesn't matter. At first there are few consequences at home or at school, since friends are a loyal lot now and eye drops usually erase the redness the smoke leaves in their eyes. As the use of marijuana turns from a want to a need, the child begins to pay an emotional price—and so do his parents.

Mood swings are the most obvious symptom. There is sunshine (or at least clear weather), then sudden aggression, then a tantrum, a retreat to his room, isolation and music louder than you ever thought possible. The goals that once were chased seem pointless now, and so does school. His clothes and hair look sloppier, just when he had learned to keep fairly clean, and his grades start to plummet, although he can still pull them up if he must. He has new friends whom you will not find very appealing and a few of the old ones who have become much like them. He gets phone calls from children who won't leave their names (there are parties to plan, drugs to be bought). Drugs can become not just a way of life but the purpose of it, even for a preteen. Mothers usually are the first to suspect drugs at this point; fathers often take another year. It is a terrible time of denial, recognition, anger and fear.

The child who is dependent on marijuana begins to use it every day, and sometimes several times a day, getting stoned before school, at recess and on the way home, although the same child would be horrified to see his parents drink gin before they went to work and at their coffee breaks.

Now comes the checkup by the doctor, with a urine test to tell you if he has smoked pot recently. You may not tell him why he's getting the test, but if he refuses to take it (or tries to use a sample from a more innocent friend), you can presume he knows his own results would be positive.

It is time to ask not "Have you ever smoked pot?" but "How much pot do you smoke?"; "How often?"; "Where?"; "With whom?" He'll be tough and evasive—and you'll be tougher. You have this encounter in his room, which you don't leave until you have had him (not you) turn out every bureau drawer; empty his closet; go through his clothes; flip his mattress; take the pictures off the walls; the books off their shelves; the turntable off its stile. And then you go together to make the same search in any other place in the house where you think he spends much time. Nothing will be sacred. And still you won't find it all and if you do it will be replaced and put somewhere else.

This is just the beginning of a long, long road to recovery, for him and for the whole family, which by then has been exposed to more lies, more scenes and more lip than any parents ever deserved. It is a necessary step-by-step process, but the price in pain is high. This scenario is by no means inevitable, however, if you protect yourselves before the fact, rather than pick up the pieces afterward.

Knowledge is your defense and, when you share it, it is your child's defense too. You need up-to-date facts, presented early, fairly and frequently, as you would present any other serious subject. Whether it's a discussion about politics or pot, you have to know enough to be convincing. There are many proven, scientific arguments against marijuana and there are more of them all the time. Much of the effect of pot is caused by delta-9-THC, its main psychoactive element, though only 5% of it reaches the brain. Marijuana also contains more than 400 other chemicals, and at least 60 of them affect the brain. Studies show that the brain cells of pot-smoking monkeys change, the synaptic clefts between neurons widen and are partially blocked and it's harder for messages to jump from neuron to neuron, which may explain why regular pot users often speak more slowly.

Marijuana addiction is harder to break than alcohol addiction. Alcohol, a single chemical, usually is gone in six hours, but since marijuana chemicals are fat-soluble and are deposited in the brain, the reproductive system and the lungs, it takes the body as long as four weeks to rid itself of all of them. The child who smokes it every weekend will still never be drug-free, since today's marijuana is ten to twenty times stronger than the one you may have tried as a teenager.

The longer people smoke marijuana, the more problems they are going to have. Emphysema and impotence can occur while the user is still in his teens. A joint is loaded with carcinogens, is twenty two times harder on the lungs than an ordinary cigarette and is a swift disaster for an asthma sufferer.

Remind your child that:

- the pot user's ability to make DNA, RNA and vital proteins is diminished.
- the immune system is suppressed; illness is common;
- the heart beats as much as 50% faster than it should;
- the lungs lose a fourth of their ability to expel air;
- chest pain is a frequent problem;
- short-term memory is damaged, sometimes permanently;
- the sperm count goes down and the sperm is often abnormal;
- the menstrual cycle becomes defective;

And for the most presuasive reasons of all:

- the breasts of boys may begin to develop if marijuana is used frequently before or during puberty;
- girls may get extra hair on their faces and their bodies if they use it at that time.

You'll make a graphic point if you remind your fifth grader of the sad fourteen-year-old down the street—the one who has gotten so withdrawn. Wonder what's wrong; how he could have changed so much. And when it's neighborhood knowledge that he is on drugs, you tell your child about it confidentially—and sympathetically. Notice the way that child doesn't talk much anymore and how friendly he used to be. His hair, his clothes, himself will be mussed and none too clean; notice that too. Talk about the way pot makes people so forgetful, school so hard and life so pointless, and when that happens, grades go down and so do self-esteem and self-confidence.

Some of these outward signs are due to the isolation that pot imposes, and your child should know that too. The conviviality encouraged by sports or clubs or even alcohol is lost with pot, for it makes people look inward. Although children usually smoke together, at least at first, they simply spend the time like two-year-olds, side by side. There is no intimacy and that means no growing up either. It takes childhood away.

An early use of marijuana binds the psyche of children as wraps once bound the feet of little girls in China. Here you have the Twelves who will age chronologically but not emotionally. Their judgment is frozen in time. At Fifteen they will make choices about sex and downers and uppers and cocaine and crack and PCP and acid with no more wisdom than they had when they first started using pot. At Seventeen there will be decisions about college and jobs, and college deans and bosses will be making a few decisions of their own. If a child didn't have psychological problems before he started using pot, he will have them soon.

The scientific facts aren't the only evidence at hand and perhaps not the most important. Marijuana warps integrity. All those years it took a child to learn about honesty and fairness and justice are turned upside down. He will learn to lie (and, if necessary, steal) just at a time when his character is beginning to jell. He feels enormous guilt. Every time he tries to quit he feels too ashamed to return to the friends and the teams that he left. To accept the love of his family makes him feel treacherous.

A Ten is old enough to know that one day he will be offered marijuana and that he must refuse it. And if he doesn't, you have to be mature enough to handle it with less emotion than you feel. Be calm; ask your child why it happened and how, and be so grave, so serious, that you won't need a punishment. That could dilute your disappointment, giving the child a reason to get angry and an excuse to repay you by using pot again. If he does experiment you might put some of his allowance in escrow (he obviously has too much money); supervise him more; monitor

friendships better; notice his accomplishments more often; and perhaps have some sessions with a family therapist, but only after you know he isn't using the drug anymore. Psychotherapy is seldom effective with someone on drugs.

You'll need to tell him that you can't police him all the time but that his behavior will inform on him if he continues. If the experiments become routine and he begins to smoke three to four times a week he will act differently—and so, he should know, will you. Many problems don't happen when a child knows his parents mean business about the business of being parents.

ALCOHOL

In the original *Mother's Almanac* we wrote, "The drunks in the park were all children once." They were also Six and Ten and Twelve. It takes children many twists and turns to get from there to here and the problem often starts early—even before they are born. Research has pretty much confirmed what was long suspected—alcoholism is basically a genetic disease.

It is also our most serious drug problem. Seventy percent of our seventh graders today have had a drink and a third of them say they drink once a week—one child out of five.

The problem is magnified when parents don't know it exists—and they almost never do. The grumpiness, the lethargy, the secretiveness are supposed to be part of "the age" and any talk they overhear about "getting high" or "partying" is regarded as harmless slang—an imitation of their elders in high school. It's also hard for a mother and father to admit that their young child might have taken a wrong turn. Drug use—any kind—is assumed to be the specter of adolescents, not preteens.

However, young children haven't fully developed; their new hormone levels are unstable and they weigh much less than adults—three factors that make them much more susceptible to drugs. Some children, like some adults, are also more susceptible than others, for alcoholism is usually inherited not just from parents but from grandparents, aunts and uncles. Just knowing it's in the genes now stops many young people from drinking too much, or even drinking at all.

Your restraint—and your respect for the power of alcohol—will help your child learn how to drink safely when he's grown. You do it first by example, drinking only a little (or none at all) and never as a means of escape, since this would invite your child to think he could use alcohol to run away from boredom, rejection or fear.

Explanations help too. Point out that it takes a healthy 160-pound person an hour to handle a 12-ounce can of beer or a 5-ounce glass of wine or a highball made with only 1½ ounces of whiskey, even though that's just 3 tablespoons. You emphasize this lesson if you always use a jigger when you fix a drink for yourself and your guests.

Heavy-handedness shouldn't be confused with hospitality. To serve a double-sized drink or a wineglass filled to the brim—or, far worse, to drink and drive—tells a child that he can trifle with alcohol too. There are too many deaths, too many paraplegics, to be casual about this any longer and, if you set a good example now, your child may follow it later. And if you don't, he surely won't.

You also need to tell your child that you drink because you like its flavor, because it makes you feel more sociable—and because, to be honest, you like its very slight effect—but that you don't drink so much that it controls your behavior or gives you an excuse to do or say foolish things. That's why, you'll tell him, you sip every drink—wine, beer or brandy—slowly enough to savor the taste and the stronger the drink, the longer between your sips.

You also make sure your child knows that you have a glass of water alongside your wineglass at dinner, so you don't drink alcohol to slake your thirst (and therefore drink too much). Although you'll only mention this occasionally, you reinforce this message when you comment on the quality and the taste of your drink, and not on its kick.

In some families the child is allowed to have a very occasional small diluted glass of wine, which can be a gentle way to introduce him to alcohol, as long as you or your husband drink and if there isn't any alcoholism in the family.

At most, this means a single glass of wine, mixed with soda, to be offered to a Twelve at Christmas or a little champagne splashed over lemon sherbet at his sixth-grade graduation party. These very limited tastes of alcohol, and perhaps a glass of wine offered at birthday dinners or family holidays when he's a teenager, will tell him how special the occasion and how careful he must be with alcohol and will help him understand that a growing child should never have wine or beer regularly. If you allowed him to disobey the drinking laws in your town, he would think he had the rights of an adult—and might try to use them by joining the gang who drink in the woods after school. The child who is permitted too much will act as wild as the child who is held back.

It can be hard for a child to say no; that's what he has parents for.

In Parents

Drugs—and that most emphatically includes alcohol—can scar a child for life, and the ones that parents take can damage him most. Alcohol is involved in half of all accidents, at home or in the car, in half of all suicides and in most family quarrels, and it is very prevalent. One out of three of us has, or has had, an alcoholic in the family—a person who infused relationships with tension and complicated plans and lives.

Most alcoholics hide the problem from themselves, and from others, sometimes for years, as the amount—and the anguish—increase. The alcoholic parent usually hurts the child most. The broken promises, the forgotten birthdays, the public embarrassments all affect a child profoundly, but it's the roller-coaster behavior that is the scariest. The child is humiliated, kissed, frightened, ignored, insulted, punished, petted, neglected, bullied, babied and maybe bribed not to tell—sometimes all in the course of twenty-four hours. Every action is extreme when a parent is drinking or recovering from an episode.

If it goes on, the aftershocks will last for life, at least to some degree. Some effects are positive, most are negative and none of them lead to great happiness. Adult children of alcoholics tend to feel different from other people, to judge themselves too harshly and take themselves too seriously. They just don't know how to have fun, because they don't know what normal behavior really is, and they overreact to situations they can't change. Although they are often extremely responsible, some are extremely irresponsible and may lie when the truth is just as easy. They also seek approval constantly and have trouble with intimate relationships because they have such trouble trusting others, yet loyalty is one of their crosses to bear. They overcommit to projects—which they often find hard from start to finish—but they can't cut their losses, even when they should.

If someone tells you that you're drinking too much—take it seriously. Only someone who loves you would confront you about it, for it is such a painful, intrusive discussion. And if, deep in your heart, you think you have a problem with alcohol—if only in the early stages—then you probably have. Call Alcoholics Anonymous for literature and go to an open meeting to listen to others, rather than a closed meeting, which is for those who know they have a problem and are working on it.

You may think your child will be ashamed of you if you say you're an alcoholic, or even say that you can't handle it or that you're afraid you're hooked. He's much smarter than that. Although he doesn't need to know any of those things, you will be closer if you share your heart. He also will be getting a fine example, for it takes courage, not cowardice, to give up something you like or need.

It would also be wise to see a nutritionist, to help you rebuild your body, and to talk with a psychotherapist too, but only after you've quit drinking, for you can't be honest with yourself when you have a drug in your system.

If your husband is the alcoholic, the "cure" will be harder because it seems as if you can't do anything about it. But you can. Explain to your child that his dad doesn't handle alcohol well; that the wanting of it is a sickness (even though he can't believe he is sick); that he'll get better when he's able to quit—and that in the meantime you'll keep right on loving him. You want to say this when you're feeling your most sympathetic toward your husband, so your voice will be kind, your words factual, yet discreet. Your child needs to know about the conditions but not the excesses.

It's important for you to go to Al-Anon meetings too, when the family and friends of alcoholics will give you both strength and information, and give it to your child too, if you and the group think he is old enough to go to the meetings. You may not want your husband to know where you're going—he certainly won't like it if he doesn't believe he has a problem—but you should tell him anyway. This admission on your part can make him feel safe enough to go public himself. And since this group, like A.A., operates as a first-name-only group, the anonymity is kept well. If you have any fears about this, there are meetings in other neighborhoods and towns. Probably no other organization has so many outlets, so many volunteers or so much credibility—and all of this help is free.

In Al-Anon meetings you learn that you play a role in the illness, and so does your child, in the ways you make it easy for your husband to drink. You are an enabler, as they say, when you do the work your husband brings home because he can't get it done at the office; when you tell the boss he's sick when he really has a hangover; when you pretend to the family doctor that the ankle he sprained last night was a simple trip on the stairs, and not a drunken tumble. The person who creates the problems should explain them. Any time you shield an alcoholic from the consequences of his drinking, you postpone the resolution and in the meantime the drinking gets worse.

And your child is an enabler too, without even knowing it. He does it by being mouse-quiet in hopes that his dad will keep on sleeping, or he hides a bad report card because it might be an excuse for an extra cocktail. It's human nature to avoid trouble but you won't make alcoholism go away by catering to it.

You also can keep a record of the family behavior to see what led up to the drinking; what was consumed and what happened during and afterward. By keeping this on a chart, you limit the information to facts, not comments.

If he won't quit drinking—or admit there's a problem—it may take a separation, or the threat of it, to make him get help, and you'll certainly have to live apart if there is physical or sexual abuse or if his verbal attacks damage your child's mental health or yours. Even if a separation is

necessary, it may only be temporary. With A.A., Al-Anon and family therapy, a marriage, once good, can be made even stronger than it was, for it will have met a tough test and passed it.

All of this teaches your child that alcoholism doesn't fade away; it's fought a day at a time. You couldn't give your child a better lesson.

PSYCHOTHERAPY

All of us need some kind of psychotherapy sometime in our lives. Talking—whether to a best friend or a good professional—gets us through those crunches when life seems to offer no hope. Death, divorce, a move, a serious family problem try the soul and can be particularly difficult for children—and for some children more than others. A trustworthy neighbor, a friend, a clergyman, a teacher—whoever cares enough to listen, without judgment—may be the sympathetic confidant your child needs, but not always. Some kind people don't know how to draw out a child's feelings and many don't have the time. Others are so close to the child, he might be embarrassed to tell them his troubles or he might think they would be hurt or upset if they knew what was on his mind.

This is the value of psychotherapy—the professional kind. It gives a child the chance to see someone who has no preconceived ideas and no stake in the consequences and who is available at the same place and the same time, week after week, to listen, to ask the right questions, to keep him on track.

The type of help available is almost as varied as a child's need for it. It doesn't matter whether your child gets help in individual therapy, in a group led by the therapist or in a self-help group, as long as he can talk often enough and candidly enough to figure out his own answers. That is the secret of any successful therapy.

You first have to figure out if your child

really has a problem or if he's just going through a stage. All children behave oddly at times, but the child in pain—or the one whose problems are getting worse—will let you know by the frequency and the extremes of his symptoms, although your standards will change with the years. Behavior that is acceptable at Seven can be a psychological problem at Eleven.

You'll know your child may need psychotherapy if he has been happy, cranky, silly, serious, energetic, lazy—which is to say, normal—and then becomes consistently angry, anxious or withdrawn. He may expect to be waited on or become apathetic or moody or wild, or he may find it hard to concentrate, to do his schoolwork, to make the simplest decision. He may behave himself at home and fall apart at school, emotionally or academically, either because school is the source of his problem or because he thinks it's a safer place to explode. Or his behavior may always be very, very good—too good to be natural. He may have no friends of his own age and only want to be with grown-ups, or he may act babyish. He may sleep much harder and longer, or more fitfully and much less—or use fantasy as his drug of choice. Or he may become fearful or spiteful or jealous or he may bully other children excessively or tattle on them or go after one person in particular in a mean sort of way.

Sometimes a child needs immediate help. This is the one who hurts himself on purpose and doesn't even complain or who threatens to hurt or kill himself or who repeatedly acts in inappropriate ways. An older child also needs prompt help if he starts lying or stealing or cheating regularly (or setting fires or indulging in frequent sex play or violence), for these are the signs of a child at war with his evolving conscience.

Most needs, though real, don't demand immediate action, however. Many concerned parents wait three to four months before making the move and find that problems often work themselves out, as the circumstances change. When a child says he has a rotten teacher, there's a very good chance he's right, since children want to like their teachers so much that they forgive a great deal of unfairness.

The idea that your child needs therapy may be harder on you than on him, as if it meant that you had failed, but it's really a sign of courage and a shortcut to happiness. A little help now is better than a lot of help later. Unless an emotional cause seems very clear, however, your child first needs a complete medical and nutritional workup. A prolonged family problem, like a separation, or a sudden crisis, like a death, can trip a physical problem, which in turn can cause emotional symptoms. Therapy won't get rid of a physical problem, even after the stress goes away, although it may help deal with the symptoms or make the healing quicker. A biopsychiatrist or an up-to-date pediatrician will look for metabolic problems like diabetes, 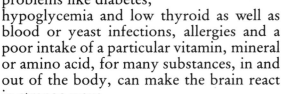 hypoglycemia and low thyroid as well as blood or yeast infections, allergies and a poor intake of a particular vitamin, mineral or amino acid, for many substances, in and out of the body, can make the brain react in strange ways.

If your child's problems don't come from his body or from some trauma in the family, he needs a psychological evaluation, including auditory and perception screens to rule out learning disabilities. After that, there's little left that could cause these problems except the patterns in his life. The child who is barely noticed at home will suffer and so will the one who is smothered with attention, which often happens when parents focus on the child to avoid dealing with their own relationship.

A child will be affected if one of his parents (or both) has a low self-esteem, is usually depressed, and is bored with life, or if the marriage is in trouble and they pull away from each other, have a diminished interest in sex, are often tense and argue a lot, or if anger is the underlying emotion in the household. The child may also react if his father acts much younger than he is or if he wants to be mothered— or if his mother wants to be cared for as if she still had a daddy to lean on. If you find that your child is reflecting some problems you or your husband might have, you'll want to get therapy too, and he should know about it. This will help him realize that it's not his job to put everything right and it will also encourage him to work on his own problems.

Your child may need only one session to sort out his concerns, six or eight sessions to deal with a single problem, or he may need prolonged attention. Some therapists begin by limiting the number of visits—a technique to make the patient work faster—but most offer only a general projection. The child should just be asked to give it his best and be assured that he can quit if he doesn't think it's helping, as long as he has one to two closing sessions to sweep away the last of those niggling worries (or change his mind and stay a little longer).

CHOOSING A THERAPIST

Choosing a therapist is like choosing any other helper, associate or adviser—you want the best. Your child will be relieved to know that this means someone who will be his friend, who is kind, who won't repeat his secrets and who will mean every compliment she gives him. The choice may be more troubling than you think.

Everyone knows of cases when a therapist has failed but most provide some help. In general, their effectiveness is on a par with that of actors, farmers, book-keepers or any other group. Many are excellent, the majority are adequate and, to tell the truth, some are quite terrible. In all cases it's the process that matters, but the best can speed it along and increase the benefits.

Ask friends for recommendations and then narrow the choices to a few who sound warm and friendly and respectful of children. They should have thorough professional training, a good deal of counseling experience, a knowledge of many techniques and, if possible, be affiliated with a teaching hospital. You and your child can either interview each one and then make a choice—the way you first chose a pediatrician—or you can give the first one a try for a month or two but be prepared to change. The first method is easier and often cheaper, even though you pay for the interviews, but in either case your child should help make the choice, for psychotherapy works only when the therapist and the child are on the same wave length.

There are many kinds of therapists. On one end of the spectrum is the psychoanalyst. He has undergone analysis himself and may or may not be a medical doctor. He probes the psyche and helps the patient dig out root fears and fancies. This therapy, which is expensive and requires a long-term commitment, is falling from favor, especially for the young. Children, it turns out, are much more resilient than doctors once thought. A psychiatrist— who is also a medical doctor—is necessary to order physical tests or give drugs to balance your child's body chemistry— such a delicate skill that he may consult a psychopharmacologist to fine-tune the prescriptions. Most children do fine with a clinical psychologist or a clinical social worker, however. The psychologist usually has a Ph.D., rather than an M.D., and the social worker has a master's degree. Both are well trained as counselors, with the social worker generally the more practical and more solution-oriented, which is good for the child above the third grade, but a young or inarticulate child may get more out of play or art therapy, individually or in a group.

Some clergymen serve as pastoral counselors too, and if they charge a fee you can expect them to have had specialized training. Other clergymen, who don't charge, may or may not have this training and may or may not have the instinct and the experience to deal with children. The school counselor, who is free, usually has an education degree in psychology and only counsels the child long enough to help him find more experienced help.

TYPES OF THERAPY

A child with deep-seated emotional problems usually needs individual therapy. However, the therapist may put him in a group if the problem isn't particularly severe or if he and other children of various ages are trying to grapple with the same problem, such as a death or a divorce. These single-topic groups may be led by a therapist or one of the increasingly popular (and effective) self-help groups. In any case, it's often easier to see our own problems when we are helping others see theirs.

Family therapy is particularly helpful to many children whose unhappiness is caused by problems at home. While working together, the situation changes, without the child feeling at fault. It is especially important in dealing with a handicap, death, divorce, remarriage and with blended families, but any family can use help when tension has been high for several months or discipline has gotten out of hand. In family therapy the child is able to establish his own identity at his own rate and the rest of the family learns what it is. Only in family therapy do the parents and the child discover how much they really love each other. By recognizing this enormous power, everyone will criticize less and compliment more, which inevitably makes the family work better.

Even if a child goes into individual

therapy to work out special problems, the family is still involved. A good therapist generally sees the parent first, to get background, and joins the whole family for a visit at home. There also may be a few family sessions at the office in the beginning and occasionally during the course of the therapy.

You'll support your child in therapy in a dozen ways, for you have an active role to play. You have to get him to the session on time, without a lot of confusion; pay the bills quickly (or see that the insurance does); and do both so graciously he won't feel guilty about it. You'll also have to pick him up promptly and treat him gently but matter-of-factly when you do. You won't ask him what he talked about, but you will give him a pep talk now and then since he's bound to feel discouraged occasionally. Changes seem to come in clumps and sometimes a child will hold back until he's sure the family has changed too or that they will still accept him.

None of this will be easy, for therapy is hard on children (as it is on adults). Anything that encourages change is always unnerving. You can expect him to hit a point in the first few months when he says that all is now fine and he doesn't need help anymore, thank you. He may be right, but it may be that he hasn't yet begun to wrestle with the roots of his unhappiness. There will be signs when he does: he will be angry with one person in the family for several weeks or months until he works through a particular problem, then switch his anger to another family member. It will be painful for each person who is targeted but there are benefits in this new honesty. Psychotherapy brings out strengths in a relationship and enables the patient to deal with the weaknesses.

Whatever the therapy, the effort is worth it. If only one person changes in a family, everyone else will shift a little bit. This is often enough to break an impasse.

THE FAMILY

Every family, like every child, is different. There may be one parent in your house or two, and perhaps a grandparent. You may have one child or many, closely spaced or spread over a dozen years, from one marriage or more— or no marriage at all.

You may be rich or poor, with a college degree or a high school diploma, and may live in an apartment or town house, on a farm or a country estate, have servants or be servants. Each element helps define your family but it gets its true identity from the people in it. The combination of individuals in your family makes it special, and you have a responsibility to make it work. It often takes a great deal of doing.

Today our homes are usually a bit bigger than they used to be, our families considerably smaller, and life—which should be simpler—is often more complex than ever. The family that is limited to parents and one or two children can be isolated from the larger community, or so involved in everything from the civic association to the school to the church that parents have no time for their children, or they may get more and more embroiled in their jobs. We have a terrible need to expand our horizons in our thirties and forties and to pursue possessions, always for those we love best. All of this can push the children away.

When you or anyone in the family spend more time pursuing objects, accomplishments and status than you spend with each other, it's time to buy less for the house, yourself and your child. If buying and paying take too much time and energy, a lot of loving gets lost. Your child may resent it at first if you have to shift your emphasis, but not for long. Studies show that a child appreciates his presents most when they are relatively few and he knows his parents saved or sacrificed to buy them (although he might not say so for years).

What a child really likes best is time and attention. They create a sense of security that enables him to rise to the challenges of the world. By talking, sharing and even quarreling with the folks at home, he develops a sense of fair play and learns how to give others their rights and to stand up for his own. This is how he learns to handle the ubiquitous problems of the great big world: envy, pride and avarice, and competition, favoritism and prejudice. It's easier to be a grown-up when you've had some help in growing.

A family not only molds the child; the child molds the family. His parents, his brother, his sister, are all slightly different people because of him. This makes the family members depend on each other, creating a family built out of loyalty and love. You'll notice it when your child accuses you of wearing an awful hat, and then defends it fiercely if someone at school makes fun of it. This is because he sees the faults and virtues of his parents as his own faults and virtues.

The atmosphere at home affects him too. If there is peace and harmony, he will admire his home and his parents—and himself—and if there is nitpicking and dissension, he will be ashamed of himself and of them. This environment will be reflected in the friends he chooses. If his choices make you uneasy, they may signify that something is amiss at home.

The parents—particularly the mother —set the tone of the household. The more openly you show your own joys, enthusiasms, fears and anxieties, the more relaxed you will be and this will spread through the whole family. If you aren't honest about both your positive and negative feelings, the negative ones will leak out and poison the family well. A child must know where tension comes from or he will blame himself—even as he denies it—and he'll become a hostile child. Give him and yourself—and everyone under your roof—the privilege of being honest. By showing that you are sensitive to the feelings of others, your child will learn to be sensitive too, most of the time.

A child needs to be free not only to express his emotions but to keep some to himself. Like you, he needs to be gregarious and rowdy sometimes, but he also needs his privacy, to mull, to daydream and just to be alone. The family home should be the place where he can feel safe enough to wander aimlessly from room to room, to watch a half hour of pointless TV or read in his room, to spread the comics on the kitchen table after school, to munch a sandwich and talk to no one at all. He needs the same sense of relief you and your husband look for at the end of your day. If you let him unwind in his own way, he'll be more willing to let you unwind in yours. A respect for privacy is not the same as a wall of silence. Parents should stay within a friendly, whistling distance.

Unfortunately, many parents find it harder to give time and affection to the schoolchild than to the preschooler because a child in the Middle Years acts so self-sufficient. You want to fight this reaction. A child needs open affection, freely given, with a lot of hugging, some honest praise and a little unconditional acceptance every day from the two people he loves most, even though he may be too self-conscious to give much back right now. You're the grown-up and you may have to give again and again, before he feels ready to respond. The obvious love of one parent can be enough, as long as the other parent isn't sitting around in cold and distant judgment. A child finds such a contrast almost impossible to bear.

Not all of the affection should come from parents. Surrogates are just fine and, at times, even better. If you don't have an extended family nearby—and most of us don't—you can extend what you have by making sure that your family has friends of many ages, that houseguests are welcome and that on the holidays you gather in those who mean a lot to you. You'll find these surrogate parents and grandparents,

honorary aunts and uncles, often give a child a new perspective on himself and are a great deal of fun too. As our old Tante Margot would growl on her grumpier days, "God gave us our family; thank God we can choose our friends."

For us, our dearest surrogate parent was Mike's godfather, Uncle Tom, who was crotchety and witty, a critic both by profession and by disposition. He was adored by all the children, not for his crankiness (he was never really angry with them) or even his wit, but because he always asked the children about themselves. He clearly wanted to know what they were doing, if only to disapprove. Because he listened to them and argued with them, they knew they were as important to him as any book or play. Even by indirection, he showed them how much he loved them. It taught us a valuable lesson. If you respect a child enough to listen to him, truly listen, you will be loved by that child.

Respect is the secret ingredient that makes a family jell, and it is infectious. When one person is accepted for what he is, he passes the acceptance on to the next and the next. Not only does each of us have the right to be ourselves, to be different and to be respected, but so does each family. If you cherish the individuality of your family, your child will enjoy going with you to the ballet in town even though your neighbors go to ball games instead. It's a matter of integrity.

A family must be true to itself, just like the people in it. This right to be different applies to all things, including discipline. Your family lives by its own limits, not those set by your neighbor, your sister or your aunt.

Other families have their own fears and fancies of course, and they're as entitled to theirs as you are to yours. This shows up mostly in the way they spend their time and their money. One family may buy many fine clothes while another gets along with hand-me-downs and basement bargains so they can have a vacation cottage or dinners out. New cars are more important to one family, private schools to another. The less you judge other families, the less they will judge yours. When a family denies itself the right to set its own standards, pursue its own interests and live by its own values it will feel at war with itself as well as with the community.

Bonding begins at birth but it grows strong when parents and children do things as a unit, not only eating most of their meals together and going on bike hikes together, but weeding the garden together and building a birdhouse. A child who is included in work as well as play will feel truly part of the family. Working and playing together should not mean that everybody does the same thing all the time, however. While your husband and your child may like to build model planes or see old Marx Brothers movies, you and the same child might paint a room together or play gin rummy.

If you have two children or more, you and your husband should have separate times with each of them and the children should also have their own special links to each other. When a Ten and a Twelve take a long trip together to see Grandma, just the two of them, they will get at least as much out of the ride as the visit.

And if you have three or more children, they need to get together not only as a group but in pairs, sharing a bedroom if they are fairly convivial (or if it's necessary) or taking an after-school class together. Just walking with each other can be a lesson in camaraderie that is never undone.

Mike, at Nine, would invent wonderful stories for his five-year-old sister as they walked to school together—stories so fine that a dozen years later Nell said, "I'll bet all the girls in the world are in love with my brother."

Love and loyalty aren't built in a day, of course, nor is there constant harmony in any household. Close friendships within a family may take years to ripen or may even go sour for a time but they grow best if a child is allowed to be his own person. In a family, where each relationship is a separate stack of blocks, there will be upsets now and then but they can be put back together or rebuilt in a new way. To do it, you have to listen to each one gripe in private about the behavior of the other. If you don't pass judgment or even offer advice, you'll usually find the griper will modify his complaints. He just needs to talk about it.

Some of this effort may seem unnecessary, but that's not true. In the Middle Years a child spends much time away from home—at the day care center, at school, at the playground, at camp—but a family is still the place where he belongs.

MARRIAGE

Remember when you married? Your expectations were so great—and so unreal. He had no flaws and he would, in his perfection, compensate for yours (if not actually erase them).

The future was rosy. The constant shortage of money would disappear in a year or two (ho-ho) and, if the in-laws proved intrusive, they could always be ignored. It was as Candide's professor promised: the best of all possible worlds. Then romance gave way to realism, bit by bit.

Your unreal expectations probably began all over again when the baby was conceived. Since he represented the best of you both, you expected the perfect baby to bring new joy to your souls and strength to your marriage. A child, you thought, would be the tie that binds and you were partly right. He did bring great joy and he

certainly bound you together more tightly, sometimes uncomfortably so. Mostly, however, baby care was fun—rather like playing house.

If you had a second baby, you no longer looked for perfection, and this time you had the pleasure of knowing exactly what you were doing and what you were doing it for. Time, or two children—whichever came first—turned you into a grown-up.

You also gradually realized that you and your husband would never be completely alone or carefree again. There was no turning back, and the road ahead looked very long. You found that the rituals of marriage changed in quite specific ways. Lovemaking may have been as frequent as ever, but those leisurely Saturday mornings in bed had to go. Instead you became grateful when the two of you found time for twenty-minute trysts between running a car pool and running a mile. Everything about your life grew fragmented, but with a little effort you and your husband stayed in touch. There was still that hour or two in the evening between their bedtime and yours that left you time to talk. This was when you put your marriage into perspective and learned to be even better friends. But it isn't always so easy now. The stress begins when the first child reaches Eight and lasts until the last one leaves the nest. Unfortunately, it will chill a little of the humor and gaiety and excitement in your life, putting pressure on your marriage.

At the risk of depressing you, you may as well know: sometimes marriage is a matter of relying on fortitude—or plain old courage. These are times when you feel a bit like the James Thurber character—the one who hated the letter O because his mother got stuck in a porthole and, when they couldn't pull her in, they had to push her out. A wedding ring can look an awful lot like a porthole now.

There's also the monotony. In the first fast-paced years with a baby, every day offered new accomplishments, funny stories or at least calamities for you and your husband to talk about. Now there is a great sameness that can color the Middle Years. Life in even the most spirited families can seem blah by comparison with the years that have just gone by.

And then there is the giving. You and your husband may spend so much time with your child—the homework; the Scouts; the coaching; the listening—that there's little left for each other. You mustn't let this happen. A marriage has an identity too and it must be bolstered. Just as your child needs to spend time each day alone with each of you, so do you and your husband need your special time too. Set aside a half-hour for this daily communion, asking your child, quietly and privately, to help you arrange it, but not at a cocktail hour before dinner. Fatigue is hard enough to handle; alcohol on an empty stomach will just make the blood sugar drop more, and make you testier. Linger instead at the dinner table with a glass of wine or a cup of coffee after your child has cleared the table, or just take a walk around the block. You'll probably say nothing important, but that's fine; it's the unity that matters.

You can also strengthen the marriage if you have dinner out together once a week, even if it's just a picnic in the park. It doesn't matter what you eat or where you eat, but that you can talk with each other without telephones, television, or any other interference—like children. Life shouldn't be a threesome (or a foursome or a moresome) all the time.

It's important that you and your husband also get away together one weekend every season—just the two of you—and if you can't afford to go away, you can at least farm out your child with friends and tell your neighbors to let you be. These interludes—in addition to the family vacation—are your investment in a stable marriage. Nothing will ever give your child better support.

When you try as hard to make your marriage as happy as you did to make your

preschooler happy, motherhood will be much, much easier. Despite your most creative efforts, however, gloom is sure to hang over the marriage sometimes. Even the best job has its grim stretches and the best marriage has its frustrations, confusions and arguments.

Children are very aware of anger and dissension, but if you and your husband make up quickly and are openly affectionate afterward, your child won't feel an undercurrent of disaster. In fact these arguments can teach your child to work out his own problems later if you and your husband learn to clear the air without recriminations.

It's often tempting for troubled parents to decide that they're doing fine but that the child is a problem. If you find yourself blaming your child or using him as the focus of your arguments, watch out, even if you talk positively about him—and talk about almost nothing else. The family is everyone's responsibility, but the responsibility for the marriage belongs to you and your husband, not your child. By realizing this and evaluating the marriage together, you keep it sound.

Despite these efforts, divorce crosses the minds of us all, sooner or later, and anyone who says it doesn't is either lying or they just haven't gotten there yet.

The time to consider divorce is when you're still well married, for almost any marriage can stay on the track if you work at it.

Sometimes you only need to analyze it to decide that no action is needed—or that you should get a job or work full time instead of part time (or part time instead of full time) or that the two of you should share more duties—a clash in almost every marriage—or that you should ignore some of the housework. These are the kinds of steps that save a marriage.

The worst problems are the ones that aren't faced. Even if you know the marriage is in serious trouble, don't separate for a day (or especially a night). Each day you are apart makes it that much harder to get back together, for pride builds the highest wall. Keep sharing the same house, the same room, the same bed. A double bed has saved many a marriage.

Poor communication is the biggest cause of divorce but running away is not the answer. If you're at that point, you need advice, you need solace, you need someone to talk to, and that someone isn't an auntie or a neighbor who doesn't know the questions to ask or have the discretion to keep her mouth shut.

You also don't need to call lawyers. It's a lot easier for you and your husband to make up without them. Once the charges go down on paper they are so cold, so angry, so extreme that they are hard to forget or even quite forgive. Instead find a therapist. Counseling may cause anguish but it won't be a patch on the hurt that divorce will bring or the counseling you'll need to deal with it. (Even with therapy, studies find that only a fourth of the parents and children in a divorce have gotten over the effects five years later. Children seldom understand just why it had to happen and they usually spend a lot of time blaming themselves (although they almost never do it out loud).)

Look for a psychiatrist, a psychologist, a clinical social worker or a marriage counselor who has good credentials and some years of experience, or go to a marital stress clinic, where the emphasis is on saving the marriage, rather than abetting the divorce. You may go as private patients or to your town's mental health clinic or a community-funded agency, where you pay according to your income (see Resources).

The quality of a therapist—no matter how much he charges—can vary a great deal and the chemistry that is right for one couple won't suit the next, so don't hesitate to change if he isn't helping you. But act. As long as you take your troubles somewhere, there is a chance to save your marriage. Nothing you do will help your child more than the support he gets from a stable, two-parent home. The same stability—or more—can be found with a single parent, of course, but a child is born of two parents and he deserves to be reared by two parents, if at all possible.

At a clinic it is usually a psychiatrist who evaluates the seriousness of the situation and the inevitable depression—to make sure it isn't dangerous—and to decide what kind of therapy would be best. One couple may do well with joint sessions, another husband and wife might need to be in a group—an idea that is not as threatening as it sounds. Here a therapist works with you and several other couples who have similar troubles, so each can see what their behavior looks like to an outsider. If the trouble runs deeper, you and your husband may be asked to see separate therapists to get rid of some of your anger before starting joint counseling, group therapy or the newer mediation sessions, where a referee—a therapist or occasionally a lawyer—makes each of you deal with one problem before going on to the next.

If your husband insists that everything is fine, or that it's bad but it's not his fault, you'll have to go to therapy alone. There is less hope here—for it's a bit like one hand clapping—but at least you can get rid of some anger and in the process you may either accept the situation or learn how to change your own behavior slightly, which will always make your husband change too.

The counseling—with both of you or

one—may take a year or more, but it's worth it. If you do have to end the marriage after you've exhausted all avenues, then you—and your child—will know that you did all you could to save it. Certainly it would be foolish to throw away a marriage that had once been happy and hopeful. It isn't a matter of sticking together for the sake of the child, but that a marriage may be stuck together again and often be better than it was before.

And when you let your child see how hard you're willing to work to repair the marriage, you're teaching him one of the most important lessons he will ever learn: some problems can't be solved, but all deserve the effort, and the more that is at stake, the harder you must try. If you can rock along you'll find a splendid joy in pulling through.

You only have a child at home for eighteen years and then you just have each other. Your love may get a little dusty in the interim but underneath it's still a treasure. If you just polish it now and then when times are toughest, it will glow for the rest of your lives.

WORKING MOTHER

Every mother is a working mother and many of them get paid for it. At least half the mothers in the country have jobs, because they want either the money or the satisfaction or both. If you've worked right along, you already can juggle your time and your energy like a pro, but if you've stayed home, you have to assess the situation again. Today the decision is usually not whether to work but when. If it hasn't happened before, it is often the year when the last child starts first grade.

You may be considering it now. Finally the duty to yourself seems to be in balance with the duty to your child and you're ready for it. The relentlessness of motherhood makes every woman yearn for accomplishments that are all her own.

To help a young child grow is a pleasure but it's a rare parent who can wrap herself

in it every waking hour. Even though you try to schedule your time between children and adults, interests and duties, you probably don't succeed and housework certainly doesn't make up the difference. Keeping house simply isn't as demanding or as satisfying as it was for your grandmother now that affluence, appliances and processed food have turned it into a part-time job. In theory this gives you extra freedom but instead you've probably found that, the more you had, the more your child wanted.

For the past six years you've known what it's like to be needed and needed and to know that, no matter how much you gave, it was seldom enough. The benign neglect of your grandmother's day went out with the drudgery. In your efforts to help your child be reasonably self-sufficient, you may have given so much that you now feel angry, exhausted and depressed. These emotions may surprise you—and your husband—but they are natural.

It's all because your child has been acting his age, year after year. He was content as a baby (for a half hour at a time); he was wild and independent at Two; rowdy and daring at Four. But he never said, "Yum-yum! Spinach!" and even when he got a lollipop he said,

"More!" instead of "Thanks!" You actually did a lot of growing in your child's early years but it seldom seemed that way. A preschool child demands not just time and energy but all the problem-solving creativity you have.

Even if you took classes, renovated your house, tended a large working garden, did volunteer work one or two days a week or had another baby or two, you still must decide what to do when the last child goes to school. It isn't the empty nest syndrome; it's the fear of an empty head. When our children move on, we must be ready to produce something more whether you get paid for it or not. Our next accomplishments will never be as great, but they are necessary.

If you haven't worked for years, however, you probably aren't psychologically ready to start a job and find many reasons to postpone it. Some of them are pretty good. First of all, you discover that you don't have as much new free time as you had hoped. If you think school means an automatic emancipation for you, you're living in what our Mike calls an F.P. (as in Fool's Paradise).

You have a brand-new set of duties now. You'll be asked to do the cafeteria watch once a month and perhaps special tutoring, and soon there will be pressure to run the carnival, make an extra cake for the bake sale and take over the Brownie troop. As an added irritation, these requests will be backed up with "All the other mothers are working."

As long as you're home all day, you'll also begin to feel responsible for the latch-key children in the neighborhood, supervising their after-school projects, bandaging their cuts and helping their fears disappear. It isn't long before you're giving twenty or thirty or even forty hours to people who aren't your own, and although most of the projects will be short-term, there is always another waiting to replace it. You'll be busy but you won't necessarily be happy. The more you're unwillingly depended upon, directly or indirectly, the more you will resent it. On top of that you may realize how lonely it is with so many neighborhood women at work, and how broke you are, as your child eats more food and wears out more clothes than he ever has before.

This is when you realize that women don't leave home just to do their own thing; they often leave home before other people's things do them in. When you reach this point, you're probably ready to work for pay. Now you have to find out how to go about it. If your money needs aren't urgent, volunteer work in a new field—or in the field in which you were once trained—is probably your best answer, particularly if you're not sure what you want to do. It's not only a great place to make business friends but it tests your abilities and your work preferences.

You can't take this or any job lightly, however. It is an intimate decision for you and your husband to make together, based on your own values and needs. What is good for the family next door may not be good for yours.

Even the best job you can get will shake up the situation in your house. Until now your husband brought in the money and you took care of the child, but when both people bring in the money the simple division has shifted. It can be wrenching. For all that we like to imagine ourselves free of the old stereotypes—the man must hunt; the woman must tend the hearth— the primitive commands echo in our souls. We may add new responsibilities, but the old ones don't go away. Even if you should make more money than your husband, he may still think of himself as primarily the breadwinner just as you may feel responsible for the sick child, although your husband gets up to tend him. We are the heirs of thousands of generations and we won't change this legacy in just one of them.

And so, if you work forty hours a week outside the house, you will come home to another job that probably will take thirty hours, and that will be much more demanding because it matters more. The din-

ner must be fixed, night after night. There is the straightening of the house; the mending; the marketing; the laundry; and then all those errands: the cleaner's is always on the list. Your husband will share the responsibilities—although seldom as much as you might think he should—but you'll still be in charge of the logistics and often feel weighted by them.

And there is still the bake sale, the clothes drive, the cafeteria watch. Never let it be said that you expect another mother to do your work. A thousand small responsibilities can turn into a monster, and this is what you must guard against. You do this by being candid with yourself and admitting that your new paid job has its benefits and its drawbacks too. It's impossible to keep house as well as before, although you're sure to do some things faster—because you must. And the house will stay tidier, because people aren't there as much.

Still those household hours that were once spread across a whole week have to be compressed into early mornings, evenings and weekends. Dinners not only can't be avoided, they must be fixed when you're as tired as everyone else. Some chores can be abandoned but some others must be delegated or shared and this is also hard. It takes enormous self-esteem (or almost none at all) to surrender our assignments.

No matter how much you want to continue the responsibilities you had or how guilty you feel when you ask others to help, a working mother can't do all that must be done and have time for her family too. When something gives—and it will— let it be the chores and not the child.

ORGANIZATION

These are problems to be anticipated before you start work rather than in last-minute desperation. You wouldn't expect your husband to work thirty extra hours after his regular job and he shouldn't expect you to do this either, but it will take

planning and organization to find solutions. Your husband—or certainly your child—won't know what all the chores are and they won't help do them unless you ask them. That's why you huddle together and write down all the things it takes to make your household function and decide who should do what and what needn't be done as often (or at all).

If a Six is clever enough to play Candyland he can wash his socks and underwear, as long as he has his own hamper or pillowcase for his own dirty clothes and you have a washer and dryer. He can do many other jobs in a household: take out the trash and garbage (if the sack is small and wrapped well); set or clear the table; load and empty the dishwasher—if you're lucky enough to have one—or scrub the pots. He doesn't have the stamina to do all of these jobs regularly but he can do one or two of them well as long as you make sure he's done the jobs each time they're assigned and change the assignment every month. This gives him the chance to learn to master each job without getting too bored.

As he gets older, he should be expected to do more jobs, more regularly and with more competence. It is, however, a fine road to walk, between giving a child too little to do and giving him too much—and therefore taking his childhood away. This is particularly tempting at Twelve, when experience and kindness and competence make a child such a good helper.

A Six is old enough to polish the candlesticks; a Seven can keep the powder room tidy; an Eight can make the salad every night; a Nine can fix dinner once a week—like tuna salad and chips; a Ten can wash the dog every week; an Eleven can mow the grass; and a Twelve can wash, and occasionally wax, the car.

A child of any age also needs the time and energy to have fun and so, in fact, do you. The preparation of a meal is much better if it is varied by plan. A fend-for-yourself dinner once a week is a holiday for everyone when each person can fix what he likes best and eat when he pleases. (This is otherwise known as a seefood dinner: if you see food, eat it.) A first grader can pour his own milk, if you put it in a small pitcher first; cook his own hot dog and dress it with relish and mustard. He also can shake popcorn with more patience than you (or throw it in a paper bag, squeezed shut, for two minutes in the microwave, if you have one). It's not a starch you'd serve for dinner but it's a good one and an apple is a super vegetable. The dinner only needs to be nutritious and the kitchen left clean for the next person.

It's also fun and easy for everyone to cook together on another night. This works especially well with Chinese food, for an Eight can stir-fry quite well—a five-minute job. If you do a big stew, a ham or a meat loaf on the weekend, there will be good leftovers, which only leaves three days to worry about. Your husband can cook one of those meals and your Nine will be making another.

Don't feel guilty for expecting your child to help; feel guilty if you don't. These are responsibilities all children should assume whether both parents work or not. A child isn't a chattel, but a parent isn't a servant either. Everyone is expected to clean up the family debris, without blame or rancor. In fact, if you work alongside your child, it becomes another bonding time, for it gives you a chance to talk about his interests. By putting his conversation first, the odd jobs will seem minor.

A Seven can help prepare breakfast and pack lunch on a regular basis and he should, for he will be more likely to eat the food if he has invested his time in it. Your child, whatever his age, should help plan the dinner menus too, for you can be sure that even a Six has opinions. By considering his advice, you are giving him the extra respect he deserves. The child who accepts more duties has the right to more respect.

He also needs as much attention as he ever did before and, above all, a good and available listener. Unfortunately, when both parents work, it is the listening—and the signs of loving—that often go first. Since it's so hard to give a child this much, you and your husband would be wise to work no more than a combined total of sixty to seventy hours a week, with either the mother or father (or a supervisor) at home during the school breaks, and at least two to three afternoons after school if he isn't in some other kind of program. A child may act wonderfully independent, but if he goes home after school, he needs to be welcomed by somebody and a parent usually does it best.

Traditionally, mothers, working part time, juggle holidays and use camps in the summer, but in some families both parents make adjustments, which is better, because the child is cared for by people with two different points of view. To give this kind of care, the husband or the wife may work a shorter week, so one or the other has more time at home, or they both change their schedules so their working hours don't coincide completely. It also may be

possible for either husband or wife to switch to a career with an office at home—an increasingly popular and practical idea. With computers and other technical tools, a lot of jobs now can be done at home on a contract basis. In fact some bosses find big-city office space so tight—and so expensive—that they will let a staff member work at home at least part of the time, but usually the staff member has to come up with the idea. Your boss may be equally open to part-time work, flextime or your sharing a job with a friend, as long as you find the friend and keep each other briefed on job orders. Time, of course, is not the only problem when the mother works.

MONEY

Money causes difficulties too. Although two people earn more than one, there may still not seem to be enough and, even when there clearly is, there can be resentments about the way it's spent or if an out-of-date budget is followed to fill today's needs. It also can cause big problems if the wife keeps her salary for herself—a carryover from the days when women kept the small amounts they earned from babysitting or sewing. If a working woman still expects her husband to supply all the upkeep for the family, she is trivializing her role and avoiding her responsibility. She might be spending every cent of it on her family, but she isn't performing equally as a parent and a partner until she puts her paycheck in the common till. Certainly most wives would be horrified if their husbands kept the money they earned.

There is less friction when working wives and husbands earn and spend money as a team. Both, of course, still need personal money beyond lunches and transportation—but this should be just a small percentage of the total family income.

You'll find your husband is a lot more willing to help you with the housework if you help him carry the financial load. The more equality you can instill into your marriage, the sounder it will be. The same is true of a family, which is why your child should be included in some of the money discussions too.

Your child needs to know the range of your income and your outgo, but don't worry. He won't tell the neighbors your business as long as he feels part of the group. If the child understands these home economics, he'll demand less for himself and be less anxious when you say you're broke—a typical worry between Six and Nine.

That's one reason why you make it clear—to both husband and child—that going to work is your own recognition of shared responsibility. It may assuage your conscience to tell your child that you only work so he can go to camp next summer—or college in ten years—but he'll feel it's his fault when you get so tired.

Accept yourself as an adult. You work at least in part because you get a kick out of the job; it's fun to be with grown-ups and the extra money stretches the budget nicely.

Even when you are the sole support and earn just enough to keep going, you're still working for yourself as much as your child. It would be especially easy for this child to feel like a burden when he sees how hard you work or how empty the refrigerator; any reminders are unkind and unnecessary. He needs to know that you would have a job even if his dad were around.

OVERWORK

The greatest danger to the working parent is not lack of appreciation but too much appreciation at work. It's easy for you—and your husband—to get so wrapped up in your jobs that the hours become too long, the evenings get buried in paperwork and you forget that your child doesn't get the same satisfaction from them that you do. Accomplishments shouldn't cost more than they're worth.

It doesn't matter whether you're turning into a workaholic to avoid the personal

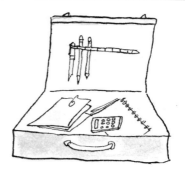

demands at home or because you always give 110% to any job you do. What does matter is your family. Somehow you have to make enough time for your child so you still know each other well. This is especially important between Seven and Twelve so he will be trusting enough to confide in you as a teenager and to confide in the person he marries.

If you and your husband can't curb your hours, you at least can include your child in some of the excitement. You may think he is too young to understand what your job is all about, but almost anything can be described simply enough, even for a first grader. If you're involved in the law in any way—as a policeman, a court reporter, a lawyer, a researcher, a paralegal—you can let your child go to a trial, whether you are part of the case or not. It will help him understand why you think it's so interesting and it will keep him from resenting your job so much.

If you're in sales, you can occasionally take a child on your rounds, and if you're a scientist you can take a child to your lab or one that a colleague maintains. A subscription to a magazine about your line of work—preferably an adult magazine written in laymen's language—is good for an older child. What any child understands best, however, is that you love him and you love your job and you want to share them both.

And if you go on one- or two-day trips, take him along sometimes, so he can picture what you're doing when you're gone next time. Every town has its point of interest and sitters, if necessary, although a Nine is old enough to entertain himself—and young enough to think a hotel room is exciting. You may think an active child wouldn't like that, but there is a lot more to investigate in a hotel than you may think, and adventure books become magic carpets. Just the plane ride, the dinner at the hotel and the time you spend together is enough to turn what would be a ho-hum trip for you into a glamorous holiday for your child, in memory if not in fact.

All of these factors—and many more—will help you decide when to start work if you haven't already. Now you must figure out what your needs are and then try to find the job, the income and the hours that fill them best. You may have to make some compromises, but it's better to adjust your goals than the quality of your life together.

After all, a family is what it's all about.

CHILD CARE

The care your child gets while you're at work is critical, for it affects the entire household now and for years to come. When the child is uncomfortable in the situation, or when arrangements change every few months, he'll become grouchy and negative and you'll start to resent your job, your child, your lot in life.

It's tempting to think that a child is emotionally able to take care of himself by the fifth grade, but that's simply not true. Every child, whether Six, Nine or Twelve, needs someone to watch over him, someone to care what happens that very day, and he needs that someone a long time before he sits down to supper.

He also needs someone to keep him out of trouble. Neither you nor he can depend on his day-in, day-out good sense until his mid-teens (and sometimes not even then). A Ten may know you're right when you warn him not to make french fries or candy after school, but he still might try, and then find himself dealing with a kitchen fire or bad sugar burn. It can happen, especially when he's with friends—even

though he promised not to ask anyone over. It's hard for him to say no if a friend comes to the door.

A lot can go on behind the closed doors of an unsupervised house and frying potatoes is among the least alarming. Marijuana, alcohol and sex have tempted too many well-reared preteens already. It isn't fair to put your own child to the test so soon. As hard as it is to find—and to pay—for the right care, even a Twelve should be supervised, by adults, by activities, and by chores, beginning at Ten, after school, on holidays or during vacations.

This child can take care of himself for an hour or so after school—and enjoy it—but he shouldn't do it more than one afternoon a week and then he should call you as soon as he gets home. You can share his day, and then you can agree on enough chores to keep him busy until you get home. As long as they are real jobs, and not make-work projects, these activities will add to the self-reliance and the sense of competence that every child should have.

It takes careful planning to get the best care. Supervision can be provided by a housekeeper—the most expensive situation—or by an "au pair," a young person who gets free room and board and a healthy stipend in exchange for some child care and housework.

Some working mothers rely on their

relatives to care for their children and this is a sensible solution, as long as it is a clear-cut, fair-minded baby-sitting arrangement with specified time and pay, even if the other parent is your own mother or sister. As charming as we think our children are, they seldom appeal as much to others unless a reasonable amount of money is exchanged. The sitter—and this includes your mother—may say she is glad to help without pay now and then but, if her willingness is abused, you can bet your child will soon pick up another set of messages.

Of all the systems that are available, family day care is often best, for when it's good it gives the child the warm, low-key structure he needs after being at school for six hours. This may be an informal program or one that is run as a licensed business, but either way it usually means a mother taking care of no more than four children, including her own. Your child will eat the same snacks as the rest of the family and do whatever they're doing, whether they're gardening, playing ball or running errands.

Larger day care centers are a possibility too (the nonprofit ones have the best reputations) and some public and private schools open early and stay open late to provide extra care.

In all cases, the first day-care arrangements—like the first grade—should be a good experience and you should evaluate the possibilities before you even look for a job. It takes time to observe agencies, after-school programs and day camps (which particularly need your appraisal) but along the way you learn what questions to ask. Each place helps you define your requirements.

Some aspects should always be considered, whatever the facility. Is it safe? Does the place have a pleasant aura? Does everyone look happy? Did your child have a good time the day he went with you? Are the problems handled well? Are many of them avoided or diverted? Do the children have interesting things to do? Do they often play outside? Does each child have a special place to hang his coat? Is there a quiet nook for a child to be alone?

Family day care calls for additional questions. Is the mother healthy and active? Can she keep up with the gang? Does she really seem to like her job? Is her house so tidy when you pick up your child that she may be spending more time cleaning than mothering? Does she limit the amount that the children can watch television and does she monitor the shows?

There are other general questions that are particularly pertinent to the larger, more formal or commercial agencies. Can they take advantage of the community resources—swimming and recreation department classes? trips to the library? Do they ever go to museums? to parades? Are snacks healthy or junky? Are the toys appropriate and in good repair? Can you talk easily with the teacher or the day care mother?

If you decide on a housekeeper or a mother's helper, you must not only interview past employers but ask each prospect to give you thorough answers about her philosophy on child care—before you tell her what you think, or she may simply agree with you. You want someone who truly thinks like you do, because she can't change her style no matter how hard she tries. Dependability also counts a great deal. The housekeeper who calls in sick at 6 A.M. brings frenzy to the working parent. You'll find there may be fewer call-ins if you offer a small reliability bonus—an extra amount if she works every day she is scheduled that month and always gets there on time.

It's easier to find the best arrangement, or the best person, if you ask every mother you meet for referrals and advice about child care, just as you do about jobs. No one knows better than the lady who's been there, or the lady who is still there.

Your child will like after-school care better if he has a say-so in making the arrangements; if he understands that you would worry if he were home alone; and that you need him to be well tended so you can concentrate on your work.

Once he's enrolled, you'll know the day care is good if he seems happy and has a lot to say about his after-school activities—most of it good. All children gripe—especially, heaven help us, the Seven—but if your child complains, be sure to listen well. It won't help to interrupt with "Oh no, Karen, Mrs. Jones is a very good sitter" or "Now, Davy, you know you really like the day care center." That just tells a child to hush.

When your child is unhappy in the day care situation—because it wasn't good in the first place, or it has changed, or he is too old for it—you have to hear him out and look for new arrangements or help him adjust or realize that the problem—and therefore the solution—is a little different than he thought. There may even be the possibility of sexual abuse, if your child seems pretty upset, withdrawn or depressed (see Sexual Abuse). Unless he feels free enough to explore his unhappiness with you—whatever the cause—he will decide that you can't bear to be wrong or that you don't think he has the right to hurt. If that's the case, he will try to swallow his pain, but it only will pop out some other way, creating tension in the family. As long as your child knows you understand, even if you can't do anything about it, he will try much harder to get along.

Even the best-run day care program gets tedious sometimes. This is when you send your child to a weekly class in something nifty, like pottery, cooking or computers, or have him join a neighborhood sports team or simply go to the library once or possibly twice a week. It's a good place for a preteen to do homework, keep out of trouble and meet new friends, like *Harriet* (that spy!) and *Gilly Hopkins*. They may be only paper people, but they will be great company.

You're bound to make some day care changes in these growing years, but the fewer the better. It's not only a great deal of bother, but it takes a lot of emotional stamina out of both the parents and the child. Of course, you will bail out of a poor arrangement as soon as you can, but with foresight you may avoid it. The careful investigation you make is the key to a wise choice. The more situations you explore, the more you realize that there are many ways to rear a child within the confines of acceptance and discipline, honor and humor. What you want is the one that reflects your family best.

SINGLE PARENT

The single parent has a tough job, no matter how necessary the divorce, how expected the widowhood or how long the separation is going to last. There are joys and other compensations to be sure, but if parenthood was demanding before, it can be overwhelming now. There is no one to spell you when your child has been sick for three nights in a row; no one else to hear his grievances, to take him to the Scouts or to rush from teacher to teacher on parents' night at school. And there is no one to help you think straight when you are lonely or scared of the directions you think this child might be taking.

You do, however, have the real pleasure of knowing that you have faced your responsibility and are doing your best. There are other rewards, even more abstract, but also real. There seems to be more honesty—and therefore more closeness—between a single parent and her child than in many two-parent families. Whatever air of infallibility you once assumed in front of your child has been discarded. Now you admit that you can't do everything, that you want his help, that you need his love. Nothing strengthens a child more than to be depended on for what he can give. The problem is in expecting too much.

A Six, or even a Twelve, is not ready to be your social companion. He may spend more time with you than he would if he had two parents, but he still should have his own friends, and you should have yours. If you don't, you will become increasingly dependent on your child, who in turn will become increasingly jealous of anyone who takes your time, especially a man. This is even more true if you decide to have your date spend the night. While this is a more common practice than it once was, it still has ramifications, in jealousy, in embarrassment and later, perhaps, in confrontations when the young adolescent wants to adopt the same behavior.

If you invite a man to live with you—a choice neither your child nor this book can make for you—the decision requires much more thoughtful consideration than it would for a childless woman, for the repercussions will be more serious. It's hard to share a house, but psychological space is much harder to share and the effort causes anxiety in everyone—including the new roomie—and some jealousy too. (see Remarriage).

It will be the permanence you expect to find in this romance that should govern your decision, since this is sure to affect your child the most. A child, particularly of divorced parents, can take just so many dissolved relationships before he thinks that all commitments are programmed for failure and will learn to avoid them altogether. This will make his twenties especially difficult—the age when he must decide to share his feelings with others, so he can continue to grow.

No matter what relationship you have with a man, your child—boy or girl—needs to have a friendship with a fatherly figure who will be a constant in his life. His own dad is usually the best person, if that is possible and practical, but your beau, an uncle or a neighbor will do. Even a high school student, paid to take your child out for one or two afternoons a week, is a good idea, as long as the person has a strong male personality.

You should, of course, be certain that this person is honest and honorable and isn't one of those birds who might make sexual overtures to your child, for the child will feel full of guilt whether he (or she) succumbs or not. The slightest idea that this may be happening would be reason to end the relationship and you must watch for it, as you would in any adult-child friendship (see Sexual Abuse). Moreover, you should talk about the general possibility with your child at least several times. Serious ideas can't be dispensed with a one-shot conversation.

YOUR NEEDS

Parenthood always has meant sacrifice, especially for a single parent. You have not only less money but less time too, for you are trying to do the work of two people. Don't try to do too much. Settle instead for the most important jobs, and enjoy them, saving some private time for yourself and some time just for you and your child. You each deserve at least fifteen to twenty minutes a day—you to read or stare at the ceiling or do your exercises—and your child to talk and be heard. And if you have more than one child, they each should have an individual visit with you, even if it's just ten minutes.

This is time spent on nothing else—without the television turned on or any glances toward the newspaper, or without stopping to take a phone call. Instead you sit with a cup of tea and you chat, as you would with any friend—telling your news so he will do the same—or looking at the rain together, arm in arm. Silence is another way to talk. The more you communicate with your child now, the more he will confide in you in adolescence. Although he certainly won't tell you everything (it's just as well), the connection should stay close enough to prevent or modify the rebellion that is so common in teenagers.

Despite all your effort, your child won't have an easy time of it either. Some studies show that a child of a single parent often gets much lower marks in elementary school than a child who lives with both parents and that he is three times more likely to get into trouble in high school. It doesn't have to be this way and it won't be if you use foresight to prevent problems.

You may have to seek psychotherapy for the two of you to stay on the right track. You also will need to take part in substantive groups that cater to single parents and their children, particularly those that have a special interest, like skiing, fishing or folk dancing. You want the kind of club where being someone is more important than meeting someone. Stay in close touch with family and friends too, even if you feel intrusive, or if it is really their turn to call you. This is no time for pride. Your child needs to feel that there are others to whom he may turn, for underneath the signs of strength there is sure to be an awful, shaking, quaking feeling—"If she goes, what will happen to me?"

GUARDIANS

Even if his dad is alive, healthy and sees him often, your child still needs to know that he would be welcome to live with him if anything happened to you. And if he isn't alive or dependable enough to be in charge, you have to make other arrangements, for your child is the most important legacy you have. Moreover, your child should be a party to these plans. Tell him that there is always the possibility, however, slight, of an accident—this will be no surprise to him—and that it is important to have him help you make contingency plans.

Ask him, in a matter-of-fact way, who should take care of him in case an accident should happen and then talk together about the strengths and weaknesses of that person. You also, naturally, suggest a name or two, but still casually and in a direct, businesslike way, settling on a person in the family if possible. Blood is not only thicker than water, its commitments are thicker than the commitments of friendship, and children need to feel as much kinship as possible and to keep as much of their cultural heritage as they can.

WILL

You have nothing to leave as precious as your children. This sample will will help you leave them safely:

I name my sister, Jane Smith Jones, as guardian of each of my minor children who survive me and of their estate, whether the children were born of this or any previous marriage or whether they were legally adopted. If this guardian dies before me, or refuses to serve or fails to qualify or resigns or otherwise ceases to serve as guardian of my children, I name my brother, Henry William Smith, as guardian instead, of both the children and their estate.

Above all, this potential guardian should be stable, preferably married, of your own generation and chosen for the love and attention and values your child would get, and not for money or position, which are superficial and easy to lose. You then discuss the situation with this person—and try not to be hurt if any uneasiness emerges. A responsible person knows that this is more than an honor; it's a critical decision. If the person you choose is wholeheartedly willing—any unexplained hesitation should give you pause—draw up an agreement, letting your child read it and encouraging any questions he may have.

The agreement should include the legal arrangements that will transfer the guardianship of your child and whatever money your estate can afford for his expenses, and one or two executors should be named to administer this trust. They should not include the guardian, however, so your child can be protected from at least two different sources. This legal arrangement should be notarized if possible, even if you haven't written a detailed will, and witnessed by two adults not named in the procedure. It will be binding until the child reaches his majority at eighteen, unless there is a successful court challenge.

This agreement is only referred to in your will but it is signed and filed with your important business papers, since you'll also want these wishes followed if you become disabled and can't make decisions for long-term care for your child.

These are cautionary steps, of course, and unlikely to be needed, as you will tell your child—and then drop the subject.

It's the day-to-day care of a child that concerns a single parent most, and it should. Not only does a child—even a Twelve—need some kind of supervision after school, but he should help to make the arrangements by suggesting how he would like to spend his time. He may not be too forthcoming, but if you listen closely to the "yeahs" and the "nyahs," and draw him out to be more explicit, you'll make more thoughtful decisions (see Working Mother).

If your child's problems are treated with dignity, he will learn to be sympathetic to yours—a trait that is often stronger in this child than in one who is reared by both mother and father.

As a single parent you are making many extra demands on your children but, handled wisely, the rewards can be greater for each of you.

REMARRIAGE

A parent's remarriage usually brings joy to a child—of a tentative sort—a great deal of stress and always some sorrow. Whether you've been widowed or divorced, the child is sure to ache a little for the life that

should have been. In the midst of your own happiness, it's important to remember his feelings, from the gentle announcement to the ceremony itself. If at all possible, let there be three months between the two, so he can get used to the idea.

You don't, of course, get permission from your child to marry, or even ask him if he thinks you should, but you do include him in all the plans and tell him where he fits. And tell him, over and over, that his role in your life and your heart will never change. To be fair, you also must point out the differences he can expect, as well as the similarities, and remind him that everyone will have to work to adjust to the threesome (or foursome or moresome) at first. To let him expect perfection in a second marriage (or any marriage) would only set him up for disappointment.

Much of the discussion will center around the wedding and the gathering afterward, with your child made to feel that his ideas and participation are definitely welcome. You may want your daughter to be your attendant or your son to be an usher and give a special reading. This is the current trend, but many children have later reported that such full participation was upsetting, even though they didn't say so at the time. It's hard for a child to be more than a spectator if he's unhappy about the marriage or thinks he'll be too emotional to keep his poise or if he feels disloyal to his father—all emotions any children of the groom may have too.

The same considerations you show your child should, of course, apply to them. Whether your children take part or not, you or the groom or the clergyman should recognize the important role they have played and will continue to play in your lives. Everything else may go by in a blur, but these words will be remembered and treasured.

Whatever you plan, you'll probably want to keep the service short and simple and the guest list small, in keeping with the tradition of second weddings. Besides, it will be emotional enough for your child. While there are often only a few guests at the wedding itself, you might want to have more for the reception, but again, keep your child's feelings in mind. Unless he has some cousins around his own age (or you have more than one child), let him invite a special friend of his own so he'll be more comfortable. It's also important for him to have a job to do—taking wraps; passing hors d'oeuvres; serving nonalcoholic punch—although he should be free to circulate at least half the time.

You'll also need to be particularly thoughtful in planning something special for your child while you and your new husband are on your wedding trip. He'll need to be with people he loves and have activities he likes, to take his mind off the changes ahead. Don't move him into your new household until you're around to answer his concerns, especially if you're blending the families in one house. Even with the world's best sitter, you'll want to supervise the merger yourselves.

And if it's your ex-husband who's getting married, instead of you, do your best to be gracious about it and help your child adjust to the idea. If it isn't easy for you— and it won't be—you can bet that it will be hard for him.

Whether it's your marriage or his, the more support you can give the children, the easier this transition will be.

STEPPARENTS

When the heavens want to test the self-righteous, they turn them into stepparents.

No other kind of parenthood has so many pitfalls.

No matter how much you love your husband, his child from an earlier marriage will, at some point, cast a shadow over yours, whether the child lives with you or not. And if you have a child from a previous marriage, he will affect your relationship too. It is folly to pretend that this isn't so or that stepparents have an easier time with girls, as some people say, or that boys are easier, as others claim. Handled well, however, both boys and girls can make your marriage richer than ever. Blending two sets of children is of course harder and, if you and your husband add a child or two, the problem escalates, at least for a while.

It is the strong, primitive link between the natural parent and the child that creates most of the tension. There are nearly seven million children in America who live with a stepparent and probably every one of them would rather be with both his natural parents instead—at least in theory. It takes these children awhile to like their new arrangements, and it's bound to be an ordeal at first. There is a silver lining. A person who cares deeply for someone can learn to care for others—including a stepparent.

The love your husband or you have for your own children is different from the love you have for each other, because the love of a child is born of protection and nurturing—and time. Every day of a child's life makes a parent invest a day's worth of love, of concern, of empathy, of expectation, of companionship. The greater the interchange, the tighter the bonding.

When you both can accept this special relationship, you can begin to establish your own bonding with your stepchildren. It will take patience and a discouragement may set in, but if you persevere you can get close to them, and you'll find that a stepparent can have a special place in the child's affection too, one which cannot be usurped. You and your husband offer each other's children something special: the love of an extra parent. Even though neither of you can share the memories of days gone by, you can make new ones, starting now, which is easier to do if you understand and respect your new children.

ADJUSTMENTS

You can't expect his child to call you Mom for a long time, if ever, and yours won't call him Dad. In fact he has all the same problems dealing with your child that you have when you deal with his, although they may be expressed in different ways. Your stepchild will be uncomfortable with you for quite a while (as you are with him), defensive about his mom, jealous of your time with his dad and anxious about his place in this new household. His uncertainty may make him sullen and wary, or he may act serene, as if there's not a ripple in his pond. This is the child who says everything is fine, always, and you may find yourself doing the same, never daring to admit that there might be problems. In the beginning you probably think there are none. There you are, a cross between Lady Galahad and Supermom, ready to save the world or at least one small child, but then you discover that wishes won't make it so.

A stepparent must first of all be candid with herself. As happy as you are to be married to your husband, it can rankle to help support another woman's child; to take care of him every weekend while his ex-wife has a holiday; to mother a half-grown family when you want to be a bride. You realize that you're more self-conscious and less spontaneous with this stepchild than you are with any adult and more judgmental too. As problems begin to surface you may think you are the only one who is affected, but it isn't true. Your stepchild will feel just as constrained as you do, reflecting all your tensions and adding at least as many of his own. Now you realize that he instinctively sets new tests for you each day while you set tests for him.

This is to be expected, and it won't stop because you sit down one afternoon and talk about it for twenty minutes and he says, "Yeah" and "I guess so" at all the right places. You can't rush love, but you can encourage it. A child whose parents have divorced or whose mother has died needs respect and reassurance. You might try very low-key family conferences and, if they don't work, there should be visits with a support group or five to ten sessions with a family therapist. This is almost essential when there are children on both sides. You'll know you've arrived when he can joke with you or ask you something "confidentially." Feel blessed to get a silly nickname or a hug around the waist. This is often as far as a child will go between Six and Twelve, for this is not a demonstrative age.

Children in the house—and that includes, most emphatically, stepchildren—make you realize that a mother's time is no longer her own and neither is her money. The lack of money—and it may be relative, but it is real—may cause much resentment between you and your husband. We all create responsibilities—and sometimes we marry them. All but the richest families know how difficult it is to support two households and, if it takes almost all your salary to pay for the other one, the tension can get high—especially if you can't afford to have a baby of your own. Even without this conflict, it's hard to work all week, put your money into a joint checking account and then see a chunk of it go for child support. You can bet your husband feels the strain too and yet you both know he must care for his child just as he would care for a child the two of you might have.

While you need to give your stepchild time and money, you must give understanding most of all. Since no one has skin more tender than this child, your own skin must get pretty tough. You can't be hypersensitive too.

A stepchild—whether yours or his—carries a special burden. There's never a

day he doesn't think of the loss of his mother or dad, if only for a brief moment, and this turns the stepparent into the rival. That's why it's best to live in a home or apartment that is new to both you and your husband, if possible. There's bound to be some shifting of bedrooms if you move into his old home or yours, and the children involved may feel that is tantamount to war. Even the neighbors may make you uncomfortable if you move into his house. It's easy to think they're comparing you with the first wife—and that they find you wanting—even if she sailed away with the plumber in a big balloon.

You also should avoid the challenges of inanimate objects if you can. When people have trouble accepting change, they often cling to the familiar. Your stepchild may think it an insult to replace the old trash can his mother left behind. You can imagine how he will feel when you use his mother's dishes—or sleep in her bed.

You cannot, of course, dispose of people so neatly, and it would be unfair to your stepchild if you could. The child will need to remain in touch with his past, and you should encourage this, in a sensible, rather limited way. It will make it easier for him to focus on your future together.

If he and his dad lived together after the first change, there was probably a housekeeper or some other surrogate mother whom he learned to accept to some

degree. Then you arrived and he felt displaced all over again. The second disruption can be much rougher on your stepchild than you might expect, particularly if this person was entrenched. Unless she was a romantic live-in, you and your husband will want to help his child maintain the relationship—if only by letters or phone calls—so he won't feel abandoned and angry. This means that you must make sure the child sends those letters and makes those phone calls. He may miss someone a great deal and yet rarely write or call the person without some prodding, even at Twelve.

It's also important for the child to keep in touch with his mother's family, which may call for you to develop a relationship with them too. Even if the first marriage ended in divorce, you probably will have some connection with her family (and with her), particularly if you live in the same neighborhood. There are always school games and plays to watch, communions or bar mitzvahs to attend, and the people who love the child best will be there to cheer.

None of this is easy.

If any in-laws or ex-in-laws make your life too difficult, you either must avoid them when you can—to keep the peace— or talk it out with the most understanding members, which is preferable. This will work better if you can explain how you feel when you're around them, without accusations. "I feel left out of the family jokes" rather than "Your family never explains anything to me." If you attack, they'll defend. The problem is exaggerated if the first wife is alive and included at your husband's family gatherings—a rather tacky thing for them to do if you object. For you it will be a matter of endurance, but don't endure to the point of sappiness. If your new in-laws act as if you were an outlaw, let your husband know it bothers you, but only do this as a last resort. He may be unable or unwilling to take a strong stand. If he won't acknowledge the problem, you have to recognize that there is other, more basic trouble in your marriage and you need a counselor to help you. If he does recognize the problems—with or without your pointing them out—you have at least a foundation for planning together to resolve them.

GUIDELINES

Even if you and your husband are doing fine, his ex-wife may use the child as a weapon to attack your marriage, getting him to carry messages announcing arbitrary changes of plans, demands for extra money or a litany of problems. Not all messages are verbal. Clothes can be used to send signals, with the ex-wife dressing the child in his most tattered jeans and shirt when he's coming to your house. It's another way to say: "You see how poor we are?"

It would be tempting to buy the child some new clothes—but don't, nor do you comment on his scruffiness. Simply ask him to wear something particularly nice—an outfit you know he has—the next time he comes visiting, so you can go someplace special. And the next time, take him to that special someplace, no matter how he's dressed. It's your job to see that he is clean and neat, not to make him embarrassed by insulting his wardrobe.

You do buy your stepchild clothes, to be sure, but do it when you're budgeted for it, or when you feel like giving him a surprise, or when he really needs something for a particular occasion, keeping it at your house if he visits often and you don't think his mother will send it back with him again. You just can't let yourself be blackmailed nor do you use clothes as a weapon yourself, buying him a sweater when you see that he's wearing a new one from his mom.

You also don't encourage the child to tell you tales about his other home or the problems there. When you, as a stepparent, refuse to play these games you help the child resist them too, for children are natural manipulators when they think their own survival is at stake—and nothing

makes them feel so uncertain as adults who fight over them. Most of all, you have to work hard at being patient.

No matter how wisely you behave, there will be resentments and resistance and the child will test you. The problems often peak around the second grade. Any Seven is sure he's neglected and undervalued, a feeling that is particularly strong in a stepchild. Since he will almost surely feel deprived of money and material possessions, it's wise to keep a family ledger to show where the money is spent, and on whom. It should dispel at least some of his grievances and it can help you be more evenhanded. A stepparent often buys more for this child than she would for her own—a generosity that comes from a sense of guilt that makes you ask yourself if you're doing enough, spending enough, hugging enough, sharing enough. To a natural parent these plaguing doubts come and go as the child moves through stages; for a stepparent they never go away.

You will naturally get angry with this child occasionally and, even if you have legitimate reason, you will feel guilty. This is useful too. A little remorse helps keep your temper in check.

If you are a mother in one complicated but not unheard-of situation, you may find yourself loving the stepchild who lives with you a shade more than your own child who lives with his dad. It's worth thinking about: all love has its wintertimes. And if that is small comfort, remember that the depths of love should never be compared, especially one's love for one's children.

It is also possible to realize that you don't like your stepchild very much and perhaps you never will. You are two distinct personalities, years apart in age and interests, and to make it worse, the child may look just like your husband's first wife. Affection isn't automatic, just because you and the child both love and are loved by his dad.

Even if the child is quite wonderful, you won't appreciate all his good qualities—nor will he appreciate yours—as long as there is stress between you. Be patient and remember: almost any two people can get along if they're willing to be honest with each other and have good manners about it.

DISCIPLINE

When one of this pair is a child, there is a need for discipline too. Fair and consistent discipline is the ultimate form of respect. It always lets the child keep his self-esteem. A good disciplinarian expects as much—or as little—of a stepchild as she would from her own. It's hard to correct a stepchild, however, especially one who doesn't live with you, but if you don't you'll find you're always at the simmering point, picking up after him like a maid and resenting it every moment.

Above all, the discipline you use must be in your own style. If it isn't, the child will hear the contradictions in your voice and won't know what you really want, which will make him angry. Any child needs to know just where parents—and especially stepparents—stand.

It's easy to go down the wrong path. You may be too lenient at first, because you're afraid someone will think you're the wicked stepmother, or too tough, because the child is "out of hand." Or you may not discipline at all if your husband says you don't have that right—a common situation and a major mistake. If only one parent gives the discipline, the child will be running the house in about two and a half minutes.

You are the codirector of the household and equally responsible for any child who stays under your roof, whether he lives there permanently, comes for the weekend or is an overnight visitor from down the street. You and your husband may not always have the same rules, but when one of you makes a judgment, both should stick to it. And you may on occasion say to the child that he may have a point, and that you and his dad would like to talk about it—alone—to reconsider and that the one who cares most about this problem is the one who will prevail.

A child doesn't have to have consistency between his parents, but he does have to know that each supports the other, if only out of respect. Whether you convince your husband or not, the child at least will feel that his complaints are taken seriously and he will take you both more seriously too. And if you change your mind on an issue, or even change your approach, he will understand if you admit you made a mistake. There's nothing a child likes better than the admission of fallibility—in grown-ups.

As long as you realize that you and the child both have legitimate needs—which don't always coincide—you can do something about them or at least figure out which ones must be endured. If he annoys you beyond measure, however, he is either trying to make you dance to his tune or he has a problem that would drive anyone scatty. Each requires a different reaction. If your approach has been thoughtful and fair, it's almost surely the second case. You, or your husband, or both, then need to ask him to confide and to listen, without being judgmental, which isn't easy either. Every family must struggle to find the rules that make it work best. They are rather harum-scarum in most families, and are sure to change as the family changes, but they are always necessary, particularly in a blended family, whether all the children live with you or not. Rules work best, however, when everyone has the chance to express their gripes and they are hammered out together. The results should be posted for all of you to follow—adults and children. If the children are expected to put their snack dishes in the dishwasher and fold the newspaper for the next person, the parents must do it too. Civilization is built on small kindnesses, and home is the place to learn them.

In addition to the family-wide rules, there should be a special set for you and your husband, including a division of child care responsibilities. Otherwise you may find yourself responsible for them all—visits to the pediatrician and dentist, teacher conferences, car pools and shopping for clothes, and you will feel overwhelmed and angry by instant motherhood. This will be even worse if your husband expects to make all the decisions that affect his child. By sharing the child care duties with you—even if he never has before—he will find it more natural to share the decisions with you.

The care of the stepchild who lives with you takes a great effort; the care of the child who comes and goes takes a greater one. All the backing and forthing needs special handling so the child can adjust to two sets of people. A stepchild must feel safe to be where he is and who he is. This is why he must be made as welcome as possible, even if it is only once a year for six weeks. He still needs to have the same sleeping space and at least a shelf or a drawer where he can leave some treasures year round—including perhaps some you may have given to him. Most children are very sensitive and, if your stepchild felt his mother would be offended if he took these presents home, he might leave them and just hope you'd understand. Please do.

Even when the relationships are quite friendly and the discipline reasonable, the visiting stepchild is sure to bring tension with him and certain patterns can make the tension worse. If you keep his schedule very full when he's with you, you may be using confusion to keep him at a distance. If you give him more treats than you can afford, you almost surely are trying to buy his affection or assuage your guilt. Even if you're not, a child will assume that you

are. As he very well knows, there's not enough money in the world to buy his love, but if he thinks you're trying to do that, he will respond to the message long before you even know you've sent it.

And if you, your husband and the visiting child make a constant threesome, you're probably more jealous than you think. What your stepchild wants and needs is not action or money but time—time alone with his dad, with jokes to share and interests to build upon. He also should have some special time alone with you. He needs an hour or so of your company, without demands or expectations—a gentle time to bake or garden or amble over to a yard sale with you.

And if your husband has several children whom you see intermittently, you both need to keep in touch with each of them individually, as well as together. If it's possible, ask each one to a visit alone occasionally, especially the child who is going through a rough patch. If these spaced-out visits aren't feasible, your husband can invite one visiting child on a special outing while you invite the other somewhere else. As long as each child understands that this is the way every family works best, they won't get jealous of each other and will get closer to each of you.

Your husband, however, may get a little jealous if you develop a special closeness with his children, and you are almost sure to resent the time your stepchildren spend alone with him. These and other bad feelings will have to be admitted, so they can go away a little sooner. The more children you have between you, the more pressured you're likely to feel.

That's why you and your husband need time just with each other. One weekend a month or at least a single Sunday should belong just to the two of you, whether you have to hire a sitter, swap the time with a friend or beg it from a relative. If you only have the child on weekends, tell the ex that you are trimming those visitations by twelve or twenty-four or

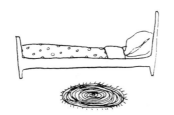

forty-eight hours a month and ask for added time in the summer or during school vacations, so the child won't feel ignored. These occasional weekends alone will give your marriage an extra measure of stability and that is important. A stepchild doesn't need another broken home.

As he gets older it may be harder and harder for him to give up his weekend activities to visit his dad and this can generate a certain surliness when he comes to your house. You can counteract this by letting him invite a friend sometimes. It makes the shuttling more bearable and saves him from a heavy dose of adult attention, which can make a preteen feel smothered.

By treating him less as a child and more as a responsible person, you'll find you think of him almost as a contemporary. You even may confide in him more than you would your own child, for you haven't had all those years to be so protective. If you can concentrate on the child, rather than the situation, you invest a bigger piece of your heart in the relationship. Your connection will be different from one you would have with a child of your own, but precious nevertheless.

The more you see him as an individual, the more he will look at you that way and see you as a friend: still a stepparent, still

an adult—but also a friend. And since friendship is the basis of any lasting alliance, you can count on its pleasure for years to come.

GRANDPARENTS

Grandparents come in all ages and while the younger ones may seem almost like contemporaries—and want to be treated that way—the older retirees need special consideration. Although they like to stay productive and active, it's often hard to do. Illness, the death of a spouse or the need to move from the family house brings them face to face with loneliness and some begin to draw back, emotionally and physically. This can make it difficult for you and your children to feel—or be—close to them.

If this is happening in your family, it may be because your parents are instinctively slipping away, for sweet dignity's sake. They burrow into a cocoon of memories, partly because the past is more vivid than the present. Depression may be so serious that even a doctor will think it's senility. It need not be this way, for children can help keep grandparents young.

It won't be the same relationship you have with your child of course, which is fine. Grandparents are no more likely to take your place in his heart than another child could take his place in yours. He will just be delighted that there are other adults—besides his mother and dad—who think he's marvelous.

The grandparents won't, however, express their affection in the same way you do and they may be much less adaptable to roughhousing, noisy games and endless prattle. There is a time for all seasons. Their energy is the main factor. No matter how much they seem to have, they probably have less than you think and you should wait for them to make a specific offer to take care of your child, except in a true emergency. To assume that their activities—even a nap in the afternoon—are less important than yours is to tell them obliquely that they don't matter much anymore.

On the other hand, your parents probably will be more likely to enjoy long, two-way conversations with your child, for they probably have more patience than you. It's time and interest that these generations give each other best. The child between Six and Twelve needs someone to listen to his opinions and answer complicated questions about volcanoes, tornadoes and the way motors run. In turn, a grandparent has a person who has never heard about selling newspapers in the Great Depression, hitting the beaches at Okinawa—or how the child's mother or father once did something silly or outrageous or ingenious.

These recollections feed a child's love of history and so do the stories that grandparents read. Whether Six or Twelve or in between, your child is Hansel and King Arthur and Kinta or Sam, who Am, Christopher Robin, Anne Frank or Nancy Drew. This is how he finds out where he fits.

It is in the history of a family, however, that a child finds his place best and no one explains it better than a grandparent, or is more willing to show the photograph albums, going through the same pages again and again with a story for every picture. And it will be the grandparent who teaches him to make the family tree—a pastime more interesting to the young and the old than to you—and explain how he is related to Great-aunt Tessie and why his cousin was removed, not once, but twice. The details and nuances that may seem tedious to you spell stability to your child. By learning now that he is part of a broad, intricate family, he will have a much stronger sense of his own identity later.

AT A DISTANCE

To remind your child of grandparents who live away—as well as other far-flung relatives and grown-up friends—hang a map of the United States or the world in his room so he can mark each hometown with a pin. This, with the addition of pictures, subtly assures the child that he will never be all alone.

The mail can affirm these friendships. Have your child address a few envelopes and postcards to grandparents on some nothing-to-do day, so they'll be ready when he wants to send them a note or draw them a picture. Somehow a child finds this idea easier when the job is divided into two parts.

A tape recorder is excellent, as long as the grandparents have one too. You can exchange tapes of just everyday conversation as a nifty auxiliary to a phone call. As your parents get older there will be many times when they want to hear your voices and yet a phone call is just too expensive—and too intrusive—for them to make as often as they would like. At least one or two of these tapes should be saved for your child to play while he's sick or you're sick of entertaining him. He also should play them before they come to visit and before he goes to see them, especially if he's making the trip alone. He'll feel comfortable with them much quicker if he's used to the sound and cadence of their voices and the expressions they use.

And that's not all. If the grandparents like to read stories to your child, you can send them a list of his favorites—even at Six, Seven and Eight—so they can read them into the recorder. And when they send a book that's beyond the skill—but not the interest—of a new reader, they can send their tape too so the child can hear while he tries to decipher the words. The closeness in a family depends on the bridges you build, not the miles between you.

THE VISIT

Houseguests are a strain and the more emotion that's involved, the greater the strain. And when you're talking about parents and grandparents, you're talking about a lot of emotions. Plan your own guidelines before anyone leaves home.

When the grandparents are the visitors, your rules should prevail—as they do when anyone visits—but accept the fact that they will give your child some special treats and jollies—some of which may dismay you. Rise to the occasion. A little outrageous spoiling is good for the soul, if not the teeth. If you feel an irresistible urge to make a big issue out of the first treat offered (or if they feel compelled to offer one on top of another), one of you is in the clutch of jealousy and is using the child to throw some zingers.

To solve the problem, stop the game. It doesn't matter who started it or how much ego is at stake, it won't continue if only one is playing. If a grandparent is the aggressor (and usually it's just one), the realization that you are not—at least visibly—annoyed will stem the flood of challenges.

Just tell yourself:

- this visit won't last forever;
- it really won't matter in a hundred years; and
- it's better to take the high road.

When you and your child visit the grandparents the strain on you is likely to be just as real, but different. Now you split your identity into yet another segment—not just a guest, a wife, a mother, but a daughter or a daughter-in-law. If you're staying with your parents you may surprise yourself by reverting to some childish ways you thought you'd long outgrown. For a daughter-in-law, the strain can be much worse. You not only feel out of the family unit, but you see your competent, confident husband turn into such a "momma's boy" he won't even pick up his socks.

It can be hard when it's not your house or your rules. While it is a relief to hand over the housekeeping to someone else, it's difficult to give up the power that goes with it. You feel displaced, which makes you uncertain and maybe angry, particularly since you now must discipline your child to fit the limits someone else has set.

If your child shows clear resentment of the new rules, you can bet he's reflecting your own attitude, no matter how well you try to hide it. Call him aside and tell him the rules bother you too, but that you have to accept them along with the hospitality, as you do wherever you visit. Even a child of Six can handle that idea, as long as you're candid with him, and you'll find it makes you feel better too.

You, your husband and your child will still have a few rules to follow: to do some of the cooking or salad making, if it's permitted, or fix afternoon tea; to clean up any mess you make as soon as you make it; to make your beds before breakfast; to set and clear the table; and to help without

ORAL HISTORY

Even a Six can be an oral historian, interviewing his grandparents on tape for vignettes about their own childhoods, their memories of you or your husband growing up and stories about relatives, how the family moved around and what they did when they settled down.

Your child will get rich stuff when he asks his grandparents how they courted and what Grandpa said when he proposed. The grandmother can sing her old jump-rope songs and the songs her mother sang to her, and pass on a verbal picture of her neighborhood and her friends and her dolls and her pets.

In recording this oral history, you'll find that both the child and the grandparents are hams enough to want their words preserved, and will like to add to the tape from time to time—five minutes here, ten minutes next week—just by flipping the cassette back in the recorder. And if you think your child might get confused and erase something important, you can borrow another recorder and copy the tape, and then he can play his own. This teaches him to use this machine well—one more competence required for a citizen of the twenty-first century.

being asked and without getting in the way. You set the pace. When a child sees his parents following such good visitor rules matter-of-factly, he will be much more inclined to do the same.

You'll also want to have very, very good manners, day in and day out—the kind you save for the boss. The more unnerved you are, the more polite you need to be. Just do a bit more than your share and then put the rest of your flexible time to good use. Neither you nor your child should just hang around. You can make a scrapbook together of the family's best recipes (or "receipts," as we used to call them down South), or ask Grandpa and Grandma to teach your child—and perhaps you—how to prune roses, decorate a cake, change the oil in the car, knit, crochet or strip furniture. Your child is at a stage when he is fascinated by small skills and to learn them from his grandparents will enrich his life—and theirs. Besides, a crotchety elder can't show off and be snippy at the same time any more than he can frown and smile at once.

You also should get out of the house often. You'll need the break and so will the people who live there. When something is needed, go get it—a quart of milk, some thread from the dime store, the clothes from the cleaner's.

Take a lot of walks too—alone, as a separate family and just with your child. And be honest with him. Tell him that sometimes you find Grandpa a bit wearing—just, perhaps, as he sometimes finds his own parents—and that you're glad to have a chance to get away with him. Don't worry; he won't tell, but he will feel honored to have your confidence. Children are much more discreet than you might think.

The movies are another good outlet, for all ages. They're usually entertaining, they're impersonal and they give everyone something to talk about (and argue about) on the way home. And if the grandparents don't want to go, you can take your child, or go alone, even in the afternoon. Country fairs, auctions and yard sales are good

excuses to go, and so are horse shows or rodeos, art exhibits, turkey shoots, oyster roasts. In most cases you probably have a bit more freedom (and free time) when you're the visitor. After all, you're just keeping your temper; not the house too.

Much of the effort you make on these back-and-forth visits is basically a matter of accepting someone else's eccentricities and hoping they'll do the same for you. And is it worth it? Absolutely. Your parents and your husband's parents are very special people. After all, they made you.

UNDER ONE ROOF

The grandparent situation is much more significant, of course, if you live with them or they live with you. Good manners, as always, will protect you, but they must be workable, workaday manners that the family has developed together to reflect everyone's interests. The rules won't be static, since people aren't static, and they'll evolve as the needs change and the child gets older, with each of you giving a little bit.

Begin by defining roles as well as rules. Ask both grandparents to pick the duties they'd like and then count on them to assume them. This is particularly important if an older relative is dependent on you, for dependence breeds resentment and anger. In a family, everybody should do his share as best he can, unless he is under eighteen months or senile.

The basic philosophy of child care will be constant, however, and it is you, the parents, who must set it. Each person in the family—parents, grandparents and children—also should understand the reason for the rules, and each rule should have a good one. You can't expect anyone—grandparent or child—to follow an edict blindly. "Because I said so" isn't enough for you and it's not enough for them.

When your mother undersands that you have sound medical reasons to limit your child's sugar intake, she may study the reports and decide that you're right: the bowl of candy in her room may be too much temptation for her grandchild to handle.

If all agree to observe a rule most of the time—and then they don't, most of the time—they're telling you obliquely that they resent it. Puzzle it out together, in a family group, probing gently and without judgment, and don't be surprised if you find that the resentment is more basic than you thought. When child care is part of the live-in arrangement, you mustn't expect the grandparent to act as a sitter whenever you want to flit. She needs as much warning as if she were paid and the right to say she's busy or just "not today" without feeling guilty about it. Everyone wants the dignity of a schedule, or at least to know that she is expected to do a certain number of hours in a week. It's a quiet, positive way to respect your elders.

The grandparent who is ill—or senile—presents a special problem. The child should share some of the responsibility but only as much as he can handle repeatedly. He is apt to feel burdened by having too much to do and by feeling different from his friends, which will make him feel guilty. He needs to know that they are perfectly understandable. No matter how fond he is of his grandfather, he's almost sure to be embarrassed to push him down the street in a wheelchair (and without his teeth at that) and yet he won't mind sitting with him in the backyard where there is privacy. A happy life is made of compromises.

It also can be embarrassing for a child

if the living room is always cluttered with tissues, medicines, the rubber ring and other sick bay paraphernalia and with nothing allowed on television but the soaps. If that happens, your child will spend less and less time at home and, by adolescence, he will be more like a boarder than a friend.

Remember: this is your child's home too. He deserves at least one specified day a week after school when he knows he can bring friends home—when Grandma and all her trappings will be in her own room. It isn't fair for anyone in the house to take over the common space all of the time.

By being considerate of your child you will have a lot less friction, and less resentment, in the house.

PROBLEMS

It's necessary to acknowledge that grandparents, treated well, don't always bring bliss. Some are simply dreadful, others are exhausting. There are also those who make fine companions for everyone but their own children. These unfortunate relationships often turned sour back when the child was between Ten and Eighteen—that critical time when the parents must let go. If they don't, they become the parents who never stop bossing their grown children around and whose grown children hate to be with them.

Fortunately, at least some of the problems can be corrected and, if you find yourself in such a situation, you should be willing to try. If you don't, it not only will continue to gnaw at your soul and keep you away from them but it will deprive your child of an important relationship that might have worked, because the problem often skips a generation.

Decide how close you can dare to be with these problem parents and then try to get a millimeter closer, and then one more step and then another. These are the same techniques you'd use to change a recalcitrant child—giving respect without obsequiousness and keeping enough room for both of you to keep your dignity.

It's possible to have a sound relationship even when a grandparent has serious flaws; a child isn't supposed to be surrounded by perfection. If one grandparent is an alcoholic, for example, you still try to give them the opportunity to know each other. You tell the grandparents clearly what you will not endure, and watch them closely when they'e together. In most cases you can find a balance.

BONDING

Parenthood follows a pattern of paradoxes: you have to let go and tie fast, all at once. The visible cord that's cut in the delivery room is the least of it. It's the invisible one that's harder to cut, but you snip it a strand at a time—when you let your Six cross the street alone (even though your heart is clutching); when your Nine earns his own money to buy the model plane (although you could easily buy it for him yourself); when you watch your child wrestle with his homework (and you're itching to give the answers). Each time you give your child a measure of independence you raise his self-esteem. At the same time the two of you weave new bonds of strength from the way you work and play—and pull—together, through the routine and the crises. This is what bonding is all about.

Every day is another day of love, a deeper investment, for parent and child. Because the effort is mutual, the reward is mutual too, which is why bonding matters so much. It strengthens both of you. While this book is written for mothers, almost everything applies to fathers too—especially the bonding. Rearing a child is a long-term, two-person job; both parents are obligated to do their full share, as different as it might be.

A child, being a reasonable person, can understand a father or a mother who must be away at work for a considerable part of the time, but a child is also a logical person. The parent who plays golf all day Saturday, or goes to the pool every day for a tan while the child is left to his own devices, or who works or goes to meetings every night might as well wear a sign that tells the child to GO AWAY. Some play must be shared. Whether it's a game of checkers or a walk in the woods or cheering your favorite team on TV, it makes your child know he is important to you, which makes the bond much tighter.

Working together has the same effect if you show your child how to do the job; if he has the right to stumble as he learns; if he feels appreciated; and if the job doesn't last too long. When the two of you are together—playing or working—you are so busy a child feels free to bring up awkward subjects. The confidences seem almost casual and much freer for both of you, because he doesn't have to look you in the eye. This is the same reason you'll also confide more easily in the car—if no one else is there—or in the dark after he's gone to bed.

Set aside a few hours each week to work or play together without either of you having a friend along—so you both can afford to reach for a new closeness. If you have other children, you may have to hire a sitter for them so you can spend extra time with the child who seems more withdrawn. The relationship you tighten now will give him a lifetime of support.

Bonding between parent and child is, perhaps, inevitable, but not all of it is positive. Some bonding is founded on anger, fear or anxiety and is just as hard to undo. Parents bond in a negative way when they foster an activity simply on the advice of a friend (or a book) and not because they like it. Artificial enthusiasm or concern bores parents and makes the child think he is the cause of their yawns and fidgets. When working or playing or just talking together, consider both your child's interest and your own. These moments should be casual and low-key and as flexible as possible.

Bonds are often tied the tightest in the lazy summer months. This is not the time to urge a child to scramble to be at the top of some sport. Instead, give him a chance to inhale fresh ideas as well as fresh air and read books that teach him nothing except a love of reading. And it is a time for camp—if you can find a good one—if only because the distance between you will make you realize how much you mean to each other.

The rituals of bonding take time and patience but the results are beyond price. Your link to your child is like no other friendship you ever will have. It is reaffirmed with each baseball game, card game and gardening session.

There are other dividends. The time you spend together also affirms your authority too. No matter how much you enjoy each other (and you will enjoy your friendship more every year—give or take a slip or two), you will still see him as your child and he will never forget that you are his protective, dependable parent. That's just as well. He can have a thousand friends.

PLAY

Families that play together really do stay together. No one wants to miss the good times. As you've probably discovered, however, play takes work. The house has to be pleasant enough for you both to want to stay in it to play cards and orderly enough for you to find the deck. Somebody's got to buy the popcorn to be popped; get the ice skates sharpened; find the soccer ball in a hurry; earn money for the cottage on the shore. No one does all the work, of course, but you'll certainly have to play a key role.

Finding the best family adventures is one of your main responsibilities, and one of the most pleasant. A child will enjoy them more if they fill his head with new language and new ideas, his nose with new smells and his stomach with new foods. Look for the firemen's carnivals and city happenings; Renaissance festivals and bazaars in ethnic churches. He'll thrive on fireworks and band concerts, country auctions and neighborhood yard sales. Whatever is different from his own culture will spark an interest. While trips to Disneyland are dazzling, it's the fun and adventures you have right at home that bind a family together.

Our children were very young when the first men walked on the moon—an adventure televised in the middle of the night—but it was not to be missed. The children went to bed, early and excited, knowing they would be awakened to watch it and toast it with a sip of champagne.

Most rocket flights are scarcely noticed now but there are other extraordinary scheduled events that can be dramatized—an eclipse, a royal wedding, a family wedding, a political rally, a transatlantic phone call to someone near and dear.

A child thrives on anticipated, contained excitement, and if there's no public or domestic extravaganza on the horizon, you can spin some possible if not probable dreams. For us it was an elaborate plan to buy a huge round cement watchtower—a relic of World War II—on the Delaware coast. It became the source of a hundred excited summer discussions over the years—first we would buy it, cheap, from the government and then we would make it into a beach cottage with a wonderful view. We would decide how to paint it and decorate it and plumb it and divide it, and whether boys or girls would get the top floor. In the winter, when the tower was out of sight and out of mind, we would consider acquiring other items of government surplus—a three-wheel post office buggy perhaps, when Kate was old enough to drive—just as we bought our old typewriters. Both the tower and the buggy proved ungettable—which the two oldest debaters had suspected all along—but the memory of the planning lingered on; it was the chance to dream that mattered.

Parents need to nurture a child's imagination with adventures and with the hope of them. A child who learns to look ahead with great expectation will do it all his life. To make this more likely, you need to encourage your child to invent adventures of his own, by listening to the whole idea before you say "No" or "We'll see." A Twelve has a hard time reaching the point, but if he's allowed to pursue his idea he'll usually decide if it's sound or silly, without your having to pass judgment at all.

Years from now you'll meet around the kitchen table and say, "Remember when you saw the chipmunk and thought it was a baby squirrel?" "Remember the old carousel on the mall?" "The boat trip around Manhattan?" "The smell of an orange grove?" "The tourist home in Zanesville?" "The heather by the sea?" These seconds will shine like moonbeams in his mind.

And you can make most of them happen.

READING ALOUD

When your child starts to read, you're going to be almost as delighted as he is. Not only has another milestone been reached, but maybe you can retire as the bedtime story reader. Dr. Seuss has worn mighty thin.

The transition is gradual. First your child reads to you, painfully picking through his primer. While you treasure that dear, halting, singsong voice, you will want to throttle Dick and Jane. You fidget, then you yawn and then you're tempted to read the newspaper headlines out of the corner of your eye. Finally you may start correcting his pronunciation at every page. If you do, he'll start reading to his little brother instead. This usually is the end of of parent-child story time, and a pity it is.

It took us a while but we finally found out that reading together offers a family one of its warmest interludes. These twenty minutes, at a regular hour, three or four times a week are glorious moments. There can also be an unscheduled read now and then, a special story you pull out of your pocket when you're on a walk together and then settle down by a tree to read it. These links are forged with gold.

Vacation trips become calm when a book is read aloud in the car—passing from one passenger to the next, or listening to audiocassettes if reading makes the riders carsick—or when you're lazing around on a summer afternoon at the beach. The bonds are tightened still more when you talk to your child about the books you are reading together—or those you're reading on your own—as you'd talk

with any friend. This shows him there is an equality in your relationship, which is another way of letting him go.

Different books are different things to different people, but almost everyone can learn, with the proper introduction, to treasure some in special ways.

At first it may be hard to lure your child away from television, without making him give up one for the other. You'll find it easier if the set is routinely turned off a half hour or so before the story hour, so the two won't be in conflict—and if you occasionally read a novel that you know will be on TV soon. The pictures in a child's mind are not only more complicated than he will get in most television plays but they are his own, and therefore better. This is a contrast he'll make when he watches the show—a contrast which will reinforce his love of books.

The kind of books you read may change as soon as your child is old enough to read for himself, for you no longer have to read the books that bore you. Now you can pick the ones you like, from C. S. Lewis to Robert Louis Stevenson. There is so much that is good, you don't want to waste time on something that one of you doesn't like. Remember, if you look bored when you read to your child, that dear, egocentric soul will assume that you're bored with him. Instead choose the books that are classics to you. They may not be on anyone's Famous List (although the best of anything usually is), but a good one fulfills the definition of a classic—a book so good you want to come back to it again and again, no matter how old (or young) you are.

Some parents get self-conscious when they read to older children and with reason. It takes practice to do it well. As the books get more complicated you have to dramatize with at least as much abandon as you displayed onstage in junior high. Switch from one voice to another to play the different parts—a good reason to start with a book that has only a few roles and little dialogue—and read more slowly, with more drama in your voice in the suspenseful parts, changing to a fast, clippity-clip pace as the tension builds. Too much description will bog down a book, so you may decide to skip an occasional dull passage, but keep those that are full of vivid similes and metaphors. They help a child conjure better pictures in his mind.

You also may decide to skip some of the racier words. The more modern books are dandy, but they may have occasional epithets which bother some parents. That's all right. If a word offends you, pluck it out.

The best books grab a child at the beginning and, if they have chapters, each one will open with a zinger and all but the last will end with a chiff-hanger. These are the books that tease his imagination, stretch his curiosity, make him laugh and cry and rattle his mind with ideas.

Good books not only help a child understand what excellence is all about, but you realize that neither the age of the book nor the age of the reader matters. As long

as the story isn't beyond a child's emotional level, it will suit him fine, even if the vocabulary is quite rich. A first grader learns to read about 350 words but he understands about 10,000. Even when he doesn't, he always can ask what something means, but he'll probably absorb new words simply by hearing them in context, the way you do when you read. This is the golden door to learning, for it stretches the mind without killing the interest.

Prose is not the only fodder for a good story hour. Poetry, written so tightly it must be read word for word, enriches a child for life. The cadence, the lyricism, the precision will make your child appreciate all writing—especially if he memorizes it—for children in the Middle Years are real hams.

The daily comics and the political cartoons are great fun to read and talk about together and even comic books are dandy, although good ones are hard to find. Look for *Tintin*, a well-drawn winner about a teenage reporter who travels the globe. With each issue taking two years to research and containing eight thousand words, a child is bound to learn.

Books, of course, are the heart of your reading and more and more are published all the time. The Caldecott and Newbery medal winners will lead you to some of the best titles and you'll find others recommended as "Notable Books" by the American Library Association.

Books like *Charlie Wonka and the Chocolate Factory*, *Charlotte's Web* and *The Great Gilly Hopkins* will build bridges you and your child will cross again and again in the years ahead, even if a certain distance grows between you for a while. As your child goes from the third to the fifth grade you graduate to a heart-stopper like *Treasure Island* or a heart-wringer like *David Copperfield*, and try to imagine your child going away to sea like Jim Hawkins or to the pub for a hunk of bread and a pint of ale for breakfast, the way David did at Eight. Both boys and girls will listen, electrified, to the adventures of Ste-

venson, and be enraptured by the graphic descriptions as Dickens weaves all the world in his stories—even the passerby "with legs so long he looked like somebody else's afternoon shadow." James Thurber and P. G. Wodehouse, Samuel Taylor Coleridge and Walt Whitman, Edgar Allan Poe and Willa Cather all help a child appreciate his own differences better.

It can take weeks or even months to finish a book, since there's no pressure to read a story, or even a chapter, every night, but that just makes you luckier: literature and loving are meant to be savored.

THEATRICALS

Each family ties its bonds in special ways. It may be intense golf or tennis games, fishing trips or wild rounds of hearts or pig, but they will matter more to your child than the fanciest gifts. One of the tightest bonds with our children was cast by the plays their father wrote for them and their friends—a cast that expanded year by year as we added more neighborhood players.

There were after-school rehearsals once or twice a week for several weeks, a few Saturday rehearsals, at least one dress rehearsal (since dressing up was so much fun), and we were blessed with a talented mother who created splendid costumes out of odds, ends and ingenuity. Finally, there was the performance itself, given for as many friends and neighbors, of all ages, as the old carriage house could fit. The actors, who varied in age from Four to Twelve, often exceeded our fondest expectations, if not their own.

To put on your own neighborhood play, you'll need a big garage; a flexible script; an enthusiastic parent to cast the players and direct them; another to organize the props and the costumes; someone else to put the costumes together; and still another to supply fruit and sandwiches for hungry players at rehearsals, and punch and cookies after the play. On that day

This is the little play that led to years of neighborhood performances.

PETER PENCE, THE PEDDLER

ACT I

It was the night before New Year's
and all through the town
Not a creature was stirring except—H. Mary Brown
(who was the mother of six).

HMB *(stirring a pot on the stove):* This soup still tastes like pistachio nuts.

PRISCILLA *(one of the six):* What do you expect? There's nothing in it but six pounds of pistachio nuts and one rotten turnip.

HMB: Thanks to your FATHER. The scoundrel left us high and dry on this miserable pistachio plantation just seven years ago today to seek his fortune in the goldfields of Alaska *(looking at her youngest and counting her fingers).*

HM BROWN, JR. *(tasting soup while her mother has been talking):* I think I taste the turnip. Other children, excitedly: How does it taste?

HMB, JR.: Rotten.

HMB: I'd better put in some more pistachios.

(Loud knock at door. Door opens. Peddler with pack enters in flurry of snow.)

PEDDLER: Good evening, madam. I am Peter Pence, a peddler peddling things that begin with *p*—pens; pencils; Pentels; pansies; popcorn; popguns; puppies; pastrami; peaches; pears; pinochle decks; partridges; pear trees; persimmons; pickles; pancakes; and pistachio nuts.

HMB *(hopefully):* Do you give credit?

PP: Only on the pistachio nuts.

HMB *(sadly):* I'll take a pound.

HMB *(then, with emotion, as she gets a better look at the Peddler):* There is something about you . . . that seems familiar.

PP: My mustache, perhaps.

HMB: That's right, your mustache.

PP: I picked it up in the Klondike. A fellow traded it for some pens, pencils and a pinochle deck.

HMB *(excitedly):* Was the fellow short but handsome with blue eyes rather close together, tousled red hair and a slight stutter?

PP: Yes.

HMB *(dejectedly):* Alas. I thought for a moment it might have been my husband, a fat brunet with dandruff . . .

PP *(abruptly):* Madam, are these your children?

HMB: They are. *(She introduces each child—Priscilla, Percival, Pam, Penny, Paula, Pat and H. Mary Brown, Jr.—and each says "Howdy;" "Pleased to meet you," etc.)*

PP *(sobbing into his peddler's pack):* How I envy you.

HMB: Don't get carried away. Feeding seven hungry mouths with a husband gold-hunting in Alaska and fifty acres that won't grow anything but pistachio nuts isn't exactly like spending the winter on the Riviera.

PP (*transfixed*): Perhaps we two can join forces. I could join you as a parent and you could join me as a peddler.

HMB: What could I peddle?

PP: Well, I've pretty well run out of *p*'s. How about *m*'s? (*pronounced ems*)

HMB: I could market marimbas; marinated mushrooms; metronomes; mice; miniskirts; maps; mugs; mints; marbles; mush; mulch; and *The Lives of the Martyrs*.

PP: Here. Let me add a few things to the soup (*tossing in some parsley and two partridges*).
End of Act One

ACT II

(*Act Two opens with the peddler and HMB about to exchange vows. The preacher, with a stopwatch in the palm of his hand, is waiting for the stroke of midnight, at which point the husband will have been missing for exactly seven years and will, therefore, be legally nonexistent. There are two children dressed as flowers girls with baskets of parsley, pansies and persimmon leaves to strew down the aisle.*)

PENNY: Ready, set, GO!

(*The flower girls start strewing. The bride and groom take three steps across the room. The preacher begins.*)

PREACHER: Dearly beloved, we are gathered here today to raffle off this new Lincoln Continental—whoops, wrong page. Dearly beloved, we are gathered here today to join this man and this woman in matrimony and if anyone knows a reason why they should not be joined, let him now speak or . . .

(*Face with large mustache appears at window*)

FACE: STOP RIGHT THERE! (*Everyone stares. Figure steps through the window, carrying a Santa Claus-like bag*).

HMB: WILBUR!

WILBUR: You recognize me?

HMB: Of course, you scoundrel. Superficially you've changed. You used to be big and fat and scruffy and now you're thin and sneaky-looking, but who else would wear an old Princeton tie stained with pistachio soup?

WILBUR: Life has not treated me gently. It has sort of worn me down. But I vowed to win through. I hunted for gold. I hunted for diamonds. I hunted for pearls. I hunted for ivory and I hunted for sapphires. And I couldn't find a darn thing. Finally I was reduced to hunting for gravel and, by golly, I couldn't find that.
I sold everything I owned: my maps, my movie camera and, finally, my mustache. Everything but my old school tie. Last month, just before I was about to be declared legally dead, I started digging one last desperate dig.

I dug all day and I dug all night. I dug Monday through Friday and into the weekend. And I dug right into the main vault of the First National Bank of Sedgway, Saskatchewan, late on Sunday night.

(*Wilbur swings his bag from his shoulder and dumps it on the floor. The bag is full of gold—mostly coins made of cardboard and yellow construction paper but a number are chocolate in gold foil. The producer may wish to add other golden edibles, such as ingots made of meringue.*)

HMB: What good is gold, Wilbur? We want a change of diet, not pocket change. *You can't eat gold!*

WILBUR: Oh yes, you can! (*He eats a coin and the children start gobbling.*)

HMB: Wilbur, you rascal! You haven't changed at all. The same old nincompoop. Welcome home!

—Tom Kelly

you'll also need some older children to dress and cheer the nervous cast beforehand and to serve the refreshments. It will mean the world to the people involved, but only if it's taken seriously (but not too seriously) by everyone involved.

In this first homemade play, many of the cast were too young to read or memorize their lines—so they didn't have any. It's a trick to remember. Even when a play does have lines, you can usually add some nonspeaking roles to accommodate the little ones in the neighborhood.

FAMILY CUSTOMS

Customs are the stuff that memories are made of—the warp and woof of the family fabric. Traditions are inherited from generations past—or consciously created for the ones to come—but customs are casual. Some evolve by chance, others by decision and every one of them affects a child. From Six through Twelve, a child is putting his mind in order, and family customs bring a sense of security and let him know where he stands.

Your family may have many more customs than you think. These customs need not be grand or quaint or unusual, but they must be your own and there must be enough of them for your child to feel comfortable and loved. There are important ones for important occasions—like the way you spend your vacation and your

holidays—but it's the everyday ones that count the most: the send-off for school in the morning, the way you break bread together and the things you say when you plait her hair.

So do the afternoon swims before supper; the family walk to the deli each Saturday; the pizza you send out for on payday. You may hardly realize these small traditions exist, but they give the starch to your child's life—something to stiffen his resolve when it feels as though his world, or his family, is under siege.

Routines, which may be boring to you, are balm for this child. You may think he anticipates the two weeks at the beach for the good times he expects, but much of the joy comes from going back to the same beach, year after year—if possible to the same cottage—and meeting the same children on their two-week vacations. Familiarity breeds contentment and repetition is the anchor, at school and at home. In these Middle Years he likes to come from school and find the same scene every day—or almost every day—and to know that the same questions will be asked and the same nods given.

As he approaches adolescence he will take variety better but will still look forward to replaying the familiar as he takes on new adult duties, just as he likes to get new and bigger, but identical (or almost identical) blue jeans every fall.

All customs, large and small, are habits and, since each imprints a child, it's important that they be good ones. If they get too costly, the child may learn to equate love with money; if they are too complicated, you may have no time for the child; if they are too standardized, he may think originality is wrong.

Some customs are simply negative. It is a custom when you eat together almost every night, but it is also a custom if you don't. And it is a custom if you never go to PTA meetings; if you take more vacations away from the children than with them; if you only say "please" and "thank you" to company. Every family has some negative ways, and that's all right, but if there are too many they will burden a child like a sack of lead. You want to cultivate the customs that support your child instead, for they make the whole family work better.

Breaking Bread

The more basic a custom, the more important it is—and none is more basic than the breaking of bread. Meals reflect the state of your own union. They are meant to be shared, for the health of the family and the well-being of each of its members. Studies show that the children who do best in and out of school are those who eat at least one meal a day with their parents, at least four or five times a week, and dinner is usually the meal that suits everybody best. In any case, it should be a warm and loving time, full of give and take and fairly civilized.

And it also should be a joint enterprise: the one who cooks the food should not also set and clear the table and wash and dry the dishes.

SAUSAGE SUPPER

SERVES: 4

Company dinners are fun, but cozy family suppers have a special appeal. A Nine can put togehter this quick and easy one-dish meal for a family supper—which will be even quicker if you keep some cooked potatoes in the refrigerator.

SLICE   1½ lbs. smoked sausage

Cut in 1″ lengths, but on the diagonal, to give this dish some class. In a large skillet.

SAUTÉ   sausage pieces
               2 T. olive oil
               4 medium onions, quartered
               4 cooked potatoes, quartered
               2 green peppers, sliced
               ¼ c. chopped parsley
               ¼ t. coarse pepper

Cook for 5 minutes. And that's that, unless your child would rather substitute 1 large can of tomatoes—or 4 fresh tomatoes—for the potatoes and serve it over rigatoni or other fancy pasta.

There should be conversation and it should include everyone, however young. A child learns to listen when people listen to him. You want to handle your family dinner as you would one with company, talking to the person on your right, and then your left, and joining in a group discussion, to make everyone feel good about themselves. Dinner actually should be an invitation for everyone at the table to talk about their day, to bring each other up to date on what happened, sharing the good and getting some encouragement to overcome the bad. Anything will be interesting to a child, as long as it's couched within his frame of reference. You'll find he has ideas on the next election; the way a move is made; the way some bosses— and teachers—can do such a good job and the way that others cannot.

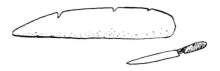

Dinnertime is supposed to create a sense of unity and, whenever possible, a sense of festivity—a toast to your son for getting a B in fractions; a favorite dish renamed to honor your daughter's new tooth. Small recognitions matter a great deal.

The style of dinner varies from family to family. For some, it's like watching a tennis match where everyone volleys at once. Sentences dangle and jokes may bounce beyond the bounds. For others, a meal needs to be an oasis of calm at the end of a hectic day. Whatever the tenor, certain rules remain the same (see Table Manners).

Different people have different staying powers at different ages and allowances should be made. A fast-eating, antsy Eight will appreciate the chance to play in his room or outdoors until dessert or cheese, and it will give you and your husband a chance to visit together. There will be years—especially when the child is between Seven and Ten—when he either wants to eat dinner at his best friend's house or have his friend eat at yours. An exchange once a week and occasionally twice, is fine but it can get out of hand. One summer when our children were either dining out or inviting in every evening, we finally had an August night when all four of them were home on the same night, and none of them had a guest. Their dad looked around the table and said, "Who are these people? I never saw them before in my life!" It turned into a festive meal, when each of us realized how nice it was to break bread with the people we loved best.

COMMEMORATIONS

Some things are so special, so amazing, that they deserve to be honored.

The Cherry Tree

A Japanese cherry tree taught us that a growing gift commemorates an event better than anything else. We drove 500 miles with the young tree on top of the car—the family present for dear Aunt Sister Teresa, celebrating fifty years as a nun. It generated much more pleasure than we expected and some old sibling rivalry too. When we drove to Indiana again the next year for Aunt Sister Helen's jubilee, we had to have a pear tree on the roof. She had made her wishes clear.

From then on, we got regular letters with each one reporting on the exceptional beauty, blossoms and strength of her tree, while commenting sadly on the slow growth, frailty and short life expectancy of the other. The nuns lived to very ripe ages and their trees outlasted them both, which taught us a valuable lesson: a living present—a plant, a tree, a kitten—keeps the joy of the gift alive.

This is as true for children as it is for little old nuns. When we gave Nell 100 tulips as a bonus for her twelfth birthday she was almost as pleased with them as we were with her.

Whether you're marking a birth, a death or a special occasion, you strengthen the bonds of the past by giving it a place in your future.

The Tooth Fairy

A Seven is delighted to find his first wiggly tooth but then may need to be reassured that the process will continue to be painless and that his body isn't going to fall apart, piece by piece. No doubt this is why some clever parent invented the Tooth Fairy. Anticipation eases the angst.

Together you can guess which day the tooth will come out and how much the Tooth Fairy will leave. It won't be much, you'll say, since the TF is as thrifty as you are. When the tooth is quite loose, give your child an apple or a caramel lollipop, which will take it out quickly, since the roots of these first teeth have been absorbed by the body when they're ready to fall out. You then whoop and holler and take his picture, but not until he's rinsed his mouth with salty ice water to stop the small amount of bleeding. That night the tooth is left under the pillow and the next morning he'll wake you, very early and proudly. There was more money than you had told him to expect but not as much as his most extravagant hopes.

Teeth will become a major subject of conversation in his school for days or even weeks. Your child will report who among his friends have lost teeth, how many and how much they got. He may also find the TF is usually more generous to the rich children at school—one small lesson in reality.

There will be other disappointments as time goes by. The Tooth Fairy often gets careless around the third or fourth tooth and takes a few nights to collect it, and sometimes your child will lose the tooth before it can be left under his pillow. This brings tears, followed by the Great Tooth Hunt and finally the joint composition of the painfully printed letter to be left under the pillow instead of the tooth, in the hope that it will bring a reward (it will).

You'll find your child will believe in the Tooth Fairy until the last front teeth have wiggled out—and the last quarter has been collected—and you will have a dear, queer collection of tiny teeth for the rest of your life.

FAMILY GAMES

There is something rich about those times when families just fool around, playing gin rummy or poker, blindman's bluff or badminton, softball or football. A game plucks the child and the adult out of their roles and puts them both on the same level. Their status, if not their ability, is equal: a gentle preparation for their changing roles, as children grow up and parents learn to let go. And games make it fun.

Water Snake

Silliness is often the sign of trust. A child who is willing to be silly in front of you is a child who trusts you. When you return the compliment and act silly too, the connection is complete.

This Water Snake guarantees it. You need to wear bathing suits and use a hose with a plastic nozzle, so the snake won't hurt anyone if it escapes. Drive a stake in the ground, tie the hose to it, 2' from the nozzle, and then turn on the water full force. The nozzle is light enough to flop the hose around in a crazy way as you both jump to escape it: a giggling, dancing sort of game on a hot summer day.

Head Wrestling

This is probably an ancient game but we like it because the man in our house thinks he invented it (and he likes it because he usually wins).

It requires two people who are near the same height—like a short mother and a tall son—and two lines, drawn in the dust. Each player plants his feet about 12" apart, toeing the line, clasps his hands behind his back and presses against his opponent's forehead with his own.

The push is on, head to head, and the winner is the one whose feet stay firmly on the floor, while his opponent hops about, or at least lifts his heel—and loses. It's a small, silly game for all ages and quick: a set-to seldom lasts more than a minute.

Arm Wrestling

Nothing makes children feel more heroic than a serious game of arm wrestling. Have a pair of Eights position their right elbows on a sturdy table, side by side, with their hands clasped tightly, and at "GO!" each player tries to press the other arm down to the table. It's a good, rowdy—and brief—interlude.

OUTINGS

The afternoons you once spent at the zoo with your Two—when she ignored the bears but loved the pigeons—or at the art gallery where your little boy suddenly peed in the fountain can give outings a bad name. It would be a mistake to be discouraged; you just expected too much or tried too soon. The child between Six and Twelve will revel in the same excursions.

Museums, factories and recreated towns like Williamsburg and Sturbridge are especially fascinating to this literal-minded, curious child. At this age, children are mesmerized by the mysteries of craftsmanship and they love to watch people work: a glassblower shaping a shimmering sphere or a silversmith as he hammers, trims and polishes a spoon. The experience will teach him respect for skill and for work, without your saying a word. A child is interested in the way fabric is loomed, cars are made, coins are minted—although highly automated production is more likely to overwhelm than to teach. It's the human element that lets the child imagine himself in the job.

Animals have a great appeal—alive in a zoo or stuffed in a museum of natural history. Usually a child wants to rush through the entire zoo or museum the first time he goes, no matter how much you try to slow him down. Let him be. The next time he'll be the one who wants to spend an hour studying an exhibit of bugs or automobiles. A child who absorbs one specialty in a large museum or visits a museum devoted to a single subject—dollhouses, rockets, gold mining, stamps—is filling a natural need for detailed information, just as you are when you visit one country in Europe instead of touring them all in a few weeks.

This focusing fulfills his need for competence. He wants to be an authority, to know all about one particular thing. Since you're not likely to be as interested in that subject, you'll get along better if you take a break from each other, with the promise to meet again at a certain place and time. A Nine should be old enough and well-behaved enough to ramble alone for a half hour and, if you agree to meet at the cafeteria, he'll not only get there, he'll probably be early.

To visit an art gallery can please a child—or bore him witless. The more familiar he is with art now, the more comfortable he will be in a gallery and the more he'll want to visit them on his own when he is older. It helps if you have some art books at home (these are often deeply discounted at a bookstore). A child either should have one or two art books of his own—there are some lovely ones for children—or be encouraged to look at yours, just by having them on the table. A young reader picks up whatever is in front of him.

It's also wise to stop in a small commercial gallery when you're running errands together or flip through the prints when you go to a frame shop. All of this makes a child feel more at home with art, so he not only will know what he likes—he'll know why.

Whether he looks in a book or a gallery, a child will more or less focus on the story and ignore the color, the style and the composition, which is one reason he finds traditional art more appealing than abstract. You can help your child focus on a particular painting by wondering out loud why the Dutchman looks so stern and what his life was like—a scenario that is easier when you point out the props in the picture that spell the story of his life. Guide your child toward a Breughel or a Grandma Moses or a Currier and Ives and he'll be entranced by the activity, especially if there are children in the picture. The more a child can identify with the art or the artist, the more he'll get hooked.

Sculpture—not in a book but in reality—also fascinates the child between Six and Twelve because he finds it easier to imagine making something with his hands than painting a picture. Besides, some of the statues are naked.

VACATIONS

The quality of a vacation depends almost entirely on the parents. One dear friend finds almost any trip is fun, perhaps because she says "Relaaaax, Alice" to calm a cranky child (whose name, of course, isn't Alice). A little humor keeps her calm too.

A vacation should take you away not only from the trappings of home but from the familiar rules, the same old arguments,

the anxieties and second-guessing. It is the time to be silly, to allow some junk food, to tell—or be told—a rather racy joke. It is the time to keep the luggage light and expect the child to carry his own backpack of necessities with good grace.

It's the time for comic books and Nancy Drew; cartoons and cop shows too (if there's a television handy); for lights still lit at midnight (ignore them) and songs sung around a bonfire.

It's the time for arm-in-arm strolls to no place in particular; for family games of miniature golf and wild hide-and-seek; for rainy days of puzzle-solving and rowdy card games; for catching fireflies and building sand castles.

It is the week or two in which money, saved so carefully, is spent profligately, and for unexpected treats—including extra pocket money—not in response to begging but for the spontaneous joy of giving it.

And it is the time to make it clear that you're on vacation too. A child would rather make sandwiches for the family supper than have you grouse about fixing dinner.

No matter how much or how little it costs, you'll know the holiday money is well spent if everyone has the chance to slow down, unwind and recast the directions they want to take. The tone is set before you ever leave home. Although the parents make the final decision, the vacation spot should be discussed by the whole family. A child in the Middle Years often wants to repeat last year's vacation, even if it wasn't much fun. This is just a sign of his own anxieties and his need for order to handle them. The more you listen to his

opinions and consider them, and the more you involve him in the plans, the more he will be at ease with the decision.

If you're going to a new place, he can study the atlas, the globe and the road map, helping you chart the roads and, by Ten, figure the mileage. Knowing that, and the speed of the car, he'll be the one to answer every time someone asks: "How long will it be before we get there?" He also can make a map of his own, drawing just the roads you'll take.

He needs to help make arrangements for the dog and the cat and be the one who runs a few inches of water in the tub, folds some heavy towels in it and puts the houseplants on them so they can drink from the bottom. And he should go around the house with you, checking the locks, the windows and the stove. This is one way responsibility is instilled and his sense of security insured.

Most of the agonies of a vacation occur either in getting there or getting back. The car can seem like a prison sometimes, especially since everyone must use seat belts. Treat your child almost as if he were sick, being careful not to let him get too tired or bored or excited, because any of these will lead to outbreaks. You'll want to pack a pillow; a blanket; a sweater; a Frisbee; some unsalted snacks; oranges (and a damp cloth to wipe sticky hands); a thermos of water; some new secondhand books—if he can read in a car without throwing up— and some taped stories if you have a tape deck or can take a tape player with you.

Ask your child to join you in singalongs—they're much more soothing than chatter—and word games, as long as they don't take more than thirty minutes. Everyone can try to think of palindromes—words that are spelled the same backward or forward—and point out odd roofs or signs or count the licenses from different states. This reinforces a child's learning and stretches it further, in a free and easy sort of way. You also may find out more about your child's education than you want to know, as we found out

when Meg insisted that she'd spotted a license from the state of Crayola.

Whatever you play, you want to listen for trouble and stop before it gets out of hand. A roadside picnic and a family Frisbee game afterward will use a child's energy on something constructive—and may get him tired enough to nap. And if you get tense and think you'll scream if you're with your child another minute—just tell yourself, "Relaaaax, Alice."

Once you get where you're going, don't plan to do too much—not even as much as you might during an ordinary busy week at home. If you do, everyone may get snappish. There is a certain tension in the air that comes from being in a new place and working out new relationships with each other, for you'll be spending much more time together than you ordinarily do. If you're on the run all day, you can expect trouble as well as exhaustion, and you also can expect it if you decide to spend a precious vacation day just hanging around a motel. A happy vacation has times of rest alternated with times of excitement—however small—each day.

Some small excitements can be dreams come true. For years Mike begged for the chance to spend just one vacation night outdoors—a promise we made—and were reminded about—from one summer to the next. He was practically Nine (in eight months) when we agreed he was OLD ENOUGH. And he wasn't the only one who had planned for it. As soon as he had fallen asleep in the sandy yard—under a blanket staked out like a tent—we touched the top of his lip with the spirit gum we had bought at the theatrical shop, carefully

covered it with crepe hair—and waited to see what an eight-year-old would say to find he had grown a mustache in the night.

Instead, he came in by midnight, feeling very young and alone, and with the fuzz rubbed off his face. Only a dirty residue of glue remained and, being Eight, he didn't notice it at all.

Vacations are made for silliness.

Eating Out

For you, a museum or a play or the view from Pike's Peak may be the highlight of a vacation, but eating out usually scores highest with a child in the Middle Years. Entire meals are remembered years later, as well as the waitress and what she said, and what *he* said in return and how much he heaped on his plate at the ice cream sundae bar.

You'll want to review manners before you go into a restaurant, so your child won't embarrass himself, and have him comb his hair and wash his face before he goes to the table so he won't embarrass you. Almost any child will behave better if he knows what's expected of him. Tell him approximately what you can afford for his meal to cost—so he can pick a suitable dish—but have him give his order to you or his dad, to relay to the waitress, in case he doesn't add too well. He should be reminded that waiting tables is hard, hard work and he therefore should keep his extra requests to a minimum, and to thank the waitress when she brings him something and when the meal is done—a child's way to tip. He also must learn that only the person who pays has the right to complain about either the food or the service, and then only in a quiet way. When a child sees that you are considerate of the feelings of those who serve, he'll find it easier to be the same. Good manners are much better for a child than green peas.

He'll get this message more clearly if you remember his feelings too, by inviting him to take part in the conversation. His behavior, like yours, will, of course, reflect the setting. Your child has probably been to fast food factories so often, you can expect him to be pretty bouncy there and he'll be more sedate at a fancier place, but you'll be broker. Each has its place in a balanced household.

When you're on the road, and on a budget, try a fast food place for lunch, a leisurely picnic or cookout for supper and that fancy place for breakfast, where you get the most for your money. Resort hotels are ideal for this and the menus will boggle his mind nicely.

Lesser Trips

Good vacations come in as many shapes as good families. One brave neighbor lady could have won the annual Good Mother Award for taking her seven children to the beach every year—and letting each one invite a friend.

They went camping, so she could afford it; they camped at the shore, so the children could spend their extra energy playing in the water; and they only stayed a week, so the vacation didn't outlast her patience. She said it was fun. It worked, she said, because tentkeeping is easier than housekeeping and because so much togetherness helped her see the world from a child's point of view.

And that's one reason for a family vacation: to remind us that a child is a person with rights and sensitivities and needs and to remind us so strongly that we remember it all year.

Parents' Vacation

Parents need vacation time together too—without a child, a dog or a telephone. The more children you have, and the more problems you have, the more you need this time. Nothing else lifts the yoke of responsibility so well as going away for a few well-spaced weekends each year, with the children safely stashed with another family. You will, of course, return the favor, but this isn't the time to think about it.

These little holidays needn't cost much—in fact, an expensive vacation may make you feel burdened—but even a few days in a borrowed cottage or at a nearby resort with off-season prices will seem like heaven. If you pack the kind of food and wine you can't afford in a restaurant, you won't mind cooking together for just the two of you.

And if you think your child will be bereft without you—think again. There may be some grousing, but a few days with another family will give him new independence and it will please the other family too. They'll know their turn will come.

WORK

Childhood is fairly new. Until the seventeenth century, children were babied—and often suckled—for their first seven years. After that they were treated like short, irresponsible adults, who were dressed in grown-up clothes and usually put to work.

We've been giving children small additional slices of childhood since then, but now the pendulum has swung so far, we try to protect our children from everything dangerous and from some things—like work—that are actually good for them. This is a big mistake. Too little work can be as hard on a child as too much.

If you are in doubt about this, look around the world. In rural cultures children have time to play, but they also are contributing members of the family. This is how they learn to be competent adults and to think well of themselves on the way.

Every child needs to feel useful; to be needed; to believe that the family functions just a little better because he's part of it. You see it in the supermarket, when the three-year-old rushes to get the cat food, and in the classroom, when all the Sevens wave their hands wildly for a chance to clean the blackboard.

Their eagerness to help won't last, however, unless it's encouraged. If it isn't, you're going to have bedlam where family harmony should be and you'll have across-the-board resentment too. If you and your husband do all the work, you'll feel martyred, your child will feel superfluous and everyone will show his anger in one way or another.

Working together is much better. It strengthens the family bonds and teaches a child the pleasure of work. Shared responsibilities are the sign of a caring family.

Work has other dividends. If everyone in the family contributes to the common good for just twenty minutes a day, you'll have a sense of fairness in the family and a much tidier house.

You want your child to learn to work for the joy of the accomplishment and not for the money it brings. This lets him grow up knowing that, if he enjoys his job, he'll earn enough to be happy, even if he's paid much less than others think he needs. This basic lesson helps him feel he is in charge of his own destiny—an invaluable lesson in junior high, when it's so hard to stand up to the temptations of the crowd.

You are, of course, the teacher. By Six your child should make his bed before he gets his breakfast—that is to say, he drags his quilt over the sheets and you hope there are no apple cores under the covers. He also sets and clears the table and helps prepare the meals in at least some small way, and occasionally in a big one. There is cereal to be put in bowls, bananas to cut and lunchboxes to help you pack. For dinner there are vegetables to scrub; lettuce to pat dry; herbs to pick. Most of the work for a meal is in the preparation, not the cooking, and a child can be a great help. However, you can't expect your child to do the most he can, day after day. He just doesn't have the same fortitude and perseverance you do.

As he gets older, your expectations get higher and your instructions more innovative. A child doesn't mind old chores so much if you can suggest new ways of doing them. The gardening he began haphazardly before Six can be a family asset by Ten when he takes responsibility for the zinnias or the tomato patch, or he does the raking while someone else mows. He should do a little daytime baby-sitting by now too, if the family needs it. Children, even preteens, aren't paid for family work, big or little, unless they have had to turn down a paying job.

There are exceptions, of course. These are the times you pay a child with a gift, if he has surprised you with a great effort, or with money, when you know he's saving for something he couldn't afford otherwise. You may even create extra work to help him reach his goal. Generally, however, a child doesn't get paid for doing work for the family, any more than you or your husband do. When everyone works, labor is its own reward.

Your child is, however, entitled to gratitude and appropriate praise, so he'll want to be even more competent. What is first-class work at Eight may barely be acceptable at Twelve. To give a blanket compliment, whatever the quality, would teach your child to discount all favorable comments. You don't praise everything but you do thank him for the effort, find some specific achievement to commend and, if necessary, send him back to do some of the job over again. He has to learn that he can't get away with bad work, or avoid a particular job in the future, by doing it poorly the first time.

As you assign jobs, you should change assignments—a bit here, a bit there—adjusting to his changing interests and the needs of the household. Some of this will be his contribution to the common good—those daily drudgy jobs that must be done—and others are the occasional quick repairs. These are the times he tightens the loose doorknob; fastens a hook on the back gate; rewires a lamp; washes all the switch plates downstairs; scrubs the copper pot.

It's true it takes time to teach and practice to learn, but there are many payoffs ahead for you both. Eventually your child does these chores with little effort or complaint, and the confidence it gives him will be apparent in anything he does. Competence, in any area, adds to his self-esteem, which will last for life.

Along the way he learns a great deal about himself. He finds out if he likes working alone or in a group, indoors or outdoors, and if he likes methodical jobs or inventive ones. As years go by, his experience in making these decisions will help him choose the right career, rather than drift into the wrong one or be nudged into it by the often unrealistic advice of relatives and friends. Not everyone should be a lawyer, a doctor or a rock star. The work your child does now will help him consider many more possibilities, and recognize the ones that will combine his talents and his interests. He may cross a half-dozen disciplines as an adult before he finds exactly what is right for him. And it all begins at home.

In the process, work welds him to his family like nothing else ever can.

THE COMMON GOOD

In a well-ordered household some work—like tub-scrubbing and bed-making—comes with an obvious worker attached. And some does not. Baseboards need dusting; refrigerators need cleaning; floors must be mopped. No particular person gets things dirty but still they must be tidied, for the common good.

While you're probably the main housekeeper, you shouldn't be the only one. When each person spends twenty minutes a day on one or more of these routine jobs, the heart of the house—the living and family rooms, the bathroom and kitchen—stay pleasantly livable, day in and day out. The weekends are for major cleaning, or for repairs or garden work, and again, every-

one should pitch in, this time for an hour or so. If they do, a household can jog along for years without too much burden on either parent.

Common contributions to the common good are the best way for you and your husband to both keep your house clean and your sanity intact. If you don't accuse your child—or anyone—of making the messes, but insist that everyone has a duty to straighten them, you'll find the work is done in a fairly good spirit. This is especially true if the work is done every day without fail and if the family squares a room together. It's a quicker, more pleasant approach and your child will learn the right way to do a simple job, partly because you stop and teach and partly because he imitates you without realizing it. Even when he works independently, there is a sense of accomplishment and pride, a knowledge that he is making a difference.

By recognizing that the family is a unit, in work as well as play, you seal the bonds still tighter.

Shining

There's nothing that appeals to a young worker quite so much as making the dingy turn bright.

FIX-IT LIST

If your house could have a wish list, it wouldn't be made up of grand designs for an expanded kitchen and an extra bedroom overhead, but a plea for Mr. (or Ms.) Fix-it to take care of all the little odds and ends. A son or daughter can take care of them just as well. And so they should.

Children can handle the overhead light that needs cleaning; the squeak on the stairs; the doorbell that doesn't work; the faucet that drips—even the paint that's chipped off a wall. A quart of paint mixed to match the switch plate will let your

Twelve touch up the bare spots in the color the walls have turned, which is much quicker, and cheaper, than painting a whole room.

Tack your Fix-it List on the bulletin board, dividing it, if it's long, according to carpentry; plastering; painting; sanding; wiring; plumbing. Some of the jobs are so quick that several can be done when the tools are used for one of them.

Work is a great deal more interesting when there is an order to it—and an end in sight.

Wiring a Lamp

Wiring a lamp gives a Twelve a great sense of accomplishment and it should: it's such a responsible thing to do. It's also the best way to explain the principle of electricity to a child, so he will hold it in the awe it deserves.

To do it right, the whole lamp must be dismantled. Unplug it and take off the base by prying off the felt and, if it has one, the lead weight. He then unscrews the nut at the base with a pair of pliers and pries off the brass sleeve at the top to reveal the ceramic socket where the negative and positive wires complete the electrical circuit and light the bulb—or cause a fire, if they touch each other. Show him how they're kept apart, by wrapping the positive wires to a screw on one side of the socket and the negative wires to a screw on the other side—the single most important safety fact he must learn.

Have your child pull the old wire out of the lamp and slip the new cord through this path and up through the brass that covers the bottom of the socket. The positive and negative wires are then pulled apart and about ½" of plastic coating is stripped from the ends. One set of these bare copper strands is rolled between the thumb and the forefinger, to make sure none of them get loose, and then it's wrapped around either of the screws, which is then tightened to hold the wires in place. The other set of bare wires is rolled together and stripped around the other screw, which is tightened too.

At this point the work should be checked by an adult, to make sure the connection is safe, and then the brass sleeve is slipped back in place, the bottom of the lamp is restored, and a plug is clipped on the other end of the wire.

It won't be long before your child becomes known as the Neighborhood Fixer.

Fixing a Drip

There are many kinds of faucets and sooner or later they all leak, usually because either the washer has gotten hard, misshapen or worn or because it needs new packing. Your Eleven can replace a washer, which sure beats a plumber's bill, but you'll have to help him figure it out and supply him with a box of assorted washers, O-rings, brass bolts and packing material.

If you have a fairly standard sink, he begins by turning off the valve under the leaky faucet so water doesn't spill everywhere (or he has you turn off your main water supply).

He then unscrews the handle at the top, pries it off and uses the adjustable wrench—with the help of a little machine oil—to loosen the packing nut (Nell says it's "Rightsy, tightsy; lefty, loosey"). He then takes the pieces apart, laying them out in the order they were installed, and replaces the worn-looking washer or O-ring with one of the same size and type and stuffs in any new packing that seems to be needed. And then he puts it all back where it came from, in the order he removed it, and turns on the water again.

And if it still leaks? Congratulate him for trying, call the plumber—and let your child watch. You may save a bill the next time.

Squeaky Floors

Have your child find the place in the floor or the stair that squeaks, by walking tiptoe back and forth and finally marking the squeaky place with chalk—a job for an

Eleven. He then hammers a 4-, 6- or 8-penny finishing nail into that spot, making sure he covers it with a section of the newspaper before he hits the last few blows, so he doesn't scar the floor.

For a classier job he can use a countersink, which permits him to hammer the nail more deeply, and then cover the depression with a little wood putty.

And if the squeak still squeaks, have him shake talcum powder between the cracks. That usually takes care of it.

Squeaky Hinges

A Six feels important when he takes the squeak out of a squeaking door—and he is. Have him first cover the floor with several sheets of newspaper and then swing the door back and forth, with his ear next to the hinge to see if he can find the dry spot that's making all the noise. When he can (or even if he can't), he squirts machine oil, graphite powder, or a silicone spray into the hinge and onto the pivot, and then moves the door back and forth so the lubricant will reach all parts of the pivot and the hinge.

When the noise is gone, your child should wipe any residue from the door with a warm soapy cloth. He's never too young to learn that a good workman completes his job.

Leaky Windows

Odd repairs interest children the most and finding—and fixing—air leaks is one of the oddest. And most important. Heating bills send shivers down adult spines and a Ten will feel like the family hero if he helps you find the places where the cold air sneaks in on a windy day.

Have him cut a 6″ square of thin tissue paper—the kind that's found in a birthday box—and paste it on his ruler. It looks like a flag, and it acts like one too. Have him run it up and down window frames, sashes, doorsills, electrical outlets, pipes, ducts in the attic and basement, and around the garage door too if the garage is connected to the house. Once located, the cracks can be filled with a caulking compound (spackling doesn't bond well with wood) but he'll need encouragement. Although he can, with supervision, manage a caulking gun for a few minutes, it takes a Twelve to do a full job. Even then he'll need your supervision and some assistance too, brushing out loose paint, plaster and dirt so the caulk will stick.

When the gaps are ready, have your child fit the caulk cartridge into the gun and cut the plastic nozzle on a 45° angle, poking a pencil into it to break the vacuum. With some priming of the gun he's ready to run a bead of the caulk, as thick as necessary, in all the cracks between the wood and brick or plaster, while you poke it in with a putty knife and make a smooth edge.

You'll need to do this outdoors too, even caulking around the outside faucets and along the base of the wall where the foundation joins the brick.

DRAFT DODGER

Not all leaks can be caulked, and your Ten can solve the problem by making Draft Dodgers to block the cold air that seeps in under the cellar door and the window sashes and sills.

This old-fashioned snake is made of any unobtrusive, heavy-duty material, like corduroy, and is as long as the sill or the threshold. Have your child

CUT material, 4″ wide

These strips are then cut to fit the length of the sills and sashes and are sewed on the machine—first lengthwise and then along one end. They are turned inside out and each tube is filled with sand—a job that needs your help. Sew the end shut as the Dodger is filled, so the sand stays where it belongs.

Your child can sew eyes and fangs on these snakes, and ears and spangles too, but be warned that if he does he'll want to give them away—or you'll want to sell them at the next school bazaar.

SEWING

Sewing is a favorite for both boys and girls in the primary years, but most boys lose interest by Ten, while most girls, if encouraged, are ready for finer stuff. You'll give your child a good introduction to sewing if you ask her to help you make something simple, like a gathered skirt—for you. Since an apprentice tailor is sure to make some mistakes, it's better for her to make the big ones on something of yours, because you're right there to repair them before it's too late. By the time the job is done, she'll be able to make something for herself—with your help—and without obvious mistakes.

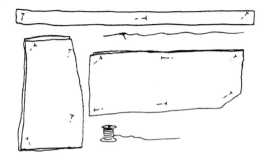

While you are her teacher, you'll be more successful if you're patient and positive and treat her like an equal, including her in every step of the decision-making. It begins in the fabric store so she'll realize that you pick the pattern and the material as carefully as you make the skirt. When you turn down styles or fabrics because they are too difficult or too impractical or unflattering—even though you really like them—she won't resent it if you have to reject some of her choices when it's time to buy the material to make her skirt.

Together you'll iron the pattern (it's easier to handle smooth paper) and iron the fabric too so it can be cut more accurately. You'll also need to teach your child to straighten the grain of the material by wrapping two or three threads around her index finger and gently pulling them out. She then cuts along this path so she won't cut the pieces crooked when she lays the pattern in place.

Only then is your child ready to pin and cut out the pattern, making sure that she has left-handed scissors if she is left-handed, so she can do the job well.

She's old enough to use the small stitch on the machine to stay-stitch all the borders 1/4" from the edge so seams won't ravel, and even to sew the 5/8" seams, starting from the bottom to the top, so the skirt will fall evenly. To sew them straight, stick a piece of adhesive 5/8" to the right of the needle as a guide. By breaking a project into its small parts, it's easy to see how much of it a child can do.

Once the skirt is sewed together, she can press the seams open so they won't be bulky inside the band, and pin and then machine-stitch a binding on the bottom to make a neat hem. She also can baste a doubled thread around the top by hand, anchoring the threads in place at one end and pulling on the other to gather the top. You'll have to even the gathers, pin them in place and then stitch them around the top by machine.

You'll also have to put in the zipper and much, if not all, of the work on the band, but your child can pull out the basting threads, sew a hem by hand and press it with a hot iron on a damp cloth to get the sharpest crease.

She may not sew much for years, but she'll find it's a bit like riding a bike and other glorious pastimes. Sewing, once learned, is never forgotten and neither is the confidence it brings.

MARKETING

The Seven, a super planner, can be a great help at the supermarket. Both boys and girls can learn a good deal about nutrition and shopping skills too. Now that your child is old enough to read he can see how you divide your shopping list to suit the layout of the store and insert your last-minute additions in the proper place—a bit of dictation he can take while you ride to the store.

As you shop, you'll help him understand that the biggest size is nearly always the cheapest (if you finish it before it spoils); that Grade A eggs are fresher than Grade B; that milk cartons are clearly marked with their expiration dates and that the freshest cartons are usually at the back of the shelf.

He'll learn—if you tell him—to choose the fuzziest peaches and the prickliest cucumbers, because they're the freshest, and to avoid fruits and vegetables that are waxed or dyed. By Nine, your child should be a practiced shopper and know that the longer the list of ingredients on a package, the more likely it is to be processed and therefore the less nutritious. He'll track down the club soda that doesn't have salt—and learn why added salt is too much—and find out that coconut and palm oils aren't good for him, even when they're just called vegetable oil.

With your help, he learns that chicken and fish are cheaper and more healthful than beef, and have fewer calories too; that fancy, solid canned tuna costs more than any other; that cheese by the wedge is cheaper than it is by the slice; that sharp

cheese costs more than mild (because it's aged longer); and that processed cheese is really more expensive because it's older and needs chemicals to keep it fresh, and because as much as half of it can be water.

If he learns the tricks of the consumer trade now, they will be second nature to him by Sixteen, when he'll have his license and can do some of the marketing for you (see Spending Money).

GARDENING

Of all skills your child can learn, gardening often pays off most. It will spur his interest in science, put him in tune with nature and help him earn money in junior high. But first he has to learn how. A child gardens best if he gardens alongside someone and that someone will probably be you. You'll both thrive on the companionship even if your garden is a batch of houseplants or a window box, but a backyard, small or large, teaches best. No lecture explains the cycle of life as well as a morning spent working over a simple garden plot.

Here the information tumbles out in easy asides, which suits him fine. Children don't like lectures at home. Your child learns when you give him last year's leaves to mulch this year's flowers, and tell him about the invisible bugs that will turn those leaves into fertilizer. This helps him realize that nothing is static and that everything, and everyone, is forever changing, in some way. It's a comforting thought, at any age.

He'll like to know that he and the trees are both breathing out and breathing in, swapping oxygen and carbon dioxide to keep each other going; that he's as heliotropic as any flower, naturally turning his face to the sun; that worms make the tunnels that let the root hairs breathe and get water—so the roots can grow—and that they help the earth stay friable.

To show your child how plants draw water from their roots, you can have him cut off the end of a rib of celery and put it in a glass to which he has added some red or blue food coloring. He'll see the color travel to the leaves in about thirty minutes—the same trick florists use to dye daisies.

What seems obvious to you often surprises and delights a child, even at Twelve. The more small bits of information you drop, the more his interest grows, for your child is as curious about nature as he is about everything else.

He'll be intrigued to hear that the roots of a tree are spread out below the earth in much the same shape as the branches above and that water carries nutrition from the soil to the leaves and chlorophyll back to the roots. And tell him, too, how nature saves water by giving some vegetables waxy leaves; that a carrot can keep water in its fat taproot because its leaves are so lacy there is little evaporation; that a cabbage stores its moisture in its thick, big, waxy leaves and its bulky stems; and that grass needs less water because its leaves are so skinny and its roots are shallow enough to catch the lightest rain. And then have him feel the bristles on the tomato stalks and the leaves which protect the plant from too much breeze—because nature knows that the more that wind touches the plant, the dryer it gets.

It's no use pretending, however, that gardening is just an effortless and informative entertainment. Every day is a new challenge. If it's not the weather, it's the bugs, but if you encourage your child to look for answers, you'll find he learns to water the plants regularly and use homemade insecticides, so only the bad bugs get killed.

The tools enthrall a child too—the pruning shears to trim the hedge, the edger to define the beds and a Swiss Army knife that lets him dig out the dandelion easier.

The more work a garden takes and the more credit you give to your child, the more pride it will bring and the more he will want to help. A garden brings one harvest a year; a child brings many more.

Testing the Soil

In gardening, a simple plant soil test—available at the garden center—explains nature best. This treated paper, dipped in a vial of soil and water, turns blue and green if the soil is alkaline; red and orange if it's acidic; yellowish green if it's slightly acidic.

The colors represent the pH range from pH 0–14, with the acidity decreasing as the numbers climb. The extremes are rare, with 4.5 representing an extremely acid soil, like peat. PH 6.5 is average and pH 8.5 means the earth is moderately alkaline. Your ideal soil is probably between pH 5.0 and pH 7.5, since most plants like a slightly acidic environment, and the extra iron that comes with it.

With you alongside, a Six can find out whether the grass needs a little limestone to make it sweeter, or the roses need some manure, or Manure Tea, to make the soil more acidic. In either case, the change will take several days.

Periodic testing is advisable because plants take nutrition out of the soil and the leaves, which would return it, are usually raked away. Testing the soil—and retesting it—will be one of your Merlin's favorite jobs.

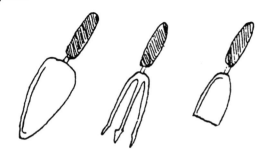

Planting

Nothing brings as much joy as planting a garden, except the dreaming that goes with it. For a child, however, bedding plants don't let the dreams last long enough and outdoor bulbs make them wait too long. That's why at least some of the garden must be planted with seeds. A child has as many marvelous images when he drops them in the earth as you have when you go through the catalogs in January.

To get a head start on the garden, your child can plant his seeds indoors in peat pots or in cracked eggshells filled with Rooting Medium, since seeds contain all the nutrition the plant needs until the true leaves appear. Some windowsill sunlight, however, will make them stronger. The plants are ready to live outside after the shell of the seed opens into what looks like a pair of leaves and then the real leaves appear.

Whether your child grows vegetables or flowers, or edges a flower bed with lettuce (a lovely show), or puts marigolds with the tomatoes to keep the bugs away, the garden will give your child a fine sense of accomplishment.

However, your young gardener probably won't even think about the garden until you suggest it, and then he'll want to sow—and reap—in the space of seven days. You can't promise miracles, but the quicker his seeds sprout, the more he will be interested in gardening—a good reason to treat the seeds before they go into the ground by softening the shells of the seeds, so they will germinate quicker. Either do this by pouring hot water into the furrow just before he plants it, or line a tea strainer with a paper towel and have him empty the seeds on it for you to pour very hot water over them. If you do it this way, the seeds should dry before they're planted, so they can be planted separately. It's a bit more trouble to make seeds sprout faster, but once you know how, it's rather irresistible. Seedlings, like babies, are the promise of tomorrow.

Propagation

By the time a child is Six, he's probably already grown sweet potatoes in water and sprouted carrot tops from carrot bottoms. Now he's ready for stronger stuff.

Layering—This curious business intrigues a child and should give you some new azaleas or rhododendrons too. First fertilize the shrub you hope to layer, and in a couple of weeks have your child bend a low branch to the earth to see where it will touch. He then strips the leaves and an inch-wide band of bark around the nearest node—that bump that will send out a shoot (if it's above ground) or a root (if it's below)—and then loosens the soil, removes grass and weeds, and buries the stripped branch in the ground, using a rock to hold it in place. Since azaleas love acidic soil, he can squeeze a lemon over the spot and bury the rind with the branch. It will probably make the soil more acidic but even if it doesn't it is a graphic way to show a child that different plants have different needs.

Do the same thing to a half-dozen other branches, since not all of them may root, and cover each with soil and then with the rocks, and then water the mother plant with another dose of Manure Tea.

After about two months your child gently pulls up a branch and checks to see if a good root system has developed. If it has 5–10 roots that are several inches long, he can cut the branch free from the mother shrub and, with your guidance, transplant the tiny new plant into a well-watered hole.

No matter how small, it will be your child's personal creation and he'll remember the glow for years.

Rooting—The plastic bag is a poor man's greenhouse, giving you dozens of new plants, but the cuttings should be treated first.

Help your Eight cut each stem just below the node—that bump where a leaf or a flower appears—and scrape about an inch of the skin. He then dips this end into the Willow Tea, so it will root better, and sticks it into the Rooting Medium, but have him pack it in firmly, so the stem doesn't rot.

Slide the shoebox into a clear, 2-quart plastic bag, close it tight and set it near a windowsill to get indirect sunlight. The cuttings need no nutrition, since they get their food from the leaves and the gentle sunlight. They do, however, need to be examined once or twice a week because the cuttings give out more moisture after they've made some roots, the way people sweat when they've worked hard. If the inside of the bag is damp in the morning and still damp in the afternoon, it's too wet. Have your child leave the bag open for a few hours to avoid disease.

Your child also should check the medium to see how much the roots have grown, transplanting when a cutting has about a 2″ ball of roots. This takes a minimum of 2 weeks, a maximum of 5, but he can make them sprout faster if he lays the bag on a warm heating pad that is covered by a cloth.

WILLOW TEA

Cuttings root better after they've had a taste of their favorite tea. To make it, have your child

COLLECT	willow leaves and stems

Stuff them in a quart jar and fill with water.

WAIT	1 week

ROOTING MEDIUM

In a pail of hot water

SOAK	2 c. shredded sphagnum moss
WAIT	30 minutes

Squeeze it and put it in a shoebox.

ADD	2 c. builder's sand

Mix together. The water in the moss should be enough to make the medium moist but not soppy.

◇ TRADITIONS ◇

Traditions provide much of the glue that holds a family together, and the more positive and constructive they are, the tighter the bonds—and yet many traditions are dropped now.

Children seem so self-sufficient in the Middle Years, so nonchalant, that they often hide the pleasure they take in family traditions until parents put them away like outgrown clothes. This is a mistake. Children treasure their old rituals and need them to get a sense of who they are and where they stand, and how their family fits into society.

Some of the best are passed down, generation to generation: the special recipe to stuff the Thanksgiving turkey (the best of a child's holiday chores) or the ones that come with your own heritage, like the making of pisanki eggs for a Ukrainian Easter.

Other traditions are seasonal and can be as evocative as the smell of honeysuckle. Picnics on Memorial Day and Labor Day, to start and end the summer, are favorites among children, because summer matters so much to the young. Going over the river and through the woods to Grandmother's house for a family reunion is another major landmark and the many small, uneventful visits amount to an equally significant impression.

Other little rituals may affect your child in ways you can't imagine, and sometimes not very well. Mike was grown before he told us how seriously he took it when his dad would clap his shoulder every morning before he went to work and say, "Hold the fort." The pleasant camaraderie of the father was the weighty responsibility of the son.

Imbalances may develop if traditions

come from just one side of the family, for this denies a child his full heritage. Your husband surely has other customs to add to yours, although you may have to ask his mother what they are. If you and your husband grew up in a fairly tradition-free environment, you can still create customs of your own. The way you celebrate holidays and entertain friends gives extra meaning to your lives.

Small religious rituals—like bedtime prayers and well-blessed sneezes—give a child a sense of serenity, and the bigger traditions of your religion can give great strength to the whole family. Even if your own faith isn't very strong, or if you attend a group whose creed makes little or no reference to God, you'd do well to take part, for it will give your child—and you—a valuable anchor as well as an elaborate set of traditions.

Simple rituals and small touches dress up any event, small or large, religious or not, and they make your family even more blessed than it is.

RELIGION

It used to be fashionable for some parents to let their children choose their own religion at a certain age—or not choose any at all. This seems logical, but it doesn't take human nature into consideration. Children need benchmarks and guidance. They need support. And they need a grown-up to tell them how to get it.

By expecting your child to follow your religion, you are asking him to take its beliefs primarily on faith. If he finds them compatible, they will be a welcome resource when he is an adult. If he doesn't, the beliefs will still provide a framework for moral judgments later. They also will give color, richness and continuity to his life, and another dimension to his culture. The celebration of your religious holidays, with all their traditions and pageantry, will bind the family and help your child define himself and his place in the world.

For all these reasons, your child—and

every child—will benefit by silence or grace before dinner, by prayer or reflections at bedtime and by going to Sunday school, church, temple or meetinghouse once a week, but don't send him alone. The child who goes to the service by himself may feel he has a license to be the clown of the congregation. It won't be long before he skips it altogether and spends his collection money on a comic book, fooling around the neighborhood—and feeling guilty—until it's time to go home again. You don't want to invite your child to be duplicitous. It's best for the whole family to go to the service together, even if your own faith is lukewarm. Consider this hour or two your gift to the solidarity of the family.

Going to the service together will remind you how blessed you are and you can emphasize the bond afterward with a family hour when you take a traditional walk, visiting the same coffee shop each week or bringing home goodies from the bakery. In each case, you're establishing a family custom and making it easier to talk to each other.

Your child will get more out of the service if you prepare for it the night before, by telling him the small things that trouble you and how you'll take them with you to the service—and maybe leave them there. Your candor will encourage him to think about the things that bother him. He may or may not tell you what they are, but it will help him think of the service hour as a safe time to look inside himself.

Your own behavior at the service must continue to encourage your child's inner self and not the part that shows. You can't do it if you spend the time correcting him—picking the lint from his jacket or straightening his tie, telling him where to find the music, when to kneel and, for heaven's sake, to stop making faces. Since every child is sure that the entire congregation is watching him anyway, this would make him still more self-conscious. There is sure to be some giggling and carrying on, of course, which you can discourage unobtrusively by having your child sit next to at least one parent. This arrangement lets you and your husband take care of three children without ever seating them next to one another. A raised eyebrow, pressed lips, a ruffle of your fingers in his hair, a hand on the shoulder when he gets antsy are all much better methods of discipline than a pinch or a threat or a whispered tirade. A few reminders keep most children in reasonable line, particularly if you often look the other way.

As for joining in the prayers and the hymns—just hand him a book and look pleased if he takes part. Many children have been embarrassed in school about their ability to read and especially to sing (although your child may not tell you for years), so their participation should be their own business. It's much more important for your child to see and hear what's going on.

The subjects that are preached about should help him feel free to talk about the big issues, including war and death—his own and yours. A child between Six and Twelve thinks about these anyway but finds it hard to talk about them without encouragement. It's particularly hard for a child to talk about God—a subject that is even more personal than sex, since it deals with the soul.

These conversations may make you uneasy, but your child needs your honest answers. Even an indecisive response, like "I don't know" or "I think" or "I wonder," will let him know it's all right to have doubts about anything, even God. A child can accept the inexplicable if he is allowed to fashion the fine points for himself. This helps him accept the practices of his religion.

Religion, particularly formal religion, isn't for everyone, but it is essential for many and your child should have the chance to become familiar with one. As an adult he is sure to face some protracted crisis sooner or later, and that's when he'll need all the extra stuffing he can get. It's much easier to seek the comforts of religion when you've known it before. It's like asking help from an old friend instead of a stranger.

It is also unfair to deprive your child of this underpinning. While he theoretically reaches the age of reason at Seven, he doesn't reach the age of conscience until he's well into adolescence. In the meantime he needs to feel that there is someone watching over him, expecting him to do his best even when he doesn't want to. Your attention and your admonitions aren't always enough to keep him in line nor is there any way you could—or should—oversee all of his activities. He needs rules to carry in his head, and a religion is a good source. Its rules will become another voice for him to hear when he's a teenager, which is a blessing. There will be times when you'll wish he had a chorus.

There is no real danger that the rules of his religion will make him into a saint, of course. He's bound to break a few of them, for rules are challenges as well as guidelines. How far the testing will go will depend on how well these beliefs are taught, for children react to the discipline of their religion as they react to the discipline of their parents. If its tenets are rigid and intense, it may inspire a child to be an adult agnostic, and if they are too vague, it may make a teenager so desperate for philosophical boundaries that he will join the first mind-bending cult that comes along. As always, moderation works best.

Basically, you're reminding your child that he has a core of goodness—of godness if you will—within himself which he can nourish and strengthen. All over the world religious customs encourage it through meditation, yoga, prayer, song or silence.

Not all families are comfortable in a religious structure, however. One thoughtful young mother—a single parent with a lively boy and girl—copied the Sunday morning ritual she learned at her mother's knee. They gathered at Grandma's to read *Middlemarch* and the Victorian classics aloud and it worked just fine. The universal truths come in many guises.

Whatever practice you follow in your house, a child needs to slow down long enough to find some inner peace.

HANUKAH

The eight-day Jewish festival of lights combines study, reflection—and play. It isn't a major holiday but it is a joyous one, and since it comes in December it offers a happy religious and cultural balance to Christmas. It also enchants children with its dreidels and gelt and latkes and presents but the small, awesome evening ceremony is what they will remember best. Candles are lit each night, starting with one and ending with eight, in memory of the time when a one-day supply of oil lasted for eight days—enough time to bless a desecrated temple.

The ceremony centers around the special Hanukah menorah—a candelabrum with 8 branches in an even row, and a taller branch in the center for the shammas—the worker candle—that is used to light the others. The head of the family lights this one first and uses it to light one other, and then he leads three blessings and a prayer of thanks. The family sings a hymn or two, each child receives a small gift and the candles are allowed to burn to their bases, to be replaced before the ceremony the next night.

On the following nights the blessings are trimmed to two and the children do the lighting themselves, with the oldest child going first. A new candle is lit each night, starting on the far right and marching closer to the left to represent a new day, until, on that final night, all of the candles are lit. That's when the parents give their children bigger presents and perhaps some Hanukah gelt (which is real money) as well as luscious chocolate "coins" covered in foil.

Aunts and uncles and cousins often join the immediate family for the prayers, the meal and a party on one of those nights. With or without a party, there are sure to be games of dreidel.

Dreidel

This fast, ancient game of Hanukah—the only time when gambling is allowed among the faithful—is deliciously rowdy. It involves spinning a square top, marked with Hebrew letters—NUN, GIMMEL, HAY and SH'IN— on its four sides, like dots on dice, that stand for the phrase "A great miracle happened there!" The letters tell the players how much to add or take out of the pot, depending on which side comes up.

N—take nothing
G—take all the pot
H—take half the pot
SH—add to the pot

The players may use pennies or candy or baseball cards, and the children decide on the number of rounds before they start—or they won't want to stop.

CHRISTMAS

Christmas is the most inclusive holiday of all. It has acquired so many nonreligious aspects that most agnostics and many non-Christians observe it and for good reason: properly celebrated, it teaches children that it's the giving that makes the getting so sweet.

By Six your child may be too sophisticated for Santa Claus but not for the excitement. You won't, of course, give him everything on his list—unless you want to rear a spoiled child—but if you choose with care, your choices will reflect his growth and taste. And if you're as Christmas-crazy as we are, you start looking months ahead for secondhand books for everybody; costume jewelry for the Eight;

an antique locket for the eldest; a box of dress-up clothes for the youngest; an old doll; and, if you're lucky, a toy from the past that can be revitalized—a scooter, a wicker cradle, a wagon, a wheelbarrow, a hula hoop. Yesterday's treasures often turn out to be tomorrow's treasures too.

Then suddenly you discover that some new and extraordinary toy—the popularity of which has never been mentioned in your house—is the Only Thing (practically) that your child wants for Christmas. Even without TV, children across the country can somehow settle on the same toy and mysteriously telegraph this information to one another—just as children's jokes and games and skip-rope rhymes have leaped around for centuries. There you are, caught once more, your fingers walking through the phone book for the hard-to-find toy of the year. In these last few days your emotions may overtake your good sense until you realize that it would take all the presents in the world to tell your child how much you love him.

Giving is at least as important as getting but it should be a truth instilled in every member of the family, not just you. Your child should be taught that the joy of Christmas is a two-way emotion. Everyone is embarrassed to receive a gift without having one to give and that definitely includes the child who can't keep up his end of the seesaw on Christmas morning.

However, he won't recognize this need ahead of time unless you tell him diplomatically. Ask your child what he's going to give for Christmas almost as often as he talks about the things he'd like to get; help him remember to save some of his allowance in October and November and to earn a little too, and help him make gifts with his own hands, by suggesting possibilities; having necessary materials on hand and perhaps, if you're making gifts of your own, let him work alongside.

His money will last longer if you take your child shopping to some of the yard sales or school bazaars, as well as to drugstores and dime stores. It's better for him to give his Uncle Jack razor blades than a scarf, if you would have to pay for the scarf, for it should be your child's gift to give, not yours. For the same reason, he should wrap his own presents, with you to show him how and then stand by, for wrapping is a hard skill to master.

Before Christmas

The best part of Christmas is also the worst: the traditions. There are so many of them. Some ideas, like Christmas cookies (decorated yet!), just seem to be there to make parents feel guilty. If they're not fun to do, or if they're not your style, or if you're too busy, forget them. They'll make Christmas worse, not better. Inedible decorations can be easier and more satisfying, if only because they don't disappear.

An Eight can be in charge of the centerpiece of fruit or flowers for the table, which look all right in practically any arrangement; the holly to tuck around the base of the candlesticks, or a garland of pine laid across the top of the mantelpiece, with a few pomegranates nestled in the curves—a favorite decoration at the White House.

You'll also want your child to help you prepare the family gift to others who have less. We've found a big holiday meal, delivered to a soup kitchen on Christmas Eve, does it best. Plan the menu far ahead and have your child help you shop for it, bake

FIREPROOFING THE TREE

Parents sleep a little easier if Christmas trees are treated with this fire retardant. First saw 1–4″ from the bottom of the tree—a job for you—and let it stand in this solution overnight, to drink its fill. In a bucket have your child

COMBINE
2 gals. hot water
2 c. karo syrup
2 oz. liquid bleach
2 pinches Epsom salts
½ t. Boraxo

Put some of this mixture in the bowl in the Christmas tree stand and add more as needed, so the bowl stays full throughout the holidays. This recipe will also keep the needles green.

the ham and the pies and deliver it to the door. Your own Christmas dinner will taste finer for it.

There are only so many Christmases when your child is still a child, only so many chances to learn what this day of giving is all about.

A church service emphasizes this message too, if that suits your religion, going either on Christmas Eve or the next morning. You can read the story of Bethlehem a hundred times, but the drama of it reaches its peak today and the crèche has a magic all its own. This is especially important at this age, when a child still thinks in concrete terms.

The crèche, the Advent calendar and the Advent wreath are all religious symbols to anticipate the birth of Christ, but the wreath has one clear advantage: a Six can make it.

The wreath is usually made of evergreens—to show that life with Christ is everlasting—and, to reaffirm the point, it's tied in a circle. Its four candles—one for each Sunday of Advent—proclaim Christ as the light of the world. Give your child a flexible pine bough and have him hold the ends together while you tie them in place,

first with wire and then with a white ribbon. He then lays the wreath on the dining-room table, fits 4 tall candles—one is pink and the other three are purple—into small holders, and nestles them in the greenery.

The first purple candle is lit before dinner on Saturday night before the first Sunday of Advent. Although every family develops its own traditions, the head of the household often blesses the wreath and gives a special prayer. From that night forth, the oldest child says the prayer and the youngest one lights this candle, which burns all through dinner every night. A new candle is lit on each subsequent Sunday of Advent—and lit again each night thereafter—with the pink candle lit on the third Sunday, to remind the faithful that this somewhat gloomy season is nearly over. Although the season isn't as serious as Lent, it is a time of prayer and some sacrifice.

There are other and sometimes more meaningful ways to celebrate Advent. Some families have a Kindness Box in the kitchen, where its members write down something they wish someone would do (or not do, like "I don't want to hear 'no' all day"). The children pull out a slip, do the small job and tuck the paper in the crèche.

Although it took us twenty years, we've finally learned one lesson well: put tangerines and walnuts in the stockings with the stuffers, rather than candy. Sugar is sure to set the child up for a letdown and so do the caffeine in the chocolate and the simple carbohydrates in the stollen. A little later you can take in a high-protein breakfast to eat by the tree. It will give you a much better day.

Christmas Day

Christmas dinner demands tradition. Whether you serve turkey, goose, ham or beef, there should be a pattern to it—even if it's the pattern to serve something new every year. Children need the most order when their days are the most confused. They also should take part in the preparation, but your child won't have the energy or interest to do much in the kitchen.

━━━━━━━━━━━━━━━━━━━━━━━━━━━━━━━

AVOCADO SALAD

SERVES 6

This salad carries out the Christmas colors with class, is quick and easy enough for an excited Nine to make, and it isn't as expensive as it sounds.

HALVE   **3 avocados**

Put each half on its own plate, on top of a lettuce leaf, and squeeze a lemon over the cut surfaces to keep the color bright. Into each well

ADD   **large spoon sour cream**
                 small spoon red lumpfish caviar

This salad is so spectacular a child may even eat it and it combines tastes and textures so well he may want to make it for other, less pressured events.

━━━━━━━━━━━━━━━━━━━━━━━━━━━━━━━

The Morning After

It takes a child and his mom several days to recover from Christmas, but it's quicker if you take it easy the day after. Give the living room a half-hour pickup in the morning and don't expect any help from your child. If he's around, you'll be inclined to fuss about the missing crayons and broken toys. Christmas is for the well-being of people, not things, and so is the day after.

You need to get out—so you don't see the mess that's left—and your child needs to move back into the big world again. He's been the center of attention so long

he'll be relieved to drift back to normal, but it takes a day or so. Boxing Day—the day after Christmas—is a good one for a traditional family adventure—a tramp in the woods; a couple of hours of ice skating; a game of soccer. To a Six, this is heaven, but even a Twelve is relieved to put life back where it belongs.

PASSOVER

Of all the feasts that meant so much to our flock, surely the seder was one they'll never forget. It was one of the greatest gifts one family could give to another—the privilege of sharing their religion, their culture.

Nothing teaches the story of the flight of the enslaved Jews, and their return as a freed people, so well as this ritualistic spring meal, when the generations gather together to celebrate the start of the eight days of Passover.

The seder is a happy, holy holiday dinner, an elegant one with candlelight and the best china, stemware and linen. It begins with the door left open and the wine poured for Elijah, the prophet who is expected each year to announce the coming of the messiah. It ends with the children's rowdy scramble to find the afikomen broken from the matzos, that unleavened bread served at the seder and throughout Passover to symbolize the flight of the Jews, so sudden they left their yeast at home.

The prayers, however, are the most memorable part of the night to a schoolchild, beginning when the youngest asks the four questions that have always been asked after the poignant query, "Why is this night different from all other nights?" The father then reads the traditional prayers over the shank bone of lamb, to remind everyone of the old paschal sacrifices; the roasted egg, for fertility; the salted water, for tears once shed; the bitter herbs, for their lot in life; a green herb, for the spring renewal, and charoses, that apple and nut mixture that serves as mortar, to remember the pyramids the Jews had to build for the Egyptians.

A fine meal follows and then the hunt for the afikomen and the present that comes with it. If you're Jewish, celebrate Passover with your children. And if you're not, try to wangle an invitation. It brings history and holiness to life.

TSIMMES

SERVES 6–8   Preheat oven 350°

This recipe—which varies from family to family—makes seder even more memorable and a Ten can make it. The meat may be served or not—it's the flavor you really want. In a large casserole

COMBINE	½ lb. brisket or chuck
	2 T. oil

Brown the meat on one side over a medium flame, then turn it.

ADD	1 large onion, sliced
BROWN	15 minutes
ADD	6 carrots, sliced thickly
	3 large peeled sweet potatoes, in chunks
ADD	¼ c. brown sugar
	1″ water
	salt and pepper

Cover the casserole.

BAKE	2 hours

Check the pot every 20–30 minutes in case it needs more water—and it probably will. You're aiming for a dish with a thick gravy when it's done and a sweet, salty taste.

EASTER

All religions celebrate spring—a new beginning, a new chance. For Christians, Easter is the exultation that comes after the preparation of Lent. If you are churchgoers, you'll want your child to experience both, for each has its special value. The child who has given up candy or sodas for forty days will have a new appreciation of life—and of candy and sodas.

Somehow Easter is more special when boys and girls have nice new spring outfits

on Easter Sunday, but do show reasonable restraint. Easter bonnets and new suits can foster competition, infecting the religious celebration with materialism which can skew a child's values. Even if the other parishioners put their children in this contest, you don't have to turn your child into a prize-winning entry. Have him wear an outfit that's nice but not spectacular—or not necessarily new. You can get him something special to wear for another occasion.

A child with a Christian heritage does deserve some of the trappings that come with Easter, however—a new book like *The Velveteen Rabbit,* or a stuffed rabbit (or a real one); a packet of flower seeds or a few bulbs blooming; and, of course, Easter eggs. Dying eggs is one of the great amusements at this age and a good family adventure.

When you hide them in the morning, include a few surprises you dyed or hand-painted when he wasn't around, and some plastic eggs filled with goodies. And if you have more than one child, write their names on most of the eggs, so the older child can't grab them all.

The goodies in the plastic eggs can hold a tiny penknife; hair ribbons; a gold cross on a chain; a small figurine; a miniature truck; some potpourri or stickers—and of course some candy.

But of all the family celebrations you're likely to have, a Polish breakfast on Easter may be the best.

Polish Easter Breakfast

An Easter breakfast is a joy; a Polish Easter breakfast is a triumph. Although the cold

KAPUSTA

SERVES 8

This is one sauerkraut dish all children love. It's a little tedious to make, but a Twelve can rise to the occasion. Into a saucepan

EMPTY	2 16-oz. cans sauerkraut
SIMMER	10 minutes

Drain the sauerkraut into a colander and wash it under cold water. Return it to the saucepan

SIMMER	10 minutes

Wash it once again, followed by a good squeeze. This process gets rid of the sour taste, and the kitchen fan gets rid of the smell.

CHOP	2 big onions

The chopping should be fairly fine. Heap the onions in a large skillet

ADD	8 oz. butter
SAUTÉ	15–20 minutes

They're done when the onions are clear and golden. If the color still isn't right,

ADD	2–4 oz. butter

In the meantime

CHOP	sauerkraut

Add it to the skillet by the handful, stirring each new addition to coat it well with butter.

ADD	pepper
SIMMER	25–30 minutes

Longer is better, but cover the pot and use a very low fire, adding a little water if it gets dry.

Polish breakfast—the swiecone—is no longer carried to church on Saturday for the priest's blessing, this midday meal is still a splendid mix of food for the body and the soul.

The table is decorated with sprigs of green leaves, in honor of spring, and a lamb molded of butter or pastry sits in the center holding the Polish flag, surrounded by sausages, hams, a cold roast—even a suckling pig. No one takes a bite, however, until the blessing and breaking of the pis-

anki—the egg as a symbol of life—and an exchange of good wishes.

Dying these extraordinary hard-boiled eggs, with patterns that look so crisp and stenciled, is much beyond the skills of most mothers and children, Polish or not, but fortunately, kapusta, another fine Polish Easter tradition, is not.

CELEBRATIONS

Life is a miracle and the younger the life the more miraculous it seems. It's a precious appreciation you don't want to lose and you won't if you help your child celebrate the special days with all the joy they deserve.

FOURTH OF JULY

If the Fourth of July didn't exist, it would have to be invented for children. From fried chicken to corn on the cob, apple pie to homemade ice cream, fireflies to fireworks, it's the magic of America that delights every child. Gather a few families together and let the good times roll.

ICE CREAM

SERVES 10–12

This is that rare combination: a pure but easy ice cream a tidy Eight can make.

BEAT	6 egg yolks 2 c. sugar

In a separate bowl

BEAT	1 qt. whipping cream

Fold the cream into the egg mixture—a delicate step which will need your guidance.

freeze	2 hours

Two hours before dinner

HULL	1 qt. strawberries

Over them

SPRINKLE	1 T. Marsala

Your child spoons the berries over the ice cream, serves the company—and gets well-earned compliments.

Fireworks

Each generation seems a little more sensible about fireworks than the one before. Thank goodness. The really big firecrackers, the small, old-fashioned ones with a wick and the round cherry bombs that caused brush fires, terrible injuries and even deaths have been banned in most places but even innocent-looking sparklers, which reach 1800–2000 degrees, can give a nasty burn even after the sparkles have died.

You don't want to frighten your child with constant warnings, but you can give him a safe Fourth by going to a big fireworks show. Sit close enough so he can smell the acrid smoke and squint his eyes at the rockets' red glare and ooh and aah with the crowd.

Or you and the neighbors can put on your own rocket show if fireworks are legal in your state. Launch them in the center of a 30–35′ circle—clear of underbrush or children—for rockets never go where they should.

After the show a Six is old enough to light some snakes and by Eight he can wave a few sparklers around if you light them; if there is a bucket of water to dump them when they're spent; if he wears shoes in case someone throws one on the ground by mistake; and if he's willing to count the ones that were burned the next day, to make sure none are in the grass, and if they are, to find them. Otherwise the lawnmower could turn them into flying missiles.

Careful parents and cautious children should give you a safe and memorable Fourth.

HALLOWEEN

Halloween is a fairy tale come true. Where else can children go door to door demanding candy, just because they look like witches and goblins? This is why you hear them planning their costumes in May and still recalling their loot in December. From start to finish, trick or treating can be a blast, even if you dress your child in your old clothes, cover his face with burnt cork smudges (a tramp) or lipstick and eye pencil (a clown) or drop a white pillowcase over the little one, with holes cut for the eyes and slits in the sides, for arms (a ghost). That was about the best we could do, but today's parents are much more imaginative. Haunted houses pop up for the day like mushrooms and sometimes haunted libraries too. The success of these parties is assured if the parents throw themselves into them.

In our neighborhood they built up the anticipation for a Halloween party at the branch library for weeks, with advance readings from appropriate books, like *The Little Witch's Black Magic Book of Disguises* by Linda Glovach; *Gunhilde and the Halloween Spell*; and the ghoulish cartoon books by Charles Addams. When the fateful Saturday morning arrived the children—and the adults—wore well-planned homemade costumes. There were gypsies and fairies and pirates and angels and rabbits, and a few stunners, like the Six who decided to be a birthday present. She had her mother help her cover a big box with gift wrap and cut holes for her head, arms and legs—so it could go from her shoulders to her knees— and she wore a big bow on her head.

Another, at Ten, painted an even bigger box red—to represent a tablecloth—and went as a Thanksgiving dinner. He had glued paper plates and plastic knives and forks and glasses on each side of the box and had

a tinfoil candelabrum on his head (but not for long). It made for a very good party.

The costumed parents and children—some a little more self-conscious than they might admit—ate apples, popcorn and cider, heard thundering poetry like "The Highwayman" and swapped ghost stories with increasing ghoulishness. And then, the party supposedly over, they were sent home by way of the dark back stairs, where one parent, hidden in an old tin locker, banged on the sides and shrieked. Others, dressed in sheets, ooohed and aaahed and made cat noises or grabbed at small fleeting ankles. The children flew down the stairs, past a candle flickering on the landing and a bare branch waving in a corner with a stuffed owl bobbing in it: a fan was blowing all.

The children were delighted—and victorious. They not only lived happily ever after, they had a costume parade to celebrate it. And the parents had a fine time too.

Staying Home

Some of the best Halloween pranks are pulled by grown-ups. They put on a show for the trick-or-treaters, being careful to pull their scarier tricks on the preteens and have the younger children help with the preparations.

One grown-up scared—and delighted—his visitors by lying in a long box, painted black, that rested on the picnic table by the front walk. When they pressed the doorbell he would slowly raise the lid of the box and, with creaking sound effects, would eerily say, "You raaaaang?"

At another house a couple played the funereal "Danse Macabre" on the stereo as the children bounded up the steps. He, in a dark dinner jacket, would open the door, and she, in ghastly, ghostly makeup and a long black hooded cloak, would glide forward proffering a large, smoking bowl. The courageous, reaching out, would find a smaller bowl inside, nestled in a bed of dry ice, heaped with candy bars. Inside of every grown-up is a child eager to get out.

And then there's our neighborhood dentist, who has a much milder routine. He changes his side garden into a Ghoul Palace, with lighted candle stubs in the flower beds, chains rattling in the background, a plastic skeleton sprawled in a deck chair, and three volunteer witches, mumbling as they stir a caldron of mulled cider on the barbecue grill. Ghosts appear from the shadows, offering peanuts in the shell and other noncandy treats. The children arrive after trick-or-treating and later bob for apples.

HOT MULLED CIDER

This warm cider is delicate enough to please young children and spicy enough for their parents. To make it, use a 3-quart saucepan and in it

COMBINE	2 qts. fresh country cider
	zest of 1 orange
	2 T. brown sugar
	3″ stick cinnamon
	1 t. whole allspice
	1 t. whole cloves
	⅛ t. ground nutmeg

Bring slowly to a boil and cover.

| SIMMER | 20 minutes |

Strain the cider and return it to the pot. Warm the cider shortly before the party begins and pour it into a punch bowl.

| ADD | 2 oranges, cut in eighths |

Squeeze them lightly, for greater flavor.

THANKSGIVING

Thanksgiving is the holiday that can bond a child to his family—and his country—more closely than any other. It's a rich celebration meant to be savored, and no one savors better than a child. Let him be involved in every aspect, from the shining of the silver to the planning of the menu and the choosing of guests. On this, the most generous holiday of all, you want to share your bounty with others.

It's also the kitchen's finest theatrical production of the year, and it plays best if everyone in the family has an active role. Have your child help you with the shopping and chopping, the setting of the table and the arrangements of fruit. There's little time to run out and play and no time to fuss, for your child should be responsible for a special recipe. The help of a Six won't be much, but the experienced Twelve is a godsend, so start the custom early.

Such efforts deserve preliminary fanfare and well-warmed plates, for serving takes a long time. George Washington's Proclamation is a good beginning, for it reminds us to give thanks for a country where we can worship as we please. Let the oldest child read it while the turkey is carved.

The blessing comes next, to remember how far and how fast our country has come (and also to keep the children from eating before everyone is served). It can be a simple thanks by the head of the table or by a special guest, or you can all join hands and sing the hymn "We Gather Together." And after that it's liberty hall.

The candlelight will help you ignore the buttermilk biscuits that are lobbed to the dog; the vegetables that go untouched; the cranberry sauce that colors the cloth; the poking and pinching of squiggly children. If you have food for a feast and a good place to serve it, children to honor your name and a dog to keep you com-

CRANBERRY RELISH

This is probably the freshest, fastest, tastiest recipe an Eight (or his mother) can make. In a blender

COMBINE **1 12-oz pkg. fresh cranberries**
      1 seedless unpeeled orange, in
        eighths
      ½–¾ c. sugar

Blend until the orange is in tiny bits, stopping several times to stir the ingredients so everything is well chopped.

ADD   **4 oz. walnuts**

Blend briefly, so the relish still has some crunch.

THE FIRST NATIONAL THANKSGIVING PROCLAMATION

Whereas it is the duty of all nations to acknowledge the providence of Almighty God, to obey his will, to be grateful for his benefits, and humbly to implore his protection and favor; and whereas both Houses of Congress have, by their joint Committee, requested me to recommend to the people of the United States a day of Public Thanksgiving and prayer, to be observed by acknowledging with grateful hearts the many and signal favors of Almighty God, especially by affording them an opportunity peaceably to establish a form of government for their safety and happiness.

Now therefore I do recommend and assign Thursday, the twenty-sixth of November next, to be devoted by the people of these States to the service of that great and glorious Being, who is Beneficent Author of all the good that was, that is, or that will be; that we may then all unite a rendering unto him our sincere and humble thanks for his kind care and protection of the people of this country, previous to their becoming a nation; for the signal manifold mercies, and the favorable interpositions of his providence, in the course and conclusion of the late war; for the great degree of tranquility, union and plenty which we have since enjoyed; for the peaceable and rational manner in which we have been enabled to establish Constitutions of Government for our safety and happiness, and particularly the national one now lately instituted; for the civil and religious liberty with which we are blessed, and the means we have of acquiring and diffusing useful knowledge; and, in general, for all the great and various favors, which he has been pleased to confer on us.

And also, that we may then unite in most humbly offering our prayers and supplications to the great Lord and Ruler of Nations, and beseech him to pardon our national and other transgressions; to enable us all, whether in public or private institutions, to perform our several and relative duties properly and punctually; to render our National Government a blessing to all the people, by constantly being a government of wise, just and constitutional laws, discreetly and faithfully executed and obeyed; to protect and guide all sovereigns and nations (especially such as have shown kindness to us) and to bless them with good governments, peace and concord; to promote the knowledge and practice of true religion and virtue, and the increase of science, among them and us; and generally, to grant unto all mankind such a degree of temporal prosperity as he alone knows to be best.

—George Washington

pany, you have reasons enough to be thankful.

Although our own family was late to copy the tradition, a personal round robin of thanks is a joyful way to end the meal—a moment of reflection when we tell each other what has really meant most to us all year. One may give thanks for health regained; another for the great new school or the finding of a special friend. But none has surpassed the solemn fervor of the six-year-old school bus rider who said, "I'm thankful that I haven't thrown up *all year*!"

GRADUATION

Graduation from sixth grade is more than an event, it's a dawning: the Age of Friskiness is about to begin. Celebrate it in a lovely, grown-up way.

LEMON ICE

12 SERVINGS

This is about as elegant as you can get—especially when spooned into a glass of very cold sparkling cider, or champagne for the adults.

BEAT	2 egg whites

Set aside when they are very stiff.

MIX	1 c. sugar
	6 T. lemon juice
	3 T. grated lemon zest
	⅛ t. salt

Fold this mixture into the egg whites, but do it gradually, so they don't lose much air.

ADD	2 c. light cream

Freeze. The egg whites keep it from crystallizing but there is so much lemon juice in this recipe that it may sink to the bottom as it hardens. Mix it once and refreeze. Drop a large spoonful of Lemon Ice in each glass.

FATHER'S DAY

When you were pregnant you may have thought that Mother's Day and Father's Day were too commercial to consider, but you're bound to be more open-minded now.

While you can hardly arrange your own party, you can help your child put on a production that tells your husband how special he is. A bouquet of daisies—for men like flowers too—is a thoughtful gift and a special breakfast will leave the commerce out and let the love shine through.

BUTTERMILK PANCAKES

YIELD: 50

These lovely, fragile pancakes are good enough to win an Eleven (or his mom) a first prize—or turn a Father's Day breakfast into a Sunday morning ritual, which is better, especially if Dad does the making. The fruit is optional.

In one bowl

COMBINE	1 c. sifted flour
	½ t. baking powder
	¼ t. baking soda
	¼ t. salt

In another bowl

BEAT	1 egg
ADD	2 c. buttermilk OR 2 c. milk, soured by 1 T. vinegar
	3 T. melted butter
	½ c. blueberries OR 1 banana, finely chopped

Dump the wet ingredients into the dry ones and mix only enough to break up the big lumps—a matter of stirring 16 times, says the source (not 17 or 15), and stirring very gently too. Oil the griddle lightly, heat it enough to sizzle a drop of water and ladle onto it dollops of batter the size of a silver dollar, so they don't fall apart the way bigger ones might. Besides—children like to brag about how many they can eat.

Although these pancakes are at their best if they're eaten as soon as they're cooked, this makes the cook feel like a galley slave and causes a lot of commotion besides. You'll find they hold up quite well in stacks on a platter, kept warm in a 200° oven.

SUNDAY BRUNCH

To children, there's something truly special about a daytime party. In return, you can expect them to give quite a bit of help.

DIPPED STRAWBERRIES

One of the most elegant, colorful desserts a Six can make is also one of the simplest: strawberries coated in chocolate.

The berries—perfect ones, of course—should be washed, dried and wearing their caps and the chocolate should be the best.

In the top of a double boiler, have your child

MELT   **2 oz. bittersweet chocolate**

Take the pan off the fire for him and let the chocolate cool slightly. He then holds each berry by its cap, dips it into the chocolate up to its waist and then lays it on wax paper so it doesn't touch another berry. Refrigerate until served on your best china plate.

COMPANY DINNER

Perhaps the best part of giving a party is the trouble you take. It's a subtle way to tell a child that friends are worth it and, if you do it in good spirit, you'll find he wants to help.

PEACH SAUCE

6 SERVINGS

This sauce is a cinch for a Nine and teaches him a cardinal rule of cooking: always marry the fruit to the wine. In this case, the almond liqueur (or the extract) complements the flavor of the pits, which underscores the fruit.

SKIN   **4 very ripe peaches**

A child can do this either by paring the peaches or by dropping them into boiling water for 60 seconds, scooping them out of the pot with a slotted spoon and slipping them out of their skins when they are cool enough to touch. He pits the peaches next, drops them in a bowl and pulverizes them with a potato masher or a mixer until they are only slightly lumpy.

ADD   **3 T. sugar**
                 3 T. Amaretto

This isn't enough alcohol to worry about, but the cost of the liqueur may stop you. In that case use

                 4 T. sugar
                 1–2 t. almond extract

CHILL   **2 hours**

Serve over the richest peach ice cream you can find.

STRESSES

No one lives without stress—good or bad—and if they did, they'd be bored silly. Stress adds variety to life: hills and valleys that make us appreciate the placidity that makes up most of our days. Unfortunately the valleys sometimes seem so deep that we lose sight of the hills.

Stress often comes with change, like moving or getting used to a new job or a higher—or lower—income. Any change is stressful and it always affects the child, sometimes more than a new school. A child doesn't look at adult changes with adult eyes and will need to be reassured.

The remarriage of a parent or a cross-country move is seldom met with joy.

Chronic stress, like a handicap or an illness or constant tension in the household, can be even more debilitating. A child in an unhappy home feels unsafe and needs extra support.

The reactions to stress—physical and emotional—are always the same and as ancient and primitive as man. When it comes, the heart and the lungs work faster, the blood sugar rises, the body sweats, the digestion slows, the muscles tense and the pupils dilate (so we can see our tigers in the dark). A child likes to know these reactions are natural and automatic, giving him the strength to either fight or flee. His body stays alert until the perceived danger goes away or he discovers that he was really safe after all.

Whether the stress is brief or prolonged, your child will want to know that his body needs more food and sleep to repair itself after the alarm has sounded, and more exercise too. A good bike ride can be balm to the soul. He'll also deal with the stress better if you help him do something he's never done before or do something for someone else. A sense of accomplishment and a little appreciation are the sweetest sedatives of all. And then there's laughter—the best of cures and the one that's most often forgotten. Everything has its ridiculous side. If you poke around to find it, your child will do the same. Friends can be healers too. If your child talks about his problems, he can sort out his feelings and put at least some of them to rest. This may not be easy to do, but when he knows that you also turn to friends—or to religion or a therapist—he will dare to be more open too.

Your child also needs to know that he can handle any stress better if he grapples with a piece of the problem each day, rather than all of it at once, and that with each success he'll cope a little better the next time.

MOVING

Some children seem to move with ease, but most do not. Meg, our dramatic one, was Eleven when we loaded the books into baby carriages, the bureaus onto dollies and traipsed seven doors up the street to the end of our city block—our flight to the suburbs. It hardly seemed traumatic, but before the day was done she had (1) called the police to report an indecent exposure she might have seen; (2) called the police to report a kidnapping she thought she had seen; and (3) said, "Call me a rabbi!" When asked why, she could only wail, "Don't you know I've always wanted to be a Jew?" Apparently, if she was going to change her room and her house, she might as well change her religion, have a bat mitzvah and get presents like her friend down the street (although she swore the presents hadn't crossed her mind).

She might have been still more anxious if she had been younger. First graders have so much change in their lives that even a new room in the same old house can upset them, although they may deny it. Most children—especially boys—try to keep their worries to themselves in the Middle Years and particularly between Seven and Nine, when they try so hard to be grown up.

Instead of asking your child how he feels about moving, talk to him about the scary changes you made in your life at his age, so he'll know he's not the only one who's ever been afraid. You may have to bring up the subject yourself when you're on a walk in the dark or on a car ride, in case there are any tears. This will let your child save face, which is so important to the young.

If you look at his worries objectively, you'll realize that many reflect your own anxieties. Moving is bound to frazzle you a bit. Although you are concerned (quite naturally) about finding a new house; a new school; a new pediatrician, a karate class and a piano teacher—and maybe, in

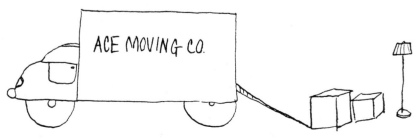

the middle of it all, a new job for yourself—try to keep your chin up and your humor high. The more positive your attitude, the more positive your child will be. It helps if you break your own work into segments, take deep breaths in between and look at the move as an adventure, even if it's coming out of a divorce or the loss of a job. Remind yourself—and your child—that change can make the family prosper in unexpected ways. Moving, like any challenge, makes everyone stretch and grow.

Even the frequent moves required by the military or some big companies can be rich experiences, but watch out for certain pitfalls. If you move often, the matter of acceptance may become more important to a child than achievement, especially for girls, for they usually need to feel accepted more than boys do. Remind your child that family values and customs stay the same, wherever you live, and so do family goals. Your house is just baggage; you carry your real home in your hearts.

There are other things you can do to make the transition easier. If you can choose the time, consider January. Your child's entry into a new school will give his fellow students such a break in the midyear blahs that he'll become the toast of the class, while a summertime move may take him into a fairly empty neighborhood, with half of the children at day camp or on vacation.

Whenever you move, it's important that your child help you pack (and unpack) his room and decide what he keeps. This is no time for you to toss away his rock collection. It also helps to keep explaining each stage of the move to your child, busy as you are, and to prepare him for his new house by telling him what time of day the sun will shine in his bedroom window and how big the room will be, by pacing off the old one. Even if he's seen it he'll need this graphic example, for children under Ten have a hard time imagining size.

It's wise to walk and drive your child through the new neighborhood before moving—either in person or by your own recollection—and then together mark a neighborhood map for the house, the school, the school bus stop, the park, the neighborhood pool, the soccer field, the dimestore, the ice cream shop, the supermarket and the hardware store. Even if he's not old enough to go around alone, he can see where he'll fit and when he gets there he can mark the houses of his new friends. If your child will be riding the bus for the first time, see if he can go home one afternoon with a school-bus-riding friend, so he'll know what it will be like. Familiarity is the balm of anxiety.

No matter how carefully you prepare for the move, he'll still be terribly anxious, for friends are especially important in the Middle Years. He needs the chance to exchange some treasure with his best friend—a toy, a book, a T-shirt—to have one-at-a-time farewells with his friends, whether he has one big bash or not, and plan how they'll phone or visit or write each other.

You can assuage moving pains later if you take many pictures of him with his friends in your house and ambling around the neighborhood and then give them to him in his own photograph album. Tape recordings with his friends, singing and horsing around, will help too. He also should have his own address book to fill out before leaving and change-of-address forms to send his friends when he arrives.

On moving day tuck a special symbol of home—the mezuzah or cross or a favorite picture—in your suitcase and hang it in the hall, with ceremony, as soon as you arrive. If you're religious you can have the house blessed once you're settled or you can go through a family ritual. One of the best: a batch of cement poured in a corner of the driveway, for everyone to scratch their names (or press their paws) on the surface. These customs are particularly good if you move often.

It's also important to give your child time to meet new children almost as soon as you arrive. This isn't as generous as it seems, for children make friends for the whole family. He'll have to be careful to be more of a listener than a talker at first, however, for children tend to brag (or sound like they're bragging) when they're in a new situation. Remind your young mover to watch out for this trap; the damage can take weeks to undo.

He'll need more than friends in his new neighborhood. Get him an official-looking, plasticized identification card with his address on it and have him learn his phone number as well as any office numbers and that of a neighbor to call in case he needs help.

Since school will be his main concern, ask to introduce your child to the principal when you register him. Even a busy person will usually take time to meet a new student, unless the school is huge and he's part of the September influx. Once he's enrolled in school, ask your child to make up a student handbook with the names of teachers, the principal and the office secretary as well as a rough sketch of the school so he'll know where to find his classroom, the bathroom and the office. It will comfort the uneasy child to realize how much he knows—and it will comfort you too.

HANDICAPS

Few things test a family's mettle more than their child's handicap. Whether the disability is caused by a birth defect, a virus or an accident, the effect can be overwhelming. You soon realize that if one person in the family is handicapped the whole family is handicapped. This may sound ominous, but adversity can make a family stronger than ever as long as you give the handicapped child the same love, rights, duties and discipline as any other child in the family. It's mighty tempting to be more lenient with the child who is chairbound or in and out of hospitals or retarded, acting either out of pity, which is unkind; despair, which is destructive; or expediency, which is counterproductive. Some-

times, of course, you need to be lenient with this child—as you need to be with any child—but if you always expect less you'll get less, which handicaps the child still further.

The more a child—any child—can do for himself, the more the parent is freed and the more the child is freed too. This brings him competence and, with it, self-esteem. He'll also get more courage. This is the bedrock he'll need to handle the problems ahead.

Unfortunately, it takes time to teach any child to be self-sufficient and when he is handicapped it takes much longer. This may seem like too much to give when you've given so much already. There's never a moment for yourself unless you force yourself to take it—and so you must. Martyrdom doesn't make anyone happy, especially the martyr. It also will make you mad not only at yourself but at your child, even though you may sublimate that anger by turning on others instead. If you have any other children, they will recognize and resent this uneven treatment, although they may not mention it: no one measures a tilt in the scales of justice as precisely as a child.

The brothers and sisters of the handicapped child often pay the biggest price, particularly in the Middle Years. The obvious difference in their family can make them feel embarrassed or isolated unless you counter their embarrassment by letting the world—and the children—know that you're as proud of your handicapped child as you are of all your children. This is a fine line to walk. Both you and your husband must not only give those ten listening minutes each child deserves from each parent each day but some extra time occasionally, even if you only ask one child to go to the store with you and another to snuggle up and read with you in your bed. This bonding is important in any family, but it's vital for the siblings of the handicapped child. By helping your other children realize how special they are, you draw them more tightly into the fabric of the family and make them want to help the child who needs it most. The urge to rally around is strong when the rallyers have been cheered. This extra attention for everybody may seem like the last straw, but you'll soon feel glad you're giving it, for the children, as they get older, will assume some of your physical and emotional burdens without waiting to be asked.

It's the worries that weigh most, however. You won't share all of them, of course, but the whole family should have the factual medical information about the handicap. Even so, a Twelve will agonize quietly over his future, wondering how he can take care of the handicapped child if something should happen to you, especially if you're a single parent. This is the best reason to tell all your children about the arrangements you've made to cover this emergency.

Many other anxieties plague the handicapped family, and you need guidance from other parents in your situation. Fortunately, there are national organizations for every major handicap and many minor ones, with newsletters, recommended books and regular meetings. A support group offers everyone, often including the handicapped child, the chance to talk about their feelings and to learn to handle them better.

The great love you feel for this child is sure to make you worry more and can stress your marriage, as it has for so many others. The divorce rate is much higher among parents whose children are physically or mentally handicapped. Talking to other parents will relieve much of this tension so you and your husband don't have to take it out on each other.

A support group is also the best place to get specialized information on education and medicine. This is where you'll find out how to get your child tested; if he can—or should—be mainstreamed into public school; how to work with the system to develop his own educational plan; if there are government grants and how to

apply for them. By discussing the latest medical information with other parents, and the odd, as well as the ordinary treatment, you have a double check in case the family doctor has missed some small critical development or is unaware of what may be a promising new theory. As the parents of an ill or handicapped child, this is perhaps the greatest lesson you can learn: if you're informed, you can usually make a more intelligent decision about your child than anyone else. Knowledge not only will make you feel more confident, but it will reassure the child, for you and his dad are the people he trusts most.

A support group will also remind you that this special child is, above all, a child, with the same needs and emotions that all children have, and that sometimes he's a handful, just as they all are. This is especially true when his behavior breaks apart and regresses before each new stage, so he can come together again as an older and wiser person (see Resources). By managing the problem, you will have an even greater appreciation of your child's abilities, treasuring his smallest accomplishments because you know the effort they took. Joy is where you find it and you often find it most when you have a handicapped child.

ILLNESS

By now you've helped your child endure sniffles and stitches, earaches and bee stings, but nothing prepares a parent for the emergency appendectomy, the convalescence from rheumatic fever, the grind of a chronic illness—or the terror of a fatal one. May you have the strength of Solomon, the patience of Job, the imagination of Peter Pan and the empathy of Mother Teresa. And because you won't reach such stellar heights, may you appreciate your successes enough to excuse your failures.

HOSPITALIZATION

There really is no way to make a child like the hospital, but you can make the experience less upsetting. This is easier to do if the stay is expected, for then he can—and should—take a tour with you beforehand and read some books about the hospital, so he will know what to expect. It's fear of the unknown that is hard for a child, and with good reason. He owns the body everyone will poke. This gives him the right to know what people will do and why. The more information you can give him about the routines, the procedures, and the equipment, the less frightened he'll be. And because every child seems to have at least one hospital emergency, he needs a book about it in his reading collection, so he'll think of a hospital in a somewhat familiar way.

Once there, it will still seem like never-never land, but your presence and your positive attitude will make him feel better, although the experience may leave him tense for weeks. The child who is hospitalized for an expected stay also needs you or your husband there as much as possible, and your other children will accept your absences better if they are given full and daily explanations.

Studies show that loving is as important as food to the child in a hospital. Even in the Middle Years he is apt to protest at first and, after a week or two, to withdraw and become apathetic, for this separation causes grief and consequently depression. This means the warming up will also take awhile. Even with your best effort, you may see your Six regress—wetting the bed, hitting his little sister—until he's worked away his fear and anger, but with your thoughtful attention he will adjust much faster.

Let there be a cuddly present on his pillow when he comes out of anesthesia and, if his stay will be longer than a day or two, see that he has some snapshots from home—including one of the cat; a flashlight to shine in the dark; a clock to know

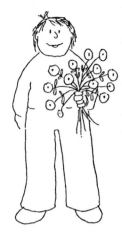

when you're coming; a handkerchief with your perfume on it; letters or cards left for the nurse to deliver several times a day and a tape player and some tapes, including one of his dad singing him good night. Even a Twelve feels mighty young late at night when he's alone in a hospital room. Colored chalk and paper, modeling clay and balloons to shape into animals all give a sick child something to do, and witty books, fairy tales and adventure stories will help to take his mind off his troubles. Library books might get lost, but you can pick up cheap copies at a thrift store.

A child also feels better if he can wear his own pajamas; has change enough to call his siblings, his friends and his teacher; and knows why you have to leave, when you're coming back and how he can reach you in the meantime. He also needs to know that his parents will protect him at the hospital, just as they would at home. This is not an idle comment. Even a good hospital has its inept interns and harassed (and harassing) nurses, but that doesn't mean you have to accept such treatment. You're buying hospital care just as you would buy any other service. It's better to insist on a second opinion or report a nurse than to have your child pay for their mistakes.

A well-run pediatric unit has certain trademarks and if you have the choice, go to the hospital that supplies them. The best program has a preadmission registration program, including time for the child and the parents to get their questions answered; a twenty-four-hour visiting policy for parents; sibling visits if the child isn't too sick or contagious and lets parents spend the night and give some of the care. A good unit also understands children and the different ways they grow; gives both educational and emotional support to the child and his family; and has a special person on staff to counsel the seriously ill. These rather unsung measures can be the difference between a stressful stay—which is inevitable—and a traumatic one.

CONVALESCENCE

The convalescent child needs to keep busy, if only so he doesn't keep you busy. Consider coloring and comic books, radio, TV and movies, adventure stories and Nancy Drews, a deck of Uno to play with a friend, and plain old cards for solitaire. If he's old enough and fit enough, he can bet 52 Monopoly dollars against the house and get back $5 more for each card he builds on the foundations. His efforts to wind up a winner will keep a Nine enthralled for hours (and teach him the gambler's woeful fate). As he gets better, see that he has more interesting books, the daily newspaper (or yesterday's newspaper), clay to sculpt, cars to race, a puzzle on a tray.

The doctor decides if your convalescent child must be in bed all the time or if he can spend time on the sofa or a lawn chair in the living room. In any case it's important for him to be as much a part of the action as possible. This is especially true at mealtimes, when he may feel his loneliest. If possible, have him eat with the family at the table, stretched out on the lawn chair with his meal on a tray, or, if he must stay in bed, see that one member of the family, or a friend, has dinner with him each night.

The meals he has on a tray are a little jazzier if there is a small treat once or twice a day: a funny note folded up under the plate; the orange juice served in a brandy snifter; the sandwich cut in a silly way;

chopsticks on a Chinese night; and a damp washcloth to use after each meal. A little preventive medicine keeps crankiness—and messiness—away.

So much attention can cause resentment among the siblings, just as the extra attention given to a handicapped child can irritate his brothers and sisters. This isn't surprising, since the out-of-action convalescent has become a handicapped child. The solution is the same: make it clear that you love the other children just as much. The special status can also cause the bedbound to become obnoxious, partly in annoyance over his new dependence and partly because he's testing his limits. Once more, work can lessen the reactions. The recuperating child can snap some beans, polish a candlestick, sort socks, sew a few buttons. Keep a plastic cloth to throw over his bed when he has work to do, both to keep his coverlet clean and to gather up the pieces easily.

At Eight he can be the family's answering machine, if you have a portable phone. Have him take messages, make whatever family calls he can handle and call people to the phone, possibly with bell signals or a tune on his harmonica, with a different ring or a different tune for each person, but out of kindness to the caller, have him muffle the phone under his pillow when he pages you. A harmonica makes a fine bedfellow—phone calls or not—because the convalescent child needs to sound off. If you have strong nerves, you can also consider a whistle, noisemakers, a horn or a xylophone.

A bedridden child is happier and easier to care for if he can do as much of his own caring as possible. For this he needs a water pitcher, a glass and tissues on his night table; a fresh litter bag pinned to the side of his bed every day; a bag of toys hanging over the headboard; some books

BEDSIDE POCKETS

A long cloth remnant across the bed, between the mattress and the spring, with big pockets hanging out on either side, lets the patient reach his possessions easily and keeps the sick bay a little tidier. For a single bed

CUT   **12″ × 84″ strip of cloth**

Hem the edges and turn up each end 12″, with the wrong sides together. Stitch these sides together and run another row of stitching down the center of each pocket, so the patient can reach in any of the four compartments for crayons and paper; pencils and scissors; a magnet and a magnifier; a flashlight and a comb; slippers and tissues.

on a rack or in another sack—but both within easy reach; a good light over his left shoulder and Bedside Pockets well stuffed to fill an assortment of needs.

The toys in his sack can include puppets (a good way for a child to act out his angst); magnetic checkers and dominoes (which means another player); magic tricks; a flashlight; tapes and a tape recorder, if possible, both to make tapes and to play them and any writing or drawing supplies you think he can manage, as well as puzzles and games. If the child is recovering from an illness rather than an accident, you can expect him to tire quickly, so the activities shouldn't be too demanding. He'll need a tray to use most of these toys. You can make a good one by cutting out two pairs of U's on opposite sides of a sturdy cardboard box, to make room for his legs, or by lowering an ironing board over his lap, with extra pillows behind him for support.

Of all his entertainments, your company will be the best. The sprawl at the foot of his bed and the silly and serious chats and reminiscences and songfests will feed his soul and yours.

PAN FRUIT

SERVES 8

Uncle Tom, our favorite gourmet, invented this simple, elegant, by-guess-and-by-gosh dessert—a tasty and nutritious treat for your favorite young convalescent, and the rest of the family too. Use 3 or 4 (or more) fresh, juicy summer fruits, cut into bite-sized pieces, but avoid grapefruit, oranges, melons, apples and pears. Fill an 8″ × 13″ glass baking dish with 1½–2″ of fruit.

COMBINE   pineapple
                     mangoes
                     peaches
                     nectarines
                     plums
                     kiwis
                     grapes
                     cherries, pitted
                     blueberries

Over it

SQUEEZE   2 limes

Refrigerate until time to serve.

ADD   banana slices
                     strawberries OR raspberries

Stir well to spread the colors, flavors and textures. Over the top

SMEAR   1 pt. sour cream

This should be about ½″ thick. Over this

SPRINKLE   ¼″ brown sugar

BROIL   3–5 minutes

It's ready when the sugar has melted—a yummy hot-and-cold, sweet-and-tangy contrast.

CHRONIC ILLNESS

Chronic illness wears you down, breaks your heart and makes you lonely, because it takes your family out of the mainstream and your child away from his band of buddies. The more life-threatening the illness, the more demoralizing it can be, but the experience can be enriching too. A serious illness makes you realize how precious your child is and, if you have other children, the special place each one has in your heart. The best you can do is cultivate a can-do spirit, accepting every problem as a challenge to be met, so your child will do the same. Life's lemons can make an awful lot of lemonade.

The chronically ill child who needs full or partial bed rest, or who is chairbound, needs the same treatment as the convalescent, but with an even heavier emphasis on self-sufficiency. Competence is critical in the Middle Years and no one needs it more than the physically dependent child.

All patients, whether they are incapacitated by mononucleosis, a heart condition, juvenile diabetes or cancer, respond better to the positive thinking around him. The less stress your child has to handle, the more he can fight the distress within himself. Relaxation techniques are helpful, especially when coupled with visualization therapy, in which the child is helped to imagine the warfare within his body and to direct the good guys to the trouble spot—a technique whose credibility continues to grow as more and more success is reported. This emphasis on the cure not only can make pain get better but often makes the cause go away. Doctors have found that patients with a will to live get well much faster, sometimes even when the case seems hopeless.

A continuing sense of growth is vital to this child. Since much of this depends on school, you'll want him to keep his connection with his class as strong as possible, with a visiting teacher to explain his work. If you can, arrange for a rotating team of classmates to bring the homework back and forth and incidentally give your child some company, for friendships do so much for the spirit. If this is hard to establish or maintain—and it may well be in a long-term illness—encourage your child to become a big letter writer, by finding him pen pals among the older relatives and children in other cities and other countries, and if at all possible, buy or borrow a computer to teach him and keep him entertained. It's also good for him to take part in a support group, talking by phone with children who have the same physical prob-

lem he does, and to have one best friend to hear his troubles.

Good nutrition is, of course, essential. Convenience foods are usually a poor idea since they seldom have much nutrition as homemade food and your child's health depends a great deal on the food he eats. Stress and illness rob the body of many essential vitamins and minerals and prescribed drugs may leach out many more. Because few doctors are well schooled in this field, you'd be wise to consult a nutritionist. He will outline a diet and prescribe vitamins and minerals suited to your child's particular needs, free of starch, sugar, colors and preservatives, which should help your child recover faster or at least cope with his illness better.

To use vitamins well, your child needs as much sunshine as possible. He also needs fresh air, and if he has allergy or respiratory problems or if you or your husband smoke, use an unscented electronic cleaner in his room. There is no point in adding to his problems.

Doctors encourage exercise, especially aerobic ones, for almost all illnesses, to give the body an extra surge of oxygen. A little bit of dancing or swimming or light weight lifting gives the blood a tonic and gives the child more energy and a greater zest for life. Almost any sport can be adapted for the chronically ill or handicapped child, such as a lower basketball hoop for the chairbound player.

All the things that are good for the ill child—a good diet, vitamins, friendship and exercise—are good for parents too, and so is the time you and your husband spend together, without any children to care for. Respite care, which provides help for a few weeks, could be the answer. Marriage is hard enough to maintain; you don't want to put it under continual stress. A pair of stable parents is the best support a child, well or ill, can have.

TERMINAL ILLNESS

The dying child needs the greatest possible support, and so does his family. If you are facing this crisis, you know that nothing will ever test you so sternly and, at times, so mercilessly.

Pediatricians generally agree that the best care is hospice care, given in the hospital, in a nursing facility, or, if possible, at home where the environment is familiar and there is less apprehension and less stress. The thrust is the same, however. In hospice care, life is not prolonged foolishly, but neither is death hastened. Instead, death is accepted as a natural, dignified process—an attitude that even a young child prefers, although he seldom talks about his going until the end is near. Studies show that hospice care helps the patient and his family feel less anxiety, less helplessness, less guilt and less trauma. This creates an intimacy that will fortify your family and leave everyone feeling that they did their best.

The patient also seems to feel less pain in hospice care, although this is difficult to assess. Pain feels different to a child than to an adult and it varies from child to child, depending on the age, the development, the sex, the culture and even the birth order. The firstborn—no matter how serious the illness—is usually more fearful, which is why he needs extra assurance and explanations before any medical procedure.

In the hospice program, a support team, made up of a doctor, a nurse, a social worker, a clergyman and trained volunteers, work with you to put the patient's comfort first. Some families also call in a thanatologist—someone who is trained to help them talk about their grief and to give the patient the therapeutic touch—that laying on of hands many medical schools now advocate to supplement pain-relieving drugs.

While institutional care may seem easier, more and more families prefer to learn the nursing techniques themselves and, with the help of their support team, take care of their children at home. You'll find it somewhat easier if you have help, and so you should. This is no time to be proud. You not only should ask for a homemaker from a social agency who can supplement the visiting nurse but call in every neighborhood chit you've ever given—and more. When people offer help, accept with alacrity. If you don't, they may not offer again, not because they didn't mean it the first time, but because they don't want to be intrusive.

Your child will like visitors for short periods of time, depending on how well he feels. Consider a team of neighborhood storytellers and musicians—arranged by one of their number. A half hour of the Hobbitt or a few tunes on a flute will give your child a daily lift while you take a nap or run an errand. You need breaks to keep up your spirits and so does your child.

Hospice home care has other advantages. It is much less expensive, both for the insurance companies that prefer these cheaper costs and for the family, who aren't dimed and dollared by the snack bar and the parking lot, and then feel guilty for resenting the money this dear child is costing them.

Whether your child is at home or in a hospital, he'll need you to be with him and to listen to him. Some of the signals he sends may be in code, if you or his brother or sister are stoic (or tearful) or if he thinks it would make you unhappy to know how he felt or he'd look like a sissy if he admitted he was scared or how much he hurt. He even might think the pain was his punishment for being bad or that he will die in his sleep, which may make him resist all his medication at night. Abandonment is the worst fear a child has, no matter who does the leaving. His secret fears turn parents into master cryptographers, better than any code breakers at the hospital. You know your child best. Even if you misread his cues, he will fare better when he is surrounded by love for this is the best medicine of all. You give it best when you let him talk about his feelings, his anger, his dreams. By being available to visit with him, even without talking much, and by looking at the funny side of his life, you let him draw the most out of it. Your child needs all the encouragement and the smiles and the silliness he can get.

Even a Six will also need to help decide about changes in treatment and how he can handle each stage better. All of this helps him accept the idea of his death. It's said that children of all ages know when they're going to die, although they won't talk about it if they feel it will make others unhappy. This acceptance is much harder for parents to achieve. The fury, the unfairness of your child's illness will sting you a hundred times a day. For this you need spiritual help, conversations with someone who's been where you're going and some counseling.

As strange as it seems, a lingering illness has a value that sudden death denies. It gives the family the chance to prepare itself, to grieve before the fact, so the grief afterward won't be quite so bad, and it gives everyone time to say good-bye.

DEATH

When death strikes a member of the family, everyone else is dramatically affected, but a child won't understand it the way you do. If he's young, he'll believe in the death of a fairy-tale witch or a TV character who suddenly spouts ketchup all over his suit, but the death of a relative or a friend is impossible. It has to be. This child is sure he can't die and neither can anyone he knows and loves. In his world, only the remote are mortal.

Meg was Six when she saw a picture of her distant cousin, dressed up as the king of a Mardi Gras krewe. Although she had never heard of the fellow before, she was very impressed, but when she learned that he was ill she was awed. She was related not only to a king but to a very sick king. Every morning when it was time to offer prayers at her parochial school she would

solemnly ask her classmates "to pray for my cousin the king, who is dying." And then it was "for my cousin the king, who is dead." Although it made for high drama—and lasted for months—it was, of course, unreal, for death is unreal to young children.

At Seven (and Eight and Nine), a child begins to understand that living things will one day die, but he still thinks that death can be outwitted indefinitely. He only starts to accept its reality and inevitability when he enters the preteens.

You help your child realize that death is natural by having funerals for his gerbils; by pinning the neighbor's obituary on the bulletin board and by taking him to the wake or the shiva, even though the younger child still wouldn't be surprised to see the neighbor come waltzing through the door.

You may be surprised to find that the more worldly Ten is fascinated by an open casket. This child is morbidly interested in seeing the dead, so long as it isn't someone he loved very much. Don't be alarmed about this. The incidentals of wakes and funerals are part of our culture and they help death seem more natural to children. It also helps if you treat the deaths of distant relations, or the distant past, with a little levity. Your child will like to hear about the preaching and weeping that went on when your grandfather died, and the excitement—and the gossiping—when the rich aunt's will was read.

The real discussions of death are matter-of-fact and frank, without fear or fakery or euphemisms. It's better to say that people die rather than "pass away"—especially since a child must pass from grade to grade—or that they "go to sleep," which could invite bedtime problems. You want your child to see the deaths of older people as you do—a regrettable but inevitable passing of responsibilities from one generation to the next.

Our flock was lucky enough to have the torch passed by an old great-aunt, Sister Teresa, a bright and saucy nun who ran a leper hospital in Louisiana for thirty years (and almost anything else she could get her hands on). We made the final family trip to say good-bye when she was eighty-five and then a trip just with Nell, the youngest of the clan, to say good-bye to the eldest. After that the children wrote regular letters to her, but in the end it was the telephone we'd arranged to have by her bed—her first private phone—that gave them their real link. They spoke with her regularly, for she was beloved, and saved money to help pay for the special call she made to her brother and sister in Ireland, who went five miles down the road to use the village phone.

The last call of all came to us at eight one morning when Teresa's best friend, in her slow Indiana cadence, said, "I knew you would want to be with us . . . Sister Teresa has had the last rites . . . I am holding her hand . . . She is breathing her last . . . This is it . . . There she goes . . . She is gone."

After the call the children ate their breakfast quietly and went on to school, sad but with a better understanding that death is part of life.

The death of the elderly, no matter how loved, usually causes less grief than the death of someone young. For a child to lose a good friend can be devastating. While a teenager will show emotion easily, a child in his Middle Years will only talk about the loss briefly or not at all. Don't be fooled. He still feels it deeply.

The death of a brother or a sister has far more serious repercussions. This loss is appalling and so is the reminder of his own immortality. Not only must he keep dealing with his everyday problems but he must wrestle with his grief (and yours). Now everything is topsy-turvy, even his place in the family. To become the first child instead of the second, or—even worse—to become the only child is very upsetting; to live without a twin is like living without a piece of himself. You can expect anger, guilt, withdrawal and poor school marks in the first year—reactions that will reappear in a younger child when he reaches the age of the one who died. A grieving child also may try to distract himself with ambitious projects or he may become super good or even try to act like the child who died, perhaps wearing that child's clothes. Some of this is inevitable, but if it seems extreme to you, he needs therapy.

OF A PARENT

The most traumatic death of all, not surprisingly, is the death of a parent. The loss, for girl or boy, can be almost overwhelming. With thoughtful guidance, however, he can be a stronger person for it. The child who can survive this knows he can survive anything.

In many cases the death is anticipated, and one parent—or both, if possible—can warn the child that it is expected. As sad as this is, the knowledge will soften the impact. You don't want to take away all hope—for hope, like love and laughter, is the medicine the terminally ill need most. Generally you want to talk in terms of comfort, however. Saying a family prayer that the ill parent will have a comfortable night or eat a good dinner tomorrow will give the child the feeling that he's doing something helpful. To help him decide which drawing, which poem, which dessert would make the best gift will give the child a gift too.

Every effort should be made now to keep life as routine and as low-key as possible; no one needs hysteria added to

the turmoil that's brewing inside. The healthy parent should help the child concentrate on his pets, his plants, his friends. The degree to which he will plunge himself into an activity now may surprise you, but when he engulfs himself in reading or soccer or even piano practice, he is simply dealing with his fears in the same furious way you might clean a closet at midnight.

To the dying parent who must surrender his (or her) young family to fortune, the stages of death are heartbreakingly acute. While passing through them, this parent must remain a parent to the end, setting the tone with grace and dignity and at a time when just a smile can be heroic. For some parents, the pain is so severe that this is impossible and the child may get furious at a mother's new and crotchety ways, a father's abrupt "Go away!" If this happens, the child may react in anger—and feel terribly guilty later.

Most terminal patients today are kept pain-free enough to deal with these profound changes constructively, however. One young mother with cancer wanted to leave something special to her three daughters and, at heaven knows what effort, she made each a quilt. Another mother, who had been known for her sharp tongue, met her diagnosis with bravery and a determinedly radiant disposition. Life had become too precious to squander—and her family was the better for it. And there was a young father who, on the long hospital nights, played the taped cassettes from home, very softly, and on good days recorded some of his wisdom and love and family history: his richest legacy.

Many people now find more solace and dignity in dying at home, but this is often impractical and most people are hospitalized as death approaches. This separation can add to a child's despair. The ordeal will be easier if the child can visit the parent even if some hospital rules must be bent, but if possible when the patient is fairly pain-free and upbeat. These visits are elixir to the parent who has so little time left to be loved and they are so good for the child. He can accept the changes as long as the patient looks tidy and smells fresh. Such visits also show him the efforts that are being made to help the parent—that indeed everything is being done that can be done—which helps to ease the remorse and regrets later. It is the unknown, the "what if?" that is so scary.

When death does come, a child has as much right to be there as anyone else, and if he is not, great care should be taken with the way he is told; if possible, the surviving parent should do the telling. It's also wise for a child—and any close survivor—to see the body before it's been beautified at the funeral home, unless death was caused by obvious injuries or the dying has wreaked great havoc. This is not as macabre as it sounds. When the spirit has gone, the body is obviously just a shell and death is more believable. This assures the child that the parent isn't going to be buried alive—a common fear among children.

If it's a family custom to have an open casket, it may be better to have it open only long enough for the immediate family to say their good-byes and then have it closed before visiting hours begin. The child shouldn't have to share this intimacy.

You'll also want your child to help choose the music or the readings for the funeral or the memorial service and to add whatever touch seems proper to him. He might like to put a memento or his picture in the casket or pick some garden flowers to leave on the coffin at the cemetery, or, as one child did, to ride alongside the driver in the hearse.

Friends and family will probably gather

at your house after the funeral, which can make your child feel lost and angry at the party atmosphere he thinks he sees. Ask a favorite adult friend of his to stay near him and take him out for a walk if he seems unsteady, because you won't be able to spend much time with him then.

No matter how well the child has been prepared for the death and how much he has helped to plan the funeral, he will mourn the loss of a parent deeply for months and probably a year. Even the young child who looks at death with a magical eye will go through the same stages as an adult, first denying it, then furious about it, then praying for a better deal and then depressed before he finally can accept such rotten luck.

There is a numbness after the death which lasts a few hours or perhaps a week. After he goes through the reactions to stress (see Stress), the child may wet the bed again and become more susceptible to infections and allergies. These symptoms may occur again later when he fully accepts the real, unchangeable truth, or when he's faced with holidays or the remarriage of the widowed parent. During these times the child deserves the tempting foods he gets when he's sick, for he is certainly sick at heart. Use a well-wrapped heating pad in bed and flannel sheets or a comforter for those sudden cold waves that can make small shoulders shudder. An extra undershirt is good by day. Earlier bedtimes help too, for fatigue is commonplace, and so are new bouts of temper; poor concentration; indecision; aggression; disorganization; hyperactivity; falling marks at school; sudden quiets. Patience and love are what he needs most.

Until the trauma is past, you can expect your child to ache just like you do, as if a weight were sitting on his chest: now each breath seems to hurt. Simply to know that this is a physical side effect of grief, and not a symptom of some threatening illness, will relieve your child's anxiety.

Now he is buffeted by anger, fear and especially guilt. Somehow he let his parent die. Every mean word he ever shouted and every word of love that went unsaid will make him feel guilty. Surely there was something he could have done, somehow. And there is the weight of embarrassment over his new status, the difference between him and his friends. Unless he has a sister or brother, he probably doesn't know anyone near his own age who has gone through the experience and who can, by his actions and sympathy, say, "I made it; so can you." He is alone in his grief, with no other small hand to hold. Anger will spill out at what seems the most inappropriate times. The contrast between his bad luck and a beautiful day can set off a tantrum over his breakfast cereal and neither of you will know the real reason.

The natural fear of abandonment is also much greater. Once one parent is gone, total abandonment seems much more likely. Even if he knows exactly where you are at all times (and he should), he may be afriad to be left alone for just a few hours, since death is always around the corner now. Nothing is safe. He also needs to know that you are healthy and doing your best to keep that way. And he needs to help you choose a provisional guardian for him, just in case you get hurt—or die. By addressing his fears, and by reassuring him, you belay the worst of them.

He also needs to know that you have enough money to get along, even if you have to get government help for a while, and that you'll do your best to stay in the same house and let him go to the same school—at least for a year. Even though you must make the final decisions, include him in this process. It is harder for a child to handle his secret speculations than it is for you, because you can draw on more information.

No matter how much he knows and how thoughtful you've been, he may be haunted by dreams and nightmares for months—and so may you—and then by day forget his sorrow for hours at a time. This can bring fresh guilt, for it is hard for a child to believe he has the right to be happy now. This is when he may try to conjure the face of the dead parent and find, to his terror, that the image has been forgotten. Although this is only temporary, it is so frightening that you should have pictures and, if possible, tape recordings around to reinforce memories.

Although your child goes through deep grief, it may not be too evident and his lack of tears may be his biggest problem, and yours. The spotlight that shines on the family now can seem so merciless, he may not be able to cry for weeks. When the tears do come, you (and he) may be tempted to believe that he indeed is shedding them for the dead animal he saw on his way home from school or because a special neighbor is moving away, but the truth, of course, is that the dam is breaking. Welcome it.

If he is not ready to talk about the pain, have him go to weepy movies or read books that give him a good excuse to cry. Reminiscences keep the flow going too and he'll soon be ready for them. Recollect the good times you had together, and then ask your child what he misses most, but do this in the dark—talking (and listening) after he's gone to bed, while you hold his hand or gently rub his back. This is how you send feelings from your heart to his.

You'll also want to give your child the details of the death, even though he's heard them before, for the initial numbness may have blocked his memory. When you share these, again and again, the reality of the death begins to penetrate. Now there will be a thousand questions—particularly if the death was sudden—and you may have to ask for answers from someone who was there. Please do. Your child will be thrilled to hear that the sound of his name brought a smile to his parent's face.

All deaths of parents are traumatic but circumstances make some of them even worse—especially suicide. In this case the surviving parent must talk longer and more often about the death, although the emphasis will be on the why, not the how, and that the deep depression probably had a chemical cause—a real probability that is sure to make the child feel better. Whatever the reason, your child will definitely need to see a therapist.

This may be necessary whatever the cause of death, particularly if the tears don't come, and if he shows serious signs of withdrawal or rebellion or if he gets very poor marks in school. While it's true that a repressed emotion may one day explode, it is more likely to freeze a child's psychological growth. Without help, he will grow into the adult who acts like a grown-up, until he's faced with a crisis, and then he reverts, emotionally, to the age he was when he suffered the great trauma.

You may find yourself giving your child so much sympathy and understanding—and getting so much in return—that you begin to depend on him more than you should. Be careful. A son cannot replace the dead father as "the man of the house" (nor is a daughter "the little mother" for her dad). Although the parent who is left may think these are positive things to say, the child will be awed by such responsibility. No matter how the family unit changes, his position in it must stay the same. A child is a child.

Although both of you will find vulnerabilities you never knew you had, you will find new strengths too. You encourage these strengths by working together while also moving along in your own independent ways. In the early months you spend extra time writing thank-you letters, solving insurance problems and dealing with the idea of too little money or occasionally too much (it's never in between), which may make you either a penny pincher or a spendthrift and not necessarily in relationship to your bank balance. While you may need to see a trusted financial adviser, your child will need a favorite adult to spend time with him, to take him to the movies—sometimes even on a school night.

And he needs you to set up low-key activities for him, so he will find it easier to confide in others his own age. Boys—and especially girls—need a good friend now. Building and strengthening these friendships is difficult at first, for children haven't worked out the ritualistic things to say about death and they feel awkward. It takes understanding on all sides. Within a few weeks you'll want to structure your child's time so he will look outward. The energetic child may become almost frenetic in his actions, unless he can pummel some of the anger from his soul. Sports will let him do this best—not team sports but the kind that make him compete against himself, like swimming or ice skating or running.

As you build new lives, you want to help your child remember the dead parent truthfully, without sanctification. To deify a parent sets impossible standards for the child when he grows up, and certainly for a stepparent. This doesn't mean, of course, that the parent who dies is ever denigrated or forgotten. One caring mother would take her four daughters to the cemetery for a gentle, reminiscing picnic on their father's birthday, so the girls could grow up knowing that the family was different but, in its way, still complete. As long as a person is remembered, he still lives.

OF A CHILD

There is no good time to lose a child. Parents who have had a miscarriage, a stillborn baby, an infant death know a grief that is almost too big to bear—and that's just the beginning. Each day a child lives makes the pain of parting that much greater.

If the death is expected, the time and energy parents have invested will demand an extra measure of grief, but if it is accidental, the rage and guilt are that much worse. If you are losing—or have lost—a child, you should know that you will heal—not completely and not soon, but you will heal.

As each unhappy family is unhappy in its own way, so is each person. Nothing is quite as individual as the way we express our grief, but there are certain universal reactions. From the moment you get the news, the grief will roll in on you in waves, first of numbness, then detachment, then weeping and then numbness again: nature's cycle that will protect you from the constant intensity of grief. It will get worse and then get better, but just knowing what to expect should bring some comfort.

The type of funeral and the style of mourning are individual matters that reflect your family and your culture. Most parents who have lost a child have found that a public funeral, rather than a private memorial service, is better, because they needed all the sympathy they could get. In exchange they had to console their grieving friends and, as exhausting as that was, at least it gave them a job to do. Whatever kind of service you choose, be content with it afterward. Even though you might, on reflection, wish you had done some things differently, it's pointless to fret. Surely your child would forgive you if he were alive; be as generous to yourself.

When you're able to take it, the numbness and detachment will wear away and you'll find yourself engulfed with pain. Falling asleep will be hard for a long time, but not as hard as waking—that awful moment, day after day, when you realize again that your child is dead. During the day, concentration is scatty and tears may spill unbidden, anyplace. It's just as well. The tears we shed in sorrow are chemically different from those that spring when we slice onions—a sign, perhaps, that our bodies don't want to keep those bad chemicals inside.

All of this puts your marriage and any other relationships within the family to a terrible test. Nine out of ten couples—even those who handled the preceding illness well—have serious marital problems when a child dies. The more grief you feel, the less comfort you can give and the more comfort you need—and yet your husband has so little to spare. This is sure to make you angry. You also clash because each of you is going through the stages of grief at a different pace, not just from week to week but day to day. Smiles and tears don't synchronize anymore and the moods of one person may anger and alienate the other. Be very careful about this. As mad as you might get, the death of your marriage will only make the death of your child that much harder to bear. Grief should be expressed in positive ways.

While the best person to share your sorrow will be your husband, he can't take it for long. Some couples find it easier to set aside a fixed time every day to mourn and grieve together. When that half hour is past, they shut the door on their pain for another day. This daily catharsis will help you put life in perspective, so you won't start expecting bad luck or carry the anger of grief into other relationships or mishandle your personal life.

There are signs that signal trouble: if you blame each other for your child's death; if one or both of you turn his room into a shrine; if you make a mess of the family accounts; if you drink or take pills to block out the pain; if you stop having sex or drift toward an extramarital affair. Any of these responses would compound the problem and so would a move, a change of jobs or a separation in the year following your child's death. Many rash decisions are made in grief. Basically, you just have to tough it out and it will be much, much easier if you have help.

The best help is probably free. There are small chapters of self-help groups, like Compassionate Friends and the Candlelighters, all over the country where bereaved parents (and grandparents) console each other and share practical advice (see Resources). Having lost children of their own, they will understand your pain and be patient enough to hear you talk about it, over and over, until it begins to be bearable.

And talking is what you must do, even if it's not your style. You need friends (or strangers) who ask, "How's it going?" and care enough to listen, but choose these people well. Forget those who try to be blithe, telling you to "Buck up!" or expecting you to agree that the child is "better off" or that he's happier in heaven or that that's the way life is. Nor do you want to be concerned with the opinions of the judgmental who look askance if you wear bright colors or go to a party (or wear dark clothes and stay home).

This sense of being judged can haunt most parents whose children died accidentally, for they are sure the death was caused by too much discipline or too little. You may find yourself grabbing for guilt over the smallest "if only," when all that matters is that you loved your child and your child knew it and that you still love your child and you're still able to love others. If guilt takes over instead, it can make you feel like a failure as a parent and make any other children in the family feel as if they've failed as siblings, for they will reflect your emotions.

Surviving children have other reactions. They frequently complain that their parents give them neither the attention nor the discipline they need. They also feel a sense of inadequacy, if they think their parents are comparing the living to the dead. To counteract this, you want to continue to spend at least ten quiet minutes a day with each child each day, to talk not about the child you lost but about the one who needs you now. Every child needs this time, but a grieving child must have it. Studies show that a child survives the death of a parent quite well, as long as he lives in a nurturing home.

You also have to help the child remember the one who died as a dear person, not a saint. Remind him of all the nice things he did for that child (he'll remember the bad ones without any help). And over and over you must tell him that everyone gets mad enough sometimes to wish his sister or brother would die and that wishes don't make it so. This gives a child the right to grieve and assures him that your love for him will help you smile again, as soon as you can.

Smiling takes practice—and so does everything else. In the first few months you will find yourself barely able to function and then you push—or somebody pushes you—and you take the first small steps back to reality: a new blouse one day; a night of bowling the next week; a bit of volunteer work, each a little step taking you further into the mainstream. You'll find you can take these steps best if you make some changes, by celebrating holidays a little differently and by taking up new projects as a family, as a couple and individually. Keeping busy, in new ways, is the key.

There will be setbacks, of course. You'll find yourself going out of your way to avoid a favorite picnic spot or a certain brand of cookies. A special family retreat will seem empty and holidays and birthdays will always be hard, but bit by bit you'll recover, a sadder person, but richer for what you once had.

DIVORCE

Divorce is what happens when there's nothing left in a marriage. There are no options. There is no hope. Counseling didn't work. Religion didn't help. The best intentions failed. You feel like you're going to implode.

You decide to divorce because you must, and you do it in total exhaustion. It is never quick, never easy, and when there are children or money involved it usually takes about five years to recover, with the most dramatic—and melodramatic—reactions occurring in the first two. And that's with some therapy.

There is the emotional separation and the real separation; the emotional divorce and the real divorce. (Unfortunately, the emotional divorce often lags far behind the paperwork), since most people now go through the legal process so quickly, and this makes the pain seem endless. This is not said to frighten you. (If you're contemplating divorce, it's important to know what to expect, so it won't hit you—and your child—quite so hard.)

Divorce brings many emotional surprises, from the moment you separate. It may be a euphoria that lifts you skyward. Why did it ever take you so long to decide? The *joie de vivre* that comes with this relief can last for several months. While one of you may feel relieved, the other is stricken by shock or denial. Who said there was anything wrong with this marriage anyway?

All of these reactions mask the sorrow that comes with divorce. The marriage is an identity in itself, and its death is as traumatic as the death of a mate and as deeply grieved. Both you and your hus-

band can expect to follow the same pattern of pain, fury and depression that you would if the other had committed suicide, for divorce is the suicide of a marriage. The longer the relationship has existed, the more it hurts to kill it.

However you react, you have to confront your grief, just as you would confront any loss. This is the way to grow from one stage to the next, until finally you can accept your role in the marriage so you can forgive your role in the divorce. Your contribution to the failure is the toughest thing to admit. Unless you married in madness or discovered that your husband was abusive or homosexual, you must unravel years of love to see how you helped to make things go wrong. It's as painful as it is necessary. By accepting responsibility for the past, you're much less likely to repeat the pattern in the future.

It doesn't make the divorce process easier, however. Even with therapy, there will be times when you get so confused and disoriented that you almost feel daffy and many other times when you will feel overwhelmed, ambivalent and depressed. You also will feel a relentless hurt and be so angry you'll find yourself using extreme verbs to describe the most everyday thoughts. You'll hate an old dress; want to murder a rude waitress; wish you could die over some trifling thing. Your sense of perspective goes askew and you may make foolish decisions about money or men or you might use sleeping pills, tranquilizers or alcohol to help you get along, a choice that only makes matters worse for you and your child. Never must you try so hard to set a good example.

Your child is your biggest concern. He's going through at least as many emotional swings as you are. He feels guilty, for children are still so self-centered in these years that they will feel responsible for the divorce; and he'll feel ashamed to be different from his friends, for children don't tell each other much about their family problems now. He'll also be very

angry and usually express it with the parent with whom he feels safer, although he'll get mad about issues of the moment and may not mention the divorce at all. Above all, he feels afraid. What's going to happen to him?

You can lessen his burden a little bit by telling him why you are divorcing. To insist that you're "not in love" anymore can be frightening to a child, who would think you might stop loving him. You don't want to explain the divorce by belittling his father or by giving your child the grisly details of an affair, but he does need some specifics, like "we fight all the time" or "Daddy worked at the office so much, we drifted apart." Because each parent will divorce for different reasons, the conflicting statements will help your child see how complicated it is.

Even if your child pretends he isn't curious or doesn't care—and some children do—he needs encouragement to express his feelings, in tears and in words, although you don't want him to dwell on his unhappiness so much that he feeds his own despair. Instead, tell your child that you love him, over and over; that his dad loves him; that life is full of adventures— good and bad—and it's how he handles them that count. This helps the child realize that he can emerge from this experience a stronger, more sensitive person, because he can choose how he plays the cards that he's dealt.

It will be easier if he knows you depend on him to run neighborhood errands to earn a little money, to help you with the cooking and to work around the house. For best results, hang a chart on the wall with the list of jobs that need doing, without assigning them but with a column for you and your child to initial when they're done. The checks become a point of pride, especially if you reward extra-good work with an exclamation point after his check.

All of this will help the child deal with his grief, but he'll still need therapy. It will give him a specific time and place to pour out his heart and to do it without hurting

his parents. Some individual sessions would be best, followed by group sessions with other children of divorce. By talking with his equals, he begins to realize that it's better to have parents who live alone in relative peace than those who stay together in war—and that their warfare is their problem, not his. You also should encourage him to tell his friends about the divorce, so he won't feel so alone, and to admit to a few of them how much it hurts.

Your own clearheadedness will give your child the example he needs. Never has it been so necessary. You have so much to do and so many decisions to make. The decision to divorce is only the first of many. The things you and your husband couldn't agree on before you separate will continue to haunt you as long as you have children in school: money, child care, shared responsibility, in-laws.

You don't want to sign anything in haste or you may feel ashamed of the demands you've won or foolish about the rights you've forfeited. Property, and particularly custody, must be settled with measured speed and in the most humane way and not to win another round. This isn't easy. With so much tension between you, it's time for a referee.

An experienced, certified mediator is usually better than a divorce lawyer and much cheaper, because her hourly fee is lower and is shared by the husband and wife. The mediator, who may be a social worker, a counselor or a lawyer, usually lowers the tension and may even be able to avert the divorce, by defining the problems in a nonaccusatory way. In either case, she starts with the easiest problem and works

on it with the couple until it's solved—sometimes in one session, sometimes in more—and then she goes on to the next. It's her job to keep the dialogue on track, searching for agreement on any point.

A lawyer may be needed to take this agreement through court for the final decree or you may both need lawyers instead of a mediator if you're going to contest each point. In this case, you can expect to pay dearly, in both money and pain. Because of the litigious nature of legal work—and because lawyers want to win for their clients—they turn complaints into charges and countercharges that often seem much harsher on paper than they did in reality. These bombshell letters can escalate your anger, making negotiation between you much more difficult in the years ahead. Divorce is tough enough without that.

You're divorcing not only your husband but your way of life. Suddenly your family budget takes a nosedive and your friends take a powder. Dividing the dishes is easy compared to dividing your friends. It's very hard for both of you to keep the same friends and the loss you'll feel will be great. You also will feel judged. Those whose marriages are troubled—whether they know it or not—may be outraged, no matter how strong and how public your case; and even if you've been very discreet, many of your friends will make moral judgments on the flimsiest inferences. Others may say nothing but soon quit calling. This can sour you or make you think that all of your friends have turned against you, but that isn't fair to them. They are probably just responding to cues you hardly know you're sending. Withdrawal is common in grief. It's important to keep calling your friends, as hard as it may be to reach out to them now. You and your child need all the support you can get from them, and from sympathetic members of your family or the clergy.

This support will help you keep your equilibrium, but beware of live-in relationships and remarriages for a couple of years.

It's not only too unsettling for a child but it's too easy to rebound into another mistake. Remarriage will probably be in your future, however, since three fourths of all divorced women (and even more men) remarry but give yourself time to know who you are. Marriages usually break up if the wife (or the husband) pretends to be someone she's not, in order to please someone else, who isn't the kind of person she thought he was. You need enough time alone to define yourself so you can know who really meets your need, and will accept you as you are.

And out of this mournful time you'll gradually find that the hurt and the anger begin to ebb and you can even talk to your ex-husband in a fairly civilized way. You won't be the same person you were before the divorce, but with effort you will be a better one, for you will have faced reality and remade your life to suit it.

CUSTODY

Custody and visitation rights are more vital, and carry more psychological freight, than anything else in the divorce negotiation. The more generous and understanding you can be about these issues, the easier the divorce will be, particularly for your child. He is entitled to have you put his needs first.

While he shouldn't be put in the awkward position of choosing the parent with whom he wants to live, he should know the plans you're making and be able to make suggestions of his own. It's traditional for the mother to be the primary parent, but an increasing number of fathers compete for the privilege. In either case the child usually stays with one parent during the school year and goes to the other for most or all weekends, holidays and summer vacation.

Other parents find joint custody is the best solution, and in the Middle Years it often is, for it helps a child stay close to both parents. Parents divvy up the week or the month, so their child moves from one to the other. This means two rooms, two wardrobes, two collections of toys and books—and parents who get along well enough to pass doctor appointments and car-pooling duties back and forth between them. These are complicated arrangements that boggle the mind but they can work well if the parents live nearby and are able to be polite to each other. Remarriage, relocation and the child's own social schedule usually cause custody to revert to a principal parent by early adolescence, however. Whatever the custody arrangements, they should be in writing—like all divorce agreements—and they must be scrupulously upheld, in word and deed.

It behooves you to respect your child's time with his dad by seeing that he is clean, neat and ready when his dad is due, and that you don't use these encounters to talk to his dad about issues between you. This would cloud the visit for both of them, making the father less likely to see the child and leading to other postdivorce problems. A father who sees his child regularly keeps up much better with child support. You'll also make your child unhappy if you encourage him, however tacitly, to tattle on his father or if you listen to complaints his father made about you. Don't get snookered into these games.

Nor should you and your ex-husband compete by plying your child with attention and gifts, a game that many divorced parents begin out of guilt and their children often encourage, often without realizing it. You'd only be teaching your child how to use people.

And if his father doesn't see him regularly—or at all—you can only hold your child tight and explain, as best you can, that his guilt and shame (or his drug abuse or his alcoholism) make it hard for him to be as loving and reliable as he wants to be, but that the two of you are strong enough to get along alone.

CHILD SUPPORT

A divorce, born of insoluble problems, will end some of them and create others, especially about money. Once the settlement is reached, you should, as pleasantly as possible, insist that it's followed, as you would any other business arrangement. Late or missing payments will only get worse if your ex-husband thinks you won't object. This will also affect his relationship with your child, because he will be embarrassed to see you and won't visit as often.

There are many ways to get the money, and most of them are usually cheaper and easier than you might think. A caseworker at the child support collection agency in your state can reclaim late child support or child support combined with maintenance (but not alimony), by having your ex-husband's tax refund intercepted or by getting an order to deduct the money from his salary, his workman's compensation, his unemployment insurance or his Social Security income, even if you live in a different state. And if these solutions don't apply, the family court in your city will bring your ex-husband to trial, wherever he lives in the United States, without your having to hire a lawyer or appear in court.

A lawyer is needed, however, to get the court to put a restraining order on your ex-husband's bank account or an attachment on his property, so he can't sell or transfer it without paying you what he owes.

CHILD ABUSE

We have probably all hurt our preschool children at one time or another with angry explosions or spankings that were too hard or unnecessary, but if this treatment goes on into the Middle Years the effect is much greater. No matter what happens or when, it seldom seems as extreme to us as it does to the children. We may get an awful feeling of guilt in the pit of the gut, but we rarely realize how much power we have and how easy it is to abuse it. Fortunately most children accept our fallibility as well as our love.

Some parents, however, are so impulsive that they cross the clinical line. Parents who are immature, unaffectionate and overly strict may physically abuse their children and, despite rather plausible stories, the bruises and breaks they inflict aren't accidental. Other parents abuse their children emotionally. They may have roller-coaster moods that pull firm land out from under their children, or they may destroy their children's confidence by repeated bursts of sarcasm, uncontained anger or periods of withdrawal—behavior that can be even more demeaning than a slap or a push.

In either kind of abuse, some children are targeted more often than others. The high-risk parent may be tempted to abuse a child for a variety of reasons. One attacks the child who is wilder, weaker, sicker or different from the others in some way or who looks like an ex-spouse now held in disregard. Another parent may be tempted to abuse her child if she has no private time to be alone, no confidante or no safe place to leave the children while she seeks a little peace. Yet another parent may lash out if the child can't meet her expectations or if the child is entering a new stage and she finds it hard to let go. Other parents use abuse to correct their children because they were corrected that way themselves. An abusive mother has often been physically or verbally abused by her husband, or was abused by her father as a teenager; an abusive father is more likely to hurt his child if he's been abused by his mother as a teenager or if his mother often hit his father. There are also high-risk times for both physical and emotional abuse: when you're getting the children off to school and getting dinner ready for the table.

The longer the abusive behavior continues, the harder it is for parents to change, which makes counseling essential, either in individual therapy or in a self-help group on child abuse (see Resources). The abusive parent must also learn to stop, mid-sentence or mid-strike, and to follow some or all of these well-tested measures: take five deep, slow breaths; retreat from the scene; put on a soothing record; do fifteen jumping jacks; meditate; take a bubble bath; call a friend or Dial-a-Prayer; write in a diary or look through the baby album—perhaps the best way to feel warm and soft again.

SEXUAL ABUSE

Sexual abuse is both physical and emotional and is more damaging, and more heartbreaking, than any other kind. Here the pleasure of an adult depends on the abasement of a child. The abuse may be verbal—the obscene phone calls or frank discussions of sexual acts. Or the abuser may try to peek in the child's window or expose himself or let the child hear or see intercourse. Or the abuser may fondle the child, touch the genitals—or have the child touch his—or try (and perhaps succeed) to have intercourse, using either guile or force.

Sexual abuse, of all kinds, is much more prevalent than you might think, since only one out of three cases is probably reported. Somehow children seldom tell and, when they do, it may seem too embarrassing for a mother to repeat. But experts think that seven or eight girls out of a hundred are seriously molested by the time they're Fourteen, almost always by a male. Although boys aren't assaulted nearly as often, no child is immune from the threat of it, nor is any culture or any class. The victim may live in a rich home or a poor one, in the city or the country, in any state and can be of any age, although children of Eight, Ten, Eleven and Thirteen seem to be targeted most.

While sexual abuse steals innocence in the most devastating, primitive way, it usually grows out of a friendly or even loving relationship. About 85% of the time the abuser is a friend, a sitter, a youth worker, a neighbor—or, more likely, someone in the family, and with increasing frequency, the stepfamily, whose members break taboos more easily because they haven't bonded yet.

The transition from affection to abuse is critical. The offenses, which seem so cuddly to the child at first, soon escalate and so does the child's guilt. Yet it is the adult who is always responsible, even when a preteen begins to practice her flirty ways on every male in the household. A child will be in her mid-teens before she can truly accept responsibility for her actions, and even then she will blame only herself.

Sexual incidents are often so minor at first that your child may think there's something wrong with her for suspecting anything, or that they are so obvious you must know (and approve). That's when the incidents get worse and the child is too embarrassed to admit what's happening. This is how the child molester escapes detection and, if that doesn't work, he has other strings to pull. He may tell her she's being a baby if she says no or, if she threatens to tell, he may say that he would go to jail or lose his job or his wife—all big threats if the person is someone the child has known or loved for a long time. And if these arguments don't work, he might threaten to hurt her, although force usually isn't necessary to keep a child quiet. Just the age and the size of the molester imply force enough.

Since children hate to admit sexual abuse, parents should know that the abuser, the circumstances and the victim all follow certain patterns, which a parent can detect.

The abuser may
- have come from a strict, authoritarian family—often with a religious or military background—where emotions were sublimated and punishment was used to discipline children;
- have been abused as a child, sexually or otherwise, or he physically abused his own wife or child;
- be a loner who only can make friends with children;

- have been charged with a sexual offense already.

His behavior is different too. He may

- drink a great deal, either to cloud his judgment or excuse it; the molester is intoxicated in a third of the cases;
- flirt with the child, and often comment on her beauty, her body and her charm, in ways that make it sound as if he's talking about an adult;
- continue to touch or tickle her, even when the child says "Don't";
- invent occasions to invite the child to his place regularly, although he has no child of his own.

Whatever the assault, it is a scarring experience that always leaves the child ashamed, angry, scared—and likely to be victimized again, for transgressions, if they seem to be accepted, are usually repeated and escalated. This is reason enough for parents to warn their children. This is almost always embarrassing. Here you are, explaining the kinky side of sex when you've barely explained the facts of life. It's like putting out the garbage: it has to be done. Both boys and girls must learn what is dangerous, with the explanations getting more explicit as they get older. Treat the matter as naturally as possible, using words like "penis," "vagina," "erection" and "anus"; this is no time for either vulgarisms or euphemisms.

You also need to explain that sickness of the mind and spirit takes many forms; that this is one of them and that such disturbed people may live in your own neighborhood and be someone who is known and accepted in the family—even a relative. Since these people usually act like anyone else, your child needs to know what to do when they don't.

This will give your child an aura of confidence that tells adults that she can take care of herself and, furthermore, she will. By first grade she should know absolutely that no one has the right to ask her to take off any of her clothes, or put a hand beneath them, or fondle her or tickle her tummy—not for love or money or milk and cookies—and by Ten she must know she's too old to sit on laps anymore. When a child knows that "accidental" body touching or prolonged tickling and wrestling is an intended approach, she can prevent its development by turning away promptly and decisively.

You also have to tell her to beware of anyone who often rubs his body against hers or pats her or who tries to give her sloppy kisses on the mouth or asks her to lie on the sofa with him to watch TV, or who undresses in front of her or exposes himself, or who wants to take her picture—naked. You not only say this directly, but you give this message when you teach your child that she has the right to offer her hand to be shaken instead of her cheek to be kissed. This tells her that her body is truly her own.

Tell your daughter (or your son) that if anyone makes an advance, whether it's happened before or not, she should say, "NO," and scream and keep screaming as she runs the other way. She should tell the first person she sees, even a stranger, and stay with him until you, or the police, arrive. There's little likelihood that two perverts will be working the same block at the same time. And if your child can't run, teach her to kick and hit her attacker in the shin and the testicles. This lets her imagine how she would protect herself. Every time she learns how to handle a crisis she will be a little safer. Here is a case where knowledge is truly power.

It's also important that your child knows she should tell you if someone molests her or even scares her—no matter who he is—and that you will understand and protect her and be discreet about it, for a child is terrified by the prospect of a big scene and what the reactions will be. She may keep quiet about an incident if she thinks her parents won't believe her, or will get mad at her, or laugh, or think she invited the advance, or that the abuser might say she permitted some liberties at first (which may be true). This can frighten a child not only into silence but into repeated involvement, and greater and greater shame, for the child always accepts the blame and deserves none of it, even into the teens.

While the abuser often knows the child, there probably won't be sex abuse at home unless there are several complicating factors. Among them:

- the family is under great stress;
- the home is overcrowded, remote or extremely poor;
- the family follows a strict, judgmental religious code;
- the family has no friends or social activities;
- there is a history of child abuse in the family;
- there is an unequal or unhappy relationship between the parents;
- the husband is deeply angry at the wife;
- the mother or the father may be away for a long time, or even permanently;
- the husband is denied sex, for one reason or another, for long periods of time;
- the family roles are skewed, with the child perhaps cooking or caring for the other children;
- the family members have trouble controlling their impulses;
- someone in the family is addicted to alcohol or drugs;
- the abuser has a very low self-esteem;
- the victim seems vulnerable, at least to the abuser;
- the abuser or the victim is mentally slow.

A mother generally knows, on some level, if sexual abuse is going on in her own home and yet she usually ignores it, as if denial could make her child safe again. If this happens, the child is truly dismayed, for she is sure her mother knows and approves. This, coupled with her now battered self-esteem, encourages the abuse to continue, get worse or spread to younger sisters or brothers.

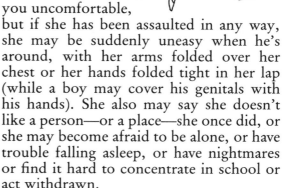

Every mother must be strong enough to consider the possibility of sexual abuse if her child displays many of its symptoms. If someone has been making surreptitious approaches, your child may act flirtatious around him and make you uncomfortable, but if she has been assaulted in any way, she may be suddenly uneasy when he's around, with her arms folded over her chest or her hands folded tight in her lap (while a boy may cover his genitals with his hands). She also may say she doesn't like a person—or a place—she once did, or she may become afraid to be alone, or have trouble falling asleep, or have nightmares or find it hard to concentrate in school or act withdrawn.

This is the child who may have extreme changes in behavior—perhaps even lose her appetite and have nightmares or wet the bed again, or she may cry often, suck her thumb, act babyish or fantasize, be withdrawn and silent or aggressive and disruptive. She may get to school early and stay late or have trouble making friends or be nervous around certain people or perhaps be afraid of someone or dislike him intensely. Or the child may act provocative or vulnerable, in a sexual way, or have an unusual interest in sex or know a surprising amount about it.

Whether the child was forced to have relations or not, she may be angry or hostile with grown-ups—especially parents—or use alcohol or drugs or start failing in school or shoplift, often trying to buy friendships by giving away the goods to other children. Or she may ask to live with another relative or say she's afraid to be alone with her father or afraid to go home or simply say that her mother's boyfriend "does things" to her.

In severe cases the sexually abused child may have physical signs: torn or stained underpants; vaginal or rectal bleeding, pain or itching; swollen genitals or vaginal discharge; vaginal infections or even venereal disease.

If your child has any of the serious symptoms or sends many of the lesser signals you must encourage her to talk. It's a scene to be played very gently and in her own room, at night, holding hands and with the lights out, so she doesn't have to face you. Tell her you're worried and why and give her time to talk and talk and many long pauses to fill. Listen well, repeating what you don't understand as a question, so she will either clarify it or agree with you. Tell her you're sorry, cry with her and hug her tight, but try not to show your shock or she might stop talking. Above all, believe in her. It will devastate her if you say, "You must have misunderstood. You know Mr. Brown didn't mean to do that!" or "How could you say such a thing about your own grandfather?" A child almost never makes up a story about sexual abuse, of even the mildest sort.

Instead thank her for telling you and be calm so she will feel free to describe the whole scene. It's one that will haunt her unless she has the chance to talk about it completely, and many times. Congratulate her for handling it well—even if a serious pass was made and completed—so she can feel she is still a good and an approved person. Tell her that you love her absolutely and that you know it's not her fault, no matter what she did or how often or how freely she acquiesced at first or if she was flirtatious. This is essential, for it will help to rebuild her self-esteem. The stronger it is, the less she's likely to be a prey to sexual abuse again.

If rape was attempted—or if it was successful—you should call a rape crisis center immediately to know how to get a medical examination and a dilation and curettage if necessary (to prevent the possible trauma of an abortion later for an older child). The center can also tell you where to get counseling and how to file charges in a way that will be least embarrassing for your child.

It is essential that you back her completely when she gives this report, both for her own sense of honor and to make the authorities believe her, but you want to back her in your own mind too. No matter what the circumstances, a child of Twelve (or even Fifteen) may not be old enough to protect herself against a child molester. It would, of course, be tempting to let less serious offenses slide, but that's not fair to other children. Most abusers repeat their crimes again and again.

You even have to take action if your own husband, or ex-husband, is responsible. Although the fairly rare pedophiliac will almost always molest again, most sex abusers may be helped if the mother openly protects the child. If a member of the family is involved and the family is intact, the agency will do its best to keep it together, unless the child is still at risk.

While you will contact the child protection services, it's also your unpleasant responsibility to speak to the offender, if you know who he is, without hysterics or accusations. Simply say that your child was frightened by him and why. He will almost surely deny it, but that is irrelevant, and so is the outcome of any pending charges. Whether he said anything or not, or did anything or not, your child is afraid of him, and therefore he must never be with her unless one of her parents is there too. It is a nonnegotiable point, even if you're dealing with a relative.

This will not be enough to soothe your child, however. She also needs individual and family therapy, many reassurances, much advice to avoid future encounters and an old-fashioned rubber wedge to stop anyone from opening her door without permission, for no matter where the abuse occurred, this child feels unsafe—even in her own room. And give her time. Let her talk about it as many times as she wants; let her know you are there—and let her be angry. This is part of the healing process. Some things can't be undone, but with help and understanding they won't hurt quite so much.

THE
WORLD

When you send your child to first grade, you give a hostage to fortune—and no one knows this better than you. Every problem you ever had in school combines with all the ones you ever heard about to make school seem pretty scary.

Age is usually a parent's biggest concern. If your child has an October birthday you're sure you're sending him too soon, and if he was born in January you're afraid he's too old for first grade. Timing usually isn't a problem for a daughter, but a son who was born in the fall may be too young, since boys usually take about six months longer to mature. When in doubt about either boy or girl, it's better to hold back than to push ahead. Starting school early won't make a child any smarter when he grows up, but it can make the growing up more difficult, for he may act younger than his classmates and find it hard to make friends. Without them he loses his self-confidence.

Parents, who are such professional worriers, have other fears as well.

• The school bus (or the walk) may not be safe. (It almost always is.)
• She may not eat her lunch. (But ask yourself—will she starve?)
• He may have trouble with his schoolwork because he's left-handed. (But so was Michelangelo.)
• The other children may tease him about his lisp. (They probably will, but not for a year or two and by then he may outgrow it.)
• The other children may dress differently. (So buy most of her clothes and school supplies a couple of weeks after school starts, so she'll know what's in style.)

The biggest fear of all comes from your heart: "My child might not need me anymore." Time will dissolve this fear. The needs of an infant, a toddler or a preschooler are piffling compared to the needs of a schoolchild, particularly at Seven and Nine and Eleven—and as a teenager your child will need you more than ever before.

Forget the "what ifs?" and concentrate instead on the pluses of school. They can hardly be exaggerated. School for the Six or Seven is the right adventure at the right time. Perfect. Nothing gives these children such a great sense of importance and responsibility. Those who had been comfortable in nursery school, kindergarten or day care find school a challenge, not a threat, although they may be surprised to lose the personal attention they used to get and to share the spotlight—and the teacher—with all those other children.

On top of that, they will be away from home six hours a day, five days a week, taking orders from grown-ups who aren't their parents and depending on strangers to be their friends. But it *will* be exciting. This is a positive age for friendships, and your child will learn almost as much by playing and working with new people as he does from his books and his schoolwork.

You and your child will be less anxious about school if you tour it together ahead of time, observing first grade through sixth to get the full picture and a sense that he will be ready for the grade he's going to enter. Your child will still have fears and doubts, however, although not the same as yours. The newness of the school is scary for the first few weeks—as it is every year—even if he has visited that classroom before. Just getting the teacher's name straight will make children fearful. The uncertainties will make them tense their whole bodies at first, and they will be exhausted at the end of each day. Your child also may cry, act babyish, shy or aggressive, while adjusting to a new teacher, new work, new expectations and at least some new friends.

287

The transition isn't easy, but your child will know you appreciate his efforts if you celebrate that first week with a Friday night supper at the pizza parlor. It's hard to overstate the impact of school on your child, even when he seems to take it in stride. A fixed schedule, including good food and plenty of sleep, is particularly reassuring because it helps the child look at school as a job—a normal responsibility of life.

Children do their best in school not because they already know their letters and numbers, not because their parents work in the PTA, not because they have the best clothes, but because, right down to their toes, each one of them knows he is Somebody. They have the physical confidence that comes from climbing and running for years, so they feel comfortable about their bodies. They have social confidence because they have spent a lot of time with other children and have had a lot of laughs. And they have gotten so much love and respect at home that they can afford to give plenty to their teachers and their classmates. School seems wonderful to this child, even if it's mediocre, but as a parent you want something better than that.

THE THREE ESSENTIALS

A good school is a happy place and it takes three elements to make it that way: a strong principal, able teachers and involved parents. They work together to develop a clear philosophy and certain distinctive characteristics: the relationship between adults and children is open and trusting; the discipline is caring and supportive; the teachers are well trained in their subjects, and the children are treated equally, so that boys get fair grades and as many smiles as

girls (even though most girls are quieter and neater and suit the teacher better) and girls have the chance to do the daring deeds that are usually given to boys. Above all, the adults expect the children to make mistakes—because they are children. In this fine school, volunteers are not only welcome but sought after, and new ideas and new materials are welcome too, as long as they further the curriculum and its teaching.

THE PRINCIPAL

The success of a school almost always depends on the skill and dedication of the principal, for she sets the standards. If she is strong and the curriculum healthy, it will suit most children and most parents most of the time.

A good principal administers well; lets her faculty help her make decisions; generates as little paperwork for them as possible; uses the intercom infrequently—so the classes aren't disrupted—and is as mannerly to the janitor and the children as she is to her supervisor and the members of her school board.

The choice of a principal is particularly important in a school that's quite big or quite small. In a big one, she must be skilled enough to handle a large budget and many problems and people, while a small school requires an exceptionally imaginative person to juggle a low budget and extend the resources of a small faculty. Here the slightest lack of leadership is felt in every classroom, for there is never enough personnel to handle the work that a poor principal leaves undone.

Ideally, an elementary school has a middle-sized enrollment—maybe 300–500 children—so the principal can visit each classroom each week and can call each new child (and each old child) by name. She will also have time and staff to create a strong cultural and economic profile of each student so she can try to get the supplemental help they may need.

In a well-run school the principal sets

expectations, for both scholarship and behavior, and lets the children know what will happen if they don't comply; but even for serious infractions the discipline is caring and supportive, not harsh or humiliating. Even a Six is too old for a spanking at home and certainly at school, where the effects would be so much greater and the shame more public.

Much discipline is unnecessary if the principal has worked with the faculty to set up good supervision in the halls and the cafeteria and on the playground. She also sees that the bathrooms are kept clean and orderly, for the bathrooms at school rank right after food in order of importance to children. If they are usually dirty or untidy or if groups of children gather there during class time, you can be sure the principal has problems. In a well-organized school, each class has a sign-out sheet—one for boys and one for girls—or a pair of accessible bathroom passes, so only one student goes to the bathroom at a time and without the embarrassment of asking permission.

Faculty recruitment is the principal's most important job. She should be allowed to choose her teachers or at least have the right to accept or reject those assigned to her. While personalities and special skills will vary, their approach to education should be roughly the same as hers.

THE TEACHER

Even the best school probably has no more than one or two good—or even very good—teachers out of four, with the others ranging from so-so to so-awful.

Good teachers reflect a good principal. If she's humane, wise and organized, she will hire teachers who are too, while a cold principal or a dim one will choose a faculty made up of the cold or the dim. Her choices are critical. The teacher is usually the third most important adult in the child's life, right after his parents. A bad teacher can be devastating, depending on the age and the vulnerability of the child; a

middling teacher neither causes nor cures much trouble; but a good teacher is a boon, a gift from heaven.

It's the personality and the skill of the teacher that matter most, and if she carries out the curriculum properly, she makes learning fun. To do this, she not only knows the subject well but is challenging enough for the brighter children and patient enough for those who are slower. She doesn't just ask for a math answer; she asks for three ways to get it.

A good teacher talks, but not that much, for she knows that in any class there are 10–15% who simply can't learn from listening alone. She also knows that some children learn best in one way and some in another, and that all of them learn by doing, so she gets them to involve as many of their senses as she can. In one lesson she may call for her sixth graders to sculpt topographical maps of the Rockies, which will make an indelible print on the tactile learners, while the next mapmaking will be with poster paints, for the visual child. These varied approaches keep the whole class busy, so no one is left out to disrupt the class. This is an important consideration, since your child will be affected one way or another.

The teacher also has organized her own material with care and knows the strengths and weaknesses of each child so well that she can give slower reading and harder math to Joel, more exercise and less art for Max and more book reports and tougher spelling for Tanya so that all the children are working close to their capacity.

A practiced teacher gets good results because she expects the best of each child, knowing that they will try to live up to her expectations. Children instinctively realize that happiness and hard work are wrapped in the same package—and so does the teacher. When their minds are well nourished, they reward her by being more satisfied and better behaved, for children just can't be happy for six hours a day if they think they're wasting their time.

While this teacher is demanding, she is

also calm, reassuring, easily amused—and makes her class feel comfortable, partly by her good manners. The children are clearly her friends and when she talks to them she looks at each one directly and finds it easy to give hugs or drape her arm over a small child's shoulder, especially if the child is not so lovable, for she knows that this one needs affection most.

Her words are friendly too. She finds something personal to say to each child each day, which is always a compliment and always true. She may notice one child's pretty braids; another's wide smile; a little boy's strength—always making comments that depend on the child's own choice and effort. Nor does she ever congratulate one child at the expense of another, for though she may have her secret likes and dislikes she has no obvious pets in the class, and no targets either. This pays high dividends. Children learn best when they work in harmony, not anxiety.

The discipline in the classroom tells as much about the teacher as the school-wide discipline tells about the principal. This good teacher handles problems well. In an hour of observation you'll discover how she deals with the wiggler, the dreamer, the child who won't—or can't—do his work.

She is always (or almost always) in control, and is not at the mercy of the attention-seeker. She may post a printed list of her main rules and penalties and then handles routine misbehavior with consistent fairness. She uses humor but

never sarcasm, sympathy but not pity. Mostly, however, she relies on well-tailored compliments to keep problems to a minimum. Like a good parent, she accepts the children for what they are, loving this one for her energy, that one for his gentleness; Harry for his wit; Heather for trying so hard. By giving positive attention to all the children, she prevents much of the trouble before it starts. And when trouble surfaces anyway—and it does—she responds with a hard look and a raise of the brow, or by chalking the offender's name on the board, without comment or punishment, erasing it when the child is clearly good again—an effective technique, but the best discipline at school, as at home, is handled quietly and if possible in private, particularly if it's serious.

Here the teacher may lay a firm hand on the student's shoulder, speak in a low voice and take him into the hall for more discussion until he's calm. And then she tells the child that the next time he's so mad he should tell the teacher and take himself into the hall for ten minutes alone. In this way, a child gains more and more control of his own behavior. This is the real goal of any discipline.

The clear sign of the good teacher is the way she handles special children—the deaf, the blind, the dyslexic, the disabled. A well-run classroom can assimilate a few children with extra needs and still serve everyone. This teacher may set aside a day, early in the fall, during which all the children in the class learn how to cope with the disabilities of the handicapped and the learning disabled. They may plug their ears and learn to sign "Hello"; try to walk with bandanas over their eyes; copy their schoolwork backward, get around on crutches or in a wheelchair. The teacher may also have them interview each other. By getting their questions out in the open, everyone can be a little more sensitive because they see how others face problems and deal with them, and can be more honest about their own.

Under the teacher's guidance the chil-

dren begin to realize that each of them probably has something that makes them different, even if it isn't obvious. A child may be weighted down by problems at home—a superbusy father; an alcoholic mother; a retarded brother—or he may be wrestling with hyperactivity or shyness or a problem of height or weight. Another child may be upset because of some difference that seems quite silly to a grown-up. We're still amazed at the problem that made our Kate weep at the start of first grade: we didn't have a purple car like the McGregors'.

The best teacher can recognize—and sometimes resolve—the hidden problems that often come from home. When a child in the Middle Years—which is to say, the Messy Years—is still neat and clean when he leaves school, he may be so lonely and fearful he doesn't play enough to get dirty. Other problems may surface at the teacher conference. You'll need to investigate if the teacher says your child is wild at school when you know he's supergood at home or that he's meek and mild in school and he's a hellion afterward.

Some children go through a bad patch because there is tension at home or because their health or their hormones are upset, but the child who can't read by the end of second grade and has a disappointing report card, time after time, either has a learning disability, a very unhappy home—or a teacher who doesn't know how to teach. This incompetent worker is found in every school (and in every office, army and factory), and it can be very upsetting to children.

If you know what you're looking for, a bad teacher is as obvious as a good one, particularly in the area of discipline. While a good teacher controls the class with her voice, a bad one uses her voice as a weapon. She either speaks so low the children must strain to hear her or she screams at a child who misbehaves. Neither is effective, particularly with the children who withdraw or clown around, for they are often troubled.

The screamer particularly upsets a class because children know injustice when they hear it and yet few of them will be self-confident enough to stand up to her. Instead they also turn on the child in trouble, and in their hearts they will be angry with themselves for doing it. This is the kind of situation that can undercut the values you teach at home and which you must protest. Honor and justice matter more than reading and writing.

You can't, of course, protect your child from all the loons in our adult world, but you must remember that the teacher isn't always right. You can find out if she is the problem by observing at school for a half day or even a full day. If you are disturbed by what you see, ask for a conference with the teacher and, if you think it's necessary, the principal (see Teacher Conference).

And if you still aren't happy about the outcome, you may try to get your school board to make changes, or even decide to choose a private or a religious school if they are available and affordable. By analyzing your child and his environment as objectively as possible, you probably can tell where the problem lies. But this is easier to do if you already know what a good teacher and a good classroom are like.

The Classroom

Good classrooms are both functional and pleasing, with plants and a live animal in

the room—if no one is allergic to them—
or at least some goldfish or pond studies.
There are clear, bright graphics for the
younger classes—perhaps with cutout figures from fairy tales or the better television
shows—and the rooms are organized to
help children find things easily and to
spark their curiosity in many ways. You'll
find a place for arts and crafts; a science
corner that invites experiments; a reader's
nook and a talker's corner. If desks are
used instead of tables, they are arranged in
clusters, rather than rows, with the strong
personalities spotted about the room to
give the quieter children a chance to shine.
By the fourth grade the classrooms get
increasingly more sedate, with pictures of
famous people and faraway places, globes
and maps of land and stars and serious
science experiments.

The children—individually and together—tell you more about the classroom
than the room itself, however. Watch them
closely, for all good classrooms have one
common characteristic: most of the children look happy to be there.

Report Cards

Although the grading system isn't great for
children in the primary years, older children like to know where they stand. They
do, however, want their reports handed to
them privately or mailed home. Some
grades are easier to decipher than others.
Pass/Fail is so broad that it tells a child
very little, even with comments, while the
1–100 grading system calls for such exact-
ness that children always find some injus-
tices when they compare their marks. Most

teachers are satisfied with the A–F system
and most parents and students are too, if
there are brief but thoughtful comments
that can be understood easily.

No matter how little you try to pressure your child about his grades, there's
going to be some moaning over them anyway, by both of you. There will be less,
however, if you ask your child what marks
he'd give himself if he were the teacher—
an appeal to his fine-honed sense of justice
now. Neither set of grades may be as high
as you would hope, but don't let your
disappointment show too much. No matter how blasé he is or how much bravado
he shows, a child is his own toughest critic.

Instead he needs you to congratulate
him for the mark he got in a hard subject,
even if it was only a C, and for the good
grades that reflect his own interests and
talents. When you praise your child for
doing his best, you help him set realistic
standards. Never forget: no one wants the
child to succeed in school more than the
child.

When you show more interest in his
work than in his grades, you encourage the
pursuit of knowledge, the excitement of
thinking. Moreover, an emphasis on
marks, either at home or school, will encourage cheating and a resentment of
school. This is one reason why you don't
give money for good grades. The good
grade is payment enough for a child's hard
work. If you were to give money or presents for an A or a B, you would be assum-
ing that the teacher's judgment was both
sound and impartial. And if you have two
children, both teachers would have to
grade with equal fairness and both children
would have to find their classes were
equally easy or equally hard. It's the effort
the child makes that matters.

At the end of the long school year,
however, you may want to follow the example of one pair of loving parents who
honored their children with an annual
brunch at a restaurant. When it was over
each child was presented with a carefully
chosen book, inscribed with a thoughtful

compliment about some special work the child had done in school that year. It was better than any payment or prize.

PARENTS

Your child still gets most of his support at home. Here, with your help, he will learn the real arts of survival: to handle his time well; to have good manners, both face to face and on the phone; to be responsible with money and supplies; to be sufficiently self-sufficient; to clean up the messes he makes; to cook; to know that the only person he can change is himself. All of his abilities and attitudes are carried into the classroom.

Children whose time and space are structured at home usually do better at school, so they should always have a place for their books, a corner to study, a set of simple encyclopedias and a dictionary, as well as fixed times to come inside, to do their work and to turn out their lights.

The schoolchild also needs a whole new routine before and after school, including a good, hot breakfast and an affectionate send-off, a nutritious, low-sugar lunch and snacks and a talk with his mother or dad when he gets home—either in person or by phone. After school he will need to have a little time alone to do nothing; a good hour of hard play; a dinner without arguments; a ban on television on school nights; a parental glance over his homework; a reminder to lay out his clothes and school needs for the next day; a few pages aloud from some good author like A. A. Milne or Roald Dahl in the primary years; some hugs and kisses from his parents; ten to fifteen minutes to read books in bed before he turns out the light; and at least nine hours of sleep a night, particularly in the first five grades.

Your child not only needs you to look over his homework at night, but he needs you to talk about it before he starts, and sometimes to help him break it into steps; to suggest possible resources; and to help him understand how to remember the information best. Where one fourth grader may need to recopy his notes to remember his lesson better, another may need to recite them out loud. A third may stamp a scientific experiment firmly in his brain by drawing a step-by-step picture or explaining it to his baby brother (see Homework).

Other help is less direct. You give it best if you make school interesting by making yourself interesting. Talk about ideas at dinner as much as you talk about family and friends. Have news and science magazines around. Show your child the editorial cartoon of the day and talk about it, even with a Six. Ask for opinions on news and on movies and give your own, without challenging his, so he can learn to make thoughtful judgments. Give him time to say what he means so he can grapple with ideas out loud. These exchanges will help him talk about his feelings too.

Use a broad vocabulary, replacing words he doesn't know with those that he does, so he can understand the new ones by their context. Big vocabularies help children remember better, because there are more pegs on which to hang new bits of knowledge, and it helps them read better too. You also help by grouping together the things that are alike: a peach and a plum; a trombone and a clarinet. These mnemonic skills help children think in an orderly way, and so does an ability to discriminate between words or colors or textures or tastes—other areas in which you can help.

Your interest and expectations do much to keep school exciting. Your child needs to know that school is his job; that you and his dad count on him to work hard; that you know he can succeed; that he's the only person he's competing against; and that he is the only one with the right to demand excellence of himself.

No matter how clever the teaching, your child is going to do some grousing about school, but it will be less if you help him accept his mistakes as well as his successes. He should know that you don't take the gold stars of school—and life—so seriously. A child who isn't afraid of a parent's disapproval will give a candid answer when asked how he did in social studies or if he has mastered his spelling words this week. You also support your child when you help him see how far ahead he is in some areas—and you do it before he notices how far he might be behind in others.

The short holiday from school in winter and the long stretch of summer come just in the nick of time. These breaks give your child time for recovery, for introspection, for patching the soul back together, but there is no use pretending: school vacations can be stressful if you have to juggle schedules and sitters. Nevertheless, be careful what you say. Your child would feel awful if he heard you say, "Oh, my God! He's going to be home for two weeks. What am I going to do with him underfoot?" Imagine how you'd feel if you heard him say that about you.

Although you don't want him to go to school in the summer unless it is necessary, he may forget some knowledge unless books are part of his daily routine. Let him have a quiet hour each morning to read on his vacation, a time at night when you read to him, and a weekly library visit, but do this in the context of life, not of school.

Just as you put your personal time and your family ahead of your work—whether it's paid or unpaid—so do you want your child to put himself and his family ahead of school. This is how priorities are set.

Parent-Teacher Conference

As Mrs. Theodore Roosevelt might have said, "Walk softly and wear a big hat." It's the sort of advice mothers need to have when they go to their first teacher conference. Few experiences are more awesome.

You not only have the normal anxiety that comes from having your child's mind and psyche dissected by a stranger, you also find yourself subconsciously squelched by the smells of wax and disinfectant; the sounds of bells ringing and children scurrying. You feel like a schoolchild again, with all of a schoolchild's tensions and fears and sitting on a little chair only makes it worse. And then, as you start talking with the teacher, you find that there is a subtle tugging between you as you each lay claim to your child. A big hat helps to remind you that you and the teacher are meeting as equals. Equality is based on respect—and it works two ways. If you give it, you're more likely to get it back.

Generally you show respect by waiting six to ten weeks into the school year before making a date for the conference, to give her time to get her class organized and to know the children. You then call and make an appointment, rather than show up after school. If there is a specific problem that needs prompt attention, however, ask for an appointment sooner and briefly tell her why, so she can pull any records she needs. In either case, call her at school (not at home) and set a time when your husband can go too if possible. It's usually much better if both parents are involved and if the child—especially a preteen—attends the conference for at least some of the time. This is no time for him to feel shut out.

Even if there is a problem, you'll want to be as open-minded about the school and the teacher as you can, so the conference will be successful. You have to assume that you're all on the same side, working to do what's best for your child.

Preparation is another key. Your

thoughts should be well organized, so you won't drift into those tempting asides that divert a meeting, and you should have a list of questions. They should include the achievements she expects your child to make—the minimum and maximum—and when. This is how you keep track of his progress in the weeks ahead. You'll ask to see the confidential school record that follows him from year to year (you have the legal right to see it and to challenge and perhaps correct any information you think is wrong or unfair) and you'll review the scores of any standardized tests he's taken. Look at the work he's done at school and compare it to the papers on the bulletin board (though not when he's around), to find out the degree to which the children must redo poor work. A fair but demanding standard is one sign of a conscientious teacher.

It's a good idea to keep notes on these semiannual conferences in a folder with his school reports and major papers, as part of the year-by-year file you keep in case diagnosticians, tutors, optometrists and other experts ever need a sequential picture of your child's progress.

While each meeting is a teacher conference for you, it's a parent conference for the teacher, and she will probably be almost as intimidated as you are. She'll react better if you both deal with a full deck. Tell the teacher your child's study habits, how much exercise he gets, how often he watches television, how well he eats and sleeps, and if there are any problems at home. Although you will be positive about your child, you need to report any troubles you think he may be having at school, so the teacher can try to do something about them. This may embarrass you, but if the teacher is a sensitive person your insights should be helpful. A parent can be loyal and honest at the same time. If the teacher makes some suggestions that you can't accept—say so. By being candid and open-minded, a better idea may emerge that should satisfy everyone.

If you can't resolve the problem, how-ever, or the classroom problems seem beyond solution, don't hesitate to ask for a conference with the principal. That's when you wear a *very* big hat.

You need to be very well prepared for this conference. Chart your child's behavior on paper so you can look for patterns; put your thoughts into words as clearly as possible; and, above all, trust your instincts. No one knows your child better than you. You'll want to discuss his unhappiness, if that's a problem, your classroom observations and your list of specific complaints, and, in fairness, the teacher should be there for at least this part of the conference.

A good principal will hear your side of the story with some empathy, defend the teacher more than you think is necessary—and then make some changes, by requiring the teacher to change her ways; by putting your child in another class; or by giving him special responsibility in school affairs, or extra time in the library, the band, or an enrichment class to boost his ego.

At home the troubled child may need a pet, or afternoon or weekend classes in art or sports or science, as well as a great deal of understanding and praise for hanging in—just as you would need if you had to stay in a bad job for months. Finally, he needs you to look for another school if nothing improves. Even a midyear change can be better than another four more months of the same. And if there is no hope for an immediate change, rest easy. A child is taught by many teachers, and most of them aren't at school.

GRADE BY GRADE

Each grade has its own style, just like each child. And, like children, they will vary but generally they follow a pattern.

FIRST GRADE

Sometimes a school seems to peak in the first grade, for this teacher is often the best of the faculty, and if not, both parent and child expect her to be so good they may convince themselves that she is.

In the first year the parents also try harder, showing up at the PTA full of good ideas and good intentions, although often with amazing misconceptions. You'll notice that every other mother thinks her child is the best, when it's quite obvious that yours is really the star. Actually, the children are all rather wonderful. There is nothing quite so heart-lifting as a schoolroom of first graders, unless it is a nursery of newborns. Each is a microcosm of hope. To the child, first grade begins as an exalting, exhausting new experience and then becomes a foundation on which to build competence and confidence.

The teacher starts the day with joy, greeting each child by name, a ritual that is so important in the first few weeks that your child may hang around outside if she's not at the door to say good morning. Once inside he is busy, busy, busy, checking everything in sight and subconsciously learning words by the labels pasted around the room: SHELF; DESK; DOOR; WINDOW; FISH.

Even when these children sit, they don't stay still, for this is a class of movers and shakers. They seem happy and excited but never quite comfortable. First graders move their whole bodies about, as if desks were made for scooching. If there were a trapeze bar in the classroom, they'd probably hang upside down and swing while writing their abc's, or at least their a's and b's. The wiggly Sixes have a hard time finishing what they start. They are always looking for better ways to hold their pencils, concentrating so hard they may bite them and chew their erasers, or they may stick out their tongues while they work and hold their pencils so tight you may find your child has a perpetual bump on his middle finger.

Much of this antsiness is caused by the trouble boys and girls, and especially boys, have in coordinating their hands with their eyes. They also find it hard to copy from the blackboard, which is why a teacher uses so many mimeographed work sheets. She also goes quickly from one activity to the next, which keeps the time lag—and the foolishness—to a minimum.

These young students want to work with numbers and letters and, with encouragement, can add a column of one-digit numbers, like 1 + 4; read the simplest books; and print in capitals, which they prefer because these letters are harder to reverse. As your child learns to read he is so wrapped up in phonics that he practices over and over on his whiches and his witches until he can discriminate between the two.

A good teacher capitalizes on their interests, with simple anagrams and dominoes; the writing of stories—no matter how the words are spelled; and the studying of small animal life under a magnifying glass.

Academic differences will soon become apparent. Most boys usually do better in arithmetic and listen to stories better, while girls usually draw, write and read better. Some people attribute this to their physical abilities: boys usually use their arms and legs better while girls are better with their small muscles—their eyes and their hands. Neither sex, however, is ready for concepts—the first grader's logic is still too primitive—but they can and should know the basics that underlie them very well. All of this is plain hard work.

Since a first grader uses so much energy

in school, he needs serenity when he gets home, and regular rituals and routines help supply it. That's why you should see that he lays out his clothes, his books, his money and permission slips at night, and gets up by his own alarm clock in the morning, dresses himself and helps pack his own lunch, while you oversee it all with as calm an air as you can muster. There is, of course, an added payoff for you. Except for the help he still needs with his slicker and especially his boots, you both will find that he can take care of himself pretty well and will carry these same skills into school.

The stress in school is social as well as academic, which may be why a well-equipped playground is so important, although many activities need no equipment at all. A playground after a big rain is as inviting today as it was when you were young. There's nothing first graders like better than nice, drippy, oozy messes. Puddle-jumping (and puddle-stomping) is still a great joy. The spontaneous play, the climbing equipment, the organized sports all give the children something to do while they get to know each other. A few of the children do most of the leading, but no one seems to mind and all but the shyest act as leaders sometimes.

The comradeship of the playground is carried into school. You'll see the children go about, two by two, like so many water bugs. The pairs change often because the friendships do too, although a few long-term attachments may begin in first grade. They are nothing compared to the feelings

a first grader will have for the teacher if she's any good at all. By the end of the year her students are all not just in love with her but passionately in love. One young poet was so moved, he went back to his school after it had closed for the summer, to print beneath his first-grade window:

SECOND GRADE

Where did all those babies go? The children in this class seem so much older. Front teeth are either missing or the new ones are too big for the face and some children are already wearing glasses. As their faces show more individuality, the size and shape of their bodies change too and their personalities become more distinct. All of this seems to make each child more anxious to look and act like everyone else.

A good teacher encourages the children to accept their differences—by displaying their handprints and family snapshots on the wall and by having them poke pins on a big map of the country or the region, to mark the places they have visited. Each child connects the pins with string and labels it with his name. The teacher also may have each child write a Self Book: the best thing that ever happened to me; the worst; my first memories; my favorite thing to do; to wear.

The teacher's interest in the child keeps her well loved and makes the Seven feel safe in school, although he may not feel safe enough to want to use the bathroom there unless he must.

This child is beset with doubts sometimes—and so are you. You've always known that the other children would never be President of the USA or even IBM, but now you realize that your child probably won't either. Problems often develop now and you'll have to decide whether they come from the child or the school. Children express their uncertainties in many ways this year and their mannerisms are as contagious as their colds. When one child in the room starts to wiggle the twitches catch on, and when a child makes an odd noise other strange noises are added. It's when they're all shuffling and snuffling that the teacher realizes she should have changed the subject ten minutes before. Second graders are willing to concentrate on a subject in class for twenty minutes at a time, but that's about it. They flit like fireflies in their casual chatter too.

Our Nell, a fifteen-year-old soda jerk on Saturdays, found herself in this helter-skelter conversation when she talked to the second grade about drugstore work during Career Development Week:

First child: "My mommy took me to your drugstore for an ice cream cone after I got my tonsils out."

Second child: "My friend from France got her tonsils out."

Third child: "I know someone who's been to France."

They like to wing it informally, but they also like repetition, returning day after day to the same lesson and moving on to the next only when they know they have mastered the last. To do it, a good second-grade teacher still nurtures her flock, but she is much more businesslike than a first-grade teacher, expecting more, demanding more.

This classroom is basically a serious place because second graders have so much to master. They must learn the difference between east and west; become familiar with capitalizations, homonyms and classifications; know all their numbers and add and subtract with the snap of their fingers. By the end of the year they must know the times tables, going first up to five and then on to ten. At Seven they are beginning to understand what numbers and letters really mean, and use them on every possible occasion.

Their spelling is taking shape but is still wonderfully inventive, and if asked to name their favorite foods they're likely to write: *lazonya; chilli* and *moshroon.*

THIRD GRADE

Things settle down in third grade. These children like school but they are so casual about it, they have to be well programmed at home to get there on time, even though they wear their watches like badges.

There are other changes too. Now they are much less jumpy but so ragtag they look like they've already jumped. Since their shirttails are sure to hang out, you may as well buy the kind of shirts that hug the body. As long as their clothes—and especially their shoes—conform to the fashion of the class, they are happy, for they still want to look exactly like their friends. At this age, they can spot a difference between brands at two hundred yards. Somehow all of this sameness merely underscores their differences.

Their desks may reflect their individuality most. Each one is intensely personal, full of the owner's special brand of junk— and possibly an old sandwich that's been stuck in the back of it for months.

On the playground and in the lunchroom, you may be struck by the ease of their manner, for they are a talkative lot. They have a great deal to say to those they admire, and they often talk in bulletins. Your child may carry this conversational style home, which makes it hard to get a full picture of how the day has gone. Instead you get an abstract but valuable glimpse of the child's sense of himself and how he fits into the school.

Third graders are in constant pursuit of

competence, but their idea of competence is not always the same as the teacher's. During the morning announcements one child may examine his hand over and over again, as if it belonged to somebody else, while another rearranges his colored pencils from dark to light, or sharp to dull. This behavior isn't born of disrespect. Third graders need to inspect, to know, to organize, to classify. The curriculum takes advantage of this by teaching the parts of speech, the prefixes and suffixes—and reinforces it with the spelling bees so many children love. Book knowledge now fits neatly into the real world and money becomes a good teaching tool. These children can understand the concept of numbers, spaces and sizes, and can divide and do simple fractions. Even the calendar begins to make sense. They will be in the fourth grade, however, before they're old enough to have a clear concept of years.

The third-grade teacher has a fascinating and demanding job. She must teach 25–30 children whose abilities in reading and math may range from the first-grade level through the fifth, which makes ability grouping essential. She also must weave values into everything from current events to fiction and console the forlorn at the drop of a tear.

This teacher acts like a good queen, with a nod here, a smile there, and always calls each child by his first name—and his last name too if she thinks he isn't sure of himself. For all her winning ways, the teacher doesn't stay on a pedestal this year, either in their imagination or in reality. Instead she often sits at one of their tables, playing games with them, or on the floor to take her turn at reading in the story circle. Even so, she keeps her dignity intact and is obviously in command of the class. All of this should create a year so nurturing, so innovative, that the well-grounded child will sail along.

If your student is slower than the others in class, however, if he looks tired and finds it hard to learn as well as his friends, he may need to be tutored or even to repeat

the third grade (see Learning Problems). Although some children make a great leap forward when they pass into fourth grade, others fall apart. Repeating, when repeating is needed, is no disgrace, but it always bothers children more than you might think and the older the child, the more unsettling the experience will be.

FOURTH GRADE

Welcome to a watershed year. Suddenly school is real and it gets more real all the time. Everything about it is different. Now there is more memory work and more attention is given to writing, style and meaning. Even the teaching may change. The fourth grader usually gets less individual help and may be shunted between two and three teachers. This can be stressful, but most children like it fine because they may see more classmates. To them, their friends are definitely more important than their teachers.

These teachers are very serious about their work—and these children are very serious about themselves. They're usually Nine now and becoming such individuals that they want everyone, including their parents and teachers, to know it. Even so, the classroom is quieter now. Girls and boys do show their awareness of each other with their smirks and spitballs, but the teacher tries to ignore them by making classwork so interesting they would rather pay attention to her, and they usually do.

Now the pupils are more absorbed and competitive, which gives them a strong need to improve on past accomplishments. There is much arithmetic, with a heavy emphasis on long division, and they now write in cursive and may plagiarize freely. This and other forms of cheating can begin to be a real problem if the teacher is disliked (or rather dull); if the work seems pointless or poorly taught or it's boring or overly hard; if there is a big fuss made about grades at school or at home; if the students don't get along well; if the seats are too close together; or if the family thinks cheating is all right or simply ignores the subject.

Cheating is also likely if the teacher doesn't speak out against it at the beginning of the year and take strong measures when it happens. The good teacher discreetly collects the papers of any child caught cheating, gives him a failing mark for them and has a long talk later to see what went wrong and to help him realize that learning is much more important than passing. This is the only way a child can learn to teach himself, and that, after all, is what school is all about. If he is caught cheating a second time, parents should expect the teacher to call them in for a conference to see if there is too much pressure at home.

Not all fourth graders cheat but all fourth graders do find that the classroom has somehow become a demanding, competitive place. The bloom is off the old school rose. To combat this, parents need to add interest to their child's life with an after-school or weekend class in science, music or art or a good Scout program—anything to keep his curiosity in high gear, for the more curious the child, the better he understands and remembers. It may be a chicken-and-egg situation, but studies show that the curious child is also more secure; more independent; more mature; more cooperative; better organized; and less prejudiced—except against members of the opposite sex.

The division between boys and girls is stronger than ever. In play the girls begin to walk about in small packs, chatting (and gossiping) and playing with dolls at recess, while boys reach their warmongering peak.

While boys and girls separate at school, however, they may play together on the playground when it's supervised or in the neighborhood, when nobody's looking. Even then fourth graders are apt to show their gender, as they did in a snow scene in our park, when a nine-year-old girl ordered a nine-year-old boy:

"NO! I'LL make the snowballs. YOU do the fighting!"

No matter how liberated the parents, some things never change.

FIFTH GRADE

This year you can almost see your child grow: he is right on the verge of simple abstract thought. His new mental leaps will shift his imagination, his learning and his humor, and all of this changes his work at school. Some boys and girls will, of course, start thinking—and working—on a higher plane sooner and some will start later but, whatever the individual level, they all are expected to learn much more this year—and consequently they will. Nightly homework is given in several subjects and the assignments are more varied. Most of the students will try hard in the fifth grade's two key areas, writing and fractions. Both call for even more memory work, which suits them fine.

Fifth graders have such hammy natures that playacting and poetry recitations are scary delights and by the end of the year they even like to solve arithmetic problems at the blackboard, in front of *everyone*. Part of this comes from their love of competition. They're ready to tackle every-thing from spelling bees to fistfights, but they usually don't want to win enough to cheat. Both boys and girls, you'll be re-lieved to know, are high on honor this year. This is part of the budding social conscience of the fifth grader, with fair play at its heart. Woe to the teacher who plays favorites now.

By the end of fifth grade they begin to test what they learn as well as each other, and the teachers must adjust to the grow-ing interests—and growing differences—among the students. The wise teacher, like the wise mother, lets the children move around easily, but she includes enough rituals and routines to give order to their lessons. Not all are academic. Art, cooking and singing please both boys and girls, while girls like ballet and gymnastics better and boys often prefer musical instruments. You'll want to arrange for some of these activities if the school doesn't.

Although your child now pulls away from you—a necessary reach for indepen-dence—he still needs to lean on someone. In the beginning of the year it's the teacher but soon he turns to friends for solace, information and advice. This is why you may see the teacher try to break up alli-ances that seem unsuitable—and you'll do the same.

The most important part of any extra curricular activity this year is the friend who shares it. These friend-ships, good or bad, are still almost always of the same sex. If you have occasional playground duty in the fall, you'll see the girls hover about in small clutches while the boys play games in one big group but the building of small boy-girl flirta-tions has begun and by spring the voices of these turtles will be heard in their land.

SIXTH GRADE

The sixth grade is the year of connections. As young minds grow increasingly analyt-ical, they link ideas and information in logical patterns. Thank heavens. This helps them understand you.

Now the preteens truly take the idea of school and run with it, although by the seventh grade you're not too sure where they're going (and neither are they). Nev-ertheless, there is—or should be—a greater air of respect and camaraderie between stu-dents and teachers as the children begin to think on a higher level.

It's a treat to watch the changes. In the beginning of the year the children will tell what happened in a book; at the end of the year they tell why. Their perceptions of good and evil, kindness and friendship help to shape their interpretations of cur-rent events. What's happening in the world now is real and far more fascinating than history. The more they understand the ways of the world, the better they fit into it. Geography can be great fun because it shows how the population and its culture is shaped by a country's topography, cli-mate and resources. A good teacher chal-lenges the different abilities of her pupils with individual and group projects.

Sixth graders are less self-conscious now and their imaginations carry them into new experiences. If by lucky chance they take Latin—which is becoming popular again in some of the better schools— they may bring it to life, parading through the halls in T-shirts, togas and tunics on their way to divide Gaul into three parts—and onstage. Now you see how this class can get out of hand so easily.

You still can help to keep order in school as well as at home by checking on his work with your child against the list of assignments a thorough teacher provides. Elevens sometimes forget what is required and when.

At school the teacher keeps her class calm by spotting the leaders around the room and building work clusters around them, but the social and academic pressures may be too much for some. This, after all, is the year when puberty is here or near. Now the sixth grader's temperature goes up and down and fatigue becomes a problem. He may find it hard to get going in the morning and be too late to eat breakfast, which just makes his blood sugar drop and his disposition turn cranky. The Eleven can be cross as a bear (and your cross to bear!) unless you see that he sets his alarm earlier and has a good breakfast and a nutritious lunch. Neither food nor sleep, however, will make this child patient with a foolish teacher. All you can do about it is sympathize. At least the children are learning another survival skill they'll often have to use as adults.

It could be worse. The children still have each other, which is why they like to get to school early. If you were around, you'd see them gather in klatches—for there is much news to exchange since the day before—and then most of them break to play. Generally the boys wrestle around like puppies, the girls skip double dutch and some children from both sexes play wall-ball or whatever is the fad of the year.

At recess the competitive games are taken so seriously that only the best players are picked first, no matter how close the friendship between a team captain and a klutz. This is fine for soccer, since girls are quite good at it, but when both boys and girls are playing baseball or touch football, most of the girls are usually chosen last (if they are willing to be chosen at all). This is seldom conscious discrimination. Boys, either by practice or genetics or both, are usually better at running and hitting—and so they like to run and hit—while girls are so much better at hopping, they almost turn jumping rope into the religion of the playground.

The boys and girls aren't ignoring each other, however. The flirtations of last year may become more intense now and the girls plot their strategies with the determination of generals. It was dear Nell and her willowy pal Felicia who reported, long after the fact, that the sixth grade had a wedding a week in the playground after lunch, and just as many divorces. A sign of the times? Not at all. Just a chance to kiss again when the preacher married them to new partners.

SEVENTH GRADE

Twelves are generally more stable than Elevens, but this may not be reflected in the seventh-grade classroom. Differences peak this year, and are emphasized if the children have been moved to junior high— a collection of boys and girls who must struggle together in their three most awkward years. Still, a well-taught seventh grade is a vibrant, thrilling place and the children can be a delight (most of the time).

It all comes down to substance, which is what these children want most. Almost all rote work should be over now as learning becomes a matter of logic, which permeates every subject. Math, if well taught, is clearly logical, and biology a jigsaw marvel, but so are the cause and effect of history. Even creative writing is logical to seventh graders when they realize that their characters must match their plots.

There is nothing a Twelve likes better than a good teacher or finds more annoying than a poor one. He knows he's more than halfway through his basic schooling now and he resents it if anyone trifles with his time. Instead he expects his teacher to be so well informed that she can answer any question in any subject, or at least give an enthusiastic "I don't know; let's look it up." Enthusiasm, for any reason, is appreciated by the seventh grader, because that's still one of the main ingredients of his personality, as it was a year ago. However, he is more in control now, more focused, and should be less of a handful in class. Part of this is due to another major bout of conformity this year, so there is less friction. A good teacher can make this conformity work to your child's advantage, by encouraging him to take pride in his work. When enough students are proud, there is a class pressure to excel.

These children are still markedly different in their ability to think in abstractions, but their strengths and weaknesses are obvious to a good teacher, for the students are always unmasking themselves. The more advanced will be those who grab for *Mad* magazine; who can understand both levels of *Gulliver's Travels;* and who sprinkle their conversation with abstract verbs like "think" and "believe" instead of concrete ones like "make" and "do."

Learning problems are also noticeable now and tutoring can be essential if a child is to keep working at grade level (see Learning Problems). Even children who still think in the most tangible terms will find the pressure rough, particularly the unusual child—the "weird" child, as he may be called. There will be less of this in a good school, of course, where children are encouraged to be more tolerant of each other, but in any case the problem is short-lived, by adult standards. The eighth grade will be much more accepting.

Wise parents monitor their children's friendships closely now. This is a prime time to try cigarettes, alcohol and pot, and almost always at the urging of the best friend.

Seventh graders take in other unwise substances: junk food. Their diet is usually atrocious, both for the poor food they eat and the good food they don't eat. You can help by nixing doughnuts for breakfast, so your child won't be tired for his ten o'clock test; by dropping one of his baby teeth in a cola, so he can see how it gets blackened and etched in a week (and realize how sodas can hurt his teeth); and by leaving peanut butter or natural cheese for his snack, so he'll play a good game of soccer after school.

Food is a primary interest this year, and so are sports—and so are members of the other sex and hearts drawn on the sidewalk. By the end of the year seventh graders are so conscious of each other that boys may grandly ask the teacher not to give them any homework over the weekend because they'll be busy with their girl-friends. (If you took a secret poll, however, you'd find that the wish was more real than the fact, by a factor of 10 to 1.)

LUNCH BASKET

As all teachers know, the waste of cafeteria food at school is awful to behold and it's not much better when children bring their own bag lunches. To carry them home is a bother or worse: some parents get quite cross to see what has gone uneaten—and how much.

At least some of the food from home can be rescued—and a little social consciousness taught—without any preaching at all. The PTA, the room mother or your own sweet self can ask permission to put a basket in the lunchroom for the children to deposit any fruit or sandwiches that haven't been bitten and to put their unopened milk cartons in the refrigerator again, to be added to the basket before the last bell rings.

Every child is welcome to take something from the Lunch Basket on his way out of school. What looks dreadful at noon with a bellyful of goodies can be quite appealing three hours later—especially to the older children. They're usually hungry enough to eat almost anything and, since they're choosing among the leftovers, these snacks are usually nutritious.

From now on you can expect romance to give school more competition, at least some of the time. It's a lovely way to go.

CURRICULA

The same subjects are generally taught in the same grades everywhere, usually with the harder subjects taught in the morning, when children are fresher. There is a year-to-year pattern too. A great deal of new material is offered in the first, third and fifth grades, while in the even years the instruction is more repetitive, because lessons learned the year before must be reinforced.

While there is a certain uniformity in the material that is taught, there are many approaches to the teaching. The best schools have a traditional base with modern innovations—spiking the old with the new—and the best teachers present it in creative ways, offering many activities that let children learn by doing.

In the early years, children want rote, drills, flash cards, spelling and grammar lessons which a good teacher handles so well (and parents so poorly), for Sevens, Eights and Nines fortunately delight in mental order. This is how they make sense triumph over nonsense. The combination of imagination and rote keeps a child thinking in the inventive way that nature intended. All of this takes so much effort that they will seem to have little originality left for such interests as art and music.

Now they spend most of their time slogging through the time tables and mastering phonetics and the basic sight reading some words require. They must be taught both the structure of sentences and the meaning of words, so that their writing—and rewriting—will be grammatical and precise and will profit by computers (if the programs are good) and by science courses. To the creative parent, this may seem like a terrible bore—a waste of precious time and a crushing of the spirit—but remember: creativity is based on sub-

stance. By the fifth grade children can understand the main concepts of math; the causes and effects in history; the origins of language; the consequences of geography.

Not all of the curriculum is taught in the classroom. Some standard school activities, such as exercise breaks and field trips, may seem unnecessary but they're not. When muscles are stretched and flexed they pump extra oxygen into the brain and recharge the mind, and field trips are a great pick-me-up, if they're designed to reinforce the lessons.

A sound curriculum is the hallmark of a good education, but the best education is still found at home and parents are still the best teachers.

READING

School has so many wonderful subjects, but to most children and parents, reading is what first grade is all about—even for those who have already learned their sounds and letters. The best readers are usually those who grow up in a book-loving household, but all children can become good readers in the first two or three years, unless they have learning problems.

Some children have trouble learning to read simply because they aren't ready for it. Boys often learn to read two years later than girls, even though they're just as smart. If they are ready for reading—and therefore ready for first grade—they can move their arms and legs adeptly, since children who can control these big movements can coordinate their eyes with their hands. They enjoy board games like Chutes and Ladders and are able to decode and memorize shapes, so they can tell the difference between *b*'s and *d*'s, recognize whole words on sight and be able to distinguish sounds. Children need good pronunciation to be able to repeat sounds in the order they're heard—a basic skill in phonics. You can help your child by reciting rhymes and alliterations together and helping him say the hardest sounds: *w; sh; th; rl; s; zh;* and *wh*. The better he can

pronounce, the easier reading and writing will be.

Skill in sequencing is especially important because it helps a child remember the order of letters and syllables, and a sense of balance affects the way he processes sound and understands it—both skills usually achieved in pre-school. The first is taught by something as simple as a stacking toy, while a child learns to balance by walking along little low walls.

To read, children must be able to track with their eyes, without skipping around, and to go from left to right, rather than up and down, the way nature intended. Etch-a-Sketch is a great game for developing this skill, especially for the child who doesn't handle a pencil well.

First graders usually learn all their letters and most of their sounds by January of first grade, which means that they know quite a few words phonetically and some by sight and will be reading by the end of the year. While some children are slower than others, they—and their classmates—should know that they'll catch up in time. A child's full skill in reading will not develop right away, however, and neither you nor your child should expect it, for reading is a slow process. He will probably be in the fourth grade before it's really easy.

Since the children will learn to read at varying rates of speed, the teacher will group them according to their abilities and you can bet that the Bluebirds (and the Redbirds and the Canaries) will all know how each group ranks by the end of the first week, without the teacher giving a hint. Never do children concentrate on anything as much as their place in this pecking order. A child can be bad in spelling or arithmetic and still feel pretty good

about himself, but if he can't read well he feels awful, for reading is the standard of excellence in the primary years.

For most children, reading improves markedly around Seven when the eyes begin to integrate images better, seeing the details and the whole picture at the same time, but if your child often squints or rubs his eyes, he may need eyeglasses or eye exercises. It's wise to correct a problem early, or at least discover the cause. If the child has trouble reading, this will usually show up by the fourth grade, if not earlier. A few children, however, can mask their reading problems so well that it isn't obvious until the sixth. You'll know your child has trouble if he isn't interested in reading at all or says he can't find anything to read and can't read it in the time that other children can. This child may be embarrassed to read out loud and makes many mistakes when he does; may have trouble reading road signs easily; and can't tell you the plot of a movie. Get help from a tutoring center or a university reading clinic (rather than a commercial speed reading class), and do it soon.

A child also may have trouble because there is trouble at home or he doesn't feel well. Both conditions will affect his concentration, and reading requires a lot of it. Nor can you expect your child to learn to read if the teacher doesn't teach well. It was Mike, a first grader with a burning need to read, who threw his book across the room and said, "Dig, Dog, Dug! How can I know?"—which led to the surprising information that the phonics teacher had taught the children their consonants very well and their vowels not at all. There are many right ways to teach reading but that wasn't one of them. A conference with the

principal put vowels back in the classroom and a year later Mike was found reading *Catcher in the Rye,* even though he couldn't make much sense of it.

A child might not read too well simply because it's hard to get a turn when there are many students in the classroom or because he's too shy to perform, particularly if he has an accent or a lisp. You can help by having your child place a ruler under each line to guide his eyes when he reads to himself and by having him read a few paragraphs a day to you, which he'll like to do if he isn't corrected very often. You may feel your gut constrict as he stumbles over each word, but most mistakes aren't worth mentioning, for children are remarkable creatures. Somehow they correct themselves automatically as they feel more comfortable with the language.

Do not, however, expect a child to absorb information when he reads it aloud as well as he does when you read to him or when he reads to himself, because he has to remember so much: to read with expression; to stop for periods; to pronounce with care. Even third graders will skip unnecessary words, simply because they're so eager to get where they're going, but since they have a great interest in possessions they'll slow down if they're given mail-order catalogs to read. They'll also like to read aloud the instructions for running the new dryer or the label on a prescription, if only because they like to tell their parents what to do.

Other children may read well, but slowly or with odd mannerisms—stopping

at every word or moving the head from side to side. The hesitant reader can read in front of a mirror by himself, as if he's giving a speech, and the child who moves his head while he reads will do better if you hold it gently so he'll only move his eyes.

If you can't find the reason for your child's slower reading, don't make a big deal of it, and don't criticize him for it. Just reassure him that he'll catch up soon, that people learn to read at different ages and that it doesn't have anything to do with his intelligence—or your love.

You encourage a child to read by talking with him about an amusing story in the newspaper, or explaining the daily editorial cartoon, as we did with Kate when she was Six. The child who's sloughing through those dreary readers needs to be reminded that reading and thinking go together. Children—and their parents—should have to endure only so much rote. Reference books help too. You can reinforce their use at school by reading maps and field guides together at home and by helping your child find words in the dictionary. Leaving messages on the bulletin board at home and reminder notes in a lunchbox about the dentist or an errand after school also may help, by reminding a child that reading is an inevitable part of life.

Your own reading aloud should continue of course, but ask the slow reader to pick up the story when you reach an exciting part. The suspense will keep him going.

The fifth grader will continue to be entranced with reading if books are part of his life and if the teacher (or his mom) adds some jazz to it, perhaps by having him find the origins of some slang words—especially if they're rowdy. There's nothing a Ten likes better than a little vulgarity.

A sixth grader who's on target may wallow in books, for he is able to understand many more words than he has in his spoken vocabulary. The interest may drop markedly in the coming year, however, if the child is too busy with baseball or ballet. You can offset this by catering to your child's special interest, with a subscription to a sports magazine or books on the dance. Anything is all right to read—mysteries, comics, *Mad* magazine, young romances—because the habit of reading is more important than the content. This reading also teaches a child to tell the difference between good writing and bad, and in time the good will win.

Present him with an interesting new paperback and ask that he give it a 20-page tryout. This will usually hook a child, if he's at the right age for it. It's worth your while to encourage reading in nearly any way you can. Since most information comes from books, the ability to read well—and to want to read well—affects a child's whole education.

WRITING

To many people's surprise, new research shows that the ability to write stories comes before the ability to read them. And that suits children just fine. They are wonderfully creative writers in first grade and even kindergarten. They won't produce polished masterpieces, of course, but that isn't necessary. The ability to express ideas clearly will stay with them all their lives, and they'll be fine, clear writers if they're properly grounded later.

Teachers and parents guide young writers best when they cheer the successes and ignore most of the stumbles. If they focus mostly on handwriting, punctuation and spelling, the child will think those skills matter more than substance and style. They matter, of course, because they make it simpler for the reader to grasp the content and recognize the turn of phrase, but no one is ever delighted by a book or a letter because it was punctuated properly or the words were spelled right. To insist on these lessons before the third grade makes the child write much slower and lose his natural originality. Instead the young should be encouraged to tell us how

they see and imagine the world around them.

Imagination and a few rudimentary tools will turn any child into a fairly decent writer and the more verbal ones into the prize winners of tomorrow. A child only needs about 10 letters, blended with pictures, to make the 42 sounds—or phonemes—in our language. While this collection of letters and words is very much his own, it is clear enough for a teacher or an aide to write her interpretation beneath the story. At first she doesn't even correct the mistakes, which may sound foolishly permissive but it works. The results are extraordinary.

Children who are encouraged to write almost as fast as they can think—without interference—usually become better spellers than other children in about two years. Their penmanship will also be just as good and they'll be much better storytellers. A child's creativity as a writer and his interest in reading are also enhanced, for the more a child likes to write, the more he likes to read. He'll organize his thoughts better and as an adult he'll want to try more professions than he might have tried, since writing is an integral part of so many fulfilling careers.

The creative process begins when the class is broken into pairs and each child talks about his story with his teammate, for children often learn best by teaching someone else. When he decides what the story is about and what pictures he'll draw, he puts it down on paper the best way he can. Even when the teacher suggests proper punctuation, spelling and revisions, he remains in charge of his own story.

If the teacher doesn't give her class the chance to write, you can do it at home. Give your child a thin, unlined journal in which to write about something that interests him, like the new baby or a new toy, but don't look into his book unless he asks you to write the story in real words. And when he seems to lose interest—and he will—give him a new book in which to write about a fresh subject in his more grown-up penmanship, so he won't be embarrassed by the babyish entries he was so proud of a few months before.

If you're not too judgmental and he's not too shy, he may underscore the words he thinks are wrong and ask you if they are and then you'll help him check his spelling in his primer dictionary. He'll know you're taking his work seriously if you praise specific aspects of it, rather than praise it indiscriminately, and if you offer to type (but not add to or edit) the exceptional one. You can even enter it in a children's writing contest. A future writer is never too young for his first rejection slip, as long as it's not his parents who do the rejecting.

As he gets older, praise the thank-you notes you have him write, but notice their originality more than their neatness, and ask him each week to tell you which library books he likes best (and why) so he can recognize and appreciate different writing styles.

The fourth grader who feels easy about his handwriting may like a pen pal, particularly if he's a bit lonely—but by the fifth grade he may lose patience with himself because he thinks he should be more creative than he is. Although you and the teacher have had him write second drafts— for good writers are basically good rewriters—you'll now have to encourage him to write third and fourth and fifth drafts as he gets older. This applies to both his letters and his essays. A weekly newsletter to his grandparents, even if they live next

door, will also help, but only if the grandparents give compliments freely and write him answering notes at least some of the time.

Meanwhile, the skills that were skimmed over earlier are given more attention. A calligraphy pen will encourage him to improve his handwriting, and the use of an electric typewriter or a computer will give him new skills and make his work much neater, which in turn will make him prouder than ever.

You add zest to his writing and his vocabulary when you use a greater variety of words when you talk. This isn't as easy as it seems. Most of us use the same small words with our growing children that we used when they were little—a sort of one-size-fits-all vocabulary. Older children need to hear bigger, more colorful, more precise words. You do this most effectively by slipping the more exact word into your conversation, where the context will make your meaning obvious. The sky is no longer clear or gray but luminous or hazy. Play with the language too. Ask him why people who are disgruntled and dismayed at times aren't gruntled or mayed at other times; point out that discourage and encourage are both part of courage and that dis-ease and disease are sometimes the same thing.

Even a second grader will find that the meanings of prefixes and suffixes can make the whole world more understandable. Teach him that circum-anything means around and he'll understand circumnavigate if he hears the older students talking about their geography lesson on the bus.

Word games, in the car or anywhere, broaden his knowledge too, or you can invite everyone to find a brand-new simile for "black as . . ." Your child will also revel in odd bits of exact information. A child likes to know that a brace of ducks or a span of mules is a pair and that a pride of lions, a muster of peacocks, a skulk of foxes or a pod of seals all mean more than two.

There are some specific ways a parent

can help a child write better and it's never by telling him what to say. You can advise him to change a general theme to a narrower one, so he won't blather; to make the first sentence of any story grab the reader's attention so he will want to read the second one; and to read his story out loud to himself, to see if the cadence is right and the meaning is clear. He can also assemble his own Word Bank, writing interesting nouns and action verbs on individual pieces of paper and dropping them into a jar. When he needs inspiration, he chooses ten slips, without looking first, and includes them in his story, a deliberate exercise of the imgination that almost always works. These tricks teach a child that he can control the language, which helps him feel more in control of his life.

The real demands begin in the sixth grade, when your child may learn to diagram sentences. This skill is often disliked by students, but it will make him write more accurately and grammatically for the rest of his life. He also will be expected to write longer pieces, and to research them. Teach him to use an index card for each separate entry, with the book and page number on it, so he will know where to retrieve more information if it's needed and so he can shuffle his information into an order. This won't be enough to put his material into a logical sequence, however.

Teachers usually like outlines—and that's an essential skill to learn—but your concrete-minded child likes to cut and paste better. Have him label each paragraph (or even each sentence) with a word in the margin to describe its substance, and then cut the paragraphs (or sentences) apart. The slips are then pasted (or taped or stapled) on blank sheets of paper with all the paragraphs on the same subject grouped together. The author who can't bear to destroy his golden words can either cut and paste a duplicate or recopy the paragraphs into their new sequence. By comparing the revision with the original, he'll see how he can throw away many words and get much clearer, tighter copy.

Revision becomes serious business in junior high, when your child should learn to read his paper over and over, looking for new problems each time. First he deletes every unnecessary word and punctuation mark and then he replaces long words with shorter ones that are just as accurate, since the best writing is the clearest and the clearest is the simplest. He then reads it for clichés and tries to substitute fresh expressions for stale ones. After that he reads it for spelling errors, and once more for punctuation, and finally he reads it out loud to himself, to make sure that it is as smooth and plain and precise as he can make it, which may mean he'll put back a few of the words and commas he had removed. By breaking the exercise into simple steps, a child discovers that this writing job isn't so mysterious after all. This helps him realize that in writing, as in anything else, substance and clarity matter more than flair, by a factor of about 9 to 1.

There will still be impasses, however. When he tells you he has an essay to write and nothing to say (and besides, he wants to play baseball), teach him the writer's ancient creed: apply the seat of the pants to the seat of the chair—and get on with it. A writer is never too young to learn that lesson either.

Spelling

Although a good teacher uses sight, sound and even touch to teach spelling, phonics still explain most words best to most children. That's why you'll hear your dear little first grader muttering about pins and pens and, in time, pitchers and pictures.

You can give him extra help at home by

writing a troublesome word in big letters so he can spell or pronounce it out loud, and have him trace it on his arm with his fingertip so his sense of touch reinforces the sight and sound of the word. Or if he learns best by hearing, he may prefer to have you recite his spelling list first, just as he will do it later—saying the word, then spelling it by syllables, then saying the word again. Reinforcement is the key to learning. He won't start spelling easily until the third grade, when his penmanship becomes more automatic. When a child makes his letters in a comfortable, sequential way, spelling comes much easier.

Stripping words into syllables will help too. The fourth grader who learns to understand and spell prefixes and suffixes will realize that most words are easy when taken part by part. The dictionary, with a little help from you, can then become his key to spelling.

Drills can improve a child's spelling and so can corrections—if he asks for them—but most parents find word games work better. Tell your child about palindromes like Otto and Anna, civic and level and how to spell some complicated word, like "complicated," and some wacky words, like gnu and knish, or how to spell it in Morse code or semaphore. It keeps the subject of spelling lively. A speller improves if he's invited to do a child-sized crossword puzzle at night while his daddy does a big one and if the family plays word games when traveling—to see how many words they can find in the word "traveling," for instance (39).

Handwriting

There are two reasons for your child to have good handwriting: to write fast and to be understood. Fortunately, those are reasons a child can understand. More abstract goals, such as neatness and good marks, won't get you very far and neither will "because I said so."

First graders who begin with printing need unlined paper, because it's hard at first to concentrate on both the lines and the letters. They move on to lined pads when they start printing in upper and lower case, but don't expect too much at first. Few children have good penmanship even after they've learned their letters because they can't yet make their fingers work well together. You can expect a girl to have fairly sloppy handwriting until she's around Seven and for a boy to take longer. This is why most schools don't teach cursive until the third grade.

You can tell if it's time to expect neater, more fluent handwriting when your child likes to work with clay and draws pictures with "clean," steady lines, and intersections that are fairly precise, and when both lines and circles have obvious reasons for being where they are. He may also be doing some simple sewing, playing with interlocking blocks and puzzles and tying his shoes with a bow. Thirty-five percent of the children have mastered their shoelaces at Six; 69% by Seven; 94% by Nine. The rest presumably go through life wearing loafers.

Even if your child doesn't have his fine skills under control, he should be expected to do the best he can, and he will, if he has little criticism and good supplies. While a thin marker is easier, the pencil—the hardest tool of all—is more challenging and children (and teachers) usually prefer them. Give him thin ones, no more than 3″ long (for an easier grip), with rather thick lead—so it won't break as quickly—and with an eraser to get rid of the mistakes.

By giving him the trappings of his

trade—good pencils and the beloved colored pencils, a pencil box and a ruler—you help a young child take pleasure in writing. Later, calligraphy pens and personalized stationery will encourage him, and so will your requests to write instructions to the newsboy; copy the list of groceries you dictate; and, of course, write his own thank-you notes.

While you don't want to tell him how to write—that's really the teacher's job—you can help the child who is embarrassed by his new cursive writing if you have him write certain cursive letters connectively. A series of *eeeee*'s, both right side up and upside down, are good and so are Greek keys and combinations of letters like *lflflflf*; *pbpbpb*; *mnmnmnmn*; *gqgq-gqgqgq*; *aoaoao*. You also can have him write "blind," by having him hide his writing hand with a piece of paper. This will make him see which letters he needs to practice. Older children will be able to read their own writing better if they're taught the reporter's trick for taking notes: to draw a line under a̲, u̲ and w̲ and above o̅, n̅ and m̅.

You'll also want to look at your child's handwriting techniques from time to time, for they can be a tip-off to other problems. Second or third graders who clutch their pencils too tightly may be overly anxious, while the one who is still doing some mirror writing or who places words poorly on a page or holds his pencil awkwardly may have some learning disability. Another child, whose handwriting is fine before lunch and nearly illegible afterward, may be allergic to something he ate.

The left-handed child may need a little special help at home, however. Gentle reminders will stop him from smudging the paper by having him make a crook of his arm as he writes. The more easily a child writes, the more he will enjoy writing.

ARITHMETIC

No subject causes such fear and loathing in children as arithmetic. Even when they like it they're apt to pretend that they don't, just to be like everyone else. Some children get a faulty start because they're taught how to add and subtract without having the chance to work with concrete examples, while others aren't quite ready to translate objects into symbols.

Other children—particularly girls—do poorly in arithmetic because they're expected to do poorly. They may have mothers who excuse their performance, saying that they are bad at math too (even though these same women may handle household budgets worth tens of thousands of dollars a year) or they have teachers who expect girls to get lower marks in math than in English because they're girls. It's better for a mother to act more competent than she feels—for an air of competence, like an aura of fear, is contagious—and it's better for teachers to expect both boys and girls to do equally well in math, because they can.

Studies show that their ability is the same until high school and then boys often pull ahead. Some experts think boys improve because they develop later, for late bloomers have a better sense of space, or that girls fall back because they tend to solve problems verbally. Most experts, however, have no idea why this difference develops or whether the tilt will continue when attitudes change.

Only one thing matters. Boys and girls study math for at least ten years and each year is built on the preceding one. They need a good foundation and a great deal of encouragement from their parents and teachers.

You can do much to make your child—boy or girl—comfortable with math without ever giving a formal lesson. Many of the rudiments of arithmetic are learned in play. Exercise is a great teacher, for a child will learn measurements subconsciously when he climbs, runs and jumps; a child's body is his first and best ruler.

Letting him keep the score in board games will teach him to add quickly—if he doesn't use a calculator—and when he helps you around the house he will learn to gauge length and depth and weight and volume—concepts that are grasped in sequence, one at a time, between the first and the sixth grades. Carpentry projects—even measuring and making a bookcase of bricks and boards—help a child translate these concepts into reality, while cooking helps him understand volume.

A calendar for his room is a help and so is a well-explained compass with well-marked degrees and a watch with an old-fashioned clock face. You also can have your child help you figure the miles you travel by car, checking the odometer against the road signs and against the measured miles. This reminds him of the precision in math. Boys and girls have to learn that they can talk or write their way around many verbal problems, but a math problem has only one answer.

Money helps children make sense out of numbers too—and there are few things that Eights like more than money. Take your third grader marketing with you, telling him how much you can spend before you start. He can compare prices against sizes, or check the unit prices and put back an item when you estimate the total together and find that it's too expensive. An Eight can even help you draw a true cash balance with your monthly bank statement—a basic how-to, why-to lesson in arithmetic (see Money).

For all the enrichment at home, children still need good solid teaching at school. Fortunately, their natural love of rote in the primary years helps them master the basic addition, subtraction and multiplication tables by fifth grade. Since each concept of math is based on those that have gone before, it's important for each teacher to know her material well. If some of them skip or skim in the lower grades, or teach these lessons poorly, your child will need extra help.

A patient, imaginative tutor is best, and preferably a stranger. If you try to teach him yourself, with drills and flash cards, all you'll get for your efforts will be tension and tears. (This is Ms. Experience talking.) You are too close to your young student; you don't know the latest techniques—and it's unfair to him. He has a hard enough time remembering his classroom lessons without having to remember your quite different ones, and then trying to put them together.

If the tutor has to come from your own family, it will be much more productive to have your child teach you, especially if you admit that you never understood some particular phase of math very well. That can only make him feel superior and therefore confident. Have him repeat the day's lesson so you can both do the same homework, but you can't use any math knowledge that he and his class haven't learned yet, which is harder than you think.

You may get something out of it too. It's surprising how much easier fractions, square root and cubic feet can be the second time around.

By the end of a few sessions you may be ready to try algebra, but your child is not. Algebra, unlike geometry or simpler math, requires abstract thinking and your child's mind hasn't taken that wonderful leap yet. This probably won't happen until he's at least in the ninth grade, more likely the tenth or even the eleventh. In the meantime, don't let your child's school push him into algebra too soon. The world does not need another generation of math-anxious parents.

SCIENCE

Science, often neglected in elementary school, can be exhilarating for a child in the Middle Years, because he can learn as much from a negative result as a positive one. If the subject is taught right, you'll find that nothing else can appeal so much to his curiosity, to his need to classify and especially to his imagination. You couldn't ask for anything better. As Einstein said, imagination is more important than knowledge.

If you have a good science program in your school, you can expect your child to have pond studies and bug studies and much more, starting in the first grade. Over the years the students may make bread and cut it open when it rises, to see how yeast makes bubbles; fill a third of a self-sealing plastic bag with water and a third with oil for an illustration of specific gravities; and make a geodesic dome out of drinking straws and paper clips to discover that triangles are the strongest geometric shape of all.

They may study erosion by filling a long plastic meat tray with a 1″ layer of dirt and mud, with a brick uplifting one end, where a few small rocks are stuck in the dirt. When the children gently pour cups of water onto the rocks, the waterfalls form rivulets and create a delta at the base of the tray. Or they make a digital clock work by connecting it to four electrodes, and sticking a negative one and a positive one into a pair of oranges and potatoes—

to discover how the acid makes a battery work. Or they stretch a piece of wool between two points and measure it under a magnifying glass to see how it swells when the weather is humid and contracts when it's dry.

Since a child learns by doing, you can see how much a good science program can help and yet science usually has a low priority. If your child's school has a limited program you'll want to push for a stronger one. In addition, you might organize a supplementary one with PTA volunteers and after-school, Saturday or summer sessions, which have begun to flourish around the country. Such programs appeal to children who want to know more; to parents who are beleaguered by day care problems and even to the volunteers because science is great fun to teach. Big city museums often have short science programs too and summer programs for the gifted. They are generally sponsored by the state, the city or the county and managed by universities.

As a parent you can encourage your child's interest by having science magazines around the house; by pointing out the daily changes in a plant that's ready to bloom (for observation is a critical skill); by seeing that your child has a magnifying glass in the first grade and a microscope around the fifth grade—or a telescope, if you're willing to study the sky with him. It's mighty hard for a novice to tell the bears from the dippers.

Your talks together about DNA, a new vaccine or whales that sing in the sea will keep him more interested in science than anything else you can do, however, as long as he does at least some of the talking. This is one more way you help him keep the lines open to his potential—and to you.

Computers

As Nell said so plonkingly at Twelve, "Anyone in my generation who can't use a computer might as well be illiterate." It's true. Computer languages, which are built on calculus, may separate the "ins" from the "outs" more effectively than anything since movable type. Fortunately, there should soon be more "ins" than ever since more and more schools are installing computers.

The real test of computer literacy is in the programming, which should be woven into the curriculum by the sixth or seventh grade. Even a much younger child can write and use simple programs and, once they do, they will know the rudiments of the newest and, for many, the most useful foreign language.

A computer not only can teach a child that he is smarter than a microchip but it helps him develop his creativity and his powers of logic. As he maps the circuits of a computer, he maps the circuits on both sides of his brain, and even the systematic use of commercial programs seems to help a child think better. The computer also has its social side, both good and bad. It helps the shy child, since students do their best at a computer if they work side by side, but it tends to encourage a formidable little computer clique that divides a class, unless the teacher blocks it.

The appeal of computer programming and computer games is not universal, how-

ever. For some reason, boys generally like these activities much more than girls do, and are usually more creative when they program. Others, both boys and girls, remain much more interested in the arts, which gives us a rich mix. The world of the future needs both programmers and artists and the twain are meeting more and more. The explosion of good software in graphics, writing and even musical composition is creating another renaissance. As our artistic children find out how much quicker they can reach their goals and how much they can accomplish—and how much drudgery they can escape—they are just as taken by this magical tool as the most math- and science-minded child.

FOREIGN LANGUAGES

The young child who is taught a foreign language is given a treasure for life. Right-handed children have their speech centers in the left side of their brain and second languages are programmed on the right—an arrangement that's sometimes reversed for lefties. When a second language is programmed early—even if it isn't used for years—the brain cells remain receptive to it and to all foreign languages for the rest of their lives. Apparently this is why Europeans, who start young and travel frequently from country to country, are usually bi- and often trilingual.

Although foreign languages can be learned later—for the brain continues to grow—most adults do poorly because they are so self-conscious about making mistakes and because they find the rhythm and the music of the language elusive. Some experts say children can avoid these problems if they're exposed to another language before they are Eight, while others think they can wait until Eleven or Twelve.

This instruction probably won't happen in elementary school, but you may be able to find a private class if your child is interested. Check the former students first, to make sure they liked it, and check

the curriculum, to make sure your child will learn the new language the way he learned his own: first he understood it, then he spoke it and much later he learned to read and write it. The child who likes a subject is much more likely to master it.

If there isn't a good class available, you might try simple foreign language records, but study it with him, choosing a language you've never tried either and tying it in with dreams of a trip you'll someday take together to that magical country. There has to be a goal. If that doesn't appeal to you, an elderly foreign neighbor might be pleased to talk his language to a pair of children, in exchange for helping him do some work in the yard: they talk as they work and you send over some cookies. You also may be able to find a Brownie leader from another country who will sometimes talk with the troop in her native tongue.

And if your child can't learn a foreign language anywhere? Don't worry about it. He'll slog through high school French just like we did. Other treasures will come his way, and they'll shine just as brightly.

HISTORY AND GEOGRAPHY

These are two subjects that are often skimmed at school and ignored by parents. Both are worth making a fuss about and should be taught separately. Geography has shaped history and history has shaped our world. Together they help teach these midway children just where they fit into it. Your child will only absorb the details at first, but the whole picture will begin to come together in the eighth grade.

Mythology is the first great way for teachers (or parents) to hook a child's interest. To a Six, the origins of fire and thunder are as riveting as fairy tales and just as plausible. Young children and old Greeks think alike. Through the early years good teachers often teach children history and geography with stories about the way their towns and states developed. They make neighborhood maps by walking the territory and study the grubby travel maps their classmates have brought back from vacation. Children are much more interested in geography and history when places and events are personalized.

The Revolutionary War tantalizes the class if the teacher reads daily bulletins about the soldiers at Valley Forge and gives each soldier a name; talks about the Lewis and Clark expedition as if it were just happening; and weaves economics into the quests of the past, so the children know the cause of today's effects. The more they understand consequences, the clearer the river of history becomes.

There is also horizontal history, which is usually overlooked. When you help your Ten find out what happened in a certain year—like 1750—all around the world, he begins to see how events impinged on each other. Playing detective inspires a child to learn more. Current events, with their human details splashed in the newspapers and television, falls into this same category and is often preferred by children, if they can give their opinions.

By the seventh grade your child may like to write the family history, from Ellis Island to your own hometown. Or draw a travel story of the family, by having him put stickers on a world map for every place an ancestor or a cousin ever lived, using a different sticker for each surname. Never mind that these relatives are no more than names in the family Bible and a few murky photographs. It's geography he's learning,

and history too, for you'll be weaving in the facts about the wars, floods and famines that made someone move along. There's nothing like the human condition to bring history to life.

FIELD TRIPS

Field trips can add depth to a school program—but they seldom do. This is because children usually regard the trip as a holiday, parents think of it as a reward and teachers find it an annoyance. This doesn't have to be. As one mother proved in a small private school in our neightborhood, a field trip can let children mesh newfound knowledge with the real world better than anything else. With a bus, a fulltime driver and a remarkably small budget, she arranged thirty field trips and events a year for the twenty to twenty-two children in each class. Some lasted only an hour, some for the whole day, and some were simply talks and slide shows, given to the class at school. The best programs often involved other parents, who explained their livelihoods as police officers, nurses, dieticians and actors and, not surprisingly, the best trips were led by the best teachers.

The program always worked no matter what the circumstances, because each trip was as disciplined as a classroom; each was designed by the teacher to fit into her curriculum; and none was undertaken until the subject had been studied for two to three weeks. A single trip often touched on more than one classroom subject. When the children would stare into the geodesic dome of a museum they would learn about history, geometry and art.

The focus of a trip should be underscored by giving the children a list of questions beforehand and either a work sheet to be used while they're there or a quiz afterward. This helps the students look at the world around them in an organized way.

A full-time field trip program can work in a private school or in a smaller, flexible public school, as long as each trip has a specific purpose and enough committed volunteers to provide one adult for every five to six children. However, any school, in any part of the country, should be able to turn workaday situations—which are often more interesting than museums—into substantive field trips. Younger children who think food is born in packages will like to see a farm, so they can see the source of eggs and milk and bread. An older class can follow up a farm visit with a harvest festival, dividing into groups to do the buying and cooking and to discuss the history of these festivals, from mythology through Michaelmas to our own Thanksgiving.

There are many other possibilities and these are among the best:

Science—When children walk in the woods and really look where they're going, they'll be investigating an ecosystem. A marsh is good too and so is a small pond. The children fill a bucket with the pond life, then study the water under a microscope and hatch the tadpoles in the classroom, returning them to the pond later as frogs. Although the children shouldn't pick wild flowers—so others may enjoy them and they can keep propagating—they can use their small, hand-held magnifying glasses to study them and the seeds on the ground, as well as the praying mantises and other bugs. The children can even find out how to make an insect zoo and have it ready, so the caterpillars they catch—if they are a certain kind—can live inside until they're butterflies.

Theater—A fourth-grade class can hear the story of *Romeo and Juliet* and an exciting passage or two—and then revel in a high school production of *West Side Story,* but again, there is a discussion afterward, to show children how the plot was updated. The universality of Shakespeare is even more appreciated by the sixth grade when some curious child discovers—and reads aloud—the bawdy lines in *Twelfth Night.* He'll win the class popularity contest—and you can bet the whole class will listen raptly.

History—Taking oral history will delight second graders if parents find interesting, articulate old people to tell them about the way it was. Older children can tour the neighborhood and draw its architecture, its buildings, streets and green spaces and see how its history fits into today.

Industry—When field trips turn from the general to the specific, things make more sense to a child. The business of making boxes or textiles is amazing; and to see a glassblower or a welder at work is unforgettable.

Professions—Children have always had a pretty good idea about medicine—and will like a behind-the-scenes tour of a hospital—but architects and brokers seem unreal unless the children see how they work.

Music—The production of sound is magic to a child—one of those abstracts in science that is touchable and tangible when children see how instruments are made; hear the startling array of sounds in an orchestra; and watch a drum and bugle corps learn to march with precision.

HOMEWORK

Few topics can cause more family friction than homework. It won't turn your house into a battleground if you remember that school is your child's job, not yours, and that homework is part of school. It's given to teach your child to work on his own, to plan his time and to reinforce what he's learned in the day.

You can teach him to skim his reading first to get an overall understanding, but he doesn't want or need you to tell him how to do the work, step by step. That would teach him, clearly if indirectly, that you think he isn't smart enough to do it on his own. And you certainly can't do any of the actual work or provide the research. If you did, you'd teach your child to lean on you—and leaners don't make good learners. You'd also teach him to be dishonest. Even a Six is smart enough to know how much of this work was his own and by Eight he'd know he was being unfair to his classmates, since the teacher grades everyone equally.

You do give some help to your child, of course, by giving him a small pad to list his homework assignments and an occasional clip from a newspaper or magazine on a subject his class is studying, if only as a token of your interest. Most of your help will be conversational, however. Ask him each day to tell you about his homework, and expect it to be about ten minutes a day, multiplied by the number of his grade. You'll do best if you sympathize a little when he moans about it, then help him understand the reason for an assignment or to consider how he's going to approach it. He'll also need to talk about it so he can clarify his thoughts before he starts and reinforce what he's learned afterward. The few questions he may have can usually be answered with prompting counter-questions of your own.

Check his homework when he's done, praising the parts that are right and penciling a light x in the left margin when there is a mistake on that line. He can either correct it or erase the x. It's his business. You may see so many mistakes—or such dumb ones—you'll be exasperated. Just give him a kiss, find something else to do and let the teacher do the commenting. Sometimes a child can learn more by failure than success and this is one of those times—especially if she makes him do the assignment again.

He'll do his homework more easily if he has an hour or two to play outside after school, for exercise gives a child extra oxygen so he can think better. He'll have to stop once or twice while he's working, too. While adults need a break every forty-five minutes, children need to stop every fifteen to thirty minutes. Just getting a glass of water or sharpening some pencils is enough.

Your child also needs a reasonably quiet and well-lit place to study where he can have access to an up-to-date globe, a set of encyclopedias and a dictionary simple enough to read the entries to himself in the second grade, and a more sophisticated edition by Ten. If he gets too distracted in his room, you might have him study where you can be nearby. Sometimes a parent's quiet presence makes the work go quicker. By the fourth grade he also should have the chance to study at the library one afternoon a week, if only because it's such a grown-up thing to do.

You help your child do his homework by what you withhold too. As shocking as it sounds, there needs to be a ban on television after dinner, Monday through Thursday evenings, even when your child says he doesn't have any homework. If you don't impose this rule, assignments will often be forgotten until a favorite show is over, and then there will be trouble. You want him to know right from the start that he doesn't play on school nights—a concept he'll have to carry through high school.

That's why most of his telephone calls on these school nights should be brief and homework-related, and if he wants to play music the volume should be low. An occasional television show or a babbling phone call is allowed, of course—you're not running a jail—but these should be rewards for good general performance, not concessions after a scene.

In the sixth grade, you'll find, your child's homework is his weather vane. You can spot trouble in time to stop it by occasionally checking the notes he takes at school, to make sure he uses some degree of precision and has a method for checking off his daily record of assignments. You don't, however, want to use long- and short-term threats to make your child study more. Admission to college doesn't depend on a third grader's homework, and if the college thinks it does, you wouldn't want your child to go there.

You'll also want to ignore the way he slouches and scooches around when he studies, as if he had a bellyful of jumping beans. That's all right. It's the homework that matters, not the posture.

THE STUDENT

The only thing more miraculous than children is their ability to learn. It's truly stunning to realize how much information they gather in these seven years, as long as the subjects are taught in an interesting way and the students are respected. Never again will they soak up so much and with such greed.

As the person who cares about your child the most, you have to see that he can meet the demands of school well, by seeing that he gets plenty of sleep, the right food, some homework guidance and your support for school activities.

You must also see that your child is at least reasonably well taught. We have put so much money and effort into salaries, textbooks and maintenance that we sometimes forget the key figure in all of this education: the student. Your student. You won't be able to prevent some things from going wrong—some things inevitably do—but your child relies on you to try to correct them and, if nothing works, to show him how to handle them with grace, and to remind him that a single school year isn't forever.

LEARNING PROBLEMS

Even the best teacher doesn't have all of the children learning at grade level in every subject all of the time—and sooner or later, your child may be the one who slips behind.

You may find that your smart, capable, adorable third grader is reading on a first-grade level or that he is a wipeout in math. It's time for a coach, not a pity party. The child who has fallen behind needs help quickly, particularly in math, where each layer of information is built on the one that's gone before. This may seem like an overreaction, but you couldn't give your child a better present, and the sooner you do it the sooner he'll catch up and the less his self-esteem will suffer. Just one or two after-school sessions a week should put him back on track in a semester.

You'll want a tutor whose work has pleased other parents—and their children; who sets goals for the child in three-month blocks and who will give you a status report every two to three weeks. A practiced tutor also should be able to recognize the signs of a more serious learning problem (see Learning Disabilities) and refer your child to a doctor or a psychologist to see if there is a physical or emotional cause and get an individual intelligence test, so

you can gauge his potential. A child's ability to learn is always affected by his health, his diet, his intelligence, his emotions and his readiness. Sometimes the child simply can't concentrate at school if the teacher is unkind or if there are serious problems at home. Anxiety or anger and fear are so scary and so absorbing that they keep a child from learning.

You or your husband may think you can tutor your child yourselves, but someone else would almost surely do the job better. Most parents have so much love invested in their child that they get mad or tense with each wrong answer, until the child feels too guilty to learn. You also may be tempted to make the sessions too long (fifty minutes is ample) and might make it the main discussion at dinner and when company comes over. An experienced tutor, however, will be perceptive enough to spot the blocks to your child's learning and will have the patience and pleasantness of a kind auntie. And why not? He isn't beset with the conflicts a parent has and he also knows how hard the work can be. Many professional tutors have had tutoring themselves.

Patience is another mark of a good tutor. He waits for the child to have a snack and a break at home, so he'll be fresh, and then he drills him on his times tables, his spelling, his reading, over and over, first building on his strengths so he will feel good about himself, and giving him a break midway so he'll learn better. By taking his time, the child learns one concept thoroughly before moving on to the next. This helps a child realize that speed is the enemy of accuracy. If you were a fly on the wall, you'd see the tutor teach your child a dozen tricks to help him associate a fact with a time, a place or a sound. In teaching math, he works with the materials with which a child feels comfortable, such as maps, geometric shapes, puzzles or games of concentration, and he may use an abacus rather than paper and pencil, to let the child focus directly on the problem.

Your own role is indirect. Encourage your child to get involved in some extra-curricular activity in which he excels, to build his confidence, and read with him about subjects he finds interesting, to strengthen your bond. Cooking together can do both and it will teach him some arithmetic too, even though it's incidental. Two tablespoons are an ounce; eight ounces are a cup; two cups are a pint, and when it comes to flour, a pint is really a pound, the world around. Seeing is believing.

The child who has been overplaced or poorly taught at school is not the only one who needs special attention. There is also the underachiever. When the amount of homework goes up—often in the fourth grade—this child slows down, but not because he can't do it. He may be hanging out with nonachieving classmates who make fun of good students; he may be a particularly creative child who is bored by the rote and routine or he may be too willful to do what his teachers require. Or he may be afraid to grow up to the new responsibilities or afraid that his parents

won't give him as much attention if he does good work or that he can't meet their expectations, so why try?

At home this child needs a well-structured life with an after-school activity in which he can shine (for underachievers are usually depressed); books that feature heroes and much derring-do (for most underachievers have no heroes); a relaxed nightly family dinner where you talk with your child as you would with a friend; and a fixed time and place to study. His homework will take longer at first, because he has to figure out new habits. He also needs a "hands-off" policy from his parents—since the underachieving child may try to use his homework to get attention—and a great deal of patience. It will take at least a year for him to change. In the meantime, ignore the schoolwork and give your child a ready smile or invite him to a game of cards for no reason, or take him camping for a weekend, just the two of you. It's better to reward a child for being himself than for what he can do.

When he brings home his papers, don't expect A's. Congratulate him for B's and C's (but not wildly so); accept his D and F papers with a raise of your eyebrow, and give no sympathy if he fails the subject and has to go to summer school. You simply assume that he has failed because he chose to fail and that if he wants to pass, he will. As tempting as it is, you don't say more—and of course you don't do any of his work for him. This tells the underachiever that his grades are basically his business and that you think he's strong enough and smart enough to carry his own burdens. If you give your child this respect, he'll try harder to earn it.

And if you put away your weapons, school won't be a battleground.

SCHOOLITIS

There is no childhood disease as prevalent and as virulent as schoolitis—that sudden (and quite real) illness that strikes a child at 7 A.M. and often on a Monday. It usually first appears about two weeks after first grade starts and the basic cause is fear. It may be sparked by a difficult demand at school, a foolish rumor, an embarrassment. Our Kate, an elegant lady now, still blushes to remember the cookies she tossed in front of the first grade, and how hard it was to go back to school the next day.

This onetime problem is typical of a child in the early grades, while an occasional child has a gnawing complaint that makes him want to stay home more often. This child likes school but—the teacher's too strict; the other children make fun; the desks are too hard; or he just has to sit still so much. These are the problems your child may not mention, but if you can get him to talk about them the ghosties usually go away. And if he won't talk, spend a morning at school just listening. Even if you don't see the problem, your child will be comfortable enough to explain it because you're familiar with his domain. He may well have a real complaint and you can do something about it.

For about one child in sixty, however, the fears are intangible and recurring and usually caused by a deeper fear—a scary walk to school or the embarrassment of having to take a free lunch or by tension at home. If you and your husband often quarrel, your child may be subconsciously afraid to leave home in the morning in case one of you might not be there at night. Generally, however, a child is simply afraid to leave the security of the home he knows for the school, with all its strangeness.

Most schoolitis isn't really serious. It's just the way a child tells you (and himself) that he needs a little more attention and affection at home. It's a good idea to give it. An occasional day off, even once a week for a month, can give a child the chance to patch his self-confidence, but if it goes on much longer, you'll want to see that he stays in bed (so he'll get well quicker)—with peace and quiet (which means no TV); without company (in case he's con-

tagious)—and is brought the blandest, most sugar-free meals—in short, a day so dull and food so dreary that school will start to look pretty good.

It worked in our house for years.

OBLIGATIONS

Good schools and good politicians have something in common. They depend on your support. Somebody has to chaperone an occasional field trip, referee a game and help at the fall bazaar and, since your child benefits, that somebody should sometimes be you.

You should, at the very least, attend some of the PTA meetings, preferably with your husband, so you can talk intelligently with the teacher and the teacher can see how the child fits into the family. These meetings can be tedious—parents do go on when their children are involved—but they're seldom as emotional or as silly as they were when your child was in nursery school. They are also much more important, for they give you the chance to understand the school's philosophy, if it has one, and to decide if the teachers are living up to it. You'll learn what kinds of problems the teachers face and see how they treat each other and if they speak of the children with respect. Your presence also shows the faculty that you care, which will prompt them to care about your child a little more. Teachers usually treat a child somewhat better if his parents are active in school affairs.

Your child will appreciate your atten-

STUDENTS' RIGHTS

CHILDREN HAVE THE RIGHT TO:

- a principal who listens to a child's complaints—even about a teacher—and who resists the public address system most of the time;
- a curriculum that includes interesting, informative field trips, movies and assemblies;
- a PTA that puts the needs, of students at least as high as those of parents and teachers;
- parents who know that if an intelligent, stable child can't learn a particular subject, it is because the teacher can't teach it—at least not to that particular child.

CHILDREN HAVE THE RIGHT TO A TEACHER WHO:

- calls them by name right from the start;
- talks with each child, rather than at him;
- knows that a happy child learns best;
- gives center stage to the children, rather than herself;
- knows that children will do almost anything they're asked, if they know why;
- pays attention to what they say, how they sound and how they move, for children speak in many languages;
- invites confidences—and keeps them;
- controls the class without mocking or spanking;
- uses praise, not threats, to encourage the students;
- has no favorites—or targets—among the class;
- believes that all children want to learn;
- stimulates independence, encourages questions and respects originality;
- makes a thoughtful lesson plan each day;
- assigns homework regularly and grades it within a day or two;
- gives work that is challenging, yet attainable;
- lets children write some reports in small groups, so they can learn teamwork;
- knows that different children learn in different ways—seeing, hearing, touching and doing—and teaches to each style;
- orders individual psychological and learning tests when needed;
- discusses results fully with the parents, and teaches to the child's strengths, not his weaknesses.
- takes a minimum amount of sick leave;
- refuses any drinks or drugs that could affect her bahavior in class;

CHILDREN ALSO HAVE THE RIGHT TO:

- school rules posted, reviewed and explained in September;
- the respect of every adult in school—from janitor to principal;
- school rules posted, reviewed and explained in September;
- discipline given quietly and privately, to leave dignity in tact;
- enough exercise to keep the oxygen flowing, the brain clear and the body active;
- a break after a test;
- a little time in the school day when they can do whatever they want—or absolutely nothing;
- a drink of water when necessary;
- a sign-out sheet, so they can go to the bathroom without embarrassment;
- a special diet if their health requires it, and special holidays if their religion does;
- supervision at lunch and on the playground;
- cafeteria food without additives and preservatives and unnecessary sugar and salt;
- a substantial lunch—free if necessary;
- vending machines that sell only fruits, nuts, yogurt, milk and pure juice, until lunch is over;
- a classroom with radiators that work; windows that are glazed; lights that don't flicker; furniture that suits the size of the children and an allergy-free environment;
- a pleasant place to eat, a playground with enough space and equipment for all ages, and a well-supplied bathroom with stall doors that lock;
- a school that's clean, inside and out;
- a sense of safety anywhere in the school building or on the grounds.

TEACHERS' RIGHTS

TEACHERS HAVE THE RIGHT TO:

- respect, without mockery or practical jokes;
- appreciation for trying—even when their efforts fail;
- smiles from their pupils when school begins and all day long;
- punctuality, by all the students, every blessed day;
- well-washed children whose clothes, hair and teeth are clean and who use deodorant if they've reached puberty;
- well-fed children who can concentrate on their work instead of their stomachs;
- well-rested children who sleep eight to ten hours a night;
- well-supplied students, so the class isn't distracted by borrowing;
- students who turn in reasonably legible homework on time and without much parental help;
- courteous children who clean up any mess they make;
- alert students who aren't under the influence of drugs or alcohol;
- a few minutes during each subject, each day, when everyone is listening.

TEACHERS HAVE THE RIGHT TO EXPECT PARENTS TO:

- encourage the child to think positively about the school, the curriculum and the teacher;
- be half as realistic about the abilities of their children as they are about the children next door;
- monitor television so their children see enough trash to feel part of the crowd but not enough to interfere with their homework;
- tell the office how to find them if needed and, if they are divorced, when each parent is in charge;
- contribute to the school and offer this help before it's asked;
- attend parent-teacher conferences regularly and at least some PTA meetings;
- tell them if the child is under stress at home, so they can be more understanding at school;
- feel free to observe the class or discuss a problem, but only by appointment;
- let teachers give their side in a disagreement with the child;
- accept their advice, if they think psychological, physical or mental tests are needed;
- go to counseling, if their child needs it too.

TEACHERS ALSO HAVE THE RIGHT TO:

- a class size they can manage;
- enough supplies, but not enough to waste;
- a free half-hour for lunch, without a single duty;
- safety at school;
- respect from their colleagues;
- a principal who knows their strengths and strengthens their weaknesses;
- a central administration and a school board who remember that children are their reasons for being and who always put their needs first.

dance too. It helps him fuse home and school, although it's nightmarish for a Six to realize that his parents will talk to his teacher and, dear God, they will talk about him. He will hardly be able to sleep until you come home and tell him what the teacher said about him, word for word, emphasizing the good remarks and toning down the bad. There are times when a child needs encouragement more than accuracy. When you show an interest in his outside life, he will find it easier not only to tell you how he spent his day but also to confide in you, and at an age when confidences don't come easily.

Attendance at PTA meetings makes parent-teacher conferences go smoother too. The better you know the teacher, the easier it will be to decipher her nuances. Listen well but remember the teacher's classic admonition to parents: "If you don't believe everything your child tells you about school, I won't believe everything he tells me about home."

Although parents seldom take advantage of it, a day—or even a half day—of observation is especially valuable and is acceptable to any good teacher, as long as it has been arranged in advance, at her convenience, and the parents keep absolutely quiet. That's when you find out if the teacher shows the children all the respect she says she does; if there are teacher's pets and teacher's targets; and if your child is keeping up with the work, adjusting well to the classroom and has a band of trusty friends. You are your own best reporter.

FUND RAISING

Every school has more needs than money, and parents must help to meet them. This may seem burdensome, but fund raising pays its own dividends. You'll learn new skills, from organizing a cakewalk to putting on a carnival, you'll meet the parents of your child's friends and you'll be helping your child get a better education.

There are hundreds of ways to do it. In one New England village the parents have sold their children's outgrown boots each autumn (an operation remarkably called the Old Rubbers Exchange), but most money is raised at bazaars selling chances, games, activities and items that come from the stove, the workbench or the sewing machine.

FRIENDSHIPS

By Six, children revel in each other's company. It's part of their great need to be popular and an instinctively wise one. The child who is socially confident now will find adolescence much easier.

Friendships are often the greatest teachers in the world—especially in the Middle Years—and they matter much more to a child than grades. And so they should. A strong friendship teaches children about charity and compassion; honor and honesty; loyalty and discretion; trust and dependability; giggles and good humor.

Above all, a true friend helps your child pursue will-o'-the-wisp dreams as if they were real, and never even laughs when they turn silly.

Meg, at Ten, and her pal Victoria knew they were ace investigators because each had been told so by her own best friend. With this assurance they decided that the gruff old cabdriver in the neighborhood was a mystery that needed solving. He lived in an unkempt house; he seldom shaved; he took his cab license from the dashboard every time he left his car; and he kept what looked like a large empty cage in the front yard. Once, no doubt, he had trapped someone inside it and he would surely do it again.

They tiptoed after this poor man whenever they saw him walking in the neighborhood. They kept written accounts of his movements, checked through his mail (until their mothers found out about it) and spun stories to each other so terrible they knew they must be true.

One sunny summer day, when Victoria's mother said she couldn't go out and Meg's baby-sitter said she could, Meg walked by herself to the FBI Building—twenty long blocks—clutching the card she had typed herself: "Meg Kelly, DETECTIVE." She knew it was only a matter of getting hired.

She asked to see her hero, Jedgar Hoover (or J. Edgar to the rest of us). When the courteous guard said the director of the FBI was busy, she said, "I'll wait." And so she did, all day long, all alone, getting madder and sadder by the minute. When she left, she put her card in her pocket, bought love beads from a vendor, decided she was a flower child for the rest of the summer and knew her friendship with Victoria would never be quite the same again. There are some things that have to be shared.

CAMP

A schoolchild has three months a year to do nothing—or what looks like nothing to his parents. By July the summer may look pretty empty to him too: most of the plans he had during the school year seem silly now. Even if the family vacation is still to come, he will complain: "There's nothing to do!"

Camp time.

Just to count on a week or two of camp—either day camp or sleepaway—can brighten a child's whole summer. The actual experience may not be as great as the anticipation and the recollection, but it will give him the chance to learn about himself and a little separation will make parents and child appreciate each other more.

These benefits depend, of course, on the child and the camp and the timing. While you may know that camp will be a great adventure, your child will be much more timid about it. Be as flexible about the decision as possible. Even if it is a necessary part of your day care arrangements, your child should know that you want him to go there for the fun of it. That's what camp is all about.

Camp is nifty just because it isn't mandatory; it isn't like school and you and your child have lots of choices. There are 10,000 camps around the country, of which about 2500 are accredited by the American Camping Association. A good one usually belongs to the ACA or is so firmly established and well recommended that it doesn't need to be.

A Six or Seven will usually be much happier in a day camp or a vacation Bible school but an Eight or Nine who's already been to day camp should be ready for a week or two at a general overnight camp. There are, of course, exceptions. The older child who is terribly shy may do better in a day camp, preferably one where he

knows at least one camper or counselor or where the neighborhood is familiar. The outgoing young rowdy, on the other hand, may be ready for a boarding camp sooner than you'd think, because he's ready for the action and activities and pranks. Some children as young as Eight or Nine will be thrilled to go to a specialized camp and preteens throw themselves into these camps with their characteristic enthusiasm, but only if the specialty of the camp captures their interests and encourages their talents.

Whether the camp you pick is a day camp or a sleepaway, general or specialized, a luxury or a bare-bones necessity for the working mother, the best suggestions will probably be passed on to you by parents who liked them and, more to the point, whose children liked them. Nevertheless, you'll still have much weeding to do to pick the one that's best for the age and temperament of your child. In all cases, set your price limit before you start looking. If you don't, you may find you and he have set your hearts on something you can't afford, and you'll either have to lower your expectations (and feel like you're giving your child second best) or you'll resent the extra cost.

The choice of a boarding camp is clearly more critical. It's especially important to know its safeguards and its safety record; its facilities for the children who get sick or hurt; the extra charge—if any—for craft supplies, special events, lessons or horseback riding. You'll also want to know its weekly menus, the activities of a typical day and whether the campers have any choice in their activities (they should). To find the answers, you'll have to use the telephone freely, asking the camp directors these and many other questions, including the ages, backgrounds and training of the staff members from the year before and those they have already hired for the next season.

A good camp has counselors who are at least eighteen or nineteen, with one assigned for each half dozen Sevens and Eights and one for every eight children who are Nine and older. They should be agile, talented, spirited and happy to be with children. In a sports camp, the counselors should be good coaches as well as good athletes, and if you're interested in a computer camp or a drama camp, the counselors should know how to work with children as well as how to write a program or act onstage.

Call some recent campers from your area—the directors should be glad to give you their names—and ask them what the place is like. The most important camper to ask, however, is your own child. From the information you've gathered, he should be able to pick two or three favorites, then you'll want to look over the places if you can. This is especially important if they are overnight camps. They should live up to their brochures—pictures can be deceiving—and you should check on the flora—and the mold. They can ruin the whole camp experience for an allergic child, so you should see if the cabin smells moldy and ask if goldenrod or ragweed will be blooming nearby.

To the first-time camper, even the most idyllic place may seem scary as the time to leave gets near, even if he's been to see it.

CAMPER'S SNACK

YIELD: 1 lb.

This makes a great snack to ship to a child at camp, and an Eight can make it the rest of the year.

MIX   1 c. Chinese noodles
1 c. raisins OR chopped apricots OR chopped dried apples
¾ c. unsalted cashews OR peanuts
¼ c. sunflower OR pumpkin seeds

Set aside on waxed paper. In a double boiler

MELT   1 c. chocolate bits

Have him drizzle this over the noodle mixture, using a spoon to divide it into small heaps as he goes, so the snacks will dry separately.

You can help alleviate much of his anxiety by stressing all the things he can do at camp that he can't do anywhere else. Be truthful about his specific fears. He has the right to know that he'll probably be homesick, just like everyone else, but that homesickness is usually cured in a few days.

In case it isn't, only enroll the first timer for a single session, and if he's particularly nervous about going away, cut a deal: a two-week camper can quit if he's still unhappy after a week, and the four-to-six-week camper can leave after he's been there for two. He'll feel relieved and you'll rest easier too, since you can be pretty sure the joy of camp life will overcome most if not all of his homesickness.

In the meantime, have him pack stationery, addresses for neighbors and grandparents and include stamped envelopes to you and his dad, of which he may send several. You'll also want to prepare a special surprise, by mailing him a letter, a poster of a comic book several days before he leaves. It will give him something to open at the very first magic mail call. Follow with letters two to three times a week—even a postcard from the dog with nothing but a paw print will be welcome—and a weekly phone call, but don't make

your news sound so wonderful he'll wish he were home.

His own news—by phone or by that rarity, a letter—may be full of woe, but much of this will be standard camp gripes, which he'll forget as quickly as he forgets a knee-skinning fall when he's home. If the problems seem more serious or if they continue from one phone call to the next or if you think his health is at risk, you'll want to talk to the director or the counselor to see if some changes can be made. You'll also want to visit him on Parents Day if you can, so you can enjoy some of the specialness of camp. A family is closer when the members share good memories.

When he comes home you'll feel amazingly tender toward this child—this stranger who seems to have grown so much, even if he's just been gone two weeks. And then reality sets in. You unpack to find he either never wore his new clothes or he stained them hopelessly; that he wore only two pairs of undershorts the whole time and that he only brought home one sock out of every pair, which means you'll only buy one color next summer.

Your child may decide that one summer of camp is enough for a long while, or he'll beg to go back year after year. In time, even the ardent camper will outgrow the allure, but the memories will linger. At one jolly Thanksgiving, our four young guests from two different families met for the first time and dazzled us with their clever skits after dinner: Jennifer and Heather and Eliza and John had all learned the same routines at camps scattered across

the country. They had learned how to make instant friendships too.

The best lessons in life aren't learned in books.

CLUBS

Clubs are a hallmark of the Middle Years, a sound and fairly painless way to teach children how to rely on each other and have a fair amount of fun as they do it. Parents organize, supervise and maintain the more formal organizations, like the Scouts, as early as kindergarten, but informal clubs begin to pop up like so many buttercups, even before the third grade. They are loose, intense and short-lived; membership is almost always limited to one sex and power is the name of their game. The membership decides who will lead, who will follow and who won't be invited at all. The groups split up and the members merge again in new ways, for new reasons, although it may be years before you learn what they are.

Meg was a self-proclaimed leader in the third grade when she decided that she would be president of a club for the chosen few and the tall pine tree at her school would be the gathering place. Members of the Secret Pine Needles would rush to reach it every morning and scramble to their appointed branches, with Meg higher than the rest to receive her daily tribute— a bag of candy from each member which was apparently the only reason for this club. She shared the candy but not always, and seldom generously, which caused her ouster rather soon, and she refused to re-join for weeks, mostly because she wasn't invited.

As children get older, the purposes of their clubs are more and more noble and usually much more grandiose than they can carry out (to Feed the World, by collecting cans of soup, which they don't know how to deliver; to Stop All Pollution in the Lake Forever, by picking up litter near their cabin on the shore for the last three weeks of summer; to Stop Drugs

Everywhere, for which they make signs for two Saturdays in a row). The clubs can make the members feel special, and even the excluded don't feel so rejected if they're kept out by club rules, however strange.

If there are no clubs, there will be cliques, particularly for girls, and cliques make outsiders feel much more unwanted. You can help the situation by helping your child understand how much exclusion can hurt and by asking her not to join in the gossip about the outsiders, although she'll find that difficult in these gossipy years. You also want to ask her to be more friendly with children at school who aren't in her crowd, to invite an outsider to her lunch table occasionally or to visit her after school or bring her to a family picnic. The child who limits herself to a tight group often finds that it gets smaller and smaller and so do her own horizons.

You also want your child to take an active part in larger organized groups—a team, a cooking class, a church or Scout group—so she learns to slide easily from one group to another and to draw friends from each one.

Uniformed groups like the Cub Scouts or the Brownies for younger boys and girls and the Boy or Girl Scouts for older children can be great, particularly for a child who is either new to the neighborhood or rather shy, and the 4-H Club, the many youth groups at church or temple and such clubs as De Molay and Job's Daughters for Twelves are all fine ways to draw children together. They also teach them responsibility and satisfy their love for order, and for rewards, and an overnight camping trip or the chance to cook around a campfire fulfills some of their love for adventure. The best of these groups encourage a child to achieve, one small level at a time, to give to others and to learn new skills that make them more self-sufficient.

PARTIES

The older children are, the greater their need for parties. Birthday celebrations are dandy but so are spur-of-the-moment multifamily picnics, movies with the gang and skating parties with cocoa and sandwiches afterward. All are outlets for young exuberance and they encourage adult exuberance too.

If you need a reason to celebrate the simple fact that you are all alive and together, remember that parties are sound preparations for the future. The child who has been to many of them will feel more comfortable when he goes to teenage parties later. It is self-consciousness that causes a socially inexperienced child to make a damn fool of himself when beer or pot is offered at high school parties.

There is an art to giving good parties and the first rule is to enjoy them. This is easy to do if you don't make big, scary productions out of them and if you let your child take part in the step-by-step plans and do much of the work. In the process he'll learn to be more sensitive about your outlay of time and money and, with his past experience and your reminders, be more sensitive to the feelings of others.

The sense of competition should be avoided in any party. A good party is much more than spending the most money or making the biggest splash. It's caring enough about friends to make an effort; it's liking them enough to put their interests first; it's trusting them enough to be silly and to let them be silly too.

The invitations can be distributed at school, but only if the whole class is invited or if he asks much less than half. Even then it would be kinder to deliver them to their homes, mail them or use the phone. Although the other children will probably know about the party, they won't feel so blatantly excluded.

There's an art to being a good guest too, which your child must learn well in the primary years, for the same rules will apply throughout his school years. You want your child to learn that if he expects to have fun, he probably will, but if he doesn't, nobody should know; that he has to say hello to the host (and the parents) when he arrives, even if he has to search them out, so they'll know he's glad to be there; that he must be polite to everybody (even certain yukky girls); that he mustn't complain about the food or the activities or publicly compare one party to another; that he has to tell the parents if he breaks anything and offer to fix it or get his parents to fix it; that he should call for a ride home as soon as the party is over, and that he always, always must say thank you to the party giver and the parents when he leaves.

No matter how well he follows these rules, however, every child is left out of some important party sooner or later. The distress will be great, although a boy may pretend he didn't notice the exclusion—a sign for you to ignore it too.

A girl tends to hurt more openly, and you'll feel the pain just as much. If you're surprised that she wasn't invited—and you're bold enough—you can call the party-giver's mother and ask if the invitation got lost, which can happen, especially if a child helps with the addresses. Or you can pet your child and comfort her and say you're sorry and that you too were sometimes left out when you were her age—and then take her to the movies so you can think about something else. Later, when the worst of the hurt is over, have a late-night talk together so she can try to figure out why she wasn't asked. This is a listening time for you, when you'll find out that she blames her hand-me-downs—or her fancy clothes; the teacher who calls on her too much—or never calls on her; the fact that you work—or that you don't. Once she's talked out, consider together whether the oversight was just bad manners, which is one reason why she must learn good ones, or whether a problem does exist and if it does, how to get rid of it.

When a child is left out, rather often, she may have a personality problem which will have to be identified, analyzed and attended to by both of you but with her leading each step of the way. It might also be that she simply needs more practice in party giving, so she'll know how to be a better, more relaxed guest. Perhaps you and the mother of one of her more popular friends or classmates can let your children give a party together. A celebration of the Fourth with fireworks or a movie shown at home, with popcorn and candy bars, is a good way to start—all techniques that work as well for a son as a daughter.

Parties have values, just like people. When children find out what they are, they learn how to give their friends a good time and how to have one too. This is another basket of sunshine that can light up their world.

BIRTHDAY PARTIES

A child between Six and Twelve takes everything seriously, especially himself, and if he had to name an essential ingredient of happiness, his birthday would rank at least as high as his books, his bike or his room. And the most important part of his birthday is his party.

This is particularly true for a child between Six and Nine and absolutely true for a girl at any age, although the parties will be significantly different at Ten, Eleven and Twelve. At this age a girl wants a party to be more sophisticated than before, while a boy may want to treat a couple of buddies to the movies or the skating rink and save the birthday cake and presents for his fam-

ily. Besides, he feels so unsure of his social graces now that he's afraid that any party of his will be fraught with small disasters. It's the why-look-for-trouble? school of thought.

When you make the effort to adjust to changing demands, you're teaching your child a little more about caring. The party you give, like the dinner you put on the table, is a gift of love and, like the meal, it is not the cost that counts but the care you take, the sensitivity you show.

In the primary years, a birthday party follows the old preschool formula: one guest for every year that's being celebrated, but this may have to be stretched a bit so your child can ask last year's best friend, who's being so dreadful now, and the child everyone else forgets. If your child can be generous about the party, so can you, but some children will still be left out. Remind your child, as always, that he mustn't talk about the party, before or after, in front of those who aren't invited. Manners that may seem obvious to you are often forgotten by the exuberant Eight.

Your child will enjoy his party most if he helps you plan the menu and the games—easier done if you can help him remember what he liked best about a party when he came home from it. A few test-marketed ideas will make him feel less anxious. He also should help choose the supplies, especially the favors. A grab bag of small wrapped gifts—one to a customer—is a good way to give them, and then you can forget prizes. He'll want to help you plan the games too, so children

INVITATIONS

A birthday party is a significant occasion and an invitation is significant too. The time and place, and any other information, like "bring a swimsuit," should be written, and either mailed or hand-delivered, for it's easy to unsettle an Eight if you ask by phone. When we invited Josh to our friend Tom's party on Tuesday at four-thirty, he asked—determined to be suave, "Is that A.M. OR P.M.?"

can let off their steam, but suggest team games or noncompetitive sports, and skip the prizes or give everyone a prize for something, instead of a favor. This reduces some of the party pressure.

If competition between children is a bad idea, competition between adults is even worse. Children don't need hired entertainment to make a party go. They need laughter, they need jokes and they need parents who want to give them a good time. They also need tapes playing in the background, especially at the beginning of their parties. If you don't play some music, the awkward little silences will make you feel like a failure as a hostess, when the problem really lies in their own lack of poise.

The best birthday parties we've given were the ones we took almost as seriously as our children did. We planned them together for weeks, choosing a theme for the party, a cake decorated and iced to carry out the theme (see Shape Cake) and some designated limits. There was a limit on the guests (it usually was broken); a firm cut-off time (always broken but not severely); and a ceiling on the amount that guests could spend on gifts, which was very low and well-emphasized to parents beforehand. It's important that the guests know their presence matters much more than their presents.

It was the Shape Cake, however, that made these parties. It takes some extra thinking, and an extra hour or two to make, but your child will think it's worth it and so will you.

Shape Cake

To a child, the best birthday cake is homemade and the very best one is a Shape Cake

to fit the theme of the party—cut, iced and decorated in three dimensions, rather than a flat cake with a picture on it.

Forget about having the talent to decorate a cake. All you need for a Shape Cake is a seven-minute icing, candy trimmings, a free imagination and a great deal of self-confidence. In exchange, you'll have a roomful of awestruck children who will believe you when you tell them that those upside-down sugar cones are really Indian teepees. Artful distraction is a big reason for its success. Colors, icing, candies and odd configurations—and especially the solemnity of your presentation—will cover up your mistakes. You're sure to make some, but let's hope you won't err as badly as we did on Mike's ninth birthday.

After a trip to an air and space exhibit, Mike and eight little boys rushed to the table for candy, pop and balloons and to see if this year's cake would match the pirate ship of Six; the train cake of Seven; the courthouse square at Eight. Too late, we saw the cake with fresh and startled eyes: the beautifully iced red rocket baked in a 46-ounce grapefruit juice can was, in fact, the largest, pinkest phallic symbol since the last Roman orgy. Some blushed mightily, a few took timid bites and all had the grace the keep quiet.

You should beware not only of phallic symbols but of cakes that look like people or animals, as we learned when one mother served a copy of her son's beloved teddy bear. You can imagine how he wailed when its eyes and ears were eaten. Instead make a cake in the shape of a cash register, a sewing box, a beach scene, an Indian village or a farm and decorate it with candies that can be stretched, twisted, cut, melted or used as they are. It's all in the way you present it and the yarn you spin.

When you make a farm, cover the sheet cake with tan icing—the dirt of the farmyard, you'll say—and sprinkle it with the smallest candies you can find: chicken feed, of course. The farmyard is bordered with candles on one side and lollipop trees on the other, their sticks heated enough to melt holes in the peanut butter cups so they will stand upright.

The barn, iced red or yellow, is on the third side and is made in a simple loaf pan, with another loaf cut in half, diagonally, to form the triangle that makes the roof. Flat chocolate bars are glued with icing to become the roof, the shutters and the open door, and the doorway is scooped away and painted with dark melted chocolate, like a shadow (you can't go wrong with chocolate), and straw of toasted coconut tumbles out. Should the seams of the roof be too obvious—even when pressed lightly with a hot knife—you sift a little confectioner's sugar on top and tell the children that there was some frost the night before.

A silver kiss hangs from a slim peppermint pole in the barnyard—the bell calls the farmer to dinner—and a haystack of toasted shredded coconut is in one corner. In another, there is the blue pond made of icing, with ducks cut out of yellow gumdrops. Never mind that they don't look like ducks; this child *believes*.

Before you make your Shape Cake, draw a sketch of it to make sure it's big enough for each child to have a special piece. You then take it to the dime store to choose chimneys, stepping stones, roofs, doors, flower tubs, wheels and cannons from the candy counter, buying enough extra candy for each guest to have a sample of everything in a separate dish by his plate. Just be sure to keep the list, so you'll remember just why you bought those particular candies.

To get the shapes you need, bake the cakes in well-greased tin cans, loaf pans, square pans or round ones—or any combination thereof. Take the cakes out of the pans after they have rested on racks for 10 minutes, trim them to suit a rough design you've drawn and put the pieces together to see how it looks. (The scraps make a nice English trifle.) You can take the pieces apart, trim them differently and join them in new ways if you change your mind.

When it's time to decorate, tell your child that the cake is a big surprise, so he

WALNUT RACES

Contests are part of birthday parties, for better and often for worse. The simplest ones can get out of hand if they encourage the children to run wild in the house. Have walnuts do the running instead.

Give your Sixes (or Sevens) half a walnut shell, empty of nut meat or woody partitions, and some cotton, felt pens, white glue, construction paper, feathers and one pair of blunt scissors for every two children. They can decorate a shell, turning them into elephants and hippos, turtles and mice.

These are then lined up on a card table, each resting on top of a marble and held back by a yardstick (and you). Have one of the children turn the table into a ramp by lifting its back legs and inserting a 3″ stack of books under each one. Give a dramatic countdown and lift the yardstick for the menagerie to start running. The race is a good mixer for children and is a sensitive solution if one of the children is clumsy or overweight or handicapped: they run, but only indirectly.

will let you alone in the kitchen. No child is as amenable as the Birthday Child.

Make a standard, seven-minute icing, which will cover the freshly cut, crumbly edges much better than a butter cream, and divide the icing into small bowls after it is beaten. Add some blue to one if you need a pond; some red and yellow together to turn those teepees orange; and some green, for grass, to another bowl—with some more green coloring in another bowl to dye the grass itself. Coconut plays many roles.

The icing, which cements the pieces together, will be smooth if you dip a knife into hot water as you work and it will be neat if you clean the knife between colors.

A Shape Cake may seem like a lot of trouble—and it is—but if you want motherhood to be an adventure, you have to make it one.

80-Minute Race

A first grader revels in rules, which is why he likes this complicated race to build a castle of blocks; to draw a picture; to jump over pillows. Even to pee! This 80-minute race combines the excitement and challenge of a scavenger hunt and a treasure hunt and needs only ice cream and cake to make the party perfect.

Whether you write clever clues in poetry or prose, the two teams will follow them, competing only to get to the right place and accomplish the right job, before they look around for their next clue and race to follow it. Each member of the winning team gets a prize, and each prize is the same.

The mother of our young neighbor Jeremy assembled the Red Team in the dining room to read the first clue, while the father led the Green Team from the other direction, taking a few detours to avoid gridlock in the middle. At one point each team had to use Jeremy's 80 blocks to make a castle with 5 doors, 6 windows and 3 floors, while at another each player had to draw a picture of a house or some trees or animals. A heap of pillows in the hall made a broad jump.

There was also a stop in the alley for each child to swack a target with a baseball bat—the least amusing stop, it turned out—and to paint two boards of the patio fence with water—the one place where both teams wanted to stay overtime. The two big favorites, however, were the juice stop, which was breathlessly needed, and the "peepee" stop, which was wonderfully ribald and just as necessary.

It took each parent four hours to write the rhymes and prepare the games. And did they think it was worth it? Absolutely. Would they do it again? Of course. But not for another three years, when the younger child reached Six.

We all give our once-in-a-lifetime parties.

Train Party

The most extraordinary Shape Cake we ever made was for Meg when she turned Seven and soulful and we surprised her with a train party at school. She still remembers every moment.

There were ice cream cones, lemonade—and a Train Cake. It was set on top of a foil-covered sheet of plywood, narrow enough to go through the back of our station wagon and the classroom door, carried inside with the help of her dear godmother and greeted with a ten-second silence. Twenty-eight little children finally breathed "Ohhhhhhhhhhh" and then timidly came forward to inspect the station house and the fifteen cars on cookie wheels with spokes made of icing, on a track of licorice whip.

They were told that, although this did happen to be Meg's birthday, the cake really was for every child who had a birthday that year and who were they anyway? As each month was called, a few children solemnly raised their hands and stepped forward until the whole class surrounded the cake to blow out the seven candles, with one to grow on.

A cake of this size is not one cake of course, but five—in this case two were white and three were chocolate—with one recipe divided between four 12-ounce buttered and floured tin cans and the others baked in four 9″ x 12″ cake pans. One of these 9″ x 12″ cakes was set aside for the station house—the cake that was taken back home intact for the neighborhood party.

The other three were cut into sixths, to make oblongs for the flatbed cars that carried the logs, the cattle, the horses, the cars and the candles. The rest were stacked in two layers to make the caboose and to hold the salt, coal, eggs, lemons and oranges and one for peanuts, for, like any good railroad, every car in the Birthday Special had a duty of its own.

The log car—a vivid yellow—carried small chocolate rolls, chained into place with the licorice whip, while the blue

flatbed held the candles. There were open stock cars—a green flatbed and an orange one—both covered in straw of toasted coconut—and fences made of broken candy cigarettes, glued together with icing. One held plastic horses, the other plastic cows, and the purple flatbed had small metal cars (chained in place in Detroit, we said)—enough horses and cows and cars for each child to take one home as a favor.

The layered oblongs included the white one labeled SALT, with clear rock candy covering the top; a chocolate-coated coal car heaped with raisins and a yellow car (marked CITRUS) with tiny French lemon and orange drops on top. The green car said PEANUTS and had peanuts on top and the EGGS car, in a super turquoise, had only its name, but still the children listened with awe. They even accepted the rather sad-looking red caboose, with its chocolate-bar roof, a railing of droopy licorice whip and a couple of caramel squares for steps.

It was the engine that looked real enough to give the children their faith. Baked in a tin can and covered with chocolate, its puffy end became the very front of the train, with a fat yellow gumdrop for the light and an orange slice for the cowcatcher. A silver kiss hung from an arc of licorice whip on top—the bell—with two old-fashioned chocolate drops from the dime store became smokestacks, with white icing smoke wrapped precariously around toothpicks. The other tin-can cars weren't as jazzy but they were fine for second helpings: a yellow car marked OIL; a white one (MILK) and an orange one—O.J.

The station house was simply a variation of the house we built for so many parties, whether we said it was like the one in *Hansel and Gretel* or that it was an old log cabin, a dollhouse or a barn. This 9″ x 12″ cake was divided into thirds—the short way. Two were layered and the third piece was cut at a 45° angle to make the roof. This was covered with flat chocolate bars—the same used for the door and the shut-

ters—and decorated with coconut (for snow) and a couple of caramel chimneys. A small gumdrop, stuck into place with the ubiquitous icing, became the door handle. The windows—iced yellow to show the lamplight inside—had tie-back curtains sliced from large gumdrops and a cross of icing for windowpanes. There was a pebble walk of candy-coated chocolates; lollipop trees in containers of inverted chocolate drops, green coconut grass and flower beds of grated chocolate.

This Train Cake takes money and time. Expect to spend the day before making the cakes, about four hours that night and another three to four hours the next morning to decorate them. It's neater if you make each small cake on a flat pan, transfer it carefully to the track when it's done, and glue the wheels in place last, using whatever icing is left to cement them in place. Hide the whole business under a sheet on the dining-room table if the Birthday Child is around. If he sneaks a peek, he won't tell.

A Train Cake also requires a certain amount of nerve. First you have to stare at the candy counter in the dime store for a half hour, asking for forty-two of that and a half pound of this and, at the end, you have to have nerve enough to tell children that raisins are coal lumps and coconut is straw. But they'll believe—and you'll feel like Michelangelo.

Pirate Party

At Eight, the most sword-brandishing age of all, Mike had his pirate party. The table was set with an old, patched sheet, dyed red; white paper plates with a skull, crossbones and a child's name crayoned on each and the usual rectangular Shape Cake. This one was cut and iced and decorated in the shape of a sailing ship—this time flat, rather than upright—with portholes and cannons and rope of licorice whip.

It was the homemade favors that decided the tempo, however. Each guest got his black velvet eyepatch—rakish and

homemade—and a red kerchief torn from another dyed sheet. Once costumed, each guest got a sword—a simple cross of 1⅜″ × ¼″ lattice strips nailed together, which Mike had painted flat black and which, of course, had no point.

After some carrying-on, the children were led to the backyard, where they took turns being blindfolded and then escorted down the steps. Here each child was spun around three times and told, in a very deep voice, to "walk the plank"—a 1′ × 6′ board that sloped from a low step to the gravel-covered patio. This 18″ slant let each child totter and fall for his friends, as dramatically as he could.

When everyone was unblindfolded, the children were given a treasure map of the small backyard, full of elaborate paces and directions. These were followed carefully and quickly led to the little wooden jewelry chest—the one from the thrift shop that said ATLANTIC CITY, N. J.—buried in the sandbox. Inside was one gold mesh bag of gold-covered coins for every child, which, with the cake, the swords and the eye patches, were quite enough for our Eights—and for us.

Elegant Party

Shortly before Nell's ninth birthday, we asked her what children she'd like to invite to her party. This dear child, who almost never complained, sounded off like a trumpet.

"Why do you say 'children'?" she asked dramatically. "Don't you know I have grown-up friends too?"

She was right, of course. If her parents could have friends who were children, surely the child could have adult friends. As she said, "That's what makes Thanksgiving and Christmas so good. Everybody is together." And so, that time and many times since, we had a party for all ages, with Nell asking a half dozen other Nines, a couple of teenagers and a few favorite adults.

A mimosa was offered to the adults in champagne glasses (orange juice with an equal amount of California champagne being the cheapest, mildest alcoholic drink you can serve), and Party Punch or juice for the children. Since Nell is our resident gourmet, the food at this party was fitting, with a proper cake—a fine Gâteau Génoise, in fact; good soft cheeses; melon cubes speared with prosciutto; and a couple of artichokes for guests to pluck and dip their leaves into a mix of mayonnaise and rough mustard.

Different children have different needs and a birthday party is a good time to fill them.

PARTY PUNCH

YIELD: 16 cups

A punch should taste as good as it looks. Like this one. In a large bowl

COMBINE
- 1 12-oz. can frozen cranberry juice cocktail
- 5 c. water
- 1 c. pineapple juice
- ½ c. lemon juice
- ¼–½ c. sugar

Refrigerate until served. You can dress up the bowl with very thin slices of lemon and drop a fresh pineapple chunk in every glass.

SIN CAKE

Preheat oven to 350°

If Nell were Nine today, she'd surely ask for this new family favorite. This elegant, easy, flour-free cake is sinfully rich. In a double boiler

| MELT | 10 oz. semisweet chocolate |

| ADD | 10 oz. unsalted butter, in bits |

When melted, remove from heat.

| ADD | 1½ c. sugar |

While this mixture is cooling, butter a 9″ cake pan freely, as well as a circle of wax paper cut to fit the bottom of the pan. In a bowl

| BEAT | 8 large eggs |

You don't even have to beat them too much. Combine the four ingredients, pour the batter into the cake pan and put the pan in a 10″ x 13″ pan. Fill the larger pan with water half as high as the cake pan, so it can steam the cake as it bakes.

| BAKE | 90 minutes |

The top may look as if it's sliding off, but it won't. Put the cake on a rack.

| COOL | 10 minutes |

Run a knife around the edge of the pan to loosen the cake, then turn the cake upside down on a flat plate or tray. Tap the bottom of the pan carefully, until the cake drops onto the plate. Peel away the circle of wax paper on top and dust the top with confectioner's sugar just before serving. With it, offer

KAHLÚA CREAM

WHIP	½ pt. whipping cream
	2 T. Kahlúa
	2 T. strong coffee
	2 T. sugar

A dollop of cream goes on each thin slice.

Watermelon Party

When times were tough, dear Aunt Kay made the living seem easy by inventing the watermelon party. It didn't cost much, and it was ideal for the Ten (or Eleven or Twelve) at that first scary boy-girl party.

The guests, in bathing suits, gathered

on the river bank—for water was essential—and watched as one watermelon after another was cut into eighths, like great red smiles, but never into circles. They don't inspire as much silliness.

The party would begin decorously enough, but after a few bites a boy would inevitably rub a chunk of melon on some girl's back and she would inevitably retaliate with a little rubbed in his hair. And then the party would go wild. Girls were chased, boys were tripped, melons were rubbed in faces, and then there was a lot of dunking in the water—routines that were gone through half a dozen times before the cake and the presents.

Not too messy and not too expensive—just good, clean, sexy fun for boys and girls who wanted to have a party together and couldn't figure out what to say. And it still works.

If there's no river or lake nearby, the backyard will do, as long as you have a hose handy.

Slumber Party

There are two kinds of slumber party. One is the giggling, all-night, preteen talkathon, usually held by girls. Here boys are the main point of discussion (with many yuks and ughs) and, with luck, these same boys will gather outside on the sidewalk to tease and taunt the girls. The other slumber party, a more recent vintage, is an Eight's imitation of her elders—where the girls giggle about teachers and boys and the girls who aren't there—or, if it's a boys' party, where there is running and whooping and something that may approach mass hysteria. In either case, there is (or should be) a curfew at midnight, which will be obeyed, more or less, if a grown-up separates the gigglers if their behavior gets too wild. You'll probably let your Eight or Nine go to a slumber party occasionally but there's no reason to let her give one when she's still so young. This party is such a quintessential puberty rite that it really belongs to the preteen, and with no curfew at all. It's just their night to howl.

Kate was just Eleven when she had her first, teaching us that the wonderful, wearying world of slumber parties hadn't changed much in twenty-five years, and judging from the slumber parties we've seen since then, they still haven't changed much. There is always a pattering of fairly big feet all night long; a house turned upside down; a late breakfast for rather subdued little girls—and a very appreciative daughter.

There are other recurring patterns. The younger children are turned out of their rooms, the father harrumphs in front of the television and there is a yummy dinner of fried chicken or pizza and, if appropriate, a birthday cake.

The real action begins after dinner and so does the chaos. You'll find snacks and sodas in every bedroom (so don't look), sleeping bags all over the place and emotions too. There will be two or three euphoric children, a few more who are just silly and at least one child who is ready to weep. She either thinks she's stuck in the room where nothing is happening and feels left out or she's in the room where too much is going on and she feels left out. This is the child who dramatically marches off with her quilt to sleep in the bathtub. Someone is bound to turn on the shower within a half hour, but that's all right; it

CHICKEN TABASCO

YIELD: about 40 wingsticks

This spicy hors d'oeuvre, served with French fries and sliced tomatoes, makes a light and easy eleven o'clock supper. On the morning of the party

DISJOINT   **4 lbs. chicken wings**

Each is cut into 3 pieces. Toss the tips in the freezer for that mythical day when you'll make chicken soup and lay the wingsticks in a large flat dish. Over them

POUR   **1 oz. Tabasco**

Roll the chicken around so there is a thin film of hot sauce covering each piece—a job to do with tongs if you have any small cut, for hot sauce can sting. Seal the chicken in a plastic bag.

REFRIGERATE   **8 hours**

Massage the bag from time to time, so the pieces absorb some of the sauce that has dripped to the bottom. Into a paper bag

POUR   **1 c. flour**
                    1 t. salt

Shake the bag to mix it, add 6 wingsticks, shake it again, put the floured chicken aside and add more. When all are coated

HEAT   **2 c. vegetable oil**

The grease is hot enough if a single wingstick makes it sizzle. Drop as many as 8 pieces into the skillet but let them barely touch, so the crust will be brown and crunchy.

FRY   **15 minutes**

You can serve these cold, but hot is better. And you can use chicken breasts, legs and thighs, for a heartier meal, but use twice as much hot sauce, marinate them twice as long, and fry for 20–30 minutes.

tells the doused she's really accepted by the dousers. This just makes her giddy and gives someone else a turn to be sad.

In between supper and bedlam, the girls might make fudge or pull taffy; try exotic facials; put on improvisational plays for your applause or elegant fashion shows, at which they wear all the makeup and evening dresses they can find in the house. The sight will be a shock. Suddenly you see that today's children are about to be tomorrow's beauties.

Kate and her friends followed the glamor routine—a party successful enough to be repeated at Twelve and again at Thirteen, when the entertainment suddenly changed. It was Mike's lumpy mattress that did it. To their amazement the girls found a stash of *Playboy* magazines between the mattress and the springs. This kept them quiet long enough to clip the most revealing pictures and pin them all over his walls, so he would be properly embarrassed. And he certainly was.

Theater Party

Many Twelves are too grown-up for a traditional birthday party but a properly recognized birthday still means a great deal (just as it always will). For this age, and particularly for girls, a theater party is the most elegant event you can conjure and the most thrilling. The memory of a certain scene onstage will last long after the same scene on the screen has faded, for there is an emotional involvement in watching a play that makes it unforgettable.

Money is the biggest barrier to theater parties, but it may be no more expensive than a movie party if you limit it to two or three friends, ask for student rates and buy seats in the highest balcony at a matinee, a preview or a college production.

If you're lucky enough to have a choice, the play should be a well-tested one, rather than something new, so you can tell the children about it beforehand. They will like theater better when they can understand at least the broad references.

To learn about the mood in Russia when Chekhov was writing or how *Oklahoma* changed all the musicals that followed (even if you have to look it up first) will give the plot an extra dimension. Almost all plays are good for this age, except Shakespeare, since it takes the finest actors to make themselves understood in such archaic language.

To give a theater party, hand each child her ticket and either drive the group to (and from) the theater or send them by bus or subway—if they're used to getting around on their own—with your child paying their fares. If possible, she also should take enough money for sodas between the acts or, for extra elegance, tea and pastry at a café afterward, where you've made reservations in advance.

The play will be a treat, but going out alone, and to the theater, is the biggest treat of all: to be a woman of the world is a wondrous thing.

PRETEEN PARTIES

This is a peculiarly poignant time in a child's life, and nothing makes it clearer than a party. All preteens go through the same round of anxieties—afraid of their audacity one moment, their timidity the next—but now the urge to socialize gets stronger for both boys and girls. It's as if they instinctively know they must practice their social skills. Although children who

grow up in or near a big city may be a little more sophisticated, nothing puts them to the test as much as even the most minor party. While it's wonderful to anticipate and pretty good in retrospect, the participation is at least a little painful.

By Eleven, and certainly by Twelve, the girls parade around a party in tight little bands, whispering to each other, drinking sodas (and holding the bottle to their lips in extraordinary ways in their attempts to be more worldly). The older girls may wear panty hose—which they hike up a lot—and redden their cheeks and shadow their eyes—often after they leave home if they're not allowed to wear makeup. The boys spend a half hour combing their hair in a careless way before they ever leave home, splash on deodorant they usually don't need and try to look incredibly casual in their new shirts.

While the girls prowl, the boys cluster, huddling together as they fool around, eating everything they see, making jokes and occasionally allowing themselves to be pushed to the dance floor—if there is one—or at least into the path of the girls they've been eyeing. There probably will be short-lived games of spin-the-bottle, a hallway grab or a stolen kiss, and regular attempts to turn off all the lights. That's Twelve for you and Eleven too: they're more inclined to test the moral code now than they will be in a year or two, but fortunately the supervision is better, the preteen is less daring and the boys are usually less sure of themselves.

Although your child probably will be a young teenager before he's invited to an unchaperoned party, you want to veto them now by checking each party beforehand so it will be automatic by adolescence. To do this, call the parent of the party giver to offer your help with some dips or chips—a tactful way to make sure the parents know they're giving a party and that they plan to chaperone.

There has been some silly business in the past twenty years, to the effect that grown-ups don't belong at a children's party. Don't believe it. If you have a party at your house, you have the duty, as well as the right, to be on the scene, whether the child is Eight or Twelve (or Sixteen) and if it's a big party there should be another couple too. When chaperones are present, there is much less reason for them. This doesn't mean you're constantly in the room with the partygoers, but you aren't hiding in your bedroom either.

The kitchen is the ideal place for you to be because you have to keep the punch bowl filled and take in the food. Choose something with many toppings, like tacos, which the guests put together themselves. You'll be taking refills into the party room all night—and the boys like to eat so much they won't even mind.

Your presence won't be a problem if you don't intrude in the first fifteen tentative minutes of a kissing game (after that, please do) and if you don't publicly criticize a guest—or all the guests. Anyone who misbehaves (and someone will) should be corrected as quickly, gently and privately as you would want someone to correct your own child.

It isn't good manners that keeps the lights on, at least dimly, or stops a war of finger sandwiches; it's the knowledge that a parent might drop into the party room at any moment. A little fear is good for the soul—and the rug.

Round-Robin Party

In a big city neighborhood, where children go to a mix of public, private and parochial schools, preteens and young teens especially need parents to set up parties and places for them to meet. The best place is a skating rink or a swimming pool, where they can be active enough to hide their awkwardness. After a couple of hours the partygoers are then driven to someone's home for two more hours of records, food and fooling around. Between school rules for children and Saturday night parties for parents, this usually means a Friday night activity from six to ten.

Parents do the scheduling, telephoning the word freely (there is nothing exclusive about these parties), and the hosts ask a few other adults over to help. This gives parents the chance to know the friends their children are making and to make friends with other parents. It also lets the younger children see how the older children act at a party, which in turn makes the older ones a little more careful about the example they set.

After a few months you can expect the parties to get rowdier as chaperones grow lax about their job and children know who's going to act foolish and how. By then the season is ready to end. It's just as well. Children don't like to swim in September or ice-skate in April.

PARTY MIX

YIELD: 60 ounces   Preheat oven to 250°

This is the kind of nibble parents fix for their children—and then eat most of it. Fortunately, it's easy to make and ideal for a card game, a beach trip and especially a party for a preteen, when the lure of sweets has begun to subside.

In a roaster

COMBINE	1 12-oz. pkg. Cheerios
	2 12-oz. pkgs. Rice Chex
	1 11-oz. pkg. slim pretzels
	8 oz. Spanish peanuts
	1 T. garlic salt
	1 T. celery salt

Mix well.

MELT	¾ lb. butter
ADD	2 T. Worcestershire sauce
	½ t. red pepper

Stir, then pour melted butter over the cereals, again mixing well, and cover the roaster.

| BAKE | 1 hour |

Stir every 20 minutes, then remove the cover.

| BAKE | 30 minutes |

Cool and store in plastic storage bags, tightly shut. If the mix gets stale, it can be crisped again in the oven at 350° for 10 to 15 minutes.

Welcome Party

Good friends—and this usually works better for chatty little girls—can give a simple party for the new girl in the neighborhood, even if she's only going to be around for the summer. It will make the child feel good and your own child feel better; it's such a friendly thing to do.

For one party we served ice cream sodas and cookies and blessed the young guest of honor, who brought her dog along. Her dad said it was essential, since she was suddenly too shy to come alone,

PECAN SHORTIES

YIELD: 4 dozen   Preheat oven to 375°

An Eleven with a gentle touch can make the world's shortest—and possibly tastiest—cookies.

CREAM	1½ sticks butter
	3 T. confectioner's sugar
ADD	1½ c. flour
	1 c. chopped pecans
	1½ t. vanilla
	⅛ t. salt

Roll the dough into 1″ balls and place them on a greased cookie sheet.

| BAKE | 15 minutes |

Cool slightly, then roll in confectioner's sugar.

OATMEAL COOKIES

YIELD: 12 dozen cookies   Preheat oven to 325°

This cookie has enough nutrition to please a parent and tastes good enough to please the Eight who makes them. In a large bowl

CREAM	1 c. vegetable shortening
	½ c. butter
	2 c. brown sugar

| ADD | 1 egg |

In another large bowl

| COMBINE | 1 c. applesauce |
| | 1 t. baking soda |

Add this to the creamed mixture, rinse and dry the bowl and in it

COMBINE	6 c. quick or old-fashioned oatmeal
	1 c. white flour
	1 c. whole wheat flour
	½ t. baking powder
	½ t. baking soda
	2 t. cinnamon
	½ t. mace
	¼ t. nutmeg

Mix well.

ADD	1 c. raisins
	1 c. chopped walnuts
	½ c. sunflower seeds

Freeze half the dough—so much baking would bore a child—and drop the rest by the tablespoon onto a greased cookie sheet.

| BAKE | 12–15 minutes |

Crisp these cookies on a cake rack.

and it turned out to be essential for the other children too. They all had dogs and the children had something to talk about. This taught us a simple lesson all over again: the party that works best is the one with a theme.

School's Out! Party

Another party—a favorite for boys—only lasts an hour or so; celebrates the end of school; gives them the chance to rehash the year's best guffaws (and outrages) and to eat super Ice Cream Sundaes. A good reason to have it outdoors.

Set out tubs of chocolate, vanilla and strawberry ice cream; bowls of sliced peaches, berries and a few bananas sliced lengthwise (in case the more adventuresome want to make banana splits); a dish of grated toasted coconut, another of maraschino cherries, a third dish of pecans or walnuts, broken and toasted, and perhaps some chocolate sprinkles or nonpareils; a bowl of marshmallow cream and one of whipped cream and two pitchers of homemade sauce.

Finally, have a big stack of paper napkins. It's the civilizing touch.

ULTIMATE HOT FUDGE SAUCE

YIELD: 1 cup

This sauce, with its intense, slightly bitter flavor, is truly the best. In a saucepan

| COMBINE | 5 T. brewed coffee |
| | 2 oz. unsweetened baking chocolate |

Cook over medium heat, stirring until smooth.

| ADD | ½ c. sugar |

| COOK | 5 minutes |

By then the sauce should be smooth and just slightly thick.

ADD	3 T. butter
	½ t. vanilla
	2 t. Kahlua (optional)

If you like a sweeter sauce

| ADD | 1–4 T. sugar |

| COOK | 1 minute |

Refrigerate in a covered glass jar. To serve hot, remove the cover and heat the jar in a pan of water and pour the sauce over ice cream: a chocolate crust. For the more classic version, use water instead of coffee and forget the liqueur.

BUTTERSCOTCH SAUCE

YIELD: 2¼ cups

This looks like liquid gold and tastes as rich. In a saucepan

COMBINE
1¼ c. brown sugar
⅔ c. light corn syrup
¾ c. heavy cream
4 T. butter

Cook over low heat and stir slowly. Drip a spoonful of sauce into a cup of cold water occasionally to test its readiness: it's done when the drops hold together when pushed between the thumb and forefinger—the soft ball stage. Put the sauce in a pitcher for pouring.

GIFTS

Children like to give presents to parents, teachers and, with some encouragement, to brothers, sisters and grandparents, because they like to be appreciated in turn. When they give to charity, however, the appreciation comes from within. You want your child to give both kinds of gifts, but the ones he gives to charity will take extra encouragement from you.

You have to set a clear example, but remember: he won't learn his phonics by watching you read and he won't learn the joy of giving by watching you write a check. The lesson is much more direct if you both bake and take cookies to the old folks' home, or make a weekly batch of soup if your church has a soup kitchen.

There are many other lessons in sweet charity. The pies you bake together for the Salvation Army's Thanksgiving dinner will teach your child more about pilgrims than cutouts, and the errands he runs (for free) for your arthritic neighbor will teach him to count his blessings. Many parents want to hide the sorrows of life from children, which is a pity. It takes exposure to make a child realize how lucky he is and eventually how much he owes others.

In the sixties it seemed as if all the discontent of the country concentrated on Washington with one demonstration after another. None had as great an impact on our family as Resurrection City—a muddy, months'-long encampment of poor people between the monuments to Washington and Lincoln—a stretch we passed every day.

To Kate and her friend Nancy, both Eleven, this was their responsibility too and they handled it in their own dear way: they went on a beggar's mission for, of all things, old wedding presents. In a frantic week they collected them, drew flyers,

PEOPLE POLISH

Blessed is the mother whose husband will give her a back rub—and whose Eight will give her the lotion to make the rub so much better. This recipe is used by the masseuses in Berkley Springs, West Virginia, America's oldest spa. It makes a splendid, and rather expensive, present for a grown-up, which you won't mind so much if you get a bottle too.

You'll have to buy the grain alcohol from the liquor store (the rubbing kind won't mix), and your child will have to collect the 6 empty 8-ounce plastic squeeze bottles he needs. They should either be run through the dishwasher or washed well and left to dry for a day.

Set a 2-quart pitcher into the kitchen sink (since some usually spills) and into it

POUR
1 qt. distilled alcohol
1 pt. olive oil

Stir the mixture well and funnel it quickly into a squeeze bottle. Stir the mixture again before filling each bottle as the lotion separates in a few minutes. Wipe the containers well and label with a reminder to shake often when using.

shined the silverplate and put out posters for the first yard sale the neighborhood ever had. The $32.72 may not have helped Resurrection City very much, but it taught two young girls the joy of giving because they did it on their own.

Children need only a few suggestions and some supplies to make gifts for their family and teachers.

THE LAYABOUT

This snaky layabout is what every note taker needs to make transcribing a little easier: the BBs make this skinny cloth tube heavy enough to hold the most floppy book open—a welcome present for a Ten to make for his working mom—and his working grandma.

Provide strong cotton in a plain, dark color, so it won't detract from the book or look dirty, and pinking shears, so it needn't be hemmed or turned inside out. Have your Ten spread the fabric and

CUT   9″ × 3½″ oblong

This is folded lengthwise and machine-stitched down the long side and one short side, ¼″ from the edge.

To fill, poke a funnel into the unstitched end of the tube of cloth and hang the tube inside a glass to catch the spillage. Into the tube

POUR   ⅓ c. BBs

Pin the end together (quickly) and sew it shut.

MERINGUE COOKIES

YIELD: 2 dozen   Preheat oven to 275°

This is a quick and easy treat, with only two tricks: your Seven has to separate the eggs and make sure the sugar has no clumps.

BEAT   2 egg whites

Beat until very stiff and into them

FOLD   1 c. brown sugar
                 1½–2 c. chopped walnuts

Drop by teaspoonfuls on a greased cookie sheet.

BAKE   15–20 minutes

They're done when they're a light, toasty brown. Spread on cake racks until they're dry and crisp.

LEMON BARS

YIELD: 24 small bars   Preheat oven to 350°

This is a good present for a Seven to make and give, but be kind: let him give some to himself.

COMBINE   1 c. flour
                    4 oz. butter, cut in bits
                    ¼ c. confectioner's sugar

Cut this pastry quickly with a portable mixer, so the pastry will be delicate, and do it in a high-sided bowl, so the dust flies less. Press the mixture in the bottom of a 7″ × 11″ pan.

BAKE   10 minutes

In the meantime

BEAT   2 eggs

ADD   ¾–1 c. sugar
                2 T. flour
                ½ t. baking powder
                juice of 1 lemon
                grated zest of 1 lemon

Beat until smooth, then spread this mixture over the warm crust and return to oven.

BAKE   25 minutes

Let cool enough to harden a minute, then cut into bars—or diamonds, if you want to be fancy. Over them

SIFT   confectioner's sugar

Or you can frost them, for fancier bars. In a bowl

BEAT   1 T. milk
                1 T. butter
                1 c. confectioner's sugar
                1 t. vanilla

Spread over the bars.

HERBAL VINEGARS

The work of summer becomes the pride of winter if you help your Ten bottle an herb in vinegar.

To make herbal vinegar, first sterilize one quart jar and one 2-quart jar by inverting them on a rack in a soup pot containing 3″ of water.

BOIL   **15 minutes, covered**

In the meantime have him

HEAT   **72 oz. cider OR wine vinegar, red or**
                  white

ADD   **4 sprigs tarragon OR rosemary OR 3**
                  sprigs basil
                  2 cloves garlic, peeled
                  2 whole hot peppers

The vinegar should be warmed enough to extract the flavor of the herbs but not enough to boil, for that would destroy the taste.

Pour this vinegar into the sterilized jars with the herbs, cover and leave them in a dark place.

WAIT   **2 weeks**

Now it's time for your child to find 6 handsome beer bottles and 6 old but unbroken wine corks, wash them all very well, remove labels and then sterilize the bottles, upside down as he sterilized the jars, along with a funnel and a tea strainer. The corks should be boiled for 3 minutes in a separate saucepan.

To finish the job, help him hold the funnel in a beer bottle, with the strainer over it, and pour the vinegar into it. To each bottle

ADD   **a sprig of fresh herb**

(This isn't necessary, but it gives a bit of class.)

Cork each bottle, wipe it well and over it

POUR   **melted sealing wax**

(This is unnecessary too, but it also adds to the charm of the gift.)

Label and give.

TIN CAN LANTERNS

The old-fashioned backyard has become a patio and it needs as many lamps as the living room. These candlelit lanterns make attractive lights, and a Ten makes them quite well.

Let him make a design of dots on some empty tin cans with a broad waterproof felt-tipped marker in whatever pattern or picture he likes, wiping off mistakes with your nail polish remover. The cans are filled with water and frozen overnight so the ice will keep the can from denting or bending when he punches out the design with a 10-penny nail and a hammer. This will make holes big enough for the light to shine through a hole on either side of the can, just below the open end, so it can be hung.

Afterward he wipes off any design that still shows, dumps the ice into the sink and inserts a long leather thong into each hole at the top, knotting the ends, so it can loop around a tree branch. Finally, drip wax on the bottom of each can and stick a short, fat plumber's candle in place.

THE ULTIMATE FUDGE

YIELD: 25 squares   Preheat oven to 350°

This makes a great batch of fudge if you have a batch of Twelves, for this old-fashioned recipe takes much beating. Just be sure they are careful when they stir the boiling mixture, as sugar can give a bad burn. Have them butter the sides of a heavy 4-quart saucepan and

ADD   **2 c. sugar**
                  4 oz. unsweetened chocolate
                  1 c. milk

Cook over low heat, stirring constantly with a long wooden spoon until the sugar is dissolved and the chocolate is melted.

When the mixture begins to boil, they should increase the heat to medium and keep stirring so it doesn't scorch. The fudge is done when it reaches 234°—that magic moment when a drop of syrup in a cup of cold water can be mushed into a soft ball (and eaten, of course).

Remove from the heat.

ADD   **4 oz. butter**
                  1 t. vanilla

Cool until it's lukewarm, without stirring at all, so it doesn't crystallize. To keep the children busy, have them

CHOP   **1½ c. pecans**

TOAST   **10 minutes**

They then beat the fudge—with a portable mixer at a high speed—until it loses its sheen and is so thick it can hold its shape when they lift the mixer—about 20 minutes. Have them add the pecans and help them pour the candy into a lightly greased 8″ square pan. They'll wait until it's firm enough to cut into squares, but only if you leave enough licks in the pot.

THE TUSSIE-MUSSIE

Any little girl would rather send a tussie-mussie to a sick friend than a card, if only she knew what it was. This old English bouquet of fresh herbs and flowers was once used to ward off fevers and plagues and in eighteenth-century America a proper young lady carried a tussie-mussie downtown to overcome the city smells. It's also been carried in celebrations for centuries— Queen Elizabeth II even got one at her coronation— while Victorians sent them to each other the way we send greeting cards. Each type of leaf, each flower, carried a sentiment of its own. Your child can choose from a rosebud for love; basil for good wishes; a daisy for innocence; dill to soothe the spirit and hinder witches; some myrtle for joy; sage for good health and long years; rosemary for remembrance; thyme for bravery; and tarragon to cure the bites of beasts (especially dragons).

Your child pokes a half dozen herb sprigs into a paper doily, with the rosebud in the center and the stems wrapped together with tissue paper.

The meanings vary with the reference books, which is why your child should include her own message. She wouldn't want her friend to think the dark purple basil meant hate, especially if her friend was sick in bed with a dragon bite.

GOOD TIMES ◇

Good times are what childhood should be all about. They set the stage for creativity and for wide-open learning. Aside from camp, where much of the fun is structured, most of the best times are spontaneous, bubbling up at relaxed moments and places that parents have helped create. A child needs time to play games of his own invention; to read and ruminate at his own pace; and to make friends, for a good friend makes good times better.

Your child will find those good times when he's allowed to collect miniature cars or animals or whatever's affordable; to use the computer or the typewriter if there's one in the house; to put on plays or have a clubhouse in the garage; to cook with permission (if he cleans the kitchen afterward); to go swimming and sledding, skating and bowling—in short, a chance to play, without the pressure of competition, unless it's what he really wants.

Variety is a factor in these good times but don't expect your child to pursue everything that's available. What delights one child will bore another. A Nine who likes puzzles, has good coordination and is a little shy may find that magic is fun and a bridge to friendships. Take him and a few dollars to browse at a magic shop. His interest may go no further than the mastery of a few card tricks, and that's fine. If it goes further, that's better. The child who develops strong interests in the Middle Years is much more likely to have a strong sense of identity in adolescence.

Books also help a child define himself, so you'll want to make sure your child has the chance to use his library card every week and to buy secondhand books at thrift shops and yard sales. Another child may need to see more movies and the adventure shows on TV, which is nothing

to worry about if they're limited to weekends and summertime. Tomorrow's writers, librarians, filmmakers and critics are getting started today.

It is their future to shape, however, not yours. As long as you realize that these interests merely indicate curiosity and possibly a talent—and not a promise of things to come—your child can feel free to pursue them all. As he grows he'll narrow his interests and by Eleven he'll concentrate on one or two of them with a passion. You'll be surprised how hard he can try when he likes what he's doing.

ROUND-THE-WORLD COOKING

The kitchen gives a child some of his warmest memories and it gives the family some of its greatest—and tastiest—adventures. There is the joy of making a spontaneous batch of fudge and the planning of a cassoulet; the silliness of a taffy pull and the orderliness of a strudel; and above all there is the richness of helping to make the family dinner together and the grown-up feeling a child gets from making his own meal. Food feeds the senses as well as the tum. The sizzles and snaps, the textures and aromas and colors imprint the memories indelibly.

Make a child feel welcome in the kitchen and he discovers the similarities of different foods and the differences of similar ones. The meatballs of Korea, Sweden and Greece are as different from the Italian variety as they are from each other. The international family of sandwiches has its differences too, but they all have one thing in common: Whether the filling is con-

KITCHEN TIPS

Scutwork chases children out of the kitchen almost as quick as impatient parents, which is too bad, since most cooking is in the preparation. Children who learn these and other kitchen hints will have an easier time, more success—and mothers who aren't so impatient.

Peeling onions is probably the worst job for a child since his eyes are so sensitive. He can chill them in the refrigerator first—cold onions cause less weeping—or slice them under running water. In any case, have him cut the root end last, for less burning.

You'll also want to teach your child to

- put the jar of sugared honey or jam into a pot of boiling water for 5 to 10 minutes so it will liquefy again;
- roll lemons hard on the counter before cutting to get more juice; and soak them in hot water for 15 minutes to get even more;
- soften hard brown sugar by baking it in a 350° oven for 10 minutes, then store it with an apple wedge to keep it soft;
- store popcorn in the freezer or wash the kernels before roasting them, which adds moisture to the kernels, makes them puffier when they're popped and gets rid of most of the old maids;
- wipe the silk away from shucked corn with a damp paper towel before boiling, pat it dry when it's done, then roll each ear in a flat dish with a little melted butter, to use less of it;
- whip egg whites in a platter with a flat whisk, for greater volume, or in a copper bowl with a regular whisk;
- toast nuts in a 350° oven for 10–15 minutes to bring out their full flavor before adding them to a recipe.

SEPARATING EGGS

Our Nell was Nine when she learned that it's much more amusing and efficient to separate an egg in the style of a professional chef.

Have your child wash his hands well and set two bowls on the table. He then cracks the egg against the rim of the counter with one hand, dropping the contents into the other hand. The white slips through his fingers into one bowl and the yolk is dropped into the other. If he separates more than one egg, he should use three bowls. One is for yolks, one is for whites and the third one is a temporary station for each white, so he can inspect it for any trace of yolk before adding it to the other egg whites, since only pure whites can be beaten stiff.

tained in some kind of bread, or served open-faced, your child can eat the whole thing. Give him the chance to make cha-patties from India, empanadas from Ar-gentina, tacos from Mexico, a French cro-que monsieur, a falafel from the Middle East, a scone from England, a Cornish pasty, a heavenly American bagel and lox and a plain old b.l.t.

The more experimental he is about making and eating foods from other lands, the more outgoing his personality will be and the more interesting the household. With your help, he even learns that every culture has its own national dish that's as cheap as it's nutritious because certain combinations, like the Cuban Black Beans and Rice, make a whole protein. Even if your child doesn't meet people from around the world—and most children don't—he'll know them better when he eats their food. It is his introduction to civilization.

MUFFALETTA

Since a Twelve thinks any good submarine sandwich is heavenly, this one should put him inside the pearly gates. It comes from New Orleans, a French town with an Italian flavor.

Your child can do it all, but you'll need to shop at a good Italian delicatessen for the hard rolls and the fresher, cheaper, tastier meats and cheeses.

HALVE   **1 small sub roll OR hard roll**

Pour some oil from the Olive Salad over the bottom half, and over that

LAY   **2 slices provolone**
2 slices mortadella
3 slices Genoa salami
2 slices ham capocollo
2 slices sopressata
2 tomato slices
lettuce
(2 thin slices onion)
3 pepperoncini
Olive Salad

Then watch him try to shut the sub tight enough to take the first bite.

OLIVE SALAD

YIELD: 1 quart

This special mix dresses that most splendid sandwich, the Muffaletta, but it can be used in salads or laid on bread, covered with Cheddar cheese and broiled. And it's also mighty easy for an Eight to make, if you don't bother with the bits of cauliflower and carrots that the purists add.

DRAIN   **1 qt. broken stuffed salad olives**

Have your child stir the olives to get rid of the last of the brine and then

MIX   **1 T. oregano**
3–4 large garlic cloves, thinly sliced

Return the olives to the jar in layers with the oregano mixture.

ADD   **2 c. olive oil**

The oil should cover the olives. Have your child jiggle a knife blade up and down in the jar to mix the ingredients better and let the flavors marry for 24 hours. The mix will keep indefinitely in the refrigerator (though it seldom has the chance).

Your child also can give small jars of this red and green mix at Christmas. Just buy a gallon of olives and teach him to quadruple the other ingredients.

CROQUE MONSIEUR

This is French and fine for a Seven to make. Heat a skillet over a medium flame. To it

ADD   **2 T. butter**

Slice a croissant in half lengthwise, and lay the freshly cut sides in the butter to heat the bread. Remove and on one side of it

PLACE   **1 slice ham**
1 slice Swiss cheese

Put the sandwich together and gently toast the croissant in the skillet until the cheese melts.

HUMMUS

A Nine can make this Middle Eastern treat to stuff into pita for lunch or as a dip for raw vegetables before dinner. In a blender

COMBINE
- 1 19-oz. can chick-peas, drained
- 6 T. tahini (sesame paste)
- 2–4 T. warm water
- 2–3 T. olive oil

Blend until mixture is creamy.

ADD
- juice of 3 lemons
- 2–3 garlic cloves
- salt and pepper

Add more lemon if needed.

GAZPACHO

SERVES 6

Spain has given us many fine dishes but none better than this cold soup. A Nine can handle it all.
In a blender

COMBINE
- 3 green peppers, seeded and quartered
- 3 tomatoes, quartered
- 2 medium onions, quartered
- 2 cloves garlic
- 1½ c. tomato juice
- ½ c. olive oil
- ¼ c. vinegar
- 1½ t. paprika
- 1½ t. salt
- ¼ t. pepper

Chill 2 hours, pour into mugs and in each one

FLOAT
- 1 T. cucumber cubes
- 1 T. green pepper cubes
- 1 T. chopped green onions
- 1 T. croutons

BORSCHT

This fine Russian soup can actually get your child to eat veggies. In a 2-quart saucepan

COMBINE
- 2 13¾-oz. cans chicken consommé
- 2 13¾-oz. cans water
- 1 c. finely chopped cabbage
- 2 large beets, peeled and finely chopped
- 2 onions, finely chopped

SIMMER
- 15 minutes

Serve hot or cold. Onto the top of each bowlful

DROP
- ¼ c. sour cream

MIDEASTERN SOUP

SERVES 6

This cool summer soup will make a Nine feel very sophisticated. In a blender

COMBINE
- 2 cucumbers, peeled and quartered
- 3 green onions

ADD
- 2 c. plain yogurt
- 2 T. fresh dill OR mint OR 1 T. fresh basil
- ¼ t. salt
- ⅛ t. pepper

Blend well. Pour into a tureen. Into it

STIR
- 2 c. milk

Let it sit for an hour and add more salt and pepper if needed—a job you'd probably rather do yourself.

QUICHE LORRAINE

SERVES 6   Preheat oven to 350°

Except for the pie shell, this Alsatian recipe is authentic—and a Ten can make it.

DEFROST	1 9″ frozen pie shell
BOIL	6–8 slices country bacon
SAUTÉ	2 Spanish onions, thinly sliced
BEAT	4 eggs
	1 c. heavy cream
	3 T. dry white wine OR 3 T. beer
	½ c. grated Gruyère cheese
	½ c. grated Cheddar cheese

Dry bacon, cut it into pieces and lay them on the uncooked pie shell, along with the onions. Pour mixture over it. On the top

SPRINKLE	nutmeg
BAKE	30 minutes

ORIENTAL RIBS

SERVES 4

This is a stop-and-go recipe, which makes it good for your stop-and-go Ten. The ribs will be easier to eat if the butcher makes two cuts across the slab, cutting almost through to the bone, twice to make 3 little ribs out of each big one. The ribs will be more digestible if they're boiled before they're broiled. Fill a roasting pan halfway with water.

ADD	4-lb. slab of spareribs
SIMMER	1 hour

This cooks the pork thoroughly and gets rid of extra fat. In the meantime make this marinade in a large baking pan:

COMBINE	⅓ c. sugar
	⅓ c. dark brown sugar
	⅓ c. soy sauce
	⅓ c. hoisin sauce
	1 clove garlic, crushed
	2 T. white wine

Drain the cooked ribs, pat them dry, cut them into individual ribs and then roll them in the marinade until they're coated on all sides.

REFRIGERATE	3 hours

Turn the ribs occasionally, then coat them once more and lay the ribs on the broiling rack, 6″ below the flame.

BROIL	15 minutes

The ribs should be turned once or twice to brown evenly—a job that requires tongs to turn them, a potholder to steady the pan and a parent to steady the delighted child.

TANDOORI CHICKEN

SERVES 6

Your Ten can make India's hot and wonderful answer to barbecued chicken.

WASH AND DRY	1 5–6-lb. roasting chicken

In a bowl

COMBINE	2 c. plain yogurt
	⅓ c. cider vinegar
	2 T. fresh lemon OR lime juice
	2 cloves garlic, pressed
	1 T. ground coriander
	1–2 t. salt
	½ t. dry mustard
	½ t. cardamom
	½ t. ginger
	½ t. cumin
	½ t. crushed red pepper
	½ t. black pepper

Make deep cuts in the fleshier parts of the chicken, poking this mixture into them and rubbing it all over the bird. Seal the chicken in a large plastic bag with the rest of this marinade and turn the bag from time to time so it's well coated.

MARINATE	8–9 hours

Do this in the refrigerator. Preheat oven to 350°. Take the chicken out of the bag and place it on a rack in a roasting pan.

BAKE	3½ hours

Baste twice with the marinade in the first 90 minutes and then baste three times with salad oil to keep the chicken moist. Your child can make a gravy with the drippings in the roasting pan. To them

ADD	½ c. plain yogurt

Stir well.

A Twelve can make the same recipe on the barbecue if he uses marinated chicken breasts, grilling them 10–15 minutes on each side, and basting them with the marinade.

Serve with rice and thinly sliced lemon, onions and tomatoes.

BLACK BEANS AND RICE

SERVES 6–8

This mild Cuban staple has countless variations, all of them good. A Twelve can make this recipe from start to finish. In a colander

WASH **1 lb. black beans**

When the water runs clear, put the beans in a 4-qt. saucepan.

ADD **7 c. water**

Bring to a boil and partially cover the pot.

SIMMER **2½–3 hours**

Add more water if necessary until the beans are tender but still intact, and then drain the beans.

MASH **2 T. cooked beans**

Set aside when the beans are a smooth paste. Into a skillet

POUR **4 T. vegetable oil**

ADD **1 oz. salt pork, diced**

FRY **10–15 minutes**

Remove from the pan with a slotted spoon and drain.

ADD **½ c. finely chopped onions**
¼ c. finely chopped green peppers
1 t. finely chopped garlic

SAUTÉ **5 minutes**

Stir in the bean paste when the vegetables are soft but not brown and add the beans and pork bits.

SIMMER **10 minutes, uncovered**

ADD **1½ c. long-grain rice**
1 t. salt

Turn heat low.

SIMMER **20 minutes, covered**

The rice should be tender and the liquid should be absorbed.

CHICKEN KIEV

SERVES 4

This classy Russian recipe is so good it deserves to be served occasionally, even though it's fried on the outside and full of butter within.

SKIN **2 whole chicken breasts**

A Twelve is old enough to cut them in half and skin them—you'll do the boning—and then to beat the chicken breasts on both sides with a meat-tenderizing hammer (or an unopened can of evaporated milk), so each breast is as thin as possible. Stray pieces of meat are stuck on each breast. In the center

PLACE **2 T. butter**
1 T. chopped green onions

Each breast is then folded up like an envelope, miraculously sticking to itself in the process. Set aside.

BEAT **3 egg whites**

In another bowl

COMBINE **1 c. bread crumbs**
½ t. salt
¼ t. pepper

Dip each stuffed half chicken breast in the bread crumbs, then in the egg white and then in the bread crumbs again and set aside. They will look like 4 large, ugly chicken croquettes.

REFRIGERATE **2–24 hours**

They can even be made the day before.

In a 10" skillet

MELT **1 lb. vegetable shortening**

When the shortening is very hot, slide in the cold, well-sealed breasts—another job for you.

FRY **15 minutes**

Turn the chicken over to brown on all sides. The only caveat: have your child remind everyone to cut the chicken carefully; the hot butter may spurt like a Yellowstone geyser.

  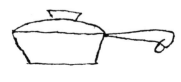

SEVICHE

SERVES 3–4

This recipe varies from country to country in South America, but it always uses the acidity in lemons or limes to "cook" seafood, without any heat at all—a nice science lesson. An Eleven is old enough to make this Peruvian salad—and like it. In a tall jar

COMBINE	1 lb. firm white fish, in ½" squares
	OR 1 lb. sea scallops, quartered
	1 c. sliced Spanish onions
	1 T. red pepper flakes OR ¼ t. cayenne pepper
	1 large clove garlic, chopped
	¼ c. chopped fresh coriander OR parsley

The slices should be quite thin, the chopping quite fine.

ADD	juice of 6 lemons
	juice of 6 limes
	2 T. olive oil
	salt

You may need more salt than you might expect, since citrus absorbs it so well, and more lemon and lime juice, to cover the seafood completely.

| REFRIGERATE | 5–7 hours |

It's cooked when the meat is white and firm but not tough, which may be sooner for the fish than the scallops. Serve on lettuce leaves.

RENAISSANCE DUCK

Preheat oven to 350°

When a child eats the food of other cultures, he can learn some history too. Let your Seven discover that classic French cooking came out of the northern Italian Renaissance. Birds were roasted in salt then to keep them from being scorched and to draw and absorb their fat. The salt works just as well on fowl today, particularly on duck, which can be greasy. It's also easy, leaving your Renaissance chef a lot of time to play. Into the bottom of a deep pot

| POUR | ½" kosher salt |

Place the 6-lb. bird, unstuffed, on its back on the salt, and then heap it with more salt until it's hidden on all sides, which makes a cover unnecessary.

| BAKE | 2 hours |

Brush away enough salt to make sure the legs wiggle easily when moved and the skin has drawn away from the ankle bone—the signs of a well-done bird in any century.

Do the next step yourself. Put on potholder gloves, dig into the hot salt and lift the bird onto a plate but let your child dust the salt away to reveal the tender, moist bird with its brown, crisp skin. It doesn't even taste salty.

Transfer the bird to a clean plate if necessary and save any dry salt for another day.

FISH AND CHIPS

SERVES 4

By the time your child is Twelve he's probably reading Sherlock Holmes and eager to taste authentic London fish and chips. While you're making the chips (which are fat french fries to us), he cuts 8–10 fillets of a dry light fish like whiting into 2" pieces and makes the batter for it. In one bowl

SIFT	1 c. flour
	1 t. baking powder
	½ t. sugar

In another bowl have him

| MIX | ⅞ c. water |
| | ½ t. vinegar |

Add the wet ingredients to the dry, stirring quickly, to make a surprisingly foamy batter. Dip the fish, one piece at a time, in the batter.

| HEAT | ½ c. peanut oil |

Since oil is still too dangerous for him to use when it boils, do the frying yourself.

| FRY | 5–7 minutes |

The fish is ready when it's crisp and golden brown. Drain on paper towels.

To serve properly, scoop a mix of the fish and the french fries into a cone made of newspaper and serve with vinegar, or the bottled British brown sauce, if you can get it.

All he'll need is a pea-soup fog.

NEW ENGLAND BAKED BEANS

SERVES 8

This New Hampshire family recipe—tested and loved for four generations—is simple and hearty, and good for a Twelve to make, when he isn't making bean jokes anymore. In a large pot of water

SOAK   **1 pt. dried yellow beans OR small peas**

Let them stand overnight. The next day

ADD   **1 t. soda**

COOK   **15 minutes**

Preheat oven to 325°

Drain and put in a covered pot.

ADD   **¼ lb. salt pork**
1 small onion, chopped
⅓ c. sugar
4 T. molasses
1 t. dry mustard
1 t. salt
¼ t. pepper

Cover with water to the top of the beans.

BAKE   **all day**

Keep adding water so the level stays as high as the beans. They're ready when your child can blow on a spoonful of beans and their skins will flutter.

ULTIMATE DRESSING

YIELD: 1 cup

While you make the salad, let your Seven make this grand dressing. It's the Italian vinegar that makes the difference. In a jar

COMBINE   **6 oz. fine olive oil**
1–2 oz. balsalmic vinegar
1 clove garlic, pressed
¼ t. dry mustard
¼ t. salt
⅛ t. pepper

Shake well.

MAYONNAISE

YIELD: 1½ cups

An Eight may want to make this great Italian-American mayo without garlic but he'll be sorry—and so will you. In a blender

COMBINE   **1 large egg**
juice of 1 large lemon
1 t. dry mustard
salt and pepper

BLEND   **2 minutes**

ADD   **¾ c. olive oil**

Pour the oil through the hole in the top of the blender, so the mixture doesn't splatter, and do it so slowly the thin stream almost breaks. When most of the oil has been added and the sauce has thickened

ADD   **5 cloves garlic**

When blended

ADD   **¼ c. olive oil**

Pour this oil as slowly as the first batch, stopping when the blender goes "thunk" each time the blades go around. If it's too thin, add a little more oil. Refrigerate in a jar to serve with beef, turkey, bologna or almost anything that isn't sweet.

PESTO

YIELD: 1 cup

This nutritious sauce is mixed into spaghetti to make it green and tasty. Have your Six make it in summer, when fresh basil is available, and make enough to freeze some for the winter. In a blender

COMBINE   **½ c. olive oil**
⅓ c. pine nuts OR walnuts
⅓ c. grated Parmesan cheese
6 cloves garlic
20 large basil leaves
3 sprigs parsley
salt and pepper

Blend until smooth.

LOUISIANA PLANTAINS

SERVES 8   Preheat oven to 350°

Plantains, those rough-fibered bananas, make an exotic dish for a Twelve to make in place of a vegetable at dinner. In a baking dish

LAY   **8 quartered plantains**

The cut sides should face upward. Over them

SPRINKLE   **8 oz. butter, in pieces**
                     ½ c. dark rum
                     ½ c. light brown sugar

Cover the dish so the steam will make the plantains more tender.

BAKE   **30 minutes**

Remove the cover, raise the heat to 400° and

BAKE   **15 minutes**

If you can't get plantains, use green-tipped bananas, but since this fruit is so tender, bake only for 20 minutes, without a cover, at 350°.

TABBOULEH

SERVES 6

This filling summer salad is a dandy introduction to the Middle East and a Ten can make it well.

COMBINE   **½ c. bulgur**
                     cold water

The water should cover the crushed wheat completely.

SOAK   **10 minutes**

Drain in a colander, pressing out all the extra water with paper towels until the bulgur is quite dry, and put it in a deep bowl.

ADD   **3 ripe tomatoes, finely chopped**
                     1 c. finely chopped green onions
                     1 c. finely chopped Italian parsley
                     ⅓ c. fresh lemon juice
                     1–2 t. salt

Stir the tabbouleh gently and well and then let the flavors marry for 1 to 6 hours. Before serving

ADD   **⅓ c. olive oil**
                     2 T. finely chopped fresh mint

It's served at room temperature on a bed of romaine lettuce.

SOUTHERN GREENS

SERVES 8

Collards (and mustard greens, kale, rape, cress and spinach) are rich in taste and nutrition. Three pounds of collards make a good mess of greens.

Have your Seven pull off all the thick stems and drop the leaves in a sink of warm, salted water, to get clean.

In a 4-quart saucepan

ADD   **2 qts. water**
                     1 ham hock
                     1 small whole jalapeño pepper
                     1 small whole onion, peeled

Bring to a full boil, then toss in the greens. Add water to cover.

SIMMER   **1–1½ hours**

Since most of the nutrition is now in the water, serve the greens with some of their own liquor. The taste is terrific.

SCOTCH SHORTBREAD

YIELD: 24 squares   Preheat oven to 325°

This is the yummiest cookie a Nine can make, because only butter will do.

CREAM   **½ lb. butter**
                     ½ c. sugar

Do this with the hands, working the dough until the fingers ache, or use a food processor, but not a mixer, because it shouldn't be fluffy at all. Into it

KNEAD   **2⅓ c. unsifted, unbleached flour**

If the dough sticks to the sides of the bowl or the hands, the butter is too warm or the dough needs more kneading. It's ready when it sticks to itself instead.

Press the dough into an ungreased 8″ × 8″ pan, smashing it down with the knuckles, then flatten with the tines of a fork pressed over the whole surface. Poke the fork through the dough many times, going right to the bottom of the pan.

BAKE   **40–60 minutes**

The shortbread is ready when it is a light tan and smells great. Put the pan on a cake rack and cut the shortbread immediately into 1½″ squares, which are small, because the cookies are so rich.

Leave them in the pan until the shortbread is cold—the hardest part of all: they smell almost as good as they taste.

GÂTEAU GÉNOISE

YIELD: 40 squares   Preheat oven to 325°

A patient Twelve can make this fine French cake if his patient mom shows him how to organize the many steps in the recipe. He should first melt the butter, sift the flour, butter a 10½" × 15½" × 1" pan, and then cut and butter a piece of wax paper to fit the bottom of the pan. Into a 3-quart bowl

BREAK	5 eggs

ADD	1 c. sugar, less 1 T.

Put the bowl on top of a saucepan of simmering water. With an electric mixer

BEAT	10 minutes

By then the mixture should be pale, thick and piling softly. Take the bowl from the pot and keep beating until the mixture is cool.

ADD	¼ t. vanilla
	⅛ t. almond extract

Now comes the tricky part.

MEASURE	1¼ c. sifted cake flour

Have him lightly sift the flour, ¼ cup at a time, over the egg mixture, barely blending it with a rubber spatula.

ADD	3 T. melted butter

Do this gradually, folding just until it's blended. Pour the batter into the pan.

BAKE	40–45 minutes

The cake should spring back lightly when its center is touched. Immediately run a knife around the sides of the cake, gently turn it upside down on a cake rack, peel away the paper and then turn the cake right side up on another rack to cool.

It can be served as a sheet cake or cut into squares, to be iced with easy, delectable Mocha Butter Frosting.

MOCHA BUTTER FROSTING

YIELD: 2¼ cups

French chefs pipe this rich frosting with a pastry tube (and Tens smear it on with a knife repeatedly dipped in hot water). In a bowl

COMBINE	½ lb. sweet butter
	½ c. sugar
	1 T. cocoa
	2 t. strong black coffee

Beat until well blended. The sugar will still be grainy but it will melt when it's spread.

IRISH SODA BREAD

YIELD: 12 slices   Preheat oven to 350°

This soda bread—a little sweeter than most—is a heart-warming treat for a Ten to make, even if it's served cold. Smear unsalted butter heavily in the bottom of a 10" cast-iron skillet, then cover this surface with a circle of wax paper. Into a large bowl

SIFT	3 c. unbleached flour
	¾ c. sugar
	1 T. baking powder
	1½ t. salt
	1 t. soda

ADD	1½ c. dried currants

Stir until everything is well mixed and the currants are well coated.

ADD	1 T. caraway seeds

In another bowl

BEAT	2 eggs

ADD	1¾ c. buttermilk
	2 T. unsalted butter, melted

Beat well, gently stir all ingredients together until barely blended and spoon the batter into the skillet. Over it

ADD	2 T. unsalted butter, in pieces

BAKE	45–60 minutes

It's done when the bread is high and brown. Put the skillet on a cake rack.

COOL	10 minutes

Remove from the pan.

CUT	12 thin wedges

To serve cold, remove from the pan, cool completely on the rack and then cut the bread. Either way, serve with unsalted butter.

THE ARTS

Art entices boys and girls in the Middle Years as easily as it did when they were Four or Five, but don't expect the same enchanting results. Originality fades in the early grades. You can blame the school's emphasis on routine and rote learning or on the art teacher, particularly one who isn't trained in art, but these aren't the main causes.

Your child's artwork is careful and restrained because he instinctively knows that this is the time to learn technique. You see him draw the same general picture day after day, with a change here and a change there until he takes the scene as far as he can and then he goes on to something else.

He also focuses on one medium at a time. Colored pencils are the surprisingly big favorite in the first grade and then your child may move on to paints or collages and come back to the pencils when he can handle them better. Most children feel at ease with two-dimensional art, while others, who have a greater tactile sense, prefer a three-dimensional challenge, like weaving or pottery, woodcarving or embroidery. A few children, who are truly gifted in art, will do everything well, although even they will do better in some areas than in others.

Your child will like to go with you to art galleries and art shows and thumb through art books from the library, but the real joy comes from actually working with different media. You support his interest by taking it seriously. Even simple questions about his drawing will encourage your child. Does the dog have a collar? Is the little boy wearing sneakers? Your attention to details will invite him to elaborate on them. Critiques help too, as long as they're positive. Appraise his work thoughtfully, and always recognize his strengths.

SUPPLIES

Some children excel in three-dimensional art and some in two-dimensional, so you need to offer both kinds. It's also better to get them from an art store—where the quality is better—but don't buy expensive ones that are beyond his skills and don't buy everything at once. That would overwhelm any child. Instead, keep adding to his art box as his interests develop. If your child doesn't take to the medium you offer, put the supplies aside for five or six months. He won't want to use them until he can make his hands work as well as his mind thinks they should.

Not all art supplies are good for children, however. The fumes from some solvents, like turpentine and acetone, and such glues as rubber cement are bad for their lungs and can trigger allergies. A rule of thumb: the stronger a chemical smells, the worse it is for the body.

Choose water-based felt markers for the Six; oil pastels—which are better than crayons for some art work—and the same

tempera you've always mixed for poster paints. Although you'll postpone oil paints until the teens, a child is ready for acrylics at Eight. They'll please you, because they're water soluble if they're rinsed away in twenty minutes, and they'll delight him, because the colors are dazzling and they also dry on the paper in twenty minutes, unless they're mixed with gel. In either case, acrylics must be applied with synthetic brushes.

Colored chalk, which was fatter and cheaper when your child was Four, is now called pastels and an Eight can handle this medium well. He's also ready for watercolors. The better ones come in tubes, and the best are squeezed from the tubes to make hard little discs and much richer colors than those that come in tins from the dime store. Your child simply squeezes a little watercolor into paper cups—one color per cup—and lets them harden for a few weeks. They're used just like the ones that come in a box.

A Nine likes to use charcoal—a little messy but worth it—for his black and white sketches and soft grade B pencils of various thicknesses. For paper, buy a spiral sketchpad of multipurpose "tooth" paper—the kind with a nubble that's sometimes called a suede finish—and a hard pink eraser.

Iron-on pastels are a great invention for the Ten, who is by now adept enough to draw and press designs on his T-shirts.

Your child will like to try his hands at three-dimensional art too. He still uses library paste and scraps, leaves and other small finds for collages at Six, and with a little help at Seven can make papier-mâché with wallpaper paste, but not with vinyl paste or the paints he uses on it will crawl away. A Nine is often a whiz with clay, especially if he has a few tools for hand building. He also can cut his own stencils with an X-acto knife—under close supervision—and indirectly learn about positive and negative shapes, and by Ten can carve a chunk of soap or a soft material, like rottenstone, with a knife.

Art supplies aren't limited to the ones he'll need to draw and carve, of course. There are, for example, the pastry tube—it's an art to decorate cookies and cakes—and needles and threads and fabric. Creativity can be expressed in countless ways, with all kinds of tools.

TECHNIQUES

Each medium has its own technique and children want to learn them well enough to know which ones they want to pursue. Your child will appreciate occasional pointers—for these are the years when he wants to be proficient in everything—or an occasional five minutes of advice, once he's mastered the basic technique.

If you have (or think you have) no artistic skill, you may have a neighbor who is willing to teach an art class and knows enough to make the lessons fun. A casual six-child, six-week class, once a week, is a great introduction to any art form, as long as the teacher has a problem-solving approach. Art, like all creativity, is based on logic.

High artistic ability depends on native talent, interest and adept fingers, but everyone has a little innate talent. Girls

generally do better than boys until the third or fourth grade, when the boys traditionally take their great jump forward.

The medium your child will like best will probably be the one you or your husband enjoy too, particularly when you enjoy it together. Consider setting up a darkroom together; baking ornaments for the Christmas tree; or making a doll's quilt or signal flags to decorate a room. These ideas may seem too time-consuming, but most art projects are the pick-up, put-down sort. Others require the parent and child to spend time together regularly and few children object to that. Katy, our grown-up daughter who drew the pictures for this book, went on sketching forays with her dad by Eight and to his "naked lady" classes by Ten. Live models didn't bother her a bit, since the setting was professional and there weren't any other children around to snicker.

There are many ways a parent can use art with a child. One divorced father and his daughter spent her two-week Christmas visit carving a wooden doll almost as tall as she was, cutting it from a pattern she had drawn. They transferred one half of the drawing to a long piece of wrapping paper, then drew the mirror image so each side would be symmetrical. He did most of the carving and she painted the face and features and made the doll a dress out of her old clothes.

This particular project would be too ambitious for most of us, but you and your child can fashion a small doll of papier-mâché, building its head on a balloon and arms and legs out of paper towel tubes, with shoes made of shiny black adhesive paper. Dress it in her baby clothes and hang it on a banner in her room for a three-dimensional picture and a sweet memory.

Coloring

Children love coloring books but parents often see them as a block to their natural originality, which isn't true for they're only using them to perfect their techniques. Accept your child's inclination to color within the lines, by giving him a splendid set of crayons and teaching him a few tricks so he'll be willing to move on that much sooner. A Six can usually learn to make tiny circles near the edges and to stay within the lines and in another year or two will learn to color evenly; to make light shadings and heavy colors and sometimes to scrape away the colors with a dull knife to make a different effect. Once he's mastered these skills he'll be ready to draw and color his own pictures and to try some new tricks. One of the best: have him cover a piece of paper completely with a bright crayon, then cover the page a second time with another darker color—even black. He then draws on the dark paper with a stylus or a dry ball-point pen, pressing just enough to leave the underlayer intact. Green leaves, gleaming through the dark covering, can be enchanting.

Drawing

Drawing is an essential of art and the basis of painting and sculpture. For you, the joy of drawing is in teaching your child to see the world around him, so he can use the eye, the hand and the memory. He'll discover that his observational skill is as important as his pencil, particularly if he's encouraged to focus his magnifying glass on a leaf or a caterpillar to capture details better.

Excursions on city streets, where you point out strange rooftops, for example, or to a marina, to show how the repeated lines of the masts and hulls make pleasing patterns, will inspire more original drawings. If you follow that up by showing him some pictures by Utrillo, and then the converging lines of a city street, he'll recognize the perspective—and never forget it.

You help a child give a sense of action to his drawings by having him watch himself move in front of a long mirror, or letting him make funny poses and draw his outline on the glass swiftly with a broad, water-soluble felt pen.

The child who is truly interested in drawing, or who wants to sculpt, will thrive in a class with a live model. By the seventh grade a group of parents can encourage the school to offer a small life class or you can hire a teacher of your own. Each child can take a turn at posing—dressed, of course—and by this demanding work learn that drawing is serious business. Once a child is involved in art, he'll find new tools and new challenges everywhere.

Painting

To artists, there are two kinds of paint—wet and dry. If your young artist is going to paint like a pro, he may as well talk like one.

Dry Paints—Pastels invite a freedom of stroke and a wider scope to the imagination. This, combined with their dusty colors, often gives a surreal look to these pictures. They are as fragile as they are lovely, however. Have your child mist the finished product with hair spray, looking the other way to avoid the fumes.

Wet Paints—A Six will keep slapping tempera on newsprint, much as he's always done, but he'll be more and more proficient until he's ready to add acrylics to his repertoire by Eight. They dry in twenty minutes (unless he adds the gel), can be thinned with water and look dazzling.

Watercolors are a complete contrast, in appearance and technique. These delicate and transparent colors must be laid on quickly and gently without disturbing the paint underneath, which is why artists say watercolors are "unforgiving." They also require a fair amount of neatness. A watercolor painter uses his brush to dribble a little pool of clean water on the hard pigment to bathe it and release the color, then cleans his brush by rinsing it in a glass of water, before dipping it into clear water so he can go on to a new color. This in itself reminds the child of the care he must take with this technique.

Printmaking

In the early grades a child can dip the flat side of a cut cabbage head onto a pad of paper toweling dipped in some tempera paint and then press it onto paper to make a splendid tree; or he can use sliced celery, a halved kiwi or lemon, but have him squeeze the lemon a little and dry it first to get a clear print.

By the fourth grade your child is ready for linoleum prints. The blocks come in many sizes; the gouges are reasonably inexpensive and they are safe as long as you teach your child that the cutting thrust is always away from his body and the cutting hand must always be in front of the hand that holds the block. As an added precaution, make a holder out of a 4″ square of wood with a 2″ lip nailed to one end, pointing down—to hug the kitchen table—and another on the opposite side, pointing up, to stop the gouge. It will look like a step with risers and will hold the block in place when the gouge is pushed into the linoleum to make a picture. When the picture is finished, the child can paint the linoleum with tempera and then press it onto the paper—a nice way to make his own greeting cards.

Sewing

Eight basic stitches make sewing the perfect one-on-one craft in the primary grades, with embroidery and knitting coming later. By the end of the seventh grade the young tailor will be able to follow a simple pattern. It's an ideal skill in many ways. Although boys' clothes are too complicated, girls can make many of their own clothes by high school, even to their own design.

Weaving

Fabric art is super for a child, even in first grade, if there is a teacher who knows and loves the craft. Weaving, with its numbered patterns, is especially good for the mathematically-minded and it can help the child with spatial problems get better. Besides—it's fun.

The teacher can make it as complicated as the child wants, from dyeing the wool with weeds gathered along the roadside in second grade to weaving elaborate banners by the sixth.

Collages

Scissors undoubtedly delight your child but they're what lawyers call an attractive nuisance. When he was little you kept them out of reach for fear of the sharp points and now you keep them out of sight so he doesn't cover the floor with snippets from the evening paper. Nevertheless, scissors bring such joy—and good artwork—that every child should have them, as long as he keeps them in the designated art corner.

To make collages, teach your child to paste any scraps—as well as leaves and glitter and buttons and string—to a sheet of paper with white glue, diluted in half with water.

CRAFTS

Crafts bring great joy to any schoolchild who is creative with his hands. He needs only time, a place to work, perhaps a few suggestions and some decent supplies, which are often free for the taking. Crafts can make use of a tremendous number of "found" objects.

Encourage your child to collect feathers, small stones, leaves and moss, as well as some supplies from around the house: heavy thread and clear thin fish line; scraps of rickrack, ribbon, buttons and sequins; macaroni and glitter; mucilage, airplane glue and white glue; mylar paper, bright tissue and old cards.

He can use these with his art supplies—the poster paints, acrylics, oils and markers; clay and plasticine; construction paper and poster board—and with proper instruction and careful supervision he can use your X-acto knife at Nine and your hot glue gun at Twelve.

Old shoeboxes, empty cigar and cigarette boxes, manila envelopes, margarine tubs, plastic containers made for the refrigerator and the sewing table all make good storage containers for these supplies.

GRANDMA PUPPET

Of all the dolls a child can make, this rough-and-ready hand puppet is often a favorite at Seven. He only needs to slide his hand inside with a thumb in one arm of the doll, the middle finger in the other and the index finger holding the head upright to make the puppet move. A steady line of patter brings it to life.

It's the making, however, that gives many children the most pleasure. An Eight can produce this Grandma Puppet, if there's an obliging grown-up—like a grandma—to lend an unobtrusive hand.

The pattern comes first. Have your child cut a square of paper, 9″ × 9″, and fold it in half, so he can draw half of the picture and the puppet will look the same on each side when it's cut. Like this:

Lay two squares of felt, 9″ × 9″, on the table, one placed precisely on top of the other to form the back and the front of the puppet.

Open the pattern completely and pin it to the felt, cutting both pieces at once with sharp scissors. The paper is then removed, the felt is pinned again and the puppet is stitched on all but the bottom side, so the hand can slip into it. Use bold embroidery thread, doubled for strength and knotted at the end, and take big, even stitches with a ½″ seam, so the edge will be tidy. The puppet is then ready for its features to be glued in place, with puffs of cotton for hair (back and front); embroidery floss for eyebrows and lashes; pink cheeks out of felt; red ribbon scraps to make the mouth; and, by all means, sequins scattered willy-nilly, for this is a silly grandmother.

FENNEL FLOWERS

Fennel—the blessing of the kitchen and the scourge of the garden—can be transformed into painted flowers for the dining-room table or snowflakes tucked on a Christmas tree. This project, saved for fall when the flowers have dried, is quick, easy and messy: do it outside with the ground and the child well covered.

Have your Six clip the flowering heads, with 4″ stems, while you cut a clean, dry half-gallon milk carton down to a height of 6″ and into it

POUR   **white latex paint**

You then take turns dipping the flowers, one by one, into the paint, deep enough for most of the stem to be covered. Lay it aside for a few minutes to drain, then gently twirl it in the air to get rid of the extra paint before laying it on fresh newspaper to dry. Wait a few hours, then break off the brown ends of the stems so the flowers are pristine and white.

If you don't know anyone who grows fennel, try any flower that dries on its stem, like a small hydrangea blossom.

BEADS

Preheat oven to 350°

Your Ten will like to make her own jewelry: it's a fun and an easy job and the number of beads will depend on the amount of cornstarch you use.

STIR   **2 parts boiling water**
             1 part cornstarch

Cover the mixture with a damp cloth until cool, then knead it for several minutes, adding salt until the mixture is firm and workable. Cover again.

REST   **2 hours**

This will make it pliable enough for your child to make a fine necklace. Roll the dough ¼″ thick, cut it into ¼″ strips and then cut it in the other direction to make ¼″ squares. Roll each square into a ball and put a big needle through it, so the beads can be strung. A piece of uncooked spaghetti will keep the bead open while it's baked.

BAKE   **20 minutes**

The beads are done when they're quite firm. While they cool

MIX   **3 parts water**
             1 part mucilage

Coat the beads with this diluted dime-store glue, then paint them with acrylics and string the beads.

BATIKS

Your Nine can make a batik with a white, all-cotton T-shirt, some wax, a stiff brush—and you. Wax can be dangerous without supervision but it's a good medium and available wherever canning supplies are sold. In a double boiler

MELT   **4 oz. paraffin wax**

Do this over 3″ of water and use a low fire—your only job. While the wax is melting, your child lightly pencils a design, like a plane, on the shirt and then slips cardboard between the front and back so the wax won't drip through. He paints the wax only over the design with a fat artist's brush in short, light strokes, lifting the T-shirt material every few strokes, to make sure it doesn't stick, while you keep reheating the wax, because it cools in about a minute. Altogether, it will take 15 to 20 minutes.

Your child then dissolves a package of dye in a large pot of very warm water—hot enough to set the dye, but not hot enough to melt the wax—then wets the shirt with plain water and gently drops it into the dye. It's removed from the dye when it is several shades darker than he wants—because it will be lighter when it dries—and laid out and rinsed under cool water until the color runs clear.

Lift the shirt carefully, so the wax doesn't crackle too much, and lay it over many thicknesses of newspaper on the ironing board. Put layers of paper towels between the front and the back of the shirt and on top of it, then iron carefully with a hot iron to melt the wax. This is done over and over with fresh paper so it continues to absorb wax and keeps the iron from getting waxy. It's done when almost all the wax has been blotted from the shirt and the design is white and clear (and probably a little crackly).

The shirt should be washed separately until you're sure it won't bleed anymore.

STARBURSTS

Back in the fifties, little girls fried marbles to make crackly, sparkly jewelry for their moms. It still works, but stand by to make sure she follows the directions. This craft only needs pendant loops from a craft shop, and marbles, either colored or clear.

Your Nine simply drops the marbles into a dry skillet, turns on the exhaust fan, turns the heat high and covers the skillet with a mesh splatter screen, to make sure they stay where they should.

COOK   **3–7 minutes**

Turn off the fire, pour cold water through the screen and the marbles will burst inside while the outside stays as smooth as ever. When cool, dry each marble, wipe with rubbing alcohol to clean them thoroughly, then glue each marble to a pendant loop with super-strength pre-mixed epoxy—a job for you. A chain or a ribbon is run through the loop, one pendant for each necklace, or your child could hang several from each ribbon.

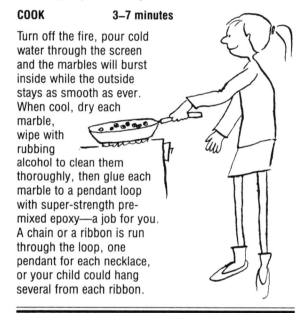

BOOKS

When a child reads, he decodes the meaning of words. When he reads books, he can decode the meaning of life. A book—or even a whole library—can never take the place of experience, but it can be a magic carpet, an open sesame, a key to a hundred kingdoms.

A book is so precious, it can make a child laugh or cry (the best do both), as it pushes his emotions—and his ideas—further than they have gone before and brings his creativity into flower. It invites a child to draw pictures in his mind and recall a sight, a smell, a touch. And it treats each child to a slightly different story, because each child responds in a slightly different way.

Whatever the plot, a child likes to read about someone mucn like himself. If the hero must tackle a serious problem, the reader wants him to be slightly older than he is, because he wants to know how to handle what's ahead. If the character is silly, however, the reader likes him to be a little younger, since a funny story isn't so funny when the hero is his own age. Instead he reads this funny book with a serious, and even satisfied air: here's someone else who feels just as he does. In the best stories, funny or sad, the children survive with their characters tested but intact. The example is well set. When a child identifies with someone who is good and noble and true, he also will feel good and noble and true—and a little stronger than before.

With gentle persuasion, the classics, new and old, appeal to the humor and fears and joys all children share, and will give your child the reading habit for life. He will be more likely to read if you have books in the house and you and your husband often read them; if books are given as presents on special occasions; if members of the family read aloud to each other; if television is limited; and if the child is allowed to read in bed for fifteen minutes before he puts out the light.

You also encourage reading if the books reflect his interests rather than yours. Don't insist that he read a certain book because you loved it as a child or "because it's a classic." Either approach will squash his interest in that particular book and probably in that particular author. You also don't want to push a book just because it will teach him virtues or skills or special knowledge, like history or geography. Any lessons should be incidental to the story and will be learned best in books that are interesting in themselves. These are the ones that will make him want to pursue the subject.

Reading shouldn't even be limited to literature, because the habit of reading is more important than the books. In fact, a certain number of junk books (like a certain amount of junk food) give your child the chance to compare and discriminate. Boys and girls who are well grounded in literature, wherever it comes from, may switch to trivial writing in their teens but they'll come back for the good stuff when they're grown. The best, it's been said, is enemy to the good (and certainly to the dreadful).

As wonderful as books are, you don't want your child to read during all of his playtime. This may even be a sign of trouble. The child who's always buried in books may be in need of friends—for children mask their loneliness in many ways— or he may be avoiding his chores. You have to help your child balance his time and his responsibilities. You also mustn't push your child to read books beyond his real understanding. With all the fine and appropriate books available, he could read two at his own level each week and have enough for years to come. What's the rush?

He will, however, understand books that are beyond his reading level, as long as you read them to him—a custom that strengthens the reading habit (see Reading Aloud).

inscribed as the donor on a bookplate inside, is another way to give your child a proprietary interest in the place. Familiarity with your neighborhood library will also make it easier for him to find reference materials as he gets older, and if you move from one neighborhood or one town to another, the new library will give him a friendly base.

You can also encourage reading—and thrift—by taking your child to yard sales and secondhand shops to buy books. Wherever he gets his books, help him look for those with bigger type and some pictures if he's in the early grades, for the eyes still don't focus as well as they will by Eight or Nine.

You also want to help him choose books as you do—by the author as well as the subject. If someone has written one good book, he probably has written others. Unlike adult books, the most popular children's books are usually the best ones, and they're usually on many lists. Look for those that have won writing awards— the Newbery or Carnegie medal or the National Book Award for children's literature—or ones that have been designated as "Notable" by the American Library Association or commended by the Bank Street College. Or look for those that have received the Caldecott Medal for art. Publishers usually choose the finest illustrators for their best books.

Because children read at such different levels in the Middle Years, the lists below are suggested in chronological order, within each category, and were chosen arbitrarily from the recommendations of a

THE CRITIC'S CORNER

Nothing pleases a Nine like a good joke book. Noah's heartfelt thank-you letter says it best: "Dear M——, I LOVE *The Laugh Book*! Where in the world did you get it? It shure has a lot of jokes. I read in it every day.

" 'Waiter, there's a fly in my soup.'

" 'Sssh. Be quiet or everyone will want one.'

"That's my favorite joke!"

Weekly trips to the library together strengthen it more and they should continue until he's old enough to go on his own. The gift of a book to the children's division on his birthday, with his name hundred children, a dozen lists, some kind librarians and my own quirks and fancies. All of them should be in your local library, even if they're out of print. And in almost every case the author who's listed for one good book has written other good ones too, so you'll want to teach your child to check the library's catalog.

Animal Stories

If a Six could read his favorite book, it would be his own autobiography, but lacking that, he'll go for books about nature, which is why Mark Trail is such a popular comic strip. Prehistoric animals have a particular appeal in the Middle Years, especially for little boys, and offer a nice bridge between reality and fantasy.

For girls—and the sexes truly divide in this category—there are realistic horse stories, like *The Yearling* by Marjorie Kinnan Rawlings, and fanciful doll stories, like *Hitty: Her First 100 Years,* by Rachel Field. Both are perfect for the passionate Eleven. Most of the books below, however, suit both boys and girls for first through seventh grade:

the Babar series—Laurent de Brunhoff
the Paddington series—Michael Bond
The Velveteen Rabbit—Margery Williams
The House at Pooh Corner—A. A. Milne
The Wind in the Willows—Kenneth Grahame
Charlotte's Web—E. B. White
The Day the Animals Talked—William Faulkner
The Borrowers—Mary Norton
The Rescuers—Margery Sharp
The Jungle Book—Rudyard Kipling
Outlaw Red—Jim Kjelgaard
Lassie, Come Home—Eric Knight
the Black Stallion series—Walter Farley
All Things Bright and Beautiful—James Herriot
Watership Down—Richard Adams
Bambi—Felix Salten
My Friend Flicka—Mary O'Hara
Misty of Chincoteague—Marguerite Henry
The Red Pony—John Steinbeck

Fairy Tales and Fantasy

Fairy tales endure because they're written on two levels—the real and the surreal— and because they're exciting; they're usually well written; they inspire the imagination; they mirror the emotional situations

a child sometimes feels—and they offer a miraculous solution. Fantasy and science fiction have the same appeal.

And to Think I Saw It on Mulberry Street—Dr. Seuss
Aesop's Fables—Arnold Lobel
The Fairy Tale Treasury—selected by Virginia Haviland
Grimm's Fairy Tales—the brothers Grimm; illustrated by Arthur Rackham
Andersen's Fairy Tales—Hans Christian Andersen, illustrated by Arthur Szyk
Roald Dahl's Revolting Rhymes
Many Moons—James Thurber
Pippi Longstocking—Astrid Lindgren
The Adventures of Pinocchio—Carlo Collodi
The Happy Prince—Oscar Wilde
Stuart Little—E. B. White
The Rose and the Ring—William Makepeace Thackeray
The Peterkin Papers—Lucretia Hale
The Black Cauldron—Lloyd Alexander
Heart of Ice—Benjamin Appel
The Hero from Otherwhere—Jay Williams
Tom's Midnight Garden—A. Philippa Pearce
Rip Van Winkle—Washington Irving
The Hobbit and the Lord of the Rings trilogy—J. R. R. Tolkien
The Wizard of Oz series—L. Frank Baum
The Hero and the Crown—Robin McKinley
The Tripods trilogy—John Christopher
The Narnia series—C. S. Lewis
The Earthsea trilogy—Ursula LeGuin
The Time trilogy—Madeleine L'Engle
Alice's Adventures in Wonderland—Lewis Carroll
Gulliver's Travels—Jonathan Swift
Peter Pan—James M. Barrie

On Mythology

Book of Greek Myths—Ingri and Edgar Parin D'Aulaire
Children's Homer—Padraic Colum
The Heroes—Charles Kingsley
King Arthur and His Knights of the Round Table—retold by Roger L. Green
Stories of King Arthur and His Knights—Barbara Leonie Picard
The Once and Future King—T. H. White
Beowulf—Rosemary Sutcliffe

And for Ethnic Folklore:

East of the Sun and West o' the Moon (Scandinavian)—P. C. Asbjornsen and J. Moe, illustrated by Hague
Angry Moon (Eskimo)—William Slater
The Arabian Nights Entertainments (Mideastern)—Andrew Lang, editor

Science Fiction:

The Little Prince—Antoine de St. Exupéry
James and the Giant Peach—Roald Dahl
The Twenty-one Balloons—William Pene DuBois
The Illustrated Man—Ray Bradbury

Feelings and Foibles:

Humor and pathos—separately or together—help a child understand his emotions, which is just what he needs. Life can seem so uncertain when you're in the middle of growing up. No one uses wit to comfort younger readers better than Beverly Cleary, and no one is as empathic to preteens (and young teens) as Katherine Paterson. Their books are among the many that show a child how to handle the biggies—jealousy, failure, divorce and death. Among the best:

Jacob Two-Two Meets the Hooded Fang (sibling rivalry)—Mordecai Richler
The Tenth Good Thing About Barney (death)—Judith Viorst
The Flunking of Joshua T. Bates (failure)—Susan Shreve
The Keeper (mental illness)—Phyllis Naylor
Dear Mr. Henshaw (divorce)—Beverly Cleary
Brave Jimmy Stone (divorce)—Elliott Arnold
The Solomon System (divorce)—Phyllis Naylor
Superfudge (new baby)—Judy Blume
Sarah, Plain and Tall (self-esteem)—Patricia MacLachlan
To Talk in Time (shyness)—Gene Inyart Namovicz
A Summer to Die (death)—Lois Lowry
Hang Tough, Paul Mather (death)—Alfred Slote
A Day No Pigs Would Die (death)—Robert N. Peck
A Taste for Blackberries (death)—Doris Buchanan
A Bridge to Terabithia (death)—Katherine Paterson

Some New Classics:

These are the evocative novels your children will be recommending to their children—along with many others in this section.

My Side of the Mountain—Jean George
Mistress Masham's Repose—T. H. White
The Young Landlords—Walter Dean Myers
J.T.—Jane Wagner
The Pushcart War—Jan Merrill
Dicey's Song—Cynthia Voigt
Harriet the Spy—Louise Fitzhugh
The Great Gilly Hopkins—Katherine Paterson
Fireweed—Jill Paton Walsh
Where the Red Fern Grows—Wilson Rawls
Island of the Blue Dolphins—Scott O'Dell

Watership Down—Richard Adams
Miracles on Maple Hill—Virginia Sorensen
Mischling—Ilse Koehn
The Slave Dancer—Paula Fox
Sweet Whispers, Brother Rush—Virginia Hamilton
The Cay—Theodore Taylor
Roll of Thunder, Hear My Cry—Mildred Taylor
Summer of My German Soldier—Bette Greene
To Kill a Mockingbird—Harper Lee
Member of the Wedding—Carson McCullers
Animal Farm—George Orwell

The Old Classics:

Madeline—Ludwig Bemelmans
Eloise—Kay Thompson
The Secret Garden—Frances Hodgson Burnett
Rebecca of Sunnybrook Farm—Kate Douglas Wiggin
Anne of Green Gables—L. M. Montgomery
The Swiss Family Robinson—Johann David Wyss
Heidi—Johanna Spyri
Hans Brinker, or the Silver Skates—Mary Mapes Dodge
Caddie Woodlawn—Carol Ryrie Brink
The Little House on the Prairie—Laura Ingalls Wilder
Little Women—Louisa May Alcott
Laughing Boy—Oliver LaFarge
Tom Sawyer—Mark Twain
The Life and Strange Surprising Adventures of Robinson Crusoe—Daniel Defoe
Treasure Island—Robert Louis Stevenson
The Call of the Wild—Jack London
Oliver Twist—Charles Dickens

Good Reads:

Some parents overlook some books because they're "just mysteries" or they're "just funny," which is a big mistake, especially for slow readers. Books that keep children guessing or laughing are the ones that keep them reading.

The Encyclopedia Brown series—Donald J. Sobol
The Amelia Bedelia series—Peggy Parish
TinTin comics—Hergé (Georges Rémi)
The House With a Clock in Its Walls—John Bellairs
Paddle-to-the-Sea—Holling C. Holling
The Snarkout Boys and the Avocado of Death—D. Manus Pinkwater
From the Mixed-up Files of Mrs. Basil E. Frankweiler—E. L. Konigsburg
A Girl Called Al—Constance Greene
The Homer Price series—Robert McCloskey
*The Education of H*Y*M*A*N K*A*P*L*A*N*—Leonard Q. Ross
The Nancy Drew series—Carolyn Keene
The World of Mr. Mulliner—P. G. Wodehouse
Adventures of Sherlock Holmes—A. Conan Doyle
The ABC Murders—Agatha Christie

Poetry

Lafcadio, the Lion Who Shot Back—Shel Silverstein
The New Kid on the Block—Jack Prelutsky
Honey, I Love—Eloise Greenfield
A Circle of Seasons—Myra Cohn Livingston
The poetry of Emily Dickinson, Walt Whitman, William Blake, Samuel Taylor Coleridge, Henry Wadsworth Longfellow

Nonfiction

Science:
The Science Book—Sara Stein
Millions and Millions of Crystals—Roma Gans
Me and Einstein—Rose Blue
The Book of Think—Marilyn Burns
The Know-How series—Heather Amery and Angela Littler
Blood and Guts—Linda Allison
Life Under the Sea—Rachel Carson
Clouds—Tomie de Paola
Unbuilding—David Macaulay

History:

Harriet Tubman—Linda D. Meyer
Pocahontas—Ingri and Edgar Parin D'Aulaire
The Road from Home—David Kherdian
Will You Sign Here, John Hancock?—Jean Fritz
Twenty and Ten—Claire Huchet Bishop
The Miracle Worker—William Gibson
Anne Frank: The Diary of a Young Girl—Anne Frank
Kon-Tiki—Thor Heyerdahl
A Day of Pleasure—Isaac Bashevis Singer

Geography:

The Book of How to Be Naturally Geographic—Neill Bell

Fun and Games:

The Philharmonic Gets Dressed—Karla Kuskin
Alligators and Music—Donald Elliott
Frogs and the Ballet—Donald Elliott
History of Art for Young People—H. W. Janson with Samuel Cauman
Sports Cards, Collecting, Trading, and Playing—Margaret McLoone
KidsSpeak About Computers—Joanne Oppenheim

References:

Macmillan's Magic Book of Words
The Golden encyclopedias
New Heritage Dictionary

Magazines:

Cobblestone (history)
Cricket (general interest)
Faces (natural history)
Owl (wildlife)
Ranger Rick (nature)
World (nature, sports and more)
3-2-1-Contact (science)

Tapes

There is a revolution under way. Books on tape are bridging a gap between books and television, and children are the winners.

A growing number of book titles are going on tape, and when they're recorded well with unabridged texts the results are excellent. They become the entertainment on long car rides—ideal for children who get carsick when they read and ride. Parents slip a tape into their child's tape player—or their tape deck—just north of boredom and bypassing bedlam. At home the older, unsupervised children of working parents can turn to these tapes in that long span before supper, when they need to hear a grown-up's voice.

Parents report that good readers not only like tapes, but they still read as much as ever. You don't want to rely on them to take over the family's time for reading aloud or playing board games, but they can be a good way to listen to a long book together, so you can discuss it and have respect for each other's opinions. This respect is a key to family harmony and it's easy when neither of you has a stake in the base.

MUSIC

Music is more important than ever in the Middle Years, for it gives these girls and boys one more way to express themselves. The preparation probably started when your child was in the womb. (Remember when you pressed a tape player right up to your belly?) You continued the lessons when you rocked him with your lullabyes and, later, when you waltzed him around like Willy. Parents foster their child's natural talents almost without knowing it, but a fully developed interest in the more complex arts, such as music, requires a positive approach now.

Concerts for children—especially band concerts in the park—are great and so is a background of music at home—classical or rock, blues, jazz, folk songs or show tunes—anything as long as it's first class. The more variety you can give a child—in style and in instruments—the quicker he can discover his preferences, and the better the quality, the sooner he'll be able to tell the difference between good and bad.

You'll also want to introduce your child (and possibly yourself) to classical music, if you haven't already, by explaining what it means (see Recommended Reading). Children enjoy music most when they know what it's all about—especially the blood-and-thunder plots that abound in opera.

By the preteens your child will be following his own music fads, imitating adolescence (always a year or two behind the times), and making you wince at his choices. Although you'll want to be as understanding as possible, you don't have to be silly. Parents police their children's music the same way they police everything else: by limiting their time and their money. If children are too busy to play this music very much and too poor to buy much, it won't be a big issue. In any case, you can expect your child to go back to the good stuff when he gets older, as long as he's enjoying it now.

TOYS & GAMES

Toys—a major joy of childhood—are as important in the Middle Years as they were in the early ones. They are, however, harder to choose.

Toys are meant to be fun, but you probably have other reasons for buying them too. Most parents naturally favor the toys they think will win out over television, or ones they feel will educate as they amuse, or those that they remember with pleasure from their own childhood. Sometimes they're intended to exorcise the ghosts of Christmases past, by giving what they once wanted so much. Such approaches can get you into trouble, for these toys may not suit your child.

By the time he starts first grade he is more of an individual and yet he not only will want to have the same things as his friends but he won't know he wants a particular toy unless they have it and they won't want it unless he and their other friends have it. (And all of them will want it if it's advertised on television.)

The toys your child will love, however, are those you've chosen to suit his own talents, particularly those that open new horizons and offer a series of possibilities. That's why the old-timers—the bats and balls; jacks and pickup sticks; the dolls; the special stuffed animal; the bike; the gym set—are still the favorites. They stretch a child's body, his mind and his imagination and some of them, like a favorite doll or a teddy, stretch a child's love. They also can get rid of anger, for a child invents scenarios that let the doll behave the way he wishes he could.

Fun, of course, is the main purpose of a toy. It's deadly to give a child a toy just because it teaches, or mainly because it teaches. Instead, a good toy invites a child to learn by making it a hoot to practice his skills and not know he's doing it. This is the toy that helps him judge distance; develop muscles; read better; write clearer; add quicker; or coordinate the movements of his hand and his eye and therefore build his self-esteem. To a child, play is work but this work is always fun. And some toys are more fun than others.

- A microscope, a telescope, a globe and a classy wooden map of the United States all help children learn about the world in an orderly way and so does a chemistry set, if you do some experiments with him, for they are hard to do alone at first.

- The toys that help children be creative are among the best, especially if they're keyed to their strengths. Children who have a good ear will like a maraca or a drum, if they're taught how to shake it or tap it to the beat of a record, and art supplies are great for visual or tactile children. Take care, however. If children are rushed to use a medium before they're ready, they'll feel inept, and if they're given too many supplies at once, they may get bored.

- Toys that foster friendships are also important because friends are so important now, making the walkie-talkie a delight between Eight and Eleven.

- Funny horns or nose masks made children giggle with abandon, so they'll always know how to laugh at themselves when times get tough. A sense of the ridiculous is as important as a sense of humor, all through life. It not only helps children cope with adversity but it helps them handle social situations.

Guilt is often a big factor when parents buy toys, because they never get as many as they want—although they usually get too many—and because they often cut back on quality. It is always unwise to spend too much, for you will resent it and your child will feel guilty when he realizes what you have done, and yet he'll continue to expect this special treatment. A mother who treats her child like a prince or a princess is very likely to be an angry mother—with an angry child. When parents take their child's dreams into consideration but still call the shots, there is a harmony in the family, a sense that everyone is in it together.

Give the toys you can afford, which may be fewer than you think, since the quality of the toy should be first rate. This subliminally tells the child that he is first rate too. It also tells him that he is capable, for quality toys don't fall apart. This will inspire him to care for them better and so will your own attention. Your child needs you to help him repair the toys that can be fixed, throw away those that are irreparable and give outgrown or unused toys to children less fortunate.

Your child should also put away a third of all but the most popular toys, rotating them so some will always seem new, and keep the rest reasonably tidy. This depends on you quite as much as your child. If you sew plastic rings on stuffed toys or cowboy hats, he can hang them on hooks on the door and window frames in his room. You should also provide shelves for the much-used toys, puzzles and books and a basket to hold the rest. You can't expect your child to keep his room perfectly but you do want him to make a regular attempt, which means that you monitor it by complimenting his tidiness when you give him a good night kiss or tell him he'd better go to his room a little earlier the next night, so he'll have time to tidy it. Finally, make sure he has a leaf rake in his closet to pull everything into a heap, which makes the sorting easier. And if he still can't put them into some kind of order, he still has too many toys.

INSIDE TOYS

These are the toys that seem to proliferate when no one's watching.

Dolls

Both boys and girls like dolls, but boys usually like them better if they're small and jointed and warlike or soft and furry and look like teddy bears. This is nothing to be bothered about, for a stuffed animal plays the same role as a dolly and both should be encouraged. They fill a child's need to nurture and care for others. These sorts of urges (and a few more exciting ones) are what keep the human race going.

A Six will hug her baby dolls—always choosing one or two favorites—but treat their clothes in the most casual way and often draw a dot of ball-point ink squarely between their legs (and be appalled when she can't erase it). Don't be alarmed. This is bathroom art, not pornography. The concept of sex is still too abstract to imagine.

While the plain (and not so plain) baby doll is best for the girl under Eight or Nine, the fancy dolls beg to be bought after that. Collector dolls thrill this child, and the manufacturers too, for this is the age when a child pines for everything that's sold in a series.

This need to collect, to sort, to classify, is one reason why paper dolls once had such an appeal and why Barbie dolls and G. I. Joe are so popular today. Although much younger children play with them, it usually takes an Eight to be adept enough to dress and care for such a frail doll. Most parents are bothered by the cost of clothes for these dolls, and the materialism they foster, but it's the chestiness of Barbie that bothers them most. While the child notices this development, and knows a bit about sex, she ignores that and instead spends hours imagining—and solving—all the social problems she thinks might loom in her future. And all the while she dresses and undresses Barbie and classifies her clothes in categories: these for day; those for evening; these for sports; those for the office—only to sort them the next month by color or cost. Children learn order and logic in many ways.

Other toys teach the same kind of thinking, as children instinctively collect baseball cards, seashells, racing cars, stamps, toy soldiers, coins, as they always have. Anything that is replicated is relished. (see Collections.)

Construction Toys

These delight children who have good control over their fingers, but they make the clumsy ones feel more awkward than ever. For those who were clever with wooden blocks, Legos and Bristle blocks as preschoolers, consider a fine-tuned construc-

tion toy like Capsela, sometimes so elaborate it has gearshifts to make it go. Those strange and awful bodies called the Visible Man and the Visible Woman are also good for the Ten, but skip the Visible Pigeon. It may be my pigeon phobia, but this toy is a bore.

A dexterous child also will like to make model planes and ships and kites (with a window open or a fan blowing, if he's using model glue). Your company will make the time go by even better, if you each have your own models and you don't tell him what to do before he asks or even give him much advice when he does. There is a time for a parent to be a teacher and a time to be a friend. It's best to be a friend if you want to be invited back to play.

Games

There are hundreds of board games—the old-fashioned kind and the electronic ones—and the best of them involve deduction, strategy or memory. Some of the newer ones are games of cooperation rather than competition, in which the players band together to reach a common goal. These deserve a share of the toy budget, but don't expect to overturn human nature in a single generation. Individual competition is still natural and necessary. The best you can wish is for your child to learn how to get where he's going honorably and happily and to apply these lessons to his whole life.

By first grade your child enjoys games for their rules as much as anything else, for this is a new and fascinating concept, although he may keep changing the rules as he plays. He will enjoy Candyland and Old Maid but needs you to forget to take advantage of a clever move so he can win sometimes. Even if you hold back, he may occasionally cheat, which calls for a new set of rules, not a lecture. Play by the ones he uses, with much jollying along the way, as if he meant the cheating to be a joke, but if he's still cheating at Eight, you quietly put away the game for another year or two until he's old enough to know that winning isn't really that important.

It usually takes a third grader to be swept away by games, and the good ones usually teach silent lessons. Sorry does a fine job of teaching children how to say it; Parcheesi, backgammon and dominoes subtly speed a child's counting; card games like hearts and gin rummy with grandfathers, and mah-jongg and Uno with grandmas teach math and loving too. A pair of dice or a deck of cards spawns a special camaraderie, and Clue and Mancola are thrilling. There is solitaire at Seven and wild, frenzied quadruple solitaire at Eight, where each player tosses his aces in the center of the table and everyone plays their cards on them, with the winner having the most cards in the community pile. Silly card games like Spit and Pig delight a child (especially when he can catch his parents) and Concentration helps him remember everything a little better. And when all seems bleak, teach him to build a house of cards.

You'll be challenging your child to checkers at Eight, Pictionary at Nine, Scrabble by Ten and chess at Twelve but, of all the games, Monopoly is king. This is because the Middle Years are perfect for order and math and Monopoly teaches both much better than teachers—or parents.

Dungeons and Dragons picks up when Monopoly ends. It's a favorite for boys but most girls—and almost all parents—ignore it. If the bug bites your son, expect it to take over his social life for a year or two, which is fine. Despite some bad press, it's a nice, safe pastime. While real estate speculation deals with complex, concrete ideas, D and D doesn't even have a board. Instead it is a mind-bending, problem-solving game that catches children as early as Twelve or even Eleven, in those heady years when they first learn to think in abstractions.

Electronic Toys

Until the microcomputer chip was invented, every type of toy that children play with today was enjoyed by early Egyptian children. The chip has changed that irrevocably. Simple video games have initial impact, but most of them get boring since they demand little skill. The home computer offers endless variations, however, if it has a good graphics program or if the child learns to program.

A computer can be a wonderful addition to the household, even if it only belongs to one person, for it can become a focal point in the family. For all the good that can come from it, however, the computer can have an addictive quality, particularly at Ten, Eleven and Twelve, when passions prevail. You can resist, to some degree, by arranging other enchantments—gatherings with one or two families for supper and charades or a ball game in the backyard. You also do it when you challenge your Twelve to a nightly run with you in the park or a running game of chess, keeping the chess board on a tray with its players in place, and taking it out for a half hour of play each night.

Exercise Equipment

An exercise mat is fine—especially if you have two roustabouts—and so is a doorway punching bag on a stand. The hanging kind, however, is too heavy for a child to punch and still feel successful. One- and three-pound dumbbell weights are good too and so are the weighted bands that clasp the wrists and ankles so easily. The seventh grader who is keen on the body beautiful will enjoy them. He can use a rebounder too if you're in the vicinity and if only one child jumps on it at once, but a trampoline must be supervised.

The Classics

Other toys are so fine and so memorable that they become the focus of childhood—the one toy that generates such intense enjoyment that it is remembered above all

others. If it's at all possible, every child should have one of these classics. It can be as simple as a secondhand Ping-Pong table or as grand as a pool table, but if everyone in the family enjoys it, it becomes the bond for all.

One of the classics is an electric train—about the only electric toy that's always safe, but it works best when a parent is a train buff too; it's too overwhelming for most children to try alone. If neither of you is prepared to get so involved, find another toy. In the right setting, however, it can brighten up an entire childhood, which roughly means from Eight to Eighty. And that's a good range to use it too. There are tracks to be rubbed with steel wool so the train will run smoother; bridges and tunnels to be built out of papier-mâché and hours of fiddling with wires to help your child make it go, which is what train fanciers spend half their time doing.

The dollhouse, the delight of so many little girls, is also in this major toy category. Probably no other toy appeals more to the collecting spirit of an Eight. Its pleasure will last for years, guiding her through childhood as she plays house and spins out her changing fantasies, perhaps with a gruff brother hanging around to help "fix things up," for a dollhouse appeals to the tough and the tender. Parents are no exception. There are many fairly inexpensive prefabricated models well worth the trouble of assembling. It takes time to find the supplies, paint the trim, paper the walls and find just the right scraps of upholstery fabric to turn into rugs, but the hours will be an investment of love as well as effort. Another bond is forged.

OUTSIDE TOYS

The best way to see that your child gets heavy exercise is to give him the toys that make him want to play hard and long outside.

Although you buy these toys, your child should be responsible for keeping them in good shape—or at least helping you do it, particularly if they're seasonal toys. It's wise to have him put them away in good condition, but he'll happily sand and wax the sled runners before the first snow and patch the raft when the weather turns hot.

The variety of equipment is tremendous and most of it is good. A wagon is dandy in the early grades, for this child is still the great transporter, and the scooter is making a well-deserved comeback. The pogo stick and stilts are fun too, although a child won't be interested in them very long.

Between Six and Twelve your child will probably want—and even need—a soccer ball, a basketball, a football, a baseball and bat, a tennis ball and a racket—if you're willing to play with him—and a Frisbee, a kite and a sled if you get snow in your area.

Bicycle

Probably no toy has such allure as a bicycle. Unless you live in Manhattan or on a mountainside, your child should have one of his own by the time he's Seven, if it's safe to ride in your neighborhood.

Training wheels turn a two-wheeler into a four-wheeler, which may make a bike less scary (especially to parents), but they don't make it less dangerous. A child really won't learn to balance on the bike until they're removed, and then there will be a few tumbles until he dares to pedal fast enough to keep it from teetering. Basically, a bike is only unsafe if it's so big the child can't straddle it and still keep his feet on the ground or if the handlebars are lower than the seat or if he becomes careless when he's old enough to ride in the street.

While a good bike should be sturdy, it doesn't need to be new, and it certainly doesn't need ten speeds unless your child is going to race it. It does, however, need a bell or a horn; some reflector tape on the fenders; a light, in case it gets dark suddenly; a helmet—and your insistence that it's worn; and a cable lock with its properly mysterious combination. Even if you live in a safe part of town, a lock reminds your child that the bike is his most expensive possession, and the light and the tape underscore the dangers. The best lectures are often unspoken.

Your child also will need a can of oil to make his bike go faster (a reason that will be much more effective than a speech about rust); a sheet of plastic to cover it or a special place to keep it out of the rain; a small bike towel to dry it if he's caught in a shower, and a pouch to hold it, along with a wrench or two. By Ten he also should have a few lessons in bike repair from an older child in the neighborhood, a book on the subject in case he forgets, a tire pump and a can of tire patches.

Skates and Skis

These are grand investments. Roller skates are a delight at Seven or Eight—either secondhand shoe skates or the old-fashioned, high-quality kind that clamp onto the shoes and can be extended as his feet grow.

Your child will beg for a skateboard in the preteens, and will borrow turns from a friend, but you don't have to encourage this sport by giving him a skateboard as a present. The injury rate is much too high, even when wearing a helmet.

Ice skates make fine sports gear, however, and for everyone in the family if you have an ice rink or a well-frozen pond in your neighborhood. Thrift shops usually are well stocked with them and they're easy to have sharpened. Cross-country skis are superb in the North, but unless you're a family of skiers, or have quite a bit of money, don't give your child downhill skis until he can pay for the lift tickets.

Guns

Without a doubt, toy guns are the most controversial of all toys. Most mothers don't want their children to have them, because they don't want to trivialize death—and life—but children, especially boys, go right on using sticks or their forefingers to play war.

There are parts of the country, however, where real guns are more acceptable. Parents in the rural areas often let their children shoot under controlled conditions. They may take them skeet shooting, join a rifle club together, give them air guns for target practice or take them hunting with a shotgun, which lets boys and girls contribute to the larder and makes them feel more in control of their lives. They should, however, follow certain rules:

- have a license, if needed;
- shoot under close supervision;
- raise the gun only at a plentiful species;
- shoot it when the game is in season;
- plan to eat the food that's killed;
- help to prepare the animal for the freezer or the table. If the child doesn't have the stomach to do that, the killing should be left to someone else.

TELEVISION & MOVIES

Many mothers fret about the effects that television and other electronic wonders have on their children, but you needn't be one of those worriers. You have far more influence than the teenage exploitation movies, the cop shows on television or suggestive lyrics on tapes, records or radio. The only hitch is an important one: you must take the time and have the patience to use that influence. If you do, you'll find the wonderful world of video has much to offer, which is fortunate, for TV is a fact of life.

It has many advantages too. It offers the younger children a bigger vocabulary and gives all children a greater sense of the world around them. It provides an easy way to introduce a child to the thrill—and camaraderie—of watching a ball game together or a science special. TV also gives you a chance to discover how your child thinks and what excites, interests, amuses or frightens him—and for him to find out the same about you. This common ground serves a real need in the Middle Years, for this closemouthed child avoids the serious issues, and yet they must be discussed again and again. "How was school today?" simply isn't enough.

You can (and should) talk if you don't agree with the direct or implied message of a particular show. Silence implies consent. Used in this way, television encourages family conversation, rather than limits it. The nightly news invites comment on child abuse, abortion, war, famine, taxes or a local election. Even commercials invite you to talk back if the sponsor recommends sugary cereal for breakfast, as if it were nutritious. Ads make it easy to point out that the toys advertised on TV often break (your child may be aware of this already) and that imitation orange juice tastes junky. You want to be careful, however, not to turn every show or every ad into a sermon. An occasional raspberry (or some applause) will do nicely. Your child will listen to your opinions as long as he knows he still has the right to his own.

The shows he watches will affect him and so will the shows you watch. Before Eight, he follows your point of view; after that he follows your example. This is a good reason for him to see you and your husband read at least as much as you watch.

We moan about the quality of TV shows and forget that most general entertainment has always been mediocre. If earlier ages seem to have passed down fine books and plays, it is because only the best

survive. There is, however, a new abundance of mediocrity, for television requires to many shows to fill all the hours on all the channels that are in use. This isn't such a big problem either. With a few new shows each season and the many available reruns, you and your child can find seven to ten hours a week of fine television to watch, which is plenty.

Everything a child does teaches him something, and if he goes overboard in any one area—like television—he loses much more than he gains. Too much TV is addictive and encourages passivity, which in turn blocks curiosity and creativity. Nor can TV teach the child how a person thinks through a problem, for everything on the screen is already decoded for him. The limits you place on your child's TV time will protect him from audio and visual overdose. The child who uses his eyes and ears passively and constantly will dull his other channels of perception. Television and movies are compelling and useful art forms, but live concerts and live theater are better, for there is an interaction between the players and the spectators.

Keep in mind: the more time a child spends watching, the less he spends doing, and it's in the doing that a child learns best. Studies show that the most successful students watch the least TV and the least successful ones watch the most. This is true whatever their intelligence, their family income or how much homework they do.

By teaching your child how to choose his entertainment wisely, he will have time for schoolwork and chores and for reading, daydreaming, art, writing, music and especially for play, the safety valve of childhood (and adulthood too). Even the ability to judge distance and space—needed in so many careers—is diminished if the child doesn't have time to build models and play with three-dimensional toys. Boys and girls use their imaginations when they play house or hospital or kings and queens, but when they watch television the story uses it for them. It's rather like eating a predigested meal.

You want to set TV rules early, not as a punishment or a reward, but as a routine. For the sake of his eyesight, you'll also want to see that the TV is at eye level, with a clear, steady image and without any reflection; that there is little contrast in the lighting between the room and the set; and that the child looks away from the screen frequently. This is particularly important for the frequent watcher.

You'll have fewer complaints if you limit the number of TV sets in your house. A child may have a radio in his room but not a TV, any more than he should have his own refrigerator. Besides, a family TV is a good way to teach sharing and to remind all the members that a TV program is a special guest, to come into your home when invited and not for round-the-clock visits. You give this message when you only let your child turn on the set for a specific show—and not to see what's play-

ing—and then have him turn it off when it's over.

It's the time a child spends in front of the set that matters most. Allow those seven to ten hours on weekends and before dinner, but seldom on school nights. Your restrictions will earn some flak, but that's the way it is in motherhood. Remember that you're taller, stronger and wiser—and you pay the mortgage.

You'll need to monitor his choices, especially in the first three grades. Children have a hard time understanding plots and delineating fact from fiction at this age and need shows with a slower pace, so they have time to reflect and consider. You can help your child choose shows that are fun and wholesome by reviewing the schedule with him once a week. Leave some TV hours unscheduled, however, so he can watch spontaneously, but with your unintrusive supervision. And by all means give him an occasional, unexpected TV treat when something special comes along, even on a school night, and let him watch a single episode of a new show so he'll feel like part of the gang at school. Not all these shows will be good, but over the long run the contrast of poor shows to good ones will turn your child into a discerning critic.

By the fourth grade you might relax the rules for a couple of years and let your child watch an extra two hours a week (although a maximum of ten is still ideal). This helps satisfy the passion that besets a child between Eight and Ten, when he studies grown-ups constantly so he will be less anxious about his own growing up. A soap opera or two won't hurt at this age, but at all ages beware of his watching a show regularly if it portrays the family in negative or silly ways or goes beyond that delicious point of fear that children love so much.

It's the violent shows—and the more violent cartoons—that can upset a child, for studies show that children who watch a good deal of them on TV often become more aggressive. Large amounts of routine violence can desensitize a child, who has no idea of the pain that would go with it, and it also can make a child see people as victims or victimizers and act like one or the other. Openly sexual shows are obviously bad choices too, for they confuse and embarrass a child, and they're even worse when combined with violence or cruelty. Any of these underlying messages can hurry your child past his true age and make him grow up with warped ideas. Children aren't as savvy as they sometimes seem. Your child is bound to see some violence, but if you ask him how he feels about it—and tell him how you feel about it—he'll be able to work through his disquiet.

You also want to point out special effects and how they're made and talk about the stunt men, the junk cars that are bought to be crashed on TV, and the break-apart bottles used in a fight. Better to shatter a few illusions than scare a child too much.

If your child is going through a mad-for-television phase, you can still get him to read by having him read about TV in the TV columns and even the gossip magazines. You also can involve him in play writing by asking him to invent a different ending to a show or to create a sitcom of his own or to write a commercial, so he can learn how persuasive words can be. For the math-minded child: have him time the commercials with a stopwatch one night to see how much of a bite they take out of a show. The more interaction you can foster, the more he will profit by television.

The television that causes the most concern today isn't television at all but movies on cable TV. They are usually uncut and unedited, and so are rental movies, which make a double impression if they're played twice in an afternoon. Even though you're careful about the movies you might rent, other parents may not be. This gives your child tacit permission to see them if they're offered when he's visiting a friend. You won't be able to police this watching easily—particularly on those endless summer days—but you do want your child to know that you're counting on him to be selective. It's mighty hard for an older child to say, "I'm not allowed to watch that movie," but ask him to encourage another activity instead—or to come on home. Even if he does stay, don't chastise him too much or he won't be so honest with you the next time, and you won't be able to undo the damage as easily.

As a general rule, it's much better to encourage movies in a regular theater, and besides, the big screen, the grand sound and the adventure itself make these movies much more fun. You have to be even more careful about movies than television, since the plots are more solid—and often more adult; they're more expensively made; the story line is more believable; and the whole scenario is usually underscored with powerful music and dazzling effects. You'll want your child to avoid pictures that have nude scenes, use bad language or feature heavy drinking or drug use, or just encourage plain old bad values. Justice and goodness are still in style.

Whenever possible you, or someone whose values you trust, should see an unfamiliar movie with a child under Eleven, so you can negate or soften its impression. Even a preteen will profit by this attention, for sometimes a movie that seems all right by the reviews will turn out to be upsetting. It depends on your child and what's going on in his life. He won't be fazed by a rebellious scene if he's feeling great about himself but he'll react poorly if he's feeling left out at school. What is cautionary to one child is seductive to another. Once more, it gives you the chance to talk about a problem in a movie if you think your child may be facing it at home or at school.

When he does see a movie with friends, either on TV or in a theater, make a point to ask him what he thinks about it afterward and which scenes were the most effective. Talk with him as you would with an equal and listen as much as you talk so he'll know he has the right to keep his opinion, just as you do. If you haven't had cross words, he may even adopt your ideas as his own.

By letting your child play family critic, and giving the movie as many stars as he thinks it deserves, he'll learn to be selective and discriminating. And when he watches at least one perfectly dreadful movie anyway—and he will—you can expect to comfort him through some serious nightmares. He may even benefit from it.

It was Mike, as Seven, who went with his big sister to see *The Three Stooges,* only to find it was *The Curse of the Fly* instead. Of course he stayed and shuddered throughout—too scared to watch for more than five minutes at a time and too scared to leave. It wasn't the end of the world, but he made it the end of horror movies. From a parent's point of view, that wasn't such a bad price to pay.

ENTHUSIASMS AND PASSIONS

The interests of children vary in the Middle Years, but the intensity they register on their emotional Richter scale differs dramatically between the early years and the preteens. In the first two grades these children usually go along with whatever is handed to them, but by the third grade they begin to pick up—and drop—enthusiasms like mad jugglers with armfuls of oranges. They have their collections, their clubs, their lessons; their very tight, if changing, friendships. The Brownie Scouts and the Cub Scouts are fun, but they're often just one more thing to do. Sports are also diffuse now, with bike riding or swimming or pickup games of soccer or baseball as well as real team efforts such as Little League. The children who take part in them often do it just to oblige and they may fret about the practice that's required, but not as much as they complain about their music lessons.

It's in the preteen years that they become passionate about something, except, thank heavens, sex. Now they concentrate on one or two interests with a fervor that may startle you. There's a reason for this. As the child begins to grow away from the family he attaches himself to something demanding enough to give him strength.

The birthday pup (or horse or cat) that would have made an Eight happy—espe-cially a lonely Eight—is heaven at Eleven. As long as the animal is new or the source of some new pursuit—like dog shows or horseback riding—this child will push himself until he has learned everything about the subject that he possibly can, and then his interest is exhausted. This usually happens about Twelve or Thirteen, although some passions continue for several more years—or even for life.

It's important to take these pursuits seriously but don't keep pushing a passion whose end has come, for your child is like you. He has the right to quit a job when he's taken it as far as he can, unless the family is depending on him to finish it. By letting your child make his own decisions about his pastimes, you're recognizing that passions are not like lessons: they have a life of their own. Nor should you act as if an Eleven's fascination with science or art is really a lifelong career choice. This would pressure a child unnecessarily. It's enough that he's discovering his native talents so that one day he'll choose the job that uses those same skills.

You also want him to do the best he can, but for the right reasons. Whether he's in a recital or a ball game, he's competing against himself, not other children, and he is winning for himself, not for you. Nor should you divert your child from one deep interest to another before the first is spent. He needs the chance to explore to the depths of himself. You only have to protect him from too many activities, too many interests. The child who is overprogrammed will feel sated and perhaps a little rejected too. He needs time to visit with his family and to be alone.

If a child can feel competent and confident in an extracurricular activity, he's more likely to go back to it in the early teen years. This is a blessing for both of you. A special interest keeps this frisky child busy and safe.

COLLECTIONS

The only way to understand why your child cherishes his collections is to remember your own. The urge to hunt and gather starts around Six or Seven—a casual, random accumulation of Things—which is focused on one or two categories by Eight, when his pursuit is almost more intense. Expect one collection to be rather grand and stored at home, while the other is usually small enough to fit into a pocket. An Eight and his collection are seldom parted. It's as if every item is touched with magic.

If a younger brother or sister gets into a collection of Barbie clothes or model planes or baseball cards—or whatever is the fad of the year—your house will echo with outrage. This may seem like silly

business, but collecting helps children learn to take care of their possessions (at least those in their collections) and to build strong friendships. Children, like parents, choose friends who like the things they do. Collecting also teaches children to think well in concrete terms, by putting the items into categories and sorting them by importance, by color, by weight, by style and by value, as they trade them with their buddies. The child who learns to arrange and rearrange tangible items in every possible way will juggle abstract ideas better in his teens.

You can get deeply involved in your child's collecting habit—but it's better if you don't. It would kill the thrill if you gave your child a full, mounted set of special pennies or seashells, when he was collecting them one by one. Instead give him a small allowance and an occasional unexpected windfall to buy another small car or miniature animal, and perhaps add to his collection on his birthday, or give him a book about it.

In time the first collection becomes a bore and your child usually goes on to collect something new, often with even greater enthusiasm, until, by Ten or Eleven or Twelve, the custom dies. This doesn't mean he's ready to be teased about a collection that's been ignored for quite a while or that he's ready to throw it away. A once prized box of horse chestnuts and acorns—the standard collection for the novice—may go unopened for two years, but it remains a vital part of his life, there on the closet shelf. It's a matter of loyalty and sentiment. Part of him will always be Seven. And aren't you glad?

CLASSES

In the Middle Years boys and girls need to learn some skills outside of school. Skills give them the added competence they crave. It may be swimming or gymnastics at Six; karate or ballet at Seven; piano or ice skating at Eight; guitar or pottery at Nine; riding or cooking at Ten; photogra-

phy or basketball at Eleven; typing or tennis or sewing at Twelve.

So much to do, so little time to do it in—and probably so little money to pay for it. Actually, your limits probably fit well with those of your child. Even at his most scattershot phase, he focuses so intently on his interests that he is likely to do better if he has only one team practice a week and only one class outside of school. When he's mastered one skill, or when he has to be a little older to go any further, his interest will diminish and he'll want to drop the old class and start a new one. That's fine. To dip into many activities, without wringing all he can out of each, would encourage him to be flighty.

Choose a class together, looking for one that will be fun and that is in line with his talents, so he'll do well and feel good about himself. When he's a preteen, you might add a class that will make life easier in high school, like typing or tennis, or open his horizons, like skiing or sailing. Even if he can't afford to pursue these sports when the lessons are over, there may come a time when he can and this introduction will make him feel more adept.

MUSIC

Music soothes the savage breast, but poorly planned music lessons can turn your child into a little savage. It isn't easy to practice every day, and for that social butterfly, the Ten, it isn't much fun either. While any child profits by some kind of music, it has to be introduced in the right way, for the right reason.

His willingness to study will depend on your attitude. He'll be accommodating if you consider music as necessary to his education as geography and history—if not reading and writing. If the main urge is yours, however, he'll accept the practice sessions with about the same grace with which he accepts homework. Not much. Music lessons will be much more rewarding if your child feels he is learning for his sake and not for yours; if he can choose his own instrument; if he is taught a few tunes by rote at the beginning (so he knows he really can make music); and if he's told what his goals are from lesson to lesson.

The official lessons in music are usually started when a child is about Eight and becomes a little more self-disciplined. The first music lessons, whatever the instrument, usually go better if your child is part of a group. Team play brings a special joy. There will be some socializing and a little improvisational playing and your child will realize that it takes mistakes to make music and that everyone makes a lot of them. This helps him put learning—and himself—in perspective. To choose the right instrument, he will have to consider his interests—and you'll have to consider your budget. A piano costs much more than a recorder. You'll also need to have a realistic sense of his ability and commitment, as well as your patience.

There are basically three kinds of man-made instruments—string, wind and percussion—and one that comes with the child: the voice. Each requires somewhat different aptitudes.

String Instruments

The string instruments come in three varieties—those with a bow, like the violin, the viola, the cello and the double bass; those that are picked, like the harp, the guitar, the banjo and the mandolin; and the piano, whose strings are struck, which makes it a percussion instrument too.

To play any fiddle with a bow, a child needs a good ear—to tell differences in pitch—and to be coordinated enough to rub his tummy with one hand and pat his head with the other. For the violin and the viola, he also needs strength and stamina. In all cases, he needs a family who can stand the sorry screeches he makes with a bow for the first few months.

The elegant harp also demands a good ear, as well as nimble fingers, but it's too expensive and cumbersome for most families to consider; the banjo is quite difficult and, like the mandolin, a little out of date, but the guitar, with its appealing folk music, is relatively easy and makes many teenagers more comfortable with their friends—a good reason to start lessons in the preteens.

Although the piano doesn't need a player with a terribly good ear, he should have a good sense of space—so he can deal with two parts of the keyboard at once; good coordination, so he can make his fingers go in different directions at almost the same time; and an ability to read several lines of music at once—the only instrument that requires such fancy eyework.

Wind Instruments

Wind instruments, which call for the player to blow air down a tube to make it vibrate, are often easier, cheaper and more fun for children than the violin or the piano and, contrary to medical myths, they don't cause physical problems. The oboe doesn't hurt the heart of a normal child; the trumpet doesn't affect the size of the lip muscles; a horn doesn't hurt the normal mouth or normal teeth (and may help abnormal ones); and woodwinds often improve, not hurt, a child's lungs. Even the child in braces may keep playing, if the practice is kept to thirty to sixty minutes a day. If in doubt, have the teacher consult with the doctor or dentist, but choose one who knows a good deal about making music as well as medicine. There's a lot of misinformation out there.

The wind instruments are many and wonderful, including the recorder, the flute, the piccolo, the clarinet, the saxophone, the trumpet, the trombone, the oboe, the bassoon, the French horn and more. Of these, the recorder is the easiest and the least expensive for a child. Another fine choice: the clarinet. A child only has to finger the keys easily and practice a bit to reach that happy time when people actually know what he's playing (and are glad that he is). The flute, that elegant instrument, is a little harder, but it's another good choice for the child whose fingers are dexterous and coordinated and whose arms are long enough and strong enough to hold it parallel with the floor. The flute—or any hand-held instrument—brings special pleasure to the handicapped child who is bound to a wheelchair.

The trumpet and the trombone are dandy choices. The trumpeter needs strong arms, because he holds the instrument straight out in front of him, and the trombonist needs long ones for those racy slides.

Percussion Instruments

And then there are the percussion instruments—not just the drums but those instruments whose names even sound like music—the xylophone, the tympani, the cymbals, the tambourine, to say nothing of the chimes and the lowly little triangle. The percussionist with a fine sense of rhythm and good coordination can learn to play all of these instruments and knows the reward of being an essential element in even the smallest band.

Voice

Singing is the forgotten instrument, and yet it is the cheapest and easiest of all. Although only 5 to 10% of children have perfect pitch—which means they remember and can reproduce any sound they hear—very few children are tone-deaf. It's true that some children may not be able to carry a tune as soon as others, but most children can be trained to sing on key, just by matching tones—high, low and in between.

If you think you have a born singer, piano lessons will prepare him well, but forget about individual singing lessons until puberty is past, his new vocal range is set and the intense practice won't damage his young vocal cords. Glee clubs, choirs and choruses are dandy, however. The choice of a teacher is critical in this as in all music lessons. One who embarrasses some children by making them be quiet, or by telling them that they are monotones, is not a teacher at all. A person's voice, like his name, shape or laugh, should never be criticized.

The Teacher

The best music teacher greatly enjoys music and brings an aura of excitement to her lessons. She is attuned to children, treats each one as an individual and is quick to try the unusual or the unexpected when her students reach the inevitable plateaus. She respects her art as well as her students and most often teaches at a music school (where lessons may be cheaper) or in her own home, rather than in the child's home, where both are bound to be distracted. This good teacher prepares for the forty-five-minute lesson and gives the pupil a thoughtful assignment afterward—clear, complete and written—so he can remember what he's supposed to be doing and why. In this, as in most things, a child should know the immediate goals set for him and the reason for pursuing them.

Look for a teacher who is well recommended by other parents—people whose children are interested in going to their lessons and are proud of their own achievements. It may take about a dozen lessons to know whether the chemistry is right between your child and his teacher. If it's not, you'll want to have a conference with her and, if the problems seem insurmountable, to get a replacement. As long as you're discreet and don't criticize the teacher to your child unnecessarily, the change should be productive.

Parents have to be as professional in their dealings with a teacher as the teacher is with them: paying when billed; having two or even three conferences a year with the teacher (but no more); calling her if there is a serious family problem that might upset the child's work; and seeing to it that he practices every day during the week and maybe on Saturday and always practices at the same time—usually after a meal or a snack, so he's not testy. Although he can take a break in lessons and in practice for the holidays, or even a summer, without real damage, it takes the regularity of a daily routine to make the lessons stick.

Try to join him for the last five minutes of his practice, not to criticize his work but to appreciate it. Neither the music lessons nor the practice sessions are wonderful but the rewards are great. Whether your child grows up to be a musician or a music lover, he'll always get a little more out of life.

GYMNASTICS

A well-supervised girl or boy of Six, with good physical and mental development and a fairly long attention span, can try any kind of gymnastics. It's almost as pleasing to hear a child talk with affection about the bars, the springboards and the pommel horse as it is to watch the performance. A child of Nine—the peak age for gymnastics—may become such a "gym rat" you'll have trouble dragging her home.

The young gymnast, like the young ballet dancer, is most likely to be small and to be a girl, although the Olympics have proved that gymnastics is one of the most demanding of all sports and boys sometimes now may make up a third of a class. Unlike many other sports, however, it's the small child—boy or girl—who does best in gymnastics, because longer legs, arms and torso take more time to rotate, and many gymnastic skills involve rotation.

Just when your child is sure she's bound for glory, her growth spurt is likely to hit and she'll lose some strength and flexibility in her upper body. This calls for the teacher and the parents to give her a lot of encouragement until she learns how to

do new and old stunts again. It isn't easy to find such a patient teacher. As usual, you'll learn more from observation than from advertisements, and more from conversations with the students than with their parents.

The best programs are often at recreation centers or suburban Y's and the less commercial gym clubs. Although many of the private centers are quire good, they may push a child to take more classes than she can handle, or to compete too soon or too often. If the atmosphere is wrong, she can be turned off or burned out.

Competition can begin as early as Six or Seven, if the child is very good, very willing and doesn't feel pushed. If your child is this good, she will have to take three classes a week for one to one and a half hours. The average child, however, takes one to two lessons a week, usually for ninety minutes each time. This will include the essential fifteen-minute warm-up, to stretch the muscles, and another five to ten minutes at the end, to cool down.

In a good program there are never more than five to six students for each teacher. If there are more, the children won't develop their attention span as well as they should, because they won't get enough time to do their floor work or get enough turns on the bar. In a bigger class the children are also likely to work unsupervised. This would interfere with safety, which you should consider above everything else. A good teacher can't let children do much on their own since a forward or backward roll can hurt the neck if it's done the wrong way.

You also want to look for consistency in the program and, above all, look for fun. That's what the children are there for.

BALLET

Ballet is a passion that afflicts many mothers and daughters and sometimes a son, if he realizes that (1) it's more physically demanding than most sports, and (2) it doesn't mean he's a sissy. Girls, however,

make up most classes in this country. It's usually the mother who introduces her young child to ballet, often reviving a long-buried dream of her own, but the child usually becomes a balletomane about Ten or Eleven, when she's mastered the rudiments well enough to feel like she can fly without wings.

If you're interested in putting your first grader into a ballet class, patience is the key. The introduction to ballet can be ardent, but it should be limited. Take her to a locally produced *Nutcracker,* let her watch the great ballet companies on TV with you and enroll her in an informal dance class where children run light and free; where they sway gracefully to the rhythms of the music and wear simple leotards with their ballet slippers or foot-seams opened and rolled up, so they can grip the floor with their bare feet.

Tap is another good and slightly more advanced outlet. It can be exhilarating to the child who finds difficult rhythms a joy to master—a conquest made all the better by her clickety shoes.

At Eight the body is ready to master the five rigorous—and quite unnatural—basic positions of ballet, but you won't want her to take lessons until you find a well-trained teacher. If she doesn't know the right techniques, your child could develop thick, bulging thighs and calves (for which no daughter would be grateful) and possible back problems. With good training, however, her muscles will be smooth and limber, her legs will look long, slim and graceful and her whole body will be stronger.

It may be hard for the novice to tell a good school from a "Lizzie Tish"—as the poor ones are known in ballet circles—but good schools and good teachers have characteristics in common. To find them, go to the annual—or semiannual—class demonstrations. This is how the better school shows off, rather than with fancy recitals where glitzy costumes try to make up for missed steps and embarrassing moments.

If the demonstration is impressive, you can arrange to watch an actual class. The good teacher—the essential element—is enthusiastic and sympathetic and she tries to give praise and criticism fairly. She also demands the best a child can give because ballet is a tough business. She expects her students to be on time, to wear their proper dance uniforms, to keep their hair neat and to do very little fooling around. In technique, you'll notice that the emphasis is on the correct body placement: carriage, poise, distribution of weight for balance. Some muscle cramps are inevitable but improper techniques produce many more.

At your interview the teacher will explain how she handles the truly talented: a good teacher can judge the limitations and the abilities of herself and her school. When she feels a child has absorbed what she knows, she will be proud to send her on to a bigger and better professional school when she's around Fourteen.

Once you enroll your child in ballet, she will need proper equipment. Students wear soft ballet slippers; leotards in the color of their class—to show the level of their ability; and perhaps a small wrap skirt for the girls. Your child will go to class one to two times a week and later maybe even three times if she loves it—and you can afford it.

After your child has had three to four years of ballet—when her foot no longer wobbles when she stands on her toes—her teacher will pronounce her ready for *en pointe* (which she'll call "on point"). Now she graduates to hard, padded, beribboned—and expensive—slippers. With these she can dance on her toes, like a real ballet dancer. Fortunately, only a professional needs a new pair for every stage performance. Now your child learns to sew her own ribbons on her shoes; to darn the shoes when they're worn; to stuff the toes with lamb's wool and stand in the resin box to scratch the soles of her slippers before she dances, so she won't slip on the floor.

If she wants to spend her life dancing professionally, you can expect the lessons to become a daily necessity. She won't need a barre at home, however. Solo practice will only reinforce her mistakes unless she is very good. Even with daily lessons, the girl who starts ballet at Eight will probably be Eighteen before she's good enough to join a company, although the build of a boy's body usually lets him reach that level in six years.

Most young dancers are content just to give ballet a fling and then go after new goals, but you can be sure they'll do it with a more graceful step than they would have had; a better posture; a head held high; and the knowledge that creativity depends on competence and competence depends on hard work. And that's the best lesson of all.

MARTIAL ARTS

The martial arts are rather like ballet for macho little boys—or little boys who want to be macho. Both are good for both sexes although parents are more likely to let their daughters take karate than to let their sons take ballet. Each type of training calls for practice and patience and gives a child self-confidence and enough self-control to carry the concentration, good manners, grace and respect into the classroom and the home.

The martial arts, however, give something ballet does not. The small, overweight or timid child will become adept enough to feel secure while the extra-rough child will be less aggressive on the playground because he finds his wits are

mightier than his fists. In all cases, the child develops the physical and psychological strength to negotiate his way out of trouble.

Martial arts—and martial sports—include boxing, which is potentially too dangerous to be encouraged, and wrestling, which is fine for a husky boy of Eleven or Twelve. The rest of the arts are from India and the Orient, each is different from the next and many movements are copied from jungle animals. The teacher may offer a particular art from India, China, Japan or Okinawa or a combination of techniques, but all are built on the same basic moves.

Kung fu and jujitsu, which are designed to make the opponent use his weight and strength against himself, are too rough for a child in the Middle Years but judo, a grappling art which uses leverage and balance, is designed to be free of danger. An adept child of Eight or Nine may master its ten sequential moves and learn how to throw his opponent in forty different ways, but it is too complicated for many children. Karate, with its punching, kicks and blocks, uses the concept of ying and yang, and helps a child learn to keep his balance, emotionally and physically. It is easier than the others and, taught well, can be great fun for both boys and girls as young as Six.

The soft-style karate focuses on internal calm and control, teaching the ability to touch an opponent without hurting him—the sign that he is true in his art. The hard-style is external and isn't meant to hurt either, but it does include the ferocious shout, to show the degree of force that's used—and to delight children, no doubt. In a well-run dojo—as the studio is called—the shihan (the teacher) combines the two styles, requiring the children to go from one to the other like an on-off switch. With these karate techniques, an adult learns to break boards and brick, but young bones are too delicate for that: a pencil is the most they'll break.

If karate seems too aggressive, consider aikido, a gentler art that teaches the pupil to use the other person's movements to his own advantage. If any of these arts are combined with tai chi, a form of breathing used to control the body, the child may be still more in tune with his own nature.

Next to a positive attitude on the parent's part, the instructor's attitude matters most. You want to find someone who is a good teacher as well as a good martial artist and who is kind and gentle and has been studying for years. The best ones, with their proudly worn and often tattered black belts, work out every day and many continue to work with an instructor all their lives. To find the best, observe at several studios, watching how the teacher treats the children and if they seem happy to be there. You also want to avoid the highly commercialized studios, where you're asked to sign a contract for your child to earn a belt, rather than on a month-to-month basis or for a longer, specific length of time. In the martial arts, as in all sports, each child should go at his own pace.

SPORTS

Sports may do more to boost the confidence of boys and girls than all other after-school activities. When children can do something well and have a chance to excel, they get a strong sense of themselves. Sports also give children a new focus and even a new vocabulary. These conversa-tions can be the glue that bonds them together.

You encourage your child's love of sports by making it easy for him to play many of them reasonably well. Basically, you're helping your child feel comfortable with his body, not just for the exercise he gets and the popularity it brings, but for good times, which is what growing up is all about.

The favorite sports today were usually the favorites in your grandmother's day—the ones that can be played at a moment's notice, often alone or with a small group: swimming in summer; sledding in winter; roller skating on the sidewalk at Six; hop-scotch and jump rope on the playground for girls and stickball for city boys, all popular games at Eight and Nine, followed by wonderful, aimless biking in the neighborhood for the Ten, either boy or girl.

You'll notice that children often make the same stereotypical choices they always did, probably because boys are naturally better at some sports and girls are better at others. Our era may be enlightened, but growing boys are still a little thinner and wirier and girls have a little extra fat—traits that affect the way they play certain games. A boy of Six is already better at long-distance running and throwing and broad jumping—a difference that is even greater by Twelve—while a girl gets progressively better at hopping, skipping, cartwheels, somersaults, relay races and the 50-yard dash. Because we all like to do the things we do best, the natural differences—and preferences—are solidly established by adolescence.

You can break down some of the inevitable segregation this causes by encouraging bike riding and horseback riding, jogging, skating, hiking, swimming, tennis, soccer, Frisbee games, kite flying and fishing—sports in which both sexes do well.

Sports, however, require more than sending your child out to swim or taking him to soccer practice. It's playing water polo with him at the pool, tossing a ball together in the front yard after supper and going to ball games together. A Seven is ready to take part in family games of volleyball, croquet and badminton and will play Ping Pong enthusiastically (but not well). Baseball, basketball and softball come at Eight and Nine and tennis whenever your child can start hitting the ball over the net—another good family game, and so are touch football, softball, golf, bowling, cross-country skiing and ice skating. When adults invite children to join in any athletic activity, they give them silent but real approval. An awkward child might not accept the invitation—at least at first—but he'll be very pleased to be asked.

Sports not only bond the family tighter but a mix of ages gives an extra hilarity to hide-and-seek, dodge ball and blindman's bluff. A child will be delighted to see his blindfolded parent walk into a tree in the backyard—or better yet, step in a cow pie on the farm, as long as only an ego is hurt—and the ego isn't his.

Even if you aren't athletically inclined, you may find yourself involved with sports if you have the sort of child who is always in motion. He'll need some kind of sports, every day, or he'll climb up and down his bunk bed, if not the walls, a dozen times between his after-school snack and bedtime. As passions go, this is pretty harmless, but he'll be much happier with an hour or two of heavy exercise every day after school. Even this may not be enough. Many children need that adrenaline charge they get from competitive sports, and superactive children have to have it. That's how they test their mettle, but be careful about this. You want your child to play to win for the fun of it, not for the glory it brings. After all, the only record worth beating is his own.

You also must use care to help your

child choose the sports that are right for him. Soccer makes a good beginning at Six, because even the most uncoordinated child can play it without feeling silly; so do swimming, gymnastics and T-ball, which is great for the eager young batter, but limit his choices to noncontact sports even at Twelve, since there is such a shortage of coaches to keep a good watch.

The best sports for your child are the ones he likes best, not those you might choose to help him overcome some deficiency. Look for those that engage his talents most, so he'll have such a good time he's sure to play well and feel even better about himself. They must also suit you. You need the time to take him to his practice and his games, and the money to pay for the paraphernalia—and perhaps the lessons—he may need.

Whatever your child pursues, see that you help him assess his strengths realistically, praising what he does well and ignoring the rest. He'll get enough knocks on the playing field. Let him get kisses at home.

TEAM SPORTS

Sometimes it's hard to know whether team sports are designed for parents or children. They do a great deal of good for both, but not always. While parents must organize the team—since children don't have the skill to do it—they tend to get too involved, which is a pity. The more parents dominate a team, the more children tend to shy away from it.

It can also be a problem when children are pushed to be too competitive too soon.

SPORTS CODE FOR PARENTS

1. Appraise your child's athletic skills—and accept them.
2. Love him for trying, and let him know it.
3. Let him play for the fun of it, not to make you proud or to relive what happened to you as a child—or what you wish had happened.
4. Encourage him to win, because competition is part of sports, and accept his defeats, so he will do the same.
5. Make sure the coach knows children as well as he knows sports and puts integrity above everything else.
6. Practice with your child if you want—and he wants—but do it as a partner, not a coach.
7. Cheer the team, not individual players.
8. Compliment the players freely, especially your child, but don't compare them or complain about them—especially your child.
9. Skip the advice and the replays, particularly on the way to the game, on the way home or at the dinner table.
10. Go to some but not all the games, so your child won't feel pressured to win.
11. Take your child's complaints with two grains of salt, but believe every success he reports.
12. Recognize the courage it takes to play a game when the whole team counts on you.

Most children under Ten like to play on a team—and win—but a loss isn't the end of the world for them, the way it can be for the passionate preteens. These players throw themselves into their favorite sports and are well rewarded for their efforts. Team sports teach boys and girls to cooperate, to depend on one another and to be reliable enough for their teammates to depend on them. For many, these teams become the focus of their lives and the games give them some of the most thrilling, and poignant, experiences of the Middle Years. This is especially true for boys, who often need to punch at each other and fool around to express their feelings, rather than talk about them, the way girls do.

Although you don't want to be too intrusive, it's a good idea to watch the coach in action before you let your child join a team, particularly if your child is younger. A good coach has certain traits. He obviously loves the game—or at least he looks like he's having a good time—and he doesn't need a lot of hoopla from parents to feel appreciated. He knows how to kick or hit or throw the ball and how to teach these techniques and, above all, he likes children and handles them much as you handle your own. He finds something to compliment the best efforts of each of them, at every practice and every game, and he never berates or embarrasses individual players. He may get mad at the whole rambunctious team but never after they've just lost a game or in front of another team.

He also coaches the team as a whole, so they'll do their best together, rather than concentrating on training a few stars, and he keeps the roster big enough to have some relief players but small enough for everyone to play at least half of every game. When the number goes beyond this tipping point, he or the parents recruit a new coach to form a new team.

Your child will like the team if it's the right sport for him, and he has a good coach, and real but lighthearted support from home. He needs you to give him time to go to practice, to see that he gets there—he has a commitment—and to go to every third or fourth game, rather than every one of them. This tells him that you like to see him play but realize that it's really his game and his team. Steady attendance makes most children feel pressured. When you do go to a game, applaud the good plays, rather than the player, and cheer the whole team, rather than your own child.

While you encourage some team sports, you'll have to discourage others. You want your child to quit any team if it is too hard for him, or if he can't get enough turns to feel successful or if he usually sits on the bench or if the coach doesn't know how to work with children, for all of this would make him feel like a loser. You also shouldn't let your child join more than one team at a time or he'll divide his time too much and feel frayed. You also shouldn't let him join an All-Star team, picked by coaches, as if he were a teenager.

He's only young once. And you shouldn't tell your child how to play the game, because this takes the fun away and your suggestions might not suit the coach.

If your child doesn't want to go to practice anymore, there's a reason. Talk about it together, to find out if he feels too much stress at home or from the coach, or if the coach or another player makes him feel bad or if he's afraid of making a mistake or getting hurt. Or if he's simply bored with the sport. There's a great division around Twelve, as the natural athletes take over on competitive teams. If your child's interest begins to lag, encourage individual sports and feel blessed that there are so many of them.

PETS

Scratch the dreams of an Eleven and you'll probably find either a ball player or a vet. This is not accidental. A well-tended animal helps a child feel loved and wanted. Everyone needs this, and always, but especially in the preteens. Even if you don't have a yard for a dog or you're allergic to cats, your child will profit by an aquarium with a few exotic fish or a canary or even a birdhouse hanging outside the window.

Animals, like ball games, also require about as much as they give. With ball games, the child must be dependable, caring and enthusiastic—and practice a little every day. With a pet, he has no choice.

DOGS

A dog can give a big, big boost to a child in the Middle Years. He is the rowdy child's rowdy companion; the shy child's entree to the playground; and every child's main confidant. Some days it will seem to him that only his dog loves him so well,

needs him so much and expects so little of him.

There's some truth in that. If only mothers didn't expect so much of their dog-owning children. Never mind how often your Eight swore to feed, bathe and walk him, forever and ever. He won't live up to the promises regularly until he's Eleven, and only then with reminders. Children just aren't as faithful to the needs of their pups as their pups are to them. This doesn't mean they love them less, just that dogs demand much more work than children can consistently give. The child who owns the dog should be expected to care for it most, but everyone in the family—especially parents—must provide backup support.

This isn't always convenient but the right dog is worth the effort. Have a whopping big argument in his presence and the next thing you know one of the battlers is petting the dog's head: the fight begins to defuse. Or have a silent, insidious tension hanging over the family and the dog will give everyone something to talk to and about.

The kind of dog you get should suit your family's way of life. Avoid shedders if you must have a tidy house and avoid yappers if you can't stand frequent, prolonged noise. If you have an apartment, consider a dachshund, not a shepherd; if you have space outdoors, go for a springer spaniel or a retriever, who'll be willing to play fetch with your child for hours. Terriers—and there are many kinds—are always ready for a romp and the low-slung Welsh corgi is a smart, devoted pet.

Every pup, including one from a fancy kennel, has certain characteristics that developed when his ancestors had to work for a living. A collie will still need to herd, a poodle to hunt. Even a pound dog, with his pound of this and pound of that, will have inherited traits. If he looks more like a Doberman than anything else, he'll act more like one too. Go to the library to find out the advantages or disadvantages of each breed. If you don't, your hearts will surely melt at the first woebegone pup you see and he may not suit your family at all.

Whether you get a purebred or a pooch, you'll pay a price. A dog with papers can be very expensive, depending on the breed and the breeding. If you get one at the pound, however, you'll save both money and an animal that might have been put to sleep but you'll still have to pay for the shots they've given him and probably have him checked by your own vet. Kennel cough and other ailments spread through pounds like colds at nursery school. You can anticipate other costs. There will be more visits to the vet for his sterilization, unless you're sure you can always get the puppies placed, and for four shots in the first six months—including one for rabies.

The new puppy, whether from a pound or a kennel, will arrive with two instinctive needs—his den and his pack. His bed will be his den. It can be a box or a basket, kept in the same place, where he will retreat to feel secure and take his many naps. Keep the bed in a small caged play area at first, and then give him more and more space to play. The family will be his pack. If you cuddle him often, the dog will know he's part of the pack and quickly find his place in the pecking order: below the baby (even if the baby arrives after he does) and above the cat, who won't care, since cats know they're above everyone anyway.

Your child should see that his dog always has clean water and 100 nutritious calories a day for every pound he weighs. It can be either canned or moist dog food and some of it can be in meat, if it isn't raw and it isn't pork. If he can't get grass he'll need fruit or vegetables and he'll need extra vegetable oil in his meals if his coat is naturally smooth or if it gets noticeably

dry. Beef bones are good as long as he's teething but when he's older they will have to be cooked for hours to make them soft, or he may splinter them and hurt his innards.

Your child should divide his puppy's food into four meals a day, rather than put it out all at once, since a dog is silly enough to keep eating the food if it's there. By six months he graduates to two meals a day if he's a small dog and three meals if he's bigger, and by eight months he's on an adult schedule, with one big morning meal and a snack at supper, so your child won't be tempted to slip food to him under the table.

A schedule will also appeal to the dog and make it easier to train him. If a dog eats on a schedule, he'll eliminate on a schedule—but not at first. Some experts say that if his water is limited to mealtimes and his owner is trained to take him outside every hour, a puppy can be trained in three weeks or less. More casual dog owners think it's as silly to train a dog in the first three to four months as it would be to train a baby. Four to five or even eight months is more like it, although Nell has been waiting thirteen years for her dear Daisy to get all the details down pat.

Begin by putting four to five sheets of newspaper all around his den—animals hate to soil this area—or beside the back door, changing them as soon as they're used, but leaving one old one underneath, so he'll return to the same place. Just don't fuss when he uses it, or he'll go somewhere else in the house instead.

You'll also need to have your child take the puppy outside, or at least lead him to his papers, when the dog wakes up in the morning, after his naps and whenever he gets agitated, walks in small circles or starts eyeing the rug. For sure success—and praise—have your child take him outside about five minutes after he has eaten, but only if he hasn't played hard with him before the meal, for this can upset his digestion.

There will, of course, be mistakes.

Your child can lessen them by making several "shake cans"—some pebbles in a tin can, covered by a plastic lid—and leaving them around the house. If your child (or anyone else) catches the puppy in the act, he rattles a shake can and says, "NO!" but this must be done within seconds, for a dog's memory is very, very short. Once you've cleaned up the accident, pour salt-free club soda on the spot, to neutralize the damage, and an odor neutralizer from the drugstore or the pet store, which alters the smell. This is critical, because a dog instinctively will mark his spot again if he can smell it—and his smell is much, much more acute than yours.

The dog must learn to follow other commands too, not to show off but to be more fun to have around. Your child should praise him for every good thing he does and only train him when he himself is in a good mood. If he's cross, the dog will think the child is mad at him, which will negate the praise. Your child will have to use the same simple commands every time, speaking each one in a slightly different way, for the dog understands tone and cadence, not words. There is the low, hard "Down!" or "No!" that keeps him in line and the other commands that are less harsh.

Begin at mealtime. To call a dog to his supper, have your child rattle the food dish, call the dog's name and say, "Come"—drawing this command out a bit. And when he arrives, the child says, "Sit," the same way, gently pushing the dog's rear to the floor, so he'll learn to sit when he's told. A slight dip of the hind legs will be all your child will get for a while—a bow to his king.

You want your child to use commands in play too, and a ball is a great way to teach them. Let him roll it on the floor, which invites the dog to run for it. The child says, "Come," leans forward and congratulates him when he gets near. He then gently takes the ball from the dog's mouth and says, "Leave," in an imperious voice, so the puppy learns to walk away

until, in time, you child can say, "Sit," before the pup surrenders the ball. It's the 1, 2, 3 sequence that a dog masters that makes him seem so smart. A new puppy will only do this three to four times, five minutes a day, until he is four to five months old. He will then be ready to learn the proper way to walk on a leash, just by adding two more commands and a check chain. This short effective collar is used to train a dog and can't hurt him as long as the chain runs from the top to the underside, to prevent choking.

For this training, the child walks with the dog on his left side, holding the chain in his right hand and balancing it lightly in his left, and checking him by saying, "Heel," smartly whenever the dog walks in front of his knee. This, interspersed with "Stay" at the curb, is about all the dog needs to learn and anyone in the family can soon keep him in control if everyone routinely uses these same commands. Let your child teach the rest of you, which will emphasize his ownership of the dog—and his responsibility.

And if you take him for a walk yourself, consider a little training of your own. Take along a few squares of paper towel, slip one under the dog's bottom when he starts to defecate, collect the stool when he's done and drop it in the trash. It's a tidy way to clean up after your dog, it will be appreciated by your neighbors and it's good training for your child. He may not willingly show such good citizenship until he's grown, however, or unless the law in your town requires it. He'll obey then, not because he is so law-abiding, but because the other young dog owners obey too. The urge for conformity has some unexpected rewards.

CATS

For those who like them—which should include the whole world—cats are the most enchanting and mysterious of creatures. They not only teach children to be generous and responsible but they use their imperious, independent ways and twenty sharp claws to get the respect they demand.

Cats aren't even much trouble if your child learns that he can't discipline his pet (and neither can you). He can only discipline himself to give the cat the kind of environment that makes it behave: enough to eat and drink, a clean litter box about four inches deep—so we won't scratch litter over the sides—and a special place to scratch.

With reminders, a Six is old enough to give the cat water and cat food once a day, milk three to four times a week and an egg on Sunday, any style. He can also clean the litter box every day with a slotted spoon, and by Eight he can wash the box each week and change the litter. If he doesn't the cat will choose the back of the closet instead, the standard revenge of the cat who is angry about a move, a new baby—or a dirty litter box.

Scratching is just an instinctive carry-

over from wilder days when its ancestors had to sharpen their claws on the bark of a tree. If you don't have a tree in your house—and you probably don't—expect the cat to use anything nappy and upright, like a chair. A scratching post is better. Even a first grader can nail an old scrap of carpet around a 1' length of 3" × 3", for you to nail a 12" × 12" square of plywood on one end, so it can stand up straight.

And then there's shedding. If the cat is a shedder—and cats usually are—have your child run a small hand-held vacuum on the sofa before company comes.

Your responsibilities, aside from nagging your child to do his small chores, will cost a bit but only once. The cat will need to be vaccinated for distemper at seven or eight weeks and again three weeks later; for rabies at four to six months. Both male and female cats should be fixed to prevent pregnancies. If you don't, the male will spray whenever he's aroused, and always on the same place, which can be death to the upholstered chair and unpleasant anywhere else. The female cat, on the other hand, will go into heat after she's six months old and no one may notice it at first. Sixty-four days later she (and you) will have one to eight kittens, a present she's likely to repeat twice a year unless she's spayed. If your cat is a female, she should be spayed at six to seven months, while a male should be neutered at seven to eight months, so he's had time to grow bigger and stronger. It isn't fair to bring unwanted cats into the world, willy-nilly.

You also may have to have the cat declawed. This is considered an infamous remedy by many cat fanciers and a commonsense necessity by others, but only if the cat is always kept indoors and doesn't need claws for protection. If the cat must be declawed, combine it with the Big Fix because it's painful and requires an overnight stay.

These measures aren't as much trouble as they sound and the dividends are worth it. A cat will give your child good company and plenty of purrs.

HORSES

Most young people—especially girls—like to ride horses, perhaps because horseback riding is a pretty sexy thing to do. That is the least of its virtues. Horsemanship brings rewards to both parent and child. Nothing teaches responsibility, or pride or the value of hard work, quite so well. To own one's own horse is, of course, heaven but it's not essential. A horse can be rented on an hourly basis at public and private stables in most cities, and someone whose child has gone away to school may be glad to have the horse exercised and cared for in exchange for free rides. The more a child does for the horse—whether it's her own or not—the better the experience will be. The lonesome child learns the joy of friendship; the extravagant one saves money to buy the trappings you never heard of; and the carefree one accepts duties like a soldier.

This is where you see how brightly passion shines. An Eleven—who had only dreamed of riding with the wind—will willingly put the needs of her horse before her own good times, whenever the choice must be made. This child is almost fanatical about giving it attention, bringing it food and water and mucking its stall on the coldest day and with little complaint. Even if she gripes, the care she takes is clearly worth it to her. She knows no one else can do it so well—or should do it. After all, whose ears hear the most precious secrets? Whose hide catches her tears? Whose back carries her where she wants to go, and lets her dream the rest of the ride?

The horse is no ordinary possession, no preferred pet. It is your child's alter ego, her magic carpet. It is the best of herself and the worst of herself. She will wrestle with its personality problems better than she wrestles with her own and learn to handle both.

If ownership is feasible, a horse is a wonderful addition to the family who has time, patience, space and money. It first takes time and patience to find a reputable owner who is willing to sell a safe, well-trained horse. Let your child visit several stables, and ride several horses at each one, before she makes her choice, for she and the animal must not only suit each other; they must be soul mates.

The purchase is the least of the financial outlay. Unless you already have a barn in your backyard, stabling a horse can be quite expensive, but a local farmer may board the horse for a reasonable amount. After that there's the cost of the bridle, saddle, combs, brushes and vet bills and more. You can count on an even swifter erosion of your bank account—and your weekends—if you let your child show her horse. Still, for the right child, in the right circumstances, it's worth every dime.

She should be expected to pay some of those dimes—and dollars—to cover the costs of the extras she thinks her horse needs. She may have to take a paper route to do it but that just makes it better. This is a good time for your child to realize that the best things in life aren't always free.

WILD BIRDS

The animal lover who can't keep a pet may like to adopt wild birds, using books and binoculars to identify them and making homemade bird food in winter.

Help me give my children the best—not of trappings or toys, but of myself, cherishing them on good days and bad, theirs and mine.

Teach me to accept them for who they are, not for what they do; to listen to what they say, if only so they will listen to me; to encourage their goals, not mine; and please, let me laugh with them and be silly.

Let me give them a home where respect is the cornerstone, integrity the foundation, and there is enough happiness to raise the roof.

May I give them the courage to be true to themselves; the independence to take care of themselves and the faith to believe in a power much greater than their own.

See that I discipline my children without demeaning them, demand good manners without forgetting my own and let them know they have limitless love, no matter what they do.

Let me feed them properly, clothe them adequately and have enough to give them small allowances—not for the work they do but the pleasure they bring—and let me be moderate in all these things, so the joy of getting will help them discover the joy of giving.

See that their responsibilities are real but not burdensome, that my expectations are high but not overwhelming and that my thanks and praise are thoughtful and given when they're due.

Help me teach them that excellence is work's real reward, and not the glory it brings. But when it comes—and it will—let me revel in each honor, however small, without once pretending that it's mine; my children are glories enough.

Above all, let me ground these children so well that I can dare to let them go.

And may they be so blessed.

◇ RESOURCES ◇

BEHAVIOR

Gesell Institute of Human Development, 310 Prospect St., New Haven, CT 06511; (203) 777-3481.

BOOKS

American Library Association, 50 E. Huron St., Chicago, IL 60611; (800) 545-2433.

International Reading Association, 800 Barksdale Rd., Newark, DE 19714-8139; (302) 731-1600.

Reading Is Fundamental, Inc., 600 Maryland Ave. S.W., Suite 500, Washington, D.C. 20560; (202) 287-3371.

CAMP

American Camping Association, 43 W. 23rd St., New York, NY 10010; (212) 645-6620.

CHILD ABUSE

National Center for Missing and Exploited Children, 1835 K St. N.W., Suite 600, Washington, D.C. 20006; (202) 634-9821.

National Committee for Prevention of Child Abuse, 332 S. Michigan Ave., Suite 950, Chicago, IL 60604; (312) 663-3520.

Parents Anonymous, 6733 S. Sepulveda Blvd., Suite 270, Los Angeles, CA 90045; (800) 421-0353.

CHILD CARE

Experiment in International Living, Au Pair/Homestay USA, 1411 K St. N.W., Suite 1100, Washington, D.C. 20005; (202) 628-7134.

DEATH

Children's Hospice International, 1101 King St., Suite 131, Alexandria, VA 22314; (800) 24-CHILD, or (800) 242-4453.

Compassionate Friends, P.O. Box 3696, Oak Brook, IL 60522-3696; (312) 990-0010.

National Hospice Organization, 1901 N. Ft. Myer Dr., Suite 307, Arlington, VA 22209; (703) 243-5900.

DISABILITIES

Association for Retarded Citizens of the U. S., P.O. Box 6109, Arlington, TX 76005; (817) 640-0204.

Federation for Children with Special Needs, 312 Stuart St., 2nd floor, Boston, MA 02116; (617) 482-2915.

National Information Center for Children and Youth with Handicaps, Box 1492, Washington, D.C. 20013; (703) 893-6061.

Sibling Information Network, 991 Main St., Suite 3A, East Hartford, CT 06108; (203) 282-7050.

DRUGS

Adult Children of Alcoholics, see your local directory

Alcoholics Anonymous, see your local directory.

Al-Anon, see your local directory.

American Council for Drug Education, 204 Monroe St., Rockville, MD 20850; (301) 294-0600.

National Clearinghouse for Alcohol and Drug Information, Box 2345, Rockville, MD 20852; (301) 443-6500.

Narcotics Anonymous, see your local directory.

FAMILY

Children's Defense Fund, 122 C St. N.W., Suite 400, Washington, D.C. 20001; (202) 628-8787.

Catholic Charities USA, 1319 F St. N.W., Washington, D.C. 20004; (202) 639-8400 or see your local directory.

Family Service America, 11700 W. Lake Park Dr., Milwaukee, WI 53224; (414) 359-2111 or see your local directory.

National Military Family Association, 2666 Military Rd., Arlington, VA 22207; (703) 841-0462.

GIFTED

Council for Exceptional Children, 1920 Association Dr., Reston, VA 22091; (703) 620-3660 (also for handicapped children).

National Association for Gifted Children, 4175 Lovell Rd., Suite 140, Circle Pines, MN 55014; (612) 784-3475.

HEARING AND SPEECH

American Speech-Language-Hearing Association, 10801 Rockville Pike, Rockville, MD 20852; (800) 638-8255.

Gallaudet University, 800 Florida Ave. N.E., Washington, D.C. 20002; (202) 651-5000.

National Association of the Deaf, 814 Thayer Ave., Silver Spring, MD 20910; (301) 587-1788.

Self Help for Hard of Hearing People, Inc. (SHHH), 7800 Wisconsin Ave., Bethesda, MD 20814-3524; (301) 657-2248; TDD (301) 657-2249.

HYPERACTIVITY

Feingold Association, Box 6650, Alexandria, VA 22306; (703) 768-3287.

ILLNESS

Association for the Care of Children's Health, 3615 Wisconsin Ave. N.W., Washington, D.C. 20016; (202) 244-1801.

Candlelighters Childhood Cancer Foundation, Suite 1001, 1901 Pennsylvania Ave. N.W., Washington, D.C. 20006; (202) 659-5136.

Juvenile Diabetes Foundation International, 432 Park Ave. South, 16th floor, New York, NY 10016-8013; (800) 223-1138.

LEARNING DISABILITIES

Association for Children and Adults with Learning Disabilities, 4156 Library Rd., Pittsburgh, PA 15234; (412) 341-1515.

Orton Dyslexia Society, 724 York Rd., Baltimore, MD 21204; (800) 222-3123.

MENTAL ILLNESS

National Alliance for the Mentally Ill, 2101 Wilson Blvd., Suite 302, Arlington, VA 22201; (703) 524-7600.

NUTRITION

Center for Science in the Public Interest, 1501 16th St. N.W., Washington, D.C. 20036; (202) 332-9110.

SCHOOL

American Federation of Teachers, 555 New Jersey Ave. N.W., Washington, D.C. 20001; (202) 879-4400.

Home and School Institute, 1201 16th St. N.W., Washington, D.C. 20036; (202) 466-3633.

National Education Association, 1201 16th St. N.W., Washington, D.C. 20036; (202) 833-4000.

National PTA, 700 N. Rush St., Chicago, IL 60611-2571; (312) 787-0977.

SEX

Alan Guttmacher Institute, 2010 Massachusetts Ave. N.W., Washington, D.C. 20036; (202) 296-4012.

Federation of Parents & Friends of Lesbians and Gays, Inc., P.O. Box 27605, Washington, D.C. 20038-7605; (202) 638-4200.

Planned Parenthood Federation of America, 810 Seventh Ave., New York, NY 10019; (800) 223-3303.

STEPFAMILY

Stepfamily Association of America, Inc., 602 E. Joppa Rd., Baltimore, MD 21204; (301) 823-7570.

TELEVISION

Action for Children's Television, 20 University Rd., Cambridge, MA 02138; (617) 876-6620.

◇ # RECOMMENDED READING ◇

(*Written for children)

MOTHER

DIVORCE

Crazy Time by Abigail Trafford (Bantam)

Growing Up Divorced by Linda Bird Francke (Simon & Schuster/Linden)

Joint Custody and Co-Parenting by Miriam Galper (Running Press)

*How to Live with a Single Parent by Sara Gilbert (Lothrop)

*The Kids' Book of Divorce by the Unit of the Fayerweather Street School, ed. by Eric Rofes (Vintage)

*Why Are We Getting a Divorce? by Peter Mayle (Harmony)

FAMILY

The Art of Sensitive Parenting by Katharine C. Kersey, E.D. (Acropolis)

Between Generations by Ellen Galinsky (Times Books)

Dr. Spock on Parenting by Benjamin Spock, M.D. (Simon & Schuster)

Traits of a Healthy Family by Dolores Curran (Ballantine)

*A Family Is a Circle of People Who Love You by Doris Jasinek and Pamela Bell Ryan (Comp Care)

MARRIAGE

How to Live with an Imperfect Person by Dr. Louis H. Janda (N.A.L.)

Married People by Francine Klagsbrun (Bantam)

REMARRIAGE

Love and Power in the Stepfamily by Jamie K. Keshet (McGraw-Hill)

*My Friend Has Four Parents by Margaret O. Hyde (McGraw-Hill)

Remarriage by Anne Lorimer with Philip M. Feldman, M.D. (Running Press)

Stepmotherhood by Cherie Burns (Times Books)

MENTAL ILLNESS

The Broken Brain by Nancy C. Andreasen, M.D., Ph.D. (Harper & Row)

The Good News About Depression by Mark S. Gold, M.D. (Bantam)

Minding the Body; Mending the Mind by Joan Borysenko, Ph.D. (Bantam)

Surviving Schizophrenia by E. Fuller Torrey, M.D. (Harper & Row/Perennial)

STRESS

Coping in the 80's by Joel Wells (Thomas More Press)

Living Through Personal Crisis by Ann Kaiser Stearns (Thomas More Press)

Necessary Losses by Judith Viorst (Fawcett)

The Road Less Traveled by M. Scott Peck (Simon & Schuster)

WORKING MOTHER

The Handbook for Latchkey Children and Their Parents by Lynette and Thomas Long (Arbor House)

The Official Kids' Survival Kit by Elaine Chaback and Pat Fortunato (Little, Brown)

Safe and Sound by Trudy K. Dana (McGraw-Hill)

The Woman Who Works, The Parent Who Cares by Sirgay Sanger, M.D., and John Kelly (Little, Brown)

The Working Parents' Survival Guide by Sally Wendkos Olds (Bantam)

You Can't Do It All by Irvina Siegel Lew (Atheneum)

CHILD

ADOPTION

The Adoption Resource Book by Lois Gilman (Harper & Row)

How It Feels to Be Adopted by Jill Krementz (Knopf)

Oriental Children in American Homes by Frances M. Koh (East-West Press)

Raising Adopted Children by Lois Ruskai Melina (Harper & Row)

ALLERGIES

Allergies and the Hyperactive Child by Doris J. Rapp, M.D. (Simon & Schuster/Cornerstone)

Coping with Your Allergies by Natalie Golos et al. (Simon & Schuster)

Detecting Your Hidden Allergies by William G. Crook, M.D. (Professional Books)

BEHAVIOR

All Grown Up and No Place to Go by David Elkind, Ph.D. (Addison-Wesley)

Child Behavior (revised) by Frances L. Ilg, M.D., Louise Bates Ames, Ph.D., and Sidney M. Baker, M.D. (Harper & Row)

The Complete Book on Sibling Rivalry by John F. McDermott, Jr. (Putnam)

Growing Up Smart and Happy by Julius and Zelda Segal (McGraw-Hill)

How to Talk So Kids Will Listen and Listen So Kids Will Talk by Adele Faber and Elaine Mazlish (Avon)

The Hurried Child by David Elkind, Ph.D. (Addison-Wesley)

Living with Your Teenager by Marlene Brusko (Ballantine)

Loving Your Child Is Not Enough by Nancy Samalin with Martha Moraghan Jablow (Penguin)

Questions Parents Ask by Louise Bates Ames, Ph.D. (Potter)

Siblings Without Rivalry by Adele Faber and Elaine Mazlish (Avon)

Solving the Puzzle of Your Hard-to-Raise Child by William G. Crook, M.D., and Laura J. Stevens (Random House)

Talk with Your Child by Harvey S. Wiener (Viking)

Teaching Children Responsibility by Linda and Richard Eyre (Ballantine)

Your Child's Self-Esteem by Dorothy Corkille Briggs (Doubleday)

BOOKS

Choosing Books for Kids by Joanne Oppenheim, Barbara Brenner, and Betty D. Boegehold (Ballantine)

Helping Kids Use the Library (U.S. Department of Education)

Eyeopeners! by Beverly Kobrin (Penguin)

The New York Times Parent's Guide to the Best Books for Children by Eden Ross Lipson (Times Books)

The Read-Aloud Handbook by Jim Trelease (Penguin)

The Uses of Enchantment by Bruno Bettelheim (Vintage)

CHRONIC ILLNESS

The Chronically Ill Child by Audrey T. McCollum, M.S. (Yale)

Home Care for the Chronically Ill or Disabled Child by Monica Loose Jones (Harper & Row)

DEATH

Helping Children Cope with Separation and Loss by Claudia L. Jewett (Harvard Common Press)

How It Feels When a Parent Dies by Jill Krementz (Knopf)

The Kids' Book About Death and Dying by the Unit at the Fayerweather Street School, ed. by Eric E. Rofes (Little, Brown)

Learning to Say Goodbye by Eda LeShan (Avon)

Lifetimes by Bryan Mellonie and Robert Ingpen (Bantam)

On Children and Death by Elisabeth Kübler-Ross (Macmillan)

On Death and Dying by Elisabeth Kübler-Ross (Macmillan)

The Seasons of Grief by Dr. Donna A. Gaffney (N.A.L.)

When Parents Die by Edward Myers (Penguin)

DEVELOPMENT

The Child from Five to Ten by Arnold Gesell, M.D., Frances L. Ilg, M.D., and Louise Bates Ames, Ph.D. (Harper & Row)

Childhood and Adolescence by L. Joseph Stone and Joseph Church (Random House)

Gifts Differing by Isabel B. Myers and Peter B. Myers (Consulting Psychology)

In a Different Voice by Carol Gilligan (Harvard University Press)

Please Understand Me by David Keirsey and Marilyn Bates (Prometheus Nemesis Books)

Your Growing Child by Penelope Leach (Knopf)

Youth: The Years from Ten to Sixteen by Arnold Gesell, M.D., Frances L. Ilg, M.D., and Louise Bates Ames, Ph.D. (Harper & Row)

DISABILITIES

Catalog of Aids for the Disabled by Nancy and Jack Kreisler (McGraw-Hill)

A Difference in the Family by Helen Featherstone (Penguin)

Everyone Can Win by Anne and George Allen (EPM)

Exceptional Parent (magazine), 1170 Commonwealth Ave., Boston, MA 02215 (617) 536-8961

Helping the Severely Handicapped Child by Phyllis B. Doyle, John F. Goodman, Jeffery N. Grotsky, and Lester Mann (Crowell)

Hope for the Families by Robert Perske (Abingdon)

The Joy of Signing by Lottie Riekehof (Gospel Publishing Co.)

DRUGS

Children of Alcoholism by Judith S. Seixas and Geraldine Youcha (Harper & Row)

Getting Tough on Gateway Drugs by Robert L. DuPont, Jr., M.D. (American Psychiatric Press)

**It's OK to Say No to Drugs* by Alan Garner (Tor/St. Martin's)

**When Your Parent Drinks Too Much* by Eric Ryerson (Facts on File)

FIRST AID

Sigh of Relief by Martin I. Green (Bantam)

GIFTED

Enjoy Your Gifted Child by Carol Addison Takacs (Syracuse University Press)

Gifted Children by Virginia Z. Erlich (Spectrum)

Teaching the Gifted Child by James J. Gallagher (Allyn & Bacon)

GOOD TIMES

Doing Art Together by Muriel Silberstein-Storfer with Mablen Jones (Simon & Schuster)

Drawing with Children by Mona Brooks (J. P. Tarcher)

The Happiest Birthdays by Michaeline Bresnahan and Joan Gaestel Macfarlane (Stephen Greene Press)

**Lollipop Grapes and Clothespin Critters* by Robyn Freedman Spizman (Addison-Wesley)

Music for Your Child by Roberta Markel (Facts on File)

**My First Cookbook* by Rena Coyle (Workman)

Quality Time Almanac by S. Adams Sullivan (Doubleday)

**Recipes for Art and Craft Materials* by Helen Roney Sattler (Lothrop)

**Scienceworks* by the Ontario Science Centre (Addison-Wesley)

ILLNESS

**The Hospital Book* by James Howe (Crown)

LEARNING DISABILITIES

The Misunderstood Child by Larry B. Silver, M.D. (McGraw-Hill)

No Easy Answers by Sally L. Smith (Bantam)

MIND

Your Child's Growing Mind by Jane M. Healy, Ph.D. (Doubleday)

Your Child's Mind by Herman Roiphe, M.D., and Anne Roiphe (St. Martin's)

MORALITY

Bringing Up a Moral Child by Michael Schulman and Eva Mekler (Addison-Wesley)

Raising Good Children by Dr. Thomas Lickona (Bantam)

MOVIES AND TELEVISION

Changing Channels by Peggy Charren and Martin W. Sandler (Addison-Wesley)

MOVING

**Goodbye, House* by Ann Banks and Nancy Evans (Crown)

NUTRITION

**Come and Get It* by Kathleen M. Baxter (Children First Press)

Parents' Guide to Nutrition by Boston Children's Hospital with Susan Baker, M.D., Ph.D., and Roberta R. Henry, R.D. (Addison-Wesley)

Superimmunity for Kids by Leo Galland, M.D., with Dian Dincin Buchman, Ph.D. (Dutton)

SCHOOL

American Education: Making It Work (U.S. Department of Education)

Choosing a School for Your Child (U.S. Department of Education)

**How to be School Smart* by Elizabeth James and Carol Barkin (Lothrop)

How to Get Your Child a "Private School" Education in a Public School by Dr. Marty Nemko and Dr. Barbara Nemko (Acropolis)

Last Chance for Our Children by Bill Honig (Addison-Wesley)

Learning to Say Goodbye by Nancy Balaban, Ed.D. (Plume)

Winning the Homework War by Dr. Fredric M. Levine and Dr. Kathleen M. Anesko (Prentice-Hall)

SEXUAL ABUSE

No More Secrets by Caren Adams and Jennifer Fay (Impact)

*No More Secrets for Me by Oralee Wachter (Little, Brown)

The Silent Children by Linda Tschirhart Sanford (Doubleday/Anchor)

SEXUALITY

*Am I Normal? by Jeanne Betancourt (Avon)

Are You Still My Mother? by Gloria Guss Back (Warner)

*Asking About Sex and Growing Up by Joanna Cole (Morrow)

*Babies by Robyn Gee (Usborne Press)

Children and Sex by the Study Group of New York (Facts on File)

*Don't Worry, You're Normal by Nissa Simon (Crowell)

The Family Book About Sexuality by Dr. Mary S. Calderone and Eric W. Johnson (Bantam)

Growing Up with Sex by Richard Hettlinger (Continuum)

*Love and Sex in Plain Language by Eric W. Johnson (Bantam)

Talking with Your Child About Sex by Dr. Mary S. Calderone and Dr. James W. Ramey (Random House)

ABOUT THE AUTHOR

MARGUERITE KELLY, the mother of four and the grandmother of two, is the co-author of *The Mother's Almanac,* a classic child care book originally published in 1975 and still enjoyed by thousands of new mothers each year. Her column, "The Family Almanac," appears weekly in the *Washington Post* and is syndicated nationally. In addition, she frequently lectures on family issues and is a trustee of the District of Columbia Public Library. She and her husband live in a rambling Victorian home in Washington, D.C.

Rabbi Nathan Abramowitz
Ellis April, M.D.
Jules Asher
Sidney Baker, M.D.
Lillian McLean Beard, M.D.
Helga Binder, M.D.
Barbara Bittner
James Breneman, M.D.
Betty Brooks
Emily Brown, M.S.W.
Blackwell S. Bruner, M.D.
Mario Cardullo
Selig Chester, D.D.S.
Garry Clifford
Mary Coleman, M.D.
Margaret Coughlan
William Crook, M.D.
Anne Crutcher
Joan Cox Danzansky
Donna Datre
Kitty Davis
Stephanie Deutsch
Winifred Dowling
Louis Dougaloff
Robert L. DuPont, Jr., M.D.
Marjorie Elson, Ph.D.
Robert Everhart
Judith Findlay
Donna Foster
Mary Flynn, M.S.W.
Patricia Frederick
Jo Anne Gartenmann
Mariana Gasteyer
James Gilbreath
Scott Goode
Ruth Graves
Elizabeth Harper, M.S.W.
Bette Glickert
Edward Grunseth
Mark Hegsted, Ph.D.
Florence Hesser, Ed.D.

Celine Penn Hickey
Barbara Hilberg
Rebecca Hirsh
Bernice Hoik
Lillian Hoik
Ethna Hopper
Faith Jackson
Willie Jennings
C. Tim Jensen
Phyllis Katz
Joan S. Keenan
Terry Van den Bossche Klein
Nora Jean Levin
Louise and Marion Lelong
Daniel and Harriet Lelong
Froma Lippmann
Dianne Lorenz
Ruth Malone
Clare Crawford-Mason
Margaret Mason
Robert Mason
Emily MacCormack
Gail McCarthy
Florence McGee, R.N.
Phyllis McGrabe, Ph.D.
Craig Messersmith, Ph.D.
Alfonsa B. Micutuan
Lynn Minton
Beverly Mischer
Minna Nathanson
Christine Getlein Nelson
Carl Nelson, Jr.
Greenie Neuberg
Joye Newman
David Nichols
Wanda O'Hagan
Mark Olcott
Virginia Penn
Ida Prosky
Audrey Pugh
Doris Rapp, M.D.

Richard Restak, M.D.
Julia D. Robertson
Lisa Romberg
Jacob Rosenberg, D.D.S.
Joan Rosenberg
Maria Salvadore
Katherine Shollenberger
Shari Ostrow Sher
Holly Shimizu
Helen Skinner
Mildred Skinner
Joanne Small, M.S.W.
Carol Smith, Ph.D.
James C. Smith, Ph.D.
Kay Smith
Sally L. Smith
John and Daphne Stegmaier
Jewell Stoddard
Franklin Stroud, M.D.
S. Adams Sullivan
Martha S. Swaim
Roger Thomas
Robert Thurston
Sarah Toomer
Kay Vogelsang
Helen Waugh, S.H.C.J.
Jennifer Wilkinson
Lorna Williams
Claudia and Hilary Winkler
Lewis Wise
Stanley I. Wolf, M.D.
Morgan Wootten
Suzanne A. Zunzer

And special thanks to

Claudette and John Best
Doremus Jenkins
Olivia Lelong
Patricia Linnell
Sarah Molumby
Bonny Wolf